Naval Leadership

NAVAL LEADERSHIP

VOICES OF EXPERIENCE

Editors

Professor of Leadership Karel Montor, Ph.D.,
  U.S. Naval Academy

Captain Thomas M. McNicholas, Jr., U.S. Navy

Lieutenant Colonel Anthony J. Ciotti, Jr., U.S. Marine Corps

Lieutenant Commander Thomas H. Hutchinson III,
  U.S. Naval Reserve

Jackie Eckhart Wehmueller

NAVAL INSTITUTE PRESS   ANNAPOLIS, MARYLAND

The photograph on page 9 of Admiral d'escadre Paul de Bigault de Cazanove
is reproduced courtesy of E.C.P.-Armées.

Grateful acknowledgment is made for permission to reprint the following previously
published material:

Keith M. Flake, "The Ten Most Wanted Men in Industry," *Vital Speeches,* May 1969
(p. 44), Mt. Pleasant, South Carolina.

David W. Thompson, "Who Is the 'Ideal' Manager?," reprinted from the January–
February 1968 issue of *Personnel Administrator* (p. 32), copyright 1968, The American
Society for Personnel Administration, 606 North Washington Street, Alexandria, Virginia
22314; $40 per year.

Susan Margetts, "How Do You Pick a Winner?," reprinted with the permission of
Dun's Review, September 1968 (p. 71), copyright 1968, Dun & Bradstreet Publications
Corporation.

Lyle A. Otterness, "He's Great in a Crisis," *Supervisory Management,* July 1962
(New York: American Management Association), pp. 7–9.

C. H. Kepner and B. J. Tregoe, "Planning to *Prevent* Problems," *International
Management,* February 1966 (p. 65), a McGraw-Hill publication.

"Correcting a Bad Decision," *Successful Supervisor,* February 1978 (p. 3), Dartnell,
Chicago, Illinois.

Roland Sandell, "Encouraging Subordinates' Suggestions," *Supervision,* October 1967
(p. 19); reprinted by permission of *Executives' Digest,* December 1967, copyright 1967
by The National Research Bureau, Inc., 424 North Third Street, Burlington, Iowa 52601.

"How to Make a Worker Willing," *Office Administration,* August–September 1968
(p. 88).

Library of Congress Cataloging-in-Publication Data

Naval leadership.
    Bibliography: p. 487.
    1. Leadership. 2. Command of troops. I. Montor,
Karel.
VB203.N39   1987   359.3'3041   87-10986
ISBN 0-87021-325-3

Printed in the United States of America on acid-free paper ∞

10 9 8 7 6 5

For in my mind there is but one honorable profession. It requires the daily attention of all faculties, the persistence of a bulldog, the compassion of a man of the cloth, foresight entrenched in previously learned lessons, the willingness to sacrifice for the good of the service all that has been personally gained or earned, and unyielding belief that it is better to preserve peace than to wage war, the self force-feeding of knowledge and new technology, the ability to blend confidence and humility, and the unyielding conviction that it is far greater to serve one's country rather than oneself. These requirements demand a foundation, and that foundation is, inescapably, experience.

The naval officer is truly unique, for he must have the capacity to simultaneously love his country, his service, his family, his shipmates, and the sea. He needs each of them unquestionably as each of them needs him. And the demands which each place on him never diminish, they only grow.

Beyond all the words and phrases of a naval officer's dedicated service, honor and professionalism must remain his past, present, and future. That, sir, is why it is *The* "HONORABLE PROFESSION."

ADMIRAL JOHN BULKELEY, USN

Contents

Contents

ix

Contents

Preface and Acknowledgments

This book was designed to be the final leadership text for those who are to be commissioned in the Naval Service; to provide instruction in leadership needed by junior officers who did not have the opportunity to review this material prior to being commissioned; and to provide information to junior officers who wished to review the concepts inherent in leadership in the Naval Service. It was first conceived in the mid-1960s. At that time, Lieutenant Colonel Robert Steed, USMC, and Professor Gregory Mann, USNA, encouraged then Lieutenant Thomas McNicholas, USN, and then Assistant Professor Karel Montor, MBA, to undertake the project. Each of 200 members of the USNA Classes of 1970 and 1971 was asked to contact 5 different officers, each of a different rank, concerning their concept of what was involved in the making of a good leader. The result was input from 1,000 officers covering 15,000 years of leadership experience. Added to this information were the results of a study on the same subject by 1,750 officers at the Naval War College, as well as materials developed by Montor and McNicholas in their leadership instruction courses. During the 1970s this material was expanded, amplified, and refined.

Between 1982 and 1986, the team was joined by Lieutenant Colonel Anthony J. Ciotti, Jr., USMC, and Lieutenant Thomas Hutchinson, USN, both of whom were leadership course coordinators at the United States Naval Academy. By this time McNicholas had achieved the rank of Navy captain and had commanded the *Barney*, the *Direct*, and the *Shenandoah*, and Montor had earned his doctorate, had been appointed a full professor at the Academy, and had served as president of the Retired Officer's Association of Annapolis.

In the 1980s Lt. Col. Ciotti and Professor Montor reviewed all of the articles on leadership that had appeared since 1879 in *Proceedings*, the magazine of the U.S. Naval Institute. These articles and many other books and publications were reviewed by Lt. Hutchinson, Lt. Col. Ciotti, and Professor Montor to strengthen the base of this book.

The result of these 20 years of leadership research and investigation was divided into 96 areas that were grouped into 10 chapters. In the next step, 90 midshipmen were selected to write on one of the 90 areas in the first 9 chapters. They were required to do a full library research project, including interviews with various officers, to ensure maximum effort regarding each topic. These papers provided the project team with a good idea of the level of understanding achieved by those soon to be commissioned as junior officers. Furthermore, the midshipmen benefited from doing the research, and additional ideas, as well as a considerable Bibliography, were developed for each chapter.

The next step consisted of contacting 96 senior officers of the Navy and Marine Corps and asking each of them to write on an appropriate area. For example, the Navy Inspector General, Admiral Jerry O. Tuttle, USN, wrote on standards in the Naval Service; Vice Admiral William P. Lawrence, USN, wrote on characteristics of a naval officer; and Admiral John D. Bulkeley, USN, President, Board of Inspection and Survey, and holder of the Medal of Honor, wrote on being prepared for emergency situations. All of these officers and the midshipmen who contributed many hours of effort to this book are listed in the Appendix; recognition of this nature is hardly indicative of the tremendous contribution they have made to this volume. Just as one should not buy a computer and then decide what to do with it, but, rather, decide what is needed and then buy the equipment, so it was with this book. We did not want to produce a book of readings; rather, we wanted to produce a book covering the areas more than 2,700 officers had indicated as being important. Thus, each of our distinguished guest authors wrote his section knowing what was in the other sec-

tions as well as the exact audience he was addressing.

After the "skeleton" book was developed, Jackie Wehmueller, editor of the beginning leadership text at the Naval Academy, *Fundamentals of Naval Leadership* (Naval Institute Press, 1984), was brought into the project. To enhance her understanding of the material, Mrs. Wehmueller reviewed many films dealing historically and currently with the operations and actions of officers and enlisted in the Navy and Marine Corps. She then edited the "skeleton" material so that it would read as if it had been written by one person, thus providing flow and continuity throughout the book. The project team conducted a final review of her work.

Since this book was intended for the education and training of junior officers, we were most fortunate to secure inputs on most areas from Master Chief Petty Officer of the Navy Billy C. Sanders, USN (Ret.), whose comments appear at the end of many of the sections in the book. To illuminate the concepts of this book further, the current Master Chief Petty Officer of the Navy, William H. Plackett, USN, came to the Academy and videographically recorded his thoughts on more than fifty topic areas.

Early in 1980 Admiral James L. Holloway, USN, former Chief of Naval Operations, suggested that it would be a good idea to put together into a single vehicle the thoughts of all the living Chiefs of Naval Operations concerning what was involved in leadership. In this way the concept of weaving into the book the ideas of former CNOs Carney, Burke, McDonald, Moorer, Zumwalt, Holloway, and Hayward came into being. The Naval Service, of course, is made up of both Marine and Navy Officers, and we were fortunate in that former Commandants of the Marine Corps Generals Shepherd, Greene, Wilson, and Barrow also participated. Admiral Arleigh A. Burke suggested that we include the thoughts of naval leaders from other countries, and so we contacted former CNOs Ruge, of West Germany, and Itaya, Nakamura, and Uchida, of

Japan. Upon the death of Admiral Ruge, the West German government designated Admiral Clausen to participate, and the French government designated Admiral de Cazanove. To increase the scope of the book further, interviews were conducted with Admirals Larson, Long, Fran McKee, Ramage, and Taylor, as well as General Rice, USMC, and Assistant Secretary of Defense Webb.

Each of these individuals was asked to comment on many of the sections covered in the book, and their comments are identified by name. It was necessary to convert their inputs, which were primarily verbal, into written format; this process involved, in some cases, paraphrasing the interviewee's words. Again, Mrs. Wehmueller was brought into the picture, first to read all the comments in their entirety so as to capture the flavor of each individual's thoughts, and then to edit and rearrange the material for use in the book. Again, the project team checked her work.

Professor Montor then combined the remarks obtained in the interviews with the appropriate "skeleton" section, and Mrs. Wehmueller reviewed and edited the material again, and the project team reviewed it again. It is our purpose to note here that Mrs. Wehmueller, during the course of this multiyear effort, moved from editor, a significant position in itself, to being one of the principal authors as a result of the clarity of her expression and her ability to rearrange material to provide a more unified approach; she also titled many of the individual sections.

The material has been read by many midshipmen and officers and has gone through multiple drafts and manuscripts. Each of the 96 sections was retyped approximately seven times. For that it is difficult to find the words to thank Janet Wingfield and Sharon DeWilde for their devotion to this project, which far transcends the loyalty that can be expected of a secretary. They worked at nights and on weekends, and met deadline after deadline. Thus, while the project team is responsible for any errors in this book, the leaders, Mrs. Wingfield, and Miss DeWilde deserve credit for making it possible. We also wish to thank Mrs. Margaret Seifert for her word-processing support.

Special thanks is given to Lieutenant Kenneth Davison, USAF, Rhodes Scholar, who conducted the interviews in Europe with Admiral Hunt (England), Admiral Clausen (West Germany), and Admiral de Cazanove (France). We would also like to thank Lieutenant Commander Norio Iguchi, JMSDF, for his liaison and translation assistance in securing the inputs from the three Japanese CNOs, and Lieutenant de Vaisseau Eric Dyeure, FN, for his invaluable assistance in arranging for the interview with the representative of the French Chief of Naval Operations, and translating documents. To General Wallace M. Greene, Jr., USMC, goes credit for the inspirational suggestion to create an accompanying loose-leaf book of cases based on the actual experience of officers relating to each of the first 94 topic areas in this volume.

Special Acknowledgments

So many people are involved in a project of this magnitude that it is difficult to thank all of those who have made a contribution. Over the years, hundreds of officers who were instructors at the U.S. Naval Academy and thousands of midshipmen have made inputs to this project and have greatly improved the final product. Through their efforts, the following individuals started, kept alive, and enabled this project to be completed: Captain William C. Nicklas, Jr., USN, who created the climate that encouraged us to start the project; Admiral Kinnaird R. McKee, USN, who, as its Superintendent, directed that the Naval Academy produce its own leadership texts rather than use civilian management/administration instructional books as the basis for leadership instruction in the Naval Service; Admiral Edward C. Waller III, USN, who brought the forces together at the Academy to finish the advanced leadership book; Rear Admiral Charles R. Larson, USN, who helped secure the support of the officers who contributed to the book; and the following Superintendents, Commandants of Midshipmen, Division Directors, and Department Chairmen, who, through their spiritual and economic support, maintained a climate for twenty years that made this book possible.

Superintendents: Rear Admiral Draper L. Kauffman, USN; Vice Admiral James F. Calvert, USN; Vice Admiral William P. Mack, USN; Vice Admiral Kinnaird R. McKee, USN; Vice Admiral William P. Lawrence, USN; Vice Admiral Edward C. Waller III, USN; and Rear Admiral Charles R. Larson, USN.

Commandants of Midshipmen: Rear Admiral Sheldon H. Kinney, USN; Rear Admiral Lawrence Heyworth, Jr., USN; Rear Admiral Robert F. Coogan, USN; Rear Admiral Max K. Morris, USN; Captain D. K. Forbes, USN; Rear Admiral James A. Winnefeld, USN; Captain Jack N. Darby, USN; Rear Admiral W. F. McCauley,

USN; Commodore Leon A. Edney, USN; Commodore Leslie N. Palmer, USN; and Rear Admiral Stephen K. Chadwick, USN.

Division Directors: Captain William C. Nicklas, Jr., USN; Captain Paul C. Boyd, USN; Captain William D. Robertson, USN; Captain James L. Anderson, USN; Captain James S. Brunson, USN; Captain Richard C. Ustick, USN; Captain John R. Wales, USN; Captain Michael C. Colley, USN; Captain Frank R. Donovan, USN; Captain R. Louis Reasonover, USN; Captain Thomas D. Paulsen, USN; Captain F. Richard Whalen, USN; and Captain Douglas J. Katz, USN.

Department Chairmen: Lieutenant Colonel Robert E. Steed, USMC; Lieutenant Colonel Charles D. Roberts, Jr., USMC; Lieutenant Colonel Don D. Beal, USMC; Commander Eugene J. Christensen, USN; Lieutenant Colonel Robert W. Howland, USMC; Commander Joseph J. Kronzer, Jr., USN; Commander William E. Smith, Jr., USN; Commander Manuel B. Sousa, USN; Lieutenant Colonel Walter E. Boomer, USMC; Commander Kenneth G. Clark, USN; Commander Neil L. Kozlowski, USN; Commander William L. Lupton, USN; Commander Julius B. Dell, USN; Professor Gregory J. Mann; Commander Thomas P. Cruser, USN; Commander Thomas H. Berns, USN; and Commander Donald J. Curran, Jr., USN.

Special recognition is due the many officers who gave of their time to prepare the materials used in this book. As noted in the Preface, these few words of recognition can hardly repay them for the tremendous effort they made on behalf of future generations of naval officers.

Introduction

On 3 July 1985, two weeks before he was to provide specific inputs to this book, Vice Admiral Friedrich Ruge of the German Federal Navy died. Admiral Ruge had been recommended for the project by Admiral Arleigh Burke, who had gotten to know him during their concurrent tours as Chiefs of Naval Operations of their respective countries. During his 70 years of adult life, Admiral Ruge saw extensive military service and was a world renowned historian and writer, as well as a university professor. As the naval advisor to Field Marshal Erwin Rommel, he was considered the person most knowledgeable of that individual's genius. The team of Rommel and Ruge, who was the naval coordinator for the defense of the Continent during World War II, prepared the defenses for D-Day, 6 June 1944.

In a foreword to one of the many books by Admiral Ruge, Fleet Admiral William D. Leahy, USN, Chief of Staff to the Commander in Chief of the Army and Navy of the United States from 1942 to 1949, wrote:

> Books from the enemy side which are the work of former enemy leaders, who have both the knowledge of what happened as well as the ability to narrate it clearly, immediately assume the stature of professional studies of first rank for all military men and statesmen as well as for the historians and general public of all countries that participated. Such a book is Vice Admiral Friedrich Ruge's history, *Der Seekrieg: The German Navy's Story, 1939–1945.* . . . And it is particularly fitting that it should be published by the United States Naval Institute, the professional society of the U.S. Navy. . . . The Germans have always been good seamen and bold and enterprising warriors. It is a comforting thought that in a possible future war they may be with us and not against us, and that the new German Navy which is now a part of the NATO Fleet in Europe is commanded by the very man who has written the book I have just discussed.

Fortunately, as a prelude to the 1985 meeting in which Admiral Ruge was to talk with her at length, Professor of Applied Linguistics and History Maria Stoffers, Ph.D., of the Graduate School of City University of New York, met with Admiral Ruge in Germany in the summer of 1984. In this meeting, Admiral Ruge provided material relative to his overall views of leadership and its instruction, as well as comments about the application of leadership. This material has been translated by Dr. Stoffers, and it provides, as the reader will see, an insight into the subject matter of this book that makes it evident why military leaders of the world recognize the contributions made by Admiral Ruge to military studies and the practice of leadership.

It will be clear from this book that the outlook on life of military leaders is basically the same, regardless of what country they serve. This probably explains why some military leaders who were friends before war could fight each other and then become friends again after the war. This is borne out not only by the Americans' acceptance of Admiral Ruge, but also by the very high regard in which Admirals Itaya, Nakamura,  and Uchida hold Admiral Burke, and he them. If political leaders could agree on an approach to life that was as consistent as that of military leaders, we might have a chance at peace.

Now let the words of Admiral Ruge set the stage for the overall approach taken herein to the study of *Naval Leadership*.

Because leadership is an art, many people are of the opinion that it cannot be taught, that it is an innate gift and therefore cannot be learned. I disagree with this strongly, for every artistic talent can be further developed. I do not see why we cannot apply this to military leadership.

The fate of the nation today lies in the hands of the armed forces, which are only as good as their officers. The more real leaders there are, the better the country will be defended. The need to educate leaders, therefore, is understood; the difficulty lies in determining what good leadership is and how good leadership is attained. I'd like to quote General Reinhard, who defined leadership as follows: "The real leader is he who can transpose his own way of warfare on to others and thus induce in them an increased awareness to act."

I would simplify this as follows: He who knows how to lead people is a real leader. We can apply this definition to any leadership, including leadership in the political arena. For the military leader, we only need to add that he has to know how to use weapons, and, for the leader at sea, that he knows how to run a ship. To lead people is, in my opinion, the most important of the three, and also the most difficult. One often talks about the *art* of leadership, but only *skill* is required to use weapons.

There are people who are especially gifted in music or in technology or in seamanship. There are others who are especially unsuited for these pursuits. We all know from our own experience that there are some who cannot, even if they try their best, conduct a good maneuver. Their ship will never go straight, and eventually these unsuited (or untalented) people decide to stop trying to be seamen and become something else. These cases, however, are rare.

Between the artistically gifted (or talented) and the completely unsuitable (or untalented) people are the masses of servicemen with numerous shades of talents, but they all learn some kind of skill. If even the artistically talented need to be educated or trained and need constantly to improve themselves, then it is evident that the persons whose gifts (or talents) are only average need to work even harder.

All of this may also be applied to leadership. The only difficulty is that success in leadership cannot be as clearly defined, is not as tangible, as success in music, technology, or seamanship. Success in leadership rests on more shaky ground. Failure in leadership often occurs late in a military officer's life, and is, therefore, much more consequential. In like manner, ultimate success in handling responsibility becomes apparent much later in a serviceman's life than in any other profession.

A medical doctor, for example, accepts total responsibility for other people's lives fairly early on. In the military, however, responsibility gradually increases. This means that the education process takes much longer for the leader than for the doctor, whose formal education ended when he received his degree. Both the doctor and the naval leader, however, learn a great deal through experience.

Every well-balanced education consists of a healthy mixture of theory and practical experience. With a functional field such as leadership, the practical aspect must, of course, be stressed more than the theoretical part. Theory usually is not considered to be very important—but that is a faulty assumption. Although theory is only a secondary means of learning, it is a useful one, and the officer has to receive instructions in understanding human behavior. This idea may not be fully accepted as yet, but its acceptance is a necessity and cannot be avoided. The purpose of this instruction is to furnish the basis for developing a general knowledge of people and troops which is so necessary in good leadership. He who wants to lead man must know man.

Before the First World War, the military services relied mostly on practical education. The results at the battlefield were excellent. But, in general, certain things were assumed which, in a longer war, proved not to be applicable because of insufficient psychological schooling. In the Second World War, we had it easier in a certain respect, because we had a strong ideological force,

the "National Socialist," which carried the whole armed forces and the people, as well. But because of this ideological force, military leaders had to assume special responsibilities, and therefore education during the years before the war was of utmost importance.

Teaching has to be impressive and has to be supported by our practical experiences and personal attitudes. Teaching must not consist solely of theory; a teacher should also speak from practical experience to the practical situation. The future officer must be given an accurate impression of the types of people he will come into contact with and how he has to treat them. He has to prepare himself personally for the tremendous differences between an 18-year-old recruit who has just graduated from high school (or has just finished an apprenticeship) and is scared of authority in general, and the soldier who has served on merchant ships or fishing fleets. The 40 or 50 year old has seen all the immoral sides of life and has no illusions left, but he can be a good fighter and even a good soldier if he is treated properly by his officer. The officer has to know that the soldier in the division can judge the officer very accurately and is often able to recognize his weaknesses and peculiarities very well.

The officer has to recognize our national virtues and mistakes, and also those of the enemy. And he must be taught which mistakes to avoid. For example, he must know that he must never talk to people with his hands in his pockets, that he cannot use bodily contact as punishment, that extremely harsh words are just as bad as an overly familiar tone, and that he should never "run after his people," since they do not like to receive overly familiar treatment. At the same time, the officer must make his people feel that the officer cares, and he must let them know that he has to be strict at times for their own good. The officer must know that, in dealing with his subordinates (who for the most part are good people), he must be *strict but fair*—he must treat them with kindness but not excessive lenience. This psychological approach should be taken in naval education, but it has to be supported by practical examples.

On the ship, the graduate must constantly be reminded of the disciplinary rules of his group, of the disciplinary consequences if he breaks them, and especially of the consequences of overconsumption of alcohol. The officer must, finally, also be very clear with himself how he would and how he should behave in difficult situations, when the limits of discipline are being reached. The goal of this instruction is not so much to give him a prescription on how to behave, but, rather, to keep the spirit alive, to prepare him for all kinds of possibilities.

I'd like to quote in this connection Lieutenant Junger, who certainly was not just a theoretician, but also a highly acclaimed "shock troop leader" in the west: "Situations with which we are confronted now we probably always thought impossible. In training, everything always happened in an orderly fashion, so that we did not have enough experience in practical areas to protect us in combat. We did deal theoretically with these things, and it would have been useful had we been instructed in such possibilities during our leadership training, just as much as they trained us in the honor code. We accepted and endured life so we could destroy whole areas for just an idea, and we were not shy about carrying out our orders. But even for that, education is necessary. They should have given us a good portion of practical education on our way, in the strictest sense of the word, as the real war demands it. Certainly the personality decides in critical cases, but there are certain ways to deal with people which one has to know about!"

The older ones among us have it in our blood. Let's see to it that the younger generation gains it, as well. To accomplish this, education for leadership must contain a collection and interpretation of war experiences in regard to leadership and its failures.

I do not remember that, in all my naval training, theoretical leadership was ever coherently taught. In the fall of 1917, "patriotic" instruction was ordered. This was the only attempt to do something for the context of the Navy itself. The necessity to instruct in leadership was not recognized as important, and was soon abandoned—the young officers who taught did not have enough experience, and the older officers did not care enough. In retrospect, I'd like to say that the imperial officer's corps was very good and that the importance of leadership in a long but rather eventless war (for the big battleships, at least) was not recognized. Today, it is best to understand that much had been done for the crews. During peacetime, the service was strongly directed toward competition, and this with great success, by introducing sports, games, lectures, entertainment, music, etc. To a large extent this was done by many voluntarily taking part in such events. During the winter of 1918–19, our internship at Scapaflow made it very clear how necessary, especially in difficult times, a carefully thought-through leadership program is. Fortunately we had in Captain Lieutenant Menche a boss who was gifted in a very special way. The outcome of neglecting leadership education during the First World War became evident only in the years after the war.

In 1918 we experienced a breakdown of discipline. It would be wrong to find excuses or even not to talk about it. The future leaders must know that such things happened, what their causes were, and how one can avoid them. Of course, one should not right away call it a mutiny when disobedience occurs. Also, here one must be realistic. Only practical examples and guidelines can give the *best* insights for future happenings. The book by Ringelnass titled *As a Naval Officer in the World War* was known by every officer. The book deals with detailed experiences in small groups and horrors such as one would never have dreamed of. As distasteful as they are, they can be explained by the fact that the author and some of his comrades were just not the general soldier type, as we were used to seeing, and that the other officers who had to deal with them had no training. Had Ringelnass been recognized for what he was, and had he been used at the right level, he could have been just as useful as he was harmful in his total ignorance of what an officer should be and do. In any case, we tried to conduct our lives within the minesweeping group in Cuxhaven during the winter of 1939–40, and in the treatment of soldiers in general, according to the motto "Never again Ringelnass," and thanks to his book, we succeeded.

It is interesting to note that, when I wrote on these areas in 1929–30, my paper was judged by the authorities, who expressed the opinion that leadership, or the leading of people, is a gift that cannot be learned. Admiral Raeder, however, did agree with me, and he suggested in his detailed position paper about my paper that the *handbook* for leadership, written by my good friend Siegfried Sorge (Class Vii/16) and titled *The Navy Officer as Leader and Educator*, be used. This book recognized and discussed the basic problems of leadership in the Navy. I am sure that this influenced the behavior of our crews, which was outstanding during the Second World War! Navy training played an important part in it. The Naval Academy kept leadership training alive, and its influence was felt in the cooperation among the various classes. There were no selfish interests in the foreground; rather, the troops were teams, were communities with mutual respect, where everyone was known well and respected. This made it possible for the crews to perform on the highest possible plane in regard to leadership.

During the years between the end of the war and the reorganization of the Navy, these leadership problems were discussed by several groups of former Navy officers. They all agreed that the principal task of the naval officer has to be leadership, the leading of people. Basic thoughts on leadership were expressed in the *Studium Generale Navale*, the general study of the Navy, which indicated that the knowledge of the sub-

ject matter of technology alone was not enough, that the officer must make it his goal to be widely educated. The danger in becoming a one-sided specialist was recognized.

During the reorganization of the Navy, a primary need was to create a corps of officers that was productive and generally well educated in regard to the Navy, one that would withstand the demands of the profession. Opposing views between an engineering officer and a line officer should not again come into play. The thrust of education under the leadership of Vice Admiral Werner Erhardt was charged with practical execution of these thoughts by means of the Naval Academy, and the ultimate goal was professionally oriented training with intellectual requirements and standards, resulting in an education that is comparable to a college education. But the most important subject should always be the behavior of the officer toward his subordinates, because he must be prepared to lead them even under the most difficult circumstances; the most important ingredient of all is the realization of mutual respect and human commonalities. This is the basis of our culture and our democracy.

One mark of a leader is the kind of leaders he produces. Therefore, every leader should, to a certain extent, be a teacher. To do this, he needs to be able to teach, which requires a certain knowledge of pedagogy. Of course, we don't want the Navy to be a seminar for teachers, but the officer must know how to conduct good classes, which means to know how to illustrate ideas and successfully teach them to the student. The officer should not, for example, try to force the student, by using military "sharp" methods, to reproduce what he was taught; rather, the officer should use kindness and patience—the qualities we need if we want to teach successfully, and the qualities that often are not present when needed. It is also necessary for an officer to be able to give speeches, which are very helpful in influencing his group. There are not very many great leaders who did not at the right time find the right words. Also, in order to give speeches, an officer must know the guidelines. The U.S. Navy has published a good book on this subject, titled *Writing and Speaking*.

The future officer must be trained to realize that not only a healthy and well-exercised body, but also a well-trained and clearly functioning mind, are prerequisites for a true leader. The academic training, of course, should have been completed on the high school level, but often it seems that it was not. It is surprising that there are cadets [midshipmen] who have difficulty in spelling, that there are young officers who have difficulty expressing their thoughts in writing, not to mention the poor style they use and their less than adequate knowledge in general areas of study. That is a problem. When general education in the high schools does not succeed, then the military must fill those voids. Of course, one does not win wars only with perfect spelling abilities, but poor spelling does show that the particular officer or soldier was not able to master the simple general principles of education. How, then, will he master difficult situations? The ultimate goal in education is the training of the mind, digesting and reproducing thoughts, especially because *wars nowadays are fought and won primarily by the mind and not by manpower*. Therefore, it is important that every good leader be well educated.

A good command of one's mother tongue is a prerequisite for giving orders and transmitting messages and for generally expressing one's self clearly. It is surprising how bad the order- and message-giving ability at many posts is and how difficult many young officers find it to express or reproduce their own war experiences. Their reports are often unclear, for the inability to report in a clear, concise, and complete manner is widespread. All this, as well as practical knowledge for life, schooling has to provide. The officer needs a good working knowledge of history, geography, and language if he wants to be successful and be respected by his troops. How, otherwise, would he inspire his troops or present a good image for them? We do not need

poorly prepared officers. The officer's academic—that is, theoretical—training should not stop when his formal education stops. This is sometimes hard when the war lasts a long time, but, nevertheless, education must be continued. The officer must occupy himself with matters other than those in the daily newspaper, because his mind needs more and his horizon has to keep widening. The better exercised the mind is, the better it can help solve the new problems that a war constantly presents us with. Training the mind saves blood!

Experience and example are essential in the practical education for leadership. Experience, of course, everyone collects by himself, but the superior must provide opportunity for others to do so. If an individual always has to do the same insignificant tasks, without variety, change, or progression, he becomes indifferent and loses the quickness and originality that is necessary in leadership.

Frequent changes within a command are not constructive, and they are to be avoided as much as the military situation will allow. One should even sometimes disregard a more ideal rearrangement if the inner strength of the troops is in question. For the development of a leader's personality, however, it is important for him to have a variety of experiences. Meaningful exchanges between the front and the command posts are valuable. Too long a stay on either post is not good. This is especially difficult in the Navy, because the command posts have to be on land.

The future officer has to be instructed in the simple forms of leadership, such as giving simple commands during exercises and seeing them carried out. It is especially important for future officers to learn how to treat the group they are leading. The superior must exercise patience when failures occur. We need everyone, and therefore we must develop every ability within every person. Some people take longer, but they will be good leaders. It should be noted, however, that an individual's basic character can only be influenced to a certain extent—there are limits. When deficiencies in character become apparent, consequences have to follow clearly and promptly. After the simple task of issuing commands at exercises is mastered, intermediate and more difficult leadership responsibilities can be taught—such as instilling in others independence and a desire to accept responsibility. This, too, must be practiced. Even if a midshipman repeatedly fails in carrying out his orders, a valuable lesson is learned.

It is important for the development of good leadership to allow the future leader to carry out his tasks independently. One should avoid intimidating a subordinate by interfering in his commands to his subordinates. It is important to know that seniors all the way up the chain of command cannot have the knowledge of all the small details of daily exercises. Interference would dampen the joy to serve and diminish the junior's accomplishments. Besides, interferences such as these contain the danger of programming failure, since a subordinate who is always controlled or treated like a child may fail when he has to act quickly and independently or give orders when he is alone and without help.

Moltke said: "The advantage a leader seems to achieve by his constant personal interference with his subordinate is only a superficial one. He only takes on an act that others are supposed to carry out; he disclaims more or less the actions of his subordinate and increases his own tasks properly!" Of course it is important for the senior at all times to *know* what his subordinate is doing. This is necessary to build the complete trust that should exist between senior and subordinate, which is the foundation for a good and ideal fighting community. This is achieved when the subordinate is convinced that the senior does not ask the impossible but leads him to success, and also when the senior is convinced that the subordinate performs on his highest possible level and that he will, in changing situations, independently act in the spirit of the senior. It is especially important for the senior to allow his subordinates to express their opinions freely, even if they are contrary to his own. The correct form, however, must be followed. It is equally important for the given commands to be carried out joyfully once they are given. Complete inner freedom and complete obedience create complete confidence, and this is the most important characteristic for keeping troops together successfully and happily.

A decisive role in the development for leadership is played by the example a senior presents. This is understood, but it deserves to be mentioned. Courage during battle, acceptance of responsibility, self-control, knowledge, politeness, attitude of service, comradeship, modesty, being well dressed, are only a few of the areas in which the leader sets the example. One of the negatives of the otherwise perfect soldier of the Prussian Army is the fact that he takes himself and other things too seriously, which makes life much harder. We southern Germans are in this respect a little luckier, and it is hoped that, in armed forces where all geographic regions are mixed together, a happy medium can be achieved.

I would like to discuss how an officer's experiences on small ships, in peace as well as in war cruises, can affect his performance. The German naval education before the war was largely geared to "acting independently," without, however, neglecting the theoretical part of training. The fleet in Cuxhaven was brought together for a week of training consisting of a series of lectures given mostly by the various chiefs of the fleet, who discussed questions like tactics, weapons, machinery, and the history of the Navy and the nation. The following year was a year of exercises and practice, divided into six-week practical study and exercise periods. The various minesweeping methods were tried out and practiced with changing commands. Besides formal drills, there were also exercises in torpedo tactics. Make-believe battles were fought, and this was very useful in the education of the senior officers with regard to tactics. These educational practices were proven correct during the war. Also, the younger officers have carried out their tasks well. They successfully carried out small minesweeping operations and battled the British successfully in the Channel. The well-functioning young officers attribute their success to their knowledge of sailing. During peacetime, the officers were trained for strong war leadership: the officers lived together with the crew on board of a ship, so that they got to know the men they would later lead. In addition, the young officers were practically trained by the captains and fleet commanders. A big peacetime problem was caused by the fleet not being used enough. The older generation of the reserve proved to have had excellent training, but the younger officers did not have the proper attitude to be officers. We had to be strict and enforce the rules. The main danger for the young officers is the alcohol, of which there is so much available.

Small units, therefore, need strict guidance that nevertheless does not hamper their relative independence. This, of course, means a lot of work in the upper leadership group in order to develop a leader's personality to be able to meet challenges of all kinds while not blindly carrying out all orders.

What a nation lacks in material goods, it must make up for with moral superiority. That is especially important in the Navy, which is built on a small foundation. This means that more is expected of a naval officer than of others. In order to stand tall, we have to develop positive personality traits as far as we can. Therefore, education for leadership in regard to troop command is the most important of all—and it is also the most beautiful of tasks.

The reader is directed to the Bibliography at the end of each chapter, as well as to the Recommended Readings at the end of chapter 10, for books and articles that complement the foregoing thoughts of Admiral Ruge. There are many theories of leadership, and the application of these theories varies, depending on whether they are applied in the industrial, government, or military arenas. Some books present the theory and allow readers to develop their own approaches. In this text, it is our aim to convey the operational experience learned over many years by senior naval officers. In the course of studying this material, readers will be able to develop their own theories of leadership and determine how these theories might work in the environment for which readers are being prepared and/or within which they operate: the world of the naval officer.

PROFESSOR OF LEADERSHIP KAREL MONTOR, PH.D., USNA
CAPTAIN THOMAS M. MCNICHOLAS, JR., USN
LIEUTENANT COLONEL ANTHONY J. CIOTTI, JR., USMC
LIEUTENANT COMMANDER THOMAS H. HUTCHINSON III, USNR
JACKIE ECKHART WEHMUELLER

Naval Leadership

1

The Parameters of Leadership and Management in the Naval Service

Introduction

In an address to the cadets of the United States Military Academy, President Harry S. Truman defined leadership as "that quality which can make other men do what they do not want to do and like it."

In other words, leadership is held to be the management of men by inspiration and persuasion rather than by direct or implied threat of force.

I personally believe that the majority of leaders are developed—not born. This belief has been confirmed by example in many individuals whom I have observed during my years of service in the Marine Corps.

Throughout your service careers, continually strive to cultivate leadership not only in yourselves, but in those over whom you may be placed, as you advance in your future careers.

During my service as a senior officer, I had frequent occasion to consider the need for men of ability to fill important positions in the higher ranks of the Marine Corps. It is difficult to analyze a successful leader, isolate his qualities and extract the attributes which, added together, explain his success as a military commander.

Over the years I came to the conclusion that most of the qualities which great military men—certainly those who have been successful leaders of American troops—have shown can be characterized by professional competence, human understanding, and sterling character.

In briefly discussing these qualities, let us first consider professional knowledge. A leader in any field must be well versed in his profession.

Yet, knowledge can be cold, academic, and unproductive of the inspiration which provides real leadership. No effective leader has ever reached greatness by intellect alone. Intellectual achievements must be accompanied by an understanding of the human individual, for, in the final analysis, he works with people.

In addition to human understanding and professional competence, the leader must also possess character. Character in my opinion is the greatest of man's virtues. It is a distinctive trait that governs an individual's patterns of behavior and is indicative of moral strength.

The question has been posed: Can the possession of these qualities of leadership be discerned in a young midshipman? Perhaps not with certainty, but there is one indication: the capacity for growth. Studies of our understanding commanders—the ones who have risen to the top—show that many of them did not stand at the head of their class.

Many had undistinguished careers as students. Some of these officers were slow in starting, but they were sure and steady in their progress. They were men who never ceased to grow and expand. Their minds were constantly reaching out as their experiences increased.

I believe this capacity to grow is a most important factor in leadership, although difficult to identify in your midshipman days. Hence, no midshipman should conclude in a moment of discouragement that he cannot rise to the top of the naval profession. To be a slow starter may not be a sign of weakness but rather an indication of latent power.

Since I am a realist, I am fully aware that all individuals do not possess equal qualities of leadership; nor can every midshipman become Chief of Naval Operations or Commandant of the Marine Corps.

However, all midshipmen who graduate from the United States Naval Academy and are commissioned in the Naval Service should become enthusiastic Navy or Marine officers dedicated to their profession.

The great military leaders of our country were men of character, ability, and dedication. They were motivated by the most noble and selfless of all emotions: love of country. Their dedication to duty in times of stress made possible the cre-

ation of this nation. In the past, each generation has proven itself worthy of this heritage.

I am confident that the midshipman of today will likewise be inspired to live up to the traditions established by past leaders of our nation, and will zealously devote their best efforts to the discharge of their inherent duties as officers of the United States Navy and Marine Corps. I can assure you it will be most rewarding.

GENERAL LEMUEL C. SHEPHERD, JR.,
USMC (RET.)
20th Commandant of the Marine Corps

As the Preface to this book states, the areas of leadership discussed herein were considered by twenty-seven hundred officers of the various military services to form the basis for effective leadership. More than one hundred senior officers who are now leading or have in the past led the nations of England, France, Germany, Japan, and the United States have conveyed their thoughts on leadership. Officers of the Naval Service come into contact with people of many nationalities; therefore, it will not be surprising to find that the phraseology and terminology used by some of these officers differs from that used in the United States. Reading these officers' thoughts as they expressed them is considered a positive experience for the reader, who will meet people of many other nations and cultures during a military career. The many individuals who contributed to this book come from very different backgrounds, but the approach to leadership that emerges transcends both geographical and philosophical boundaries. It is the purpose of this text to help all officers establish a personal style of leadership based on the thoughts of successful leaders who have preceded them.

1. Successful Leadership

Only after reading this book and learning from years of experience will the junior officer be ready for higher command; however, we all must start somewhere. There is no magical approach to leadership, no shortcut to the top, but if it were possible to sum up leadership in a single sentence, this statement by General W. H. Rice, USMC, which echoes centuries of leaders, would do so: "Know yourself, know your troops, and know your job!" You are advised to observe leaders, both officers and enlisted; you will find that all good leaders share certain patterns and certain traits, and, conversely, that some leaders make mistakes that you should avoid in your own career.

Admiral Robert Long, USN, in discussing how a selection board works, notes:

Overall the entire promotion system of the military is fair and equitable in the long run, about as fair as it is humanly possible to make it. I have been on several selection boards in my career, and, looking back on those experiences, I'd say it is relatively easy to pick out the top performers and essentially eliminate what we used to call on the selection board "the pack." You'd say, "An officer is in the pack," meaning that an officer is sort of a run-of-the-mill, mark-one officer, though those officers have a fair chance of promotion in time up through commander.

Someone has said of my career, "You must have had all this planned ahead of time." I can quite honestly say that I was somewhat surprised every time I received another star, pleased, but somewhat surprised. I also during my career never consciously asked for any specific assignment, other than I wanted assignments that rotated me from sea duty to some challenging shore job (and that normally meant Washington, but not always) and then back to sea. But some officers plot and plan for years: they want to get this particular job or they want to be that officer's aide. My advice would be that an officer seek demanding jobs, because those demanding jobs are known to the selection board. Seek demanding jobs, try to do well in those jobs, and play it like you're going to stay in the military for at least thirty years, and then whatever happens I think that officer would be prepared for higher rank. Also, if the officer would elect to leave the service, those are good habits.

Field Marshall Bernard Montgomery, of British army fame, had good advice on how to pursue leadership: "Get your major purpose clear, take off your plate all which hinders that purpose and hold hard to all that helps it, and then go ahead with a clear conscience, courage, sincerity, and selflessness."[2-14]*

A junior officer in today's Naval Service wears many hats. Depending on the officer's assignment, background, and training, the officer may have one major job with minor collateral duties or a primary job and several collateral duties. Either way, the junior officer must manage time to be able to concentrate on several major areas: first, being a leader of the unit (which can be made up of any number between 5 and 150); second, being a manager of both equipment and personnel; third, being a counselor to those in the unit; and, finally, developing the officer's own professional growth, not only within a specialty, but generally as well.

*Footnotes refer to the Bibliography at the end of the chapter. The first number is the number of the source, and the second number indicates the page being cited within that source.

DEVELOPMENT OF A LEADERSHIP STYLE

Leadership is the key to a productive unit, whether it is a radio shack on a frigate, a missile division on a *Trident*-class submarine, or a squad on a night deployment. Creating conditions that motivate troops (including senior enlisted), giving decisive commands, being available to answer questions, and setting an example in dress and demeanor, all are keys to being an effective leader and, in turn, a good officer.

Rear Admiral Jack Darby, who has served as commander of submarine forces in the Pacific and as the Commandant of Midshipmen at the Naval Academy, once pointed out that new officers will be exposed to many types of leaders and many different leadership styles. He explained that observation is an excellent way for new officers to develop their own style. He suggested that individuals carry two imaginary bags, one for acceptable styles and one for unacceptable styles. After graduation and the early years of duty, young officers can reach into the "good" bag, and not use the material in the "bad" one, which, though unused, will not be forgotten. In this way, junior officers will be sure not to develop the styles of leadership they find to be unsuitable or with which they are uncomfortable.

MANAGEMENT OF MATERIAL AND PERSONNEL

Management of material and personnel is another critical area of duty for an officer. Good management, in concert with effective leadership, is the mark of an excellent officer who is a valuable asset to the Naval Service.

Young officers need to understand that when they first report to a unit, they will not know everything about the equipment. While Navy schools are excellent, all graduates of Navy schools are not experts. One ensign who was the communicator on board a *Trident*-class submarine reported that his new duty station was like a spaceship to him. Only after studying for many hours and asking many questions did he understand the ship's abilities and, more important, its place in the operation of the command.

What some young officers fail to understand is that part of their duty as leaders and managers is to listen to the advice of their enlisted members, especially the senior chief or sergeant. These individuals understand the inner workings of the equipment and procedural operations, and they can be at least as helpful as a technical or administrative manual. Asking them questions and watching them operate is as much a duty of an officer as completing assignments on time. Senior enlisted understand the service, including the promotion and selection process, and they have seen many examples of success and failure. The officer who listens to advice in everything from leave requests to school dates will find that the unit or division runs more smoothly, as officer and enlisted keep each other informed.

The pride that individuals have in the unit will often be evident in their willingness to talk about its capabilities, thus providing a ready source of information for the officer. Like officers, enlisted personnel have collateral duties and can help an officer in specific areas, such as repair parts and publications. The officer who takes the time to ask questions and learn from enlisted personnel will be a more competent officer.

As officers become more senior, the scope of their collateral duties will increase. They may be assigned as the public affairs officer, the intelligence officer, the training officer, and so on, and each duty entails staff work. Checking the weekly and monthly maintenance records, completing weekly destruction reports, or following through on submitted requisitions in the supply system are part of staff work. To complete staff work, an officer has to take the time to check the details, from spelling and grammar to the accuracy of instructions. The officer must also issue follow-up reports to seniors to answer their questions. Checking to make sure that paper work is complete, and persevering to follow it all the way through, are important parts of an officer's duty.

KNOWLEDGE OF AND ASSISTANCE TO TROOPS

Knowledge of troops. To be an effective leader and manager of people, an officer must do some homework. A commanding officer of one unit once asked all the officers at Officers' Call if they knew the names of their subordinates' spouses . . . of their subordinates' children . . . or of the commands the personnel had been at previously. The commanding officer also asked whether the officers had recently looked at each division member's jacket and pointed out to that individual anything that may have been missing. Getting to know people *as people* is vital to the success of the unit and the officer.

Admiral David McDonald, former American Chief of Naval Operations (CNO) points out that there is a significant adjustment difference between operations aboard ship and

shore-based operations in that, with the exception of religious orders, there is no other profession where individuals not only work together but live together. The term *shipmate* means so much. You work with others, you eat next to them, you establish a camaraderie, and then of course you learn that the most important thing is how to get along with others. Whether you agree on social and political issues or not, you can still get along, and that's a very important lesson to learn.

Understanding how enlisted members get promoted is another duty of an officer, who must secure an explanation from seniors as to how the promotion and advancement system works and how enlisted members communicate with those who determine their assignments. Understanding programs for potential officers which become available to enlisted members is also important. It is an officer's duty to help subordinates and to discuss with them their logical alternatives as well as to refer them to the command career counselor. When an officer shows an interest in a subordinate and the subordinate's family, the subordinate is likely to be a happier and more productive member of the Naval Service.

Counseling. An officer's duties in counseling are many. If the officer listens and shows interest when a member of the unit has a professional or personal problem, the officer is contributing greatly to keeping the unit operating. Of course, this does not mean that the officer should try to take the place of the chaplain or the doctor. But when subordinates need immediate assistance, an officer should listen to them. Sometimes the openness of someone in authority is all that is necessary to make a person's burden seem lighter. On this theme, it is imperative that a division officer understand naval programs such as Navy Relief and the Drug and Alcohol Counseling System. When a subordinate has a problem, the officer should be prepared to tell that person where to go for help. The nearest Family Service Center and the local chapter of Alcoholics Anonymous can be invaluable.

It should be made clear to the person who comes to the officer that the officer will do everything possible to help the person. When someone is scared or needs legal assistance or a plane ticket to fly home because of a death in the family, the officer must remain calm and try to help as much as possible. Before an enlisted member starts to explain a problem, the first question out of the officer's mouth should be "Have you talked to the chief?" Keeping the chief informed in situations like this will pay big dividends later.

Keeping others informed. Along with showing interest in the careers of personnel, a good division officer supports and uses the chain of command. Keeping seniors and subordinates informed is vital to a smooth operation. An example is the situation that presents itself to the officer of the deck on a ship that is underway when a piece of gear breaks. It is that officer's duty to let the department head and chief know what has happened. Chances are the chief already knows and, if necessary, is trouble-shooting the problem down in the spaces or lending assistance to the first class. Assuming a noncatastrophic failure, the officer of the deck will inform the department head before calling the captain, as the department head is responsible and will want to be ready for a meeting with the captain, either immediately or the next morning at breakfast. A division officer must realize that keeping the department head informed is more important than letting the department head sleep.

As one navigator put it to a communicator on a *Trident*-class submarine, "It is your job to let me know when something goes out of control any time of the day or night. Uncle [Sam] pays me for 24 hours a day, 7 days a week, 365 days a year, and I need to know." The navigator went on to explain that the department head must have all necessary information so the department head can be ready for daily meetings with the executive officer (XO) or be ready to answer questions from the supply officer. Information allows the officer to update the equipment status report. Just as a division officer is responsible for the division, the department head is responsible to the captain for the way the department is operating. Any change in status needs to be flagged immediately.

PROFESSIONAL GROWTH

An officer has important duties that are self-concerned. Professional growth is indispensable to the success of an officer and the Naval Service in general. Professional growth is achieved by going above and beyond the qualification cards. An incredible amount of important information can be learned about torpedo systems, for example, by an officer who conducts a simple question-and-answer session with a watch stander. It is a good idea for an officer of the deck (OD), during an after-watch tour, to learn something new. (An after-watch tour takes place after the OD is relieved; in it, the relieved OD tours the ship one last time to allow an experienced "eye" to look for anything unusual.) Whether the ship is a patrol hydrofoil or a *Trident*-class submarine, there is always something new to learn.

Officers can profitably spend time assimilating information about the way various opponents operate. One can never know too much about potential enemies. Countless intelligence publications describe everything from air tactics to the range of the enemy's weapons. Surface warfare officers can study the enemy's identification characteristics; a submariner, the enemy's acoustic signature; and Marines, the enemy's battle tactics.

By questioning things, an officer will become more competent, make the organization more efficient, and make the Naval Service stronger. This does not mean questioning every report or every piece of information received. However, the officer who asks a sonar technician to explain how sonar can separate the different types of machinery used by trawlers or merchants will be in the sonar compartment for hours. The information is there; the officer just has to dig for it.

These, then, are the major areas in which an officer in today's Naval Service has responsibilities. The officer has many other duties, as well. The attractive thing about the military profession is that the job is varied and never boring. There is always a contact to dodge, a report to write, or a qualification card to complete.

The foregoing discussion, and the rest of this book, is intended to prepare the officer for a first assignment. There is generally more than one acceptable approach to preventing mishaps and solving problems, and officers should be deliberate in developing a style that will meet the goals and follow the directions indicated by their seniors. The end result will be a rewarding career for a great nation.

A few final thoughts about word usage are in order here. The reader will note that up to this point there has been a scrupulous avoidance of the words *his* and *her* in the general discussion of an officer's duties, actions, and responsibilities. This is so because we want to recognize that both men and women have contributed and continue to contribute to the military service. Most books use the words *he* or *his* in describing the roles of officers and enlisted, and sometimes this creates the impression that only men contribute to their country. Women such as Medal of Honor winner Mary E. Walker and Rear Admiral Fran McKee (whose words are quoted herein) are among the legion of women who have also served their country.

Both male and female officers serve in the Navy and the Marine Corps, and therefore both sexes are represented by examples in this book. *He* and *his* are often used, in our current culture, to indicate men and women. We believe this facilitates communication. However, it must be remembered that this usage is *still* changing. Because leadership includes making decisions, it will not seem unusual for us to make a decision early on in this book. Therefore, wherever the words *he* or *his* appear, the reader is asked to remember that *she* and *her* are implied.

Master Chief Petty Officer of the Navy Billy C. Sanders, formerly the number-one enlisted person in the Navy, provides officers with the view of the enlisted community on the points made herein. Enlisted people are the people you will lead. If you want them to follow you, it is highly recommended that you heed MCPON Sanders's remarks, which appear at the end of many of the sections of this book.

2. The Basis of Leadership

PERSONAL EXAMPLE

The father of our Navy, John Paul Jones, gives us a good start in understanding the requirements of effective naval leadership. Jones's words on leadership have become hallowed, and rightly so:

He [a leader] should be the soul of tact, patience, justice, firmness, and charity. No meritorious act of a subordinate should escape his attention or be left to pass without its reward, even if the reward is only a word of approval. Conversely, he should not be blind to a single fault in any subordinate, though, at the same time, he should be quick and unfailing to distinguish error from malice, thoughtlessness from incompetency, and well-meant shortcoming from heedless or stupid blunder.[54-22]

John Paul Jones wrote of the need for naval officers to be gentlemen as well as mariners. To a gentleman, courtesy (tact) and honor are of paramount importance.

For Field Marshal Montgomery, leadership involved "the capacity and will to rally men and women to a common purpose, and the character which will inspire confidence."[44-10]

There are very few traits that can be found in all successful leaders, but proper personal example is one such trait. In their responsibility to set a good personal example, leaders are on duty 24 hours a day. People in charge must constantly be aware of their actions as they relate to leadership. It is noteworthy that, at the Battle of Trafalgar, only 6 of Admiral Nelson's 30 captains had previously served with him, but his enthusiasm spread to all, with great result.[32-67]

Assistant Secretary of Defense James Webb believes that

a leader who does not have the respect of his people, whose people do not believe  he is operating from a system of values, will find that his words are considered meaningless by the people he is leading. If the individual lacks credibility, his leadership will be ineffective. Furthermore, an individual who cannot accept responsibility for his own acts cannot even begin to be a leader.

Whether he is a squad leader or the nation's president, a leader must always follow certain principles. One of them is knowledge—knowledge of the subject matter of his leadership, knowledge of the individuals he is serving and the individuals who are serving him, knowledge of human motivation. A leader must also develop a strong character, including moral responsibility. A leader who has character displays absolute integrity on the issues that surround his unit's mission, as well as humility before his subordinates. Character involves courage—not just physical courage, but also moral courage, which involves being able to face an issue and be unyielding if that issue involves principle.

Another principle of leadership is that every individual must develop a style of leadership that suits his own personality. Patton couldn't be Bradley, and Bradley couldn't be Patton, and if either of them had tried to be the other, he would have failed as a leader. Leadership also requires vision. A leader must be able to see where he wants to take the people he is leading.

A leader who follows all of these principles—knowledge, character, personal style, and vision—will be an effective leader, whether he is tying together 3 or 236 million people. But he must first convince his people that he embodies the principles they respect. Personal example is the primary way to illustrate this. For the President of the United States or an admiral, many of the demonstrations of personal example are symbolic. Many of the things he chooses to do are meant to send a signal to his people concerning his beliefs and feelings. In hostile situations, personal example often means that the

officer must not ask his people to assume risks that he personally would not assume, and in many cases the officer must be willing to assume more of a risk just to demonstrate to them that he has the credibility to give them the orders that are required.

Poor followers are poorly led. When there is a problem with morals, appearance, performance, or a hundred other indicators, the culprit is very often at the top. Even if the commanding officer (CO) has the expectation for excellence, excellence will not be a reality as long as the CO sets a poor example. The leader who is in the habit of demanding sacrifices from followers but is unwilling to suffer the same hardships personally will soon be in charge of an ineffective, unmotivated mob. If a unit is having a problem with personal appearance and grooming, the boss needs to have the shiniest shoes, the best haircut, and the sharpest uniform in the outfit. The leader who is unkempt, overweight, or sloppy has no right to expect more than that from the troops.

Two quotes worthy of mention in this regard are: "Respect yourself and others will respect you" (Confucius) and "First find the man in yourself if you will inspire manliness in others."[41-144]

Some leaders lose sight of the fact that example is a vital element of leadership. Because leadership is a full-time job, leaders let down a little now and then. This is inevitable, because all leaders—indeed, all people—are subject to the stresses of life. But how much they let down, where they let down, and with whom they let down is all-important. Timing is everything.

Thus, officers should strive to set a good example for those they lead. They should live up to their own expectations and abide by their own standards. They should not demand from others what they do not demand of themselves. Admiral Teiji Nakamura, former Japanese CNO, comments that he believes that

personal example is the most vital factor in leadership, although a commander can't

be assured of constant success through personal example only. Personal example, of course, does not mean that the leader serves as a role model for the jobs performed by subordinates. The higher the level of the commander, the more different the content of his task is from the content of his subordinates' tasks. Still, the commander who does his best to execute his tasks, volunteers for difficult assignments, and, particularly, is unselfish is setting the most desirable personal example. His sincerity in wishing to share his fate and lot with subordinates is certain to be felt in their hearts.

An old Chinese teaching for rulers says, "You should concern yourself with the future of the people before they begin to do so and should seek your own pleasure only after the people are assured of their happiness." This applies to commanders. An officer should never rest before his subordinates, whenever they are attending to tasks ordered by him, even in cases when he cannot take the lead.

The more severe the battle, the more important the personal example. A commander should stand at the head of his subordinates when he is forced to throw them into the jaws of death because of operational necessity. Even if his overall mission prevents him from being at the head, he is required to have the resolution and preparedness to follow his subordinates as soon as the situation permits. If he lacks this resolution, he should not order them to execute such a dangerous task; if he does, success can never be expected.

One of the reasons why Admiral Isoroku Yamamoto obtained the profound confidence of officers and men of the Combined Fleet was that he always had such resolve, which was felt by his subordinates.

Admiral Paul de Bigault de Cazanove, former French Commandant Chief of the Atlantic Theater, sums it up with these words:

The officer must not be of the type who says others should do one thing, and he does the opposite. Your personal example is the best teaching you can give to others. You need to know your profession, for personal example means far more than appearance and capability. It means inspiring others by your example to do more than they otherwise would have attempted.

MORAL RESPONSIBILITY

Few characteristics of leadership are as difficult to define and yet as important as moral responsibility. Webster defines *moral* as "relating to principles of right and wrong in behavior." In *Command at Sea, moral* means what is *right*, considering: integrity, sense of duty, and obligation to one's country.[41-143] History is replete with examples of what results when a leader fails to take moral responsibility; often the penalties for unethical behavior are severe. Unfortunately, the adage "You rate what you get away with" will be around for a very long time, unless officers take a stand.

Admiral de Cazanove suggests that
you cannot live in two different worlds, but rather must meet the same standards in both your personal and your professional life, for without a high sense of

9

moral responsibility, you will negate everything you may have achieved by your personal example in other areas.

A sense of right and wrong must be instilled in leaders from the outset. A leader who has a reputation for doing the right thing without regard to personal consequences will be followed. An officer who develops a reputation for being morally weak and always taking the most expedient route will find that his ability to lead is severely handicapped. An officer must consistently do the right thing, even if this is not always easy. At times leaders must make decisions that will be unpopular. At times the course of action a leader chooses may seem unreasonable to others. But the leader cannot be dissuaded from what he knows to be right. The greatest form of cowardice is to know what is right and not do it.

To illustrate, imagine that you are the XO of a ship and enlisted advancement results have just arrived. Those who have earned advancement are frocked to their new rate with all of the appropriate fanfare and ceremony. Among them is a young, newly frocked second-class petty officer. His family attended the ceremony and is extremely proud of his accomplishment. One week later, your first-class personnelman comes to see you with a very sad look on his face. He informs you that there was an error on that second-class petty officer's paper work and that, instead of making the cut by less than one point, he has actually missed advancement by that amount. You ask who knows about this situation, and the personnelman says just the two of you know. If you say nothing, life goes on as before. If you make your findings known, the young petty officer and his family are devastated, and the command gets a bad name. It's your move—what do you do? You know what is right. Despite the pain it may cause, you have to make the right decision. If you do not, *you* will know that you have done something wrong, and the *personnelman* will know that you have done something wrong.

Moral responsibility and ethics can be viewed as a pyramid. With a solid base, it is very sturdy and would be difficult to topple. If the officer allows it to happen, however, that base can be chipped away over time. At first it is small things, but the officer becomes desensitized to this sort of activity, and gradually infractions escalate by degree. Before long, travel claims are being falsified, thus cheating the government during permanent change of station (PCS) moves, or maintenance records are doctored in order for a division to pass an inspection. Soon the ethical pyramid is unstable, and it may topple at any time.

Unquestionably, there are times when being ethical is more difficult. Ultimately, however, the officer has to make a completely personal choice and live with that choice and himself. The pyramid can become stronger, or it can topple.

Admiral Nakamura sees "moral responsibility from two standpoints, one as a person and one as a commander."

In the personal context, moral responsibility includes an individual being aware of his actions based upon his conscience or social standard of morality, even though he is not strictly accountable for that action by law or regulations. For example, General Maresuke Nogi once lost his regimental color in a battle when he was a regimental commander. Though he was not prosecuted because the authorities judged the situation unavoidable, he felt his moral responsibility for that incident deeply throughout his life, and this feeling became the decisive factor in all of his actions.

A commander should shoulder moral responsibility for all operations and administration under his command and also for the guidance, supervision, personnel administration, and welfare of all his subordinates. As his level of command becomes higher, a commander needs to delegate his authority to his subordinates and, accordingly, put the primary responsibility on them. But never does this mean that the responsibility of the original commander has been canceled. Power can be delegated, but responsibility cannot be.

Legal responsibility is regulated by law. Whether stipulated or not, the legal responsibility of the original commander to guide and supervise the subordinate commanders to whom he has delegated authority exists all the time, and all moral responsibility, including the selection of appropriate commanders and the suitability of the delegation, remains with him.

Both personally and in leadership, legal responsibility indicates the minimum requirement; what is required further is the moral responsibility, the level of which differs according to one's sense of morality or the moral standard of contemporary society.

Generally speaking, it can be said that the higher the level of moral responsibility, the better the armed forces. Taking this concept too far, however, can lead to ill-advised attitudes and actions. The harsh dealing with prisoners of war in the old Japanese armed forces and the precept that a captain of the Japanese Navy must go down with his ship are examples.

So it is important to remain moderate, while enforcing the standards set. In other words, it might be good to add special considerations to the specific characteristics of the fighting force to make its standards more severe than the standards generally accepted by contemporary society.

General Louis Wilson, Medal of Honor holder and former Commandant of the Marine Corps (CMC), explained how he reconciles the conflicts imposed by being a moral individual who must fight fiercely to destroy an enemy.

I believe in the Ten Commandments and in a higher being, and I'm not trying

to get religion involved in this, but in life there are adversary relationships. When a child is born there may be an adversary relationship with the mother, there are adversary relationships between siblings in the family, there are adversary relationships when a child goes to school—competition and striving for advantage—so it is in a town, community, state, and nation. Therefore, why should we think that somehow after we get beyond this that conflict will stop? War is nothing but an extension of failure of political discussion.

At each level there is an increasing use of lethal weapons. Lethal weapons being on the one hand sticks with children, and on the larger scale the destruction of a nation's economic condition with striving for advantage by certain nations. Our business is that we understand conflict and we take an oath that we will protect our country and not make policy. This started in the city states in the earliest times, when people with capability and a willingness to band together to protect the cities got together while the cities were going after economical and agricultural pursuits. This has expanded to what it is today, and so in fact, if our country, which we believe in, is attacked, or if it's in the interest of our country, up to a point, that we do this, then our killing is a logical extension of our need to prevail in war.

GOOD LEADERSHIP REQUIRES GOOD MANAGEMENT

A successful organization is usually well managed; management is an integral part of leadership. Usually leadership cannot succeed without well-executed management, and successful officers must be competent in both their managerial and their other leadership skills.

While doing the right things and requiring the same of subordinates is important, this is not in itself the secret of success. The naval officer's job must also be done efficiently, effectively, on time, and within budget, and using personnel properly so that they are not diverted from more pressing or important assignments. General Montgomery said that men are more likely to follow a leader whom they feel is competent than one who is considered incompetent. However, General Montgomery also said that a leader must exhibit enthusiasm, confidence, determination to persevere, a knowledge of human nature, and self-control.[44-11]

The leader must remember that a division on a ship or a squad in a company is no more important than the larger unit, and, furthermore, that it cannot be successful at the unit level unless all possible efforts have been made to ensure that the larger unit has received all the help the subordinate unit can offer. An individual cannot be considered successful, and a unit cannot consider itself successful, if the parent organization is in trouble. Thus, when an officer finds that his unit has taken every action necessary to be successful, his next responsibility is to offer help to the next higher unit or to a lateral unit. The officer should determine whether the overall unit will work better if he lends personnel or takes on some of the responsibilities of the other organization. For example, a division officer might well help out another division officer to ensure that the overall mission of the department is accomplished.

Admiral Arleigh Burke, former American CNO, described his relationship with his driver, Hamilton.

> We'd be alone lots of times, and I usually read when we went back and forth, but every once in a while I'd talk a little bit, and he'd give me a hint that some-

thing was wrong in the way things were going. He would hear about something wrong, and I'd check into it. It was, and I'd tell him about it— "We found something cockeyed"— and thank him for it. He was the most humble man I've ever known and he meant it. It wasn't one of these false things. That man taught me an awful lot about human nature. He was very good with people. I didn't want to lose my ability to drive a car, so every once in a while I'd put him in the back seat. I'd get up and drive the car. One time we went to Quantico, and I went in the gate, of course, I said, "Hamilton, put my cap on." "Oh no, Sir," and I said, "Damn it," and we went through and it went fine. He was very much embarrassed about it; he said, "Admiral, you can't drive this car unless you promise me," and I said, "All right, I won't go through any more sentries."

> But he'd tell me about people, and he never told me anything bad about anyone in his whole life, I mean, he just couldn't do that. He would tell me about the situation that was bad, and it was up to me to find out who was behind it or what was behind it, not him. But when people were in trouble he would let me know. Humility is a great asset and there's not enough of it around.

In the modern Naval Service, management skills are more important than they were in the past. It is no longer possible to manage from a "wheel" book or from the back of an envelope. Today's officers grind out POA&Ms (Plans of Action and Milestones), cost-benefit analyses, decision theories, and personnel productivity and efficiency studies—to name just a few. Management by Objectives, the One-Minute Manager, and others claim to be the best approach to management. Management guidelines, formulas, tricks, and regimens abound, and they are fine as far as they go. But a naval officer must be a leader in addition to being a top-notch manager. To Admiral Nakamura, "good management, in the military, means conducting all jobs relating to the preparation and support of the fighting strength of the combat force effectively and efficiently, with an aim to contribute to that strength." Admiral Nakamura believes that, to achieve good management, we should take care to do the following.

1. Make efficient use of limited resources (men, money, material, time, etc.).
2. Design the cycling of the job (organization, planning, execution, examination of the results, and improvement) suitably and effectively. In particular, it is important to design a cycle that is appropriate and will facilitate the execution of the task.
3. Use good judgment concerning the ordering of task priorities.

The merits of leadership and the merits of management could be discussed at great length. Clearly, what is needed is a balance of both approaches to mission accomplishment. The person who is too far along the management scale tends to concentrate on the mission and not enough on the people, while the leader who cannot accomplish the mission is of limited value to the organization. The effective leader/manager does not lose sight of either the mission or the crew.

An overemphasis on management in the Naval Service could lead to the development of good managers at the expense of developing good leaders. The organization must not swing toward "bottom-line" mentality, wherein the end justifies any means. The payoff, in this approach, may be the largest number of inspections successfully completed, the best retention figures,

and the greatest number of underway days. All these are viable goals for a naval officer, but how the officer attains them is critical.

These goals, even during time of war, cannot be attained without regard to the human element in the management/leadership equation. Personnel must believe that the unit's leader cares about them as individuals. This does not mean that an officer must demonstrate genuine concern for the welfare and advancement of the crew by pampering them; however, Nelson was known to pay especially great attention to the health of his midshipmen, and it is often said that he ruled by love instead of fear.[32-68]

It is in the area of welfare of personnel that leadership and management may be at odds. A naval officer who is long on management skills and short on leadership abilities may attain the bottom-line results, but at a great human price. Working conditions under such officers may be intolerable, because the troops are regarded as machines. This attitude may be successful in the short run, but in the long run, it will prove disastrous and take its toll on the troops.

TACT, DEPENDABILITY, AND A SENSE OF HUMOR

Tact. The officer quickly learns that subordinates will acknowledge the senior's rank by showing deference, but what is desired is that all hands do everything possible to support the mission of the unit, which in turn supports the ship or regiment, which in turn supports the Naval Service and the country. It is all well and good for officers to know what they are doing and convey that to subordinates, but they must do so in a way that tells subordinates that they are seen as part of a team, and not as slaves who must carry out the will of the most senior individual. For their part, juniors would do well to note an anecdote of Admiral McDonald, who related that

a senior officer told him that he might be the dumbest officer of his rank in the Navy, but if he was, maybe he couldn't help being dumb, maybe he was born that way. But—he said—even though he might be the dumbest, he knew that he was the most polite officer of his rank and even a dumbbell could be polite, and he hoped that I'd never forget this.

The best rule of thumb for dealing with seniors is the Third Law of the Navy: "Beware what you say of your seniors. Be your words spoken softly and plain. Lest a bird of the air tell the matter, and so shall ye hear it again."[54-39]

Admiral Nakamura defined *tact* this way:

I would say that the basis for acting with tact requires being able to read the feelings or thoughts of other people and trying to think as they do. Being tactful requires avoiding delicate subjects and expressions that might be offensive to others. Tact should never be an excuse for lying or cheating, except on the battlefield against the enemy.

The purpose of being tactful is to facilitate an individual's role as an officer serving his country, military service, and unit. Tact should never be used for the purpose of enhancing one's career or for other self-interested purposes.

General Wilson suggests that tact is something that sometimes is misunderstood and misused.

It doesn't mean that you should never reprimand subordinates, of course, but it means, I believe, that you should not reprimand subordinates in front of their juniors or in front of their seniors. They should be reprimanded in private and praised in public. I think that tact embodies those terms.

When a subordinate who has been making an honest effort makes a mistake, the officer must take action to avoid repetition of the mistake, and he must do so in a manner that will not affect initiative, effort, or quality. When a subordinate makes a mistake, then, the matter must be handled with tact. The senior must make it clear that it was a particular action of the subordinate, and not the subordinate, that created a problem. The senior may indicate displeasure with a particular action but should not indicate that the person is not liked as an individual. The individual who made the mistake has probably already spoken harshly to himself, if he is a dedicated individual, and thus the senior may only need to provide feedback on how to avoid the problem in the future. It has been said that tact is the unsaid part of what you think.

Admiral de Cazanove feels that

it is more important now than it was years or centuries ago that people at all levels of command be treated as human beings. You must show your consideration for all people, and act toward them as you would want them to act toward you. While it may be difficult at times, if you are tactful and polite, you can say almost anything to anyone. You must give your opinion as to whether something is good or bad, and if you do so with consideration for the listener, your message will be appreciated, even though the person may not like what he hears you saying.

Dependability. Admiral Nakamura suggests that

the primary factor in classifying an officer as dependable or not is his sincerity. An officer who is unselfish and honest, does not embellish the truth, and tries to accomplish his mission by giving his best is dependable and useful, even if he has some obvious faults. It is possible to guide him to offset his faults or to give him a post that is most suitable for his merits.

On the other hand, an officer who does not report matters unfavorable to himself, patches up the truth for the moment, and plays both ends against the middle can neither be dependable nor work together with others, regardless of his many merits.

Admiral de Cazanove makes the point that

you have to be yourself and not completely rely on others. In dealing with seniors as well as with subordinates, you must be consistent, show your confidence in them as you expect them to show it to you, and do what has been assigned to you. In addition, you show your dependability by never bypassing the chain of command. It is the worst thing to do, because the one who is bypassed feels he is of no use and thus will not do anything.

Sense of humor. The ability to retain a sense of humor will help anyone to retain his perspective on life. Imagine you are on the bridge of a destroyer. As conning officer, you are bringing the ship alongside the pier in Lisbon, Portugal. The CO and the Portuguese pilot are standing behind you. The phone talker asks the CO if he wants the two tugs, which are running upriver with you, to come alongside. The CO answers "No" emphatically. The phone talker relays the message and then asks the same question. The CO again answers "NO," but now his forehead is furrowed and the veins in his neck are standing out.

You continue your approach. The tension is mounting. Now the phone talker, who has become very timid, repeats the same question about the tugs. The CO comes unglued and almost eats the phone talker alive. In order to bring some order to this chaos, do you: (1) Ignore the situation and conn the ship? (2) Tell everyone to clear the bridge so you can concentrate? or (3) Ask the captain if he wants the tugs to come alongside?

This incident actually took place, and the conning officer chose (3), which served to break the tension. Everything turned out well, and the CO was able to laugh at his reaction to the tug situation. (The tugs came alongside anyway.)

General Wilson also thinks that a sense of humor is important.

If you don't have a sense of humor, the people you're trying to influence will think you are pompous. After all, the word is *influence*, not *impress*. They cannot know everything, but the leader wants them to do their best and to give him their best advice so that he is able to make a decision based upon the advantages and disadvantages of each problem that is presented, and therefore he needs to elicit their support. People are afraid of a leader who has no sense of humor. They think that he is not capable of relaxing, and as a result of this there is a tendency for that leader to have a reputation for pomposity, which may not be the case at all. Humor also has a tendency to relax people in times of stress.

Admiral Nakamura suggests that in the military, particularly in severe circumstances, humor is essential. It might be the best refreshment to change the mood, soften the tension, and restore the calm. It is necessary, of course, to take care regarding the timing in specific cases. A commander who has a good sense of humor can generate personal magnetism, which quite usefully supports his leadership style.

In this complicated world, it is not likely that anyone—civilian or military—will go along without meeting a challenge, or even adversity. It is therefore incumbent on all individuals to see themselves as part of the larger plan of life, the plan they are not the center of, no matter how important their particular contribution may be. In this regard, the service adage of trying not to fall on your sword is a good one, for it recognizes that one should try not to make errors even though the attempt will not always be successful.

A successful naval officer, then, must have a sense of humor. If he is unable to laugh at his situation and himself at the right time, he is in for a very long tour and a longer career. The downfall of some potentially great leaders has been caused by their inability to see the humor in life and to react appropriately. Few people

15

enjoy the company of someone who is always a buffoon or a clown, but neither do they relish spending time with someone who is always serious.

Secretary Webb comments that
humor shows rapport among people, a shared understanding, and it develops naturally in a unit that has cohesion. Combat is filled with bittersweet humor. Faced with a very difficult order, one guy might turn to another and say, "Well, you know if you give a . . . you aren't worth a . . . . All right, we'll go do it." In this kind of exchange, people demonstrate to one another that they understand one another and that a bond exists among the members of the group.

Humor acts as a lubricant to keep things moving and operating smoothly. The most efficient and effective organizations are those in which people enjoy going to work. They work because they *want* to, not because they *have* to. When things are not going well, people look to the boss. If he is overwhelmed by the situation, down in the dumps, surly, short-tempered, and downright humorless, then his subordinates are very unlikely to be upbeat. Even when he is down, the officer should try to smile. He needs to get the job done, he needs to be effective, and he also needs to be pleasant. Being professional and smiling are not mutually exclusive.

Obviously there are times, usually in an emergency situation, when direct, positive action must be taken, when doing otherwise would be inviting disaster. It is only when the boss consistently regards routine situations as emergencies that trouble arises. When the boss is running around in circles and his people are right behind him on this race to nowhere, the unit is not likely to be very productive.

A career in the Naval Service should be fun. If people do their job and confusion is kept to a minimum, there is no reason for people in the Navy and Marine Corps not to enjoy their work.

A large part of that enjoyment stems from a balanced perspective, which, in turn, results from working for and with people who have a sense of humor.

PERSONAL STYLES OF LEADERSHIP

Admiral Burke points out that the concept of leadership is different for every person.

There is very good leadership for very bad causes. Hitler, for example, is considered by some as a superb leader. Some Communists are good leaders. Gangs and the Mafia have a very good leadership campaign; their leaders do what they are supposed to do, or they are dead. But this is not what is meant by leadership in the Naval Service.

In the service, there are many different kinds of leadership, but in general terms, leaders in the service are those who can get their people to do the right thing at the right time for the good of their government. Leadership is understanding people and involving them to help you do a job. That takes all of the good characteristics, like integrity, dedication of purpose, selflessness, knowledge, skill, implacability, as well as a determination not to accept failure. Furthermore, different situations will require a leader to use different combinations of his leadership qualities.

But there is no prescription for leadership, and no leader is always a good leader. General MacArthur, for example, was one of the best leaders this country ever produced, but he did not *always* do the right thing, though he usually did. The object of leadership may be stated as having a system whereby a leader recognizes what is good for the good of the government, for the good of the nation, for the good of humanity, and recognizes the qualities he has and what he can do within his own limitations. He cannot do, and should not attempt to do, the impossible, but he should not fail to attempt something that might be extremely difficult and may be possible.

An individual should pipe up because in his judgment someone is doing something wrong, but he shouldn't pipe up just because he disagrees. The most valuable officers I've ever had were the people who checked my judgment. I chose my deputy vice-chief of naval operations in each case because they were strong men with different ideas and I knew that they would tell me what they thought was wrong. We had a conference every morning and they would tell me what was wrong, and it was the hardest part of the day. They weren't always right, and sometimes I overruled them (more often than I should have, probably), but still they told me, and we're still very good friends, probably the best friends I could have. I trust them absolutely.

To get a person, particularly a young person, to tell you when he thinks you're wrong is very difficult. In war, for example, the commander and above of any combat unit will have to make a lot of snap judgments, and they can be very important judgments on very minor things, like your rate of gunfire: you're going to get hits or you're not going to get hits, depending upon this simple thing. You don't have time to analyze, you must do something because of your training, which is based on instinct as much as anything else.

If you've got time, it's a good thing to ask someone: "I want to do this. What do you think?" He gives you an opinion off the top that is as real as he can make it. Usually he's looking for something wrong. That's what you want him to do, you want

him to discover if anything is wrong with your decision. But if he always states that you are haywire, he's not much help. You want his good judgment of what you're doing. A good officer can be of great help to a senior if the senior will ask.

General Wilson believes that the only way an officer can demonstrate his leadership qualities is through personal example. We've often heard it said that those who are least likely to be good leaders are those who say "Do as I say, not as I do." I believe that an officer has to demonstrate through personal example, personal appearance, weight control— those qualities he expects in his subordinates. I for one have never believed that you should ask any person to do anything that you wouldn't do yourself.

I believe that the guiding qualities for a person are those that begin in early youth, in the home, the church, the school. These are the influences that determine our basic qualities, that we build our careers and our future lives on. Sometimes people in leadership positions start to believe that somehow they're infallible. Nothing could be further from the truth, as we know, and we have to guard against this, and I think it helps to know that we are all mortal. We are, and we do make mistakes, and we have to admit those mistakes and seek guidance from the Almighty in whatever we do.

I do not believe that good managers or good leaders are born—I believe they are made. Since I retired from the Marine Corps and have been involved in the business world, in several of the large corporations of America, I have found that the word *leadership* is rarely used in the business world. But whatever word is used— *manager*, *executive*, etc.—it means *leader* in the military parlance. In fact, of course, we're all a part of our background, and I believe that the word *leadership* implies much more than any other word that I have ever used in the business world.

Obviously, a good leader is a good manager, but a good manager in the narrow sense of the word is not necessarily a good leader. Managers imply to me those who are more of an administrative sort, whereas leadership implies all the broad aspects, which is getting others to do what you want them to do even though they might not undertake the task of their own volition.

I have found that most people like to have former military people work for them after they have finished a service career, because they have those qualities of dedication and work, initiative, and a day's work for a day's pay, which is not always found in a working person who progressed in another lifestyle.

MCPON Billy C. Sanders: *Personal example plays a big role, especially within the enlisted com-*

munity. We have leadership manuals and things of that sort, and we speak leadership, but nothing speaks louder than personal example. The enlisted community looks at its officers to lead, and if they see an officer doing something that they know he should not be doing or doing something that counters what he has been speaking to, the officer will lose credibility, and it will be very difficult to earn it back. The officer is expected to live up to the ideals that are inherent in military life: be dependable, act with tact, and keep a good sense of humor. Being dependable is the key, and officers must be the same way every day;

enlisted must be able to depend on the officer responding to like situations each time the same way, and if they are not able to, then we have a problem.

3. The Steps to Mission Accomplishment

Accomplishing the mission within the capabilities of the unit and the resources allowed while maintaining high morale is the goal of every naval officer. An astute officer can become an achiever by applying basic management and leadership principles to the organization of which he is a part. The new officer begins this process by becoming as professional in his billet as he can.

KNOW THE JOB

The basis of successful leadership is making things happen through people, but first the leader must know his job. The team he is working with will give him some "slack" for being the new officer on board, but that slack is rapidly used up if the officer does not move out smartly to learn all he can. In the long run, his division will not care whether he is a "hail fellow well met," but they will care whether he knows what he is doing, especially in difficult or dangerous tasks, when they will look to him to keep them out of trouble and to get them safely home. Admiral Takaichi Itaya, former Japanese CNO, believes that

only an enthusiastic leader can accomplish

a mission and instill in his subordinates a full understanding of the importance of the mission. Together with encouraging them to feel a sense of pride, *after* accomplishment of the mission, he will try to get them a collective material reward.

He will fully prepare the necessary material, work to overcome the difficulties associated with accomplishing the mission, and build a spirit of unified cooperation. In 1934, when Admiral Itaya was an ensign, he took to heart the teaching that "whatever the task, after one has decided to tackle it, it must be done gladly. I think that this was effective in carrying out my mission."

PLAN THE MISSION

Accomplishing the mission requires planning and monitoring. Planning is the development of action steps needed to achieve an objective or goal. Ability to plan is closely related to the other skills required of naval officers, such as anticipating requirements, establishing priorities, and meeting deadlines.

Planning is required to accomplish any task assigned to a division, whether that task is routine or emergent. The officer should attack routine and emergent assignments the same way. A planned maintenance schedule (PMS) for a radar is an excellent example of a routine plan, because it outlines action steps and specifies the frequency with which they are to be taken. Preparations to integrate a large number of midshipmen into a work center to ensure a maximum learning experience is an example of an emergent task that an officer in charge of at-sea summer training might have to handle in a relatively short period.

The first step in developing a plan is analyzing the task. A division officer should separate an upcoming engineering propulsion plant inspection into sections, such as training watch standers, practicing emergency drills, and upgrading material conditions. The outline for the plan should include training and testing sessions for all watch standers, casualty control drills to see how the team reacts to emergencies, and continuous emphasis on material readiness. The plan should be flexible enough to handle the changes

that inevitably will occur. This should be a long-term plan rather than a compressed, crisislike schedule.

IMPLEMENT THE PLAN

Once the plan is set, the officer has to consider priorities and prepare to meet deadlines, because he will never have the luxury of working on only one task at a time. The Naval Service is much too dynamic an organization to permit single task operations, and the officer has to learn how to keep several "balls in the air" simultaneously. It is a skill that starts with a plan, just like organizing homework and professional responsibilities at school. Last-minute preparations rarely camouflage the lack of a routine approach to tasks. A methodical "daily" effort that includes (in the engineering inspection example) training, drills, and maintenance will produce well-qualified and motivated operators as well as an efficient engineering plant. As the inspection approaches, little extra effort should be required, because the long-term, consistent, daily effort will be evident. Crisis management and its negative impact on morale must be averted wherever possible. The chain of command is the vehicle used to implement the plan. Through the chain of command, the officer issues orders that ensure that each individual involved with executing the plan accurately understands his role in accomplishing the task.

MONITOR PROGRESS

A good plan must continually be monitored, and here is where young officers most often run into "shallow water." The Navy adage that you get what you *inspect*, not what you *expect*, has been hewn out of unhappy consequences for officers who do not monitor the work they have assigned from their plans.

In the engineering inspection example, monitoring is accomplished through evaluations of training seniors, through emergency drills, and through reports of material conditions, as well as through on-site "viewing" by the officer and his leading petty officers. If this evolution indicates that the necessary proficiency in drills has not been reached, the original plan should be modified. For example, the number of practice drills could be increased. Since there is no "free lunch," allotting more time for drills will impact on the other parts of the plan, such as maintenance, and, once again, the officer will have to evaluate his priorities and make judgment calls on his adjusted schedule. The officer should never just assume that a plan is working; he must monitor effectiveness by following up on it by becoming personally involved.

MOTIVATE

Given a basic objective and armed with a plan of action to achieve it, the officer uses leadership to get the mission done and to maintain high morale while doing so. Mission accomplishment and high morale occur in tandem: in other words, good leaders get the job done *and* maintain high morale. Admiral Fran McKee, USN, points out that

the primary concern of most naval officers is getting the mission accomplished, and that is almost an impossibility without a high degree of morale. There is no magic formula that will produce high morale, but the individuals who are on the teams you happen to supervise, whether they be at a junior level or a senior level, have to be well informed about what they're doing. I think they have to realize the importance of the job they're doing and their part in accomplishing the mission. People must understand the part they play.

I find that most sailors want to be a part of the winning team and they want to

make things work. Because of this and their spirit of ingenuity, there are few things that they cannot accomplish when they are inspired. If they have a thorough understanding of the job, and have been well trained for it, they generally have a sense of pride in getting the job done, and if every member of the team is pulling his or her own oar in the same direction, the mission is then much easier to accomplish.

Naval history is full of remarkable examples of inspirational leadership. Outnumbered and outgunned naval forces have frequently achieved victory through the daring, guile, and resourcefulness of the leader. This type of leadership may be significantly different from the day-to-day leadership required by a division officer. In other words, leadership is situational, and the appropriate style or approach varies according to the situation or the set of circumstances.

The ability to get others to respond is a primary leadership requisite. Some very bright and conscientious young officers flourish in their early days in the fleet, but, because they lack the ability to get others to respond, they gradually fade out in their middle years. At the beginning of their careers, they are judged solely on their own performance in the tasks they perform, but as they move up in rank, they are increasingly required to delegate authority and to create in their subordinates a strong desire to do what they have been directed to do. The lesson here is clear. The least an individual can learn to do as a division officer is to delegate effectively. The ability to inspire others to perform is more difficult.

MAINTAIN MORALE

Admiral James Holloway, former American CNO, notes that high morale is not a guarantee of mission accomplishment, because other factors influence a unit's ability to carry out its task.

In combat, for example, enemy action

may prevail, and therefore the unit will not be able to carry out its assigned mission. An outfit with high morale has a much higher probability of achieving its mission than one with low morale does; furthermore, it will carry out its mission more effectively and efficiently than a unit with low morale will. During the Korean War and the Vietnam conflict, the aviation outfits that had high morale, that had pride in their unit and confidence in their professional ability, would get pumped up before a mission, just as a football team does before a big game. They had enthusiasm, they had dedication, they had a desire to do the job right, and as a consequence, when they got in on the target, they would press home their attacks to the minimum range consistent with the weapons delivery techniques, regardless of enemy opposition. Of course, the closer they got to the target, the higher probability they had of scoring hits, so those units with high morale usually came back with the mission accomplished: they had destroyed a bridge or a truck division. Those units that did not have high morale looked on a mission not as something to get done, but as something to attempt; after that, their main goal was to get back.

Probably the greatest example of how low morale has caused a tremendous reduction in military capability is the Iranian Air Force during the 1980s conflict in the Persian Gulf area. The Iranian Air Force had very poor morale because their planes were down to about 20 percent of what they originally had, most of their equipment did not work, and they had taken high losses.

Intelligence indicates that the pilots were flying level at fifteen and twenty thousand feet and dropping their bombs. Their planes, F-4s, the Phantoms, were designed to be used in diving attacks at a very low level, but the pilots simply did not care. Their morale was destroyed, so they went in and just checked off one more mission.

MAKE THINGS HAPPEN THROUGH PEOPLE

Every officer in the Naval Service will at some point work with those who are "gate keepers," or custodial leaders. Their interests are short term and their horizon close aboard. Officers will also see the "managerial" leader, who is getting the job done but is putting the emphasis on the management of his organization, not on the inspirational elements. Finally, they will meet or work for the "charismatic" leader, who not only gets the job done but also makes things happen through people.

The charismatic leader started out by knowing his job and the personnel assigned to him, and by planning, setting priorities, and meeting deadlines. But this officer also was able to communicate to the division what the command goals were and took the time to explain why certain tasks were required and where the unit, team, ship, aircraft squadron, was headed and how it was going to get there.

As a consequence, this officer created within the division a common vision and high expectations. This leader also worked to make the division feel stronger than they were and more in control of their own destinies. This leader was seldom let down by the trust he had in his people or by the expectations he had of them. He was usually "for" things rather than "against" them. He used competition to advantage, but for the most part he worked at developing cooperative relationships rather than competitive ones.

In the charismatic leader's division, organizational conflicts were resolved by mutual confrontation among the chain of command rather than avoided or solved by an unyielding decision made by the "boss." This division was not a democracy in which decisions were made by majority vote; however, the charismatic leader's decisions were made in an environment of trust. The team had confidence in the leader and had begun to get the results the leader had led them to believe they could get in the first place. The result was a team effort in which individuals attacked tasks and enjoyed the opportunities to be tested and to do something well.

No one in the charismatic leader's division lost sight of responsibility, authority, and accountability. The leader had been able to accommodate and use these basic tenets to get the job done. More importantly, the leader had been able to articulate a vision or a mission congruent with the needs and values of the people who worked in the division. The charismatic leader had achieved both—task accomplishment and high morale—and had, in the end, promoted goal-oriented thinking and behavior.

PROVIDE TRAINING FOR PERSONNEL

Admiral Elmo Zumwalt, former American CNO, explains that

mission accomplishment in an operational unit can be thought of as a matrix over

time. In any given year, an officer will need to meet a series of short-term objectives— getting ready for a fleet exercise, getting ready for deployment, etc.— and at the same time address

the problem of having an extremely successful unit overall, in terms of maximum

effort toward battle efficiency. Preparing for mission accomplishment requires that the officer consider other ramifications, such as long-term schooling requirements of his people and their capabilities in terms of their becoming assets for other ships or divisions as well as their suitability for higher positions. These considerations must be fitted against the backdrop of the situation in which the officer is operating.

Admiral Zumwalt described how the military scenario has affected the training of individuals.

In the immediate post–World War II period, we had many chief petty officers and a lot of seamen, because all the experienced middle grades had left us, and we were able to think in terms of having lots of schooling because we did have some very highly experienced people to keep things going while these youngsters were out getting their training. On the other hand, in the fifties and early sixties, we were stretched very thin for petty officers in all categories, and we had to be much more guarded about long-term training. Once the Vietnam War became the primary consideration, we had the problem of meeting all of these other objectives while keeping our eye on the significant overriding objective or mission of being ready for a specific, highly structured contribution to that war. In each case, therefore, one plays the personnel situation quite differently. In one case, the long-term schooling, and in the other case, maybe compressed schooling.

Throughout it all there is absolutely no question in my mind that if one has to err, one should err in favor of doing those things that make it possible for individual capabilities to be improved in an atmosphere which has sufficient fun and zest to allow them to enjoy contributing to the mission. That, to me as a commanding officer, always meant that I was willing to take some risks with immediate readiness in order to ensure that everybody was getting the maximum leave, some risk with the immediate objective in order to make sure that there was as much schooling as was necessary to motivate, paying particular attention to making sure that each group of people understood the overall mission. For example, I used to think that it was just as important for the engineers to understand what we were trying to accomplish in a specific shore bombardment exercise as it was for all of the gunnery personnel.

In summary, the leader must apply fundamental principles of management and leadership as he learns how to accomplish tasks with his team. A naval officer attacks his tasks with a plan, develops that plan while considering both resources and priorities, and then monitors the plan to accomplish the desired results efficiently. Leadership is the ability to influence people so that they willingly and enthusiastically strive toward achievement of unit goals. Leadership is situational, meaning that the approach used varies based on the circumstances encountered. It starts with knowing the job thoroughly; setting the example; and taking care of personnel, gaining their confidence, and making them feel stronger than they actually are.

Using an understanding of the human needs and motivational factors, naval officers can inspire and direct their people under normal or adverse conditions. Properly motivated, people will shortly start performing as if they were as good as their leader has made them feel they are. Hard work and high morale are compatible. One final note: en route to charismatic leadership, some individuals acquire the reputation for being lucky. Like avoiding accidents, luck isn't just something that happens to an individual, but is, rather, the result of careful planning. People like to work for people who are *good* at what they do and who make their *own* luck.

4. The Components of Integrity

While there may be some disagreement as to whether there is one overriding characteristic of a leader, there is worldwide agreement, among military leaders, that an officer must act with integrity at all times. The outward example the officer sets is constantly observed by his subordinates. He is the model of behavior by which the group he leads is most influenced, and therefore his conduct must be of the highest quality.[36-63]

Integrity of character is the basis for the first article set forth by the United States government for naval officers. It states that "the commanders of all fleets, squadrons, naval stations, and vessels belonging to the Navy are required to show themselves as a good example of virtue, honor, patriotism, and subordination."[7-2]

Admiral McDonald makes the point that "integrity can be best ensured by telling the truth, so that you will never have to remember what you said." Admiral Lawson Ramage, Medal of Honor holder, adds that integrity "is of prime importance in all cases. Without integrity, no officer can command the loyalty, respect, or confidence of either his juniors or his seniors."

LOYALTY, HONOR, AND HONESTY

Admiral Karl Clausen, former Commander of North Sea Forces for the Federal German Navy and, simultaneously, NATO Commander of the German North Sea Sub-area, acknowledges that

the realization of integrity, an ambitious quality, is difficult. The law for the Forces in the German Bundeswehr (Soldatengesetz) contains a number of virtues that are demanded from everyone. Beyond that, there are rules that should be followed by every citizen.

To realize and practice the multiplicity contained in this word *integrity* will always be a task that must not be considered easy. The substance of the internationally known saying "Nobody is perfect" is, in fact, serious. I think that, above all, the following possibilities give guidance to an officer:

A religious commitment.

Continuously striving to meet all requirements one is asked for, as perceptible endeavors produce effective results.

Keeping one's eyes on examples that demonstrate the significance at which the word *integrity* is aiming. With this I am thinking less of abstract contents or definitions than of living or historical examples who give steadiness and stimulation for personal review and guidance [in German: *Leitbilder*].

VIRTUE

Virtue represents the individual's "bravery to endure and bear up against evil and danger, as well as to go forth and face them." It is the courage to seek daring enterprise. "The brave man is not he who feels no fear, but he whose noble mind its fear subdues."[7-2]

Captain James A. Graham, USMC, won the Medal of Honor during the Vietnam War for conspicuous gallantry and intrepidity at the risk of his life above and beyond the call of duty. Captain Graham led his company on an assault of an enemy-occupied position. While crossing a clear paddy area toward the assigned objective, his company came under heavy fire, which inflicted many casualties. Two platoons were able to withdraw, but one remained under severe fire from two concealed machine gun positions. Seeing this, Captain Graham personally led a squad in the destruction of one of the machine gun sites. This enabled the platoon to remove many of their wounded. In the face of enormous odds,

Captain Graham ordered the withdrawal of the rest of the platoon while he stayed with a man too seriously wounded to be moved. He held off the enemy while the platoon moved to friendly lines. In his last radio transmission, he relayed that about twenty-five Vietnamese had surrounded him. He died while protecting himself and the wounded man he chose not to abandon. Captain Graham's dedication and display of outstanding qualities of leadership and indomitable fighting spirit saved the platoon from annihilation.[67-819]

Secretary Webb reminds us that

no matter what position of responsibility a person is in, there will be pressures and temptations to take a shortcut or to yield to someone else's will. Where principle is involved, an officer must be deaf to expediency. This means that the loyalty and the trust of his boss and the loyalty of the people under him are more important than shortcuts or possible favors one might receive.

An officer must be absolutely "straight." If he lies to his boss, his people will lie to him; if he works a deal to get something done, basically pulling the wool over his boss's eyes, everyone under him is going to believe that is the way to get things done.

The organization will be a workable, functioning structure only if it is based on absolute integrity. If an individual commits a false act, even if it is not something he could go to a court martial on, he must be reprimanded so that other individuals who know about the incident will not be adversely affected. If he is not reprimanded, the fabric of the unit may fall apart.

Secretary Webb recalled this incident from his involvement with officer candidates in the Marine Corps:

Back in 1970, if you came through an officer training school and you failed to make it, you spent four years as an enlisted man in the Marine Corps, you went down to Parris Island. I sent an individual in my platoon down to Parris Island because he lied to me about a simple thing, about smoking a cigarette. I asked him if he had smoked a cigarette. He said no, but I knew he had. I said, "I'm going to give you ten seconds to think about that," and I asked him again, and he said no, and I said, "You're on the next train south." There was a lot of confusion among the people in the platoon about what I had done, and I explained that this individual had knowingly broken a regulation, and I realized that everyone some time or another does break regulations. But if you fail, as a person of honor, to acknowledge your mistakes, you don't deserve to be an officer, and that's a distinction that has to be maintained.

As do many other seasoned military officers, Admiral Long places integrity at the top of his list of leadership principles.

If I were prioritizing leadership principles, I would list integrity as the most important. I have observed literally thousands of officers over my time in the United States military. For the most part, these officers have had good professional training, have been energetic, and usually had a high degree of integrity. Many times an officer is called upon to act as an advisor to a senior, and I believe in those relations that the element of loyalty is obviously required, and certainly an element of knowledge of the subject is necessary, but I think the element that I prize the highest is the individual's level of integrity. I think this is particularly important as an officer proceeds in his naval career, for there are many opportunities for an officer to deviate from standards, and I think that it is important for an officer not only to actually act with

integrity, but also to give the perception that he has good integrity.

For Admiral de Cazanove, integrity means respect for oneself, loyalty to one's country, and being just and honest with others as well as oneself. Whatever you are doing and wherever you are a military leader, you must have integrity, or you will not accomplish much in life.

Admiral Burke observes that officers who concentrate on doing their jobs will in all likelihood make steady progress in their careers. Officers who concentrate, instead, on scheming to get ahead may find that their attitude restricts their advancement. Overambition will kill your friends, and a person is supported by his friends—in the service, in civilian life, in any other job—he is supported by his friends and the people he works with. If he starts being highly competitive and maybe doing just a little bit of throat cutting on someone else to get a little advantage, his friends soon know about it. People don't do anything by themselves, things are done with a group of people. So this aspiring to too much can lead to too much *me* and to destroying the support you get from other people.

The officer who begins to pay more attention to himself than to the Naval Service compromises his leadership ability. The officer should not go around getting publicity for himself. It's right when you see something wrong to bring it up, but you have to bring it up properly, you have to work for the good of the organization and not for your own good. Individuals who are trying to correct something don't encounter animosity unless they are doing it for their own purposes.

There are quite a few people who start looking like they're going to be pretty good. They're good starters, but they don't finish the race for one reason or another. They don't end up being pretty good. There's one criteria that you can use to tell when a man is slipping. I was looking back over some of my friends I thought were very good when we were young, but they didn't turn out well, and they seemed to have one common denominator that came about the middle of life, usually, they started talking about themselves instead of their cause, their duty, or something like that. "I am good," not "We are good." "I did this." It isn't that he's wrong, maybe he did do it, but if his mental attitude starts shifting from his cause to himself, he is no longer good.

I don't think men change very much in what they do. I don't think a man would say, "Now I have completed my contribution" and then stop or slow down. I don't think he could. I think, rather, he would continue his contribution, but he might start overly crediting himself.

"INTEGRITY," BY ADMIRAL ARLEIGH BURKE

The classic treatise on the subject of integrity was written by Admiral Arleigh Burke in a letter to Professor Karel Montor. This treatise was published in the October 1985 issue of *Proceedings* and is produced here in its entirety. Brief definitions cannot do justice to this most important topic. This article, while it does not cover all aspects of integrity, will provide the reader with a good frame of reference for further thought.

"Integrity"

First you find yourself overlooking small infractions that you would have corrected on the spot in the past.

Soon, you are a participant in these infractions. "After all," you say, "Everybody's doing it."

All too soon you find yourself trapped: You no longer can stand on a favorite principle because you have strayed from it.

Finding no way out, you begin to rationalize, and then you are hooked.

The important fact is, the men who travel the path outlined above have misused the very basic quality and characteristic expected of a professional military man, or any other professional man for that matter: They have compromised their integrity.

This quotation, from a plaque hanging in the office of the Chief of Staff, Marine Corps Development and Education Command, Quantico, Virginia, is remarkable in its simplicity and truthfulness. My old college dictionary defines *integrity* as (1) an unimpaired condition; soundness; (2) adherence to a code of moral, artistic, or other values; (3) the quality or state of being complete or undivided; completeness. As synonyms, it lists *honesty* and *unity*.

These are good definitions, but they are not very exact. They allow a great deal of leeway because the descriptive words may mean different things to different societies, different cultures, and different people. What is integrity for a Japanese may not be so for an Iranian. What is integrity for a cowboy may not be considered integrity by a minister (the disposition of horse thieves, for example). Integrity also varies widely among individuals in the same group. Probably no two individuals have the same ideas about all aspects of integrity. The point is, there exists no absolute definition of integrity.

Since no two people have the same values, how does a person acquire integrity, a code of conduct, a set of standards by which to live? How does a person develop a sense of obligation toward others, whether they make up a civic group, a military service, or a country? Most individuals' standards are learned when they are very young, from family, associates, and other contacts, from reading, and from watching television. It is well to remember, though, that families with high standards have had children who rejected the beliefs of their families and turned out to be first-class scoundrels. The reverse is also true. People with integrity have come from families that have lacked it. Perhaps this does not happen often, but it does happen. The point is that it is impossible to guarantee that any one person will acquire integrity. Development of integrity depends primarily on the individual.

There will be wayward priests, crooked politicians, and wicked naval officers. In a highly moral organization, people who fall below the standard will eventually be recognized and removed from the organization. In an organization of lower standards, they may be punished but still tolerated. In an immoral organization, such as in a criminal family, they will be measured by their contribution to their organization.

Individuals are responsible for their own integrity. They will be influenced by many people and events, but, in the end, their integrity quotient is of their own making. People are responsible for establishing their own standards, and their choices determine the kind of person they will be.

The integrity an individual should look after is his own—not his neighbor's, his subordinate's, his senior's, or his associate's, but his own. You can try to influence people to accept your views, but whether they do or not is up to them. A society or an individual may force rules on others, but no one can ensure that integrity will be inculcated. Only the individual concerned can accomplish that.

The integrity of a society or a group is approximately equal to the lowest common denominator of its people. When the standards are lowered for an individual, the standards of the group or society to which the individual belongs are lowered. Sometimes standards are raised in groups, but more frequently there is a gradual disintegration of standards.

Since the integrity of individuals varies, an organization cannot maintain an absolutely uniform integrity; not even sequestered groups can accomplish this. A general level of integrity can be approximated, but individuals may deviate greatly from the norm, even in organizations that try to keep standards high.

In these days of high-speed teaching methods, young people receive guidance from their families and literally dozens of other groups. They are even given computerized, capsulized advice. Developing individuals observe the people who dole out the plentiful and diverse guidance, and the observations they make influence their acceptance of what is right or wrong, good or bad. The following example is frequently mentioned in regard to education: If merit and capability are not requirements for success in the teaching profession, then young people are likely to judge that merit and capability are not important. Likewise, if developing individuals observe that people with known moral defects, or people who are known to be crooked or liars, are accepted in society without penalty, they might well conclude that integrity is not worth their effort, either.

Still, individuals determine what convictions they want to have and what they want to do about them. They continually adjust what they think is correct, what they want to learn, and how much effort they are willing to devote to each subject. Individuals determine who to like and who to avoid, who to admire and who to emulate, and make decisions about what is important and how to go about self-improvement. Individuals also determine what obligations they are willing to undertake on their own volition.

Since individuals create their own integrity, it follows that integrity is not fixed permanently. Integrity is a variable in one individual, among individuals of the same family and society, and among different societies and cultures. Integrity may be changed throughout life as individuals determine what actions they are willing to take to improve themselves and their integrity. Deciding how much integrity individuals want to develop is one of the most important decisions they make, whether they are conscious of the process or not. The basis of all education is learning to make judgments. This holds true for developing character as well as for becoming expert in any particular field. Individuals' judgments on material matters can be based on what other people have developed, and so can their judgments pertaining to integrity, but the final choices in both areas are made by the individual concerned.

Olympic athletes have devoted nearly all their efforts and time—often their whole lives—to becoming expert in their chosen field. If a person wants to become one of the best gymnasts in the world, that person ought to start training by the age of three—or maybe before. Since many people find that their dreams exceed their natural capabilities, they will make the sound judgment not to continue to try to accomplish the impossible, but to restrict themselves to what they can do well. The lesson must be learned early in life that very few people can ever be number one. This insight is part of learning to make sound judgments.

Individuals who get away with schemes not to mow the lawn do not increase their sense of obligation very much. When individuals decide not to make the efforts necessary to learn arithmetic or calculus, it is not likely that they will be very good in any profession requiring a knowledge of math. The young person who fools around at the piano, not really trying to learn, is making the choice not to be a piano player. If people worked as hard at learning academics and professional knowledge as they do at performing in athletic contests, it is probable that the world would be a better place to live.

It must be understood that a judgment on anything is not irrevocable, although action taken as a result of a judgment, such as hanging the wrong man as a horse thief, frequently has irrevocable consequences. A person with low grades can see the light, for example, and decide to become more proficient in math. If desire is there, most things can be accomplished. It takes more effort, more time, more determination to correct an original wrong judgment—but it can be done. Grandma Moses became a great artist after she decided to try painting later in her life.

Of course, individuals can alter their integrity.

Too frequently the alterations are on the side of lowered standards, as has been demonstrated in a number of professions and in government. The crux of this is that individuals make their own integrity by reason of their own decisions, choices, and judgments, and they change their integrity by the same means. At the same time, people should make judgments on other people's integrity gingerly. The many different concepts of integrity held by different individuals, groups, and cultures should be treated with all due respect.

Some of the most vicious wars in history have been fought in the name of religion by societies that had very strong—and very different—convictions concerning integrity. They disagreed on what was right, on their basic mode of implementing what was right, and on their bibles or the equivalents thereof, and thus, each side resolved to force its views on the other side. Both sides were absolutely certain they had the monopoly on integrity, and that the other side had no integrity at all.

The extended upheaval in Lebanon is primarily based on different views of religion: what is right, what is good, and what is the word of God. These differences have been exacerbated by greed, desire for power, and self-interest. The Middle East (like a number of American cities) is full of strong and conflicting views on integrity and full of people who do not seem to have much integrity. Some leaders in the Mideast appear to be scoundrels, liars, selfish in the extreme, and generally without socially redeeming features. It is likely that few people in this country agree with, or understand, their philosophy, and that fewer still would stand for any attempt to force that philosophy on them.

Keeping our own integrity up to par is problem enough. We are responsible for our own conduct; we are not responsible for another's integrity. If we have made the normal number of correct judgments during our lives, we have probably concluded that we should not try to interfere with the religion of others or to determine what is right or wrong for them. We should not interfere unless another group tries to force its views of integrity on us or our organization. Then we must resist, or the other group's efforts will appreciably lower the standards of our organization. In relation to the naval profession, in particular, the following observations are applicable:

— Integrity and motivation are necessary in naval officers, but competence in the profession is also essential.

— Good intentions are most desirable, but nothing can be built or done by good intentions alone—except maybe paving the road to hell. Performance is required. Good intentions may help get performance, but the required end product is performance, not "I meant well."

— Integrity, or lack thereof, is not always discernible. Many people practice successfully to appear to have great integrity, or more than they do have. They can fool many some of the time. But always guard against making a final judgment on another's integrity based only on his own statements or on what appears to be.

— Be wary of self-proclaimed virtue. Do not rely on other people's evaluation of their personal integrity. Perhaps if they had integrity, they would not be their own press agents.

— The marketing of reputations for integrity is a good business. Many leaders have made good livings allowing their reputations to be used to represent organizations with no or poor reputations of their own.

Despite the cynical tone of these observations, most people and a large percentage of naval officers are people of integrity. They are honest; they are reliable; they are professional, and they do have good professional ethics. Have faith in your fellow officers, but be ready if one of them is less valiant, less competent, or less honest than you thought.

All of us can learn from the past. As wise as Moses was, he had difficulty hearing the disagreements of all the people who came before him. The people wanted Moses to settle matters between them and make known to them God's decisions and regulations. His father-in-law, Jethro, observing that Moses was having great difficulty handling the work, suggested:

> Be thou for the people to Godward, that thou mayest bring the causes unto God. And thou shalt teach them ordinances and laws, and shalt show them the way wherein they must walk, and the work that they must do. Moreover thou shalt provide out of all the people able men, such as fear God, men of truth, hating covetousness; and place such over them to be rulers of thousands, and rulers of hundreds, rulers of fifties, and rulers of tens. And let them judge the people at all seasons; and it shall be, that every great matter they shall bring unto thee, but every small matter they shall judge; so shall it be easier for thyself, and they shall bear the burden with thee. If thou shalt do this thing, and God command thee so, then thou shalt be able to endure, and all this people shall also go to their place in peace. (Exodus 18:19–23)

The point is that, when considering weighty matters, an individual can be helped greatly by turning to and relying on others for support, for no one individual has all of the knowledge necessary to be 100 percent correct all of the time.

One question to be considered is, "What should an officer do when he thinks that a senior is lying to the next senior officer in the chain of command?" Certainly a junior officer who believes a senior is making a mistake—any serious mistake, not just a mistake with regard to integrity—should inform that senior officer. For example, suppose that the officer of the deck has the conn, and he orders "Come to 080." The junior officer of the deck believes that it is an incorrect order, and he tells the OD right away. The OD rechecks and either corrects the order or tells the junior officer that the order will not be changed and why. This sort of exchange is common in the Navy. Usually the senior will ask for the junior's opinion as a matter of training, if for no other reason. Seniors do not want to make mistakes, and they appreciate being informed of an error before any damage is done.

Thus, it is a good habit to question suspected errors in normal operations. An officer, however, does not often deliberately lie to a senior.

This example illustrates how important it is for a naval officer to have experience in making judgments. There are, unfortunately, no general guidelines that can be laid down for the contingency of lying. The appropriate reaction to lying depends on circumstances, which are unpredictable. If a junior officer believes that a senior is lying, the junior officer must ask himself questions. Is the junior officer sure that the senior is lying, or is it possible that he is only guessing that the senior is lying? Is it possible that the issue involves a difference of opinion? Could it be a question of interpretation? Finally, does the matter have significance?

The junior must judge whether the lie will have an effect on the organization. If the junior concludes that the senior is lying on a significant matter, and that the senior's integrity is involved, then it is the duty of the officer to tell that senior that the matter will be reported to the next senior in the chain of command as well as the reasons why the junior believes the report is necessary. It is particularly important for an officer to confront a senior accused of dishonesty or another breach of integrity, and to advise that officer on the intended course of action, before he besmirches the reputation of that officer.

The decision to accuse is never to be taken lightly. An officer who accuses peers or associates of any kind of wrongdoing knows well, before he utters the first words of accusation, to expect judgments from shipmates and perhaps from larger groups on the appropriateness of the charges made. This is in accordance with the old adage: "Judge not, lest ye be judged."

Therefore, when the junior starts wrestling with his conscience to make the judgment on where his duty lies, he should resist impulsive actions and even consider searching out a second opinion. Friends in the unit will likely take the issue seriously, or at least the more conservative ones will. There may be one or two who have

noted the alleged misconduct themselves. I suppose that this sort of a drum-head court martial without the presence of the accused would come to a general conclusion, one way or another. Still, the final decision is in the hands of the originator of the charge, and that individual must make the final judgment on what should be done, no matter how much advice was sought and received from others. The decision belongs to the officer—and no one else.

Matters such as these are difficult for a junior officer, a Chief of Naval Operations, or a president. At the Naval Academy, in the year just before they graduate, midshipmen are taught the relationship between duty and honor: "We serve the country first, our seniors second, and ourselves last." The future officers are counseled on honor versus loyalty in the Naval Service, and specific attention is given to the difference between a professional and a careerist. These definitions are given: "A military professional is someone who upholds the highest standards and serves the country with unquestioning loyalty; the professional is not motivated by personal gain. . . . A careerist is someone who serves the country in the best way fit to further his own career." It is noted in this lesson given to our future officers that the careerist is more likely to fall into the zero-mentality syndrome, to be someone who would choose to cover up those things that might draw discredit to his own unit. The professional takes on the issues directly and does not swerve to avoid criticism. These matters are never easy for the officer, but he must take on the issues to fulfill the obligations he holds to country, service, unit, personnel therein, and self.

As a junior officer on a battleship, I was once involved in a delicate situation that I did not handle properly. I recount it here so that others may not need as much time to learn when the proper action should be taken in such a situation. On a Labor Day weekend I had duty as one of three officers of the deck. My relief did not return to the ship on Monday morning to relieve me, so I stood his watches on Monday without reporting anything amiss. When the derelict officer showed up on Tuesday, he told the senior watch officer that he had made arrangements with me to stand his watches before he left for the weekend. That was not true. He simply took the chance that some dope would fill in for him. I did not do anything about that misstatement, either. Within two years that officer was dropped from the rolls of the Navy for a similar offense. Had I reported him the first time, he might have been jolted out of his expectation that there would always be some volunteer who would step in to carry his part of the load.

There is also the question of what to do about a "whistle blower." The answer involves knowing whether the individual has made an honest effort to correct the wrong by using the chain of command channels that are available. A clever whistle blower can parlay an error into something that produces publicity and promotion that is not deserved. Recognizing the media's hunger for material to present to the public should cause any person to ask, before he blows the whistle, whether all possible steps have been taken to correct the situation. The Naval Service is an organization made up of people, and people are subject to making mistakes, but it is important for the public to know that efforts are being made to find mistakes and to correct them. It is wise to wait before making a judgment until you know why the usual steps were not taken or why those steps were not successful. It is also wise to listen and not make a premature judgment. Every organization needs good internal checking, internal policing, and internal corrective apparatus, just as every organization needs an external inspector, an external check, and means for external correction.

It is suggested that codes of honor and integrity must not be so rigid that they are beyond the capability of human beings to follow. I believe it should be the personal responsibility of individuals to decide whether to report lying, cheating, and stealing, and that they should do so

only after completely scrutinizing their own conscience regarding integrity. When a person steals a pencil, perhaps absent-mindedly picking it up from someone's desk, the observer should have the discretion to judge whether the theft should be reported. A person can dream up many examples and possibilities, most of them minor, when there is no doubt that a theft, a lie, or a cheating incident has occurred. But the incident may have been so inconsequential that an individual of good conscience could interpret it as not significant enough to be reportable.

In summary, we must instill in individuals a sense of personal honor, an obligation to their organization and other groups, a desire to keep their own standards high and to keep the standards of their organization high. This sense of honor gives real meaning to the feeling engendered from belonging to a "Band of Brothers," and to other nostalgic emotions that are essential to a taut, high-standards organization. However, an honorable person should have the option of determining whether to believe that others are honorable and whether to take appropriate action in each case. The appropriate action is not usually reporting the offender to the senior, but confronting the suspected culprit with the charge first. What should be done must be individually decided at every step. A fixed rule that insists that a person never squeals on a classmate, a shipmate, or a buddy is just as wrong as a rule that says that everything that could be construed as lying, stealing, or cheating should be reported to a senior.

Likewise, it is also important to comment on the issue of "pleasing the boss." "Greasers"— those who play up to their bosses strictly for personal gain—do not last very long in the service, because their method of operating is discovered and disliked, and they are discharged. But also keep in mind that bosses are pleased to have confidence in the competence of their subordinates, and that there are few subordinates in any profession who do not want to please their bosses. Bosses have been put in positions of responsibility and authority because their bosses think the individuals know what they are doing—and what their subordinates, in turn, should do. What pleases the boss is usually getting done what should be done. It is proper that all officers of the Naval Service should want a reputation for contributing to the improvement of their service. There is nothing wrong with that. Every unit's effectiveness is determined by the way the bosses, and everyone else in the unit, do their respective jobs. The reputation of the Naval Service, the unit, and the individuals in the unit depends on overall unit effectiveness.

Since the boss usually desires a reputation for being a capable officer, including being a capable leader, it is laudable in a subordinate to want to please the boss. There is certainly nothing wrong in pursuing that trait, unless pleasing the boss results in turning in a poor performance. It is usually not too difficult for the boss to recognize insincere support. Greasing seldom works in a classroom, and it succeeds almost as often in the fleet.

Each of us must make his own decisions about the meaning of integrity. I suggest that officers who want to be ready for the difficult decisions of life study the great military leaders of the world, their similarities and differences. Frankly, there is no shortcut to wisdom. Rules to cover all situations do not exist. All of us must find our own ways. Our ability to make the best decisions at the time will certainly be influenced by our knowledge of the past, our consultation with others, and our ability to "see" the future. At the moment of decision, we will have to use our best judgment on what we in turn will do about it. Good luck!

MCPON Sanders: *A naval leader should do a job simply because it's a matter of personal integrity, pride, and loyalty to country. Personal integrity is the key, and we in the enlisted community expect our leaders to respond in this type of manner, to take on tasks not because someone is pushing them, but because the job needs to* *be done. As a matter of fact, many enlisted people do not think of our officers as having someone directing them to do the job. We think of the officers generating the tasks themselves. We're talking about doing a job right and on time because of personal integrity.*

5. The Components of Professionalism

The difference between having a job and having a profession is that an individual who has a job is only responsible for it during hours he is in the work force, usually 8 hours a day. He does his job because he gets paid to do it and has been assigned to do it. An officer has a profession, which means that he lives it 24 hours a day and that everything he does during that 24-hour day, whether it is in the work place or at his leisure, is done as a naval officer, and he is responsible for his conduct, his behavior, and his work at all times. "Professionalism means the competence to perform functions inherent in the naval profession at a uniformly high standard."[70-33] An individual in a profession does not work because a task has been assigned to him. He works because he has pride and likes what he is doing. He lives what he is doing.

PRIDE

Admiral Thomas Hayward, former American CNO, explained how he thinks pride is developed.

Success breeds pride. One will seldom find an individual who is proud of himself  who is proud because he is beating the system or getting away with something. He probably is proud because of what he is achieving, what he's part of. So the individual has acquired a record of achievement based upon the goals that that individual has set for himself or herself, and that probably interrelates very closely to the success which the unit has accomplished. One could be part of the division or a squad or an office that has enormous pride because it is so good. More than likely it's a soundly based pride in that office or division because there's a lot of motivation inside the unit itself and the unit has pride.

It ultimately leads to whether you have pride in yourself and the ship and the unit, and are you proud of the Naval Service? That pride is often associated with the fact that you know people respect you because you're wearing a uniform, you respect yourself because you're in uniform, and you respect that because of what's being accomplished, you're part of a very important assignment that the country has placed upon the Naval Service. Certainly throughout my service in the Navy there's always been a major demand placed upon people in the armed services, and there is always pride that goes with the accomplishment of something tough. If it's easy, you're not going to generate the same element of satisfaction. The tougher the job is, the more you're going to bear down, the better people perform, the good people show up better, their talents come forward, they stand out more obviously, and the old result is success, and that leads to pride, and that's what we're striving to do, satisfaction in one's self, satisfaction in the Naval Service.

An officer always feels that he is part of the profession, and he is always concerned about what he does. He knows that he is representing himself and the Navy or Marine Corps in everything he does. So he performs because he likes serving and is proud of his profession.

Admiral Zumwalt hypothesizes that there may be two classifications of leaders,

those who are martinets, or drivers, and those who lead by persuasion and example while placing a minimum of emphasis on the disciplinary structure, which of course must be present. The type of leader who is the martinet can have a very efficient ship, but it may lack that special esprit that makes the ship come through against all odds. Time and time again as I came along, there were examples of squadrons in which the ship led by the martinet did not make out quite as well in individual battle efficiency competition as did the ship that was led by someone who led by example.

EXPERTISE

"Expertise is the most effective tool for improving personal group performance and minimizing morale problems."[14-16] To ensure that he does his job as well as possible, the officer should, according to Admiral Zumwalt, understand it, and to understand it, he should obtain an understanding of the various parts of the job through both observation in an operating situation and deep study of the specific system, whether it be engineering or gunnery or combat information center (CIC). He adds to his knowledge of the system by learning the individual jobs of the people subordinate to him, and he also adds to his leadership ability, because he can better understand the individuals and their problems, which affect him as he tries to operate as a subset of an operating system. By learning his job through his people, an officer is likeliest to be able to visualize all of the contingencies that may suddenly confront them, and therefore confront him as their supervisor. Admiral Zumwalt testified to the merit of this method of learning.

When we first had radar installed on my first destroyer in World War II, I was made electronics maintenance officer knowing absolutely nothing about electronics other than cursory work that we had had at the Naval Academy. I therefore felt somewhat like a fifth wheel as a couple of highly qualified radar technicians did the repair work, but I made it a point to be with them whenever something was out, whether it was in the middle of the night or middle of the day, in order to observe their problems and gradually to absorb enough of the technology that I was able to understand the systems. It's hard to say how much that helped me with regard to my primary job, which was CIC officer, but nevertheless it did make me much more capable of knowledgeably responding to comments of the commanding officer as he addressed the amount of time that the radar technicians were taking to complete their repairs.

"The professional officer needs to be sufficiently well grounded in engineering principles to make sound judgments without relying entirely on the advice and counsel of others."[14-61] "Advanced technologies in weapon systems, communications, and propulsion, together with a paucity of trained sailors and a societal attitude which spurns the hardships of sea duty, demand the presence of a technologically and technically competent manager-warrior on the bridge."[26-21] "All officers . . . should subscribe to and read their own branch journals. However, officers should not restrict their reading to their own branch journals."[28-49]

LOYALTY TO COUNTRY

Officers believe that what they are doing is worthwhile, is good for the country and for other people, and will make a difference. Their careers are not just something they get paid for, they are something that really make a difference in the world, whether the officers are serving on a submarine on patrol on a remote station underwater somewhere or working in the Pentagon to obtain resources to keep the military strong.

This involves loyalty to country, which to Admiral Hayward means

> belief in our fundamental tenets of liberty, including freedom of choice and opportunity. If you do not have this belief you are certainly in the wrong place, and should not be in uniform. It seems to me, if there's a basic loyalty to this country, then you believe in what your Commander in Chief is trying to accomplish. We all have a conscience, we have a point of view, but we also have to recognize we aren't totally right, we might just be needing a little bit of guidance, and the Commander in Chief might have a purpose in what he's sending us out to do.

PLEASURE IN WORK

In every case, officers believe that their contribution is an important one. There is no better feeling in the world than waking up in the morning and looking forward to going to work because you enjoy what you are doing and you are proud of what you are doing. Admiral Fran McKee offers that

> enjoyment, having some fun, is a vital ingredient in getting the job done. There are some tasks that you are charged with doing that may not be too enjoyable, but you can make most of them enjoyable because of the interrelationships of people on the team who are trying to do the job. When that enjoyment of accomplishing something is missed, then people are very unhappy, and as a result the job doesn't get done as well. When enthusiasm is present it's amazing what people can accomplish, and usually enthusiasm is a result of pure, unadulterated enjoyment.

SELF-IMPROVEMENT

Another point that separates the naval profession from other professions is the consideration that an officer has a responsibility to self in addition to a responsibility to the Navy or the Marine

Corps or to the command. This is not a selfish responsibility, because an officer who takes seriously the responsibility he has to himself is a better officer. To carry out this responsibility, an officer must set aside a certain amount of time each day for study, for learning, for self-improvement. He must take time for himself, whether it is time to study for a formal qualification on board a ship or whether it is time to read or think or do other things.

Part of a naval officer's responsibility to the profession is a responsibility to grow. It is very easy to put that responsibility aside and work full time on the duties of the job, but taking responsibility for his own growth will make an officer more valuable in the future and make his contributions more meaningful. An officer should never feel selfish for setting aside time for personal reflection and growth. One note of caution from General Wilson:

> Somehow officers at an early age and on up through the ranks get into their minds that there are certain jobs that they must have in order to move through the ranks to achieve flag and general officer status. Now they do this either by talking to their friends and those whom they admire or by looking at the biographies and lives of people who have had certain jobs in order to move through the ranks. I have never believed that this is true.
>
> Except for some personal things that I think should be taken into consideration and that should be looked on with compassion—the birth of a baby or an unfortunate situation where a child or a spouse needs special medical attention—I believe that an officer should take his assignment, do absolutely the best job he can, and prepare himself at that time for the next higher rank in that job. Not only should he do that job, but he should learn the job and the responsibility of the next higher rank as best he can so that he can take over in case the present incumbent

should be incapacitated. But mainly he should do the job well and quit worrying about so-called ticket punching and whether he has to go to the War College when he's a major or has to have a ship to command when he's a commander: "I've got to do this because if I don't get this, life's just passed me by and I'm dead and I've got to look for other jobs." Nothing could be further from the truth. The fact is that there have been officers who have made flag and general officer with every kind of assignment, and I'm convinced that their seniors look upon the job they do and how they do it and not what experience they may have had for six months. You've hit a very sensitive subject with me, because I have been so insistent on this over the years, and I have no reason to believe that it is not true now in the military, nor do I have any reason to believe that it is not true in the corporate world. People have achieved chief executive officer status in the corporate world from doing a job well. There are people in finance who have been at the lowest end of the scale when they started off with a company—General Electric, General Motors, and others—and yet they have moved by virtue of their experience into other companies, have been hired by other companies because of the job that they have done and the reputation they have developed. Basically, advancement comes from dedication, hard work, interest, initiative, and enthusiasm.

Admiral Hayward states why it is so important for a naval officer to know his job and to strive for self-improvement.

> Knowing his job is a clear, basic requirement for a division officer. How could you possibly lead your people in any constructive sense if you don't have a grasp of what is expected and whether you are missing certain technical elements

or even leadership elements? You are constantly involved in self-improvement, so that's a given. If a division officer, a commanding officer, a Chief of Naval Operations, is not always trying to understand the brutality of his responsibilities clearly and constantly to improve upon the performance in meeting those responsibilities, he isn't going to be very successful. I don't believe you're going to become a successful senior officer without a natural instinct for self-improvement. I think one of the most exciting things about the Naval Service is the unlimited number of opportunities to stretch one's capabilities, to learn about something of particular interest, develop an additional skill, or take on an additional challenge. The very successful are the people who are constantly working at improvement. Take, as an example, Admiral Rickover. Nobody who has ever observed the man ever saw anybody who was so intensely involved in learning more, always picking up some more information, working to know something more thoroughly in a wide spectrum of talents. I think that's true of a division officer, a watch officer—in fact, technology today is moving so fast, if you aren't trying to improve beyond that which is just around you, you're going to be left on the trail, the bright guys are going to go right on by you. If you don't know electronic warfare or aren't striving to know electronic warfare—I don't care what your other jobs are—if you don't end up understanding the combat information system, if you don't have a feel for the engineering requirements of the ship, all put together with those leadership demands, the hot shots are going to leave you in the dust.

Admiral Kazuomi Uchida, former Japanese CNO, suggests that

an officer's professionalism should be

demonstrated not only by his military skill but also by his humanistic superiority. That contributes to the effectiveness of a leader. In order to ensure professionalism on a high level, an officer should include the "read widely and think deeply" step in his daily routine. However, an officer should not love his desk and ignore the maxim "Always on the deck."

A young person of diligence and integrity can accomplish whatever he wants to. Certainly, pride and loyalty plus personal humor greatly affect and encourage subordinates, thus proving the leader's own performance.

Admiral de Cazanove notes that

Charles de Gaulle would say culture is the true school of command. Things are never given to you, and you have to go out again and again, preparing yourself for what may come your way. Let me tell you a story of my first meeting of the enemy when I was nearly 20 years old, commanding a PT boat in the 1942–43 time frame. I fought the enemy with this boat under my command, and we were in a lot of trouble, and I had to do something. I saw that my crew obeyed all my orders, which greatly impressed me and helped me to think that what I was doing was right. From this confidence displayed by the crew, I realized that all the prethinking, planning, and "What if?" thinking that had gone on before battle paid off as the crew followed my orders and we prevailed. You must rely on your imagination, professional competence, and prebattle work that you have done. You will find that your imagination and rank will increase in proportion to the amount of preparation you have gone through.

SELECTING AND UTILIZING STAFF MEMBERS

When they are selecting people for staff positions, most senior officers look for proven professional excellence, people who have done well in the past in their specialty area, whether it be in aviation, submarines, field units, or surface ships, and people who have a good reputation and are well thought of. They also seek people who can communicate, especially on the telephone. In dealing with senior people and with people in all levels of the government, it is extremely important that staff members be able to convey clearly their senior officer's thoughts and ideas, as well as represent the institution in a very professional, diplomatic, and friendly manner.

People on staff who are proficient in their own areas and are respected for the fact that they are doing a good job do not have to wear the stars of the senior officer. People will be responsive to them in a professional environment because they will understand the staff members. Staff people who are good know what they are doing and that they are part of the team.

A senior officer should give his staff self-confidence. He must communicate with them so they understand his thoughts and his goals. Then they will be able to speak for him realistically, and if they are challenged by someone, the senior can back them up.

Treating staff members with respect. It is also critically important for the senior officer to treat his staff with respect—in a public forum, a meeting, a conference, or a private setting. If he treats his staff with dignity and respect and shows in little ways that he appreciates their capabilities, then others will get on board and follow his lead. If he treats his staff like servants, then he will find that others treat them like servants, too, and they will not be able to do an effective job for him. A senior officer must be sure that his staff members have the respect of others. However, as Admiral Burke points out, you do not have to treat people equally. You can't. Many times the people you mistreat the most are the people who are the best, because you give them the tough jobs, the jobs that have danger in them, the jobs that require great skill, and if they fail, then they will have a mark of failure against them, and a man who has never had that responsibility doesn't have that mark. So you mistreat your very good people by requiring higher performance of them. It's not fair to the individual, but it sure is fair to society, and this is a secret of the service.

We must live by standards, and when a nation, society, or organization lowers its standards or output, it eventually fails, because others can do it better or cheaper as a result of their maintaining standards. In our educational system, the value of high school and college degrees will be less a mark of accomplishment if standards are allowed to deteriorate. Thus, our schools must maintain their grading requirements and require teachers to meet standards or the entire nation's future will be imperiled. For the officer, this means not accepting the minimum. There is a saying that if the minimum were not good enough it wouldn't be the minimum. This approach is unacceptable in the service if we are to keep our accident rates down, present a posture of capability to the world, and prevail when called upon to defend our country. It is a challenge for an officer to correct an enlisted or officer when standards are not being met, but that is part of being a professional and must be done.

Challenging and guiding staff members. One technique an officer can use to build his staff is to challenge individual staff members. According to Admiral Giovanni Torrisi, Chief of Staff of the Italian Navy, "In order to make a complex and distinct organization such as the Navy function well, it takes continuous training."[66-35] The officer can let people work to the limits of their capability, so that, in addition to the tasks in their formal areas of responsibility, they take on as many additional tasks as they can. The senior officer can ask his staff to give a little more, and a little more, and a little more, until he sees they may be in danger of becoming overloaded or working too hard or getting into an area where they may not be quite as effective. Then he can either redelegate or do some of the work himself. The senior who allows his staff members to stretch their capabilities generally discovers that they have a greater capacity than he expected, and that they are much happier when they are working than when they are sitting back feeling unproductive. Admiral Zumwalt suggests that

> morale can be thought of as a significant subset of individual capability. Seaman Smith can be a moderately good petty officer if his morale is poor, but he can be a very good petty officer if his morale is high. The capability of an individual and the capability of a ship can be enhanced by some 20 to 30 percent if morale is high. Morale, then, which certainly is a significant contributor to mission performance, is a large part of capability.

A senior officer can help individual staff members to feel that they are doing something important to contribute to the mission of the staff by holding regularly scheduled staff meetings. The senior can critique the previous week and talk about where the staff is going during the current week, what the major issues are, what he is trying to accomplish, both long and short term. He can read a list of the critical issues he is concerned about and things that he wants to stay updated on and things that he wants to make happen that week. Through these meetings, staff members stay informed about what they are doing, why they are doing it, where their senior is trying to go, and what the senior considers important.

Allowing staff members to participate in plan-

ning. Participatory management, in which the senior officer brings his advisors in and lets them give their opinions as he is formulating policy, has three advantages. One, staff advisors are able to speak their mind; everyone likes to participate in policy formulation rather than just being dictated to. Two, the senior officer often picks up very valuable ideas that make the policy more effective. And three, once the senior has made the decision and decided where he is going, then all of his pepole have a vested interest in the senior's success, because they participated in making the plan. The officer who believes he is the most brilliant person in the world and does not need any help whatsoever and so just sits back and dictates will create an environment in which people skeptically stand back with their hands on their hips and say "I hope he falls on his ear because he didn't ask me about this." A team effort is created by involving people in planning. In this way everyone works together, and people do meaningful work and have a chance to make things happen.

6. Self-Discipline

"The totally dependable man—who will fulfill his responsibilities under any and all circumstances in the absence of direct and immediate supervision—is the one who has achieved the ability to discipline himself. It is such men who carry on the battle when their leaders and shipmates have fallen."[45-153] Secretary Webb insists that

> self-discipline is a trait that every officer must develop. Some people, through other activities in their lives, have naturally developed the sort of self-discipline that can make them function in a stressful environment. Others may need a structured period of indoctrination in order to ensure that they are self-disciplined.
> Self-discipline is only one part of an attitude that affects many aspects of lead-

ership. The plebe system at the Naval Academy, the officer candidate system in the Marine Corps, and boot camp in the Marine Corps develop that attitude through indoctrination, through example of the leaders, and through anecdotes that individuals can measure their experiences and aspirations with.

These institutions also perform as filtering devices to make sure that individuals who do not possess the ability to function in a stressful environment do not pass through the system and become responsible for the lives of other people. Individuals are placed in situations where they have to react, they are exposed to stressful environments in a context that is new to them. Many very intelligent people can function in what is for them a moderately stressful environment, say an academically stressful environment, but are less capable of performing if they are placed in physical discomfort. By the same token, a physical specimen might not hold up well if he is put up against the bulkhead and harassed. The indoctrination system exists to measure the ability of individuals to perform under stress, and in this way it also assesses their attitude, including how much self-discipline they possess.

It is useful to think of this attribute as encompassing two facets. The first covers what the officer should do, and the second, what he shouldn't. Stating the former in more precise terms, an officer must carry out his responsibility in a superior manner, even when it conflicts with his personal desires. The latter can be stated as personal, self-applied restraint from things and excesses that do not fit in with ordinarily accepted rules of society and the Naval Service.

The practice of self-discipline is a key not only to command success, but also to mission accomplishment. It does the military little good for a commander to be successful within his own organization if such success does not contribute positively to the overall mission. The brutal fact is that there have been times when the failure to exercise self-discipline has cost lives and contributed to battle reverses. Admiral Clausen notes that self-discipline

is required everywhere, but for an officer beyond usual measure. Many examples can be visualized. For instance: self-preservation in conflict with duties; cowardice in conflict with reasonable action; tiredness in conflict with vigilance. The problem is to overcome one's own weakness in order to get self-control and, through that, self-respect. Self-discipline prevents losing one's temper. Self-discipline can be learned during peacetime. It is a question of the will winning over a lack of self-control.

There are no simple recipes for how to increase self-discipline, but I think there are many possibilities during the education and training of aspirant officers. Officers can practice and exercise strength of will; practice to eliminate emotions; practice to overcome anxiety, timidity, and nervousness. I think that sporting activities are very significant in this endeavor.

This discussion is divided into four main sections. In the first, the emphasis is on the officer; the second concerns relationships with subordinates; the third explains how one goes about developing self-discipline. A summary of the components of self-discipline is presented in the fourth section.

SELF-DISCIPLINE IN THE NAVAL OFFICER

The first step for the officer is, through reading and discussion with others, to determine what is the right thing to do and then, despite any possible reluctance, to do the hard right rather than the easy wrong. In setting his standards, an officer needs to choose a mode of behavior which requires no less of him than he requires of others—otherwise his very standards will be cause for discontent. Once the correct course of action has been determined, advance preparation is necessary to ensure that any hardships that may be encountered can successfully be met. Since individuals are not born with behavior patterns, it is necessary for them to anticipate the types of situations they will encounter and then resolve in advance the action they will take so that it may be done without hesitation; quick action generates confidence in others.

A very important part of the concept of self-discipline is the carrying out of orders regardless of the individual's opinions of these orders. When a commander discusses a decision with a subordinate, the latter should state his honest opinion, but once the decision has been made, the subordinate must carry out the orders with spirit and enthusiasm, as if they were his own, even if they conflict with personal desires. Individuals can follow a commander who has strength, but if the subordinate officer detracts from the leader, the troops will in turn lose confidence in their ability to accomplish the overall mission and lose enthusiasm for carrying out their assigned tasks. "The officer who expects unflinching obedience and cooperation from subordinates will do well to give the same obedience and cooperation to his seniors."[45-153]

The officer must be extremely flexible and be able to adapt to changing routines easily, recognizing that situations are constantly changing and that to keep going blindly in the same direction may lead him off a cliff. An officer is not just someone who is carrying out the master plan of the Naval Service; he *is* the Navy or Marine Corps, and thus he must be constantly alert and prepared to make modifications in daily routines which will support mission accomplishment. Sometimes the hours will be long and the call to watch irregular, which contributes to frustrations. It may help to remember that "these are the times that try men's souls—the summer soldier and the sunshine patriot will in a crisis shrink from the service of their country." The Naval Service, even during peace, must operate as if the nation is at war, because of the sensitive nature of and the danger inherent in exercises and maneuvers. Death can result even if there is no enemy within a thousand miles, if anyone reduces his vigilance for a moment and allows his link in the chain of command to become weak.

The commission you hold and the standing orders from the captain do not specify each and every action and assignment with which you are charged, because an officer is expected, as a member of the Naval Service leadership team, to be willing to take on jobs that he might be able to avoid—for when such jobs are avoided, it is quite likely that no one else will fill the void, and a job left undone today may lead to disaster tomorrow.

The hard right often requires great moral courage, as the action to be taken may be very unpopular—but if popularity is your goal in life, then a naval career should not be. Admiral Long makes the point that there are

certain qualities that officers have because they are born with them, and there are other qualitites that they have because they acquired them during their life at home, at school, at the Naval Academy, or in association with other people. Obviously an officer cannot do very much to change his physical appearance and, in some cases, his physical ability. His inherent intelligence level cannot be altered very much, either. But qualities such as self-discipline can be acquired.

It would be nice if every officer came into the Navy with a high degree of self-discipline, but most people are not particularly well disciplined early on in life. As he enters into the responsibilities of commissioned service, however, an officer needs self-discipline. It becomes increasingly important, not only to his professional life, but to his personal life, as well. Without self-discipline, officers will have difficulty finding the time to meet their many obligations.

The Naval Academy is a place where a midshipman can learn self-discipline. The rigors of being a plebe may be unpleasant, but they will generally instill a certain level of self-discipline that will carry an officer throughout his naval career and beyond.

An officer must guard against being so self-disciplined that he acts in an unbelievable manner. He should not be so disciplined that he lacks flexibility and the ability to communicate and lead people. Self-righteous individuals are uncomfortable to be with. As in most things in life, a balance must be struck, so officers should seek to maintain an appropriate level of _____ without making everyone _____table in their presence.

T____ _____ for the good of the profe____ _____imself will find that a "milita____ ___y—the respect of his peers, ___ ___ce of his subordinates, and the _____is counsel by his seniors—will be his reward.

SELF-DISCIPLINE AND RELATIONSHIPS WITH SUBORDINATES

One key to an officer's relationships with subordinates is that he sets the example for them. The fact is that if you are ineffective in disciplining yourself, you will be even more ineffective in disciplining your subordinates. Few things will disgust people more than an officer who is a "do as I say" rather than a "do as I do" person. Subordinates find it difficult to accept discipline from someone who cannot discipline himself. They feel that he is asking more of them than he is willing to do himself and, since the officer has the greater rank and pay, they conclude that his action and requests are unfair and are not representative of what the Navy really wants, and therefore they don't obey his orders to the best of their ability.

The officer should be a model for his troops, but he must be careful not to make requirements or set standards that are not within the realm of possibility. Through discipline of self, the officer will secure the loyalty of his troops as they recognize that his pride in the way he does his job, along with his maintenance of a good appearance, is respected by his peers and seniors. All people want to be on a winning team. They know that the officer who has earned the acceptance of his peers and seniors will be well treated, and this treatment will in turn allow him to take better care of his troops. The result is a team effort, with the troops helping the officer and the officer helping them.

You must at all times remember that you *ARE* the Naval Service, and its good name can be affected by your actions. The men will see all officers as they see you. Thus, even physically you should be in better shape than the average sailor or Marine in your command, thereby winning the respect of your troops and generating their enthusiasm for the performance of their jobs. Admiral McDonald remarks: "In order to be a good leader, one must look like one; i.e., neat in appearance, hair cut, shoes shined, shoulders thrown back, and looking PROUD." Remember, "Sloppy officers cannot gain the high confidence and respect necessary for real efficiency and discipline."[47-148]

An officer who gripes, procrastinates in carrying out his assignments, or seeks praise for his accomplishments will not be respected by his troops. He must be a Rock of Gibraltar, for the troops will reason that, if the officer is not getting a good deal or is not recognized for his work, how will they, as lowly sailors and Marines, make it? People do in fact learn by what they see, and procrastination by an officer, for example, will be accepted by the troops as a mode of behavior. Self-discipline necessitates on-time reporting for watches and appointments, and meeting the deadline for filing reports. An officer's every action is observed by the troops and sets the standards for their behavior.

Setting the example means not being the first one off the ship when liberty call is sounded.

An officer is assumed to be doing an important job and to be on duty all the time, as opposed to standing specific, measured watches. The responsibility of command dictates that officers complete their assignments and responsibilities before they pursue their own pleasures. It is well to mention here that enlisted are well aware of what an officer does ashore. Even if he is not in uniform, the officer is known as the person who is supposed to be the leader, and if he exhibits behavior that is inconsistent with the image the troops have of a "good" officer, then all his work and actions on board ship will be for nought, for it will be seen as a facade of convenience. Self-discipline takes many forms, not the least of them staying nearby when the troops are working late. The officer should find something to do, as the men will put out for someone who shows the way by his own self-sacrifice. The maintenance of an officer's own good health is another matter of self-discipline, and when an officer deviates from the norm for naval officers, the troops quickly notice.

Unless this relationship with subordinates is achieved by the officer's good example, morale will be low, appearances will be sloppy, and bad performance will result in the unit. It is axiomatic that mast cases result from a lack of self-discipline. If the officer does not exercise it, his troops will think that self-discipline is unattainable, and so they will not try to be self-disciplined but will excuse their actions by rationalizing that they cannot be expected to do any more than their officers are capable of doing. When an officer leads his troops by providing examples of self-discipline, they will willingly follow, and mast cases will be few and far between.

DEVELOPING SELF-DISCIPLINE

The first step is to know yourself, for, unless you understand your own machinery, you cannot very well expect to control yourself. In addition to taking the basic courses and reading the basic books in leadership and psychology, you should consult with friends and listen to the comments that are made to you and about you. When you talk, listen to what you are saying and try to determine why you are saying it. Are you saying what you think the listener wants to hear, or are you saying what you think? By using a feedback system within yourself, you can observe your actions and then analyze what motivates them.

Self-discipline can definitely be acquired, though not easily. To accomplish the task, you must determine your faults and seek improvement. Think ahead and be aware of the consequences of your actions, and if the results are not consistent with your goals for self-discipline, then take a different approach. The main point is to set goals and accomplish them—develop a code and live by it. An officer has a great deal of power, so it is necessary for an officer constantly to review the way he is connecting himself with the people around him. Does he support the Navy line, or does he short-circuit its intentions? Planning in advance to meet the rigors of command and putting forth the best effort to complete an assigned task successfully are both signs of effective self-discipline.

The "good" officer realizes that he cannot run everything himself and will delegate to subordinates the authority to accomplish the mission. This delegation of authority is itself an example to the troops that they are a part of the team, a team that requires active participation by its members as well as by its leader. The old trick of counting to 10 is a good one, because an officer who loses control of himself also loses the respect of his troops, for they reason that, if he cannot control himself properly, how can they depend on him to control what they have to do without letting his emotions interfere? The same holds true for living within one's income. Everyone knows to the penny what every other person earns. The officer who lives above his means is demonstrating, in one of the many possible ways, that he does not have self-discipline in everything he does.

Where little direction is given, the officer must take the action that the situation requires and thus, by setting the example for his troops, develop in them the spirit of getting the job done, rather than "leaving it to George" or letting it fall between the cracks. Self-discipline, then, involves loyalty and dedication; the officer must be able to relate to others without necessarily being moved by their conduct or their opinion. The officer who makes the hard right choice will find that his troops avoid making the easy wrong choice.

THE COMPONENTS OF SELF-DISCIPLINE

Admiral Lawson P. Ramage suggests that self-discipline is founded on a thorough

knowledge of the goals set by one's command and pursuing those goals to the best of one's ability. To be a good follower, one must endeavor to emulate the best characteristics of successful leaders.

One of the greatest leaders who ever pulled on combat boots was Lieutenant General Lewis B. (Chesty) Puller. General Puller knew the necessity of looking and acting in a sharp and military manner. As a lieutenant, he was chosen to handle the Marine drill detachment at Quantico. The Marines had not done well in the national drill competition in Boston for years, being shown up by drill teams from the Army, Navy, and Coast Guard, despite the reputation of Marines as sharp marchers. With Lieutenant Puller in charge, the Boston drill competition was ruled by the Marines. One sergeant remembered: "Puller won that cup all by himself. He didn't look like flesh and blood, he stepped out so smartly and proud and soldierly that it was like watching a mechanical man. He just carried them on his

back, and it was hard to keep your eyes off him to watch the ranks."[21-51]

The officer must be careful regarding the outward manifestations of his self-discipline. Misapplied, it may take the form of arrogance or stuffiness, with a resultant negation of all that self-discipline would normally accomplish. An officer should take pride in his ability to control himself, but if that ability is lorded over others, they will resent it rather than respect it. By trying to see yourself as others see you, you will be better able to judge the extent to which you have achieved self-discipline. If others cannot see self-discipline in you, then it probably does not exist. To help you achieve it, associate with people who set an example, for "life is a stage and all the people players"—we have to learn to exercise self-discipline, and watching and emulating others makes that job easier.

A job must be done right, not because the skipper is watching, but because it is the right thing to do. By acting properly in public and demonstrating ethical conduct, your own self-discipline will instill confidence in others. An officer must be above reproach and set an outstanding example, and he will find that behavior will be contagious to subordinates, peers, and seniors, and that the rewards of accomplishment and greater command will follow. Admiral Fran McKee reminds us that

you have to be disciplined to be a naval officer. There may be times when you are called upon to accomplish an assignment instantly or within hours or days. You've got to discipline yourself to accomplish that task on a specific schedule or to complete it with other tasks during a given time period. I think you also have to learn to be a good follower before you can learn to be an effective leader. There is nothing like walking in another person's shoes, and when you have walked in his or her shoes you have a keener understanding of what a realistic pace is supposed to be. If you discipline yourself during all your experiences and learn the lessons well, you can then be better prepared to assume the mantle of leadership.

FOLLOWERSHIP IS A FORM OF SELF-DISCIPLINE

In May 1984 the Commandant of the Marine Corps, General P. X. Kelley, USMC, presented the commencement speech for Norwich University's Class of 1984. In his address, the Commandant stressed the importance of leadership and followership in our society. Included in his remarks was the following.

An ingredient as essential as leadership to a free society . . . is what I would like  to refer to as "followership." To me, "followers" are the backbone of any great nation or organization, for without loyal, dedicated "followers," there can be no effective leaders. And without effective leaders, no viable organization could survive.

To put "followership" in perspective, I have been a "follower" for all of my 34 years as a Marine. As a platoon leader I followed the leadership of my company commander, as a company commander I followed the leadership of my battalion commander, as a battalion commander I followed the leadership of my regimental commander, as a regimental commander I followed the leadership of my division commander, and even today, as the Commandant of the Marine Corps, I follow the leadership of the Secretary of the Navy, the Secretary of Defense, and the President of the United States in his constitutional role as our Commander in Chief.

Conversely, while I have been a loyal follower for some 34 years, I have been in command positions for something less than one-quarter of that time.

"What is this thing called followership?" Let me try to explain.

First, and probably most importantly, "followership" is the ability to place the health and well-being of an organization ahead of personal ambition. In a book entitled *The Armed Forces Officer*, published in 1950, the year I was commissioned, this point was made as follows: "In all human enterprise, the whole is greater than the sum of the parts. The citizen who thinks most deeply about his country will be the first to share the burdens of his community and neighborhood. The man who feels the greatest affection for the service in which he bears arms will work most loyally to make his own unit know a rightful pride in its own worth."

"Followership" is the ability to know where and when to articulate one's views on an issue, and then to have the loyalty and devotion to carry out a final decision on that issue with a "cheery aye aye," even when that decision may not be to one's liking. In this regard, I am reminded of a technique used by a now retired Marine general officer who told me that shortly after he was commissioned he had what he believed to be just and sufficient cause to question certain orders issued by senior officers. He decided there and then to keep a little "black book" that contained the circumstances surrounding every order he disagreed with, so he would not make the same mistake as he advanced in rank. To be fair, he also agreed with himself to cross out an entry if he subsequently had reason to agree with the contested order. The distinguished officer told me that, upon his retirement after over 40 years of service to his country, his "black book" had only a handful of orders which had not been crossed out.

I am not suggesting that the system is perfect, but I am saying that as the Commandant of the Marine Corps in 1984, I am issuing orders that I would have questioned as a young captain in the mid-1950s. I can only hope that some young captain with a little "black book" in 1984 will ultimately find cause to cross out his disagreements.

"Followership" is the ability to have the same allegiance and loyalty up the chain of command as one would expect to flow down the chain. Said another way, it is the provision of the same loyalty to one's seniors as one would reasonably anticipate from one's subordinates.

"Followership" is a strict adherence to a personal code of conduct which upholds the standards and values of the organization. This needs little elaboration, for it is the bedrock of a healthy and wholesome society.

Admiral Ramage offers that

juniors will follow if they have confidence in their seniors and if the seniors do not demand the impossible. I think the senior has to realize the limitations and the capabilities of those who he is commanding when he issues orders and not to ask for the impossible.

"THE NO NAME COMPANY": SELF-DISCIPLINE AND FOLLOWERSHIP

Self-discipline and followership, when combined in the same individual, form the basis for military leadership, as exemplified in this abridged version of the Vietnam story about "The No Name Company" which appeared in the January 1985 issue of *Marines*.

My R & R in Honolulu with my wife and child was like stepping through a time warp when compared to the horrors of war I had left only days before in Vietnam. A radio broadcast cancelling leave for all military personnel and ordering everyone to return to duty in Vietnam took me back through that time warp sooner than I had expected. I knew my wife wouldn't question why I believed I should return when no one knew I had heard the broadcast. No one knew but the two of us . . . and she realized that I had to go. We both knew that it was the Corps, the Corps, the Corps.

DaNang was always confusing, but on my arrival, I found chaos. Over one thousand military personnel, mostly Marines, were milling about, not knowing why their emergency leaves, R & R, or end-of-tour rotations home had been cancelled. The airport was a collection of people who were supposed to leave and people who were coming back, and no one was going anywhere.

Activity several hundred yards down the airfield caught my eye. A steady sortie of helicopters were landing, and Marines hurried out to discharge the cargo, which was stacked like cord along the edge of the taxiway in the hot Vietnamese sun. I watched for a while before I realized that the cargo being unloaded consisted of large black bags. Black plastic bags. Body bags. From that distance I counted several dozen. Whatever was happening was heavy with death.

That day at DaNang there was a loud chorus arising from the uncertainty and frustration of those who had left and then had been brought back early. In the midst of all the commotion, a tall Marine colonel tapped me on the shoulder and said, "Captain, I need to see you in my hootch."

I entered a strongback hut a few yards down the flight line and found five other young Marine officers. None of us knew what was about to happen. The colonel explained that the communists had launched a major offensive, which we now call the Tet Offensive. Regular North Vietnamese Army (NVA) regiments were headed straight for DaNang, which until then had been similar to a rear area. DaNang was short of defenders, and we were going to provide extra defense. We were to be company commanders.

"I think you ought to know, sir," I advised the colonel, "I am a Comm O." The other officers responded similarly, and not one was an infantry officer.

"That makes no difference," the colonel said, "you're all Marines."

I knew then that I had a job to do, so I didn't stand around to chat with the other five officers who were in there as to what was going to be done or how it was going to be accomplished.

I walked out of the hut, grabbed the first sergeant and said, "Top, I've got a problem and I think you can help me solve it. We're going to have to form some companies here and what I'd like you to do is to have this mob fall into three ranks." Top said, "Aye, Aye, Sir," turned around, and at the top of his lungs yelled, "Fall in!"

Just as they were trained to do, these Marines who had been milling around became a military formation by falling in facing this first sergeant in three ranks. That's the way they were taught to do it. That's what I expected to happen. This mass of humanity began its transformation into a fighting unit.

He turned back to me and said, "Now what do you want me to do, Sir?"

I said, "I'd like you to have them count to 13 three times."

They counted down. We then had a random selection of three platoons of Marines. I began to think I would need a couple of admin types, maybe some corpsmen, some people who know logistics—I was flashing back to all I'd been taught about organization for combat in Basic School 12 to 15 months earlier. I asked him to get me some Marines for a headquarters group. He did, and then he dismissed the rest.

At that point I didn't have any officers, so I asked my first sergeant to pick the ranking staff NCO in each platoon and make him a platoon commander. I then called these platoon commanders front and center. They made quite a group! I had a master sergeant who was a cook,

a baker by MOS; another master sergeant who was an intelligence chief; and one who was an admin chief. I had no one with an infantry MOS. The only one I knew was the baker. He was one of the most dedicated Marines I had ever known from the standpoint of believing in a support role, believing that his mission was just as important as the guy out on the point. Master Sgt. Cook was his name and, even though he was a baker, he would soon be on the point.

He and the other platoon commanders came over. I explained the circumstances to them and told them that we had been tasked to form a provisional rifle company. That's what the colonel had called it, "A provisional rifle company of III MAF." Since we were the first company formed, I gave us the name of 1st Provisional Rifle Company of III MAF. I told them that was what we would call ourselves. I asked the platoon commanders to get organized, to assign squad leaders and fire team leaders, and to get the names, ranks, and serial numbers of all our personnel. They did so and I had admin types put together a company roster. This process, from the time I started talking to the first sergeant until I had a platoon roster, took 20 minutes.

I went back to the colonel and reported to him that I had formed my company and asked what we were to do next. I heard him offer defense of the medical battalion, and I figured that if I had to get shot, I would rather be where someone could take care of me. It would be a mutual relationship: if we took care of them, they would take care of us.

The colonel said, "All right, that's where you'll go, to the medical battalion. You will be in defense of their perimeter."

I said, "Fine. But we don't have any weapons." It was 1600, and he directed me to take my new company across the road to the mess hall for hot chow and advised me that by the time I returned, the weapons would have been delivered. The Top marched them to the chow hall and had them back in one hour for muster.

The company returned a little happier; they had food, a little bit of organization, and they were all accounted for at muster. No UAs. They still wondered what was going on.

As I learned information, I shared it with them. I think it is important to keep the troops informed. I told them that we had a mission and I thought it was important that we do it and do it to the best of our abilities because we were Marines. They responded without any grouching or grumbling. I explained that the weapons would be arriving shortly, and that we would mount out on "six bys." The colonel had since told me that we would be trucked out to the medical battalion which was on the other side of Hill 327, "Freedom Hill."

About the time I finished talking with them, up rolled some six bys, and in the back were big wooden crates full of brand new M-16 rifles. The troops were impressed with rifles that had not been fired and were still in crates. I was uneasy. They started passing rifles out just like you'd pass out beers at a party; come down the line and get one. Every Marine got one, including me. We were also issued five magazines, rounds for the magazines, and a cleaning rod. We placed the magazines inside our jackets, since we didn't have any web gear; we were not issued helmets or flack jackets, either. All we had were our jungle utilities.

I still didn't know the extent of the enemy situation, but after the gear was issued, I knew we were in a whole lot of trouble. After they issued me all this gear, no one came up to ask me to sign for it. That's trouble. When a military organization doesn't ask you to sign for gear, especially weapons, you know that people are more worried about getting the job done than having the paper work taken care of.

When we arrived in the medical battalion area, I reported to a Navy captain who, when he saw me, was the happiest person I have ever seen. He didn't have many personnel to help him defend that area. I told him what I was there for and asked him to show me his positions and

what he had for defense of the area. The dug-in positions had sandbags that could have interlocking fire. If we had been going to be there longer, I would probably have done much more with it. It was a position that had been there for a long time; it was adequate but nothing to write home about.

The first sergeant and I decided to handle the defense by placing two platoons on the line and keeping one back as a reaction force. I did not send out any patrols, because I had no maps. We were on 50 percent alert on the positions. One person was to be up all the time in all the positions. Being a "Comm O," I established something similar to a gun loop on artillery. We hooked in a telephone loop that went around the perimeter that we were defending and back to me, so I could talk to anyone at any of the phone positions. We had never worked together, we didn't know each other from Adam's house cat. If they got nervous about anything, I wanted them to talk to me before they did something. I told them not to just go shooting up the place. "I want good fire discipline, and I want you to talk to me about it first. If you see something or hear something, talk to me."

We got the phones, wire, and other gear from the medical battalion. With the medical battalion's entrenching tools we improved our positions so more people could be up on the line. With a North Vietnamese Army regiment coming, I wanted to have plenty of firepower. We got it all done before it was completely dark. I was amazed that we were able to accomplish so much so quickly. Then again, I was working with Marines. If you ask Marines to accomplish something, they do it.

We set in for the night, and I periodically checked the lines. Soon the NVA began to probe. We were mainly probed by fire. Several fights erupted to our front with the units on our flanks. We maintained very good fire discipline and never gave away our entire position, since we did not return fire until I ordered it, and I only ordered it when we were being attacked. I only wanted to return fire when there was sufficient volume of fire coming in to justify it. I figured the enemy would not know our strength as long as we maintained fire discipline. In thinking about it later, it is amazing that we could maintain fire discipline with a group of men who had never fought together, and had only been an organized unit since shortly before supper. We did not even know one another's names.

It was to our advantage to keep our positions concealed until it was necessary to fire final protective fires. I was impressed with the troops. During the course of the night we never cranked off the first round. We took many rounds in the positions, but never in sufficient volume to justify firing all along our line.

Came the dawn and we were still there; life went on. The Navy captain was all smiles and couldn't tell us enough how he appreciated us. He provided rations and water and repeated thanks. While we caught up on our sleep, the medical battalion was hard at work, as incoming casualties were crowded all over the area. The rest of the day was spent improving our positions and checking on the troops. No one seemed to be nervous. Belonging to the 1st Provisional Rifle Company helped relieve the tension caused by the confusion, disappointment, and frustration of missing R & R, leave, and rotation.

The second night was a repeat of the first. Random incoming fire, probing minor fire fights, and excellent fire discipline by the 1st Provisional Rifle Company.

On the third day a messenger came out and told us the alert was over: "They are not coming; I don't know what happened to them." The answers to all my questions were the same, "I don't know." All I could find out was that we didn't have to be there anymore. We were ordered to return to our units.

I called the company together, and everyone who had answered the company's first muster was still there. I told them we were being relieved, and that I appreciated everything they had done. We got back on trucks and returned

to the air strip. Supply personnel were there to pick up all our gear.

After we turned in our gear, we had a formation and I thanked these Marines one more time. All the individual baggage was stacked in a small warehouse, just where we had left it before departing for the medical battalion area. We retrieved our baggage and off we went. Those leaving the country checked out flights. I went to flight operations and caught a ride back to Quang Tri, and reported back to my unit.

It is fantastic to see that it does work. I never felt we had done anything heroic or had turned back the thundering hordes. Our presence may have diverted the enemy to some other area or made them reconsider their action. The roster was written in longhand and never typed. No entries were made in any service record books of the duty, and to my knowledge no record has ever been made of the existence of the 1st Provisional Rifle Company.

The 1st Provisional Rifle Company was formed out of chaos, existed on a tradition of training and discipline, took hostile enemy fire in trenches without helmets, maps, or artillery support, and was disbanded without any record. It functioned as a fighting unit because every man there knew he was part of the Corps, the Corps, the Corps.

MCPON Sanders: *A key to all leadership is that the individual must understand and discipline self. We must understand what it means to follow, and, as the senior, understand what the subordinate is thinking about. You must know in advance that the crew will follow you if they are given an order in a battle situation or an emergency. If you can follow the direction of your senior, you will know what it means to be in that situation; therefore, when you give orders you automatically think about the impact on the person who must carry out your direction. I think that you'll be able to give orders much, much better if you understand the makeup of the person you are giving the orders to.*

7. Characteristics of a Naval Officer

JUDGMENT

Good judgment is based on very thorough personal knowledge in the officer's area of responsibility, broad knowledge in various fields, and innate intelligence. General Robert Barrow, former Commandant of the Marine Corps, thinks that

> judgment, a critical element in leadership decision making, has two components.

One is knowledge. A leader cannot make a judgment if he is unfamiliar with the subject about which the judgment must be made. In military affairs, it is particularly important for a person to be as knowledgeable about his responsibilities as he can possibly be.

The other component is common sense, which is an attribute that individuals attain through experience. We have all pretty much said that there's no such thing as a born leader, that one can become a leader by study and self-analysis and instruction and by example given to him by others, and that's quite true. However, there are some qualities that I don't think can be learned, and maybe one would not necessarily have been born with them but somehow acquired them over a long process, and common sense is one of them. I've known officers who were as knowledgeable about their responsibilities as they could possibly be, but the point is, when they were put in divisions where they had to use good judgment, they were often found wanting for the simple reason that they didn't have the quality of common sense. It's simple. It's almost too simple. When you're driving down the road and you see someone spill a bag of nails in front of your car, you don't drive through it, you drive around it, because somewhere in your experiences you learned that you might get a flat tire. But surprisingly, there are people who would drive through it. They don't have any common sense, they don't know that nails puncture tires or whatever it is. Because common sense is a quality that canot necessarily be learned, one would then concentrate on the other component, which is knowledge. So I would say to an officer who needed to improve himself in that area that he needed to be better informed so that he can make a judgment based on the knowledge of his job.

Admiral Clausen believes that good judgment is based on a broad platform of capacities. Logical thinking is insufficient for an efficient officer. The higher the rank of an officer, the more trained and experienced in judgment he must be. The ability to make a reliable judgment is a distinctive mark, especially of an admiral.

We are living in a time when the conception of life and military profession and the theoretical substances of both of them come more and more under the influence of intellectuality. In this development, the component of intellectual valuation of almost everything very often carries weight to a degree that distorts judgment, especially where leadership is concerned. (Not everything is subject to precise analytical analysis.)

Therefore, I think that the quality of judgment of a naval officer is based, first of all, on the foundation of his *personality*. This finding is not a new one—certainly it was known during the days of the Kriegsmarine—but knowledge of it should go deep into the consciousness of any naval officer. Secondly, I think judgment is based on *competency*. Competency implies technical knowledge and manifold abilities and also, I think, a certain amount of experienced proficiency. Judgment can be improved by training to a certain degree.

The officer in command must take care that subordinate officers and enlisted personnel are employed in a duty or task according to their abilities, talents, and predispositions. This truism is very important, as shown by the cruel reality of war. No one must be promoted within any hierarchy into a step, a stage, or a grade of inability [this is known as the Peter Principle].

Many mistakes were made during the war, with very bad outcomes. The areas and levels of judgment differ, but the same principles and factors are always effective. And if a decision has to be made, an individual should at least know how to regard and evaluate a situation in order to come to a reasonable, sound, and substantial judgment. (In former times, known in the German Navy as Lagebetrachtung mit Entschluss [that is, what, where, when, why, and how].)

Admiral Jeremy Taylor, USN, describes judgment as

the crucial element in decision making. In order to solve a problem, you've got to reach a decision, and the quality of the decision is tied directly to the quality of the judgment. Judgment, of course, encompasses many things. I'd put it under the category of experience. You have to be out there and do things and learn by trial and error, and that sculptures your judgment. You have the knowledge that you get from books, from others, and then there's this basic quality that comes to some and not others: called common sense, it is an instinct about things.

When you roll all of those into one, you have a quality called judgment, and when a problem is put before you, you will come up with a solution. The quality of your solution has your mark on it, and you will be graded accordingly. What you're looking for are people with good, solid judgment. It's a crucial part of a fitness report, I might add.

A great deal of study and personal application is required to acquire knowledge, but knowledge allows the officer to weigh the relative importance of events and determine the proper course of action. Admiral Burke also believes that

judgment is a factor in deciding whether to demand that a problem be corrected or to make a note of the problem but not spend time on it. Minor problems must be brushed aside if the organization is to function smoothly, and the correction of problems is dependent a good deal upon the importance of the problem.

You cannot keep heckling on minor things. A lot of minor things go haywire and there is no need to make a great big fuss about a minor thing. That is a judgment factor; some people might not think it's minor, and if it's a question of integrity, it isn't minor. In general, minor things should be mentioned but not escalated in importance, unless the same mistake is repeatedly made. In that case the rule should be enforced or done away with. But as long as the rule is on the book, and performance is possible and needed, the rule should be followed. You

may never get the very best of everything, because you don't have that much
time to refine things, so if something is
pretty good and it will do the job and if
there isn't any direct competition, you
may have to take that or have a tremendously long delay.

Having a very thorough base of personal
knowledge in a particular field can help a person
to be imaginative and creative, because once
someone knows a field thoroughly, he can start
thinking of better, more efficient ways to do a
job. He can be creative in the sense of improving
the approach to performing or to command.
Admiral Thomas Moorer, former American CNO
and Chairman of the Joint Chiefs of Staff, says
that

people being led expect their leader to
have a considerable knowledge about the
problems in which
they are involved,
so one of the first
requirements for
effective leadership
is knowledge. A
leader quickly
becomes aware
that his people are
watching him to
see how he per-
forms under certain circumstances and
how he reacts to unexpected things, so
the leader simply must conduct himself to
the best of his ability and in a way that
indicates that he understands what he is
doing.

While his people are observing him,
the leader should observe the way the
people he is leading react to what he
does. If necessary, he can take time out
then or later to explain to them just why
he did what he did.

As the association between the leader
and the led continues, the led will have a
growing confidence in the leader who has

convinced them that he knows what he is
doing. It is very important for a leader to
work on this kind of influence, because
once he gains the confidence of his people, he can rest assured that they will be
loyal and dependable and will do their
best.

Before judging the ability or judgment
of a junior officer, a senior officer should
observe how the junior performs under
several different circumstances. A sound
appraisal of judgment cannot be made
simply on the basis of one incident. This
is particularly true of very inexperienced
officers, because they are continually
being exposed to new situations. An officer who at the onset is a little uncertain of
himself may well exercise excellent judgment once he is given an opportunity to
perform and gain confidence. An important point to remember is that different
individuals acquire good judgment at different times in their careers.

During his career, the naval officer will
have an opportunity to watch changes not
only within a service, but within the
country and internationally, as well. All of
these changes will impact on how an officer feels about his career, but he should
be careful not to make a hasty judgment
concerning his career, because he cannot
prejudge what the situation is going to be
ten or twenty or thirty years hence. When
my class was commissioned, for example,
the country was in the Great Depression
and newly commissioned married officers
were paid $125 a month. After three
major wars and a strong economy, my
position and circumstances changed dramatically. I recall some advice my father
used to give me: He said, "No matter
what you do, I have just two things that I
want you to remember. One is you must
always find ways to enjoy what you do,
and two is you must do your best to per-

form better than anyone else." I think those are two good, solid guidelines for any young person to follow.

IMAGINATION

Imagination requires the use of words, and of course a child who never learned to talk could not imagine things to do, because he would not have the words to imagine them. General Barrow believes that imagination has application in peacetime and in times of war. Imagination is that mysterious element that some people have a great deal of and others have very little of. People can be encouraged to develop imagination, however. Their leaders can tell them to explore beyond the immediate answer that comes to them when they are faced with a problem; they can tell them to reach out, not to feel bound by convention or anything else, to do the unusual or think of doing the unusual.

General Barrow described imagination as "an almost uncanny ability to conceive things that others have not thought of. I've known Marines, officers and enlisted, who could just reach out. It didn't rest in the knowledge of their job, it didn't rest in having an unusual amount of intellect, they learned to be imaginative by not restricting their thinking."

Admiral Moorer offers that imagination can be defined as

thinking all the time, and that certainly is a major requirement on the part of an officer. This is particularly true with respect to officers in the Navy, because naval operations are conducted in a mobile situation, and people are embarked on an unstable platform that is at the mercy of the weather and the sea.

A good officer of the deck or a good squadron commander or a good skipper of a ship must always have his brain turning over what can be called "What if?" questions. What if this happens? and What if

that happens? These questions will help him visualize what might happen and how he might best react if it does. It takes a great deal of imagination to predevelop a solution that he might choose to follow in the event he is faced with a certain problem, but a good officer is prepared with a solution, because he has imagined the situation beforehand.

Admiral Clausen states that

there are, of course, many examples that demonstrate the necessity and utility of imagination in the different fields of the military and naval profession. There is the imaginative faculty during a planning phase, and perhaps even more during the course of an operation, which is of inestimable value. But the process of transposing imagination into feasible reality requires a masterly command of professional skill. There is a boundary where imagination may glide off into unrealistic reflections and a world of fancy ideas, a boundary that, being passed over, would land someone in an uncontrolled area.

General George C. Marshall, who later became Army Chief of Staff and then Secretary of State, was a person who was able to reduce complicated military problems into relatively simple concepts. He stretched subordinates so that they were able to grasp the complexities of command.[46-96] Admiral Taylor says that imagination, like common sense, is

in some and not in others. People without imagination have tunnel vision. They don't widen their outlook and search for other opportunities, they don't gather information from other places and then put it into that little computer that runs between their ears and come up with some intuition. People without imagination are reluctant to take initiative. There are some people who live by the book and do not understand how to apply judgment, to take a little risk here and there and go outside to try to bring in a new idea.

The more someone learns about a subject, the more creative he can be in his approach to it. Sir Nicholas Hunt, Commander in Chief of the British Fleet, values independence of mind over all other attributes. He thinks that

the development in an officer of an independent mind must be a cardinal feature

of his training and education. Imagination and individuality are also essential, and can be suppressed by too stereotyped a pattern of training. While the encouragement of important qualities—

loyalty and the recognition of discipline, for example—is of course essential, an attempt to mold character according to a prescribed pattern is the way to waste talent.

An example of individual thought took place during the battle of Saratoga in October 1777. After a day of seemingly uphill struggle, the American lines were exhausted and were starting to give way. At the crucial point of the battle, just as the Americans were starting to turn and flee, a division commander, General Benedict Arnold, made a snap decision. He would ride forward and attempt to rally the Americans and turn a rout into an attack. He was able to do just that. As he did so, he was able to take advantage of a weakness in the enemy lines and capture a fortified position. Paying the price of a broken leg, General Arnold secured the victory at Saratoga due to his swift independent thinking and sound judgment.[22-251] Admiral Robert Carney, former American CNO, observes that

it often seems in wartime that appropriate leaders naturally come forth, just like when a group of people are washed

up on a deserted island and the person who knows about survival and what to eat and what not to eat emerges as the leader. This same individual might be helpless in an urban setting,

however. The fact is that certain circumstances breed leaders, and this is no reflection on those who do not lead under those particular circumstances.

Admiral Carney further related how he judged leadership ability.

When I was chief of staff to Admiral Bristol up in a North Atlantic shipping protection outfit, I had a lot of young officers, lieutenants, lieutenant commanders just made, and I didn't know much about them, so I systematically set about giving each one of them a task. They'd say, "What am I supposed to do?" I said I didn't know what the problem was, just that there was one and they should go see what the problem really is and see what they could do about it. There were some who came back not only with the bacon but with the whole pig, and there were others who came back baffled. That's all I needed to know about them. One of them was going to be a journeyman all his life and the other one could very possibly be a good leader.

ANALYTICAL ABILITY

To make a good decision, it is necessary to gather as much knowledge as possible on the subject involved. But a sound decision cannot be made without well-defined short- and long-term goals and objectives, because a sound decision enables an individual to advance toward the fulfillment of those goals or objectives. It is often useful to lay out the varying alternatives when making a decision. Sometimes an officer might choose to have members of his staff follow alternative courses of action, and then the officer can make a sound decision as to the course of action that will best lead him toward the goal. Obviously, then, an officer must know what his ultimate goal or objective is before he makes any decision. Admiral Burke reminds us that "you take a chance every time you make a decision, because you may not have enough information, and thus the importance of having trustworthy people who share the same professional background."

> General Barrow believes very strongly that effective leaders can make "seat of the pants" decisions when time is pressing. I'm sure that there is someone in this world teaching leadership who would say to his students, "Make sure that you approach every decision with the components very thoroughly thought out in a carefully labored-through process"— which is another way of saying "methodical"—and they may reach the right decision, but it's too late. The instructor has done them a disservice to say that's what you have to do in *every* instance.

The analytical ability of a junior officer, according to Admiral Moorer,

> becomes apparent to his seniors as they watch him over a period of time. The junior may be a supply officer or an operations officer or a plans officer, but in the course of finalizing the papers that he prepares on his assignments, the junior officer will reveal his ability to analyze and perform.

Admiral Clausen discerns that

> to take an object apart into logical components is an ability of thought which must be learned by a naval officer, especially one in staff duty. It can be learned through discussion with others who are more experienced. The power of distin-

guishing between and evaluating components and factors, and the ability to separate essentials from immaterials to the subject, requires soberness. And this is the point where the character of a naval officer and his education become a connecting link to logical thinking.

Admiral Taylor sees analytical ability as a process much like geometry:

> As I recall from the old days, you have some basic facts that are available to you, and you use your judgment to select some good assumptions to fill in the gaps. You identify the problem clearly—and the way you do that, in my experience, is to gather the best people you have working for you, brainstorm with them, ascertain the facts, discuss the assumptions, and then, using your analytical ability, lay down the essential elements. Work yourself toward a series of alternatives, and from those alternatives pick out the one with the greatest chance for success. You have analyzed the problem and you have developed a solution to pursue and thereby set a goal for an organization, and you have a lot of people on board. That's analytical ability from my standpoint, and I think that holds up as a subspecialty of operations analysis in the Pentagon and in the fleet.

IMPECCABLE PERSONAL BEHAVIOR

From an ethical and moral perspective, an officer's behavior and standards must be impeccable. Midshipmen are not to lie, cheat, or steal, and an officer's word is his bond. In other words, a naval officer is to be completely truthful and honest. Admiral Moorer reminds us that

> naval personnel are exposed to public scrutiny all the time, and consequently their conduct in terms of moral standards and social standards must be maintained at a very high level, because they are

serving their country. People are often quick to criticize, so service people must maintain the current high standards of the organization. Today's technology, in which the Naval Service is the front runner, requires very intelligent people and very motivated people who are concerned about their reputation. It should be remembered that if they get a bad service reputation and sooner or later choose to leave the service, the bad reputation will follow them.

The naval profession requires a great deal of moral courage, because it is not always easy to take a course of action, particularly an unpopular one, but moral courage means doing the right thing in all situations. It is easy to equivocate, to rationalize why a particular course of action need not be taken, but it takes a great deal of moral courage to stand up and take a course of action that is not going to be well received. Admiral Long remarks that

loyalty to seniors involves not blindly supporting seniors by being a "yes man." It means an officer tells seniors precisely what he believes and gives them his own recommendations, that he has the courage to tell them information that may not be particularly pleasant. If after he has done that his senior decides to take a different course of action, then loyalty involves carrying out those instructions, assuming they are lawful orders.

Being truthful, honest, and having the moral courage to do what is right regardless of the consequences are all important elements of an officer's personal behavior, and they are at the center of his conduct.

There should be little difference in the minds of naval personnel between what they do when they are on duty and what they do when they are off duty. The service person's actions on and off duty are seen as one. Therefore, an individual's fundamental approach should remain the same whether he is on the job or in a private setting. The same principles should govern his actions. This is particularly important in a family setting, because the ethical standards set by the parents determine how the children develop.

In General Barrow's experience, those whose personal behavior was beyond reproach made the best leaders.

I think that one's personal conduct has a direct bearing on the subject of leadership. I know that when people speak about certain leaders of the past, they'll laugh and say, "Of course, you know he likes to booze it, but when the time came for him to exercise good leadership, he was there," or they'll bring up whatever the conduct might be that's unattractive or inappropriate. Well that, to me, is stretching the facts a little bit. I doubt that they were complete in their leadership capabilities. They may have served well in specific times and places, but those other things detracted somewhere from their effectiveness, and mostly from the area of simple respect.

You rarely can fool the troops, as they say, and whatever an officer's doing that is morally wrong will ultimately leak out. After all, let's just take an officer who has a 200-man unit that he's responsible for, let's take the Marine Rifle Company or something approaching that. He had a pretty difficult time getting to know all of them well, but they know him. There is a kind of barracks-room analysis by each person who looks at him—and they all do—and that makes a contribution to a mosaic. But a surprisingly accurate picture of him is painted.

Leaders are being looked at, analyzed, judged, very much more than they realize. Ultimately the moral weaknesses of an officer will be revealed to those he had expected to lead, and for every one person who might shrug his shoulders and say "So what?" there are several others who have less respect for him, and therefore he degrades his effectiveness as a leader.

Looking at it from the other angle, if I have officers working for me, and one of them shows some moral flaws in his personal life, naturally, just like the people who work for him, I lose a certain confidence and respect in him, too. I begin to think that if he would do that, why should I trust him with the lives of these young troops I'm about to assign him to be responsible for?

Additionally, General Barrow believes that an officer must be impeccable in his approach to every aspect of his job and life so that those who look up to him for the leadership he is supposed to provide do not see any flaws. His subordinates must never believe that they can do something that is wrong because their leader is doing it. An officer does not say, for example, "You cannot use this government gas in your vehicle" and then put government gasoline in his own vehicle. It goes almost without saying that the leader has to be the one who does what he is supposed to do and never does those things that he does not allow his troops to do.

Admiral Clausen thinks that
every nation's navy should have a clear conception of how its naval officers should behave and should reinforce that concept as necessary and suitable in order to make everyone conscious of the image of the navy on the whole and of its officers. In doing so, the education should aim at a prototype of an officer in the form of a human personage, as to both his profession and our society. The explanation of what has to be understood by this definition "officer as a personage" has to be convincing and clear-cut and should be implanted in every officer's mind as both a concrete and a symbolic figure who is highly ranked and whom an officer should emulate during his entire career. I do agree with Admiral Nelson, who admonished a midshipman: "Observe that you have to be a seaman in order to become an officer and you can't be a good officer if you are not a gentleman." [Translated by recollection.]

The young officers should have a goal which can be reached in a rather short endeavor. They must always want to emulate this example during their entire careers, and when they get to a higher rank as a result of this striving for a rather high-ranked goal, they must give in return an example to the junior officers. I think this combination of the goal given to the junior officers and, on the other side, from the high-ranked officers, is very good for officers on the whole.

Admiral Taylor suggests that "basically the rules for personal behavior are very clear and they hold good at every level." Admiral James D. Watkins, former American CNO, told the following to Admiral Taylor.

First of all, to live the Ten Commandments. If you live the Ten Commandments, I think you're in pretty good shape. I would add another one: it is an important part of every officer's life to live the Golden Rule. You can't lead if you don't live the Golden Rule, and if you live and lead by the Golden Rule, then you will have set personal behavior rules that will be very easy to live by. If you commit a felony, you're out, if you commit a misdemeanor, you're probably out. Before you do something, think about this: how will it look in a newspaper column?

And as Admiral Taylor remembered the conversation, Admiral Watkins said, "Well, it isn't all bad. It isn't over if you get your name in a column," because I guess some of his best friends and maybe the admiral himself have been in Jack Anderson's column. But then there's the bottom line for everything we do regarding integrity and personal behavior, and that is to ask yourself, Can I defend myself in front of the American people? And so it's a case of let your conscience guide you, but know also that there are a few basic rules to follow that will keep you straight and in good shape.

A midshipman might well ask himself, before he does something, Would I be proud to announce my actions at the King Hall Anchor, with my family, professors, friends, and the brigade in attendance?

MILITARY BEARING AND FORCEFULNESS

Military bearing. An officer leads largely by example, and the key element of example is appearance. For General Barrow, military bearing brings to mind more than just standing tall and straight and looking like a leader. In fact, it involves

demeanor or a command presence, exhibiting confidence and poise, coolness, steadfastness. It inspires people to want to work for you, it makes them feel like everything is all right, because you look like everything is all right. A leader should not be a hail fellow well met, slap him on the back, glad hand, or that kind of person; however, it is helpful to have a demeanor or a personality that projects a certain warmth, confidence, and optimism.

President Reagan has it, that's one reason he got reelected. People like him, he has a warm glow about him. I've been in his physical presence a number of times, and I'll tell you the kind of person he is. If you didn't know him from Adam, and if you were in a roomful of people and he came in, sooner or later you would ask

someone "Who is that guy? I'd like to know him." Bearing is that calm part of the picture of the individual that one gets visually, and it's very important. The fellow who looks gloomy—maybe it's his personality to want to think deep things and furrow his brow and look down at his feet, and he may be brilliant—but the people around him look at him and say things must be going to hell, and they lose confidence. It's not nearly the fellowship you have with the fellow who's exuding that spirit.

Admiral Clausen cautions that

"military bearing" should not be a habit of mendacious fuss and theatrical appearance and thereby approach the neighborhood of a "farce." This bearing should and must be interpreted in our profession as an expression of social manners. Although the spirit of our time sometimes curtails an explicit bearing in general and sometimes causes its wasting away, it still remains that military bearing and physical fitness and self-control are the exterior expressions of an inner carriage.

In some parts of the Western world, a uniform, no matter for what purpose it is used, has lost its traditional popularity. This seems to be the fact, especially in the armed forces of some countries. The meaning of wearing a uniform has obviously changed in those countries. This new attitude is to be seen sometimes in the uniform's maintenance and condition.

Admiral Taylor observes that

the leader has to look the part. There is little disparity in definitions of *military bearing*, and I have definitions for the words that go with the fitness report that I hold up every once in a while to see that I am using the picture that is used by others who are on selection boards. To me military bearing is the picture of a leader. He has to look the part, people have to say, "Yes, there's someone I'll follow any-where."

An officer who is trim and fit and wears a sharp-looking uniform is setting an example for others. When he appears smart to his subordinates, the officer enhances their feeling of confidence toward him, makes them more receptive to following him. There have been military leaders who were overweight or did not wear their uniform well, but officers such as these are starting out with one strike against them. They have to be extraordinarily capable in other areas to compensate for the lack of smartness.

Being trim and physically fit is an important element of everything that officers do, because it is an indication of the overall makeup of an individual. An individual who has the personal discipline to keep himself fit and trim and to require that uniforms be clean and well tailored and to give attention to his appearance is a disciplined individual, and his discipline will be manifested in other ways. Research at West Point indicates that cadets who went on to become effective leaders had usually scored well in areas of military bearing, appearance, and tactics while at the academy.[30-623]

Forcefulness. If an officer is dynamic and enthusiastic, this is clearly conveyed to his subordinates. It rubs off on them and enhances their zest and enthusiasm for doing their job. This is one reason it is very important for an officer to be enthusiastic and dynamic in his approach to his job.

General Barrow finds that

a leader does not necessarily need forcefulness in the delivery of orders, but he often needs forcefulness in arriving at that point. In other words, an effective officer who sees that something needs to be done does not wait for someone to tell him to do it. When he moves to do it on his own, he is displaying a form of forcefulness.

Furthermore, the forcefulness that he demonstrates in the accomplishment of a task will motivate people, and they will probably get the job done quicker and better and will probably maintain high spirits while doing it, because forcefulness is related to enthusiasm if it is used correctly.

Admiral Clausen remarks that

there is no doubt that a naval officer, in his appearance, his bearing, and the content of his statements and views, should be definite and clear-cut. Only in this way will his posture and attitude be unequivocal and will he get a reputation for what we call "radiation." This should find its expression when the officer is practicing his duty. As squadron commander, I adjusted the daily duty to a so-called "3-H-Programme" in order to let everyone know the general course I was determined to steer. "3-H-Programme" stood, in German, for "*Herz-Härte-Hingabe.*" These words translate as: Heart (having confidence in and affection for the crew, along with concern for their care and welfare); Hardness (a symbolic expression of providing all hands with a challenge); and Devotion (developing motivation in the crew so that they are ready to serve their country without always having to convince them of the true necessity of their task).

Conviction will bring motivation. An example of combining the concept of forcefulness with motivation is Gustavus Adolphus, King of Sweden in the sixteenth century. Adolphus was a strict disciplinarian who was ruthless in regard to his subordinates' inefficiency yet at the same time was able to maintain the well-being of his soldiers by ensuring that they received good equipment, plenty of food, and good pay. As a result, his army gave him its fierce loyalty and a series of successes on the battlefields of Europe. Adolphus's son, Charles XII, in contrast, did not follow his father's example. Charles held his men in low regard, and, as a result, his army was utterly crushed by the Norwegians.[38-21]

Admiral Taylor states:

I have lived by the axiom—attributed to Frederick the Great, although George Patton speaks of it very well—that fortune favors the bold. If you don't have the quality of forcefulness, I'm not sure you would be able to charge through others. I'm basically the Bull Halsey type of guy. I think of the choice as one between warrior and wimp. You must have a way of projecting what you have inside you. You put trust and confidence in your people, and then you get in front of them and hope that you have set an example. You lead out there in front and you are forceful. It's worked very effectively. It goes back to "The bold will inherit the leadership jobs." Of course, if you're bold and dumb you won't survive, you'll make all kinds of mistakes and our selection processes will move you off the track. So, before you get too bold, you want to be sure that you're right, that you've done a good job at deciding which course to take, and then, once you do that, don't back off, but press on.

Of Nelson, it was said that his penchant was for audacity. His tactics were audacious, and, as a result, his men were audacious. His tactics were bold, and he personally exposed himself to danger in battles.[32-69]

Forceful backup. Thus far, this discussion of the concept of forcefulness has considered only the approach a senior takes with subordinates and peers. But it is important to recognize that commanding officers expect their subordinates to speak up when something is wrong, like the little boy in the tale of "The Emperor's New Clothes" who dared to tell the emperor that he was wearing no clothes. The term *forceful backup* is used to describe that process whereby the subordinate, either when he is given an order or when he notices that something the senior did may be wrong, will speak up and bring it to the attention of the senior and *forcefully argue his position.*

Seniors expect and want their subordinates to let them know if they don't agree with a plan or action, and they would like to know before something goes wrong, while there is still time to make a correction. Just because the senior does not at first accept the new idea or approach is no reason to back off; rather, the subordinate should make additional arguments, presenting them in a forceful way so that the senior knows the subordinate has studied and is committed to the idea being offered.

However, it must be remembered that once a full discussion has taken place and the senior has been provided with all possible ideas and approaches—and he still makes the decision to go with the original plan—then it is the duty and the obligation of the subordinate to accept the senior's plan and both carry it out and support it as if it had been the subordinate's plan originally. This is another way seniors and subordinates express loyalty to each other. The senior always looks for the ideas of the people he leads, and subordinates, in addition to providing inputs—forcefully at times—support the senior in the final decisions that are made. After a subordinate takes on board the plan of the senior, he should in turn present it to his subordinates as if it were his own. The subordinate's subordinates should never know that there has been disagreement over a policy in the chain of command, unless all hands were involved in the discussion.

SPEAKING ABILITY

The ability to speak clearly and articulately is important to an officer from the very beginning of his career. Most of the communicating a junior officer will do will be in a small group setting, often in a one-on-one setting. Nevertheless, coupled with their personal appearance, the ability of officers to communicate will determine other people's evaluation of their capabilities as leaders. There have been effective leaders who were not good communicators, but they were good leaders *despite* their inability to communicate. General Barrow observes that

> for people who have to have a group of other people do what needs to be done, effective speaking is a powerful instrument, and it is an instrument that can be acquired. People can be trained to be effective speakers and to be forceful speakers. They can learn to make eye contact, to choose their words carefully, and to use good grammar and diction. An individual's speaking ability affects his leadership ability, but it also, as with military bearing, reflects on the organization he serves.

General Barrow described the way people commonly react to a good and a poor speaker:

> If you are testifying before Congress on Capitol Hill, if you speak to the senators or the congressmen effectively, whether it's your prepared statement or answers to questions they give you, they conclude that the Marine Corps has good leadership at the top because of the way this fellow came across to them. They think, "This guy must be a good leader because I asked him some tough questions and he was forceful and straightforward and forthrightly gave me those answers." Conversely, if he goes out and mumbles around, they may never say it, but somehow deep in them they think, "Is that guy a Marine? Is that what all Marines are like? Then they're not what I thought they were. I thought Marines were aggressive and forceful and stand up there and tell it like it is." Speaking forcefully, speaking effectively, can influence a broad spectrum of people, not just those who are being led.

Admiral Taylor opines that

> it doesn't do you any good to have a great mind and great ideas if you're not going to project them. You will have to stand up and talk to people if you are going to lead

them. Look them in the eye and tell them. If you don't have anything important to say, then you're going to fall flat, but you're still going to be ahead of the person with great thoughts who can't get up and say what's on his mind. You have to be smart, industrious, and bold, and when you're bold, that to me speaks to the fact that you're willing to stand up and get counted and speak out. Speaking is an essential part of leadership. It's a case of just getting up, telling them what you're going to tell them, telling them, and then telling them what you've told them and sitting down.

Young officers should take every opportunity to speak in public, to get up on their feet, because public speaking is just like any other skill: the more you do it, the more effective you become. In his early years, an officer will have to devote much time to writing out a speech and reviewing it very thoroughly before getting up and communicating publicly, but as time passes, he will be able to speak extemporaneously. It is important for a young officer to get as much practice as he can in public speaking, because that will lead to improvement. Officers can also take courses in public speaking and seek the help of individuals they admire. The officer may be able to get a friend to convey to him how well he is doing, so he can continue to improve.

Admiral McDonald observes that

> a naval officer will make public appearances on many occasions during his career. A neat appearance, proper conduct, and the ability to communicate on his feet will lead to success on these occasions. The first two attributes are easily attainable and are vitally important, because when an individual steps before a group of people, the first things they notice are his appearance and his conduct: Are his hands in his pockets? Are his shoes shined?

> Personal appearance is a simple matter

of paying attention to details, but without conscious thought, these details will be overlooked. When he talks, an officer's ability to convince others that he means what he says and his ability to get across to them the points he is trying to make are crucial.

People want to be led by strong officers, and since in a public appearance an officer cannot convey his strength individually, through a firm handshake, for example, he must do so through appearance, conduct, and speech.

Writing Ability

Writing is a skill that is improved through practice, so officers should seek every opportunity to write and therefore to improve their technical ability to write. Imagination and the desire for self-improvement play a large part in the effectiveness of an individual's writing, as General Barrow explained.

Some people know the mechanics of how to write, but they are not very good writers because they don't have the imagination to add the appropriate descriptive phrase, adverb, adjective, whatever it is that makes this thing live a little, makes it more readable, more appealing. I don't think you necessarily can teach just anyone to be a professional writer, but you can help them improve. I would encourage young officers not to draw away from the normal approach to writing tasks but to accept them as a challenge to create, just as any other artist does.

Rarely is rewriting unnecessary. Write it, read it, and, as a consequence of reading it, write it again and work it and rework it and get suggestions and get it critiqued. Don't just say, "Well, he wants me to tell him something in writing, so I'll just give him whatever comes to mind," and then use lower case and upper case inconsistently and write in incom-

plete sentences. Inattention to detail causes the person who reads the writing to say, "I thought this guy was smarter than this. This is a terrible piece he gave me, full of all kinds of errors. He doesn't express himself very well, shows no imagination. It just doesn't flow well."

There was a period when some people thought that the only people who needed to know how to write were those people who were majoring in English composition in college. The answer to that is that everyone needs to know how to write. I don't know of any area of endeavor that won't somewhere along the way require you to put it down, explain the engineering thing you're doing, or whatever it is.

As an officer becomes more senior, writing ability may make a difference in his assignment or even promotion. If those making that decision say, "You know, that individual can really write. He used to do some beautiful staff work for me," he may get the nod. Or "You know, he's a heck of a nice guy and a good officer, but don't give him anything that requires him to write, he just can't hack it"—that's thumbs down. Writing ability can limit you. It may take a while to get there, you may be well up the ladder, but it may be the thing that limits your achievement.

A young officer should use military writing manuals, for they give good guidelines on how to write effectively, and he should encourage others to study them to improve their own writing ability. Courses of instruction are provided in various areas throughout the military, and they are taught by very capable instructors.

Admiral Taylor views writing as who, what, where, when, why, and how, and it's just as important to know the facts in analyzing a problem as it is in mathematics to know the theorems and formulas to get a solution to the problem. When you sit down to write, to put your thoughts down, if you're going to make a contribution in this business, you've got to be able to make it good, articulate, cogent, and a hard-hitter in order to make your point, and if you can't, then you're going to get washed away. Every writer, every successful guy in the E, D, and down to the A ring in the Pentagon or out in the fleet and in the Corps is a writer. If you can't write, then practice and just keep at it.

Officers should use every opportunity to improve their writing ability; in fact, one of the responsibilities of a junior officer is to write effectively. Officers should not confine themselves to writing routine communications, but should try to be imaginative and creative in their writing. They should use good form and try to convey enthusiasm through a dynamic style rather than trying to make *every* communication routine and conform to the military style. The way people write can reflect their personality and their leadership style. For this reason, officers should practice writing and work to make their writing style more creative and dynamic. This assumes proper grammatical use and correct spelling. Don't be the poor writer who is responsible for the failure of his subordinates to advance because their abilities and accomplishments were not adequately described.

SELF-IMPROVEMENT

In summing up his thoughts for midshipmen on areas of study, Admiral Long offered this opinion of the areas a midshipman should concentrate on for service in today's Naval Service.

My own view is that the present curriculum of the Naval Academy results in our turning out highly trained and professional officers for the Naval Service. I think it is important that we all have an appreciation of what we are trying to produce at the Naval Academy. First and foremost, I believe that we are trying to produce offi-

cers who are prepared and qualified to lead combat units in the Navy and the Marine Corps. We need to understand that many of the responsibilities of young officers revolve around highly sophisticated technical equipment. Therefore, for an officer to be able to discharge his responsibilities when he enters the fleet, he must have a sound background in science and engineering in order to be able to understand the systems he's dealing with, and he must also be able to communicate with the people he commands as a division officer or platoon leader, as the enlisted personnel are working with the same complex technical equipment.

Admiral Clausen concurs with this position by remarking that

a naval officer without sufficient technical control is not imaginable. That is to say, he must know at least the technical working principles of gears and equipment in order to operate with it and to know exactly the capacity or efficiency of these technical instruments. In most cases, he will leave repairs to technical specialists.

Admiral Long continued:

I fully appreciate the need for naval officers to have a broad education, including an appreciation of history and political science, along with the ability to write and speak. I think it is particularly important as officers go up through the ranks that they become more proficient in writing and in speaking, because the facts of life are that the more senior you become, the more involved you will be with pleading cases before Congress or seniors and in the management of large forces ashore or afloat. I fully support the idea that every officer should have an appropriate exposure to the subjects of history and politics and acquire the ability both to write and to speak well. However, I do wish to emphasize that I think it is possible to retain our excellent technical education while improving the communication skills of our midshipmen.

Admiral Clausen, in taking a similar approach, sums up his thoughts by saying that,

in spite of having so very many abilities and experiences that resemble a handicraft, the profession of an officer requires that the officer's mentality comprise educational and intellectual cultivation. By this process, power of mind, the will, and the connection of feeling/soul/heart can be developed. The continuation of studies in these different fields is required of an officer in the manifold aspects of his profession. It is self-evident that a well-educated officer cannot do his duty without speaking and writing abilities, which he has to improve continually. In the military field, the language should be clear, succinct, understandable, direct and to the point, sober, and I think these should not be forgotten by officers when they are writing papers or speaking with their troops.

According to General Barrow, self-improvement is

knowing that you can be better than you are in knowledge of the area of your responsibility, all the way down to including how you look. It's a conscious awareness, without being self-centered, that you have certain responsibilities and you should always be striving to be better at them than just routine, "Ho hum, I've got this job, so that's all that matters."

People think somehow, when they've been assigned a command, for example, that all of their machinery that is supposed to come into play to make that thing click is going somehow to be given to them, and that the mere fact that they've got the job means that the wisdom is just going to flow out and everything's going to be fine—and that is not the way it is, that's a fact of life.

Self-improvement can be achieved in so many ways. It can be achieved in study, not only in the area of your responsibility, but beyond that, so that someday, when someone says, "Who knows anything about . . . ?" and they name some off-the-wall thing, you can raise your hand and say, "I know something about that." We should not always apply ourselves just to the areas of our responsibilities, we can reach out in other areas. In addition to studying formally, individuals need to have a conscious awareness of the need to be better.

CORRECTING PERCEIVED WRONGS

General Barrow states that

most young officers come to their assignments with a fair amount of schooling in the leadership requirements for that job and their rank. They have been required to study to be an officer, and they expect to serve in the company of others who have also studied to be an officer and who reflect that study in their performance. But some of these young officers can expect to encounter seniors and peers who are violating some of these principles of leadership by doing things they should not be.

The newly commissioned officer who observes this behavior in his fellow officers may become disillusioned. He may feel as if someone has let him down because not everyone in the military is behaving as he thought they would. What should the young officer who is confronted with this situation do? He may, as a new officer, have to bide his time and try not to become too disillusioned over the actions of a very few.

As he advances in rank and gains self-confidence and comes into contact with exemplary officers, an officer will know even better what good leadership is and what is right and wrong. At this point he may decide that he must take action regarding the officer who is not using good leadership principles. Doing so requires extraordinary tact, and the best method for proceeding varies according to the situation.

When he observes a simple flaw in a peer's approach to leadership, the officer can often approach him one on one, subtly or not, depending upon his relationship with him and the kind of personality he is, and speak to him in a way that would tell him he needs improvement in that area. With a senior, the officer can sometimes speak to the individual in the third person; in other words, by speaking about a hypothetical person in a hypothetical situation—"What if . . . ?"—convey to the senior that he believes the senior has used poor judgment in his leadership.

Those who are senior to the individual with the aforementioned problem need to involve themselves. General Barrow described how he reacts when a problem goes uncorrected.

When some incident occurred way down the chain, the first thing that came to my mind was "How could that have happened?" I sure wasn't asking how did it happen that someone junior to the situation didn't find out, didn't report it or do something about it. I was asking how it could happen in terms of the level of those above where it happened. How could they not somehow have anticipated it or headed it off before it got to be more serious? Many of the things that happen in command are telegraphed well in advance, they don't just pop up.

General Barrow further related how, after waiting 30 years, he was able to change something he had been opposed to all that time.

I tell them all the time, if you don't like it, stick around and change it. That's a simple, cryptic way of saying you'll get to

be senior and you can change it. I have done that. I harbored some things I didn't like for thirty years, and when I became Commandant I changed them. I'll give you an example.

In 1953 or 1954, along in there (I was a young major at the time), the decision was made in Headquarters, Marine Corps, that Marines serving in the Far East would be on unaccompanied tours. That meant that married officers and married enlisted would go out there for a year without their families, and that they would do it repeatedly if they were careerists. If there was reason to do it, you might have understood. Now I'm speaking as an individual, I'm not saying that what I said was widespread in the view of others, but I felt that it was a bad thing to do.

The people who made that decision, interestingly enough, in more austere circumstances and circumstances that had some element of risk and hazard involved, had had their families with them in places like Santo Domingo and Haiti and the China station, Shanghai. The other point is, they would make these decisions, but they wouldn't have to execute them, they had become too senior to be going out and taking their turn in the barrel. One of the things they gave as a reason for an unaccompanied tour was that dependents would become encumbrances, they would get in the way, and these Marines would be able to train harder, be more deployable, wouldn't have to worry about momma and the kids if they pulled out and left. Then there were some arguments that officers staffing schools should have their wives out there, but the young enlisted couldn't have theirs.

I harbored for thirty years, almost, a feeling that this was wrong, and I did my turn out there, and then I went out as the first general officer in the history of the Marine Corps with his family authorized west of Hawaii in 1969 to be the Commanding General of the Marine Corps Base, Camp Butler. I served there for three years, 'til 1972, and during that time I once again could see firsthand the frustrations and the problems attendant to the perpetuation of this unaccompanied tour business. Along with the unaccompanied tours you got the problem of no job continuity, people turning over all the time, serving for twelve months and then somebody else taking your place. You also challenged the morals of some officers by the temptations that were there.

It was a bad show, and the more I saw it the more it gnawed on me. As a brigadier general I remembered back as a major the decision on the Far East. Now to change it required some other things, you couldn't just change it, you had to be assured that there would be adequate housing and these other kinds of things, but you've got to take a first step sometime, and I encouraged an increase in the accompanied tour numbers when I was there, and several years later, after I got back, I was certain I could make correct decisions. So we did increase the numbers, but we didn't go all out, and early in my tenure as Commandant, I was on a Western Pacific trip and I learned that the Japanese government was willing to go beyond building things quid pro quo. They were willing to finance support facilities in exchange for our defending them, in a sense. So while I was out there, I said, "We are now going to have accompanied tours on Okinawa," and somebody said, "To what extent?" I said, "To the maximum extent possible, which means officers and staff NCOs who are careerists." I stated that we would only be limited by the availability of resources to

support it, but that we were not going to wait until resources got put in place, because we weren't going to take this subject and study it to death, which would have taken two or three years. I said, "We're going to do it," and it got back to Washington before I got back, and when I got back everyone was running around saying, "You know, we've got to do something about this." So they formed a task force to implement my decision. So when a young officer sees something he doesn't like, one thing he can do is wait around long enough to change it.

THE PROMOTION SYSTEM AND THE NAVAL OFFICER

With a look to the officer's future, Admiral Moorer comments that

the Navy promotion system is one of the fairest of the service promotion systems. For instance, in the selection process, not only does an individual get more than one opportunity before a selection board, but he is never required to appear before the same people twice. Consequently, no one individual could, in effect, prevent him from being promoted.

By and large as he goes up the ladder of rank, an officer in the service, particularly in the Navy, develops a service reputation, and senior officers certainly hear from other senior officers and others about young Jack Jones, how he's an up-and-comer. But young officers should not spend their time trying to impress seniors. On the contrary, they should spend their time trying to impress those who work for them, because the people who work for them, not the people they work for, make them look good. In this way an effective leader will gain recognition for his ability to motivate others and put their abilities to work for the Naval Service.

Admiral Moorer explained why the promotion system must always be followed to the letter.

I've had several contacts with people who think it's very simple, that the Chief of Naval Operations can promote anyone he chooses. During the time I was Chief of Naval Operations, the President called me on the phone and said he wanted me to promote his cook. By and large the stewards in the White House were within the Navy, and this cook was a first-class petty officer. At that time, as I recall, we were having competitive examinations for promotion, and we had thirty or so first class who had passed the examination but only six vacancies, and the President's cook was one of the ones who did not pass the examination. So when he told me to promote his cook, I told him that I couldn't do it. Now as the Commander in Chief, the President can promote anyone to any rank, but he didn't want to do that.

I said, "Mr. President, what am I going to tell those who passed but didn't get promoted, that you asked me to promote one who didn't pass?" I said, "That will destroy the entire promotion system, and thus I cannot promote him. You can promote him, if you want to, but it will have to be a political promotion." I said, "I'll tell you one thing that I'll do, I'll send over a good cook who is every bit as qualified as the one you have, and then we'll send your man to school, and then later, if he passes the examination, he'll have a good chance for promotion, but he's not getting promoted now."

This is very important for young officers to know. You cannot make exceptions or toy with the promotion system of enlisted or officer personnel, because the minute you do that you are almost like a municipal political system, where you're not making the decision on the basis of qualifications. That spreads through the entire organization immediately and will change attitudes and in some cases will significantly lower morale and in other cases make people get out of the Navy or get out of the organization, whatever it happens to be. This is just as true in any executive pyramid that exists, whether in a corporation or whether in a military organization, so you must be meticulous about how you conduct and make promotions, because that's one thing that spreads like wild fire, and you can't slip somebody in and hope no one knows about it. It just doesn't work like that.

SUMMARY

Admiral Moorer, in summarizing the concept of leading by example, pointed out that a leader can gain the support of his people by telling them specifically what should and should not be done. (This does not imply how to do it—just what it is necessary to accomplish.) People do not like receiving orders that leave them uncertain of what is required of them. The officer who allows his people to carry out his orders in a halfhearted way is sure to lose their respect and, as a consequence, lower their morale, because people like to have set limits, and they like to know they will be required to follow orders completely and to the best of their ability.

The self-disciplined officer imposes on himself certain personal standards and maintains them to produce a military bearing that commands respect. Military bearing is sometimes described as smartness, and, in a sense, the officer maintains a shipshape personal appearance. He stands up straight, wears shined shoes and a clean and pressed uniform, and responds to people with courtesy. He does not use wishy-washy terms in discussions. All of these things combine to constitute military bearing.

In the exercise of any kind of leadership, the officer must have the capacity to convey to others by voice what he wants them to do and why he wants them to do it. While it is difficult for many people to stand up in public and make a speech, the individual who volunteers, when a naval officer is needed, to make a speech will find in time that he has overcome his stage fright and mastered speech making. Every naval officer at a very early time in his career should seek every opportunity to get on his feet and speak to a large group. An officer can also work on his speaking ability by standing in front of a mirror and speaking into a recorder and then observing his performance and doing everything he can to improve it.

The officer who has command of a unit must be able to talk to the people he is leading in a succinct and articulate way. They will form an opinion based on how well he communicates with them, so he must communicate well. For this reason, effective public speaking is a capability that a young officer should seek to acquire as fast as he can.

To improve himself and better prepare himself for a career, the young officer should pursue knowledge in many directions. A young officer going aboard a ship or joining an organization may find himself at the beginning with what he considers a narrow assignment. Rather than complain that he is not being challenged, the officer should take the opportunity to seek knowledge. On board a ship like an aircraft carrier, for instance, there are a large number of technologies to explore, such as nuclear power, the aircraft, the catapults, the gear, and all kinds of communications and electronics. The challenges are unlimited, in fact. [Editor's note: An officer's fitness report will be positively influenced by his outstanding performance of collateral duties, which may be one way of distinguishing him from other front-running individuals.]

A young officer who really wants to improve himself has to find out what his friends are doing and find out as much as he can about their particular assignments. If he continues to do that through his career, he will be an excellent officer. When he gets on a staff, for instance, he may be the operations officer, but he ought to find out what the supply officer is doing, what the planning officer is doing, what the communications officer is doing, and so on. For example, he should not wait until he is assigned in the communications office to learn about communications.

MCPON Sanders: *It is very important that officers realize that they are being observed at all times, and they should conduct themselves properly not only on the job, but also when they are on liberty or anywhere else. Their behavior in public is very important, because if they don't conduct themselves properly they will lose the respect of the crew, and once they lose that respect, they will find it very hard to maintain credibility or gain respect in the future. Enlisted personnel communicate quite well within their community, and an officer's misbehavior is most often a topic of conversation.*

In the area of being able to write in an effective manner, the officer must be able to put on paper, especially with respect to evaluations, exactly the words that describe how the sailor performs. If they are good performers, you must be able to say why they were good performers and do not ever lose sight of the fact that the people who will be reading the evaluation, when it comes time to determine the sailor's service career, will be master chiefs. Enlisted selection boards are inherently made up of master chiefs, and if you use words or terminology that is not normally familiar within the master chief rank, if you use what I would say are dollar-twenty-five words when you could use nickel words and make it just as clear, then you are not writing effectively. Remember, in writing, to give it the effort you would want if it were impacting on your career.

8. Naval Standards

STANDARDS FOR READINESS

Admiral Holloway points out that
the United States Navy has established a complete system of standards and evaluations for almost every evolution that a unit is expected to perform in an operational sense. For example, a ship is supposed to be able to achieve a certain percentage of hits per gun per minute in gunnery. There are even standards for something as mundane as replenishment at sea, or underway replenishment: a certain minimum time is established as a standard for the ship to get the first line over after coming alongside the oiler or the ammunition ship. To ensure that the unit is performing well, the commander has to schedule evaluation evolutions, and careful records of them must be kept. Through these evaluations, it is how close a unit comes to matching the standards that are established for it that is evaluated.

Readiness is defined as the capability of a unit to perform the mission or function for which it was organized and designed. In its broadest sense, readiness is the degree to which the landing force, carrier battle group, ship, squadron, department, division, or branch is ready to carry out its mission to wage prompt and sustained combat at sea or on land—and win.

A naval officer must continuously assess his unit's potential capability to fulfill the assigned combat mission responsibilities by comparing the unit's readiness with established readiness factors. A naval officer, by personal example, inspi-

rational leadership, dedication, and professional performance, must comply with and strive to exceed the established standards of supervision, safety, effectiveness, appearance, and training of others to enhance materially the overall readiness and combat capability of the Navy and the Marine Corps.

Admiral Nakamura believes that
the only way an officer can evaluate whether he satisfies the requirements laid upon him is through the results obtained by the team of which he is the leader. He should evaluate precisely the actual state of readiness, safety, efficiency, and economy of the team, his own attention to and efforts to improve these factors, and the results of his efforts. Of course the circumstances under which the team has to work greatly affects the results. Still, trying to improve the conditions or to adapt to them is one of the important capabilities required of an officer.

Basically, readiness is comprised of personnel, material, and training resources. These resource areas are normally compared to a standard, analyzed for deficiencies, and then upgraded as necessary to meet the standard. Speaking to these points, General Wilson comments that when he was Commandant, he had a basic theme on which he spoke to the troops when he visited bases, and this basic theme was readiness, quality, and standards of conduct.

Readiness, of course, led them all. The basic mission of the armed forces is to fight our country's battles. We must never lose sight of that. We are given ancillary missions, and properly so. But a commander must never lose sight of the fact that he must be ready at all times, under all circumstances, to fight our country's battles. It's not his business to make policy, it's his business to do what he's told to do within the concepts of morality and the Constitution, and therefore his primary job is to ensure that his unit is ready to do what his basic mission is. For instance, an infantry unit should be ready to fire and take objectives. An artillery unit should be able to fire, have plenty of ammunition, and hit the target. Aviation supports the troops and is ready to get close enough to hit the target in support of the infantry.

Personnel. To determine personnel readiness, it is necessary to compare the authorized strength of personnel by grade/rate and skills necessary to perform the wartime mission of the unit (the standard) with the available personnel on board.

Secretary Webb believes that

one of an officer's most important functions is developing and maintaining the combat readiness of his people. In Vietnam, newcomers joined the unit that was already in the field, and there was very little time to train, because the units operated constantly. For sixty days at a time, the units constantly moved out, set up a company patrol base, dug in, patrolled, and then moved to another spot. In a nine-month tour of duty, standdown time was only a couple of days here and there. It is an exhausting environment. For months, no more than two or three individuals at a time were able to sleep, because of the watch schedules at night.

In that combat environment and living environment, as far as leadership went, the trick to readiness was mental freshness. The leader had to try to get his people the creature comforts that he could, this was their home for a year, if they survived long enough. For example, the leader could break out his PRC 25 radio battery so that the Marines could listen to a transistor during the day. Morale boosters such as this allowed the troops to relax but did not affect their jobs.

Everything about the combat environment has to be dealt with in an absolute

sense. If an individual knows that his senior is making every effort to get him the small comforts, then he does not mind being forced by circumstances to perform continuously in an alert way.

The officer's credibility is also very significant in the combat environment, because day after day he must order individuals to take action in which they may take a bullet. In a war of attrition, this is a very difficult challenge, and many times these orders must be given abruptly—for example, the unit is moving across a paddy area and a ridge line opens up; the officer does not know whether there are 4 people or 400 people up there, and he must tell an individual scout to go up there. That individual must trust the officer, he must believe that the officer is a person of sound judgment, that he has knowledge, that he is not going to waste the individual's life.

This bond, this rapport, must exist between the officer and his men. One way to establish this bond is for the officer to sit down with every man in the platoon every day, if possible. The officer can sit around and talk to his people, make sure they are getting mail, make sure they are getting paid, make sure that if they are eligible for a promotion the paper work is going on it, listen to them gripe, and so forth. They may ask questions. When George Washington brought Von Stuben over to train the rag-tag American army, Von Stuben told Washington that the Americans always want to know why. If the officer takes the time when he has it to answer those questions, and if his subordinates can measure him and know that he knows what he is doing, then the officer has credibility already built in, so that when there is no time to ask questions and he points a finger at someone, that individual will stand up and go.

Officers in a noncombat situation must be able to walk away from their jobs at any time, they must not love the position more than the responsibility. It is nice to ride in a first-class cabin, but the officer has an obligation to stick his oar in the water. He must be able to say the things the boss needs to hear; if a bad situation exists, the boss must hear about it. People in power are by the nature of their office insulated, and therefore they need individuals around them who will tell them the truth, and they must encourage those individuals to do so.

During war, the operational military as a whole, and particularly the sea services, operate in a dangerous, highly active, unsafe environment. One of the functions of a junior officer in that environment is to understand the job of everyone in his command. Here is a story that illustrates the importance of this function.

When I went through Basic School after I was commissioned, we learned every weapon in a Marine infantry battalion, including the 3.5 rocket launcher, which was this relic of Korea which had an electric trigger device. A year later, after I had spent my time as a rifle platoon commander, I was a company commander, I had a 3.5 rocket section in my company. The thing about the 3.5 rocket launcher was, since it was electrically fired, sometimes the gunner would pull the trigger and the rocket would not fire. There was a set safety drill where you waited for a while to see if it went off, and then you were to take the unexpended round out and put it in a safe place because sometime later the thing might go off.

Well, when I was a company commander this happened. We were prepping an area and my 3.5 rocket guys pumped one round that didn't go off, they waited the right amount of time (this is called an immediate action drill), they pumped it again and it didn't go off, then they took it out and laid it right in between the feet of the gunner and started to put another one in. I was probably fifty meters away, and I went running over screaming at these guys. There was an abandoned foxhole there, and I said, "Get rid of that round," and they said, "Oh, lieutenant," and I said, "Don't give me that, put it in the hole," and they said, "What's with this guy?" and they took it and they put it in the hole. I walked about ten steps away and it went off.

The officer who knows all of the systems also knows how to enforce them, and he can prevent people from getting hurt. When he establishes his credibility as someone who knows what is going on, the officer increases his credibility as a leader. It has been said that a naval officer's weapons are his people, and if he fires his personal weapon he has lost control over his unit. In an infantry environment, that is absolutely true. If the officer develops a close personal relationship with his people, if he is doing his job right, then he begins to realize that the expenditure of one of his people for reasons that are not of the utmost importance to carry out the mission is a loss that is going to stay with him for a very long time.

Equipment readiness/supplies on hand. To determine material readiness, compare the operating status and quantities of wartime combat-essential equipment, support equipment, and organic supplies which are prescribed to perform the wartime mission (the standard) with those possessed by the unit. (This area will be more thoroughly covered in chapter 9.)

Training. In peace and in war, training is a primary naval objective that is surpassed in wartime only by the necessity for victory, for which training is the essential preparation. Modern ships, weapons, and aircraft are useless without

well-trained crews. Obsolete equipment, however, has performed very effectively in past wars
when operated by skilled and courageous personnel. An officer's training of subordinates must
be based on a plan, the objectives of which should
be understood by those who execute it. Aboard
the unit, the training objective is to develop a
well-organized team capable of maintaining and
operating the unit at its maximum effectiveness
during peacetime operations and in combat.

Compare the requisites for a fully trained unit
(standard) with the present level of training.
Inspections not only ensure that the work is
completed and the proper training achieved,
but also show the men that their boss does
take an interest, and this will make them strive
harder.[47-174] Results of training exercises, evaluations, operational readiness evaluations, technical proficiency tests, intertype fleet operations,
type training, and refresher training should be
carefully evaluated. Admiral Holloway suggests
that,

> after plans are made, the command ought
> to keep very careful records of, for exam-
> ple, how many times this officer of the
> deck had the conn coming alongside; how
> many times he anchored the ship; how
> many rounds were fired in short-range
> battle practice; how often the guns were
> fired under full radar control. There are a
> limited number of steaming days, and
> there are a limited number of rounds of
> ammunition that can be fired, and the
> officer needs to make sure he is getting
> the best out of every round fired and
> every hour steamed.

All of these actions should contribute to
the long-range objective of having the unit
as battle-ready as possible. The successful
commander knows what he has in the way
of resources (his budgetary limitations),
and he knows what his objective is (his
course is charted) through his plan, and
he matches the two. Through his plans
and his records, a good commander can

tell any day just where he is, how far he
has progressed along the line to having his
outfit fully combat-ready.

There are many ways a leader can keep
his plan and his record in front of his people. During wartime, commanding officers
of ships or aircraft squadrons often sus-
pend large plexiglass boards in the operations or ready room. The boards indicate
the number of hours each pilot has flown,
how many bombs he has dropped, and
what his bomb score is. This keeps the
information at the officers' fingertips, but
it also constantly reminds the pilots of
their records. The poor bomber pilot who
has a low average might be embarrassed,
but he no doubt will make maximum use
of his flight hours and his bombs to get
out there and try to improve his average.

STANDARDS FOR SAFETY

Admiral Holloway reminds us that
military service is a very dangerous
profession, and safety cannot be guaranteed. In naval aviation, for example, there
is a saying that the only way to be perfectly safe is to keep the planes in the
hangar. Nevertheless, the Naval Service
mandates that safety precautions be taken
wherever and whenever possible.

What are the rules for ensuring that the
maximum degree of safety is factored into
a unit's concept and its operations? First,
the unit must know the rules for safety—
how to do things properly; second, the
unit must train and practice those rules;
and third, there must be a discipline in
the command of that unit so that individuals will carry out the safety provisions
that they understand and have trained in.
The third factor is sometimes overlooked,
but it is the most important of the three.

Admiral Holloway had this to say about the
importance of discipline:

> Going back to my experience in naval

aviation, I remember in my early days right after World War II, when I think we were going through a transition, we lost a lot of planes and pilots through flat hatting.

What is flat hatting? That's flying as low as you can without hitting the ground, and that can be pretty low and that can be pretty dangerous. It's very exciting, and although it was illegal, pilots enjoyed it, and they would go show off before their girlfriends and other friends, and a lot of pilots "bought the farm," as the expression goes, flat hatting. There's a lot less of that now and it's because of discipline. Pilots were court-martialed. There is a much stronger sense of responsibility, I think, today than I've ever seen before in my roughly forty years in the Navy. But that's a very important factor that we must not overlook. A ship's skipper may try to get his ship back a half-hour early by taking a shortcut, which really isn't safe because he's not sure exactly what the depth of the water is and thus runs the risk of scraping the bottom. This is really a breach of discipline because he probably knew better.

The objective of safety is to enhance operational readiness by reducing the number of deaths and injuries to personnel and losses and damage to material from accidental causes. Safety, like training, is a command responsibility and therefore is implemented through the chain of command. Each echelon of command and supervisory level has responsibilities, both in training and in day-to-day supervision of routine as well as specialized tasks. It is not a safety program itself that makes a unit or crew less hazardous, but rather the planned and coordinated activities of the crew acting as teams and subteams within the framework of a program.

An officer must ensure that education and training programs contain a systematic approach to the promotion of accident prevention, both

in the unit and in off-duty activities. Accident prevention awareness and education should be tailored to the many variables and events involved in the unit's schedule so as to pique interest at appropriate times.

The best policing system is one of self-policing by both officers and enlisted personnel. Complacency, haste to complete a job, and the "it-can't-happen-to-me" attitude all tend to militate against the effectiveness of a self-policing system in the safety area.

Safety standards and regulations are based on standard procedures and precautions to minimize risk. These standards are based on guidance from higher authority in various instructions, technical publications, watch instructions, and unit regulations.

The safety organization must continually monitor the measures taken to ensure that the unit meets or exceeds the established safety standards and criteria. General Wilson points out that

we deal in weapons that are very dangerous. In training day to day throughout the armed forces, we have practically all of the dangers that are inherent in a weapons war. Safety is so important because, if there are accidents, we lose the value of the person who is injured, and we also lose facilities and the medical personnel who could be doing other things.

Furthermore, as one person is disabled this has a tendency, of course, to disable the whole unit, because each person has a niche and a job. It's so important for leaders to understand that they must ensure that their people know that they are not just a cog in a machine, that they have a particular job to do. In a rifle squad with thirteen men, if there are just twelve, the squad is disabled to whatever extent this person performs his job. Whether he's an aircraft mechanic or a tank mechanic, an injured man disables his whole unit. So safety is important for an individual, but it is also important for the unit, because we must always keep in mind the importance of readiness and the unit's ability to perform its mission.

STANDARDS FOR EFFICIENCY AND EFFECTIVENESS

In striving for a high state of readiness and war-fighting capability, a naval officer must constantly compare the effectiveness and efficiency of the unit to established standards. "How can my unit best accomplish its purpose?" should be a question the officer frequently asks himself. Setting goals and performance standards, conducting evaluations, and initiating actions to improve the unit's performance are part of the career responsibilities of a naval officer. He must strive to measure the effectiveness of his unit continually. An officer must be concerned with attaining goals, maintaining high standards, and pursuing the economic use of resources.

Admiral Holloway reminds us that

to ensure that the unit is operating at maximum efficiency within budgetary limitations, an officer must plan carefully and keep very accurate records. Planning is one key to the success of any organization. The successful commander has a yearly plan, a quarterly plan, a monthly plan, and a daily plan, and he also has plans of what to do if he has to deviate from those plans. There should never be any time in any organization for which plans have not been made.

The further into the future plans extend, naturally, the less valid those plans are. Those in the Naval Service need not be slaves to plans; when circumstances change, individuals must adapt. But usually it is not necessary to pull alternatives out of thin air, because alternate courses of action generally have been discussed. Those in command should ask themselves, "What should we do one year from now if such and such happens? We

hope it doesn't, we won't look for it, but if it does, this will be our course of action."

Effectiveness is the comparison of results with purpose. These questions tell the officer how effective he is within a unit: What are the right things for me to do? What did I actually accomplish? Did I get the right things done? To determine efficiency, the officer must ask: Was my leadership or were my other activities economical or wasteful in using the available resources of people, time, energy, and materials in the course of achieving results? In other words, get off of the routine and on to the problem or problems.

General Wilson thinks that

efficiency and economy go hand in hand, and during war it becomes a matter of judgment. But economy in peacetime operations is very important. There is a tendency for troops to believe somehow that there is a source of supply that is never ending, and nothing could be further from the truth. The more rank one receives, the more responsibility, the more one has to understand that these sources are finite, and that the American people should have no reason to expect that a member of the armed forces would be extravagant in his use of taxpayers' money and funds, which are represented by vehicles, ships, airplanes, rifles, uniforms, and food. A service person should not any more take more food than he can eat because it's there than he would when he is in his own home or when he is doing his own finances. Now, when the time comes for war, then you should husband your resources to the extent necessary in order to assure victory, which is the ultimate aim. Then you have to use what you have to use in the way of resources and, indeed, lives, weighing the objectives against what would be the alternative.

In developing leadership strategies and priorities, and in confronting new situations, an officer must always find a balance between efficiency and effectiveness. This kind of flexibility and thought leads to superior performance by an officer as well as to enhanced unit readiness.

STANDARDS FOR PERSONAL APPEARANCE AND PERFORMANCE

Admiral Holloway affirms that

personal appearance is tremendously important in leadership, because no one admires a slob. Comedians amuse a great many people, and have hordes of fans, but their mission is not to lead, it is to entertain. We tend to respect people who are sharp, clean-cut, athletic, and fit.

People will talk about the leader who habitually does not have a clean shave, lets his hair grow a little long, and wears rumpled khakis, but these people are successful leaders *in spite of* their appearance rather than because of it. They are so good, so smart, so able, so courageous, that they are able to overcome their sloppiness. The Naval Service is led by people who can do the job right and who can inspire other people to do the job right, not by people who cut a dashing figure.

It is very important for officers to recognize that, since they will no doubt be transferred, they must lead in a manner that will be consistent with the manner of those who take their places in the future. An officer who motivates his personnel through his winning personality alone is not doing his successors or his personnel a service. Because of the way the Naval Service is organized, an officer must be ready, and his people ready, for the next person to come along and take over.

U.S. Navy regulations require that "all persons in the Naval Service shall show in themselves a good example of subordination, courage, zeal, sobriety, neatness, and attention to duty." Any person in a position of leadership must con-

tinually demonstrate these qualities to perfection; to do less is to diminish that person's effectiveness in direct proportion to the lack of effort. An officer cannot demand of others more than he is willing to give himself.

Admiral Nakamura says that

there is no doubt that proper personal appearance is a quality which a leader should maintain. Even if he is an insignificant-looking person, he should dress neatly and tidily, as well as keep a bright mood. This is one way he can obtain the respect and affection of his subordinates.

In severe situations—in the battle or in the storm—people look at their commander's face. His resolute but calm appearance under such conditions stabilizes and encourages them.

Of course we should not forget that personal appearance cannot be substituted for substance. Subordinates will have learned what their new leader's character is within three days after his arrival, regardless of his personal appearance.

Regarding personal appearance, Secretary Webb says that

the way an officer wears a military uniform is a signal to his people, just as how he salutes is. The officer who fails to wear his uniform with an appropriate degree of correctness is indicating to his people that he lacks the sort of self-discipline that he may be asking them to acquire in a number of other areas. In the military environment, everyone knows what the distance between the pocket and the first row of ribbons is, where the insignia is supposed to go, whether the tie is dimpled, and whether the tie is centered. The officer who does not dress properly is signaling that he is not going to demand correctness in other areas. How an officer dresses also indicates how he feels about himself. Even when he is not in uniform, an officer should spend time on his personal appearance, because a good appearance will make him feel better about himself, and that will help him perform better.

For Admiral de Cazanove,

your personal appearance shows others the amount of self-respect you have. By your personal example of appearance, you also show others how much regard you have for regulations. The first time I saw General de Gaulle, in July 1940, I and the other young boys of my age were impressed, and thought that having someone so tall as he would be better than someone who was short—though we must not forget that Napoleon was a short man. Sometimes appearance may help, but, of course, it is not enough. However, physical appearance should have no effect on your self-respect and your way of wearing the uniform and adhering to regulation.

STANDARDS FOR SUPERVISION

Admiral Nakamura comments that

it is quite important for a commander to maintain close contact with his subordinates. He should put in an appearance as often as he can. This is especially important in the case of young officers.

The higher the level of the commander, the more extensive his responsibilities, making it more difficult for him to make on-the-spot appearances. He should, however, make every effort to show himself. Even when he is unable to maintain close contact with all of his subordinates, the commander can show his concern for them by making contact with a portion of them, who will quickly relate the contact to the rest. Particularly when the force is fighting under severe conditions, the appearance of a high commander on the spot produces an immeasurable effect on the morale of the force.

A fine leadership cliché is "deputize, recognize, supervise."

Supervision is best defined as the careful watching and directing of others to accomplish the mission within the capabilities of the unit. The good leader should never pass on an order by saying "So-and-so said to do this." Personnel cannot respect or be loyal to an officer who does not accept the responsibility of his position and is not loyal to his senior officers.[1-100] The naval officer who attains a high degree of success will be adept at obtaining maximum efficiency from subordinates through effective supervision. A good supervisor will use most of the following techniques to accomplish the unit's mission.

Giving orders. Give clear and complete orders. When possible, explain the reasons for the orders and the decisions involved in making up the orders. Determine that instructions are understood. Delegate responsibility for specific tasks to subordinates. Do not attempt to do all the work personally. Do not give orders and directions in minute detail, but leave some discretion and authority to junior officers, petty officers, or staff and noncommissioned officers. Follow through on orders to ensure that they are obeyed fully.

Encouraging subordinates. Today's Navy requires well-trained individuals, and officers must, therefore, treat subordinates as the valued assets that they are. This is not to say that the troops are to be pampered or spoiled, but, rather, that their welfare must be the concern of their leader. Before a person can be of use to the Navy, though, certain requirements must be met. For example, clothing, food, and living spaces have to be provided.[47-23] Points to keep in mind are: Administer a reprimand or disciplinary action in a constructive manner. Do not reprimand or criticize in front of others. Reward subordinates with praise or a recommendation for promotion when they have done an outstanding or exceptional job. Welcome, consider, and discuss ideas and suggestions of subordinates. Make use of competent advice; do not refuse to consider or discuss suggestions; offer constructive suggestions for improvement.

Show interest in the welfare and morale of subordinates. Take responsibility for fair treatment of subordinates. Accept responsibility for actions of subordinates. Give credit to subordinates: a pat on the back sometimes goes a long way.

Admiral Holloway suggests that native intelligence—the ability to look at a situation, evaluate it, and then make a sensible judgment—is one of the necessary attributes of a good leader. An officer must be smart enough to know what his subordinates ought to be doing and smart enough to know whether they are doing it well. Sometimes an officer hears sailors saying, "Ensign So-and-So is no darn good," but that may mean he is the best ensign aboard because he is tough but fair, and the ensign's senior officer must be intelligent enough to sift what he hears and properly evaluate the ensign.

An officer must know how his subordinates are performing in a professional sense, and then he must know how best to counsel them. He can take them aside and say, "You know, you really don't understand your people," or "You're spending too much time on the books and not enough time out on the deck watching the crew. It's a thankless task chipping paint, but, you know, if a sailor does a good job chipping paint he ought to get a pat on the back for it."

An officer must also have a concern for his people, for the ability of his organization to do its mission, and for the security of the United States. The officer needs to be concerned that the individual, for example, has an opportunity to get ahead in life and in the world and in his career. But the higher concern is a concern for the good of the service, and while a senior

may like a young officer and think he is a fine young man and has a nice family, the senior should not give his subordinate good fitness reports and push him ahead if he is not able to handle the job, because to do so would be to show improper respect and lack of concern for the good of the service.

Do not accept credit for the work or ideas of subordinates. Loyally support policies and actions of seniors and associates to subordinates. Do not complain about, or argue against, the policies and actions of a senior to anyone except the senior.

Using time and personnel. Consider various alternative approaches when planning the accomplishment of an assignment. Do not request more specific instructions from your senior when all necessary facts are available. However, if in doubt, it is better to ask than guess. Schedule work; manage your own time and that of subordinates after considering all important factors. In assigning responsibility for tasks, consider the capability and experience of personnel rather than only their availability.

STANDARDS FOR ADVANCEMENT IN RATE

The real value to the Navy or Marine Corps of all personnel preparing themselves for promotion is that it improves combat readiness. Thus, officers are not just "looking after their personnel" when they closely supervise and encourage their preparation for promotion: they are at the same time improving the efficiency, performance, and readiness of their units or crews.

How fast an individual is advanced in rating depends, to a large degree, on that individual. The ambitious person who seeks opportunity in the Naval Service will find it and will move steadily up the ladder. Getting ahead involves more than merely waiting out time in grade. Officers must manage, advise, and counsel their personnel to ensure that those capable of accepting more responsibility meet the objectives for advancement.

To qualify for advancement, each individual must have the needed length of Naval Service or time in grade and the necessary marks in proficiency (ability) in rate and conduct. He must have satisfactorily completed required training or correspondence courses and, when required, have completed courses of instruction at specific Navy or Marine Corps service schools. Additionally, he must have qualified in the practical factors for his rate and met the military requirements for his pay grade, have been recommended by his commanding officer, and have satisfactorily passed a servicewide examination (Navy) for advancement to the rate involved.

INVOLVEMENT IN EXTRA-MILITARY PROGRAMS

Each and every naval officer should extend himself into the local community, time permitting. Actively participating in community service organizations or youth athletics or enrolling in advanced academic degree programs not only broadens the officer and improves his leadership techniques and professional skills, it also enhances the community's impression of the Navy or the Marine Corps. General Wilson remarks that

it is very important to participate in programs off base if you are on independent command. If you are on a base and there are a large number of people, you should obviously have extracurricular activities. Whether or not you want to move into community affairs is up to you and your spouse. I'm talking abut your spouse, too, who is a large part of your career. I will say here and now that if your spouse does not like the service and feels that your job competes for your affections, then you should seriously consider seeking another profession. However, experience indicates that the officer who involves the spouse in the military community will have a help-

mate who avidly supports the Naval Service.

An officer should enlarge his horizons by participating in Navy Relief, Red Cross, and all of those things, or he should move into community affairs. Make the community know that he is interested in them, and the community will then become interested in him. Too often communities feel that, "Well, the military may be all right. I like the officers. They all look like a fine group of people. They talk a strange language, say 'Yes, Sir,' cut their hair. But just about the time that I've come to know them, they're transferred, so it's best to leave them alone. They never participate in anything. They have their own little world out at the base, and they live their lives and I live mine." The fact is, if we allow that to develop we are hurting ourselves, because the community would know the service better, they would support the service better, understand the problems of service people better, if service people had more contact with them. Unless service people communicate with civilians in the community, a riff develops, and the service should take the initiative, because service people gain by closer relations with civilians. Service people can then understand what the civilians are thinking and are not stuck within their own little worlds they so often get into.

Admiral Holloway offers that

the higher an officer's rank in the service, the more he becomes a member of the community, and the broader his interests, the broader his character and personality become. Extracurricular activities such as staying abreast of current events, reading good books to stimulate and improve the mind, and getting involved in an athletic program or a fitness program to maintain

physical fitness are essential. Other outside activities, such as singing in a glee
club or coaching Little League, can also
help develop an officer's potential. An officer should never become so involved in
outside activities that he neglects his military responsibilities, however.

Involvement of ship personnel in activities in foreign ports is considered official
business. For example, it is good public
and foreign relations for the young officers
and sailors of a ship docked in Naples to
play basketball against the local Neapoli-
tan police squad.

MCPON Sanders: *We should not be so busy at
getting the job done that we forget about the
needs of the sailor. Make sure that they do their
rating exams or courses. The officers should
ensure that the crew prepares for advancement
and makes the right wickets along the way.
Sometimes you will have sailors who say that
they do not care if they are not promoted to the
next pay grade, that they are going to do their
four years and get out. Well, this may be true,
but it's darn sure going to be true if we don't
help them to advance. After four years of service, if they are at the same starting block that
they were when they first came in, naturally
they're going to get out, because we really have
never tested them or tried them or put them in
a position where they have to think for themselves. So I think that we need to stress to officers that they must be aware of what their people are capable of doing and make sure that
they perform to that standard, and one way
is to make sure that they prepare for advancement.*

9. Performing under Pressure

The mission of the Navy as defined in Naval
Warfare Publication No. 1 (NWP1) is "to be
prepared to conduct prompt and sustained
operations at sea in support of national inter-

ests,"[59-78] and therefore an officer must be able
to lead in the stress of combat as well as in the
less stressful peacetime environment.

WHAT KIND OF PERSON PERFORMS WELL IN
COMBAT?

Immediately after World War II, an international group was convened to try to determine
why some men performed well in combat while
others did not. In "Men against Fire," it had
been stated that only about 20 percent of men
in combat would get up out of their foxholes and
engage the enemy. The others would lay down
in their foxholes and would not take action. Often
their performance depended more on their leader
than on their own inclinations. What is that
ingredient in leadership that will make troops
enter battle and risk their lives? Secretary Webb
offers some of the answers by pointing out that,

> to function in an emergency and stressful
> environment, the officer must know him-
> self. He must have thoroughly examined
> himself and must know where his
> strengths and weaknesses are. The worst
> time for an officer to discover a flaw in
> himself is during a crisis. In the plebe sys-
> tem and in the boot camp environment,
> the individual has many opportunities to
> find out about himself. In addition, every
> time he does something that requires him
> to make hard decisions, when he has the
> opportunity and is not in a stress environ-
> ment, the officer should sit back afterward
> and ask himself what he did wrong,
> because there is always room for improve-
> ment. It is said that every successful life is
> in reality a series of minor failures. The
> individual who is going to grow mentally
> and is going to understand himself must
> constantly evaluate himself so that when
> crisis does occur, he will not discover
> something about himself that he had not
> known before.

The aforementioned international body was
organized to ascertain what qualities make up

leaders whom troops will obey. The group concluded that leadership was not predictable; before troops were "bloodied and gutted," no one could say who would be a natural leader. There was no peacetime measure of combat leadership ability. Even strong peacetime leaders sometimes failed miserably as leaders in combat. Some ship COs had nervous breakdowns and turned their ships over to their XOs to take them back to their home bases or the United States. They couldn't hack combat. Most of these men were older; in their eyes, they had more to lose, and they thought of being killed more than the younger generation, which had not yet learned the finality of death.

Admiral Ramage, speaking to this, said:

> I don't think there's any way that you can judge who is or who is not going to be successful in time of war. I was just an average Joe along with Sam Dealey (USNA 1930, Medal of Honor), serving in the same submarine division. He was a very quiet and unassuming chap. Both of us came up for qualification at the same time and both had difficulty convincing our respective skippers that we were ready. We both made it on the second try. Now, Sam was probably the most courageous and innovative skipper we had but to look at him you would never pick him out of a crowd, nor would I ever have been singled out for any special attention. It is just inherent somehow that when you meet a situation head on you handle it instinctively. I think that if you are concerned about your own welfare and safety, that is, if you're going to worry about not being successful, the odds are already stacked against you. Self-confidence is all important.

Even officers of the rank of commander have "failed to engage the enemy although the enemy was made known to them." They were sent home. In the invasion of Normandy, some generals and officers failed as combat leaders and were relieved or "sacked." And there were enlisted men who just loved to have "command" of a 20-mm or a 40-mm gun and engage aircraft or small combatants. They were the natural-born leaders. One flag officer recruited only football players for his squadron. He believed that these men had been tested and had proved their courage. It didn't turn out as he had predicted. When it came to facing the enemy on the bloody field of battle, with life itself at stake, these men showed no more courage than anyone else. No person knows how he will perform in combat.

In the first moments of combat, reactions can be confused. The first instinct is usually one of self-preservation, involving "flight" rather than "fight." But most people can overcome this reaction, shape up, and commit themselves to the responsibility of leadership. The leader must engage the enemy and persuade his men to do the same. Rear Admiral Kostev of the Soviet Navy has written that, on board a ship, there should be an atmosphere of "vigilance and poise aboard with every crewman ready to cope with any difficulties involved by the swiftly changing situation."[37-377] A good leader will rally his men when they are pinned down . . . and, above all, he will lead them in attack after attack . . . that is a "must" in leadership. To do otherwise would be cowardly.

PREPARING FOR COMBAT: INSTILLING CONFIDENCE IN SUBORDINATES

Admiral John Bulkeley, USN, Medal of Honor, believes that

> an individual must have confidence in himself and have no self-doubts; he must have confidence in his weapons; and, further and most important, he must have faith and confidence in the leaders above him.

> You, as naval officers and leaders, must instill this confidence in your subordinates. You must establish a relationship with your subordinates early on, before the time comes for action. Explain to

them, if possible, what your objectives are. Show them by your actions that you believe in your mission and its place in the overall picture.

Prior to combat, "the commander and watch officers must make a thorough study of enemy weapons and equipment, his operational and tactical views, and the forms and methods of his actions."[37-377] "It is said that the United States has traditionally bred officers with initiative and daring, capable and willing to take chances. In peacetime, the combat conscious leader must work at encouraging initiative from his subordinates. This flows naturally from confidence in his men, mutual trust, and a willingness to listen to and implement others' suggestions, balanced, of course, by an insistence on compliance with orders. Initiative is the essence of confidence."[59-80]

On a number of occasions General MacArthur stated that, "for men to move into combat, they must have absolute confidence in their weapons and in their leaders." He also said that the unfailing formula for the production of morale is patriotism, self-respect, discipline, and self-confidence in a military unit. This must be combined with fair treatment and appreciation from without. Morale cannot be produced by pampering or coddling an army and is not necessarily destroyed by hardship, danger, or even calamity. Though it can survive and develop in adversity that comes as an inescapable element of service, it will quickly wither and die if soldiers come to believe themselves to be the victims of ignorance, personal indifference, or ineptitude on the part of their military leaders.

When a naval officer is faced with making a decision in combat, he must fulfill his obligations to his conscience and his country. He cannot afford to neglect either.[57-47] In too many cases during World War II, the senior officers were not known by name or sight by men in the ranks. This is one reason General MacArthur showed himself right up in the front, with the men engaged in actual "shooting." A leader who hides from combat will not have the confidence of his men.

At Corregidor, when the air raid sirens sounded, General MacArthur headed for the shelter of Malita tunnel. He walked calmly and never ran. He had often said that there was not a bullet made to kill him. He never showed any fear. His men were proud of his courage and were confident in his leadership. MacArthur was a natural-born leader.

In addition to General MacArthur, other examples of leaders are Admirals Nimitz; Halsey; Spruance, the quiet man; Lockwood, the most capable; Donitz of the German Navy; and General Rommel, the great battlefield commander. Then there were Eisenhower, who was firm; Montgomery, a master of military planning; General Patton, almost a Rommel, and a natural-born leader. All had different instinctive techniques, and all were well developed and experienced in combat.

THE PERSONALITY FACTOR

Different leaders, of course, have different characteristics. People do not lead on a set group of principles, but, rather, develop a demanding style, a tough style, a persuasive style, or whatever style best suits them. Admiral Long points out that

a junior going into the fleet assumes a greater responsibility than almost any other person of comparable age. A young officer, 25 years old or less, can be placed in charge of the movements of a large ship, a very expensive aircraft, a platoon or company of Marines; he can be placed in charge of literally hundreds of men and women. It is in this particular role of a younger officer that the qualifications of professional training come to bear. There is no substitute for an officer knowing his job, or excuse for not knowing it.

In the past there has been a notion that to be a good naval officer and an effective leader, to set forth basic objectives and measure if those objectives have been accomplished, one need know only the principles of management. But, in fact, officers need to know their subject matter, because when a young officer goes on active duty in the fleet, many of his responsibilities revolve around extremely complex, highly technical machinery and equipment. The officer must have a certain understanding of the aircraft, ship, submarine, or combat system. Without that necessary technical understanding, he will become a follower and not a leader.

It is particuarly important for officers to have an understanding of their equipment if they are involved in hazardous positions such as flying an aircraft, serving on a ship or submarine, or serving in the combat forces in the Fleet Marine Forces. It is in this type of environment that an officer must take necessary, quick, and correct action if he is to avert casualties and avoid disastrous damage to his ship, aircraft, or equipment. In this particular regard the knowledge and professional training of an officer is critical.

In squads or small ships, camaraderie is vital. The different personalities of those in a unit must be melded into a workable team. All the individuals know one another, one another's personalities and habits, and when they have a close relationship, they will rally and become a tight organization that will react and attack when instructed to do so by a good leader. "A truly closeknit fighting team is potentially the warship's strongest human resource."[2-107]

It should be understood that "the natural-born leader" is a genetic concept to which everyone does not subscribe; there is no agreement on this even among the contributors to this volume. What can be said is that there are men and women of strong personalities who will lead under all circumstances, and there are others who will follow.

USING INITIATIVE AND INSTINCT IN AN EMERGENCY

We must teach all hands by example. There are many different examples, and all of them are worthy of study. An example of an emergency that was handled promptly and correctly by a well-trained crew is a fire that occurred aboard the USS *Guam* on 19 July 1981. This amphibious assault ship was conducting flight operations underway when a CH-53 Sea Stallion attempting to land collided with another CH-53 already on deck. The blades hit an H-1 Huey as the Sea Stallion crashed to the deck. The three aircraft were in flames, and fuel spread the fire down the deck elevator and into the hangar bay. The *Guam* executive officer, Captain L. D. Presnell, stated that "some of our most junior people . . . took charge, did the job they were trained to do, and more." The fire on deck was extinguished in ten minutes. Damage was minimized in the hangar bay by the same quick reaction. Only 54 percent of the ship's petty officers and chiefs were in the area at the time of the accident, and most of those fighting the fire were young sailors and marine reservists. Said Captain Presnell: "We were dependent on junior petty officers and non-rated personnel stepping into leadership roles. They proved the value not only of having a core of chiefs and senior petty officers, but of training the next generation of leaders."[48-33]

When the time comes for action, take action— *early, decisive,* and *effective* action! If you lead your troops before battle, they'll follow you in battle. Admiral McDonald comments:

Seldom will a service person get in trouble by using his own initiative unless in so doing he is knowingly violating a policy that has been set by his senior. Most seniors are very forgiving when a junior fails for the reason that his approach did not happen to be the right one, because they would rather see a young officer use his initiative and make a mistake than do nothing. From the commander's standpoint, there is a certain satisfaction when one of his subordinates does do something on his own and does it right; the commander can say to himself that he helped train that fellow a little bit.

I'll never forget my operations officer. Once, he did something on his own which was absolutely wrong in my book. I said, "Boy, you sure did fall through the crack that time. Now let's turn it around and do it this way." But I could practically have patted him on the back because waiting and getting permission up and down the line would not have been good, either.

A naval officer's job is to lead his forces into battle. That is the number one job, the operational job. But he has a number two job, which is the managerial job. It is close to number one, but it must take second place. Certain management tools are necessary at sea, but most of them are used ashore. Most of the important management jobs of the operational Navy officer will be either with a base, or perhaps more importantly, in the Pentagon. Compromise is a management tool that will be used in the managerial job more than in the operational job, because the officer's duties in a managerial job will lead to contact with people in other areas.

Admiral Ramage does not believe that there is any certain way to prepare for emergencies.

One must try to anticipate the most probable contingencies and know his job thoroughly, both of which will enhance his self-confidence and ensure his initiative. Concentrating on and reviewing past history are helpful to recognize the potential hazards. Only self-confidence and trust in one's juniors and seniors alike will ensure composure and effectiveness. To determine a young officer's ability to act decisively and effectively, he must be handed increased responsibility at every opportunity. In other words, if you're going to bring a youngster around you've got to throw responsibility at him, and as fast as he can take it.

As to suggestions on getting the job done and not worrying about one's possible demise, let me say that, first off, I never stopped to consider the possibility of my being killed in action; that is the first thing you put out of your mind. You have a job to do and your full intent and effort is devoted toward meeting this situation when it comes on. In submarines we were quite different than I think any other branch of the service, because we had a chance there either to engage in combat or to avoid it. Usually you had two choices. Because you were the first one at bat, either you attack or you don't attack. In the early stages of the war some of our submarine skippers in the Far East collapsed because they were not mentally prepared for combat operations and, of course, their bases had already been taken over by the enemy.

The first problem you have to face, of course, is changing from a peacetime attitude to a combat attitude; in other words, psychologically you've got to make a complete turnaround. You never fired a shot in anger, you never killed anybody, and now you've got it facing you, so that's the first hurdle you have to get over. From there on, your whole intent and effort are directed toward accomplishing your mission, never once thinking that it's going to fail. You've got to have the courage of your convictions and self-confidence and, as I said, you've got to figure out what you can do, what you can't do, what you can get away with, what you can't get away with.

I was always looking and trying to find an opportunity to attack, going to extremes to get into position to attack, never once trying to avoid attack, though once I did. I had attacked a ship twice and both times the torpedoes had failed. Subsequently, I found myself face to face with this same ship, but this time we were in a narrow, shallow strait where I was preparing to lay mines. So rather than compromise the mine field and lay myself open to certain depth charging in shallow water with no means of escape, I deliberately withheld an attack. Taking the initiative to start the attack, you've got one leg up and have the advantage by having first crack, but then you've got to keep following it up, ensure that you maintain the initiative. Once you lose the initiative and the other team comes to bat, then you're in trouble; the idea is to stay at bat as long as possible until the game is won. Don't ever turn it over to the other guy. I think that's the essence of it. I would always encourage my troops to do their best, to use their initiative in everything, and I also felt that I had an obligation to them because they were down there working their hearts out. They expected me to do the job, so I owed them something as much as they owed me, and it's that sort of a combination of respect and trust that carries you through.

10. Other Requirements for Effective Leadership

DEVELOPING PHYSICAL AND MENTAL STAMINA

For most officers, the most effective form of leadership is by example. Senior naval officers know well that a unit soon reflects the personality, courage, discipline, integrity, sharpness, and other characteristics of its leader. It can be said that *management* is the science of matching resources against requirements, and that *leadership* is the art of resolving the difference. Peo-

ple are the most important resource an officer and leader has to work with, and anything that will increase their contribution to accomplishment of the unit's mission will be of great value. Few individuals push themselves hard enough to explore the limits of their capabilities. Therefore, most people are capable of doing much more than they think they can or are now doing; a vast potential exists for improved production.

Thomas H. Huxley expressed it this way: "Perhaps the most valuable result of all education is the ability to make yourself do the thing you have to do, when it ought to be done, whether you like it or not."[10-10]

If an officer wishes his subordinates to be hardworking, dedicated, and diligent, then certainly one of the best ways to motivate them is by providing an inspirational example in his own behavior. Conversely, laziness in a leader can only beget laziness in his subordinates. Each officer will encounter situations where duty demands that he go without rest, delay meals, and forgo satisfaction of other physical and psychological needs. Who has not heard someone say in admiration of an officer, "He would not ask his people to do anything that he would or could not do"?

People can be pulled much more effectively than they can be pushed. The leader bears responsibilities that cannot be delegated but that also cannot be carried out without the dedicated efforts of his subordinates. This gives him an incentive to lead, and it also places great value on the continuity of his observation and direction. The commanding officer is usually his own best lookout, not because his aging eyes are better, but because no one is better motivated to look out than he is. Keeping your men healthy, therefore, is a quality-of-life issue and a responsibility of all commanders from the highest echelon down to the squad level.[25-10]

Units with the best operational reputations usually have commanding officers who spend a great deal of time awake and personally involved in the tactical picture. Commanding officers have extremely broad areas of responsibility. Those areas that he does not periodically visit, view, or review are not likely to maintain the standards he sets. As in civilian life, this translates to long hours of hard work and high levels of physical activity, especially at sea.

General Wilson says that

a good physical condition is a primary requisite for military service, and it makes no difference what your job is, whether you're a radio operator on a submarine or whether you're a member of a special forces team that parachuted behind the enemy lines before your landing operation took place. Good physical condition makes you do the job better, and you also feel better. Inner strength is also required. I believe that you must be so dedicated that when the difficult times come, as they do to us all, you have the dedication to stay with it and see that the mission is accomplished despite the fog of war, as it's been described. For that, nothing except good judgment, long hours of training, and dedication to your work will see you through to victory.

The leader's physical stamina, his ability to perform over prolonged periods of time and under adverse conditions, will frequently make the difference between mediocre results or failure and complete success. His ability to "set the example" by being the first on station, by being diligent in ensuring that all is ready for the next evolution, and by invariably being prepared for contingencies will set the tone for his subordinates and peers. The leader who neglects his health and his ability to function at top physical efficiency will find himself unable to influence his subordinates at the critical time.

Admiral Burke believes that "stamina—the ability to operate under pressure, the ability to operate without sleep, the ability to just stand on your feet or do physically strenuous things— is very important." Admiral Clausen sees this as a positive challenge and observes that

the profession of a naval officer calls for all aspects (forces) of a human being (physical, intellectual, and psychosocial), which makes the profession especially attractive. It is self-evident that physical stamina must be trained for and preserved in a progressive age, the more so since physical fitness is of importance for the balance of all human forces. Training for endurance and power to resist should be included with exercises to withstand difficulty, so that stamina skills will not be forgotten.

Obviously, physical stamina alone is not enough to assure an officer of success. Perpetual motion does not exist in physics or in biology. Even the best physical and mental conditioning cannot obviate fatigue, only delay its onset. The symptoms of fatigue—such as irritability, anxiety, and loss of mental acuity—must be recognized and dealt with in self and in others. Tough-minded, forehanded decisions reflecting the finest judgment must be made on how best to spend the stamina coin of the leader and his subordinates in mission execution.

The "iron man" who remains on station simply to provide a presence during preparations for an exercise or during casualty restoration may find himself operating at severely reduced efficiency or may not be able to function at all when he is most needed. Personal injury and high stress may exacerbate the officer's difficulties in keeping his thought processes logical and dispassionate. The leader must also be alert for deterioration in the performance of his subordinates, be aware of their limitations, and act to ensure that they operate efficiently and correctly.

PUTTING OTHERS BEFORE SELF

The leader who fails to subordinate personal needs or desires to the needs of the organization will not succeed. Unselfishness in the leader's actions is an absolute prerequisite to earning the respect of subordinates. He must demonstrate with every action that his first concern is for the mission and his personnel. His people must know that their welfare and performance are his first priority, and that his decisions are based on sound judgment rather than on his personal needs or desires. Admiral Itaya sees it as a matter of

the leader maintaining a strong body and mental stamina at all times. In particular, if he does not maintain his physical strength, then he will not be able to build mental stamina. Many years ago in the [Japanese] Navy, it was said, "Put a uniform on a stomach and an admiral is born." ("Stomach" meant that a man with a keen appetite was a healthy man.) One must use restraint and get appropriate exercise and rest, for most causes of illness are stress (anguish) related. Also, one must be careful to avoid personal and economic trouble.

"Lead by example" and "Duty before self" are among a leader's rules, and are considered the most important. From this it follows that a leader should work harder than his subordinates.

The operative word in leadership is *integrity*. A leader must have integrity in his interpersonal dealings, in his professional conduct, and in his personal affairs. Integrity also applies to the maintenance of high standards of conduct and performance. However critical he may be of the product or of his subordinates, if the officer is seen as being even more critical of his own work, his people will amost invariably work harder to accomplish tasks in a manner in keeping with his high standards. The effective leader considers his integrity his most important attribute and will not compromise it for any reason.

WORKING HARDER THAN SUBORDINATES

If the leader accomplishes all of the above, he will find that he is routinely working harder than most of his subordinates. That does not mean that he has to spend hours and great physical effort on trivial tasks simply to demonstrate how hard he works, or that he has to stay at work unreasonably late and require the same of his people. That sort of activity will have counterproductive effects, both in deteriorating morale and in fostering an unhealthy sense of competition between the subordinate and the leader. Admiral Burke suggests that

good leaders do not necessarily have to work harder than everyone else. Admiral Mitscher was a fine leader who didn't work very hard. He was a frail man, and he recognized his physical limitations, so he kept his work within his physical capability. Even so, he could stay up for long periods, and he could think pretty well, but he did not try to work very hard. He took the big pieces, he reviewed the situation all the time, he did sometimes fiddle with little things, and he expected his pilots and his subordinates to be qualified. Other people, like his chief of staff, were required to ensure that certain things were all right.

Many good leaders do work harder than everyone else, but I do not feel it is necessary in every case. Often it depends on what his assignment is. In fact, there are many very poor leaders who work very hard on things that they should not be working on, and a leader who does a job his subordinates should be doing is not a good leader.

General Wilson believes that an officer must work as hard or harder than his people, but that

an officer's hard work differs from the hard work his people do. Hard work for an officer is not necessarily getting out with a pick and shovel, hard work is not necessarily having an officer crawl through the woods with his rifle in his hand. That's hard work to a private, and it would be even harder work to an officer who was not used to it, but in plain fact, if an officer did that, then he would be neglecting other jobs that he should be doing and for which he is getting paid. So I think that hard work is many things. Hard work is deep thought, hard work is putting on paper what is in one's mind, hard work is weighing advantages and disadvantages to make decisions.

An officer may be sitting in an air conditioned office while the troops are out marching on the parade ground. They are working hard on discipline, and he is working just as hard, because he would be less efficient if he was out under the sun doing the same thing. These things have a tendency to be looked on as not hard work by those who are juniors, but in fact as one rises in rank he learns that this hard work is mental work, physical work—depending on what you have to do—and long hours.

Now that is an interesting question, long hours. There are people who put in long hours to impress their seniors and who appear to have the weight of the world on their shoulders, coming in at five o'clock in the morning, leaving at eight o'clock at night, and hoping someone will see them to say "He's hard at work." Well, that's foolish, of course. He could well be playing golf in the afternoons and improving his physical condition or his mental condition if in fact he had nothing to do at the office. I have never been one to believe that one should stay at the office from 8 to 5 or from 6 to 6 or whatever it is just to be there. So as a result, when the time comes, I expect people to work 24 hours if necessary. The circus has a term for it that says "What you make in peanuts, you lose in popcorn." If you are to be a successful officer, there is no question that the hours that you put in will be much longer than 8 to 5. How you put them in, how effectively you put those hours to work in the accomplishment of your mission, is what's

important, not the hours you work by punching a clock.

Effective use of resources demands a sense of priority which allows the leader to differentiate between the necessary and productive and the unnecessary and trivial. Spinning wheels and working simply for work's sake will uselessly deplete the energy available and will, in the long run, detract from the benefit derived from more positive attributes. The effective naval leader will find that he will work harder than his subordinates as a natural byproduct of paying attention to detail, making sure that both his subordinates and he are prepared for evolutions, and providing direction and motivation to those under him. There will be no artificiality to his actions, and their merits will be evident to all.

The leader who has the physical and mental ability to carry on under fatiguing conditions and has the will to act unselfishly and to work harder than his subordinates possesses the keys to success. He will earn the respect of his subordinates, peers, and seniors, and he will be the most effective officer possible. He is the physically fit, sharp-looking, mentally tough individual who regards his integrity as his most prized possession, and who sets the finest example of the work ethic to everyone in his every action. He is the prototype naval officer.

All of the foregoing needs to be kept in mind by the upper class as they train the plebes. Secretary Webb suggests that

the person who is involved in plebe indoctrination should keep in mind that there is always someone else evaluating the job that is being done. Perhaps the individual should make that person the mother of the sailor or Marine whom the plebe is going to have to lead if he ever goes to combat. Precommissioning training must be able to assure her that if a midshipman cannot handle stress, he is not going to be in a position to make decisions that may get her son killed.

MCPON Sanders: *Officers must have the physical and mental ability to carry on under fatiguing conditions. They should also be aware of the stress on the sailors and divide the work equitably if at all possible. We may never be able to be fully prepared for emergencies, but one of the things that we should think about is, What would I do if I had an emergency with this, or what would I do if I have an emergency with that? Therefore, if you mentally test yourself on the task at hand, then I think that you would have instinctively prepared yourself to act in times of stress or emergency, but you must always think before it happens. Be aware of potential hazards, know what to do, study or take courses, CPR courses, do everything you can to prepare before something happens. Test yourself every now and then and say, What would I do if . . . ? I think if you do that once or twice a day, you will basically be prepared when the real situation occurs.*

11. Objectivity

Making Decisions: The Impact of Facts and Feelings

Secretary Webb points out that
> both facts and feelings enter into decision making. When an officer is making a decision under stress and has a time constraint, he must combine the facts that are available with what his own intuition tells him. One thing a leader should always remember is that he will never have all of the facts, and there may be someone under him saying, "Wait a minute, Sir," someone whose input will make a great deal of difference. A good leader appreciates someone who speaks up and volunteers information.
>
> Conversely, a good leader, one who feels a sense of responsibility to the peo-

ple under him, will also speak up and take the risk that one may not want to hear what he says and may retaliate. If things are not right, the officer must say so, and if someone under him who has credibility with him says something, he should listen carefully. Some people who make it to positions of authority, for some reason, particularly in a stressful environment, believe they do not have the duty to listen.

Secretary Webb gave an example that points up the consequence of this attitude.

> During my last two months in Vietnam, I was assigned to the "three shop" (S-3), the operation shop, and we would get the Night Activities Report of all the units in the regiment. A rifle company was planning a night move into an area I knew to be dangerous, as it was a place where my company had hit a box mine and been ambushed many months before. At the time I was a first lieutenant, I had nine months in the field, I had walked every square inch of the regimental area of operations, and I knew most of it like the back of my hand. I went to our regimental S-3, a lieutenant colonel in charge of training, and explained to him what had happened before, and he said, "Well, what would you have them do, lieutenant?" and I said, "Move them in through this other area that I knew very well and instead of having them move all night, have them take off at six in the morning, they will be across phase line green by 0800, and they won't have to go through that dangerous area." He basically said, "Well, that's why I'm a lieutenant colonel and you're a first lieutenant," and they went through the suspect area, and within 300 meters on the grid map where my company had lost nineteen people. They lost six killed and fourteen wounded. In combat, one can never be sure about the

results of any one action; however, listening to subordinates may prevent such disasters.

On a puristic basis, it can be said that an officer should consider fact and avoid letting personal prejudice or expediency affect decisions and actions involving subordinates. However, if this is taken literally, the officer may incorrectly become indoctrinated to rely solely on "Just the facts, ma'am" in situations involving subordinates.

It is the opinion of both officers and their civilian executive counterparts that leaders/managers do attempt to ascertain "fact" when confronted with a problem requiring their action. Both naval and civilian leaders are often highly trained technically, and, because of their talents and abilities, are promoted and put in charge of groups of people. In technical specialties, problems are generally caused by mechanical, electrical, electronic, or hydraulic equipment component and/or system malfunctioning or failure to function. Though many technical problems are extremely difficult and challenging to solve, they are probably the easiest to understand and lend themselves best to gathering facts without considering personal prejudice or expediency. For this reason, these individuals' skill and training may lead them to search for "fact" as the best way to deal with people.

There are other types of problems, situations, and circumstances, however, which do not lend themselves to such handy fact-finding. For example, operational problems and people problems are much more difficult for the officer to work with. "Operational" means such things as policy, organizational structure, problems stemming from laws and regulations and their application, deployment schedules, problems in the functional specialties between divisions and departments, and so forth. "People" problems are caused primarily by the behavior of an individual or a group of people. This category, people, usually involves the least tangible and least factual variables of all. Human behavior may at times seem vague and its causes ambiguous, whereas the substance of operational problems is somewhat more concrete, and technical problems lend themselves most easily to solution through factual information alone.

The point is that "facts" are not always available, ascertainable, or acquirable, and it must not be assumed that only facts are useful. Officers may not be fully aware of all the personal prejudices and biases they have that may color their decisions or get in the way of their making appropriate decisions or taking appropriate actions. As to expediency, if it means subordinating moral principle for the sake of facilitating an end or purpose, it is bad. However, it can also imply usefulness, fitness, pragmatism, suitability, and other positive means for achieving desired results, in which case it is good.

How, then, to proceed? Some of the time the best anyone can do in a difficult situation, especially one involving people, is to work with probabilities rather than with "facts." Not only may facts be difficult to ascertain and open to multiple interpretations and impacted by situational variations, but they may also be affected by individual perceptions. Despite our best efforts to be fair, honest, and exact, we may, because we are human, delete, distort, or generalize "facts" and thereby fall victim to our own subjective bias or biases. Seeking the "facts" also puts one in the position of looking for "truth," and, in the process, of becoming caught up in the polarities of right/wrong, good/bad, black/white, and the entire spectrum of either/ors. This most often leads to assessing blame, finding "the one correct" answer (when there may be many), and setting up a scapegoat rather than getting to the cause of a situation or particular behavior.

Considering the foregoing, the earlier puristic statement is revised: The officer must consider as many facts, opinions, perceptions, and assumptions as time and the situation will allow in making decisions and taking actions involving subordinates. Officers need to be aware of their own bias or biases during the data-gathering process and the impact such data and their interpretation may have on the final decision or results.

The following exercise is included to pique awareness to our blind spots in our data-gathering processes and to shed light on our prejudices, as well.

THE "F" INCIDENT

Please read the sentence set out in the box below:

> FINISHED FILES ARE THE RESULT OF YEARS OF SCIENTIFIC STUDY COMBINED WITH THE EXPERIENCE OF MANY YEARS OF EXPERTS.

Read the sentence again and, as you read it, count the number of times the letter *F* appears. In pencil, lightly write the number of *F*s you find here: _____

How certain (on a scale of 0 to 100 percent) are you that you have correctly counted all the *F*s in the sentence in the box? Before you answer, read the sentence once more and count all the *F*s. Now indicate your degree of certainty: I am _____ percent certain.

Complete the following statement*: I am _____ percent certain that the sentence in the box printed above has no more and no fewer than _____ *F*s in it. I am willing to stake my professional reputation on this fact. _____ (Initial with your initials.)

Before we divulge the "facts," let's examine an *F* Incident scenario.

You are a division officer. Your division is made up of 20 people and includes 1 chief, 1 first-class petty officer, 2 second-class petty officers, and 4 third-class petty officers; the rest are seamen.

* Before you complete this statement and initial it, feel free to read the sentence and count the *F*s again. Do you still see the same number of *F*s? Now go back and complete the statement.

Your division's minority breakdown is 4 blacks, 2 Hispanics, 1 Filipino, and 4 women. Since you have taken over the division, work has gone smoothly and very few problems have come up. One day, however, you receive a request from one of the POs, a black female named Smith, to speak to you. You know Smith to be a good worker, but you have also picked up scuttlebutt that she sometimes "mouths off." You tell the chief to have her come see you.

When PO Smith appears, she seems upset and proceeds to tell you about the *F* Incident, in which she saw seven *F*s but no one will believe her. As it happens, *F*s are very crucial to her job and she is 100 percent certain that she saw seven and no more or fewer. She feels she is being harassed by one of the second-class POs (white, male) and the first-class PO (Hispanic, male), because they say there are no more than three *F*s and they are tired of putting up with her big mouth. You listen and ask appropriate questions. Finally, you tell PO Smith that you will look into the situation and get back to her.

You begin to check out the incident by talking to your E–7, Chief Jones (white, male). The chief knows about these situations (he has been in the Navy 11 years), and he tells you that PO Smith is obviously mistaken. He has had numerous *F* Incidents, and there were never more than three *F*s. He adds that there were usually five *O*s, but only three *F*s, "for sure." Besides, he tells you, PO Smith seems to be a bit of a troublemaker. Probably it would be best to let the matter drop. No need to make a big deal of it. Chief Jones, in your opinion, is a real "straight arrow" guy. He is a bit more authoritarian than you are comfortable with, but you can live with that.

You are considering taking Chief Jones's advice and letting the matter drop when you accidentally overhear an exchange between one of your seamen (white, male) and the other second-class PO (black, male). They are talking about the *F* Incident. The seaman says he is certain that he found five *F*s, and the PO2 says that it is impossible, that there can't be more than three *F*s. The seaman persists, saying that there are at least five *F*s and maybe more. The second-class PO tells the seaman in emphatic tones to knock off his nonsense and get back to work. He accuses the seaman of hanging around PO Smith too much and says he had better "cool it" before he gets labeled a troublemaker, too.

At this point you decide that you should check further into the *F* Incident. During the next couple of days, you engage in a quiet but systematic gathering of data (or facts, if you prefer). Each time you have occasion to interact with one of your crew you ask how many *F*s he or she has noticed. What you discover is that 14 of 20 saw three *F*s, 1 saw four *F*s, 2 saw five *F*s, 1 saw six *F*s, and 2 saw seven *F*s. You are puzzled. You ask to see the *F* material, and at a quick glance you find _____ *F*s. (Insert the number here that you actually found earlier.)

Questions for Discussion

1. How would you resolve this situation?
2. How do you account for the differences among your crew members?
3. Before you check how many *F*s you found, which crew member or members had the most credibility or influence with you? Explain.
4. How do you know or determine what is fact, opinion, or prejudice?
5. Can an officer deal effectively with subordinates using anything other than facts? Justify your response.

COMMENTS AND IMPLICATIONS

General Wilson reminds us that
we are all a product of our background, but this does not mean that decisions based on that background are necessarily right. We sometimes have to resist the experiences we've had, successful or unsuccessful, in our past in order to ensure that we make proper decisions in the present. We cannot simply say, "Yes, I remember now, ten years ago something

happened and this was the result and I'll do it again."

The facts are that times change, technology changes, weapons change, but basic human nature doesn't change. A leader must keep up to date on every aspect of his job, weigh all facts, and seek other people's advice.

Officers of the rank of lieutenant commander, major, commander, or lieutenant colonel are often in command positions and have a staff. They simply must use that staff to good advantage and ensure that staff members participate in the decisions that are made. The commander seeks his staff's advice in logistics and intelligence and operations and personnel; he seeks their advice and lets them know that their advice is needed and considered, but that, finally, he must make the decision. A good leader, if he has to go against a recommendation of his staff, calls them in and thanks them for their input and explains his decision to them. And they may like it or they may not like it, but they deserve an explanation, and a leader by all means should let them know why he did not follow their advice. I believe they will work just as hard the next time to give the officer good advice, because they appreciate him letting them know why he didn't take their advice this time. If the officer does take advice, I certainly believe that he should give credit to the other members of the staff. To repeat an old homily, there is nothing that cannot be accomplished if no one cares who gets the credit for it.

Admiral Uchida offers that,
when making decisions about subordinates, officers should first think of their subordinates' success and human happiness through their careers. It is important for the officer to let them understand that there is no predetermined personal course

in the Navy, that individuals who work hard and persevere can accomplish a great deal and attain advancement.

The *F* Incident demonstrates how we, as human beings, form *scotomas*, or blind spots. A scotoma is a sensory blocking out of parts of our environment and is caused by conditioning or prior expectation. We develop scotomas to the truth about the world and ourselves because of our preconceived ideas and conditioning. This causes us to see what we expect to see, hear what we expect to hear, and think what we expect to think. The result is that we develop blind spots to the "Truth"; that is, we sometimes gather data, often quite factual, that agree with what we already believe, and we overlook or tune out or omit anything that contradicts our position. Awareness of this tendency is useful, but more important is a willingness to listen to and look at other perspectives with a mind open to learning. (Note: The number of *F*s in the sentence can be found following MCPON Sanders's remarks at the end of section 14. Before checking, you may also wish to count the number of times the letter *O* appears. Write the number of *O*s here: _____.)

RESISTING PERSONAL PREJUDICE

In discussing the progress the Naval Service has made toward eliminating prejudice, as well as the need for officers to overcome their personal prejudice, Admiral Hayward comments that,

> in the period 1965 through 1985, the nation has gone through a very dramatic adjustment to the social structure, as equal rights for women not only has been recognized but also has become a very important part of our daily lives. Along with human rights and civil rights, and the real understanding of the racial issues, the ethnic problems that we have tolerated in our country for two hundred years have rapidly come to the surface, and we've had to deal with them. We have

been successful to some degree, though it's probably accurate to say that the generation of naval officers entering the service in the second half of the decade will be better prepared to deal with prejudices in a social context than those of past year groups, because they've lived through the transition and are much more comfortable dealing with the interpersonal relationships that might affect religion, race, sex, nationalities, and the like. I hope that's true, and my observation tells me that's basically true.

I reflect back on the days when Admiral Zumwalt was Chief of Naval Operations and we almost had mutinies aboard ship because there was such a rapid movement toward black civil rights in the country, and we had a very large percentage of blacks aboard ship in the wrong divisions and the wrong rate structures; gross prejudice being applied unconsciously. If we had been really conscious of it, we wouldn't have tolerated it. The great mark that Admiral Zumwalt left on the Navy was his ability to bring that to focus very, very rapidly and cause the naval officers and civilian leadership to recognize the enormous deficiences that existed. We corrected it quite quickly, much, much faster than otherwise would have been done in my judgment, by placing requirements upon the officers and chief petty officers to get with it.

So let's hope that the concept of personal prejudices has gone away, but prejudice is still going to be there in the sense of personalities. There are a few nasty people still around and personalities that just clash, and that will always be true. It's going to be very difficult for leaders to lead well if they can't deal with those prejudices. They've got to set them aside, they've got to learn how to deal objectively with the human being despite the fact that they may really have a difficulty communicating with or interfacing well with that person, whether that person is a senior or a junior. Some prejudices may always exist, since we are human beings and thus will fail in our ability to be perfect to everyone—it's not natural. So the stronger leader is the person who's going to be able to have that self-discipline to be able to control that in a fair way in the manner in which he goes about leading other people or working with and for other people.

Some people are very good at being terribly decisive and making a decision, and others are very deliberate and may never make a decision; but naval officers are required to make decisions under many different kinds of circumstances. Most situations do not require an officer to be so decisive that he fails to pay attention to the people around him. He needs to listen to their advice and include them in the determination of the solution. Especially when he is involved in the decision-making process, an officer needs to overcome his prejudices and listen to what a person has to say and give him credit for a certain amount of judgment.

There are situations where there is no time to wait for input; in these situations an officer's experience will come heavily to the fore. The decision made will be a good one or a bad one based upon experience level and knowledge base.

An example in which prejudice (underestimating the capabilities of another culture) affected the outcome of a military battle is the famous Battle of the Little Big Horn. "The tactics of the Indians that day resulted in their doing to Custer exactly what Custer had planned tactically to do to them. And they had the leaders, the arms and the overwhelming forces, none of which facts were known or appreciated by the Seventh Cavalry. Their members had been underestimated;

their leadership and fighting capacity undervalued; their superiority in arms not even suspected. The Seventh Cavalry paid the penalty for national stupidity."[13-29]

MCPON Sanders: *The officer must not allow expediency to influence decisions and actions involving subordinates. It is difficult to control one's prejudices. Doing so requires a person to work at it and to be very objective, and if you can abide by this, you are on your way to being a leader in any endeavor, whether it be military or civilian.*

12. Accountability

"The crewmen want to trust their new Captain to deal with them fairly, and they want the security of knowing that the Captain is a skilled warrior who will bring them home from battle."[17-42]

Thus far, the concepts of integrity and responsibility have been examined in great depth. There is no need to try to decide which concept is the more important, because the special trust placed in those in the commissioned ranks dictates that they "do it all"—that is, that they try to meet all of the requirements placed on them and perform their assignments in an exemplary manner, making sure that all actions necessary are taken to ensure mission accomplishment and the building and maintenance of a military team that will prevail over all obstacles.

This concept is embraced by Admiral Carney, who observes that

one of the most important factors in leadership is seeking responsibility and accountability. The naval officer must assume full responsibility for his unit, for everything that happens to the unit he is in charge of or commands. Traditionally, the captain takes the credit for everything that is good and the blame for everything that is bad.

An individual's sense of responsibility

should apply in his personal life, as well. Those in command, whether of a ship or of a corporation, value individuals who seek out responsibility and who are accountable for their actions.

Accountability, then, is another key concept for officers. The Random House College Dictionary defines *accountable* in terms of (1) being subject to the obligation to report, explain, or justify something; (2) being answerable; and (3) being capable of being explained. Admiral Nakamura remarks that

> an officer should take full responsibility for all of his actions, even when he is following orders or instructions from his senior. If he tries to escape that responsibility, he will forfeit the entire confidence of both his seniors and his subordinates.

Remarking on the importance of accountability, Vermont C. Royster, a noted journalist, once wrote: "On the sea there is a tradition older even than the traditions of the country itself. . . . It is the tradition that with responsibility goes authority and with them both goes accountability. . . . This accountability is not for the intentions but for the deed." Royster was writing of the collision between the USS *Wasp* and the USS *Hobson* in April 1952, and he stressed that, in the military, when someone was held accountable for a certain action or event, it was not the intentions, no matter how kind they were, that mattered, but, rather, the outcome of the action itself.[31-24]

KEEPING SENIORS INFORMED

"Subject to the obligation to report" means that an officer is required to keep his senior advised concerning all actions, especially those that might result in embarrassing questions being put to the senior by someone outside of the organization. Certainly officers are known for their ability to do many things almost simultaneously, and to do them right. In such situations, the officer is only too glad to let the boss know what

he accomplished. However, there will be times when a mistake has been made or necessary action has not been taken, and the officer also has a responsibility to report such events and circumstances to his senior at the earliest practical moment.

People have always been concerned about making mistakes, but today there seems to be a concern that one mistake will be the end of a career. Admiral Burke refuted this idea and suggests that,

> if an officer makes a mistake, he should let the boss know first, so that the boss hears about it from the officer responsible rather than from someone else. Furthermore, after an operation, the officer should analyze it to see how it could have been done better so that others can do it better.
>
> Sometimes a mistake helps a career. Very few people have been promoted after being taken off the promotion list, but I was. My wife and I went down to look for a place to retire. We were all through. If it hadn't been for an honest President, I would have been through. Lots of times people make a mistake and it helps them. Why? I don't know, exactly. Not just because they admit it, but maybe because they do something about it, maybe because they inform people.
>
> You learn a great deal about life by making your mistakes early. When I was a chemical engineer, I studied a course called Equations. Essentially, what goes in has got to come out, what comes out has got to have been put in. It was a very good course, and I remember that nothing comes in for free. Everything that comes out of a thing was put in it somehow, and the question is how to control what goes in. When anyone reports that something is going haywire, or he thinks something is a little bit wrong, you ought to think

about it a little bit, you ought to recognize that he's got a reason for saying so. It may not be important, or he may be wrong, but he's got a reason, and it ought to be checked. A lot of things go haywire because they haven't been checked early enough or they were checked and nothing was done about it.

There are people who have a tendency to answer only those questions that are asked, and not to volunteer unpleasant information about themselves or anyone else in the organization. But being an officer is not like being on a quiz show or playing twenty questions. Seniors should never be expected or asked to guess the facts, implications, or expected results of an officer's actions. An officer should always be honest, forthright, and forthcoming; to be less is to be an incomplete officer. Officers should provide information to a senior just as if they were the senior in the situation and wanted to know all the pertinent details. This requires reciting all events leading up to the event, the event itself, and both realized and expected results of the event.

In effect, all officers are expected to have moral courage and to realize that the good of the Naval Service and the country come before their own well-being. The future of the country is far more important than the future of any of its members. The reputation of the country is far more important than the reputation of any of its members. Certainly it is not easy to tell others when a mistake has been made, but the officer who always does so ensures that his seniors and the Naval Service itself will spread his service reputation, which will describe him as someone of complete honesty and candor. Thus, someday, when he is thought to have made a mistake and he has not, his innocence will be believed on the basis of his own words. This special trust is one of the major rewards of being an officer—someone whose word is his bond. An honest officer can be relied on and thus can be given assignments that are challenging.

Any type of command in any service carries with it a great deal of responsibility, but in the Navy especially there is one position that should become the goal of every officer in any naval specialty, because it represents the pinnacle of responsibility and authority and accountability in the military and civilian sectors of the United States. "In each ship there is one man who in the hour of emergency or peril at sea can turn to no other man. There is one who alone is ultimately responsible for the [safe] navigation, engineering performance, accurate gunfire, and morale of his ship. He is the Captain."[17-39]

TAKING RESPONSIBILITY FOR THE ACTIONS OF SUBORDINATES

Trouble cannot always be avoided; nor are all mistakes identifiable in advance. Thus, officers should remember that they will be judged by seniors who have "been there before" and will understand if something is not quite right. Seniors will know that possibly there was no way to avoid the trouble, or that one of the junior's subordinates was responsible by doing something against the junior's instructions or without his authorization. In this regard, it is useful to note that an officer does not need to explain to others that a mistake was made by a subordinate, first, because the senior is responsible for what his personnel do, and, second, because every senior has been a junior and thus understands that things do not always proceed as planned.

Admiral Nakamura believes that

the degree of a leader's responsibility for the actions of his subordinates differs according to the situation. Do the actions originate from the will of the subordinates themselves, or from the leader's orders or instructions? Are the subordinates directly under him, or do they have intermediate commanders? And so on.

For the actions taken in pursuance of his orders or instructions, a commander should be accountable fully. For actions originating with his subordinates or even taken against his instruction, a commander cannot escape his responsibility to lead and supervise.

If the subordinates are not directly under him and he is leading through intermediaries, a commander has an indirect responsibility to lead and supervise, but even in that case his moral responsibility remains at all times, and legal responsibility is his in some cases.

Providing Complete Explanations for Mistakes

Written explanations and justifications to a senior should be complete, leaving nothing to his imagination. Omitting something is just as much a violation of personal honor as reporting something inaccurately. The writer should try to read the report from the standpoint of the person who will eventually be reading it, and he should ask himself questions that might come to the person's mind. Is the report complete? Does its sense depend on information that is not included? Does it leave in doubt who made the mistake? Has the writer taken 100 percent of the responsibility for all his actions?

Being "answerable" means that the individual has an obligation to volunteer information, even though it may be detrimental to him. At all times an officer should be reviewing his action with the thought of relaying to a senior any information that will allow that senior to do a better job or put him in a position to help his own senior do the job better or increase the possibility of mission success.

Officers do not normally work to a specific job description, and their duties are not usually prescribed in anything approaching exact terms. An officer is an individual whose life is dedicated to country, and thus he is expected at all times to be observing all events and circumstances and to react by providing inputs and actions that will help the mission to be met. In this context, the officer may by omission due to forgetfulness; oversight; other, more pressing, duties; or interfering instructions, events, or circumstances either fail to take an action or avoid taking one, or take the wrong action. Being answerable means that the officer has a solemn obligation to volunteer an explanation for all events in which he is involved without having to be asked to do so.

A Leader's Actions Must Be Justifiable

Finally, being accountable means that the officer does things that are "capable of being explained." He does not do things without rhyme or reason. The officer carefully thinks out every action to be taken with respect to its effect on others and the mission, and with respect to his own authority to take the action in the first place. An officer should never take an action if he cannot justify it on the grounds of military propriety.

Admiral Fran McKee, in commenting on this general area, offers that

probably nothing is more important in the realm of fulfilling your job as an officer than being responsible and accountable for the decisions you make and the actions you take. You are ultimately responsible for everything that happens in your division or your department or your ship or your command or wherever it is, so it never stops, it goes on and on. You can assign people to do certain things, but you can't give that responsibility to them.

We should all be held accountable for what we do, and while the leader has the ultimate responsibility, everyone should be accountable for his or her own actions. Each sailor has an assignment that is part of the big picture in accomplishing the mission, and it is necessary to rely upon each individual in meeting that goal. If each person is held accountable, the leader can then have more confidence in the ability of the crew to accomplish the mission.

An officer has two beings, an official one and a somewhat more informal "personal being."

However, even when an officer is in civilian clothes and out in the civilian community, he is responsible for meeting the requirements that are placed on him as a military officer. Officers shall be honest in their dealings; not "use" their position as officers to influence others; and, in appearance, bearing, and speech, reflect only the highest credit on the Naval Service.

ACCOUNTABILITY HELPS DEFINE THE LEADER

Admiral Holloway amplifies this point by observing that

> the commissioned officer is distinguished from the horde, and always has been, as the individual who makes the judgments and takes the responsibility. An officer is not an officer because he gets more pay or because he went to college and the other people did not. He is an officer because he has assumed certain obligations, and these obligations can be very difficult.

During the Korean War, the Marines were desperately trying to hold the Pusan perimeter. In one battalion alone, 22 second lieutenants doing their job were killed because it was their responsibility to see that the troops stayed on the ridge line, it was their responsibility to see that the counterattacks were made. The responsibility is the officers'.

An officer should be meticulous in the handling of his private and personal affairs, as people whose personal habits and personal life are unattractive generally are not admired. Part of integrity for junior officers and midshipmen is to pay their bills on time, to carry out their personal obligations. When an individual fails to do this, his subordinates and his seniors will find out, and the ability of that individual to command and lead will be impaired.

Drinking is an accepted social custom, but drinking too much is clearly an abuse of an individual's physical well-being. A person who has had too much to drink also often appears very foolish. And while it is a good idea for an officer to come by the division picnic, where the personnel can relax and perhaps can get to know the officer better, sitting down and getting drunk with the troops is never a good idea for an officer. The officer who does this loses the respect of his personnel and may eventually have to be relieved of his command because of it.

The "accountable" officer is aware that he is known to be a member of the military by general knowledge and through ID cards. Others will judge the entire service by the actions of one individual. Thus, the accountable officer acts in a way that can only bring credit to the armed forces as well as to himself. "If you can't discipline yourself, obey regulations, . . . or accept the consequences of your own actions, you not only can't lead, it's immoral for you to try to lead."[63-10]

Because officers are officers 24 hours a day, if the country needs them while they are on leave or vacation, it is their obligation to go immediately to their home station or the nearest military installation for duty. In an emergency, many people may be trying to get to places of safety, and those in charge of directing traffic and individuals will, of necessity, have to give priority to those trying to reach their duty station. The military ID card is the only official means of verification, and therefore all military individuals are required to have it with them at all times.

An officer must remember that if he owes a debt, it is not entirely a private debt. The government has no obligation, but in this country commanding officers are expected to act against officers who fail to meet their obligations. Thus, an officer is expected to live by the highest ideals of John Paul Jones, and not become involved in matters he would not be glad to see reported in the newspapers. While officers are expected to have a social life and a family, they are also expected to be paragons of virtue and to remember at all times that they are models for their subordinates. They are also individuals who give the entire country a feeling of safety because of their dedication and high standards. Admiral Nakamura says that

> it is quite important to the establishment and maintenance of a relationship of confidence for a leader to meet personal commitments strictly. An officer who breaks his commitments not only will lose the confidence of others, he will also render very bad effects on the confidence between the upper and the lower ranks in the system and thereby render leadership difficult.

If, through poor planning or unexpected tragedy, an officer finds himself in difficulty in financial or other personal matters, it is best, if family and friends cannot help, that the officer bring the matter to the attention of the senior so that, first, the senior will be prepared if he is asked by his own senior for an explanation of what is going on, and, second, the senior may through his resources try to secure help for the officer, as well as the understanding of others who are involved with the officer. Just as a banker does not go around in shabby clothes, which would make depositors think that the banker might abscond with some of the money, an officer must avoid doing anything that would give the impression of wrongdoing, not caring, or being insensitive to the thoughts and wishes of others.

An officer is accountable, responsible, and expected to carry out his duties with integrity, dispatch, and competence. It is because of these expectations that officers are held in such high regard. This is a trust that has been earned by those who went before, and that new officers are obligated to uphold in the future. You can do it!

MCPON Sanders: *The leader must be accountable "period"! I think that accountability is something that we have gotten away from in the last few years. We tend not to make decisions on our own, we do it by committee, and when* *you do it by committee, then no one person is accountable. The leader must be accountable for actions and decisions made, regardless of their outcome, and meet personal commitments promptly and fully. I couldn't stress this more.*

13. Completing Assigned Tasks despite Adversity or Personal Distaste

"Discipline is the sacrifice of a man's comforts, inclinations, safety, even life for others, for something greater than himself. It is the refusal to be the weak link in the chain that snaps under strain."[55-66] "Discipline is the proper mental attitude which causes an individual to understand the necessity for obedience and have a firm desire to comply."[71-72]

The acceptance of a commission in the Naval Service simultaneously implies acceptance of all tasks that might be assigned and their timely completion, despite personal distaste or inconvenience. In this regard, the officer must remember that "no man is an island," that the result of his efforts form the basis for action by others; in a very real sense, the team of which we all are a part is no better than each of the individuals who contributes to task accomplishment.

General Barrow, in discussing the importance of officers completing assigned tasks on schedule in spite of obstacles, said that

> completing assigned tasks is a clear measure of an officer's confidence, motivation, or ability to do the job. His seniors, to whom he is expected to render this task completed on time, will inevitably draw conclusions from his performance. If I gave someone a job to do and I figured, well, that isn't beyond his capability, and he has time to do it, and he fools around and doesn't do it, I'd think, well, he's not very good, and I might try to find some way to forgive him the first time, I might even help him conjure up some excuses.

But if it happened more than once, I'd figure, wait a minute here, we have a loser on our hands.

As for distasteful jobs, I've had some of those, but I was not in the business of saying, "I like strawberry and chocolate and don't like vanilla, and somebody else can have that." There are times when you just have to do whatever you are told to do.

A quote from the *Message to Garcia:* "My heart goes out to the man who does his work when the 'boss' is away, as well as when he is at home. And the man who, when given a letter for Garcia, quietly takes the mission without asking any idiotic questions, and with no lurking intention of chucking it into the nearest sewer, or of doing naught else but deliver it."[33-10]

Admiral Itaya suggests that

if a task is beyond an officer's capability, or if there is insufficient time to accomplish it, and this is cause for a lack of enthusiasm, then it is necessary for the officer's senior to correct the situation by assigning him help or allowing him more time.

However, if the task is undesirable simply because the officer will get his hands dirty, or if he finds that he will get no recognition, or if he is depressed because of a long separation from family and friends, and for one of these reasons he refuses to do the job or wants to quit, he should never be permitted to do so.

It is well to consider that all tasks required of an officer are vitally important, or they would not have been assigned in the first place. Certainly a combat assignment is not without its dangers, yet the purpose of the Naval Service is to support our country in both defensive and offensive roles as established by the Commander in Chief, the President of the United States. It is this realization, if taken on board, that will enable an officer to be enthusiastic about each assignment. The attitude of an officer is infec-

tious and will profoundly influence the performance of everyone he comes in contact with.

"An officer can be a power for good or a power for evil. Do not preach to them—that will be worse than useless. Live the kind of life you would have them lead and you will be surprised to see the number that will imitate you."[71-18] More than one hundred years ago, at the First Battle of Bull Run, the following conversation, which illustrates this principle, took place:

> STAFF OFFICER: General, the day is going against us!
> STONEWALL JACKSON: If you think so, Sir, you had better not say anything about it!

This is not to say that operations will always go smoothly, but rather to emphasize that the tide of battle and the will of individuals is a matter of will and psychology, and that when subordinates see confidence in their seniors, they share in that feeling and thus can affect the tide of battle.

GENERATING PERSONAL RESPONSIBILITY THROUGH KNOWLEDGE

When an officer receives an assignment, the first question he should ask concerns the desired completion date and time, and the second concerns the importance and relevance of the task to other projects and actions with which the unit or organization is involved. It is important that officers know as much as possible about a task so that they can feel that it is their own and therefore take full responsibility for it, just as if they had generated the task themselves. Furthermore, they will be in a position both to explain the task and to motivate others in seeing that the assignment is completed expeditiously and efficiently.

Through obtaining an overall understanding of the importance of the project, the officer will obtain a sense of responsibility that will give meaning to his efforts and overcome any feelings of distaste he had for the task. The importance of physical conditioning, for example, is well known to all officers, yet maintaining a sound mind and body requires extensive physical exertion that at times entails some physical pain. In addition, maintaining proper physical condition requires setting aside time for workouts and/or participation in physical sports, and this, too, can be inconvenient. A naval officer knows that the results of these efforts are worth the personal sacrifice, however, and so he applies himself to the task.

Admiral de Cazanove suggests that, simply stated, one should do the task assigned one, without regard to how one feels about it, for all jobs are important to meet our ends. One of the requirements of being a leader is to present tasks to subordinates in a way that they will be persuaded to do their very best and be persuaded that the job assigned to them is really important. In the French Navy we have both nuclear and conventional forces, and it is important that everyone realize that both classes of ships are important—even though one may be in a role of supporting the other. People in the service must realize that they are part of supporting the defense policies chosen by the government, and that, for example, if there were only nuclear forces without other supporting forces, our total defense position could not survive. It's important to realize that without the knowledge by others that we do have a complete complement of supporting forces, our forces would not deter or dissuade anyone, and, thus, all personnel must be helped to realize that everyone is important to the defense of the country. I remember when I was very young and training at the academy in 1940 on board an old battleship, and my only duty was to clean the lavatory. I was with a young friend, and he said he didn't think we should have to clean the lavatory. I pointed out to him that it was as important to do this job as

one that seemed more central to the operation of the ship, for in so doing, we were developing the approach to life of doing every job to the very best of our ability. Whatever you do, you should do it with the same faith and confidence as you would those jobs that require greater professional knowledge.

TURNING "BAD" JOBS INTO "GOOD" JOBS

If officers will remember their obligation to the Naval Service team and the dependence others place on them, they will have no trouble placing the completion of tasks as their first priority and, in doing so with a willing air, they will find that the task is in fact "tasteful," for it provides an opportunity to contribute. The question of personal inconvenience will never arise, for officers will recognize that what is best for the unit also accrues advantages to the individual. Therefore, the timely completion of an assigned task is both rewarding and fulfilling, and the question of personal inconvenience is secondary not only to the organization, but also to the individual. Admiral Taylor remarks:

I have thumb rules that are easy for me to stick to, and one of them is, if you're not having fun, you're not doing it right. Sometimes you're going to get stuck having to do something you don't want to do, and what you have to have is a broader picture and a good, positive attitude about things. Up to that point when a decision is made, what you're being paid to do is ask the boss "Gee, why are we doing this?" You have to size up the boss— some will accept that a little better than others. I've been very fortunate, because nine out of ten people that I worked for wanted to hear other ideas.

So up until the decision is made you give the benefit of your experience and your input, and then when a decision is made, you salute and you execute the decision with absolute loyalty. You participate and you just say "I am having a good time," whether you are or you aren't, and you will absolutely make a heck of a contribution and find you are having a good time.

This discussion can be illustrated with a story by Admiral Burke, who related how, as a young officer, he came to understand that even "bad" jobs can be turned into "good" ones.

After one year of serving in rotating assignments, I was assigned permanent duty as an assistant turret officer. Well, immediately after I got that job—which was a very good job, since I could learn to be a turret officer and there was a lot to do—I was given a lot of special assignments.

In those days the double bottoms of ships had not been initially considered very important, but in time it was realized that they should be inspected and, thus, double bottoms were important. They rusted and they had to be taken care of, and all those new battleships, such as the *Arizona*, built in 1915 and '16, were in terrible shape and were going to fall apart.

So I was given a crew of all the evildoers in the ship. In those days liberty was granted by the executive officer, not port and starboard watches, on the basis of conduct, and the people with good conduct had a free gateway. People with bad conduct had no liberty whatever. I got all the latter people, and this group along with me were to clean the double bottom. It was a dirty job, but we started with the bow and we went back. I got a couple of tough petty officers, too, and it took me about six weeks to do this job, and it was a miserable job, and when I got through I went back down to the gunnery officer, and told him that the job was finished and it was hard. He said, "Is it a good job?" I said, "Yes, Sir, I'd like to have you

inspect some parts of it." He said, "No, if you said it's good, it's all right." He said, "Do you have any recommendations on how to keep them up?" And I said, "Yes, Sir," and I told them to him.

Then he said, "Now, tomorrow morning, I want you to report to the shore patrol officer at six o'clock on the dock in San Pedro." My face fell, and he said, "You don't like that, do you?" and I said, "No, Sir, I don't," and he said, "Perhaps you better have a cup of coffee and we'll talk about it, so sit down." He said, "Why don't you like that?" and I said, "Because there's nothing professional in it at all. Anybody could do the job. If I do it I won't increase my professional ability. It's just one of those things like this double bottom job. Anybody can do that, it's just a question of having to do it." He said, "Well, you recognize, of course, don't you, that there are jobs in the Navy that some don't want to do, but have to be done well just the same?" and I said, "Yes, Sir, but I'm getting a lot of them now," and he said, "Well, you also recognize, don't you, that a man does well if he likes what he is doing?" and I said, "Yes, Sir. Yes, Sir, that's fine." He said, "Well, Mr. Burke, you're going to get these jobs. If you learn to like what you've got to do, you might become a good officer someday. But," he said, "You'll have to learn to do every job well." I tried it out for three or four months, and I found he was right. I *was* going to get those jobs forever and ever, or he was going to break my back. It was the best thing that ever happened, because I never had a bad job thereafter, it was always good, there was always something that you could do about the thing. He told me, "Until you learn what you have to do, and you do it well, you'll not amount to much."

There was a lieutenant at the Naval

Academy in the Seamanship Department right after World War I, an ex-chief boatswain's mate. He was a tremendous chief boatswain's mate, and he used to take us out for sailing instruction. Once we were in a fifty-foot motor launch, under sail. Those things are very cumbersome and wouldn't come about very well, so we were heading for the beach, and this lieutenant called out, "Throw over the anchor. We'll have to anchor," and a man in the bow says, "Sir, there's no line on it and there's no chain on it." The lieutenant said, "Throw it over anyway, maybe we'll lose some of it." Now that sounded silly, but there was never a boat that left the dock thereafter that didn't have a line on it. That was good instruction, but that was for my class. Now they will say, you tell anybody "Throw it over anyway, it may do some good," they'll know exactly what you're talking about.

MCPON Sanders: *The leader should properly complete assigned tasks on schedule in spite of possible personal distaste for the task or personal inconvenience. If we face tasks that are before us and act on them as they come up, then we will not make a hasty judgment later on. It's very important for us to do that, because if we don't, we will have a bigger challenge every day, and it will include yesterday's unfinished work.*

14. Evaluating Leadership

General Order 21 defines leadership as the art of accomplishing the Navy's mission through people. It is the sum of those qualities of intellect, human understanding, and moral character that enable a man to inspire and to manage a group of people successfully. Effective leadership, therefore, is based upon personal example, good management practices, and moral responsibility.[47-4] This is a good definition of leadership. But what measurement, if any, can be made of leadership effectiveness? Admiral Zumwalt described how he rated officers:

In judging subordinates, I've always tried to keep in mind as I viewed each individual how I felt he fitted in, in comparison to all of the others I had known at his age and rank and level of experience, and to avoid diligently trying to compare him to those who were more senior and more experienced. Further, I tried to view him in the backdrop of what was going on around him, whether he was able to withstand the trauma of leaving behind loved ones and the worries that go with that and, notwithstanding the sorrow that he felt, to persevere and to be a good leader and to make it clear to subordinates that he was getting some fun out of his job. I always put a great deal of emphasis on the ability of the individual to deal with an emergency, the common sense with which he addressed new problems that were beyond his experience, and particularly to observe whether he was willing to disclose fully the problems that were confronting him to the extent that they represented potential problems to his senior.

If he honestly analyzes himself, an officer will know better than his rating senior how well he has done a job. At the end of a particular exercise, the officer who was in charge of a team, for example, can ask himself how well he did as a team leader. He can also go over the exercise verbally with the team, discussing how it performed as a group. Often an officer can judge his performance as a leader from the suggestions and comments that are made by his subordinates. As he goes through the critiques of the team, the officer should pay attention to, first, how well the overall effort went, and, second, how that reflects on him.

101

At the end of each completed exercise or evolution an officer should sit down and record the lessons learned, the pluses and minuses of how well he prepared for that exercise, so that the next time around, he can do better. The officer should ask himself, where could I, by greater diligence, greater prescience, greater planning, have done this overall operation better?

Not all judgments concerning the leadership of a command, a department, or a division are empirical. Experience—both good and bad—is an imprecise yet generally valid criterion for forming opinions on subjects that are vague and ill defined. A bad experience can cause an individual to discard a particular course of action, when in fact the problem may not have been in the course of action, but in the method or techniques used in implementing it. An individual who wishes to improve his leadership ability must continually review his leadership qualities and make self-appraisals. A midshipman or young officer has had very little experience, so how can he measure his effectiveness as a leader?

MISSION ACCOMPLISHMENT AS A MEASURE OF LEADERSHIP

The overriding consideration in assessing the effectiveness of a particular military unit or its subdivisions is not leadership per se. It is mission or task accomplishment. Mission is the uppermost criterion in any organization. How well or how professionally the job is done is the bottom line in any leadership evaluation, whether it is a soul-searching self-appraisal or an opinion formed by juniors, peers, or seniors. It follows that leadership is an integral yet distinct part of mission performance. The best leadership in the world fails if the unit does not succeed in its mission; the military is still suffering pangs from the Vietnam War. On the other hand, success in the mission does not guarantee that leadership was effective and proper. History is full of

examples of authoritarian leaders whose style would not fit into the present-day military.

Morale is a vital but quantifiably elusive factor in determining unit readiness to accomplish its mission. The cliché "A happy ship is a fighting ship" is not necessarily true; happiness can also be a self-satisfying and dangerous state of mind. Rear Admiral H. E. Eccles, USN (Ret.), a distinguished military scholar, has conceptualized two types of morale in today's Navy; one is called weapon morale, the other, soda fountain morale. "The concept of *weapon morale* is that high military morale is developed primarily by rigorous discipline, hard training, confidence in one's leaders, one's weapons, one's ability to use them, and above all by pride in one's ability to accept great risk and hardship. . . . The concept of *soda fountain morale* is that high military morale is created or at least greatly stimulated by luxuries, privileges, and fringe benefits."[26-247] It should be obvious which is more effective, both in war and in peacetime readiness to deter war.

OTHER INDICATORS OF SUCCESS

Admiral Clausen suggests that

to determine whether he has been successful, an officer can consider, above all, the following aspects:

1. Whether and how the commanding officer, during the entire time of his command that his officers and enlisted personnel followed him, measured up to given orders and instructions. Whether and how he succeeded in carrying out his mission in general and how his officers and enlisted personnel showed obedience and conviction.

2. Whether and how ship and crew reached the preparedness and readiness for action. How they reacted in different places and during different situations when they were presented with different scenes of action [in German: "Gefechtsbilder"] and combat practices.

3. How they managed the conse-

quences of an arising situation, especially in case of an emergency.

4. Whether the atmosphere on board ship showed a good mood, perhaps even cheerfulness, and whether the subordinates were of a mind to carry out their duties.

This, combined with personal contacts on different occasions and open-forum talks and an honest and detailed summary written in the final report, gives to the officer a distinct and clear knowledge of how successfully he has done his work.

While I respect the value of statistics, I think it is dangerous to rely solely on statistics in evaluating qualifications. I think it is important for an officer to know that he is living together with people and that his task is to be a leader of them. That is to say, on the one side, he must live at a certain distance from the people, but, on the other side, he must have a rather narrow relationship with them. The outcome of these relations is that people must know the officer is senior to them, must know that he does his job with fairness, and I think the outcome is confidence between the senior and the subordinate.

A midshipman or junior officer can use several indicators to make the self-appraisal that is important to his or her professional development. Some of them are:

Unauthorized absence. In a unit with good morale and positive leadership, the UA rate is lower than it is in a unit that lacks these qualities.

Special requests. With good two-way communications, the need for special consideration disappears. High morale, firm and fair leadership, and mission accomplishment equal job satisfaction.

Captain's Mast (Art. 15 UCMJ) or office hours. There is such a thing as report chit leadership, and it is the antithesis of the type of leadership naval officers should be striving for. In a properly led unit, the use of mast for punishment should be limited. Court martials are by definition a punishment, and punishments are the "results of a failure of discipline."[23-122]

Safety. Occurrences of serious and minor personnel injuries should be few. Pride and professionalism go hand in hand with safety on the job.

Awards. Recognition within the Naval Service is the area most neglected by junior officers. Awards should range from the simple verbal "Well done" for task accomplishment to letters of commendation and formal medal awards for exceptional performance of duty. If the officer is doing his job, the trend for awards in his unit should always be upward.

Inspections. The results of each of the many and varied inspections conducted internally and by outside agencies should be better than the results of the preceding inspection. The list of inspections may seem endless. Here are but a few: personnel, preventive maintenance, space cleanliness and preservation, operational readiness evaluation, nuclear weapons, operational propulsion plant, and underway material. Inspection results are key indicators, since they closely relate to unit readiness and ability to accomplish the mission.

Training is defined in the *Naval Division Officer's Guide* as "a primary naval objective surpassed in wartime only by the necessity for victory, for which it is the essential preparation."[47-90]

A word of caution: The young officer can easily succeed by relinquishing leadership to higher authority through report chits, which "pass the buck" up the chain of command, by ignoring the true nature and needs of his people, or by letting the massive assistance and inspection schedule control his people's time to the detriment of both mission and personnel. There is sufficient time in a day for sailors and Marines to accomplish all they are *required* to do.

Here are some of the questions that distinguish good leaders from ineffective leaders: If we were tested in war tomorrow, would my unit and personnel be ready? What can I do to improve that readiness? How can I balance my efforts between personnel and mission so that I will not drive out of the service those people we will need to fight if war does not come for several years? And, most important, am I the sort of leader I would follow into battle? These questions cannot be asked only at the end of the tour; they must be asked continually.

Admiral Hayward believes that

a positive attitude is crucial in achieving success. If I had to pick out one characteristic that I would want to have myself or hope that I was able to produce in the people I work with, it would be the concept of having a positive attitude about their work, about what they're trying to accomplish and what they are accomplishing. I'd like to deal with the negatives as tasks to take on that will lead to further success. I think it's absolutely critical that one be able to develop within one's peer groups, and certainly one's subordinates, a positive attitude, and that goes to whether you're working with just two people or four or ten or hundreds of thousands. It is critical that you have a positive attitude about what you're doing and what you're trying to accomplish and what the groups are trying to accomplish.

Hopefully you're able to lead people in a positive fashion that will build into a

success-oriented organization, and they do go together, there isn't any question about it. If you have a negative attitude in a unit, you will not have success, and the leader has to turn that situation around. The leader has a very difficult challenge if he has a lot of people coming in and asking for transfers. He better understand why and be able to deal with that, and I guess one might say there's another element there. If you're the next senior up, you had better be wise enough to know what the cause of that negativism is and remove it, even if it's the division officer or the division chief who is the problem.

MCPON Sanders: *If the officer, upon reassignment, can honestly and positively answer the question, "Are the people I have just left better for my having served with them?" then the leader has done the things that should have been done and not only held himself responsible and accountable but also taught the people who worked for him to be accountable and responsible for certain segments of the work. If you can answer the question in the affirmative, then not only have you made sure that they did the job at hand, but you also prepared them to take on bigger challenges.*

The correct number of *F*s in the *F* Incident is seven; the correct number of *O*s is five.

Chapter 1 Bibliography

1. Andrews, Lincoln C. *Military Manpower*. New York: E. P. Dutton, 1920.
2. Appleton, Daniel S. "Shipboard Training: The Team's the Thing." *Proceedings*, Oct. 1983, p. 107.
3. Assagioli, Robert. *The Act of Will*. New York: Viking Press, 1973.
4. Ayling, Keith. *Old Leather Face*. New York: Bobbs-Merrill, 1945.
5. Basilisk, John. *Talks on Leadership*. London: Hugh Rees, 1941.
6. Beardon, William, and Wedertz, Bill. *The Bluejacket's Manual*. 20th ed. Annapolis: Naval Institute Press, 1978.
7. Belknap, R. R. "Military Character." *Proceedings*, Jan. 1918, pp. 1–14.
8. Bellows, Roger. *Creative Leadership*. Ed. Dale Yoder. Englewood Cliffs, N.J.: Prentice-Hall, 1959.
9. Best, Hugh, *Red Hot and Blue: An X-Rated History of the American Revolution*. Lahaska, Pa.: New Hope, 1976.

10. Blegan, Carl W. *Troy and the Trojans*. New York: Praeger, 1963.

11. Bliss, Edwin C. *Doing It Now*. New York: Scribner's Sons, 1983.

12. Brett-James, Antony. *The Hundred Days*. New York: Macmillan, 1964.

13. Brininstool, E. A. *Troopers with Custer*. Harrisburg, Pa.: Stackpole, 1952.

14. Brooks, Leon. "Surface Ship Command Qualification: Who Needs." *Proceedings*, Sept. 1981, pp. 60–61.

15. Buell, Thomas. "The Education of a Warrior." *Proceedings*, Jan. 1981, pp. 40–45.

16. Burke, Arleigh A. "Young Officers and Leadership." *Proceedings*, Jan. 1975, p. 4.

17. Byron, John L. "The Captain." *Proceedings*, Sept. 1982, p. 39.

18. Campbell, Dennis C. "Techniques for Effective Leadership." *Army Logistician*, Nov.–Dec. 1983, p. 49.

19. Carmun, C. C. "Qualifications for Leadership." *Proceedings*, June 1921, pp. 857–75.

20. Chenard, John H. "Needed: A Better Yardstick for Battle Readiness." *Proceedings*, Mar. 1973, p. 118.

21. Davis, Burke. *Marine! The Life of Lieutenant General Lewis B. (Chesty) Puller*. Boston: Little, Brown, 1962.

22. Decker, Malcolm. *Benedict Arnold: Son of the Havens*. New York: Antiquarian Press, 1961.

23. Department of Defense, Armed Forces Information Service. *The Armed Forces Officer*. Washington, D.C.: U.S. Government Printing Office, 1975, p. 122.

24. Dunn, R. Letter to the Editor. *Proceedings*, Feb. 1981, p. 21.

25. Dyer, Travis N. "Why Physical Fitness?" *Air Defense/Artillery*, Spring 1983, pp. 10–12.

26. Eccles, Henry E. *Military Concepts and Philosophy*. New Brunswick, N.J.: Rutgers University Press, 1965, p. 24.

27. Elliot, Gary E. "Let's Emphasize High Physical Standards." *Marine Corps Gazette*, Jan. 1983, pp. 26–27.

28. Garland, Albert. "The Case for Professional Reading." *Armor*, July–Aug. 1983, p. 49.

29. Goode, William J. *The Celebration of Heroes*. Berkeley and Los Angeles: University of California Press, 1975.

30. Gouldner, Alvin W., ed. *Studies in Leadership*. New York: Russell and Russell, 1965.

31. Greenbacker, John E. "The Cruel Business of Accountability." *Proceedings*, Aug. 1977, pp. 24–30.

32. Horsfield, John. *The Art of Leadership in War: The Royal Navy from the Age of Nelson through World War II as a Case History*. Westport, Conn.: Greenwood Press, 1980.

33. Hubbard, Elbert. *Message to Garcia: Being a Preachment*. East Aurora, N.Y.: Roycroft Shop, 1899.

34. Hwang, John, ed. *Selected Analytical Concepts in Command and Control*. New York: Gordon and Breach Science Publishers, 1982.

35. Kagen, Donald; Ozment, Steven; and Turner, Frank M. *The Western Heritage*. Vol. 2. New York: Macmillan, 1983.

36. Kelly, J. M.; Patton, G. D.; Downs, J. F.; and Corini, G. J., eds. *Leadership and Law Department NL 303 Book of Readings*. Annapolis: U.S. Naval Academy, academic year 1983–84.

37. Kostev, G. "Ship's Combat Systems." *Soviet Military Review*, Feb. 1981, p. 377.

38. Law, Bernard. *Viscount Montgomery of Alamein: The Path to Leadership*. New York: G. P. Putnam's Sons, 1961.

39. Leaf, Walter. *Troy: A Study in Homeric Geography*. London: Macmillan, 1912.

40. Mack, William P. "Education and Professionalism." *Proceedings*, Oct. 1983, pp. 40–47.

41. Mack, William P., and Konetzni, Albert H., Jr. *Command at Sea*. 4th ed. Annapolis: Naval Institute Press, 1982.

42. Malone, Dandridge M. "Able and Willing." *Infantry*, Mar.–Apr. 1983, pp. 9–11.

43. Mason, John T. Interview with Commander Richard A. Stratton. Annapolis: Naval Institute Press, Dec. 1976.

44. Montgomery, Bernard. *The Path to Leadership*. New York: G. P. Putnam's Sons, 1961.

45. Montor, Karel, and Ciotti, Anthony J., eds. *Fundamentals of Naval Leadership*. 3d ed. Annapolis: Naval Institute Press, 1984.

46. Mosley, Leonard. *Marshall: Hero for Our Times*. New York: Hearst, 1982.

47. Noel, John V., Jr., and Bassett, Frank E. *Division Officer's Guide*. 7th ed. Annapolis: Naval Institute Press, 1977.

48. Novotney, John. "When Leadership Counts." *Naval Aviation News*, Dec. 1981, pp. 33–35.

49. O'Brien, William V. *The Conduct of Just and Limited War*. New York: Lippincott, 1982.

50. Patton, George S., Jr. *War as I Knew It*. New York: Bantam Books, 1980.

51. Petraeus, David H. "Building Morale through PT." *Infantry*, Mar.–Apr. 1983, pp. 11–12.

52. Pocalyko, Michael N. "The Fleet Nugget." *Proceedings*, July 1983, pp. 70–74.

53. *Principles and Problems of Naval Leadership*. 2d ed. Navpers 15924A. Washington, D.C.: Bureau of Naval Personnel, 1964.

54. *Reefpoints*. Annapolis: U.S. Naval Academy, 1983.

55. Roskill, S. W. *The Art of Leadership*. London: Collins Clear-Type Press, 1964.

56. Sandoz, Mari. *The Battle of Little Big Horn*. New York: Lippincott, 1966.

57. Schrantz, Paul R. "War, Morality, and the Military Professional." *Proceedings*, Sept. 1983, pp. 46–51.

58. Schultz, Duane. *Hero of Bataan*. New York: St. Martin's Press, 1981.

59. Stavridis, James. "War, Peace, and Leadership." *Proceedings*, Aug. 1983, pp. 78–80.

60. Stewart, G. V. "Followship." *Proceedings*, May 1943, pp. 631–35.

61. Stockdale, James B. *A Vietnam Experience: Ten Years of Reflection*. Stanford, Calif.: Hoover Press, 1984.

62. Stokesbury, James, and Blumenburg, Martin. *Masters of the Art of Command*. Boston: Houghton Mifflin, 1975.

63. Stratton, Richard. "Leadership: Getting Things Done—Through People." Interview. *All Hands*, Sept. 1982, pp. 10–11.

64. Thompson, Henry L. "Sleep Loss and Its Effect in Combat." *Military Review*, Sept. 1983, pp. 14–23.

65. Thompson, Sir Robert. *War in Peace*. London: Orbis, 1981.

66. Torrisi, Giovanni. "The Spirit and Continuity of the Navy." *Proceedings*, Apr. 1980, pp. 34–39.

67. United States Congressional Committee on Labor and Public Welfare. *Medal of Honor, 1863–1968*. Washington, D.C.: U.S. Government Printing Office, 1968.

68. Uris, Auren. *Executive Dissent*. New York: AMACOM, Division of the American Management Association, 1978.

69. Williamson, Porter B. *Patton's Principles*. Tucson: Management and Systems Consultants, 1979.

70. Winnefeld, James. "Quality of the Officer Corps." *Proceedings*, Sept. 1981, pp. 33–38.

71. Wolfe, Malcom E., and Mulholland, F. J., eds. *Selected Readings in Leadership*. 2d ed. Annapolis: Naval Institute Press, 1960.

72. "World War II." In *World Book Encyclopedia*. Vol. 21. Chicago: Field Enterprises, 1976, p. 396.

2

The Responsibilities and Qualities of Leadership

Introduction

What Is a Leader ?

A leader . . .

. . . knows where he (and his group) is going and how to get there, or, if he doesn't know how, he is willing to let his subordinates in on (1) the ultimate goal, (2) proximate goals, and (3) the path(s) thereto, and to enlist their support.

. . . trusts his followers to be loyal, to have intelligence, to know their jobs and be able to carry them out without nitpicking supervision. Even if they do not possess all these characteristics, he treats them as if they do—and, surprisingly enough, they either will have them or will acquire them.

. . . treats his followers like human beings, respecting their feelings and abilities as well as their limitations, treating them not as objects but as cooperative persons who are able to make useful contributions to the task(s) at hand.

. . . is truthful with his followers. If he cannot explain all the reasons for commands he must order them to follow, he lets them in on as much as he can and is not too proud to let them know that there are factors beyond his control.

. . . is in control of himself and his actions, feelings, and emotions, which he does not regard as excuses for venting frustration on others.

. . . is not one who expects that he has, or will have, all these qualities—but he's in there trying, even if this means letting his subordinates in on the effort, letting them know their help is wanted and appreciated and will be accepted.

. . . practices—and sees that his entourage does likewise—the elementary aspects of courtesy, such as saying "Thank you" and giving praise for jobs well done and for an individual's best efforts.

That is what a leader is. All others are managers. No one has ever followed a manager to the absolute limits, to the loss of his own life.

And a leader, especially a military leader, must be able to ask this of his followers. If he is what he is supposed to be, this will not be a problem. If he is not, no rules, regulations, structures, or coercive practices can force his subordinates to pass this ultimate test of loyalty.

15. Leading by Example

There is a phrase describing the essence of a naval officer which has fallen into disuse. That phrase is "service reputation," the unwritten, unspoken, unlisted net assessment of an officer's pluses and minuses. When naval officers were less numerous than they are today, an officer knew most of the other officers and privately ranked them according to their service reputation. Perhaps the size and complexity of today's Navy and Marine Corps prevents a "familiar" appraisal of and by each member of the officer corps. Perhaps modern management information systems distract officers from what truly matters to them about other officers, whether they be junior, senior, or peer. But, in their hearts, all officers know that their behavior and attitude have a profound effect on everyone they work with. Admiral Uchida agrees that

> an officer's behavior considerably influences other individuals, particularly his subordinates. Regardless of an officer's personality or style, he must be always unselfish and fair to subordinates so that they never lose their reliance on him. An officer's humanity is perceived through his behavior, and it is this which moves others.

THE POWER OF POSITIVE RELATIONSHIPS

The relationship between an officer and his people has an effect on his and their performance. When crew members of a ship that has been deployed too long complain proudly about the hardships they are undergoing and develop a kind of a spartan pride, they probably have a good relationship with their commander. The morale of a less well led crew can be expected to deteriorate progressively under exactly the same circumstances.

An officer can develop a great deal of camaraderie with his people without destroying the discipline that is so essential in any kind of an evolution, particularly in wartime. Admiral Zumwalt recounted this episode of his career:

> I had the honor of commanding the world's first guided missile frigate, the USS *Dewey*, and because it was the first of the class, I was given the cream of the crop from the Bureau of Naval personnel. The heads of departments were superb, and because they were superb and very sure of themselves, they were not the least bit hesitant to come up and discuss with me in very vigorous terms things that they thought could be done differently. But when the chips were down in any evolution and I gave the directive, there was instant and total obedience. The fun was always recognized as just part of the business of having a good team spirit.
>
> In order to do an optimal job, an officer needs to believe that the Navy is worthwhile, that the service is something of which he is proud. He need not view the institution as something sacred and unchangeable, nor should he assume that every cog in that vast institution works with anything like perfection. He can be positively critical of those areas that need fixing, but he must have a dedication to the overall mission of the Navy and to the concept of the life of service in readiness to defend his country and be a good officer.
>
> In the wardroom or in the staff, an officer should do his best to be a good corporate citizen of that unit. Where there are personality clashes, he should do his best to understand what makes the other fellow tick. There are compromises that need to be made in order for an officer to

be a good overall team member, but there is also a very clear line beyond which he should retire when he runs into the occasional "bad apple." There may be someone on the ship or in a unit who has a very negative attitude and who can be extremely disruptive, and counseling and corrective action regarding this individual is the responsibility of the officer next higher in that individual's chain of command.

THE POWER OF A POSITIVE ATTITUDE

In discussing the importance of a positive attitude, Admiral Hayward related this story.

There's a great story about Admiral Red Ramage and how he won his Medal of Honor with the *Parche*. He wouldn't stop and think about, "Gee, what will happen if we get hit or get sunk?" He kept in mind what he had to do, and that was to sink the enemy. It may have been in his mind sometimes in his tactical decisions about what is the risk he's taking, but if caution is the character of a person, that person's probably going to be too cautious for a fast-moving Navy tactical engagement. The way you overcome that, if you are an individual with a cautious nature (because you can be born that way), is to force yourself into training situations, and the Navy tries to do that, tries to expose you to enough training encounters that you develop self-confidence. Through meeting somebody, you want to help them arrive at that point, so in the debriefings you don't dwell on the person's negatives, except in the constructive way, and you help them accentuate what they did right, so they will get back out and do it again and keep working on it.

Now a few people wash out of flight training, you know, it's just going to happen. Some of them wash out because there's a physical inability to perform that particular kind of a mission, others wash out because they don't have the motivation; there's a lot of difference between whether you succeeded or didn't succeed in that sense. So it seems to me as though a TACCO (Tactical Coordinator in a P-3) has one and only one responsibility, and that's to learn his job so well he's got the confidence that he's going to hang in there, and if he loses a few, okay, but he makes the most of them and keeps a good reputation for pressing on.

An individual cannot be effective in any way or successful in any way at any level in the Navy if he does not have the capacity to take on the task of setting the example, and behavior is a basic element of setting the example. The crew has a right to look upon their leader with respect, but the leader has to earn their respect and work to keep it. The quickest way to lose respect is to set a bad example through gross behavior. This includes doing the kinds of things that some may think are macho or funny, but that in the long run are going to undermine the morale of the command and the leader's pride.

SETTING THE EXAMPLE

An officer's behavior, both on and off duty, is noticed by shipmates and helps define their perception of him as an officer and a leader. The famous naval officer Admiral Marc Mitscher is a prime example of a man who led by example. So great was Mitscher's concern for the training and welfare of his men that he was able to retain their final ounce of effort and loyalty. He was "a bulldog of a fighter, a strategist, and a seeker of truth."[7-53] Similarly, officers cannot help but note the behavior of their people on and off the job, whether they are full-time personnel or drilling reservists. The old adage "an officer is on duty 24 hours a day" has even more significance in the era of the total force.

Working with and through others to further the mission of the command and, consequently, the mission of the Navy and Marine Corps, is a vital aspect of an officer's job. Self-serving actions must be secondary. For example, although cooperating with other individuals and other organizations may be desirable to accomplish specific tasks, cooperation should not be an end in itself. That is, peer pressure to "go along" or "get along" with a situation that is ethically or morally wrong must be resisted. To yield to such pressure is to do a disservice to the Naval Service and to the service reputation of the officers involved. Admiral Hayward cautions that,

> whatever his position of leadership, an individual who believes that he can conduct himself in a way that is not gentlemanly is making a significant error of judgment. Senior officers whose personal behavior was not "up to snuff" have never progressed very far in the Naval Service.

A leader needs to work at getting along with people without compromising his beliefs. He can stand firm on an issue he feels strongly about without creating a problem, however. The boisterous, loud, tough actor is not the "right kind of guy" to follow. Generally speaking, while there are some who become very good officers who chew people up and spit them out with ease, the finest officers learn how to deal with every human being as a human being and can dress a person down properly, up in the right circumstances, and congratulate a person correctly under other circumstances. In short, the successful officer learns how to deal with difficult situations without ever compromising his principles in the process.

Recognizing the difficulty of reconciling the principles and ideals of the Naval Service with the reality of car payments and sick children is part of being a leader. A successful leader understands the personal history of each of his people, knows from what segment of society each person is drawn, and understands the job of each person. A naval officer cannot begin to earn respect unless he possesses that kind of knowledge, and he cannot expect to keep it unless his behavior is impeccable.

To Admiral Zumwalt, the episode that might be most useful in demonstrating the painful choices that an individual has to make in complex situations where duty is not necessarily clear transpired during the 1973 war, when

> it became clear very early on that the Israelis were likely to be overrun because they were not able to count on the replacement of their equipment by us— we weren't moving the equipment forward fast enough. I went to see the Secretary of Defense, and told him that my judgment was that this was likely to happen. He said, "I agree, but my hands are tied." This seemed to me to be playing at war without being aware of how difficult it is to change the momentum of a battle. The President had become quite unavailable to the chiefs by that time, and I therefore concluded that something had to be done and that I'd better do it.
>
> I went to see Senator Jackson and gave him this information and urged him to call the President, which he did. The President directed that the equipment be immediately sent forward, which in my judgment made it possible to turn that war around. In what I did, I took action that the Secretary of Defense had not taken, and yet my conscience at the time led me to believe that it was the necessary action, and even in retrospect I believe that it was an appropriate thing to do, even though in so doing I certainly ran the risk that the judgment would be made that I would be dismissed from office. [Editor's note: It should be understood by the reader that this represents a decision made by an officer with decades of experience.]

Admiral Zumwalt tells of his experience as commander of our naval forces in Vietnam, when he presided over the command of the brown-water navy, coastal surveillance forces and the craft that were involved, and the rivers and canals and the aircraft assigned thereto.

As one would expect on board ship, I found that in order really to be able to understand the situations that my very young brand-new naval officers, commanding officers, were experiencing in their small craft, and to be able to understand how effectively to use them, I had to get out and be with them. So I spent a number of evenings in ambushes with them patrolling the rivers and canals. In discussions with them when we were out in ambush, I came to understand the limitations both of the equipment and of the people, and the very great capabilities of both, and I was able to visualize a lot more of the possibly otherwise unforseeable contingencies with which we might have to deal in major campaigns operating out of Saigon.

Based on the knowledge that one gains from those operational inputs, it was possible to have detailed discussions with the personnel on my staff in Saigon and to prepare ourselves mentally for the fast decisions that we would have to make. Fast-breaking events took place when we took a new blockade along the Cambodian border and other places. I think that it's fair to say that we were able to foresee the general nature of almost every action or counteraction that the enemy might take. Incidentally, one of the things that we proved to ourselves was the age-old principle that you can get away with almost anything by surprise, and you can probably do the same thing a second time, but you better not try it the third, because by that time a wise enemy has pretty well learned to adapt to it.

The key to being a good staff officer is to have had the operational experience that makes it possible to understand the problems of the commander's subordinate operating units. The officer who goes to the staff of the admiral of a cruiser-destroyer flotilla is far more competent to help that admiral carry out his responsibilities if he has served on one of those cruisers or destroyers or a similar type. This is also true for those who are more logistics oriented, such as supply officers. A staff officer must also make frequent visits to the operating units and have a meticulous sense for those details that are essential to operational efficiency. He must be able to distinguish them from those details that could be categorized as simply minuscule.

A requirement for anyone who aspires to high rank is to read beyond the literature required for him to do well in his own particular job.

INSTILLING A POSITIVE ATTITUDE IN SUBORDINATES

After the Vietnam War, enlistment and reenlistment rates were way down. Admiral Zumwalt, who had been asked to address the problem, decided to approach it from the standpoint of morale.

I concluded that things were so bad, and the social fabric of the country that was supporting our armed services was so bad, that one had to take a revolutionary approach. I had for many years been waiting for my opportunity to strike a major blow in behalf of equal opportunity, and I was also a firm believer in the fact that women have as much capability as their male counterparts. I had just come from 20 months in command of our forces in Vietnam, where I had found that the most ruthless and cunning enemy I had ever had to face were the Vietcong women, and I concluded that dealing with the sexual differences in the Navy was timely.

It was also clear that to me, again as a result of my wartime exposure to the wonderful young men who were fighting in Vietnam, that there were some other very serious problems in the Navy. We were in the brown-water Navy when I was in command, at one time taking casualties at the rate of 6 percent a month, which meant that in any given year's tour your typical officer or sailor had nearly a three-quarters chance of being killed or wounded. I visited with 10 to 15 thousand of them in the Delta, and I visited with hundreds of the wounded in the hospitals, and I don't ever recall being taken to task about the war, but I recall many times being asked, "Why is it that I, who volunteered to join the Navy and volunteered to fight in Vietnam, am not permitted to look like my peers with a beard or a mustache or with sideburns?" It seemed to me, in looking into this needed revolution, that it was a small thing to give those patriotic individuals that privilege. Indeed, upon being reminded that Navy regulations had always authorized neatly trimmed beards and mustaches, it suddenly dawned on me that senior commanders were violating Navy regulations, and the Z-Gram in that regard merely said "Obey Navy Regulations."

Such things as beer in the barracks, black beauty aids in the Navy Exchange, the requirement that nobody be kept in line for longer than 15 minutes (instead of those very long lines that we used to have to wait through), were all designed to give our men and women, in the midst of a very unpopular war and surrounded by a hostile society, the feeling that they were needed and wanted and were the kind of individuals who deserved to be treated that way. And the bottom line, I think, is

quite clear. By the end of four years our reenlistment rates were above 30 percent, nearly quadrupled.

MCPON Sanders: *A positive attitude toward the Naval Service is so important. I don't believe that I have ever served with an officer who bad-mouthed the Naval Service and also was a success. Ninety-nine percent of them were poor performers, and they had serious flaws. The good officers take responsibility for the things they have to maintain and the orders they follow. I've heard junior officers say, "Well, the reason we've got to do it is because the captain says so, or the skipper wants us to stay late," and they are not taking the attitude that the reason they are doing this is because the job needs to be done and they are making a decision to get it done. A few junior officers are poor leaders because they act embarrassed, as if the Naval Service is making them do something that they would not normally do. When an officer does that, he's lost the respect of the troops.*

16. The Chain of Command

One of the most important elements of military organization is the chain of command. Admiral Nakamura sees the chain of command as

the fruit of the wisdom and experience of mankind which has been devised over a long period of time to help the services conduct complicated and extensive operations and/or administration effectively and systematically under a unified command. Today operations and management cannot be executed appropriately without this basic system.

In simple terms, the chain is the pyramid structure of communications, authority, and responsibilities which allows every individual in an organization to know what is going on with those below and what is expected by those above. It is the conduit for the orderly direction of command activities and provides a two-way communication flow. It is only as good as the people in it, all of whom are key links. Admiral Holloway points out that

> everyone involved in an operation must know what the senior is thinking and what his plans are. By sending orders down the chain of command, those involved make sure that the word is spread. By reporting up the chain of command, everyone between the person who is doing the job and the person who ordered it done knows what is being accomplished so they can adjust their actions accordingly. Uninformed individuals can take actions that are unsupportive and may even be in conflict with the operation. For this reason, the chain of command must be followed, and the chain itself must be well established; a tortuous chain of command that includes elements that do not need to know the information that is being passed indicates a deficiency on the part of the commander.

BYPASSING THE CHAIN OF COMMAND

The chain of command can be bypassed only when it is absolutely essential in the judgment of the individual who is going to bypass the chain that doing so is necessary for the national good. The apparent simplicity of this description does not do justice to the concept's crucial role in shipboard life. In addition to being a mechanism for promulgating orders and for "getting the word out," the chain of command is essential for maintaining good order and discipline, assessing combat readiness at each echelon of command, and delegating authority for action. Every officer in the Naval Service is an active participant in the chain from two aspects: from his seniors downward and from his subordinates upward. Each of these aspects encompasses different responsibilities.

General P. X. Kelley observed that, during his first year as Commandant of the Marine Corps,

he was struck by the number of Marines who felt that they needed to go outside the chain of command to resolve a personal problem. In far too many cases, research had indicated that the problem could have been solved within the chain of command by Marines in positions of leadership and responsibility.

While General Kelley was addressing his deep concern over this subject at Headquarters, Marine Corps, the words of his distinguished predecessor, General Wallace M. Greene, Jr., 23rd Commandant, were brought to his attention and were found to be as applicable today as they were in 1967.

General Kelley enjoined all commanders to give this White Letter the widest dissemination possible, and observed that, when individual Marines felt compelled to go outside the chain of command in the future, he would from time to time ask the question: "What actions were taken by the chain of command to solve the problem?"

A03C-jpp
3 Nov 1967

From: Commandant of the Marine Corps
To: Commanding Generals and Commanding Officers

Subj: Leadership and the Chain of Command

1. Since the founding of our Corps, continued success in war and peace has made the name Marine synonymous with soldierly virtue, military proficiency and professional pride. This legacy, passed on through generations of Marines, has been built on the cornerstones of camaraderie, discipline and esprit de corps.

2. Every Marine, from his first days in the Corps, is thoroughly indoctrinated in a way of life in which Marines take care of their own; one where each Marine may have complete reliance on his fellow Marine no matter the

circumstance. One of the means of instilling this camaraderie and trust is to insure the opportunity to all Marines to express constructive criticism, grievances, and recommendations via the existing military chain of command, further to see that its availability is understood and exploited.

3. Discipline is not simply unhesitating obedience to orders. Certainly in the combat environment, response must be swift, sure and predictable. However, this requirement is not in conflict with suitable consideration of innovational recommendations prior to action, nor of professional criticism and review after. All Marines have both opportunity and responsibility to contribute to our administration, techniques and procedures. This is especially true with respect to matters which bear on the daily life, safety, and effectiveness of Marines. In part, it is through this process that we progressively improve. This rational dialogue is most useful and effective when it is conducted within the organizational structure.

4. Recently, there appears to be a growing tendency for some Marines to project problems, which could be resolved by internal Marine Corps measures, into avenues or to authorities outside of the Marine Corps chain of command. I do not mean to imply that any Marine is prohibited from communicating with anyone with whom he may desire. However, in almost all such cases, the query is eventually forwarded to the Commandant for response and action, whereas in reality most of these problems could be, and properly should be, resolved by a command level much closer to the situation than we are in Washington.

5. Paramount in the exercise of their duties, all commanders must continue to create, through traditional Marine Corps leadership, an atmosphere of faith, trust and reliance on one Marine for another; a feeling of esprit, protectiveness and interest which causes the junior, by choice and with confidence, to turn to his immediate senior for advice and assistance, assured that he may expect every reasonable effort to provide the appropriate information, counsel, action or remedy.

6. As I see it, we must positively impress upon all Marines that every commander in our Corps, from the Commandant to fire team leader, is vitally and genuinely interested in the health, welfare and professional ability of his Marines and that Marines of all ranks who have either a problem or constructive criticism to offer may best obtain action by utilizing the existing chain of command to express their thoughts. Utilization of the chain of command, in most instances, presents the most efficient and expeditious means for each Marine's suggestions and concepts to receive the attention and consideration which they merit, toward the end that those concepts and suggestions which so merit are translated into action. We must insure a broader understanding that this is so.

WALLACE M.GREENE, JR.

The chain should never be so rigid that it inhibits imagination, innovation, flexibility, or good judgment. Situations will occur—and not necessarily only during combat—in which it is appropriate to bypass the normal chain of command and report an emergent situation directly to the executive officer or the commanding officer. Under such circumstances, an officer should inform his immediate seniors at the earliest opportunity of the situation that has arisen as well as why he reported it directly and what steps he has taken to reconcile it. This is not done just out of respect for seniors; it also keeps key leaders of the command fully informed. Admiral Fran McKee concurs that

probably one of the better-established tenets of naval leadership is following the chain of command, and I think it's necessary that that be done as a general rule. There are certainly times, because of expedience or unavailability of an individual, when you can't do that, but that doesn't preclude going back after the fact to keep your seniors informed or your juniors informed. Everyone is part of this great wheel that's turning around to accomplish something, and if a couple of spokes don't know what's going on, then the wheel doesn't turn in proper balance and you're in trouble. So I think as a basic tenet the chain of command should be followed if at all possible.

Examples of circumstances in which an immediate senior might be bypassed are changes in the tactical situation or equipment casualties that might affect the ability of the command to meet its mission. Another exception would be an unsafe or an immoral situation that was deliberately being covered up by the next senior in the chain. A junior is obligated to ensure that higher authority is apprised of such impropriety. A junior must support the best interests of his command and uphold the moral obligations of his commission. This may require making a request that an immediate senior pass critical information up the chain of command. If such recommendations are unsuccessful in bringing about a resolution, an officer may be obligated to bypass his chain. Fortunately, situations of this sort are rare. Nevertheless, junior officers are expected to place the safety and operational readiness of their commands above loyalty to an immediate senior if there is a question of negligence or impropriety.

General Wilson advises that,

> if someone is given an order which he believes to be morally indefensible, he has every right to bypass the chain of command. I cannot help but think of the My-Lai instance in Vietnam, where indiscriminate killing of civilians was ordered, and it has not been recorded that there was any protest. Now that's very easy in combat, and we must be careful not to condemn people for this, because this is a fine line.
>
> I'll give you an example of an experience that I had in the past. We went into a Vietnamese village in which there was nothing but women and children, all the men had gone, and as we left the village, five of our men were killed—fired at from holes in the ground which are generally near the trees. The next day we went by,

and suddenly there was fire coming from the holes, and we went in, lost a few men, and there was no one in the town but women and children. There were these tunnels in Vietnam by the hundreds through which the enemy could move about.

> There's a point in time when a commander has a moral obligation to the parents of sons under his command, and he cannot afford to continue to take those casualties, yet on the other hand he knows that if he directs that artillery fire or air strike on the town, he's going to kill women and children. Now, what do you do? What do you do, Lieutenant Jones, in this instance? Is this morally defensible or not? I think it's a judgment that one has to make, and you can be criticized in the papers either way, for being a poor commander to take casualties and not take care of your men and for wantonly disregarding the lives of American soldiers, or, on the other hand, for killing women and children.
>
> I have to say to you there is no answer. I'm not here to tell you that it is black and white, and I don't believe anyone else can. It's a situation that calls for good judgment, and those decisions have to be made. But when you make the decision, then you've got to live with it.
>
> If you say go ahead and bomb the village, very well, but there may be a lieutenant who says, "I cannot go along with that, and I hereby submit my resignation," and he leaves the scene and goes back to division headquarters and says "Not only am I submitting my resignation from the service, but I'm going to the newspapers and I'm going to report this." Therein lies the problem for each person. Each person, though, cannot fight the war himself.
>
> These are the hazards of command. If

you would be a commander, you have this responsibility you have to assume yourself. You cannot push it up and you cannot push it down, and if you're not willing to live with those decisions, then you ought to seek another profession.

From time to time, seniors also may direct action to a junior who is not directly below him in the chain. Similarly, on occasion, a senior may convey wishes or important information in informal situations such as social events. In doing so, as a matter of convenience or practical necessity, a senior expects that the person receiving such information or direction will subsequently convey it to interested parties. The chain provides a system of checks and balances. If key people are bypassed, the guidance they normally provide may be lost. More important, someone in the chain may know why such an action should not be undertaken.

Admiral Nakamura believes that
it is a basic principle that military personnel give orders and instructions and report or offer opinions through the chain of command. The violation of this principle invites confusion and exerts a negative influence on leadership. But it is permissible to bypass in the following cases:

1. When it is perceived that crucial timing will be interfered with by strict observation of the chain of command.
2. When it is necessary and suitable to bypass in order to simplify communications on routine affairs.
3. When seniors direct a bypass, recognizing a special necessity because of security or other reasons.

When the chain of command is bypassed, the commanders bypassed should be informed concurrently except in the case of (3) above. When it is not possible to inform them concurrently, they should be informed as soon as possible.

Admiral de Cazanove believes that
it is important that the chain of command never interfere with proper operations. Orders are to be clear and simple and understood by everyone in the chain, for bypassing will interfere with properly coordinated operations. Sometimes it may be easier, for more-junior officers, to go straight to the person detailed to do the job instead of passing through the proper petty officer in the chain of command. This is not to be done, because the individual who is bypassed will just be inclined not to do anything further when called upon at some future time. You cannot tell someone he is not important at one point of time and then that he is important at another point of time. It must be clear that everyone has a job to do and that each person has to get the order from the one he is supposed to get it from, and not from someone else. Of course, in emergency situations it may be necessary to bypass the chain of command, but in that case, those bypassed should be informed as soon as possible as to what transpired.

THE IMPORTANCE OF ACCURATE INFORMATION

When faced with a difficult decision, a commanding officer is reassured by the knowledge that the information given him accurately reflects the existing situation. In a combat situation, in which the captain's decisions must be based on a rapid assimilation of information, survival may depend on accuracy. But accuracy is equally important during his daily routine, as the commanding officer evaluates the morale, climate, and combat readiness of his ship and crew. A critical input comes from his officers and petty officers in the chain. The responsibility of the commanding officer to know his command makes good communications with those below him essential.

Senior officers should exercise control through

policy rather than through detailed procedures, for it is important to allow a subordinate to handle the details of a specific task if he is capable of doing so. An example of this can be found in the *Marine Officer's Guide*. Remember the old promotion-examination question for lieutenants, in which the student is told that he has a ten-man working party, headed by a sergeant, and must erect a 75-foot flagpole on the post parade ground. Problem: How to do it. Every student who worked out the precise calculations of stress, tackle, and gear, no matter how accurately, is graded wrong. The desired answer is simple. The lieutenant turns to the sergeant and says, "Sergeant, put up that flagpole."[25-374]

Under normal circumstances, formal dialogue takes place primarily between the commanding officer and the executive officer regarding administrative matters, between the commanding officer and the department heads regarding operational and administrative matters, and between the commanding officer and officer of the deck (conning officer) or tactical action officer regarding the tactical disposition of the ship. In every case, those briefing the commanding officer must rely on their experiences and the information they have obtained from subordinates to advise the captain correctly. Thus, the chain depends on a series of valid reports.

These reports must include the bad news as well as the good. Sometimes junior officers make the mistake of believing they are expected to solve all problems themselves. Therefore, they do not want to inform their seniors of a problem until it is under control. While it is better, as the old saying goes, "to come with a solution rather than be part of the problem," it is both an obligation and common sense to bring those with greater experience into the problem early. In addition to familiarity with past problems and their solutions, seniors usually have greater access to resources and the clout to generate necessary assistance. More important, seniors must be aware of weak areas in their commands in order to direct the command's activities effectively. When

in doubt, it is better to err on the side of keeping seniors fully informed in a timely manner, especially when conditions are deteriorating.

Junior officers must have the courage of their convictions and inform a senior when the senior's perceptions are believed to be in error. Candor and honesty are essential at all times. This is not, however, a license to question authority, to lack tact, to be inappropriately stubborn, or to step outside the bounds of discretion. Fortunately, most senior officers can readily determine whether a subordinate is speaking his mind or is inhibited and only saying what he believes his boss wants to hear. The latter types serve no one well. A fighting team needs to have everyone thinking, communicating, contributing, and cooperating. One trait of American naval officers that many of our foreign colleagues admire is the readiness of juniors to "call it like it is" and to speak up when they believe there is a better way. The trust, confidence, and instant responsiveness of the chain of command that is required in emergency situations is not meant to foster blind obedience.

Sometimes, limited experience and lack of confidence cause newly commissioned officers to rely too much on their chiefs and leading petty officers for initial solutions to problems and to transmit these recommendations to their seniors (department heads) without supplying their own input. No matter how inexperienced, an officer should not underestimate his importance in the chain. A junior must always apply common sense, dig until a problem is understood, and give a personal best judgment. Constant interaction with seniors and subordinates in the chain will quickly broaden experience and enhance knowledge.

MAINTAINING THE INTEGRITY OF THE CHAIN OF COMMAND

We frequently speak of the integrity of a system, usually meaning the ability of a mechanical or electronic system to function reliably under a wide range of conditions and stresses. This is equally true for the communication and control system defined by the chain of command. Within military organizations, the integrity of the chain of command is a direct reflection of the character of the officers and sailors or soldiers who comprise the organization. Where the integrity of even one officer or petty officer within the active link is weak—whether through lack of moral courage, a self-serving attitude, or limited understanding—the system will deteriorate. Officers in authority will not have an accurate assessment of the capabilities and limitations of their command or the benefit of the best judgment of their subordinates. Consequently, the success and morale of the unit could suffer.

When the chain of command is not used properly—when the chain is bypassed downward under normal circumstances—there may be several detrimental results. First, the bypassed persons will feel that they do not have the confidence of their senior, and they may harbor resentment, up and down. Second, it may make them hesitant to act in a similar situation in the future. ("Didn't the boss handle that without reference to me last time?" they may ask themselves.) Third, a senior officer does not help subordinates by doing their work for them. They can be instructed and guided as necessary, but they should never be cut out of the chain of command. Finally, the senior should be training himself for higher, not lower, command. [45-197]

An active chain of command should also ensure that each person knows his place within the organization and that individual efforts contribute to achieving the overall goals of the command team. A shipboard division in which the members receive conflicting commands from their leading petty officer, their chief petty officer, and their division officer cannot be managed effectively. Similarly, contradictory priorities from the commanding officer, the executive officer, and the department head breed confusion. It is imperative, therefore, that priorities originate from a single source (however many centers of emphasis there may be) and that each individual feels personally responsible for his contribution to the overall success of the command.

SPAN OF CONTROL

Span of control means that there is a limit to the effective supervisory capability of any one individual. The span of control typically is three to seven people, though it may be higher. This following illustrates the importance of the chain of command. A rifle platoon commander has 30 to 50 people under him, a company commander has between 150 and 200 people, and on up, to those who have several million people under their jurisdiction. All of these officers must directly supervise a number of people, each of whom in turn supervises several more.

Secretary Webb suggests that,

> whenever possible, a leader should choose people to work for him whose strengths compensate for his own weaknesses. These people are in diverse ways mirrors of different parts of that leader's personality and professional acumen. In turn, the leader should allow those he supervises to choose the people they want to work for them. The person in charge may want the final say in whether an individual is offered a position, but the person who will be supervising that individual knows best whether he can work with him or not. [Editor's note: Of course such leeway is not always possible, and sometimes it is not desirable—for example, if it would result in significant friction between members of subordinate supporting units.]
>
> Once he has selected his staff, the leader should trust them fully to perform their responsibilities and see that they are rewarded for doing so.
>
> Rewards can take different forms, but, as Napoleon said, the general's reward is not a bigger tent, but command; in other words, the ornaments of leadership should not override the responsibilities.

THE CHAIN AS A TWO-WAY CONDUIT FOR
INFORMATION

When the chain of command works, it is an
admirable institution. Secretary Webb recalled
how it worked in Vietnam.

> I got to Vietnam, and the very first
> patrol I went out on, I said as we were
> walking along something like, "Hold it
> up," and a column stopped, and I said,
> "Get on line," and they were on line. I
> mean almost before I could get the words
> out, that's how fast it was, and it was
> because they used the chain of command.
> I would say something and the squad
> leaders would say it, and the team leaders
> would repeat it, and it was done, I mean
> within seconds. It was marvelous.

A senior must take time to pass the word down
the chain. Sometimes a senior's initial concerns
are satisfied, but juniors receive insufficient
information about why, ultimately, certain decisions were made or about what is going to happen. Juniors deserve the courtesy of being kept
well informed. In most instances, the crew should
be told why policies are adopted; all parties who
have responsibility or could help with a problem
need to hear about it. It is also easier for them
to be team players when the objectives are
understood.

It is also important to consider at what level
in the chain various decisions should be made.
Some issues cannot be delegated. However, giving authority to more junior officers and petty
officers often enhances efficiency, teamwork, and
a sense of responsibility.

A commanding officer or department head may
deliberately probe into what is going on at the
"deckplate level." A wise commanding officer
will not totally depend on what comes to him
directly through the chain of command and must
be alert to "filtering" of information by his subordinates. Commanding officers are encouraged
to talk to their men, to meet with their chiefs,
to tour their ships frequently, to hold captain's

calls with the entire crew, and to keep their eyes
and ears open. At the same time, a junior can
be assured that the commanding officer will keep
informal comments in perspective, that he knows
his people, and that he will avoid undercutting
the officers and senior petty officers in his own
chain of command. Tasking should flow through
the chain.

MCPON Sanders: *We tend to have a better chain
of command going up than we do going down.
I think if we kept the sailors better informed of
what is happening in their organization, it would
make them feel part of the organization instead
of being just workers. They are contributors and
contributing because they want to. If they are
kept informed, they will know why something
has to be done without having to ask or wonder
why. While I would agree with the concept that
unless emergency situations dictate otherwise,
the chain of command should be followed, I do
think that sometimes some of our junior officers
use the concept as a crutch by waiting for the
chain of command to make a decision and get
the job underway, as opposed to taking some
initiative and responsibility and starting the job.
Follow the chain of command, but don't use it
as an excuse to put off directing that necessary
action be taken.*

17. Standing by Seniors and Associates

"Authority and responsibility is invested in the
captain of a ship, and the unequivocal requirement is made for obedience to his command."[4-189]
The concept embodied in this quote serves as
the basis for the following discussion of the naval
officer's obligation to support both his seniors
and his associates in their policies and actions.

A fundamental assumption every leader must
make, regardless of his station in the chain of
command, is that every leader above him is
morally motivated to carry out the mission and,

whenever and wherever possible, to carry it out in a manner that serves the best interests of the officers and enlisted who make up the Naval Service. A professional tasking that does not spring from this premise will probably result in an undertaking that falls short of the intended goal in some respect. Guided by this assumption, an officer comprehends that his response to commands, orders, and other official taskings from higher authority, no matter how challenging they are or how many man-hours they require, must be rapid and unquestioning. This is the essence of military discipline.

Most dramatically, an officer's instant and wholehearted response to commands in combat or in critical damage-control situations is passed rapidly down through the ranks and can result in saving a great number of lives or a ship, submarine, or aircraft. There is a great difference between leadership and command. "A leader is a commander, but a commander is not necessarily a leader." A person can be given a command by an official order, but he cannot be given the qualities of a leader. He is a leader only by the use of his own qualities. [43-145] In a less dramatic sense, a like failure to respond with utmost vigor, aggressiveness, and professionalism to a firing exercise, a man-overboard drill, or a flight-deck barricade drill could well cost a ship and the crew the Battle "E" after arduous months of planning, training, and striving for that ultimate operational recognition. The Battle "E," incidentally, is an award that every ship or squadron must set its sights on during each competitive cycle if, to paraphrase a popular recruiting slogan, a command is going to be "all that it can be."

DEMONSTRATING LOYALTY

Recognizing the motivation and intent of officers in command is part of a precept of good leadership: loyalty. The last thing a good leader wants or needs is a "blindly" loyal subordinate, but an informed and loyal subordinate is highly valued. Loyalty works both ways. Loyalty to one's own organization and personnel is just as vital as loyalty to seniors. If a leader is proud of his people, if he has in them the faith that real loyalty demands, they will return his support and backing a hundredfold. [46-34]

An interesting exposition on the subject of loyalty is provided by Admiral Clausen.

Loyalty is one of the most noble qualifications that can be held by humans. An officer owes his seniors and his country loyalty. In this lies some danger, because there will always be those who try to take advantage of it. This and history explain why, in the German Bundeswehr, all the particular aspects of loyalty have been defined by law [Soldatengestz], in order to make plain the limits, which must not be passed over. The following conditions should be known to all officers:

1. The law must describe exactly the manifold virtues specified in the catalogue of duties.
2. In the forces it must be clear: Although a catalogue of duties is demanded from everyone, especially from officers, these duties and virtues cannot be demanded unconditionally. They have to be derived from principles and fundamental rules of constitution and existing law.
3. Officers must be brought up with a critical mentality. Above all, they should be conscious of intentional and unintentional possibilities of misleading. That implies that they must be informed on civics.

The education of German officers before the war is a warning example. They were educated according to a law of 18 June 1921 [Wehrgesetz], which said: All members of the military service (officers, soldiers, seamen) are not allowed to participate or take an active part in politics; are not allowed to participate in any kind of political election; are not allowed to participate in political parties and political events, meetings, or assemblies; and cannot be elected into a political function. This law was made in the time of the young German democracy, 1921, as a guide especially for officers. I was brought up in accordance with this law very correctly. The law was cancelled, to my knowledge, in 1944. Its result and effects were fatal.

DISOBEYING ORDERS

The following statements by Admirals Hunt and Burke should be viewed in light of the fact that the comments and recommendations were made by very experienced officers. Admiral Hunt provides guidance from his position as leader of the British Fleet.

It is very important—increasingly so as an officer gains in seniority—that he understands what responsibility for his actions means. The more independent his position, the more he must be prepared to regard his orders as nothing more than guidelines. I call the process of learning to judge when this applies "training to disobey." The history of war gives us many well known cases of great successes being achieved by those on the spot who have followed their own instinct in contradiction of their orders; and equally of failures or disasters which have followed from slavish obedience to orders which were no longer—or never were—apposite. Battles have been won and lost on this account alone.

If an officer disobeys his orders, and proves to be right, he should be promoted. If he does so, and is wrong, he should be ready to take responsibility for his actions. But those who then decide his fate should distinguish between energetic initiative (which may yet be an invaluable

asset for the future) and the characteristic of poor judgment (which may be a grave liability).

Admiral Burke says that,

in combat, a leader must always think in the enemy's terms. When he thinks as he imagines the enemy is thinking, he can often discover how to prevent the enemy from doing what he ought to do. The enemy will also try to think like the U.S. officer, so the U.S. officer sometimes must do the unexpected.

In going over some battles with Admiral Kuzoka, a Japanese commander, I found that he knew more about what I did, about our tactics, than I did, because he studied it. He had his charts, photographs, all the other data, and he knew exactly what we did. But he one time said, "You did not follow your own doctrine. How could you operate and not follow your doctrine?" It was a doctrine, it was not an order. It was a normal thing to do, the most logical thing to do. It had been studied very carefully. "But," I said, "I knew you had our doctrine, you must have, and I figured that you probably had it, so I didn't do what the doctrine said. I did something else, I split my forces and arranged a big surprise." He said, "How can you disobey orders?" I said, "Those are not orders." The Japanese were rigid in their operations, and we were not.

These views of senior officers are provided so that junior officers will understand the complexities of command that must be considered by their seniors and thus will be able to follow orders loyally by having confidence that their seniors' orders are designed to win battles and minimize loss of life. On this same subject, Admiral Long comments that,

if decisions made are contrary to an individual's personal beliefs, he has several acceptable options available to him. First, and the one most recommended, is for the individual to enunciate the reasons why he thinks the decision or the policy is not correct; he should always recommend an alternate course of action. If the issue is of great magnitude and an officer cannot in all good conscience carry out the decision and is unable to change it, then he clearly has the option of resigning or retiring.

Back in my own life in the Navy, there were times when I was sorely tempted to turn in my chit and resign because I felt so keenly. Most of those issues dealt with decisions of seniors affecting my own family life, and also decisions that affected the welfare and morale of the people under my command. In those instances I did object to the policies and decisions that were being made, and when those decisions were not changed, I must admit that I was tempted at that time to turn in my resignation. As a matter of fact, at one time I did write out my resignation and was argued out of it by my wife, and on reflection, I'm glad she did.

Every officer will be faced with difficult decisions during his career in the military. But no one should take a drastic action without a great deal of thought and consultation with others.

General Barrow gave two examples of situations in which he deliberately disobeyed orders he disagreed with.

I happened to belong to the school that says there are some circumstances in which an officer can refuse to do what he is ordered to do. There are some people, surprisingly, who say you are to execute whatever it is you are told to do without question, even though it is distasteful and you don't want to do it; they say it is your duty to do it, etc. I'd say normally that's true, but, this world being made up of imperfect people, you're going to have people give you wrong orders. Just to oversimplify it, if someone said, "I want

you, Captain Barrow, to take your company and jump over the cliff," obviously I would not obey. But it doesn't really have to be that blatantly stupid, it can be something much more subtle than that.

When I was involved in the Seoul [Korea] operations, for example, I had a company that was out in front of all the other companies in an irregularly shaped line in the heart of Seoul. I had an eerie feeling that something was not quite what it should be; the area that we were going into just looked dangerous. There was this intuitive thing that said don't go blindly charging ahead because something's wrong down there. So we very carefully positioned ourselves, sought proper cover and protected it, and we watched with binoculars the area below us and in our zone of action, and all of a sudden we saw significant movement, enemy movement, back and forth, repositioning themselves to give us a welcome party in many, many greater numbers than us. Had we gone into this, we would have been going into a real trap.

It was an ideal situation to employ a support in arms, we wouldn't expose a single Marine on the ground to enemy fire, but we would blast the enemy with artillery, mortars, long-range water-cooled machine guns, and anything else we could think of. And that's what we did, we brought up all these forward observers and controllers of these kind of weapons and started pouring in on them, and as we did they, too, had to seek better cover and expose more and more of their presence. Meanwhile my boss (I'm a captain, my boss is a lieutenant colonel) has me on the radio saying, "Move out," and I'm trying to tell him that what I'm doing is a lot more important than me saying "Everybody move out," which would get a lot of people killed. I told him what we were doing was accomplishing a mission in the sense that we were killing the enemy and were going to be able to go into that area without ourselves getting seriously hurt. He implied such things to me as, "If you don't move out at once, you may have a new battalion commander," which was his way of saying, "They are really putting the heat on me for you to move out."

I thought I was going to go nowhere, so I turned my radio off, which is a form of disobedience, and I got my most articulate platoon leader, the guy who was persuasive and forceful, who was an effective speaker, and I didn't need to tell him what the circumstances were, he happened to be the platoon leader of the third platoon, he could see for himself. I said, "Go back there and find the command post or the battalion and entreat our commanding officer to come up here and see for himself." I said, "I'll leave it to you to persuade him. Tell him what we're doing." Lo and behold, he did just that, he convinced him that what we were doing was the right thing, more important than obeying someone's orders. [Editor's note: We see here how Captain Barrow avoided repeating the disaster portrayed at the end of the movie about the WWI Battle at Gallipoli.]

I may as well digress here and say that the orders to move out came from way up the line and had to do with orders we got that night about moving out, all beholden to someone's idea that Seoul should be retaken on the third month anniversary of its falling. If there was ever a stupid thing, it was to make a military decision based on some anniversary. There are no military considerations in that at all, but that's really what somebody was doing. Some general way up the line was saying, "Let's give MacArthur a prize. Three

months to the day that it fell, we're going to take it back, so move out Marines, move out," and you know Marines are very obedient, so it's easy for a regimental commander to say move out when he hasn't seen any reason not to, and then the battalion commander the same thing, but when it got down to me, I didn't blindly say, "Yes, Sir," because I had something else going on, and I balked. I didn't move out, and that's what you get paid for. You see, there are people who would have moved out when he said, "I'm telling you to move out, attack, go forward," and there are many Marines and others who would say, "I've got my orders. We've got to do it." But I believe it is a matter of judgment. Now this is a touchy business. When do you not do something you're told to do and be prepared to take the consequences? Suppose he came up there and said, "God damn it, I told you to move out, and I don't give a damn what you're doing, you're relieved." I would have gone to my dying day thinking I did the right thing, but he could do what he wanted to, get rid of me if he wanted to.

To complete the story. The lieutenant brought him back and we were then almost in the anticlimactic part of what we were doing without supporting arms. We were about to cease, and yet there was sufficient going on that he got excited and jumped up and down and said, "Let's get more artillery, let's bring in more mortar," and we almost felt like saying, "Well, for God's sake, if you could have just been here about an hour ago, you would have really seen what it was we had as targets." So I'll just say I survived that, I didn't get any criticism or anything else. I've done that sort of thing several times in my career, simply not doing what someone told me to do, and I had to maybe sometimes stand there with my heels together, and if I believed I was right, that's the way it was.

About one time I will never know whether I was right or not. This same battalion commander had a good reputation for being a fair man, he was a prisoner of war during World War II and escaped to the Philippines. He was a Naval Academy graduate and had a good record. He took over the battalion in Camp Lejeune, this was 1949, the year before Korea, and I had just taken over a rifle company about the same time that was at Little Creek, Virginia, so we were miles apart and had never met. I didn't know that the first thing he did after he took over was to say he wanted to go up to Little Creek and see this company that I happened to be in command of. My company was involved in the evaluation of submarines carrying troops and an amphibious tractor and other things, and we'd go under and surface and do all kinds of things to see how quickly we could move x numbers of people. We did many tests and drills. It was a group that was involved in something different.

One day we were not doing any of this evaluation, it was sort of a clean-up everything day. A lieutenant colonel from the headquarters that I was responsible to, a staff officer, had sent a classmate of mine, a captain, to tell me that another unit, a battalion-sized unit, Marine Corps, had moved out of some barracks not far from where we were and left it in a horrible state of police and that he was directing that Captain Barrow and his A Company, 1st Battalion, 2d Marines, go over there and clean it up. That's wrong. I mean, that's wrong on his part to do that. It required an outfit that, it looked to me (I had just gotten there), was pretty squared away and had its own area cleaned to go

clean up someone else's mess. So I balked at that. I told the captain, "You go back and tell the colonel I'm not going to do it. We didn't make the mess, also we're not going to do it." He came back in about twenty minutes and he said, "Man, the colonel is furious. You've got to go up there and see him."

What would have been the outcome normally? Would I have gone there and been chewed out and still have had to do it, or would I have been able to talk him out of it? Would I as a young captain saying, "Sir, I should like to come on out and talk about this, there's a morale issue involved," have been able to talk him out of it? Well, as it turns out, as I was waiting outside his office, down the hallway came this lieutenant colonel with another officer I knew with him, and he stopped and said, "Colonel Hawkins, this is one of your company commanders, Captain Barrow." The battalion commander, as I said earlier, had come up to see us in our training. We hadn't seen him, but he had just arrived, maybe within the hour. He greeted me cordially and I did him respectfully, and he said, "Everything all right? You got any problems or anything?" and I said, "Yes, Sir. I have a problem." So I told him about this incident, which was proper, since he was my battalion commander and someone senior to me out of my chain was about to pull my chain. He didn't get angry, but he said, "Humph, Captain, I'll take care of that." It turns out that he was a classmate of this lieutenant colonel who was after me, but he was also senior to him, and I'm going to assume he went in there and said to him, "You know that's not the right thing to do, making that outfit go over there and clean up somebody else's mess. Why don't you make sure they send a contingent down here to do it or make some

issue out of it, but don't go and do that."
I don't know what he said, but the point
is, I didn't have to face that music.

Now think about this story. Everything
has transpired within the earshot and eye-
sight of several people, my officers, first
sergeant, company gunnery sergeant,
clerks, and whoever else is around close
enough, and their antennas are quivering.
"This young new captain we've got has
done something none of us ever heard of
before. He told another captain to tell the
colonel he wasn't going to do something.
What in the hell do we have here?" They
knew what the task was and "By God, this
young captain ain't going to make us go
over there and clean up somebody else's
mess. He has said he wasn't going to do
it, and then a little while later he's been
sent for. We're going to have to do it, but
he sure is standing up to them." I came
back and never said anything, and I would
guess, being a judge of human nature,
that my stock went up considerably. I
didn't come back making any claims about
anything, I certainly didn't tell any stories, but I didn't want to say, "My butt
was saved. I ran into the battalion commander and he took care of it." I didn't
need to say it, so I didn't say it. Maybe I
exploited the situation for my own benefit. But that's not why I did it. I did it as
a matter of principle.

You can just imagine what those young
Marines were saying about that new captain. "Here's a guy who stood up to them.
Not only that, but they sent for him, he
came back, and we still didn't have to do
it, and it looks like he's in one piece and
he's still got his job." That was an example of standing up for principle, even
though we might have had to do it. An
additional point is that the good consequences of standing tall on morale issues
can sometimes be of marvelous value to a
commander. You do it because it's right,
but you also end up getting a followership
that becomes even more intense.

On the subject of a junior advising a senior of
his disagreement with policy, Secretary Webb
stated that

many people benefited when I spoke up
to correct a wrong. In Vietnam, we had
an area called Liberty Bridge, and eight
miles away there was this place called An
Hoa, which was a combat base, and there
was a dirt road that connected the two
where a convoy ran twice a day. Because
the dirt road was occasionally mined,
every morning two rifle platoons whose
duty rotated provided flank security out in
the weeds while the engineers swept the
road for major mines. But you know the
Vietnamese, the VC, were not stupid, and
they realized that if they put a mine
inside the road it was going to be found,
so they started booby trapping both sides
of the road, and we averaged a loss of a
man per day in this small platoon that
averaged 28 people on the flanks.

I had been in Vietnam not very long,
maybe a month or so, when my platoon
got this mine-sweeping flanks security.
These guys were always saying, "Well,
you know somebody's going to get it
today, it happens all the time." My people moved along and I lost a guy in the
right flank the first day, and I came back
and I started talking to my company commander about us and I said, "It's really
silly, you don't lose anybody on the road
and yet in the flank security, for the guys
on the road, you're always losing people,"
and I went out the next day and I lost two
guys on the left-hand side, then I went to
the battalion commander, and I said,
"This is crazy, you know, count the casualties that you've had, Sir, and you know
for the sake of possibly losing somebody
on the road, we're guaranteeing three and

four hundred people a year out on the flanks," and he had me write a proposal, which was rather unusual in the field of Vietnam, but I got together with my company commander and we wrote a proposal and we changed the policy so that we were allowed to send patrols out and set up sort of outpost positions on the side of the road, and the casualties stopped.

Good officers who believe strongly that something is wrong have the courage to say they will not do it, and generally they will be listened to, although at times they will not.

The officer who believes he has to present himself in different ways to different people will end up wrapped around the axle. If he understands himself and is able to live with himself, then the officer only has to say it one way, and that makes life much simpler. The officer who adheres to his value system generally is at peace with himself and is willing to take the consequences for his beliefs and tenacity.

MAKING UNPOPULAR ORDERS PALATABLE

The Naval Service is becoming increasingly expensive and sophisticated, both in terms of combat and engineering systems and in terms of the ever better educated and trained officers and troops who provide the vital human link in the war-fighting equation. Leadership in the modern Naval Service is, more often than not, beyond the capacity of any single human being. Good and wise leaders at each level in the chain of command, therefore, are receptive to constructive and knowledgeable inputs from subordinates when the situation warrants. A junior officer should express his dissent to his seniors in private and in a frank and full manner. He should never be open in his dissent or air "dirty laundry." Of course, after discussing the matter with his seniors, he must faithfully and loyally execute the order and impart his full backing of the policy to his subordinates, whether he agrees

with it or not.[Chap. 1:41-144] The effective leader will readily accept and weigh such inputs with knowledge already at hand, and then make his decision and issue appropriate direction and guidance.

The direction or guidance handed down may not be what the subordinate leader recommended or hoped to influence through constructive input, but this is where "the rubber meets the road," where loyalty comes firmly into play. An officer who sets the example of loose criticism, especially in the presence of enlisted men, cannot be surprised if he gets from his men only a similar lack of loyalty.[48-34] The subordinate leader is duty bound to run with this order as if it were his own and to "make it happen!" When an officer receives direction from a senior officer which he considers wrong or unfair or which he knows will be less than favorably received down in the ranks, he must confidently draw from his reservoir of leadership "tricks" and from the well of rapport he has established with his subordinates to get the job done properly and in good time.

While commands must be carried out in a prescribed manner, and Standard Operating Procedures are to be rigidly adhered to unless operational necessity dictates otherwise, a subordinate leader, more often than not, will have the option of carrying out orders or other taskings in the manner he deems to be in the best interests of the Naval Service. An imaginative and resourceful leader can often soften the overall impact of an unwelcome order or task.

EARNING THE LOYALTY OF SUBORDINATES

Admiral Ramage, in talking about training troops for combat and following orders, noted that

there may be an occasion to question the policies of your seniors, and, if so, you must be ready to offer substantial reasons therefore and similarly listen to subordinates if they question your orders. If unable to settle the differences, you have to seek further advice and counsel; in other words, there are times when you say, well, that's not going to work, and I did this at times with Admiral Felt when he was vice chief and he would have everything all prepared. He'd studied all the references to some problem and he'd made up his mind the action that should be taken and he called in all of his staff officers and said this is the way it is going to be, and I'd say, well, I don't think so, I think we should approach it a little differently and so on, and he'd listen and say, well, I think you're right, and many times he'd say, you're the only guy that ever takes exception. Well, it can be done and seniors will respect you, and likewise, in all my commands I had staff conferences and I conducted them almost like a TV show, I'd ask the individuals questions, throw the problem out, let them respond and get their input, because nothing succeeds like success. If staff officers find that their suggestions or recommendations are accepted and acted on, it increases their ego and their ability and eagerness to participate further.

To this, Professor Montor said: "It sounds like what in effect you're doing is training. You're building in subordinates a responsibility to think, probably knowing that sometimes they may have said something to you which you didn't agree with, but the fact that you didn't hit them over the head and say 'Get out of here' in turn made them realize that they could have confidence in saying what they thought and you'd listen, even if you wouldn't necessarily always accept what they had to say." Admiral Ramage continued:

Well, the only way you're going to build the strength of your command is by enhancing the responsibilities of all the individuals associated therein. I carried this a step further when I had command of the First Fleet. I was very much concerned about all these vast operations

orders we used to have in the amphibious force, with each level of command issuing their own supplementary operation orders covering every last detail. They became so voluminous they became confusing and self-defeating. I often compared them to Shakespearean plays where every actor knew ahead of time when he was going to be on stage, what his lines were, and when he would be off stage just standing by. It was very unrealistic, to say the least. So I called in Admiral Colwell, ComPhibPac, and General Krulak, CGFMFPac, and told them we were going to run this next amphibious exercise without an operation order. Instead, a Letter of Instructions (LOI) would be issued giving the Task Force Organization, task assignments and time of getting underway. From that point on the exercise would be directed by dispatches in accordance with a scenario prepared in advance by my staff. Ships would assume full readiness conditions upon getting underway and assume actual wartime conditions. That is, minesweepers would have to proceed ahead and sweep for mines already laid in advance. Then they would have to take suitable antisubmarine measures to avoid submarines awaiting their sortie. Next, they would have to man their anti-aircraft batteries and take targets being towed by planes under fire. And eventually the surface support ships would be turned loose to conduct shore bombardment on San Clemente Island. During the night, ships had to be on the lookout for surface raiders exiting from San Clemente. Also, an active air search had to be maintained as occasional bogies would make unscheduled attacks throughout the night. Every effort was made to simulate actual wartime conditions and to put the onus on each command to react to each situation in accordance with doctrine.

Specific directives were sent to the Task Force Commanders requiring them to initiate certain actions. This in turn would result in further directives being originated and passed on down the line, calling for individual initiative and imagination at each echelon of command. This put a tremendous premium on communications and served to impress everyone with the importance of this essential adjunct to successful operations. Many other innovations were injected into the scenario. For example, up at Camp Pendleton, where the landings were made, the Marines had tried to simulate conditions to be found in Vietnam as closely as possible. They had built several native villages—no one was allowed to speak English—only Spanish was permitted. The natives were not too cooperative, and it took quite a bit of ingenuity to accomplish necessary tasks. Everyone entered into the spirit of the enterprise and came up with many original contributions.

This type of operation was so successful and so realistic that it was followed in all subsequent fleet exercises. In each one, special emphasis was directed at some particular aspect of operations, such as: communications, guided missiles, ECM/ECCM, NTDS, AAW, ASW, and strike warfare. All facilities both ashore and afloat were utilized in order to provide all realism possible.

"Loyalty is in no way merely a blind and servile service to the letter of the regulations."[46-33] One officer remembered a story that illustrates this. He had to tell his carrier's crew, during transit home from an arduous seven-month deployment, that the type commander had informed him that his staff had determined that preparation for a unique, out-of-home-port, service-life-extension overhaul, scheduled to begin six weeks after the ship's arrival home,

would require ten hours of ship's force effort every day of the six weeks at home, including the day of arrival:

The fact that it was summer and married crew members' children were out of school and looking forward to spending time with their long-absent fathers, and that the local beaches were crowded with distractions for the unmarried crew members, certainly did not make my 1MC (public address) announcement any easier. I followed up the news with a challenge to the crew to figure out a better way to execute the tasking than the type commander's staff had formulated, and we would do it our way. Needless to say, the minds of my 3,500 crew members went into overdrive, and the results were even more impressive than I had imagined: first of all, we were able to carry on with the normal post-deployment 50 percent leave policy during our first 30 days at home; second, by a huge consensus, the crew elected to go with a unique 0700 to 1300 workday, forgoing lunch and other workday-associated personal needs that would normally be satisfied during a standard workday, until after the 1300 secure.

In doing it our way, we were able to satisfy the type commander's requirements while coincidently ensuring that the best interests of the crew and their families, and, in the long run, the best interests of the Navy, were served.

Admiral Long discussed how priorities differ in peacetime and during times of war.

One of the principles of command says that the mission comes first and the welfare of our people comes second. I do subscribe to that view in critical wartime situations. Obviously, the situation or the scenario dictates the priority of what we are doing, and military officers need to have sufficient flexibility in their own thinking and decision making to accommodate varying priorities. In wartime, where the accomplishment of a mission is critical, I would certainly subscribe to the view that that mission is of primary importance. However, in peacetime, one of the principal jobs military officers have is to maintain the readiness of the force. The readiness of the force clearly starts with personnel readiness, and that involves retention of trained, experienced personnel, and that in turn is dependent upon the welfare and morale of individual people. Therefore, an officer in a command position must, in my view, in peacetime always be concerned about the welfare, the morale, the training of his own people as necessary, because that concern is absolutely fundamental to achieving a high personnel readiness.

Beyond personnel readiness is, certainly, material readiness of an individual unit, whether it's an aircraft squadron on a ship, a submarine, or a Marine battalion. In peacetime, material readiness becomes quite critical, and it's the responsibility of all levels of command to ensure that the fleet or force is not driven or operated to such a high degree that material readiness and personnel readiness decline to an unacceptable state. Here we must seek a balance of fleet readiness that is dependent to a large degree on achieving adequate operating time, which includes adequate steaming hours, adequate flying hours, below which the overall readiness of the fleet declines. Obviously if we drive the fleet to the degree that personnel are never in their home port, never have an opportunity to maintain their equipment, never have an opportunity to see their family, then in that situation, and certainly in peacetime, personnel readiness goes down, retention goes down, and overall operational readiness goes down, and that is a situation that is not in the best interest of the United States.

"DAMN EXEC," BY LT. COMDR. STUART D. LANDERSMAN

The manner in which orders are relayed down the chain of command is another leadership issue. The following sea story, "Damn Exec," by Lt. Comdr. Stuart D. Landersman, was originally published in the January 1965 *Proceedings* and addresses the issue in a most effective manner.

"Damn Exec"

The Norfolk wind was streaking the water of Hampton Roads as Commander Martin K. Speaks, U.S. Navy, Commanding Officer of the USS *Bowens* (DD-891), stepped from his car, slammed the door, and straightened his cap. As he approached the pier head, a sailor stepped from the sentry hut and saluted.

"Good morning, Captain."

"Good morning, Kowalski," answered Commander Speaks. He took pleasure in the fact that he knew the sailor's name. Kowalski was a good sailor. He had served his entire first cruise in the *Bowens* and did his work well.

The Captain noticed that, over his blues, Kowalski wore a deck force foul weather jacket, faded, frayed, dirty, and spotted with red lead. "Little chilly this morning," said the Captain as he walked by. "Yes sir, sure is," replied the sailor with his usual grin.

As the Captain approached his quarterdeck, there was the usual scurrying of people, and four gongs sounded. "Bowens arriving," spoke the loudspeaker system, and Lieutenant (j.g.) Henry Graven, U.S. Naval Reserve, gunnery officer and the day's command duty officer, came running to the quarterdeck. Salutes and cheerful "Good mornings" were exchanged, and the Captain continued to his cabin.

Lieutenant Graven looked over the quarterdeck and frowned. "Let's get this brightwork polished, chief."

"It's already been done once this morning, sir," replied the OD.

"Well, better do it again. The Exec will have a fit if he sees it this way." said Graven.

"Yes sir," answered the OD.

As soon as Graven had left, the OD turned to his messenger, "Go tell the duty boatswain's mate that Mr. Graven wants the brightwork done over again on the quarterdeck."

Later that morning, Captain Speaks was going over some charts with the ship's executive officer, Lieutenant Commander Steven A. Lassiter, U.S. Navy. The Captain had just finished his coffee and lighted a cigarette. "Steve, I noticed our pier sentry in an odd outfit this morning. He had a foul weather jacket on over his blues; it looked pretty bad."

"Yes sir. Well, it gets cold out there, and these deck force boys have mighty bad-looking jackets," the Exec said.

The Captain felt the Exec had missed his point and said, "Oh, I realize they have to wear a jacket, but for a military watch like that, I'd like to see them wear pea coats when it's cold."

Lieutenant Graven was talking with a third-class boatswain's mate on the fantail when the quarterdeck messenger found him. When told that the executive officer wanted to see him, Graven ended his discussion with, "There, hear that? He probably wants to see me about the brightwork. I don't care how many men it takes to do it, the Exec told me to be sure to get that brightwork polished every morning."

The executive officer indicated a chair to Graven and asked: "How's it going these days?"

Lassiter had always liked Graven, but in the past few months, since he had taken over as senior watch officer, Graven seemed to have more problems than usual.

"Okay, I guess," Graven replied with a forced grin. He knew that things were not as they used to be. It seemed strange, too, because everyone on the ship had been so glad to be rid of the previous senior watch officer, that "damn" Lieutenant Dumphy. The junior officers even had a special little beer bust at the club to celebrate Dumphy's leaving and Graven's "fleeting up" to senior watch officer. Now the Exec was always after him. The junior officers didn't help much either, always complaining about the Exec. Maybe the Exec was taking over as "the heel" now that Dumphy was gone.

"That's good," said the Exec. "Here's a little thing that you might look into. These men who stand pier watches have to wear a jacket, but the foul weather jacket doesn't look good for a military watch. I'd like to see them wear their pea coats when it's cold." Graven had expected something like this, more of the Exec's picking on him. He responded properly, got up, and left.

Graven told his first lieutenant: "The Exec says the pier head sentries can't wear foul weather jackets anymore. If it's cold they can wear pea coats," he added.

"But the pea coats will get dirty, and then what about personnel inspections?" asked the first lieutenant.

"I don't know," Graven shook his head, "but if the Exec wants pea coats, we give him pea coats!"

"Pea coats!" said the chief boatswain's mate, "Who says so?"

"That's what the Exec wants," said the first lieutenant, "so let's give him pea coats."

"The Exec says pea coats for the pier sentries when it's cold," announced the chief to his boatswain's mates.

A third-class boatswain's mate walked away from the group with a buddy, turned and said, "That Damn Exec. First I got to have all my men polish brightwork on the quarterdeck, now they got to wear pea coats on sentry duty 'stead of foul weather jackets!"

Seaman Kowalski's relief showed up at the sentry booth at 1150. "Roast beef today," constituted the relieving ceremony.

"Good, I like roast beef," was the reply. "Hey, how come the pea coat?"

"Damn Exec's idea," said the relief. "We can't wear foul weather gear no more out here, only pea coats."

"Damn Exec," agreed Kowalski. "Captain didn't say nothin' when he came by."

"The Captain's okay, it's just that Damn Exec. He's the guy who fouls up everything," complained the new sentry.

Seaman Kowalski had just gone aboard the ship when Captain Speaks stepped out on deck to look over his ship. The quarterdeck awning shielded the Captain from the view of those on the quarterdeck, but he could clearly hear the conversation.

"Roast beef today, Ski."

"Yeah, I know, and we wear pea coats from now on."

"Whaddaya mean, pea coats?"

"Yeah, pea coats on the pier, Damn Exec says no more foul weather jackets."

"Well that ain't all, we got to polish this here brightwork 'til it shines every morning before quarters. Damn Exec says that too."

"Damn Exec."

Captain Speaks was shocked. "Why 'Damn Exec' from these seamen?" he thought. It was easy to see that the executive officer had passed the order along in proper military manner. It was easy to see that the junior officers, leading petty officers, and lower petty officers were passing it along saying "The Exec wants. . . ." That's the way orders are passed along. Why? Because "it is easy."

"All ship's officers assemble in the wardroom," the boatswain's mate announced on the loudspeaker system. Lieutenant Commander Lassiter escorted in the Captain. The junior officers took their seats when the Captain was seated. The executive officer remained standing. "Gentlemen, the Captain has a few words to say to us today."

The Captain rose and looked around slowly. "Gentlemen, we are continually exposed to words like administration, leadership, management, capabilities, organization, responsibilities, authority, discipline, and cooperation. You use these words every day. You give lectures to your men and use them, but if I were to ask each of you for a definition of any of these words I would get such a wide variety of answers that an expert couldn't tell what word we were defining. Some we probably couldn't define at all. We still use them, and will continue to use them as they are used in the continually mounting number of articles, instructions, and books we must read.

"If I were to ask any of you how can we improve leadership I would get answers filled with these words—undefined and meaningless.

"If we listed all of the nicely worded theories of leadership, studied them, memorized them, and took a test in them, we would all pass. But this would not improve our ability as leaders one bit. I can tell a story, containing none of these meaningless words, that *will* improve your leadership.

"In 1943, I was secondary battery officer in a cruiser in the South Pacific. In my second battle, gun control was hit and I lost communications with everyone except my 5-inch mounts. I could see that the after main battery turret was badly damaged and two enemy destroyers were closing us from astern. At the time my 5-inch mounts were shooting at airplanes. I ordered my two after 5-inch mounts to use high capacity ammunition and shift targets to the two destroyers closing from astern. 'But Mr. Speaks, we're supposed to handle the air targets; who said to shift targets?' my mount captain asked.

"There were noise and smoke and explosions that day, but the explosion that I heard and felt was not from a shell, but from those words of the mount captain.

"Those attacking destroyers got a few shots in at us before we beat them off. Maybe those shots found a target and some of my shipmates died. I never found out. There was too much other damage.

"I thought over the battle afterward and realized that this entire situation was my fault, not the mount captain's. I may have been responsible for the death of some of my shipmates because up to that day I always gave orders to my subordinates by attaching the originator's name to it.

"What does that mean? It means that it was the easy thing to do, to say, 'the gunnery officer wants us to shift targets.'

"In this peacetime world you may say that we no longer have this struggle on a life or death basis. Quick response does not mean life or death now, but it might tomorrow, or sometime after we've all been transferred elsewhere and this ship is being fought by people we don't know.

"Whether you're cleaning boilers, standing bridge watch, or administering your training program, it's easy to say 'The Exec wants' or 'Mr. Jones says.' It's the easy, lazy way; not the right way. You can sometimes discuss or even argue with an order, but when you give it to a subordinate, make him think it is coming from you.

"Giving orders the lazy way is like a drug. Once you start saying 'The ops officer wants' you will find yourself doing it more and more until you can't get a thing done any other way. Your men will pass along orders that way, too, and it will become a part of your organization right down to the lowest level. When some problem arises and you want action, you'll get 'Who wants this?' or 'Why should we?'

"Each of you ask yourself if you have given an order today or yesterday in the lazy manner. I think almost all of us have. Now ask yourself if that order really originated with the person who gave it to you, or did he receive it from a higher level? We never really know, do we, but why should we even care?

"In almost every unit the 'lazy' ordering starts on a particular level. From personal experience I can tell you that this can be an exact measure of the unit's effectiveness. If it starts at the department head level or higher it's a relatively bad outfit, and if it starts at the chief's level it's

a relatively good outfit. You can find the level below which it starts by hearing a new title preceding a primary billet. 'Damn Exec' means that the executive officer is the lowest level giving orders properly. 'Damn division officer' means that the division officers are taking responsibility for the order.

"Here I am using some of those words, responsibility and authority, those undefined terms we want to avoid, but perhaps we have helped define them.

"To be more specific, every officer does some 'lazy' ordering, but we need to do it less and less. We must try to push the 'damn' title down as far as it will go.

"Let's push the 'damn officer' down all the way to the chiefs and below, then we will have a Damn Good Ship."

MCPON Sanders: *We must be very supportive of seniors. That doesn't mean covering up anything, but if you speak down about your seniors to subordinates, you're not really building yourself up, in fact you're also tearing yourself down. If you have a problem with a senior I suggest you talk it over with your peers and then address the matter up through the chain of command. While that may not always be easy, and sometimes you may not be able to do it at all, never take it up with subordinates, because they cannot do anything about it.*

18. Carrying out Orders

There is little rational argument that can be raised about the role and legitimacy of discipline in a society or its separate parts. It is the stuff and substance that turns an unruly mob into a cohesive body of men, banded for specific objectives. Discipline is a major advantage to a unit in battle. Discipline takes many forms, and the military record is replete with demonstrations of the obvious fact that the disciplined fighting force, be it an army or an individual, almost invariably carries the day against the undisciplined, even though the latter might be superior in numbers, machinery, or terrain.[4-188] This section concerns discipline as it relates to obeying orders.

There is no magic formula for achieving promotion and success. In chapter 1, it was established that an individual must learn to be a good follower in order to be a good leader. It follows naturally that the leader should comply with the decisions, the orders, and the directives of seniors and begin assignments as promptly as possible after they are received. Admiral Itaya stated that

> an officer must always fully comply with the decisions, orders, and directives of his seniors. However, this must be on the proviso that these orders and directives are within the authority of the seniors, that they are legally and morally appropriate, and, furthermore, that they do not exceed the capability of the recipient.

An example of a military force that went beyond the bounds of morality is the SS, who were so self-contained and so driven to carry out their duty that they were ignorant of the harm that their actions caused. When the tribunal charged his *Einsatzgruppe* D with averaging 340 killings a day and peaking at 700 per day for as long as 30 days at a time, Ohlendorf, to the horror of those in the courtroom, showed that he was proud of those figures. He told [the prosecution] that he did his duty as best he could at all times.[29-60]

Admiral Itaya continued:

> An officer must bear in mind that his seniors have one more level of responsibility and have greater information. Regardless of this, if these orders and directives cannot be complied with, the officer will state his view to dispel doubts. When the situation is impossible to resolve, the way is open for him to appeal to a higher level of authority. However, in such a case he should be prepared to accept responsibility for the disruption that this will cause.

Modern business and management courses teach us that leaders are democratic, autocratic (one person rules), or participative (a group or committee acts as a body to give directions) in their approach to solving problems. These approaches form a practical basis for developing an individual method of managing and leading. However, it seems that leaders and subordinates both forget at times that they live and function as military members in an autocratic system by personal choice. All of them raised their right hand and swore, among other things, to obey the orders of those appointed over them. This oath commits them to meet obligations and fulfill responsibilities not encountered by those outside the military. Admiral Long emphasizes this point by stating that

> command involves responsibility, and responsibility is something that an individual either has or does not have. People who are in the chain of command must clearly recognize that they can delegate most or all of their authority, but they can never divest themselves of their responsibility. The commanding officer is 100 percent responsible for what goes on in a missile division; clearly the gunnery or weapons officer is 100 percent responsible; and the division officer is also 100 percent responsible. An understanding and appreciation that responsibility is absolute is critical to an officer doing his job.

If an officer's boss gives him an order that is clearly unpopular with the troops, he should nevertheless pass that order on as his own. Junior officers must recognize that their loyalty to the commanding officer of their ship, squadron, or battalion requires that if they disagree with a commanding officer's order, after they have had an opportunity to express their disagreement, they take the order and carry it out as their own, whether their disagreement altered the order or not. The military system has worked successfully that way for a long time, and it should continue to work that way in the future.

When a senior gives an order, the junior has an obligation to act promptly and to make his best effort to carry it out. If a live steam line breaks and steam endangers those around it, the rudder fails, or they are told to take that hill, military personnel do not want a vote taken on what their actions should be. Lawful orders, no matter how trivial, should be promptly obeyed. Every order has a significance to the overall effectiveness of the ship. Combat-sustained damage, fire, flooding, collision, and other material- and life-threatening hazards are constant companions and will ever remain so aboard ships of war. Only well-prepared and carefully trained crews can assure survival in times of emergency. Instant obedience is a vital force in their conduct, as anyone who has been to sea can vouchsafe.[4-196]

When there is no emergency, the same idea applies during day-to-day operations. Seniors expect prompt action to the best of their juniors' ability. "Nothing lowers the effectiveness of a unit faster or further than acceptance of disobedience or deliberate poor performance."[8-128] At the same time that juniors are being judged and evaluated by their seniors, their subordinates are watching to see how they respond. If junior officers procrastinate or grouse, how can they expect their subordinates to behave any differently when the juniors direct subordinates to accomplish a task? Admiral Taylor described how officers can best decide how quickly they should begin to implement a command.

> The decision is a function of time: How much time do I have before the problem is in extremis? If it is a sudden red light in a cockpit, you've got to do something pretty fast. If it is something due next month, and the decision is made, now it's time to press on and get the job done better than the other fellow can get it done, just taking into consideration all the other factors involved there.

What you're going to do is size up the problem and get a plan of attack. Get yourself some milestones. You want to use the time that's available to take in more input so that the quality of the decision is better—where you have time, you're inevitably going to do better. Using factors of judgment, I think that the successful naval officer is not going to bite his pipe or go to the powder room or do a lot of dilly dallying. He's going to go to work with everything he's got to come up to the fastest possible way, even for those things being done next month, he's going to get a plan. Sure, its a plan from which you can deviate, but don't wait until next week and procrastinate. Start right now doing things in a quality way, whatever you decide the plan is going to be and how you're going to get there to solve this problem. Just get in the habit of doing things now and keeping your mind open to gather more facts.

Furthermore, when carrying out an order and tasking sailors and Marines, an officer must be enthusiastic, forceful, and fully committed and make it seem as though the task is his idea. When he can't make it look like his idea, he must show outwardly complete commitment and loyalty to his seniors and emphasize the positive aspects of each task. This will often require that he use his imagination and squelch his own ideas or his disagreement, but it will promote unit cohesiveness and provide the best example of the loyalty an officer expects his subordinates to show him. Admiral Clexton noted: "[Subordinates] will do their jobs the way you want them to, the right way, as long as you train them properly and then continue to insist on quality compliance."[15-1]

Procrastination is defined as deferring action, prolonging, or postponing. Thomas Carlyle writes, "It is one of the illusions that the present hour is not the critical, decisive hour." Leaders must be decisive and responsive. From a practical standpoint, since they are going to have to do the job anyway, they may as well do it cheerfully, well, and promptly. Doing so can only help their own image and that of their subordinates and, most important, contribute to the accomplishment of the mission and the unit's reputation for efficiency. Officers are not leaders or even good followers if they do not live up to the ideals and traditional values taught during their precommissioning training. General Wilson is a firm believer in complying with the decisions of a senior.

If you have a responsibility in any field as a staff officer or as a commander and you are asked a question, you forcefully and articulately as possible give your position. As a result, if you are able to convince your commander, fine. If you are not and he makes a decision, you should be given one more chance to say, "I hope you realize these things, Sir, which I want to reemphasize," and if at that time he overrules you, it's your responsibility to say, "Aye, aye, Sir, you have my wholehearted support and cooperation in carrying it out." I'm not talking about morally indefensible things, which are practically nonexistent.

I think it certainly is not the mark of a good leader or the mark of a good student to wait too long to begin an assignment. Sometimes individuals say "Well, that's so far in the future, it won't happen on my watch. I'll be retired when that comes up. Why should I begin it now, even though I think it's a good idea." I'm reminded of the story of a commander who wanted to have trees planted near the parade ground, and his staff officer, a G-4, came in and said, "Well, General, we'll get around to those trees sometime, but they'll take twenty years to grow," and the commander very wisely said, "In that case, we'd better get started this afternoon." This applies not only to planting

trees, but to other things and other good ideas. Long-range planning is so important. What would have happened to our country if our forefathers had said, "Well, I think this taxation without representation is probably unfair, but who am I to jeopardize my life and my fortune and my sacred honor for such a foolish thing as that?"

Most of us have seen the movie or play "Mr. Roberts." Was he a good naval officer? He was certainly loved and revered by his subordinates! Should he be respected? We could conclude that the answer to both questions is no, since Roberts did not show or build loyalty toward his commanding officer. Nor did he indicate that he was enthusiastic and positive about carrying out his orders. He was not able to hide his disgust and lack of respect for the commanding officer. Lastly, except for his sacrifice for their liberty, he did not make the jobs or lives of his subordinates any easier. Maybe on his ship these things were impossible, but it is difficult to conclude that Jim Roberts even tried.

Admiral Hayward explains that

the Naval Service is a profession of such a wide variety of responsibilities and interests and technologies that there is almost no job that does not have more tasks and challenges in a day than there is time to do them. Generally speaking, if someone does not like his job, there is an underlying problem with the individual, and that needs to be addressed; it usually is not a question of whether the job is a good one or not.

Obviously, some jobs are much more demanding and more enjoyable than others, and an individual attains the better ones by performance. An individual must do well, because his success is based on how well he is accomplishing his job. His seniors will look at how well he performed before determining whether they throw him into the fire or the next tough job or a job that is less demanding. So the first responsibility is performance.

Regardless of what the job is, an officer can make it a challenge in almost every circumstance. There are jobs that do not follow the career objectives that the individual has. He might want to be an engineering officer very strongly, and if he does not get off to postgraduate school and get his degree and get into that segment, he is not meeting his career objective, and therefore other jobs will be less satisfying. That individual may even leave the service because he is pursuing the wrong track there. But, on balance, if someone wants to be a specialist in a given area, the Naval Service tries to get him there if he works hard enough at it. The individual who wants to be a generalist and strive for command positions, as do most naval officers, must perform well in what he is doing and he will end up in that exact position.

An officer should strive to let his detailer know what he wants, perform well enough so that the detailer will be responsive to his need, and keep working to stay in the track that he has established in his own mind. If he does not like the job, the first thing he should do is examine whether he is doing a good job of it. Next he should see if the cause of discontent is related to personality problems or leadership issues rather than to the quality of the job per se.

It is entirely possible not to like a job because of the kind of individual who is supervising. If the individual finds poor leadership and poor morale within his unit, he may want to join another outfit, one that is on the fast track. Or he can take it as a challenge instead of as an excuse. He can stick his shoulder to the grindstone and turn that situation around. That really is the challenge of the top-

notch leader. Someone with tremendous potential will get in there and fix the problem. Even if he is a junior in the system, he can generate a positive vantage and work on the problem areas.

In assessing a job, the individual must understand his own capabilities, look at the assignment with objectivity, and then make the most of the situation. Odds are that he will not have too many bad assignments with this attitude.

Naval leaders must exude confidence and enthusiasm and take seriously the phrase in their commissions which mentions special trust and confidence. They must attend to professional activities like mess nights, dining-ins, and dining-outs, and they must understand the customs, traditions, and history of the Navy and the Marine Corps. Naval leaders do all these things and much more because they could not stand the embarrassment of being thought of as less than professional. However, the statement of Rudolf Hess, the commander at Auschwitz who stated the following at Nuremburg, must be remembered so that our officers do not repeat such mistakes: "We were all so trained to obey orders without even thinking that the thought never occurred to us to disobey. Someone else would have done it anyway. You can be sure it wasn't always a pleasure to see those mountains of corpses and smell the continual burning, but Himmler ordered it and had explained its necessity. I never really gave much thought to whether it was wrong."[29-83] What we do must be morally right—if you are in doubt, discuss the matter with your senior and further up the chain of command if necessary.

In the same light, a military professional disdains those who procrastinate or do less than they are capable of doing. They demonstrate a good sense of timing, and because they know their own limitations and those of their people, they listen to advice from those above and below but take full responsibility for a decision, good or bad. If the outcome of a decision is bad, they must never pass the buck. When the outcome is good, they must always try to pass praise and commendation on. If they attain command, the reward for loyalty, moral courage, and smart performance, they must count their blessings and then work harder than anyone else in the unit.

MCPON Sanders: *The naval leader should comply with decisions, orders, and directives of seniors, and begin assignments as promptly as possible following receipt of them.*

19. Criticism and the Naval Officer

It is not possible for perfect officers to work for perfect leaders and lead perfect followers, because no one is perfect. For this reason, constructive criticism—the ability of one person in a naval hierarchy to improve the performance of another through objective, corrective comment—is a vital element of a leader's work. The ability to deliver criticism smoothly, to receive criticism with equanimity, and to elicit criticism where it would be helpful are leadership skills that must be cultivated.

General W. H. Rice points out that many successful naval officers consider seeking responsibility and taking responsibility to be a key of successful leadership. Young officers should not be afraid to take responsibility because they are afraid of making a mistake. Some young officers put off making a decision because they are afraid they will make the wrong decision. But it is far better that they do *something*, even if it is wrong, than do nothing. If their decision

is based on the facts as they know them at the time, if they have taken all this information and used their judgment and knowledge to make a decision, then their seniors will almost always back them up 100 percent.

This does not mean that officers should make a decision out of nowhere just to do something. They must address the facts before making a decision. But if they have done so and they still make a wrong decision, the seniors will likely support them. In addition, the officer who makes a mistake will learn from it and is unlikely to make the same mistake again. That is the value of experience. No one expects an ensign or a second lieutenant to have vast experience, so ensigns and second lieutenants will very often make mistakes. But their seniors will back them up, because their seniors recognize that the only way young officers can gain experience is to be allowed to take responsibility and make decisions.

Seniors get to be seniors not because they're nice guys, but because they were selected to the rank they hold through a conscientious program. They have been selected by a senior board of officers who have the experience and the knowledge to choose tactically and technically proficient people. A staff officer's responsibility is to use his judgment and his experience to provide advice to the senior officer. But once the decision is made, the staff officer's position is to do his part to execute it. Seniors will listen to subordinates who are known for having common sense and good judgment, but seniors look at problems from a different perspective. Seniors look at a larger picture than young officers are able to look at, so young officers cannot expect the senior to accept their recommendations every time. When they have the time, seniors should explain their rationale for their decision, for these explanations are part of the education and experience that young officers need to gain.

ACCEPTING CONSTRUCTIVE CRITICISM FROM ABOVE

Everyone in the Naval Service has a boss—bosses, in fact. Bosses can be expected to have more experience and broader responsibilities than those who work for them. Critical comments passed down the chain of command to the individual officer and leader are the mechanism by which leaders both exercise their responsibility and try to help their subordinates past rough spots.

An officer must pay attention to what the boss tells him. He must pay attention, even if the comments are phrased in the nicest way, are barely critical, or are only slightly corrective. A pleasant civility in delivering course corrections is often displayed by senior naval officers (and this approach is worthy of imitation by their juniors), but course corrections they are, nonetheless, and the boss certainly will note and correct a failure to respond to what he intended to be critical comment.

An officer must pay attention, even if criticism from above is a constant diet. Some commanding officers are screamers, some are nit-pickers, some occasionally attempt to revisit scenes of former glory by doing a junior's job (a junior will get a lot of help from these types). But that does not change either the junior's relationship with his seniors or his responsibility to respond to their comments. An officer should stay tuned to the leader who talks softly, and not tune out the one who talks incessantly.

Finally, an officer should not rely solely on his report of fitness for a clear picture of how he is doing and where he needs to improve. Far more useful than the fitness report itself is the chat that goes with it. An officer should ask his boss how he is doing and what areas he should

concentrate on—and he should be responsive to the answers.

OFFERING CONSTRUCTIVE CRITICISM TO SUBORDINATES

Setting standards is an integral part of the naval leader's job. Standards of readiness, standards of appearance, standards of training, standards of safety—standards, standards, standards. And having established how things should be, the leader must use courage, forehandedness, and zeal in holding the high line. That means effectively passing critical corrections to subordinates.

Having passed them, an officer must make them stick. It takes tenacity and patience to lead most people. The young officer must understand that there are subordinates who have neither the ability nor the dedication to perform as directed, and this can lead to frustration in attempting to effect change through criticism. One of the characteristics of the poor listener is that he is usually a good bluffer. Seldom willing to admit that he hasn't listened, he will fake understanding and take a chance—often with disastrous consequences.[6-50] An officer can impose great pressure on a subordinate, but the young leader must keep in mind that it is the outcome that is important, and so his actions should be aimed at achieving the goal, not just exercising authority.

Effectively criticizing junior enlisted personnel is by no means as challenging as delivering criticism to his chief by a young division officer or to his staff NCO by a platoon commander. Chiefs and staff NCOs are easy people to be afraid of, and even if that dimension is not present, a young officer often thinks that criticizing the chief or staff NCO is presumptuous. Nonsense. The chief is pleased to have the help of a young officer. If there is something he needs to be told, then the junior should tell him.

In all this, courage, confidence, a strong sense of responsibility, and a keen awareness of the sensitivity of all persons to criticism is absolutely necessary. In short, an officer should set standards, monitor performance, and—through effective leadership, including critical comment—make the right things happen.

Performance counseling. Corrective criticism usually means fixing problems on a case-by-case basis. Beyond this, however, a leader is responsible for regularly reviewing the performance of individuals.

Sometimes in the Naval Service a career enlisted person or officer falls short of being the best performer he can be. The sailor or Marine has talent and seems motivated but does not seem to be able to "get it together." The good leader will do his best to improve this person's contribution, but it is a frustrating task, often causing the leader to wish he had had a good shot at this sailor or Marine in his formative years.

The fact is that many below-par performers continue to be promoted, yet they remain ignorant of the fact that their performance is not (and may never have been) up to snuff. They were not monitored, counseled, and steered properly early in their careers. Their leaders were too busy or too uncaring or too uncourageous to hold up their end of the leadership burden and regularly review performance. *Regularly* means *as necessary*, but, at a minimum, at least monthly.

Performance review may be very challenging for a leader and, frankly, it takes guts to do it right. Some followers may prove to be impossible to help, but most respond to guidance. Many of the prospective "unfixables" will respond to early, fair, and firm counseling. The sound leader will regularly review the performance of the individuals in his charge and take action to make these individuals as capable and competent as they can be.

ACCEPTING AND OFFERING CONSTRUCTIVE CRITICISM UP THE CHAIN OF COMMAND

Admiral Uchida notes that,

in principle, an officer should welcome any suggestion made in the spirit of good

will and honesty. By so doing, the officer will foster better cooperation and submission, thus enhancing his corps' morale.

There will, however, be occasions when he cannot adopt those suggestions, for various reasons that are difficult to make public. An apologetic attitude harms the officer's dignity and authority, so he should be straightforward at all times.

It is best if others, by observing the officer's daily work, come to believe that he is always the superb decision maker whom everyone can fully trust.

The wise leader quietly solicits comments from the subordinates whose opinion he values and also regularly samples the organization to obtain knowledge of what the troops are saying and doing and worrying about. A certain openness to criticism from below can be very helpful here; the inputs serve both as valuable corrective comments and as a measurement of how well or how poorly various policies are understood. All too often the word passed from above either never gets to the nonrated personnel or has been significantly altered on the way down the chain of command. General Barrow points out that,

when a junior officer speaks forthrightly and confidently, his seniors will almost always consider his suggestions. The junior who is taking part in a discussion and sees that a decision is about to be made can usually find the right moment to say, "May I make a suggestion, Sir?" Then he must convey his confidence in his ideas by speaking effectively.

The officer can also put his suggestions in writing. Seniors are more likely to spend time considering ideas that are expressed in readable and persuasive prose. Even if the senior officer does not implement the junior's idea, he will make a note of how effectively he presented it. In addition, the junior who writes his ideas down has a record of them and thus can pass them on to others.

To make sure these nuggets passed up from the troops are useful, the leader must do two things. First, he needs to accept that the comments may have a low validity factor. That's OK. If the problem is one of misperception in the ranks rather than less-than-perfect leadership above, the inputs from below can serve as valuable intelligence on how well the message is being transmitted and received. Second, he must maintain an even composure as the comments come in, at least to the extent of keeping the conduit open. It takes courage to tell the boss he is mistaken; close that conduit once and it is closed forever.

Admiral McDonald, wanting to emphasize that it is appropriate for an officer to speak up, gave this example.

> In later years, but long before I'd become CNO, a flag officer I was working for said to me: I will probably seldom ask you for your advice, but if I do, I want to know what you are thinking not what you think I'd like for you to think. Subsequently, as a commander, I was attending a conference of high-ranking officers, one of whom (not the one mentioned above) I was working for. Many views were being expressed on the subject at hand and not all were in agreement. Ultimately the vice admiral who was chairing the meeting asked for my views. I expressed them, rather vociferously and in direct opposition to the previously expressed views of the vice admiral. Following the meeting, the flag officer for whom I was working chided me a bit and said I shouldn't have talked to the vice admiral the way I did. Shortly thereafter I left my job and went out to the Pacific as air officer and later executive officer of the *Essex*. Upon being detached some time later (after I had been selected to captain), I was advised that I was being sent to Ford Island on the staff of the vice admiral to whom I

had talked so rudely, and at his specific request.

The young officer should also be prepared to make appropriate critical comments to his seniors. Tactfully, sensitively, but courageously, the junior officer in a command relationship owes the senior his best judgment, opinion, and advice. Indeed, in certain situations, a principal responsibility for the junior is careful second judgment. Executive officers have this relationship with their commanding officers. Division officers do well to see that their department heads get their best advice, and platoon commanders should do the same for their company commanders. A simple fact in the Naval Service is that "good followers give their best judgment to their leaders—and good leaders listen." However, it must be remembered that there is such a thing as subordinate power and authority, which is the ability to make decisions based on one's own thoughts, which may or may not be in favor of the senior. An excellent example is when General Theodore Roosevelt, Jr., discovered his troops had been landed on the wrong beach on 6 June 1944, D-Day, World War II. There was little opposition, but the only way they could move inland was by a narrow road cutting through swampy ground. If the enemy attacked while his soldiers were on this road, the result would be disastrous. On the other hand, if he waited until a faraway superior told him what to do, it might be too late. "We'll start fighting the war right here," Roosevelt told his subordinates. His divisions moved forward, and their success contributed tremendously to the Allied cause. Had Roosevelt been a weaker man, a tremendous opportunity for victory would have been lost.[63-9]

DESTRUCTIVE CRITICISM

Officers of the Naval Service, even ensigns and second lieutenants, occupy powerful positions. Irresponsible criticism from a unit's officers can destroy unit integrity and the effectiveness of the individuals in the unit. The conscientious young officer will dampen ward-room "bitch sessions" wherein the Navy or the Marine Corps, the command, or the command-ing officer are being harshly criticized, and he will attempt to stifle a mean putdown of a fellow officer or an enlisted person of the command.

To be useful, criticism must be pointed some-where, toward some corrective improvement. Constant, idle complaint is a pernicious habit that an occasional wardroom will inflict on itself. Kill it in the crib. Kill also the urge to hammer some poor sailor or Marine in public. Matters of safety and primary operational urgency require immediate corrective action by a leader, but most times and most circumstances permit operation of the classic rule "Praise in public, censure in private." Unless it is your purpose to destroy forever the effectiveness of the person you are correcting, regard the rule as sacred.

SUCCESS THROUGH COOPERATION

Admiral Burke described how he learned that success is most often achieved through cooper-ation.

I was very fortunate, because I entered the Naval Academy completely unpre-pared, as I only went two years to high school. When I got into the Naval Acad-emy there were a lot of little things that I should have known that I didn't, so I stood way down in the bottom of the class, and I had a rough time, barely mak-ing it. Well, I got through because class-mates helped me. They would spend the time on me in teaching me things that I should have known, and everyone helped me, including professors sometimes. I learned that no man can do very much by himself, that a man does a job and 90 per-cent of what he's credited for doing is done by someone else. It's either done before him or after him.

Now this happened over and over again, everyone knows it's true, but it

takes a long time to realize that any job that is done, is done by a group of people, so you've got to be careful not to think that an individual by himself is all that good. A lot of it is, you happen to have a good chief boatswain's mate, you happen to have a good vice chief, you happen to have a well-trained crew that you inher-ited from someone else, or you happen to have a kid with bright eyes who could see very well and he saw something that no one else could see and reported it.

I was on many boards when I retired from the Navy, and one time I objected to a movement of a plant in England of one of the companies I was with. I objected because I didn't know enough about it. Well, I didn't know enough to say no, but I put in my reservations just the same. They went ahead and moved the plant from the outskirts of London up to the east coast of England. They spent a lot of money, they had to build a plant up there. About a year after they got the plant built, people wouldn't move. Since I had objected, they asked if I would mind going over to England and taking a look, so I went over and talked to a few people. In two days I found out what was wrong. What they hadn't considered was that the British people don't move. They liked their job where they had it, and they wanted to live there. Their grandfathers lived there, and they were not going to move up the east coast. So they had to get new people.

This new young fellow who had put this superior plan in was a brilliant man, but I called up and said, "I've made the deci-sion. You've got to fire this young fellow and get him out of here because he can't run things, no matter how good he is technically, he can't run it because he doesn't know people. You've got to call that old guy back who is retired for age and get him to come back." Well, he came back on a contract for two years at the same salary that he had before, but the important thing is that at the end of two years he would retire. If he had made a success, he would get a big sum of money, I think a half-million dollars or something like that. If he didn't make a success, he didn't get anything more than his pay. The company jumped at that, and of course he made a success. This whole thing hinged on a very minor thing: they had forgotten that they weren't dealing with Americans in the moving thing.

MCPON Sanders: *It is recognized that it may be difficult for a junior officer not to show resentment when a senior enlisted is making a suggestion about a plan that the officer had put together. While they may not speak from the same educational view as the officer, senior enlisted do speak from experience, and sometimes the experience is a little bit better than the book learning the officer has received. While you don't have to follow the suggestions, do listen to them, and at least recognize that the suggestions and comments were given in good faith, and weren't made to make fun or put down your thoughts and ideas.*

20. Moral Responsibility and the Naval Officer

> *"God grant that men of principle shall be our principal men."*
> Thomas Jefferson

A naval officer is morally responsible for all aspects of what happens to his unit. The basis of this principle of naval leadership is codified in Article 0702.1 of Navy Regulations, 1973, which provides that: "The responsibility of the commanding officer for his command is absolute, except

when and to the extent, relieved therefrom by competent authority." This rule of absolute responsibility, and its corollaries of authority and accountability, have been the foundation of operational efficiency and effectiveness throughout the history of the Naval Service.

Today's officer must also be aware of the moral, financial, and cultural dilemmas faced by his personnel. He is morally responsible for their welfare. All commanding officers and others in authority in the Naval Service are required to show in themselves a good example of virtue, honor, patriotism, and subordination: to be vigilant in inspecting the conduct of all persons who are placed under their command; to guard against and suppress all dissolute and immoral practices, and to correct, according to the laws and regulations of the Navy, all persons who are guilty of them; and to take all necessary and proper measures, under the laws, regulations, and customs of the Naval Service, to promote and safeguard the morale, the physical well-being, and the general welfare of the officers and enlisted persons under their command or charge.[49-58]

According to General Montgomery, "the four cardinal virtues" provide a good guide for moral responsibility and leadership. These are:

1. *Prudence.* Refer all matters to divine guidance. Outcomes are impartiality, wisdom, and tact.
2. *Justice.* Give everyone their due. Outcomes are religion, obedience, gratitude, integrity, and good will.
3. *Temperance.* Pursue self-control for the highest development of human nature and for personal and social needs. Outcomes are purity, humility, and patience.
4. *Fortitude.* Follow the spirit that resists, endures, and triumphs over temptations of life. Outcomes are courage, industry, and self-discipline.[Chap. 1:41-13]

Absolute responsibility is imposed upon a commander by positive force of law in the form of a written regulation, but the scope of command responsibility is based upon more than just codified legal principles. A commission as a naval officer should not be viewed as simply a contract of employment between a person and the U.S. government which creates only legal obligations on the part of the individual in return for monetary compensation. More importantly, the oath of acceptance of a commission as a naval officer must be viewed as a pledge to contribute to the common good of our society as a way of life, making the commitment both legal and, to a much greater extent, moral. The rewards for moral commitment are not necessarily tangible. Officers of the Navy and the Marine Corps, having traditionally sought positions of high trust and confidence in the service of their country, often find that the greatest reward is the personal satisfaction of command. Along with the authority and perquisites of command go the responsibilities of leadership.

Conscience

Responsibility has been defined as the state of being answerable for an obligation, fulfillment of which is dependent upon an individual's judgment, skill, ability, and capacity. While legal responsibilities are imposed by law or contract, moral responsibilities are recognized and enforceable by an individual's conscience. The conscience can be thought of as the ethical layer of the human personality, which provides people with inherent values about the difference between right and wrong. Like other facets of human character, the conscience is influenced and developed by many sources: family, religion, education, standards of the community, and the ethics of the Naval Service and the nation. An individual assumes moral responsibilities because of the compulsion of conscience, not because of possible legal retribution. For example, you may see a person drowning in a lake. Although you may have no legal responsibility or duty to save that person, you have a moral obligation to render assistance, because the society in which you live has placed a high value on human life. In attempting to help such a person you have assumed a responsibility demanded by society, while failing to act would be a refusal to accept such responsibility.

Service as a naval officer is a noble profession that demands many virtues: unselfishness, a sense of duty, honesty, courage, obedience, loyalty, and integrity. While society demands many of these attributes from all people, every one of them is critical in a military context, for, without them, a unit could not operate. An officer who is driven by these underlying values cannot help but do the "right" thing, despite the fact that another course of action might be easier or less dangerous to career aspirations.

It is often necessary for naval officers to address moral considerations in the conduct of their duties. In particular, they must always be concerned about the moral welfare of their personnel. If naval officers were to adopt solely a contractual view of their responsibilities as commanders, they might find it relatively easy to attempt to divorce their military functions from moral considerations. War could be thought of and conducted as a business. Since the primary tasks facing a military leader are the development of strategy, tactics, and weapons systems which will efficiently destroy real and potential enemies, the body count becomes the bottom line. The theory is similar to the adoption of a contractual view in the teaching profession. This concept sees the role of the teacher as a transmitter of purely objective knowledge, packaged and distributed; here, the grade point average is the bottom line. Neither approach accepts responsibility for forming the character of the people being led, and there is no predicting the uses to which their weapons or knowledge may be employed. This is a chilling thought in an era of genetic research and chemical weapons. Leadership is not an impersonal, value-free operation. Approaches that ignore the critical moral aspect of leadership must be viewed as incomplete.[64]

MORAL COURAGE

Failure to act in our example involving the drowning person, although not punishable criminally, may indicate the lack of an element that is inherent in moral commitment and assumption of responsibility. This element is moral courage. Without moral courage (as distinguished from physical courage), the officer's ability to lead others is impaired. An officer must possess moral standards in both thought and action, which includes speaking out when he believes he is right. Firmly adhering to a code of moral values is the basis for integrity, which is essential to strong leadership.

Training for the armed services places an emphasis on readiness to accept responsibility, because leaders must learn the meaning of moral courage early in their careers. If officers fail to learn this when they are young, they will not be prepared for the heavy responsibilities of high command, where great moral courage is demanded in a variety of situations. One moral situation that a commander may be confronted with was described by Vice Admiral William P. Mack in his retirement speech, delivered upon completion of his duty as the 47th Superintendent of the U.S. Naval Academy:

> As I complete 42 years of service, I would like to leave to the Brigade of Midshipmen a legacy of one idea which represents the distillation of that experience: The one concept which dominates my mind is that of the necessity of listening to and protecting the existence of the "Dissenter"—the person who does not necessarily agree with his commander, or with popularly held opinion, or with *you*. Unfortunately, history is full of examples: then-Commander Mahan, whose novel ideas of seapower fell on barren ground; then-Commander Sims, whose revolutionary (but correct) ideas on naval gunnery ran counter to those of his seniors; then-Commander Rickover, who fought a lonely battle for nuclear power. All eventually succeeded, but *not* with the help of patient, understanding officers. Regretfully, each needed help from outside the uniformed Navy. We cannot afford this way of life in the government or in the Navy in the future, for the intervals given us for discussion and decision will be increasingly shorter. You may ask: What can you, as a midshipman or junior officer, do about this? My answer is that time will go by for you, as a busy naval officer, very rapidly. Before you realize it, in a decade *you* will be the young commander called upon to give your honest (and, perhaps, dissenting) opinion. In another few years, you will be the senior officer charged with preserving and using the dissenting opinion of another.
>
> The point is: To begin at this early age to cultivate an open mind, to determine to hear all arguments and opinions, no matter how extreme they may seem; and, above all, to preserve and protect those who voice them.

In the daily life of the junior officer, small acts of moral courage are constantly demanded in the administration of justice, in making decisions, which, though known to be right, will probably prove unpopular, and in the acceptance of responsibility, particularly when things have gone wrong. Every time an officer turns a blind eye to a situation or behavior that he knows to be wrong, such as a minor breach of discipline, the officer is in fact refusing to accept the responsibility of his office and is exhibiting a lack of moral courage. A succession of even minor failures may strike at the roots of an officer's personal integrity, and destroy his ability to lead.

An example of a succession of moral failures which led to disaster is the West Point cheating scandal of the mid-1970s. One hundred and fifty-two cadets were dismissed or resigned after plagiarizing on a take-home exam. An internal investigation found that entire companies had gone "cool on honor," in part because they felt that the academy's honor code had become trivialized by being used as a tool to enforce petty regulations. Instead of working within the system to effect changes in regulations that they believed to be unfair or unneeded, the cadets took what appeared to be the easy way out: they disregarded rules they did not like. Classmates tacitly agreed among themselves to ignore the honor code, and the resultant spiral of disobedience led to disaster.

Integrity no doubt comes more easily to some people, and some are more prone than others to live up to the standards they know to be right. Yet integrity is vital to the leader, and the lack of it will be detected quickly in a person in a position of leadership. Naval officers should never forget that they often command young and impressionable people who, even if they are older than or close to the same age as their officers, look to them for guidance. Every act of moral courage is in fact a victory over one's self and provides an example for others to emulate. On the other hand, to give way to one's innate fears or selfishness is to place one's self in danger of developing moral cowardice. Officers who are unwilling to make the effort themselves have no right to demand it of others.[56-49]

With respect to the officer being a member of a profession that at times may be required to prevail over an enemy, Admiral Zumwalt believes that

> the mission of the armed services is best described as being so ready to kill that they won't have to kill, to be so ready to win that they won't be attacked. It seems to me, after all, that the fundamental responsibility of a democratic nation is to have armed forces of sufficient strength that those, in tandem with an enlightened foreign policy, can produce peace on the terms that are reasonable for our democratic way of life.

Admiral Holloway says that

> an officer is responsible in a moral sense

to what happens to his unit insofar as he has control. As an example, assume a platoon is in a blocking action to permit the withdrawal of the battalion. The platoon could very well take heavy casualties under such a circumstance; in fact, the leader could lose the entire unit. The leader cannot be held morally responsible for the losses unless through a lack of judgment or professional skill he failed to employ his platoon in the best possible way to carry out the mission, or unless he attempted, after making contact with the enemy, to withdraw. Those are the only circumstances under which he could be held responsible, because he had control of that, but the fact that he was put in a blocking position, was left behind as the rear guard, was beyond his control. The moral responsibilities of that could go all the way to the President who declared the war in which he was fighting.

Moral responsibility is difficult to define and regulate because it depends on what a person is made of. No amount of thought, desire, education, or experience will make an officer fit to assume command and exercise moral leadership unless they are accompanied by a conscious, unremitting effort at self-control and self-improvement. Moral responsibility is active, not passive. It is more than just not doing bad things. It is an ongoing process of personal struggle against weakness, expedience, and self-doubt, and its rewards are strength of character, resolution, and confidence.[49-61] Admiral Hunt believes that

> there is a very clear need for a military officer to have an understanding of fundamental principles. Perhaps I could give an example. It may be in certain types of warfare that there is a temptation for an officer to use force on some other person, for example, torture, which would normally be of horror to him. For example, if somebody is picked up in the street and you know that he has vital information,

there is very often strong motivation, especially in the heat of warfare and battle, to get that information out of him by one means or another or to tell somebody else to make sure he gets the answer. Unless you think about these problems in advance, the chances are that that's what you'll do. So I think that a military officer must have a very clear idea of what is right and wrong before he's faced with these problems, and then when he comes to these problems he doesn't step down the wrong line. I would never ever allow anyone in my organization to break the moral code in that sense, I would never give instructions to do that, and I'd never do it myself—at least that is my view. When faced with a particular problem I can understand that, in the heat of the moment, people might look in a different direction, but I think that would be absolutely wrong.

ACCEPTING MORAL RESPONSIBILITY

The commander's responsibility for his command is absolute. Admiral Nakamura observes that an officer is morally responsible for what happens to his unit. He must he held accountable for its safety, well-being, and efficiency, both legally and morally. Every day tests the strength of character, judgment, and professional abilities of those in command. In some cases, commanders will be called upon to answer for their legal responsibilities in a court of law. Virtually every day, however, officers in the Naval Service will be answerable for their moral responsibilities to their unit. A naval officer should want it no other way, for the richest reward of command is the satisfaction of having measured up to these highest of standards.

In view of the experiences of civilization just before and during World War II, the words of Admiral Clausen are particularly meaningful:

Responsibility, in a very short explanation, is the necessity or the obligation to give an answer for one's own activities or those of others. In order to undertake responsibility, a naval officer needs human and technical qualifications and competence in the task conferred on him, which include knowledge and experience. For a commanding officer, the responsibility is comprehensive, indivisible, not transferrable, and continuous.

In a difficult situation or during a war, the holder of responsibility comes very often into conflicts, and he has to decide between different duties. To deal with all aspects there are powers given to the holder of responsibility written in the law and in instructions, orders, regulations, etc. By this means he can carry out his task of leadership.

Although this is certainly correct, I do have some additional views from my own experiences.

1. I do not think that the holder of responsibility should cling only to regulations and paper work. Responsibility must go into very abstract places: into the human conscience, into the character, into the mentality, into the holder's power of comprehension. [Editor's note: Traits that lessen an officer's ability properly to care for the welfare of his personnel are self-interest and extremes in professional dedication, which lead to "mindless commitment."][10-35]

2. Responsibility needs the mutual confidence between the leader and the subordinates. This correlation of authority and confidence is especially indispensable during a war or during a difficult situation.

3. Subordinates are not human beings who can be programmed and disposed of in an automatic way. Subordinates have a body *and* soul. That implies that each subordinate who has to carry out a task must be guided to think or, better, to think under consideration of all necessary

contingencies, so that he is in genuine connection with his leading officer and the task.

These three additional views make it clear that naval officers must be able to cope with a reality that is never as chemically clean as simulated by theory. Therefore, an inadequately or overly intellectual naval officer will be hindered when he has to act as leader of personnel on board ship. In the profession of a naval officer, very many circumstances (especially by development of technique) have changed and shall change in the future, but the qualifications that are required of the leader will not differ from those that have been valid for centuries.

HONOR

Admiral Clausen discussed honor in the context of moral responsibility:

The word *honor* became, after the war in Germany, in connection with the profession of an officer, discredited. To be outspoken, I never understood exactly what people meant. Obviously they did not want officers to have or own a "special honor" in the same way that they did not like to have the maintenance or cultivation of the idea of an "elite." Now, I think it is not as simple as the ideas behind these words as treated by the public, because these ideas make an enormously high demand that most members of the public would not be willing to meet. A wrong sense of honor is, of course, detrimental to the officer's profession and would be disastrous.

As the honor of profession imposes the highest commitment/liability/obligation on an officer, and futhermore his profession requires him to observe a number of virtues, it seems to me no surprise that a naval officer needs in a well-meant sense a conception of honor that is based on the interest of his profession. A naval officer has a very special job that can't be compared, for instance, with a baker's job. That does not mean that a baker should be respected less.

As the Naval Service becomes increasingly more dependent on technology, its officers may well be increasingly tempted to judge success in terms of systems efficiency—the managerial position—rather than in terms of personal values. No doubt these criteria are vitally important within the context of any complex organization, but the danger arises when the system is emphasized at the expense of the men and women who make it work. [49-58]

Admiral Clausen continued by opining that to serve the country must be an honor. I cannot imagine an officer without this interpretation. An officer will be entitled to this concept of honor only if he is educated accordingly and is willing to follow the virtues prescribed to his profession: to serve faithfully; to exercise loyalty, uprightness, veracity, bravery, sense of duty, discretion, comradeship; to perform carefully all duties, especially where subordinates are concerned, etc. These virtues can be learned in theory. That is not of sufficient use. The concrete application of these virtues in practice is of decisive significance. Therefore, an officer must be observed during his career carefully and criticized in permanent reports with regard to his character, his personality, and his conduct. When this is done seriously, then the result will be expressed in bearing and reputation of the whole community of officers, and I am convinced there will be no difficulty in attaching the word *honor* to the right place.

MCPON Sanders: *The officer is morally responsible for all aspects of everything that happens to his command.*

21. Responsibility and the Naval Officer

One of the differences between leaders and those who follow is the propensity on the part of the former to seek out situations in which they can contribute and take charge as necessary, as well as their willingness to accept responsibility if something goes wrong. In addition to seeking out opportunities in which their experience can be brought to bear in directing the actions of others, officers are expected immediately to accept responsibility for carrying out any assignment made by their seniors. To Admiral Itaya, responsibility is

> our most important asset. A man without responsibility does not have the character to be a member of the organization. Such a person is a detriment to the unit and of no value. During a shelling in World War II, what kept me going was my sense of responsibility. One could say that responsibility was my spiritual savior. One of my superiors told me, "It is not necessary to be ashamed of being afraid. But, be ashamed of acts of military cowardice. One can do nothing more than devote one's self to fulfilling his responsibility."

Admiral de Cazanove believes that

> an officer shows he is responsible by, first, searching for responsibilities. The worst thing for an officer to do is spend his time in the service without seeking out additional responsibilities. If you are going to be an officer, then you should work at being a leader, and sneaking around trying not to be in trouble is not the way to be a leader. In addition, you must develop this desire for increased responsibility in your subordinates. The more responsibility you give to others, the better it will be for the job, and you will grow by the very act of thinking about and assigning responsibilities to others. In

other words, you will increase your own capabilities and ability to take on additional responsibilities by learning how to maximize the use of everyone in the organization. Of course, you must always accept the responsibility for everything that takes place in your unit, and, when passing out directions, you should take the responsibility for giving the directions and not say that the troops have to do something because someone else made the decision that something had to be done. You must act as if it was your own personal idea and not the idea of the boss. This is an intellectual necessity.

The size of armed forces makes it impossible for any one individual, no matter how talented, to wage and win a battle alone, and thus it falls on the team, made up of subordinates and their leaders, to put forth a maximum effort to prevail in battle. Of all the responsibilities of a junior officer, mission accomplishment is and must always be the highest priority.[70-45] While individuals are not born with the desire to excel and to meet the requirements handed down by their seniors, this desire can be learned, and it is the responsibility of the senior to train and educate subordinates in such a way that they will want to do all that is requested of them as well as take initiative when and where necessary to ensure that the overall objectives laid down by their leader are met.

General Rice described the best attitude for an officer to develop regarding his responsibilities:

> As an individual advances in any organization, his risks get higher, partly because his subordinates increase in number. An officer gets paid for taking responsibility, and the higher in rank he goes, the more responsibility he will have. He should never shirk from taking responsibility, even though in every officer's career there may be some very unpleasant duties.

This is not to say an officer is expected to volunteer for unpleasant duty, but if he is given an unpleasant assignment, he will, if he is a true professional, get on with it. He will not moan or complain about what he has to do; rather, he will do it better than anyone ever expected it to be done. This is what marks that officer as a true professional, and marks him by his seniors as an individual who has a future, who will not shirk responsibility. This officer will have self-satisfaction, and very likely his senior officers will congratulate him on the job he did. This, of course, is a hallmark of good leadership: telling people they have done a good job as freely as telling them they have done something wrong.

Volunteering

While only a few people learn in school to volunteer information and their services, officers are expected to keep themselves apprised of the needs of their seniors, subordinates, and peers and to offer to help them in any way. Those in the Naval Service are a part of a team in which no member or unit can consider itself successful unless the next higher or adjacent member or unit is also enjoying success. One of General Patton's fundamental principles of leadership was that your men always serve with you, not under you.[70-9] Officers are evaluated by the enthusiasm they show to seniors in making themselves a part of the overall organization. According to General Patton, the most important thing to keep in mind in picking the right leader is to base the decision on ability, not friendship.[70-50] "School days" may have put the stigma of "apple polishing" on anyone who appeared to show an above-average interest in studies, but the officer will soon find that when he diplomatically offers to help, and keeps his offer low key, his senior will gratefully accept the offered aid.

Admiral Moorer observes that,

in the Navy, the ultimate assignment is one of command, whether of a fifty-foot minesweeper or a ninety-thousand-ton aircraft carrier. An officer who is seeking command indicates by his actions that he is willing and eager to accept responsibility. Once he takes command, of course, there is no question about who is responsible.

In a staff situation, responsibility for, say, an operation is more diffuse, but in the final analysis the commander is responsible. The commander, in turn, of course, is watching all the people who are working for him on the same basic problem.

In the Naval Service there are many opportunities to seek and acquire responsibility, and the young person who is eager and willing to accept responsibility will find that his service reputation reflects his attitude. During the war, for example, certain pilots would volunteer for night raids because they liked the idea of being in charge, even though it may have been of only two or three aircraft. And these pilots developed a fine reputation.

Officers should constantly try to improve their professional knowledge and capability, and thus an officer is rewarded for volunteered effort with an increase in his knowledge, which in turn means that others will select him for assignments that require the knowledge and understanding he has accumulated. The additional understanding gained by a junior officer through his volunteered efforts is likely to be rewarded by even more jobs. Thus, the enthusiastic professional officer who seeks out responsibility will find that he is just the kind of person his seniors like to have around, and that when "good" assignments and opportunities to represent the command come up, he will be selected, because his senior knows that this individual's actions will reflect favorably, not only on himself, but also on the senior who selected him.

THE DYNAMIC OFFICER

General Barrow states that

> everyone has known someone who can be a good leader for a specific occasion, to meet a specific requirement, or at a specific time, but before the event started and when the event is over, he is asleep on the bench. That is his style: He does a great job when he is called on to do it, but only then. This individual has narrowed his capability.

> An officer who is a complete officer— not one who sleeps most of the time while waiting for a call to duty—is dynamic. He seeks out responsibility by using his imagination to find things to do beyond the requirements of his assignment. Very few orders limit the officer's search for responsibility by saying "Do this and nothing more."

General Barrow described a dynamic officer:

> Don't be willing to say, "Well, I've read all the orders, and it looks like all I have to do is make sure the place is opened up at eight o'clock and everything is secure and no classified material is on the desk and all the parking lots have been cleared out at seventeen hundred." If you want to be that kind of person, fine, but you won't get anywhere. I'm surprised you even got in in the first place. I think that whatever you've been told your job is, whatever you know it to have been historically, traditionally, or whatever your orders say, implicit in that is one enormous array of unstated things that you can seek out to do. Some of them will come to you by suggestions from subordinates moving about and listening.

> There is just no end to things a dynamic officer wants to do. This often draws a distinction between a mediocre officer and an outstanding one. The compliments that the dynamic officer often gets paid by a senior are along the lines of: "Boy, he's something else. That guy not only does everything he's supposed to do, but he can always find some things that need to be done and does them so well." The only limit is you cannot intrude on others or overburden your subordinates to the extent that all you're doing is making yourself look good at their expense.

If you are comfortable in being a commander, if you are comfortable in being a leader, you should be willing to bare your soul. Say "I believe in this, this, and this, and I don't believe in that." As regimental commander, you gather the staff and maybe the battalion commanders, if they are around, and often at night, when you are involved in combat in the field, you just talk and you get messages across, such as the necessity to seek out responsibility. You convey those kind of messages which you would not put in an order. You wouldn't say, "I expect every man in this command to seek out responsibilities," but you can encourage it to by speaking to the subject, and you set the example sometimes. They say, "The colonel seems to think things need to be done, and nobody else did them, so maybe I ought to go look for some things that need to be done." You reward those who do with praise, which encourages others to say, "The colonel paid Sam a compliment about doing this thing that needed to be done. Maybe I ought to go look for some of those things."

An officer can quite easily avoid additional assignments: by not being around much, by looking at the floor when a senior is asking for help, by making "a big deal" of all the work he has to do. Leaders rarely have time to cajole people to take assignments, and they find it discouraging to ask someone to do something and have that person turn them down. So the officer who wants to establish the reputation of not being available and of not wanting to do extra work will have no trouble.

Good officers do not want to make mistakes, and when someone helps them learn from a mistake, they are grateful. In the long run, they will feel pride in themselves for compensating for an error. As the commander of a destroyer, Admiral Carney helped one young officer learn responsibility.

> I required each of my officers to maintain a journal. I had one young officer brighter than hell and lazier than hell, and he got way behind on his work, so I told him he was restricted on board until it was up to date, and he said to me that he would have his journal ready by Saturday. I said, "Unfortunately, that won't be useful as far as you're concerned because I won't be here Saturday, so you can have the weekend aboard ship." So I came back Monday, and I was in the Army-Navy Club talking to the clerk at the desk. There was a gentleman standing beside me, he turned around to me and he said, "Are you the skipper of the *Reed*?" I said, "Well, yes, Sir, I am." He said, "Then you're the one who put my son under hack for three weeks." Well, I thought, what's this old guy trying to do, trying to tell me how to run my ship? I got the hair up on the back of my neck right away and I said, "Yep. He didn't measure up to my requirements and I wouldn't turn him loose until he did." He said, "Well, thank God somebody took hold of that brat."

In a basketball game, suppose one player always hangs back near his own basket. His fellow players will exclude him from most actions because they have learned he is not dependable, and the coach will soon thereafter remove him from the game. A reference to sports with respect to offi-

cers doing their duty is made several times in this volume, and this is one appropriate point to remark that officers are team players who not only seek out responsibility, but also eagerly accept responsibility when it is offered by their seniors, or even when they are asked to do so by peers and subordinates. Accepting responsibility is another way officers can earn psychic income, the amount of which is limited only by the desire of and the time available to the officer who looks for ways to contribute to his organization.

DEVELOPING A SENSE OF RESPONSIBILITY IN SUBORDINATES

An officer can develop a sense of responsibility among subordinates in a variety of ways, but the most effective method is for the officer to demonstrate by example that seeking out and accepting responsibility is the way to succeed. For example, when an officer receives an assignment from his senior, he can show his pleasure in the assignment to his troops; they, then, will know the proper attitude to take when they are given a chance to contribute. The officer who acts enthused and quickly gets started on his work sets a tone that will filter down quickly to the rest of the organization. The officer who volunteers himself and his unit to help with the overall mission also sends a message to subordinates that the right way to play the game is "One for all and all for one." While it is certainly not necessary to reward every voluntary action with a three-day pass, a few words or a short note to the individual who has excelled in an assignment beyond his normal duties will build a sense of loyalty in the individual which will last for a very long time. General Rice believes that

> it is bad practice for a junior officer to dodge responsibility. There are opportunities for a young officer to take responsibility, and he should not wait for someone to ask for a volunteer, he should step forward. The young officer who sees a need

and decides to take charge, to say, "I'll do that," and does not wait to be told, will learn the value of looking for ways to get involved.

An officer gives his subordinates a sense of responsibility by giving responsibility to them. That is a difficult thing for a senior to do, because he has to sit back and give someone the assignment knowing full well that he could do it faster and better himself. But the officer who continually does things himself is doing a disservice to the people under him. So, even though it may be very difficult to sit back and let someone else do something, that is the only way subordinates can be taught to make decisions and to take responsibility.

Once he has assigned to subordinates the responsibility for a task, the officer must hold them to it and make them responsible. He cannot slack off. If he expects something to be done, and he has given subordinates the responsibility to do it, he must hold them responsible. He should not say, "Well, they're young, and I should not have expected that much." If they make a mistake, the senior should let that mistake teach them. He should let them know what their mistake is.

RESPONSIBILITY CANNOT BE DELEGATED

While officers can delegate to subordinates specific authority to accomplish an action in their absence, it is important to remember that responsibility cannot be *delegated*, although responsibility for a mission may be *assigned* to someone else. In other words, although someone else may be given responsibility to see that a certain task is undertaken and completed, the responsibility for the success of that action still lies with the senior officer involved. After Gettysburg, General Robert E. Lee sent a note to Major General Cadmus M. Wilcox, making this point: "Never mind, General, all this has been

MY fault; it is I that have lost this fight, and you must help me out of it in the best way you can."

Thus, a division officer is responsible for everything that happens in his unit. He cannot make the excuse to his department head that the order was passed down correctly but the troops failed to get the job done correctly; this does not relieve the division officer of his responsibility for proper completion of the task. In the first case, making such a statement will quickly lose the officer the loyalty of his subordinates, who have done their best to succeed. Second, it will make the officer look weak in the eyes of his senior, for the officer will be indicating that he is not willing to accept responsibility. All department heads were at one time division officers, so they are fully aware that, no matter how good the officer is, he is not capable of doing, nor should he do, everything within the unit, and that he must rely on his subordinates, not all of whom the officer chose. So, while department heads know that officers are responsible for what goes right or wrong, they will usually take the factors involved in an unavoidable failure into account, making it unnecessary for the junior officer to ask for special consideration.

ACCEPTING THE RESPONSIBILITY FOR MISTAKES

If an officer has taken every step possible to train, educate, and inform his unit of its duties and of how it is to meet unexpected emergencies, and he follows up with constant practice and opportunities for subordinates to improve their performance, a failure will not end the officer's career, but will be seen for what it is: an unavoidable happenstance. Officers must remember that it is critically important for responsibility to be accurately placed in the service. Only in this way can seniors determine what areas require further attention, so a disaster can be avoided in the future. The work responsibilities of officers are certainly extensive, and time does not usually allow for protracted investigations into what went wrong and why. Thus, officers are expected immediately to volunteer information concerning events with which they were involved, knowing full well that the Naval Service's mission is inherently dangerous and is subject to errors due to enemy action and the minute details that must be handled, even during peacetime operations. An officer should do the best he can, always look for methods to improve his performance, take responsibility for his own actions and those of his unit, and above all, seek out every opportunity to volunteer his services to do what is best for his unit, the Naval Service, and his country.

Admiral Clausen offers the following in this regard:

Although incidents during a war normally produce lessons preponderant in tactical, technical, operational, and other details, there is one incident that made me more pensive in a general way. This incident happened when I was sunk in 1943 in the English Channel as commanding officer of one of our fleetsweepers (crew of 110) after an engagement with *Hunt*-class destroyers, and I lost half my crew, either dead or wounded. This incident gave rise to a great number of lessons learned, which led me to evaluate, to the benefit of my activities, my time in the Bundesmarine. Out of these more general lessons learned, I shall point out those which might be of interest in this connection.

1. Leadership on board is not the business of one person (the commanding officer) only, but a task of teamwork of all kinds of superiors on board a ship in their different fields and roles of activity. The commanding officer, as holder of the responsibility, is in possession of the key to the ignition and of the control of this process in order to direct and to control the manner of how the crew has to be led. He must find the way to transfer his

intentions, imaginations, and ideas of leadership to his officers, chief petty officers, and petty officers and, via this chain, to the ratings.

2. The significance of all petty officers in the field of leadership, training, and education is eminent on account of their permanent and direct contact with ratings. The former Kriegsmarine has learned in this regard very much after the revolution in 1918. The proximity of contact between officers and men became more and more narrow, perhaps even enhanced during the Nazi-time, because no group of society is able to separate from the spirit of the times. This happens always and everywhere and must not be mixed up with identification.

Nowadays we find ourselves, with regard to petty officers, in a development stimulated by alterations mainly in the field of increasing technics [the study or science of an art] which have caused a change of tasks. These tasks are of a different nature than the tasks in their former practice in their former capacity as superior of groups and thereby as mediator and generator of discipline. It is not possible to ignore sometimes that under these new aspects there are petty officers who try to withdraw into the position of a technical expert or skilled specialist only. This problem cannot be excluded from officers, especially because theoretical education carries more and more weight. The integration of leadership as one component of education must be observed emphatically. An officer must have a sense of his people and their complexity in modern times. After all, a military leader has to be a competent, personality-oriented person in the practice of this profession, and not a theorizing matter-of-fact person.

3. Although the significance of "leadership" has been recognized for years, its

integration was repeatedly contested. To me it seems there is no doubt that "leadership," "training," and "education" make *one* unit, in which one of these components must not be separated from others. It is this unit only which guarantees the object aimed at: readiness for action of a naval unit on the combined basis of technical knowledge, efficiency, and spirit of personnel.

4. As these principles existed in the Kriegsmarine and worked rather well during the war, it has been suspected again and again that this state of affairs has been achieved by ideological indoctrination. Therefore it may perhaps be useful when I state in this connection that I did not experience one hour of [state-sponsored] "ideological" education during my career in the navy. Therefore it has to be stated that morale and fighting strength at that time already resulted from the quality of leadership. The standard spirit and readiness for teamwork was enormous.

Apart from the question of personal contact with the crew of a naval unit, it seems to me that under the circumstances of today, willingness and obedience must be obtained more than in former times by means of conviction in order to get a sincere or upright readiness for operation as the expression of an inner attitude.

5. There have never been written so many books and articles on leadership, morale, and team spirit as there are today. In former times the daily practice was always of more importance than writing and thinking on it. We are living today in a time of almost inundation by theoretical contemplations, considerations, and analysis of almost every activity which, in former times, have been considered an uncomplicated part of naval life.

I do not declare myself against it, because the development we are experi-

encing calls for tribute. But I may quote a remark from a German essay, which should dispose a naval officer for thoughtful reflections: "The excessive application of science impairs the practice-oriented thinking and acting."

MCPON Sanders: *If the leader accepts responsibility, then the majority of the time he will hold his subordinates responsible, which in turn will help to develop leadership traits in subordinates. Keep in mind that when a leader does accept responsibility for something, he is also making a commitment for his subordinates, which may sometimes be good or bad from the point of view of the subordinates. If you're just coming back from a cruise and you jump out and make a commitment for your subordinates when they were expecting to go home to their loved ones, you may not be properly exercising responsibility if you have not considered the plans of subordinates. This problem can be avoided by doing as much maintenance and repair as possible at sea, so that port time will not require the full crew on board.*

22. Authority and the Naval Officer

Admiral Charles R. Larson, USN, points out that

we need to develop an officer corps that, within the triad of responsibility, accountability, and authority, has an ethical code that ensures that officers always do what is right and always use authority properly. Junior officers need to see that their leaders always act in an appropriate, proper, and legal way, so they will have confidence, when orders are issued, that those orders will be legally constituted and that authority will be properly used. We need to have an organization whose members must react to orders. In my view, the only reason for not obeying an order would be if that order was illegal or immoral. If we build a foundation that ensures that we do have a code and a corps of people who are honest, who react properly, and who never abuse that authority but use it for the good of the unit and for the mission, then we'll never have an organization where people have to force that authority on people or say "You have to do this because I'm the boss." It will be an instinctive reaction to follow their leadership, and it will be an environment where people know that the right thing will be done.

The ability to exercise authority properly is one of the most important qualities of leadership. Authority can be broadly described as the freedom granted by seniors to allow individuals to command or influence the behavior, thoughts, or opinions of others. Proper uses of authority in the military are based on officers' ability to "show in themselves a good example," support the establishment of the Naval Service and all that it stands for, support and enforce the laws and regulations, and "promote and safeguard the morale, the physical well-being, and the general welfare of the officers and the enlisted persons under their command."[67-33]

The authority of an officer over subordinates rests not only on the officer's legitimacy due to his position, but also on his legitimacy due to acknowledged high moral qualities, strength of character, and capacity for leadership. General Barrow believes that authority must never be abused:

Having authority, you are able to compel people to do whatever it is you ask them to do, and it's very easy to abuse

that by asking them to do things they shouldn't do, or that don't need to be done. It is demeaning to them and may even be illegal. Certainly you shouldn't ask someone to do something just because you have the authority to more or less compel him to do it.

For an American citizen, authority can only be legitimately exercised in a spirit of liberty. An admiral in the Naval Service expressed it this way: "The American philosophy places the individual above the state. It distrusts personal power and coercion. It denies the existence of indispensable men. It asserts the supremacy of principle." Admiral Uchida suggests that

an officer's authority should be of such magnitude that subordinates are devoted to performing their duties as he orders. An officer's authority will be extended when he commands his subordinates from the most important spot in the battle line, following the noblesse oblige doctrine himself.

An officer sometimes must, whether it is wartime or peacetime, give subordinates difficult directives to accomplish. The officer should do everything he can to assist them until they understand that the directives they received are in the best interest of their mission and until they feel honored to have been selected as the task members.

However, it can also be argued that authority, properly exercised, reinforces discipline and enhances the necessary military virtue of obedience. Mahan makes this point: "The duty of obedience is not merely military, but moral. It is not an arbitrary rule but one essential and fundamental; the expression of a principle without which military organization would go to pieces and military success be impossible."

Obedience in a positive sense, then, means the uniform adherence of everyone concerned to a set of rules, customs, and conventions which balance individual freedoms with protection of the interests and requirements of the unit or society as a whole. Thus, discipline and obedience result from the proper exercise of authority, which enforces adherence to the rules. Both discipline and authority are essential for the orderly and effective coordination of effort toward shared goals. The common goal of every naval officer is that of getting the "people to do the Navy's job effectively."[24-80]

THE BASIS OF AUTHORITY

The authority vested by law in the military leader is very real. While authority is inherent in a leader's position relative to subordinates, in practice it is based on other factors, as well. As noted earlier, it is derived from the moral qualities and character of the leader. It is also based on the leader's personal abilities, professional knowledge, and humility—recognition that the leader does not and cannot know everything that his subordinates know.

The authority of a military leader is strengthened by quiet resolution, the willingness to take necessary risks, and the moral courage to accept full responsibility for decisions. A leader must be as ready to accept full blame when things go wrong as he is to share rewards with subordinates when things go right. For subordinates, recognizing authority means submitting themselves to an authority that has demonstrated the right blend of fairness, impartiality, and humanity. It is the leader himself who induces the compliance with his orders.[71-35]

ETHICAL ASPECTS OF AUTHORITY

Good leaders have an ethical claim to authority. The leader who worries only about the personal gains that he can derive from his position has no such claim. Rather, the ethical claim goes to the officer who only asks where his duty lies and then seeks steadfastly to carry it out. Troops will not follow an officer they know in their hearts to be promoting himself at their expense. While they may give their obedience, they will not give

their complete loyalty. Without such loyalty, both up and down, a military unit's effectiveness is degraded, particularly in combat or other situations where lives may be at risk.

In the exercise of lawful authority, then, an officer should be a professional but not a careerist. That is, he should seek always to do those things necessary for the good of the service and the nation as opposed to what is perceived to be good for his career.

Admiral Clausen offers the following:

Authority depends upon several values: proficiency, decency of character, convincing personality, mutual esteem, etc. There is always a correlation between authority on the one hand and trust on the other.

If it will be possible to inculcate attitude and bearing (which must be appropriate with our time) into a type of person, and he disposes of the necessary qualities of leadership, I would call such a personality in our language a *Herr*. I am inclined to think that this would be one educational aim. According to my experiences, subordinates are more willing to accept authority from such a type than from any other type one may think of. It would be absurd, if not dangerous, to have a wrong picture in mind. I understand the German word *Herr* to be a type of gentleman who is modest, well-educated, self-confident but reserved, hard-working, and devoted to life and always ready to bear privation for the community, etc. A *Herr* is the result of a profound education, which would be ineffective if this officer at the same time would not work at self-education. These attributes sound, probably, high-flown. They are used in order to outline the contour of this type of person in general.

If this is the type of officer a navy is striving for, it should determine first of all which are the characteristics of a modern *Herr*, because he will always be a reflected image of society. After that begins a detailed education, which must convince the aspirant of the trust put in officers; otherwise, the education remains superficial. The rule applies here again: Theory of education must be directed at real conduct of life; it should be known to each officer where the navy is aiming.

DELEGATION OF AUTHORITY

One time-tested method for a military leader to build strength within his organization is for him to identify within it individuals of initiative and energy, and then associate his authority with theirs. This act makes it clear to others that these subordinates are speaking and acting in the leader's name. To be able to do this well is one of the keys to effective leadership. The ability to delegate authority, to put it into the most capable hands, and thereafter to support these individuals in their efforts is a valuable leadership asset. Admiral Fran McKee described how she determines how much authority to exercise over others.

A lot depends on your knowledge of the people who work for you. I think it's very important that you are able to know who is capable of doing what. I keep going back to accomplishing the mission. I guess that's the first thing that we are always concerned with, regardless of what specialized area we may happen to be in, but training is a very important part of that, and that's a responsibility of the leader. You must see that all the people are properly trained to accomplish the job they do, and you must provide them with the circumstances to accomplish that training, and then you dispense the job assignments depending upon who has what capability.

Explicit orders to some people are more called for than they are to others, because

if you have an individual who's not well informed or does not have the experience that other people have, that individual needs a little more guidance or more close supervision than others. There are other people you can give an assignment to and you may not see them for a week, and they report back to you and it's accomplished.

An officer who is unable to delegate authority is not a leader. More than evidencing a lack of confidence in his subordinates, he is betraying a lack of confidence in himself and his own abilities. If an officer cannot delegate authority and is mistrustful of all power except his own, he will not be able to command, even in peacetime. In combat or in other difficult situations, his unit at some point will surely break down. "The effective leader will therefore be conservative in his use of power and he will bend every effort to bring about its eventual distribution among the members of the group."[39-80]

Command is not a prerogative; it is, rather, a responsibility to be shared with all subordinates capable of carrying out the implicit details of orders that may be given in only the most general terms. The leader who is unable to delegate the authority to carry out such orders erodes the flexibility and teamwork his unit needs to win on the battlefield. Admiral Burke, when asked by Professor Montor how much authority an officer should give someone when he is asking that person to do something, replied:

Give him complete authority, absolutely. If you don't give him authority, don't let there be any bones about what you're not giving him; make it clear, not only to him but to everyone else.

Dr. Montor then asked: "In other words, give him the same power you would give to yourself if you yourself were doing it?" and Admiral Burke replied:

More to the point, if you don't have trust in him, then restrict him, but restrict him so that everybody knows

what the restrictions are so that he is
not responsible for your restrictions,
so that you know who's responsible for
what.

THE PROCESS OF AUTHORITY

The personal responsibility of military leaders
is as important as the authority that is vested in
them by law. The manner and completeness with
which they accept and discharge that responsibility indicates to a large degree their capacity
for leadership.

It is not easy to get people to subordinate
themselves willingly to the command of authority. To assist leaders in accomplishing this, the
military has a body of longstanding and refined
rules and regulations. These have evolved to
produce in personnel military virtues such as
accountability, integrity, selflessness, loyalty, and
bravery—virtues that can spell the difference
between victory and defeat in battle. But rules
and regulations are worthwhile only if the
authority underlying them is properly exercised
and enforced.

To exercise authority properly, leaders must
be both demanding and dynamic. Leaders are
charged with the responsibility and authority to
uphold the rules and regulations by demanding
that they be followed, and they must enforce
conformance when doing so becomes necessary.
The leader's consistent enforcement of authority
will serve to ensure that the standards and habits
formed in peacetime are predictive of performance in wartime.

Officers can exercise authority in either a positive or a negative way. Authority that is exercised in a positive sense, in fulfillment of the
responsibilities inherent in the leader's position,
is generally well accepted by subordinates and
is supportive of discipline and obedience.
Authority that is exercised in a negative sense—
that is, applied arbitrarily in order to enhance
the leader's personal goals at the expense of his
subordinates—is often accepted by subordinates, but in a grudging way. In the long run,

negatively exercised authority is destructive of
discipline.

Authority may be used arbitrarily when the
leader has little time—as in combat or emergency situations—to weigh the strengths and
weaknesses of a range of possible choices. However, in most leadership situations, authority is
exercised in a more predictable and more proven
manner.

The best leaders tend to be those who are
expert in the proper exercise and delegation of
authority. They are exacting perfectionists in
regard to performance of duty, maintenance of
discipline, and attainment of the loyalty of subordinates. They are authoritarian, but at the same
time they constantly evince concern for the personal welfare, interests, feelings, and rights of
their personnel. The military leader who strikes
the proper balance between exercising authority
and taking care of subordinates can expect to
meet with success.

The foregoing clearly provides the overall view
of the Naval Service. The following remarks by
Admiral Burke are provided to remind officers
that they are expected to think, for it is impossible for seniors to spell out in advance all the
actions expected of juniors.

> Everyone has authority, but not every-
> one is willing to use it. Nearly all people
> in the Navy stay too closely inside their
> orders. They circumscribe themselves on
> what they can and cannot do. What is
> needed quite frequently is for them to go
> a little beyond. You get into trouble that
> way if you're wrong, but you can also do
> some good things if you're right.

Admiral Burke explained why it is important
for individuals to take authority and exercise it.

> The President is ultimately in com-
> mand, but he can't know everything, he
> can't be told everything, he doesn't have
> time. So what the President has to be
> dependent upon are his people doing
> things that they ought to do without even

informing him, because he doesn't have time to be informed of minor things, yet he should be kept informed of those things he should know about.

Particularly in a combat situation, not necessarily in battle, if you have to ask for permission, it may be too late. What can the President or other people back here know of your particular situation? Sometimes you have to take authority. But you can't start a war, you can't be the wild life major and start World War III. There are many times when, if the subordinate can make the decision and do a job, he can do it, but if he has to ask for authority to do it, nobody can do it, because there's nobody who has the authority without a great big confab that takes four days, and then it is too late. Taking authority in certain situations is like handling a ship with the division commander aboard the flagship. The division commander has nothing to do with controlling your ship, the captain is in command of the ship. The captain gives the orders to the ship, but the division commander gives the orders to the division, and the captain of the ship accedes to those orders. But if he is in a torpedo attack or an exercise of a torpedo attack, for example, and the division commander has given a certain course and the captain of the ship sees something wrong, he's got to give orders to the ship right quick. He can go right to a left stop, back full, not always just to avoid collision, but to do the right thing. He's taking authority that is not his, that is his division commander's. Over and over again this happens, particularly in combat itself, where people do things that they aren't authorized to do. Sometimes it's wrong, sometimes it's absolutely wrong and a lot of people die because of it, but more people will die if people never do what they are sure is right and should be done.

MCPON Sanders: *There may be a tendency among weak leaders to use authority improperly. They may try to get things done that will benefit them, and they do so using the authority an officer has. In seeing this happen in the past, I can tell you that no one has been fooled, especially not the enlisted community. We teach the enlisted to follow the rules and regulations and, especially, the orders of our officers, which places a special requirement on the officers not to ask for anything which is either improper or to the officer's personal gain. You have to be very careful to make sure that, any time you use your authority, it's done properly.*

Chapter 2 Bibliography

1. Ballou, Sidney. "Faulty Communications." *Proceedings*, Feb. 1929, pp. 89–98.
2. Bass, Bernard M. *Leadership, Psychology, and Organizational Behavior.* Westport, Conn.: Greenwood Press, 1960.
3. Beardon, William, and Wedertz, Bill. *The Bluejacket's Manual.* 20th ed. Annapolis: Naval Institute Press, 1978.
4. Bekkehdal, C. L. "Discipline and the Profession of Naval Arms." *Proceedings*, May 1977, pp. 186–201.
5. Black, James M., and Black, Virginia T. *The Front-Line Manager's Problem-Solver.* New York: McGraw-Hill, 1967.
6. Boyd, Bradford B. *Management-Minded Supervision.* New York: McGraw-Hill, 1968.
7. Burke, Arleigh A. "Admiral Marc Mitscher: A Naval Aviator." *Proceedings*, Apr. 1975, p. 53.
8. ———. "The Art of Command." In *Leadership and Law Department NL 303 Book of Readings.* Ed. J. M. Kelly, G. D. Patton, J. F. Downs, and G. J. Corini. Annapolis: U.S. Naval Academy, academic year 1983–84, pp. 125–29.
9. Burton, John Wear. *Deviance, Terrorism, and War.*

New York: St. Martin's Press, 1979.

10. Callahan, D.; Stromberg, P. L.; and Wakin, M. M. *The Teaching of Ethics in the Military*. Hastings-on-Hudson: The Institute of Society, Ethics, and the Life Sciences, 1982.

11. "Calley's Story." *U.S. News and World Report*, 8 Dec. 1968, p. 4.

12. Carrington, James H. *Command Control Compromise*. Annapolis: Naval Institute Press, 1973.

13. Clexton, E. W., Jr. "Trust and Confidence." Commanding Officer's Memorandum no. 20, USS *Dwight D. Eisenhower* (CVN 69), 21 Feb. 1984.

14. Collins, F. C. "The Loss of Leadership." *Proceedings*, Apr. 1975, p. 53.

15. Dahl, Robert A. *Modern Political Analysis*. Englewood Cliffs, N.J.: Prentice-Hall, 1970.

16. Daniels, Anthony J. "Evaluation Systems and Superior-Subordinate Relationships." *Military Review*, Jan. 1972, pp. 3–8.

17. Dean, B. C. "Authority: The Weakened Link." *Proceedings*, July 1971, pp. 48–52.

18. Diggins, John P., ed. *The Problem of Authority in America*. Philadelphia: Temple University Press, 1980.

19. *Disciplinary Regulations of the Armed Forces of the USSR: The Officer's Handbook—A Soviet View*. For sale by the Superintendent of Documents, Washington, D.C. Moscow, 1971, p. 167.

20. Dornbusch, Sanford M., and Scott, W. Richard. *Evaluations and the Exercise of Authority*. San Francisco: Jossey-Bass, 1975.

21. Gibson, James L.; Ivancevich, John M.; and Donnelly, James H., Jr. *Organizations*. 4th ed. Plano, Tex.: Business Publications, 1982.

22. Gillan, Richard, ed. *Power in Postwar America*. Boston: Little, Brown, 1971.

23. Hasson, Raymond E. "The New Breed of Sailor." *Proceedings*, Mar. 1979, pp. 41–46.

24. Hazard, John. Editorial. *Proceedings*, Apr. 1981.

25. Heinl, Robert Debs, Jr. *The Marine Officer's Guide*. Annapolis: Naval Institute Press, 1977.

26. Helms, R. E. "Shipboard Drug Abuse." *Proceedings*, Dec. 1975, pp. 41–45.

27. Holland, W. J. "Command at Sea." *Proceedings*, Dec. 1976, p. 18.

28. Hollander, Edwin P. *Leadership Dynamics*. New York: Stein and Day, 1982.

29. Infield, Glenn R. *Secrets of the SS*. New York: Free Press, 1978.

30. Jacobsen, K. C. "The Stranger in the Crowd." *Proceedings*, Sept. 1974, p. 33.

31. Janowitz, Morris. *The Professional Soldier: A Social and Political Portrait*. New York: Free Press, 1971.

32. Johnson, Spencer, and Blanchard, Kenneth. *The One Minute Manager*. New York: William Morrow, 1982.

33. Kattar, R. J. "The First Commandment of Leadership: Love Thy Soldier." *Military Review*, July 1980, pp. 65–68.

34. Keenan, P. C., and Tarr, C. W. "People: The Navy's Most Critical Resource." *Proceedings*, Nov. 1976, p. 45.

35. Knowels, Malcolm, and Knowels, Hulda. *How to Develop Better Leaders*. New York: Association Press, 1955.

36. Krieger, Leonard, and Stern, Fritz. *The Responsibility of Power*. Garden City, N.Y.: Doubleday, 1967.

37. Kuhne, Michael D. "Can Do! Should Do?" *Proceedings*, Mar. 1977, p. 86.

38. Laffin, John. *Links of Leadership: Thirty Centuries of Military Command*. New York: Abelard-Schuman, 1970.

39. Lindgren, Henry Clay. *Leadership, Authority, and Power Sharing*. Malabar, Fla.: Robert Kreiger, 1982.

40. Loye, David. *The Leadership Passion*. San Francisco: Jossey-Bass, 1970.

41. Mack, William P. "The Need for a New Morality." *Proceedings*, Dec. 1975, pp. 30–33.

42. "The Massacre at Song-My." *Life*, 5 Dec. 1969.

43. *Military Leadership: Supplementary Readings*. West Point, N.Y.: U.S. Military Academy, Department of Tactics, Office of Military Psychology and Leadership, 1962.

44. Montgomery, Bernard. *The Path to Leadership*. New York: G. P. Putnam's Sons, 1961.

45. Montor, Karel, and Ciotti, Anthony J., eds. *Fundamentals of Naval Leadership*. 3d ed. Annapolis: Naval Institute Press, 1984.

46. Munson, Edwin Lyman, Jr. "Leadership for American Army Leaders." *Infantry Journal*, 1941.

47. "The My-Lai Massacre." *Newsweek*, 24 Nov. 1969.

48. Noel, John V., Jr., and Basset, Frank E. *Division Officer's Guide*. 7th ed. Annapolis: Naval Institute Press, 1977.

49. O'Hara, M. J. "The Challenge of Moral Leadership." *Proceedings*, Aug. 1977, pp. 58–62.

50. "An Old Sailor Tradition." *Proceedings*, Apr. 1975, pp. 42–45.

51. Peers, William A. *The My-Lai Inquiry*. New York: Norton Books, 1974.

52. Powers, William H. "Almost beyond Human Endurance." *Proceedings*, Dec. 1977, pp. 60–69.

53. Reed, B. *Personal Leadership for Combat Officers*. New York: Whittlesey House, 1943.

54. Reynolds, Clark G. "Youth and the U.S. Navy." *Proceedings*, July 1973, pp. 26–34.

55. Rocap, Pember W. "Who Was Tangled in the Chain When We Threw It Out the Window?" *Air University Review* 25, no. 4 (1974): 75–80.

56. Roskill, S. W. *The Art of Leadership*. London: Collins Clear-Type Press, 1964.

57. Slocum, John W., and Hellriegel, Don. *Management*. Boston: Addison-Wesley, 1982.

58. Solley, George C. "Trust, Confidence, and Obligation." *Proceedings*, Nov. 1981.

59. Soper, M. E. "Officers for the Eighties: A Challenge for NROTC." *Proceedings*, Feb. 1975, p. 40.

60. Stavridis, James. "Closing the Gaps in Naval Leadership." *Proceedings*, July 1982.

61. ———. "On Leading Snipes." *Proceedings*, Jan. 1981, p. 74.

62. Stivers, E. R. "The Mystique of Command Presence." *Proceedings*, Aug. 1968, pp. 26–33.

63. Vance, Charles C. *Boss Psychology*. New York: McGraw-Hill, 1975.

64. Wakin, Malham M. *Military Leadership: In Pursuit of Excellence*. Ed. Robert L. Taylor and William Rosenback. Boulder, Colo.: Westview Press, 1984, p. 55.

65. Walzer, Michael. "Two Kinds of Military Responsibility." *The Proceedings of the War and Morality Symposium*. West Point, N.Y.: U.S. Military Academy, pp. 20–29.

66. Ware, Hugh C. "New Tools for Crisis Management." *Proceedings*, Aug. 1974, p. 19.

67. Watkins, James D. "The Principle of Command." *Proceedings*, Jan. 1983.

68. White, Jack. "The Military and the Media." *Proceedings*, Jan. 1983.

69. White, William S. *The Responsibles*. New York: Harper and Row, 1972.

70. Williamson, Porter B. *Patton's Principles*. Tucson: Management and Systems Consultants, 1979.

71. Wrong, Dennis H. *Power: Its Forms, Bases, and Uses*. New York: Harper and Row, 1979.

3

Planning for Mission Accomplishment

Introduction

The planning of any operation is a complex process requiring extensive coordination among individuals, staffs, and units. The officer who has the responsibility for planning must orchestrate the effort, anticipate future operations, provide an outline, establish goals, and ensure that an executable scheme is prepared.

The leader must consider the mission at hand, the level of conflict, the scope of responsibilities, the force and systems available, and the rules of engagement that are in effect. He works with these factors to satisfy a specific aim or purpose—or, in the event of a general plan, an agenda of objectives—and disseminates the information he has concerning these factors to everyone involved in the planning process. This initial step is perhaps the most important, as it establishes the basis for all future planning actions and analyses.

Sometimes it is necessary to contact all involved units, staffs, or personnel indirectly. In this case, message or electronic mail is the most convenient method and should be used if possible. However, this is not nearly as effective as a face-to-face "kick off" briefing with representatives from all units.

An initial planning conference introduces everyone, facilitates early discussions, permits personal and professional relationships to develop, and enables the leader to state his objectives, policies, and philosophies clearly with respect to the task assigned. When a conference is arranged, people do not have to try to interpret written messages from individuals they do not know. Information exchange among participants is also generally improved as people get to know one another.

The roles of all concerned must be clearly identified. Staffs, units, and personnel with unique expertise must be given appropriate planning assignments. It is equally important to recognize when outside assistance is required, such as in areas where there is little in-house experience. The scope of modern naval warfare has broadened so dramatically in communications, electronic warfare, wide-area ocean surveillance, long-range missiles, antisubmarine warfare, etc., that an outside expert is brought in more often than not. The leader must recognize this early on and request assistance in a timely fashion. His knowledge of the abilities of assigned organizations is fundamental to his ability to analyze deficient areas and strike out smartly to put together a strong team. It boils down to a basic leadership tenet: The leader must know his personnel to facilitate a coherent planning effort.

The first step, naturally, is to stipulate the initial direction, but no leader, and certainly no navigator, is subsequently going to retire to his cabin and assume there will be no deviations to course. Frequent follow-on working sessions are necessary to monitor the planning process and audit the progress. There must be a mechanism in place to check whether actual performance is related to estimated activities. Unless it is checked continually, planning can result in considerable thought without direct results.

In sum, the leader must set the agenda, identify the planners, set targets, establish a monitoring mechanism, and commit resources to support the planning process. Planning is a prerequisite to follow-on operations. The leader must be involved in planning as the major participant, not in settling on details, but in setting the tone and guiding the operational elements.

In an overview context, MCPON Sanders points out the importance of bringing senior enlisted, whether the chief or the first-class or second-class petty officers, into the planning discussion early on. An officer has personal needs and goals and career aspirations, but if he does not take into account senior enlisted leaders and their experience and include them in the development

of the plan, then he is going to fall short and cause resentment in the ranks.

23. Setting Goals

Most people enter the Naval Service for reasons other than to become managers and leaders: a life at sea, excitement, sleek jets, exotic ports of call, smart uniforms. Once they arrive at their first duty station, however, it soon becomes apparent to them that the Navy or the Marine Corps has bigger things in mind for them. Very quickly they are challenged by a broad spectrum of duties and responsibilities that often are individually complex and seemingly unconnected. In a single day, for example, an aviator can be totally absorbed in mission planning for flying and fighting a thirty-million-dollar F-14; laying out work programs or counseling personnel; attending lectures on a wide variety of subjects; running a charity campaign; serving on a qualification board—in short, carrying out the duties of the complete naval officer.

In their first assignments, officers tend to look to experience—to the chief petty officers, division officers, and department heads—for guidance and leadership. These individuals can help officers sort out their priorities. From the beginning, however, the burden for success rests squarely on an individual's shoulders. How quickly and capably officers are able to use the tools of their profession is determined to a great extent by how well they learn to understand their personal aspirations and how effectively they identify their goals or objectives.

LONG-RANGE, MID-RANGE, AND SHORT-RANGE GOALS

Objectives or *goals* are defined as "that toward which effort is directed; an aim or an end." It is convenient to think of objectives as capstone (long range), horizon (mid-range), and stepping-stone (short range). Capstone objectives are objectives individuals can early on more often sense than

define with clarity: writing the great American
novel, leading a major command or corporation,
attaining great wealth. Horizon objectives are
those that individuals can see, that they can define
with some precision, and that are within their
reach if not within their immediate grasp: earning a master's degree, earning command at sea,
and attaining a promotion. Finally, the stepping-
stone objectives are more closely related to the
tasks at hand: doing a job properly, earning qualifications, buying a first house. Within each of
these broad categories, individuals' objectives
need to be arranged in a hierarchy that reflects
what to them is most important—their priorities.

Admiral Carney notes that
> long-range planning is an essential service
> function, and it is something to which
> everyone can contribute. A junior officer
> who has a bright idea can submit a letter
> that can go on up the line and finally wind
> up on the CNO's desk. The focal point of
> future planning is the Naval War College,
> which uses games to put some of the
> future-based theories to the test.

Admiral Clausen suggests that
> a planning scheme should be valued more
> as guidance than a rigid instruction that
> has to be followed stupidly. According to
> my mind, the following principles should
> not be disregarded.
>
> 1. Missions and their planning must be
> realistic as to the object in view during all
> phases of development and, above all, in
> the period of performance. The whole
> process must be under constant review.
>
> 2. Although it depends on the mission,
> generally the naval officer in charge of the
> performance should not be narrowed into
> an unalterable pattern and thereby
> become an instrument of implementation
> only.
>
> 3. An officer in command must be able
> to make independent decisions within the
> scope of his mission.

> 4. In setting short- and long-range
> goals, the planner should first of all start
> with great soberness from the facts of the
> prevailing situation, the urgency of the
> object in view, its necessities of details,
> and the factor time. When transferring
> these factors to the performers' possibili-
> ties, the realities become distinct to the
> planner. And this is to me the most
> important fact in the setting of short- and
> long-range goals.

The distinctive benefits of setting goals include:
(1) the planning of purposeful and integrated
work is made easier; (2) goals serve as standards
for purposes of control, and they play an important part in motivation of personnel; and (3) the
establishment of goals requires consideration and
answers to the questions who, what, when, where,
why, and how. It should be noted that meeting
the goals set by higher authority has priority
over unit or individual goals, and that steps must
be taken to ensure that, in meeting short-range
goals, individuals do not compromise long-range
goals.

ORGANIZATIONAL GOALS

Admiral McDonald points out that
> a young naval officer's first goal should
> simply be to become the best officer in
> the United States Navy. One way he can
> achieve that goal is to do each and every
> assignment given him to the very best of
> his ability.
>
> When people set only personal goals,
> they become self-interested rather than
> service-interested. Individuals who go to a
> particular school or try to attain a certain
> type of duty solely in order to get pro-
> moted may be disappointed. In many
> instances they did not want that school or
> that duty at all, and when they get there,
> they do not do very well, because they
> are not interested. Of course an officer
> must have individual goals; he should be
> very careful in setting his goals to make

certain that the goals he is setting are not being determined by what he thinks he should do in order to get promoted. He should do the things that will lead the Navy to benefit from his services. If he serves to the best of his ability, promotion generally will follow.

Organizational objectives and an individual's responsibility in helping the organization meet those objectives are usually well laid out in Navy Regulations and in station, ship, or organizational manuals, and by commanding officers. The successful naval officer will establish as a first priority meeting organizational responsibilities by effectively performing all assigned duties. At the same time, however, he will survey the present and the future from all aspects, and identify his personal objectives both within and beyond the present organizational framework. The officer will develop a habit of failure if he makes a decision and then does not carry it through.[34-39] Developing a clear sense of where an individual is going—determining objectives—is largely the responsibility of the individual, and the importance of this responsibility cannot be overstated.

Admiral Taylor refers to *The One-Minute Manager*,[10] which counsels the manager to set goals, reward achievement, and punish failure.

> In setting the goals, we're a great organization for management by objectives. We have little brass rings, the Battle E, the Commodore's Cup; whatever it is, we're a very competitive bunch of people. We've been recruited because of our competitive spirit, because war is a competition of sorts. And so you must set goals that are stated clearly, and get the little milestones in between and get people working toward those. Now you ask, how do you set short-term—that's a milestone—and long-term goals? Say "We will win the Battle E, and here's what we have to do to do that." Then you go do some studying and you get everyone, your department heads, your commanding offi-

cer, involved. If you're a division officer, maybe the goal is less than that, it's a case of not losing any airplanes, it's a case of putting all the ordnance on target, whatever it is. There's always something coming up, some exercise you can use as a goal, and then you have to get everyone down, get them on board, and press on as a team toward that goal and get that feeling inside of "I am a part of a team." The achievement of short-term en route to long-term goals is the way we do our business, and if you understand that, then you're ahead of the game.

PERSONAL AND PROFESSIONAL GOALS

In attempting to determine their personal aspirations, individuals will find that they do not have a single objective. Rather, for every individual, there is a complex family of objectives that serve as building blocks to a successful career—indeed, to a successful life. Admiral Moorer affirms that,

> in setting personal goals, the young officer should decide what specialty he would enjoy and would succeed in. He needs to decide whether he would prefer operational or managerial assignments, and then choose a specific setting: aviation, submarine, surface ship, Pentagon, etc. From there on, he should plan to acquire as much knowledge as he can about that specialty.

Unfortunately, individuals seldom take the time to think through their objectives or test their priorities. Yet priorities, along with principles, serve to guide individuals' actions and their lives. And, while having a clear and firm set of objectives and understanding priorities will not assure success, defaulting on objectives—"going along with the flow" without discipline—seldom produces self-satisfaction. More frequently it results in frustration and unhappiness. Admiral Carney offers that

> an officer who has an idea that he believes

worthy of open discussion or presentation must indulge in a little self-examination. He must ask himself whether it is an original thought, whether it has been dealt with elsewhere, and what the bibliography of necessary research would be. If it is sufficiently relevant to merit being published, or the officer is convinced that he has something that is worth saying in public, he should proceed.

Very few people are able to identify their capstone objectives early in their careers; however, if they devote a little time and effort, they can construct a list of short-range and mid-range goals to work toward. Early in their careers they can rearrange their list dramatically—their objectives and priorities can be easily changed as new options and interests appear. As they proceed through life and their options begin to narrow, their list must become more evolutionary. But, at the same time, they will begin to see more clearly their capstone goals and to work more directly toward achieving them.

NATIONAL GOALS

On a national level, the subject of goals has also to be considered in a context of what is best for the country. Admiral Moorer had this to say on the subject:

> When an officer is down in the lieutenant commander level, he has got to believe his squadron is the best, and that the Navy's better than the Army and Air Force, and that in the Navy, if he's a submarine officer, his submarine can lick all the other submarines. You've got to have that kind of feeling among the junior officers. But once you get up into senior captain or flag rank, then you've got to broaden your outlook and take a joint look at what's required for all the services, because we have the unified command plan, which, simply, is built on the assumption that in any kind of major conflict, all the services would be involved.

MCPON Sanders: *Everyone should set short-range and long-range goals, not only the junior officer, but all of our chiefs and enlisted, as well, if they are going to be successful in life. If we just have long-range goals, we may, unfortunately, not get there, for sometimes we don't have a road map, and that's what the short-range goals are for.*

24. Introduction to Planning

An effective officer in today's growing and increasingly complicated Naval Service is a talented planner and a sound manager as well as a skilled and inspiring leader. Many will argue, with substantiation, that in past conflicts this has not necessarily been true in the heat of combat—that there were war fighters and war planners and also managers, who served both the tactician and the strategist.

A comparison between Generals Eisenhower and Patton may be drawn to illustrate the other side of the argument. General Eisenhower was a consummate planner and strategist, General Patton a consummate fighter and tactician. But while General Eisenhower was unquestionably a leader and an inspiration to his Allied staff in the War Room, was he not also a manager of plans, ideas, and vast quantities of vital warfighting resources? Was General Patton not a manager of regiments and battalions and the logistics necessary to sustain his drives into enemy territory, as well as a very visible leader on the firing line?

While such distinctions provide material for an interesting and prolonged argument, suffice it to say for now that U.S. service academies always have been and always will be in the business of educating and training combat leaders who are equipped with a wide range of personal attributes as well as technical and mechanical skills. Traits desired in military leaders run the gamut from morality, courage, and sound judgment, through planning and managerial ability, to tactical and strategic thinking ability.

There is no such thing as a "combat manager." The Naval Service has recently recognized its need for astute managers in the Washington arena by establishing a new breed of naval officer, the Material Professional. Positions in the fleet, at the cutting edge, are reserved for war-fighting leaders. There are similarities between leaders and managers that should not be overlooked.

Admiral de Cazanove states that he agrees with the necessity of planning even if things never go as planned,

> but individuals must go through the reflective process to ensure that they are well prepared. You must also involve others in the planning process, for one person cannot think of all the things that have to be done. On the other hand, having made a plan and spent a lot of time at it, one must not be overly tied to that plan should the situation dictate that changes are in order. The British had no plans to prepare for war with the Argentines, and maybe because there were no plans they were able to succeed—but I don't think officers should take this as meaning they can win without plans. It is probable that all of the planning they did do in their training helped them to adapt quickly to the new situation and prevail.

SETTING GOALS

Like a good manager, a leader must set goals for his unit and himself, and make plans to accomplish those goals. The naval leader is responsible for everything his unit does or fails to do. It is therefore no accident that the leaders who succeed are the ones who plan ahead and avoid embarrassing, perhaps even deadly, mistakes. Admiral Moorer advises that,

> in planning the goals for his unit or division, department, or ship, an officer should be thinking about its operational

readiness for war. The services are expected to maintain national security through deterrents, by which it is clear to a potential enemy that, no matter what action it takes, it will be forced to accept the consequences because of the operational readiness of the military forces of the United States. Then, if deterrents fail, the services must be prepared to fight the enemy. Therefore, operational readiness in every respect, including logistics, is the primary consideration in planning.

Discipline is mandatory if operational readiness is to be achieved in a military service. The captain or the commander or the officer in charge has, according to Navy Regulations, the authority, and he has to exercise it fairly. He must make certain that everyone knows what the rules are and that no exceptions will be made unless extenuating circumstances dictate. And he must consistently enforce rules; he cannot make a special case out of one incident and then expect everyone to obey from then on. And the officer can never violate his own rules.

RECOGNIZING PROBLEMS

The first hurdle for any leader is to recognize problems that must be solved if goals are to be attained. This is not always as easy as it sounds. The leader must study every situation in enough detail to identify the problems and separate them from their various symptoms. For example, a squadron division leader who is evaluating the performance of the pilots in his division must determine whether Lt. (jg) Jones's poor airmanship during formation flying reflects a complacent attitude or is the result of insufficient practice caused by a cutback in flying hours due to budget constraints. If the problem is attitude, what is the cause, and how can it be corrected? If it is training, given the fuel constraints, how can Lt. (jg) Jones's proficiency be improved? Again, before the leader can take positive steps to correct a problem, he must pinpoint what the problem is, rather than merely attack the symptoms.

FORMULATING A PLAN

The general plan. Once the problem at hand is defined, the leader must formulate a general plan to solve it. The task can range from a limited training plan to a full-blown battle plan. Throughout this phase, leaders would do well to keep two easily remembered principles in mind. They are: KISS, "Keep It Simple, Stupid," and P7, Proper Prior Planning Prevents Particularly Poor Performance. These principles may sound trite, but many leaders, young and old alike, have landed in a heap of trouble by failing to keep them in mind during both planning and execution.

The detailed plan. Once he has formulated a general plan, the leader must follow with a more detailed plan that includes allocation of time and resources. Such a plan may take the form of a checklist. A wise leader makes a conscious decision regarding the importance of each and every item on his checklist and the order in which each item should be addressed. If his planning method is to start at the final outcome and work backward, he can formulate a general timetable, remembering that time is a resource that can be more important than fuel, food, or ammunition.

Contingency plans. In formulating the detailed plan, the effective leader visualizes as many alternatives as practical and weighs the advantages and disadvantages of each. He cannot, in most cases, plan for every possible contingency, but he can easily consider several most probable scenarios. Finally, the astute leader always asks himself what the worst possible thing that can happen is, and then he makes a contingency plan for it, regardless of how improbable its occurrence is. Through this act, he avoids becoming a victim of Murphy's Law. "Although human error is the major cause of accidents in almost any field of endeavor, the reasons for human error vary from seasickness to negligence and improper planning."[39-59]

Standard Operating Procedures (SOPs) are valuable time savers, but only when they are truly *standard*. Operations become very confused when someone uses a SOP that is not widely understood. A SOP that is understood by one squadron, ship, battalion, etc., may not be understood by other squadrons, ships, or battalions. It is best to use only those SOPs that are utilized every day and that are understood by everyone.

As mentioned, there is a practical limit to the number of contingency plans a leader can make or reasonably expect his subordinates to remember. A simple technique that will often help bridge the gap between the plan and an unforeseen occurrence is to ensure that everyone thoroughly understands the ultimate goal, so they can respond to changes in such a manner as to assure mission accomplishment rather than detract from it. It is incumbent upon the leader to brief the people who will participate in carrying out his plan and to designate a qualified alternate leader.

No matter how well thought out a plan may be, it is only as good as the results it produces. And, while the plan may be flawless, the human equation must always be kept in mind. It is essential that every plan be rehearsed as often as necessary by the people designated to carry it out. Even if it is impractical to rehearse the entire plan, the most critical segments of the plan should be rehearsed to the maximum extent possible. Any planner who believes his plan is too good to be misunderstood has forgotten what it is to be human.

A SAMPLE PLAN

The extensive requirements that go into planning even the simplest carrier air-wing strike projection mission serve as a good example of what a planning sequence can entail. Figure 3.1 illustrates the numerous factors that come into play when a strike projection mission is assigned. In this era of contingency response planning for possible retaliation against terrorist actions, the

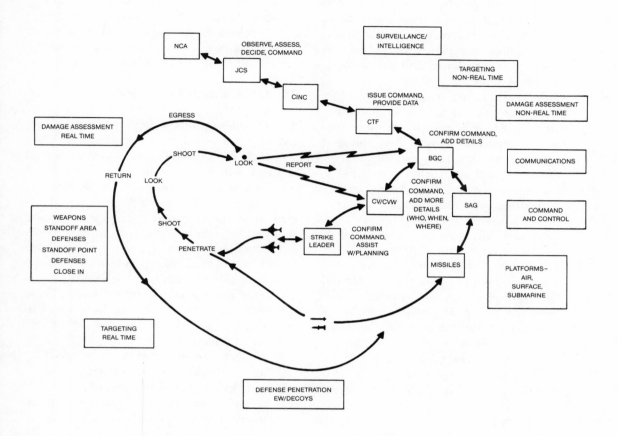

Figure 3.1   Strike ASUW Required Capabilities

National Command Authority normally initiates assessment of alternatives, decides on strike options, and issues orders down the chain of command as reflected in the inner, clockwise, series of boxes. Each commander in the chain of command adds appropriate details, such as rules of engagement and reporting requirements. Ultimately the on-scene commander refines the strike plan based on latest intelligence and other local factors and turns the execution over to the strike leader. TACAIR strike leaders and cruise missile shooters carry out penetration, battle damage assessment, and

reporting functions. The counterclockwise boxes outside of the strike lines represent functions that every strike leader must take into account in planning and executing a strike. Not shown, but potentially having at least equal weight in planning considerations, are available logistic support, state of training of the strike crews, and tactics development.

Planning such a strike is a complicated procedure that must be completed with utmost dedication. Failure to plan thoroughly can lead to fatal results, even in peacetime training.

Those aspiring to lead sailors and Marines in

harm's way must develop leadership qualities and skills that will assure success in combat and safe and effective training in peacetime. Understanding the importance of proper planning, and appreciating its complexity, will help an officer develop these skills.

Admiral Larson reminds us that,

in any planning for mission accomplishment, you have to realize that there are no new missions. Many of these things have been done before, so review some of the past operations, review past plans, look at lessons learned, and incorporate all of that into your initial planning. And then you have to prepare your crew, communicate with them, explain to them what the mission is, what you're trying to accomplish. Get your subordinates involved in the planning and training so that your people are cross-trained, so that you have backups in case of losses, or you have people ready to step into the fray. You need to develop good communications within your crew and within other units, so that you know how you fit into the total plan and how your ship interacts with other forces. Also, you need to have contingency plans. I always ask myself, What's the worst thing that could go wrong in this plan? or What's the worst case? or How would I react? or What if? You need to train your subordinates to think the same way, because if you think things out in advance, it will be hard for you to be surprised. And then you have to decide how you will change your plan if things do not work or things do not go well. You have to understand how you will evaluate your success and, if you're not doing well, at what point you will change. Then, in either changing your plans or moving for a higher level of success, you need to keep the other echelons or other units informed, so that you will continue to work as an integrated team.

But I think the foundation of that whole thing is getting that crew prepared, getting them thinking about contingencies, getting them cross-trained, and getting them behind the mission of your unit.

25. Obtaining Information

A good leader continually seeks information that will improve and update his skills. There are seemingly endless sources of information—good and bad, structured and informal, planned and happenstance—but the leader should strive to discover the sources that will assist him in his goal to attain improved performance. A few thoughts the officer might keep in mind while evaluating himself are: (1) We can always learn from each other. (2) Any person who thinks he is indispensable already isn't. (3) Know what you know and know what you do not know. These principles, set down by General George S. Patton years ago, are still pertinent today.[59-3, 38, 108] Admiral Nakamura suggests that

an officer has the information he needs if he can decide his course of action, develop detailed planning, and follow through along sufficient objective grounds in any operation or administration. This does not necessarily mean the officer will have all the information there is, because, regardless of the remarkable progress in the means of collecting information and in C^3I [Command, Control, Communications, and Intelligence] systems today, it is very difficult to obtain all the information on a subject in a timely fashion and to arrange and evaluate it, especially when the information gathered is contradictory.

An officer must realize what information he wants to have to make a decision, and then try to obtain it. Furthermore, he must be prepared to make decisions and to act with insufficient information.

The division officer may be the best example

of the leader who can "make or break" himself through his capacity to seek out information; only by educating himself and developing the kind of expertise that abounds within his organization among his subordinates, peers, and seniors can this officer succeed. In order to have a successful career, the person entering the fleet today as an officer must first be a successful junior officer. To do this will require continuous hard work, self-education, and a concern with the big picture.[30-128] The division officer whom personnel immediately respond to is the one who is open to the guidance of those who are more skilled and knowledgeable, and who honestly seeks to develop his own expertise. The qualities that are evidenced in the person striving toward this goal are self-confidence mixed with humility, honesty, enthusiasm, and an ability to put people at ease so that information can freely pass among them.

Education is not necessarily tied to a formal learning-teaching relationship; it is often accomplished at a personal level. The civilian phrase for this type of education is on-the-job training. Have you ever heard the cliché "trained but not educated" in reference to the kind of learning done at the Naval Academy? This is incongruous, because a good naval officer—that is, a true leader—is indeed well trained, but his *training* is the most sophisticated *education* in the world. He listens, absorbs, studies, and practices over and over, in a seemingly endless course of development. This kind of activity is essential to the leader. The ideal is not to be well trained once, but to be always in training! Of course, leaders must have other qualities, such as good judgment, maturity, and sensitivity, but the desire ever to excel and go higher, refine and improve, is one of the most dynamic leadership qualities.

DOCUMENTED SOURCES OF INFORMATION

The leader's documented sources begin with the instructions and directives he encounters in performing his duties. This source tells what he is required to do, but not in every case does it tell him how to perform the actions necessary to meet these requirements. This lack of information concerning the "how" leads the officer to review references that his basic instructions lead him to. Thus, the leader consults a pyramid of information, beginning with the detailed data of his specific requirements and flowing down to a wide base of supporting and substantiating documentation. The leader must determine how involved his research into the supporting documentation needs to be in each instance.

The good leader does not confine his knowledge and ability to his positional requirements; rather, he recognizes that his development requires him to broaden his knowledge of the Naval Service and its function in the defense of the nation. The rationale for a broad base of knowledge is exemplified by a detachment, in which a leader can find himself fulfilling responsibilities other than his usual ones. At this time, he should have ability and knowledge in sufficient depth to fulfill the duties required to make the detachment operate smoothly and efficiently.

The publications that are available for the officer to review provide another source of documented information. These publications include those issued specifically for the naval officer (*Proceedings, Naval War College Review*, etc.) and those intended for the professional military officer which are not specifically tied to navy requirements (*Armed Forces Journal, Military Business Review*, etc.). Civilian professional publications (*Harvard Business Review, High Technology*, etc.) inform officers about emerging trends that will change the future of the military and the world. Biographies of great military leaders provide insight into techniques that have worked in the past, in many instances under the duress of combat. In this book, the Bibliographies at the end of chapters 1–9, and the Recommended Readings at the end of chapter 10, provide additional information for the officer's benefit.

UNDOCUMENTED SOURCES OF INFORMATION

Admiral Moorer offers that

listening to several points of view is part
of how a leader evaluates a plan. When
the President is presented with several
defense plans and he must choose one, for
example, he listens to the director of the
National Security Council, and then a representative from the Defense Department, and then people such as the
Secretary of State, the Secretary of
Defense, and the Chairman of the Joint
Chiefs of Staff. He listens to all of them,
and then he spends several hours thinking
about what he has heard before issuing a
memorandum saying, "The President has
decided that we will execute Plan A."
Then it is the responsibility of everyone in
the executive branch to carry out their
part of that plan. That is how it happens
in the apex of the government, and by
and large that is the way any leader
should choose a plan. After he assesses
the situation and gathers input, he has to
exercise his judgment.

One person cannot possibly think of all things
at all times. Also, everyone is stronger in some
fields than in others. It is, therefore, sensible
for a decision maker to elicit ideas from different
persons, subordinates and co-workers alike. And
it is essential that the decision maker create an
atmosphere of exchange that is free of restraint
and authoritarianism so that people who are asked
to express their views can do so honestly. In
today's dynamic Navy, the officer must remember the words spoken by Ben Franklin nearly
two centuries ago: "No one is thinking if everyone is thinking alike."[59-103]

Only in a democratic social setting can solutions and ideas be examined equitably. A leader
is almost always in a position to solicit many
ideas. The planning process involves examining
ideas in a search for a solution, and, during the
planning process, the leader should create an
open forum to draw on the individual expertise
that exists at all levels in any field. Because of
their wealth of knowledge and experience, the
senior petty officers deserve a position of special
trust and confidence.[32-63]

Of course, an officer may be required to
implement a decision previously made, may be
under a time constraint, or may be in a situation
that demands authoritarian decision making. But
even then a good leader involves subordinates
to some degree, so that they believe they have
influenced the decision. Even though the course
may have been predetermined, the officer can
create a platform for ideas by letting several
alternatives be proposed—and making sure the
predetermined course is presented as one alternative. If the predetermined course is obviously
the most logical or intuitively the best course,
the leader may let his subordinates "choose" it.
Or he may make the final decision as part of his
prerogative, knowing that he has the support of
fair competition behind that decision.

Peers. Undocumented sources of information
are the knowledge and experience of people.
Like the documented sources, the undocumented sources can be divided into several
groups. First are the officer's peers. Whether
military or civilian, these personnel are on the
same level as the leader and are experiencing
similar problems, performing similar actions, and
fulfilling similar responsibilities. This is the group
with whom the leader can discuss his tribula-
tions and successes, and they will have similar
experiences to share.

Seniors. The next group is made up of the
officer's seniors, those who have authority over
him, whether it is legitimate (CO, XO) or positional (school instructor). Members of this group
normally have additional years of experience and
training that have provided them with insight
that the junior officer has not yet acquired. In
achieving his command, the CO, for example,
held many positions, and his greater experience
gives him an understanding of what can and cannot be done. In the example of the instructor,

although he personally may not have experienced the positions and been required to fulfill the responsibilities, he has heard a multitude of comments and solutions from students during his class discussions.

Subordinates. The final group of undocumented sources is comprised of subordinates, the personnel over whom the leader has positional or legitimate authority. These are the people who in most cases will carry out his directions and perform the actual efforts for him. The leader will know what is to be done to attain successful performance, but at times his subordinates will better know how to do it. For a leader to be successful, he must have the support of and be able to use the knowledge of his experienced subordinates. In the case of the junior officer, the subordinates he searches out will normally have had many more years in the service than he has had, as well as the experience of having performed under various leaders with different leadership styles. The vast knowledge of these people cannot be ignored by the leader. Admiral Nakamura believes that

> the extent to which subordinates should be involved in the planning of operations differs greatly according to many factors, such as the size of the force, the time limit of a mission, the capabilities of the commander and the subordinates, and so on. Generally a commander would decide the course of action and his staff would lay out the details and distribute them after receiving the approval of the commander, although the commander should obtain his subordinate commanders' views if he thinks it necessary or valuable to do so.

In all three groups of undocumented sources, the officer will find knowledge of how to accomplish tasks and missions. To uncover this knowledge, the officer must sometimes find personnel who have previously performed the action or fulfilled the responsibility. His effort to determine how others have performed in the past will pay off by showing the officer the "easy way" to accomplish his objective. Through this effort, the officer can, while still complying with existing instructions and regulations, eliminate a percentage of the administrative and bureaucratic delays that are normally encountered by naval personnel.

To achieve success in the performance of his duties, a leader must be able to take advantage of all the information sources available to him: the documented sources (regulations, instructions, and publications) and the undocumented sources (the personal knowledge and experience of his seniors, peers, and subordinates). The good leader incorporates the available sources of information into a data base that will help him to develop and attain good performance.

EVALUATING SUBORDINATES DURING PLANNING AND EXECUTION

The good leader recognizes that he is fully responsible for the quality of both the plan and its implementation. He is responsible for building his subordinates into an effective decision-making group. The leader is accountable for everything resulting from a group decision, including execution and final outcome. Involving subordinates in the planning process takes time and resources, but the investment will be returned many times over. Not only will the leader improve his own skills and those of his subordinates, but he will also attain a commitment from his subordinates to support the plan, because they helped develop it. Also, execution of a plan developed in this way will normally take less time than execution of a plan in which subordinates played no part, since those responsible for the plan's execution were involved in every step of its formulation.

The subordinate who is involved in planning is encouraged to understand the program's and the unit's "big picture" and to feel that he is a viable part of the program and an integral part of the unit. As a member of the team, he would be more likely to feel comfortable presenting and defending his own opinions. While evaluating subordinates' creativity and innovativeness during discussions, the leader will also have the opportunity to evaluate how they handle constructive criticism.

The leader should be careful not to provide too much negative criticism, as this could cause a subordinate to be reluctant to participate in future discussions for fear of opening himself up to more criticism. The fear of repeated negative criticism (especially if the planning session involves other people in addition to the leader and the subordinate) could produce an outcome that is directly opposite to what the leader desires. Conversely, if a subordinate receives positive feedback in front of a planning group, the subordinate's development will benefit. More important, the leader will be able to assess the subordinate's abilities and limitations, for, through the subordinate's actions during the planning and execution phases, the leader will have the opportunity to observe the subordinate's leadership abilities and his interaction with the other members.

A leader should alter the written work of subordinates only when it is essential that he do so (e.g., to correct obvious grammatical errors or to bring the written work into conformance with command policy). Watching a document proceed through the chain essentially as he wrote it is a very satisfying experience for the document's author and will provide him with a sense of having positively influenced command performance. Another way leaders can assure each person that he is a valuable member of the command is to provide subordinates with feedback on the disposition of their inputs and recommendations.

By involving subordinates, a leader reaps other benefits, as well. For example, the leader will be able to optimize the use of the resources available to him. He can take advantage of all the insights and additional information possessed by his subordinates.

To involve his subordinates fully in the planning, the leader must totally understand the pro-gram himself, so that he can provide subordinates an in-depth briefing concerning constraints and objectives. In conjunction with this briefing, the leader has the opportunity to discover discrepancies in his planning and obtain subordinates' inputs on any shortcomings or gaps. Involving subordinates in this way allows the leader to make sure that the personnel who will perform the actions fully understand the leader's objectives.

Once he has assured himself that his subordinates understand the goals of the unit and the plan for implementing them, the leader is able to monitor the performance of subordinates, tracking work-in-progress against standards or milestones set during planning. Monitoring provides the leader with two major evaluative benefits. First, comparing performance to a set benchmark provides an excellent evaluative tool for the leader to use in counseling subordinates on their strengths and weaknesses: Did the subordinates perform as planned and achieve the desired results? Second, it allows the leader to evaluate his own communication skills: How well did he make his subordinates understand his requirements?

CHANGING THE PLAN IN LIGHT OF NEW INFORMATION

General Rice makes the point that,
in making a decision, an officer considers inputs from staff officers, logistics officers, and communications officers, weighs the pluses and minuses, looks at his options, and then makes the decision. It is his responsibility to make the decision based on intelligence from several sources as well as his own instincts. If an officer makes a bad decision, he should not hesitate to change his decision. Or if, as time goes on and the situation changes, the decision needs to be changed, he must change it. He cannot get locked in, make one decision and stay with it, because situations change. Part of being an officer

and a leader is being able to grasp a multifaceted, changing situation and not hesitate to alter a decision, which may mean
the difference between victory and defeat.
The great generals and admirals did not
hesitate to change a course of action and
thrust out in another direction or move
troops.

Young officers look to their seniors to
see how they grasp the situation, and see
how they make decisions. They will listen
to the captain and the colonel and wonder
if they would make the same decision.
They will listen to all the information, and
they might say to themselves, "If I was in
charge, what would I do? Would I do the
same thing that the colonel is doing?"
That is part of self-education and self-discipline. Sometimes the young officer
believes he knows more than his senior,
and when he find out that he does not, he
has contributed to his self-education in
another way.

Rather than waiting for the senior to
say, "Tell me what you think," the young
officer can tactfully offer his own thoughts
on the subject. In fact, as officers move
up in rank, they come to depend more
and more on those around them. Seniors
cannot possibly be familiar with all the
details of everything that goes on, and
that is why they have a staff and delegate
authority on certain things. They have to
rely on their staff and their subordinates.
It can be disastrous for subordinates to
refrain from speaking up when they know
something the senior needs to know but is
unaware of.

THE EFFECT OF TECHNICAL INFORMATION ON
PLANS

Planning encompasses many aspects, including technical considerations. Admiral Moorer
points out that,

unless the weapons work, there is no
point in being in combat—in fact, it is
very dangerous to be there—so an officer
must concentrate on the training of personnel and the maintenance of the weapons systems and those systems that
support the weapons systems, like communications. In combat it is essential that
these systems function as they were
designed to function. For this reason, an
officer must understand how weapons
work, and he must ensure that they are
properly maintained and that the people
who are going to use them know how to
use them.

Admiral Moorer described how certain individuals he knew prepared for combat.

In the beginning of World War II, I
was flying a patrol plane and we were
ordered to the Philippines, but before we
could get there the Japanese captured
them, so we wound up in the Dutch East
Indies. In any event, when we left Pearl
Harbor, we put a spare of everything in
the airplane: one generator, one starter,
one air speed meter, etc., and the people
who flew the plane knew how to install it
and how to work it. For instance, the
radioman could be sending out a message,
and if something would happen to the
gear he could, just by listening almost,
tell exactly what vacuum tube had failed
and reach in there and fix it. By November of '42, just eleven months after the
war had started, five of these enlisted
men were officers, who were further promoted in follow-on years. That is an example of what I mean by making sure that
your people understand the equipment
and understand how it works. Many times
after you get into combat you can expect a
major expansion of the force, and therefore you're going to have to rely on the
people who already know how the equipment works to teach new people how to
work it so they can take their place.

A young naval officer should have technical curiosity. He should want to know how technical things work, because that will stand him in good stead the rest of his career, whether he is the CNO testifying before the Congress as to why the Navy needs something or a lieutenant in a destroyer.

In evaluating a combat plan, an officer must first take into consideration the actual situation, which includes the physical readiness of all of the units involved, the capabilities of the opposition, and the basic elements of the fight: concentration of poise, the timing involved, the weather, etc. There are many, many things that apply, so while, for example, one plan may be more reasonable if the weather is good, another plan will succeed better if the weather is bad.

MCPON Sanders: *In the search for information on a problem at hand, most of us do quite well. We go to manuals and books, but are perhaps weak in involving subordinates in planning and seeking them out for information. They are a source of information that perhaps goes untapped for years. We have junior petty officers, mid-grade petty officers, and even senior petty officers whose knowledge goes untapped until they make chief; suddenly they are discovered to have great wisdom, although they had this knowledge prior to putting on the chief's hat. In addition to the officer learning a great deal, by involving subordinates in the information-gathering process, he has an opportunity to pay them the dues (of recognition) that they have earned. When receiving constructive criticism, the officer should not take it personally. Perhaps what the enlisted will say is correct, perhaps not, but if you take it as a personal attack to your integrity, to your knowledge, then you've lost and there's no way for anyone to win.*

26. The Planning Sequence

Any successful operation begins with the commander. He starts the process by exercising his lawful authority and using all the resources and means available to him to accomplish the mission. These include leadership skills and management actions such as planning, organizing, staffing, directing, and controlling. If the commander is to be successful, he must follow a step-by-step process in these areas. "The will to do comes from the confidence that one's knowledge of what requires doing is equal to that of any man present."[60-164] In other words, there must be a sequence of Command and Staff Action (see figure 3.2). This sequence is a planning sequence, and it is initiated when the commander receives a mission (step 1).

Admiral Larson believes that keeping those within the organization informed is very important:

When I was an executive officer of a submarine, and also a commanding officer, I used to meet with my crew at least once a week, and I talked about goals and objectives, where we were going, why we were training, what we were trying to accomplish, and what our schedule would look like for the next several months. And then the subordinates would take over and try to incorporate those broad goals and objectives into a ship's training plan and into divisional training plans. It's also very important to answer questions, to take questions from the crew, so that they have a chance to air any grievances they have, and then they are totally on board with where you're going and what you're doing. I used to do that at sea, once we got out there on the operation. About once a week I would sit down at sea and, as classification would allow, I would discuss how we were doing, where we were going, and our progress toward meeting those goals and objectives, or those mission objectives. Once you get your unit ready, or your crew ready, then you need, certainly, to transmit that status to higher authority. In the training phase, I used to send a weekly message to my operational commander that talked about each of my units. It would talk about our goals, where we were going, what had happened that week, and what I had planned for the future. Of course, you need to have a mechanism in an operational sense to transmit changes to higher authority if your plans change or you have perturbations in your mission accomplishment. I found that free and open communications are very important—not a message that tries to make you look good, but an honest appraisal that identifies problem areas, suggests solutions, and indicates how you're going after them to get that unit right on top.

Today, more than ever before, particularly because of numerous modern-day scientific improvements, speed and mobility are decisive factors in all operations. This applies not only on the battlefield itself, but also in the paper work that is necessary in order for troops to get to the battlefield and sustain themselves there. Paper work is often necessary; however, many steps in the planning sequence can and sometimes must be accomplished via thought processes. Although the planning sequence is initiated by receipt of a mission, an outstanding commander, obviously, is continuously involved in planning for every mission that is likely to be assigned to his unit(s), ship(s), or aircraft. The longer and more complex the operation, the longer and more complicated the planning process becomes. Manuals, books, and Standard Operating Procedure guides can be invaluable assets to the commander for planning purposes. However, officers should "be innovative and not always go by the book." Once he lends himself

to predictability, an officer becomes vulnerable, and once he exposes himself, he increases the enemy's ability to defeat him. Admiral McDonald points out that, "in emergencies, time will not normally permit an effective analysis of the situation, but, regardless, the leader must show composure and act decisively."

In a proven course of action, after the commander receives the mission, he must analyze it (step 2). He does this by developing specific tasks that will later allow him to accomplish the mission. He will spell out some of the specific tasks in his operations order, but some of them must be deduced by subordinate commanders based on their own knowledge of tactics.

As the commander analyzes the mission, he also tries to determine the information requirements (step 3) in the area of operations (AOA). Things he considers during this step are the relative combat power of the enemy and the friendly forces, and the capabilities of each.

Obviously, the commander cannot know or integrate all this information. Therefore he must use his staff. In step 4 he gathers information from his staff and from higher, lower, and adjacent headquarters. The commander must make assumptions to cover gaps, but these assumptions should be validated later, if possible. Many of these steps will be going on concurrently; in fact, they must be in order for the sequence to be completed.

Based on the first four steps, the commander moves into step 5, his planning guidance (what he believes to be important).

From this guidance, his operations officer, in concert with the other members of the staff (both general and flag special staff, e.g., communications officer, liaison officer), proposes courses of action (step 6). Proposed courses of action by the commander's staff can sometimes be announced before the commander issues his planning guidance.

Step 7 is the formulation of staff estimates, which must be based on a coordinated effort of

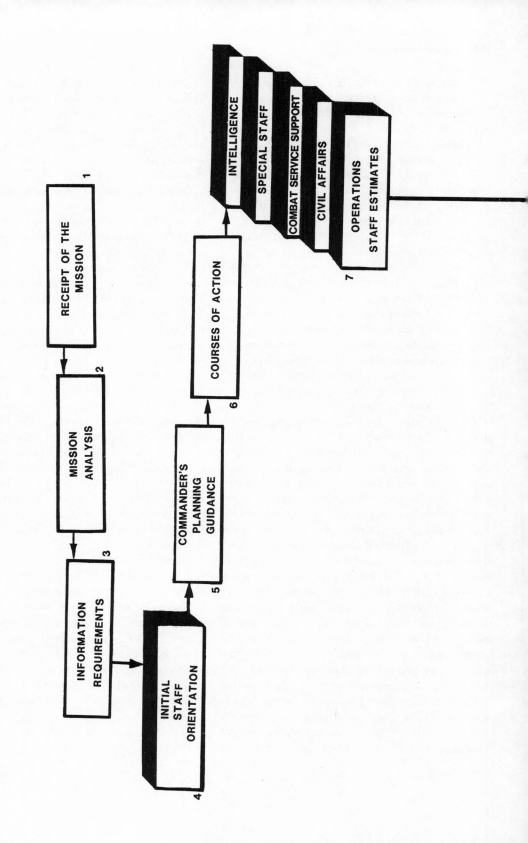

1. RECEIPT OF THE MISSION

2. MISSION ANALYSIS

3. INFORMATION REQUIREMENTS

4. INITIAL STAFF ORIENTATION

5. COMMANDER'S PLANNING GUIDANCE

6. COURSES OF ACTION

7. STAFF ESTIMATES

OPERATIONS

CIVIL AFFAIRS

COMBAT SERVICE SUPPORT

SPECIAL STAFF

INTELLIGENCE

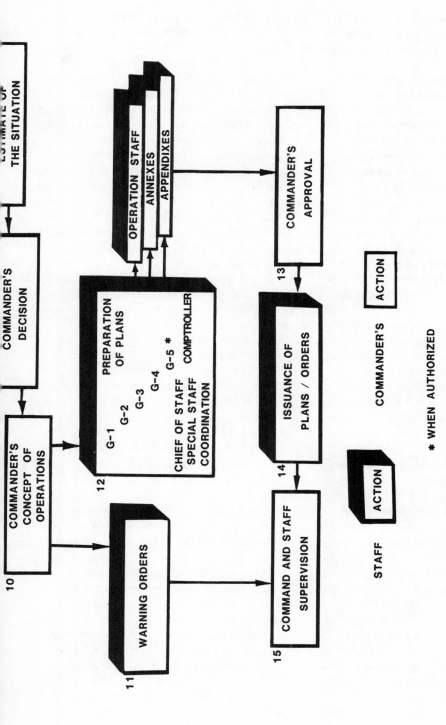

Figure 3.2 Command and Staff Action
SOURCE: FMFM 3-1, *Command and Staff Action* (a Department of the Navy, U.S. Marine Corps Publication).

all staff sections. Just as in a team sport, military action planning requires team effort in order to produce winning results. Admiral Long notes that

> most individuals who have achieved in the Naval Service would readily admit that they were successful, in part, because they relied heavily on the advice and intelligence and wisdom of people who were under their command as well as their peers and seniors. When an important, complex issue arises, it is a good idea to seek inputs from several sources. One of the worst things an officer can do is become the captive of a single source of information. Instead, he should gather information from a variety of places. He will be able to evaluate the source and the quality of the information and then make a judgment concerning it.

> It is absolutely essential that an officer make it clear to his subordinates that he does not want them to become yeasayers. He must be able to tap their intelligence capabilities and their initiative and their imagination, as well as gain their loyalty and support; to do this, he should encourage them to express their ideas and to tell him when they think he is wrong. That does not mean they should be encouraged to refuse to obey or carry out his orders; rather, before the order is given, they should give the officer their best advice and knowledge.

Once they are completed, staff estimates are given to the commander, who considers them and then makes his own estimate (step 8) based on his analysis and what he considers to be the most favorable course of action. He then announces his decision (step 9). The commander amplifies his decision in step 10 by stating his overall concept of operations. This concept is the basis for issuing warning preparation orders (step 11) and unifying the subsequent development of detailed plans and orders (step 12).

Plans are normally submitted to the com-mander prior to being published as orders (step 13); however, if the situation is urgent, this step may be omitted. The last two steps are issuing the plans or orders to the executing units (step 14) and supervising the execution of the orders (step 15), which is a continuous process.

These proven guidelines or similar guidelines can only help ensure an officer's success on the battlefield, whether on land, at sea, or in the air. Proper planning by a commander can ulti-mately determine victory or defeat. To ensure that he has victory on his side, a leader must carefully plan his combat operations, making effective communication of his desires a prereq-uisite for effective leadership.[5-128] "Effective communication can be defined simply as the simultaneous, identical understanding of the content and intent of a message by the sender and the receiver."[5-112]

Regarding the foregoing, Admiral Ramage suggests that,

> to achieve mission accomplishment, a leader must be thoroughly familiar with the objectives of the mission and the capa-bilities and limitations of his command, including his personnel, weapons, and equipment; in addition, he must consider the weather, the time, etc., and ensure that other individuals and organizations are completely aware of his intentions.

> Now, to elaborate on that, submarines were a rather special case. At the start of the war, they were sent out independ-ently with orders to proceed to a desig-nated area, conduct offensive patrol for thirty days on station, and return. Wolfpacks, comprised of three subma-rines, required a bit more coordination. They normally operated on parallel courses within a 60-mile square. They would all move either north, south, east, or west one degree of latitude or longi-tude in accordance with a prescribed schedule. Once contact was made, all sub-marines closed and took station, one on either bow of the oncoming target, while

the third took station astern in order to destroy any damaged stragglers. That was the general concept of operation—very simple and uncomplicated, to say the least. We each knew where we were supposed to go and what we were supposed to do. On the other hand, in the case of fleet operations, it was far more complex, as many more units are involved and things happen much faster in comparison.

27. Courses of Action

Courses of action—their examination, adjustment, rejection, and, ultimately, adoption—are part of the commander's everyday life, in peace or in war. Nonetheless, they are most often thought of within the context of combat, because that is when the pressure is greatest and the price of error most unforgiving—for those for whom the commander is responsible as well as for the commander himself. The commander must uncover the specifics of a proposed action. These specifics will be readily apparent if the task is simple. However, a more complicated operation, such as a reconnaissance mission, will require the leader to question seniors and subordinates to find a specific goal or set of goals for the mission. Hence, the primary step toward planning involves defining objectives.[43-405]

THE PRINCIPLE OF THE OBJECTIVE

There are numerous truths associated with courses of action, but there is one fundamental, unvarying principle, and that is that any course of action worthy of consideration must focus entirely on mission accomplishment. This may be called the principle of the objective. If that essential principle is not followed, failure is foreordained. This may seem to be an obvious point, hardly worth mentioning, yet any serious study of warfare will reveal example after example of commanders adopting courses of action which

had nothing to do with the real objective. Ask yourself whether you are attacking the basic problem or merely its symptoms.

The Union's much abused and heavily used Army of the Potomac is an excellent case in point. George McClellan's campaign on the peninsula was aimed at seizing Richmond and failed because McClellan could not cope with Robert E. Lee's Army of Northern Virginia. Later, the hapless A. E. Burnside started for Richmond, was stalled by the Rappahannock River at Fredericksburg, and ultimately was forced to assault Lee frontally at Marye's Heights in order to continue his move to Richmond. He never came close to success. Mr. Lincoln gave the army to General Joseph Hooker and told him that Lee's army, not Richmond, was the objective. Hooker, in an initially brilliant effort, maneuvered Lee out of his Fredericksburg positions, but then he developed the "on to Richmond" mindset and left himself open to a crushing defeat by Lee. Finally, in Ulysses S. Grant, Mr. Lincoln found a general who understood the objective.

Commanders at all levels, from patrol leaders to battalion commanders and upward, must continually develop, assess, and select courses of action. The more senior the commander, the larger the staff he has to assist him and, usually, the more time he has to reflect on the various courses. That does not necessarily make matters easier. In truth, regardless of the level of command, the unwary can easily be led away from the objective.

THE HUMAN FACTOR

Many tasks, distractions, and obligations compete for the time and energies of commanders. The indecisive commander can readily use these to rationalize his lack of active participation in the identification of potential courses of action: "Let the staff do it. I get paid to make the decisions." The commander who operates on this basis has tacitly yielded command, because his only input will be to select from courses or options suggested by others, and these options may well be nothing more than a series of staff compromises.

A commander may not be able to sit and argue each option through; indeed, he probably will not be able to do so. What he can and must do, though, is identify courses he wants to examine and then devote his free moments to sifting the problem through in his own mind. His staff may be best suited to amplify information—for example, tonnages, timetables, rounds of ammunition—while he will deal in personalities. He will consider the capabilities of his subordinates, of adjacent and senior commanders, and, more often than might be expected, of the enemy commander.

In addition to stamping his own personality—his leadership—on the courses of action, the commander must be acutely sensitive to his staff and how staff members normally interact. He must know his people and their strengths. For example, Who are the dominant personalities? Who is normally conservative? Who will probably push for adoption of the high-risk, high-gain courses, regardless of the situation? Who may tend to compromise when perhaps he ought not do so? How much control does the executive officer or chief of staff exert over them? In short, how can he get the best out of his team? He alone is responsible, but he needs to utilize fully the talent available to assist him in fulfilling his many responsibilities.

SIMPLICITY

The principle of the objective and the influence of the human factor on it are fundamental in selecting courses of action. Another principle that should be inherent in courses of action is simplicity. It can be argued that the more senior the level of command, the more complicated the course of action. This is not necessarily true, however, because simplicity is relative, so that what is a simple course at one level may be complicated at a lower level.

War is confusing enough without injecting further complications in the form of intricate courses of action. Overambitious courses of action can be expected to draw attention away from the objective; invite failure in execution; fritter away forces; rely on critical timing factors; or create confusion for the lower echelons of command. Most damning of all, the mistakes resulting from intricate courses of action may be capitalized on by the enemy.

A severe Japanese weakness during World War II was their penchant for involved plans. There is probably no better example than the concept of operation which Yamamoto adopted at Midway. His objective was to destroy the U.S. Pacific Fleet, particularly the carriers. His concept included long-range aerial reconnaissance and harassment bombing of Pearl Harbor; a submarine reconnaissance screen; attack and invasion of Midway; attack of Adak and seizure of Attu and Kiska; and a mopping up of Pacific Fleet remnants. Too many objectives, too many timing requirements, and far too much reliance on American forces doing what the Japanese assumed they would do.

In the final analysis, Yamamoto's course resulted in a complex failure; his vastly superior force was thoroughly defeated by a significantly inferior one. Nimitz was immeasurably helped by the fact that the United States was intercepting much of the Japanese message traffic. This gave him the advantage of surprise, but many people at the time thought that Nimitz was relying far too much on the radio intercepts, which may have been deceptive. Many also attempted to counsel him away from his objective: the destruction of the Japanese aircraft carriers. But Nimitz won because he stuck to his objective, knew his staff, had confidence in his commanders, and was well aware of his enemy's penchant for complicated operations.

THE INFLUENCE OF FACTS AND OPINIONS

Admiral Holloway points out that
  briefings are usually for the purpose of
  presenting facts in a succinct, useful fash-

ion. Opinions are often important, too, however, and they can be incorporated into a briefing as long as they are identified as opinions. As a member of the Joint Chiefs of Staff, I always differentiated between fact and opinion in my presentations.

On those occasions when I was acting chairman, we were very meticulous in making sure that the President and the National Security Council understood what was fact and what were our views. For example, I might come in and say, "Here is the situation." Then I might say, "It is the view of the Joint Chiefs of Staff that . . . such and such. Mr. President, I generally agree with the other chiefs with this exception, . . . and my personal view is that . . . so and so." Now what the chairman has done is give the facts to the National Security Council. He presents the consensus and then gives his own views if they differ from those of his colleagues and he believes they are important.

Finally, when he is evaluating courses of action, a commander must use his judgment regarding the accuracy or relevance of facts that are available to him. Under some circumstances, all of the information he is receiving may be totally suspect. Certainly not much of what Admiral Nimitz had to ponder before Midway turned out to be good information, yet he took what he had and used his considerable strategic and tactical judgment to formulate a plan. Waiting to get "all the facts" before acting is a luxury few—if any—combat commanders can expect to enjoy. Whether to execute a course with the hard information available or to wait for more information is a decision that almost every leader operating under duress can expect to have to make. Admiral Carney makes the point that

the person who knows the most concerning any subject will rise to a position of leadership like cream in a pot. Leading

from a position of ignorance is self-defeating and will prove to be a disaster for everyone concerned, so an individual who seeks responsibility must be as knowledgeable and as informed as he can be.

MCPON Sanders: *I have found in the past that many times people will have a good idea, but when asked why, what, when, and what made you think of it, the suggester wasn't prepared, and often the good idea just faded away. The leader should do the homework, and prepare for possible attacks on his thoughts, and if he has done his homework, his hard efforts will pay off.* [Editor's note: While officers may be expected to staff an idea completely before presenting it, and to present the idea in writing, offering pros and cons, the officer should not expect that same degree of completeness from his enlisted subordinates. If he hears them out, he may be able to "catch" a good idea by supplying some of the needed staff work.]

28. Budgeting Funds, Material, and Personnel

Planning often presents a challenge to young officers. Predicting the future is always difficult and frequently impossible, while reconstructing past planning efforts in order to develop trends is not always possible or helpful.

General Rice observes that,

to economize in the use of personnel, material, and money, the officer needs to use management techniques. He can take management courses and supplement what he learns with experience. Maybe he has run into the same type of situation before—for example, he knows what it takes to run a headquarters, and, even though his experience does not match what someone else says it takes to run a headquarters, he can manage—and his experience and his education, as well as the expertise of staff officers, will help him use his supplies to best advantage. In the area of supply management, an officer almost always must rely on input from experts, who have taken postgraduate or special courses in this area.

An officer can expect to receive personnel cuts, so he must use initiative and planning to see how he can still accomplish his mission, even though he has fewer people. He also should not hesitate to advise his seniors if he cannot accomplish the mission as assigned without additional resources. "Can do" is a good slogan, but it has also gotten people killed, so the officer must determine through his experience and education when he must acknowledge inability to proceed.

BUDGETING FUNDS

Everyone has at some time established a budget for allocation of personal funds. How well people are able to plan ahead and use their money to accomplish or attain the things they want to is determined by how well they have addressed the demands on this scarce resource.

When individuals begin budgeting funds that are not their own, they discover that, very often, these funds are "funny" money: money that is backed by a system that never seems to be synchronized with the "real" world. The individual who designs a lean budget, with no frills, may suddenly discover that he is forced to take a cut. The next time, he pads his budget, and then he is given an increase that he must spend in a short time. As a result of these experiences, he spends more time trying to gauge the spending climate than he does developing a workable plan.

Regardless of the budget climate—whether funds are expanding or shrinking—the economic use of the dollars entrusted to a naval officer's care is an imperative. An officer can only use these funds wisely if he has identified and prioritized his needs. The naval officer should

always know where he would spend the next, and, possibly, the last, dollar. Admiral Burke discussed the importance of budgeting both time and money.

There are two things that I think maybe people now are negligent about: (1) They do not have a sense of the value of time or money. (2) They will postpone things from today to tomorrow or next year, when they should be done now. Things cost a lot more when people do not do them properly, and somehow we can't get the word across. We need a sense of value.

Young officers are sometimes careless with their money. They believe they must have a lot of things: car, radio, television. And they are sometimes careless with the Naval Service's money, too. When I was a kid, when you went aboard ship you were given a pencil, and you didn't go back to the gunnery officer and get yourself another pencil. When you lost it, you had to buy a replacement pencil. You turned lights out on the gangway so that you could win your engineering competition. While a few electric lights made only a little bit of difference, what it did do was cause everyone to be cost conscious.

Planning for the use of allocated dollars is the easiest of an officer's budgetary responsibilities. The more difficult and more important areas are material and personnel.

BUDGETING MATERIAL

Officers in the Naval Service have been entrusted with a vast array of sophisticated equipment, and this equipment must be managed to maintain operational readiness and training availability. Commercial airlines minimize the ground time for their aircraft, since no revenue is created when the aircraft are not hauling passengers. The Navy's challenge is different. Naval officers have to ensure that equipment is ready to perform at full capability at any time.

Yet they cannot let equipment idle in pristine condition while they await the "big moment," because the equipment has to be used to train the people who will fight it. If the division officer does not manage his material properly, not only his division, but also the supply department, will be inefficient. [44-217]

Thus, two competing equipment requirements must be addressed in any equipment use plan. Economic utilization of equipment must be balanced with the requirements that the equipment be maintained, that it be available for training, and that it be utilized at a rate that does not shorten its life expectancy or exceed the logistic support available for that rate of use.

BUDGETING PERSONNEL

The most important asset officers need to utilize economically is personnel. Without the individuals who make up a unit, none of the equipment could operate, and the duties of the division could not be accomplished. For that reason, the division officer should devote the main part of his attention toward the efficient use of his personnel. [44-14]

The greatest mistake officers can make is to assume that, since personnel are a full-time asset, they can be managed carelessly. Nothing is more unmotivating for a sailor or a Marine than to sit around under the pretense that his services are needed, and then never be called into action.

The division officer should always assign attainable objectives. Personnel must have something to "shoot for" in order to perform at maximum efficiency. If the goals are too far-reaching, success will not be imminent. If the officer divides the goals into small units, the men will see success along the way, and they will be more apt to work efficiently as each small goal is attained and refuels their drive. [44-33]

Properly constituted duty sections exist to provide manpower for emergent work. When careful thought is put into duty section rosters, seldom will additional people be needed for task completion. Duty sections can be used more economically and efficiently when their members are given a list of tasks that they can accomplish during the duty day. Training is another area where substantial gains in productivity can be made, particularly in damage control PQS (Professional Qualification System). An officer must make it clear that he is interested in what takes place during a duty day. Weekend duty sections in particular often benefit from attention to managerial needs.

General Greene's December 1984 article in the *Marine Corps Gazette* provides insight into the development of the fire team, which for more than forty years has shown the value of personnel utilization planning. Fifteen years in development and containing concepts stretching back three thousand years, to the four-man fighting team of Greek Marines employed by Ulysses in cleaning up the Aegean Sea, this article demonstrates that officers can develop further economy in personnel utilization when they accept the challenge and try. (The following excerpts from the article are applicable in this context.)

Early in the Nicaraguan Campaign (1927–1933), it became evident that a small point sent ahead of a Marine patrol to act as an advanced group could easily be lost on forking trails. Frequently, the enemy separated the point from the patrol by a cleverly devised ambush and annihilated it. The traditional formation of placing an automatic rifleman in the forefront of the patrol, or at the spot in the patrol where the attack was expected, so that his fire could immediately be directed by the patrol leader, resulted almost invariably in an inconclusive firefight. The first concentrated fire from an ambush usually made a casualty of the automatic rifleman if he was near the front or an exposed flank.

As a second lieutenant stationed at the Marine Barracks in Portsmouth, N.H., with "day on, day off, duty" as officer of the day and consequently with time to study my profession, I enrolled in this course and was fascinated to discover the part which the so-called "fighting team" of four men had played in small unit patrol actions. I deduced three things: (1) it helped ensure the continued operation and advance of an automatic weapon in combat, (2) it provided an established triangular maneuver organization of three teams for the squad, (3) it would serve to develop a large number of small unit leaders in any Marine Corps organization.

In answer to the rising emergency in China, I was hurriedly transferred to the 4th Marines in Shanghai in 1937 to become the assistant to then Major Edson—the hero of the Coco River patrol in Nicaragua. I talked with Edson a great deal about his combat patrol experiences and my peacetime adaptations with the four-man fighting team.

By trial and error, I shifted personnel within the company until each team was finally composed of four men who liked or respected each other. I billeted each team together in the same squad bay. I assigned them guard duty, police work, athletics, as teams. I encouraged them to go on liberty together and to help each other at all times. The best man in each team and so recognized by his teammates was designated team leader. All members of the team in order of rank or recognition were taught to automatically take over as team leader in the event of casualties and to keep the automatic or special weapon in action at all times. If three men finally became casualties, the fourth with the weapon would join the nearest team.

I wish I could tell you just how the men responded to this scheme of organization and leadership. It was as if, being sports-minded American boys, they were joining an athletic team—in this case a four-man fighting team. The individual teams were designated by numbers or let-

ters, and we often trained by calling out football-type signals to indicate a maneuver by the teams. These men and these teams, through their own enthusiastic, shared, and dedicated effort, eventually won the competition for the best company in the 4th Marine Regiment.

Later, during the Marshall Islands operation in World War II, I came to realize from association with the 22nd Marines in the attack against Eniwetok Atoll that patriotism and sacrifice were measured and understood by the individual Marine in terms of the fighting team in which he served. He could not let the other team members down, and consequently he did not let the Corps and his country down. Struck by a heavy Japanese mortar, cannon, and machine gun fire and also, through error, by some of our own supporting naval gunfire, as it landed on the western beaches of Parry Island, the 1st Battalion was thrown into utter confusion, in which control and communications were temporarily lost. In the melee, the fire teams, knowing what they were supposed to do, automatically took over and fought forward until the unit commanders could reestablish command.

Thomas E. Lawrence, of Arabia fame, had laid down the principle upon which guerrilla fighting tactics were based. He tried to formalize the principles of guerrilla warfare in much the same way that principles had been standardized for regular combat. The most important feature in such fighting, according to Lawrence, was that the guerrillas, usually inferior in number, had to operate with few casualties in order to keep up both their strength and morale. Under this disadvantage, they had to avoid massive troops or allowing themselves to be drawn into large-scale battles. The basic tactic of the guerrilla group was to strike and run, to destroy lines of communication rather than to conquer territory or kill the enemy. The second main feature of Lawrence's thesis was that whenever two men were together in guerrilla warfare there was one too many! This principle of course was a subsidiary to the first. Here he overemphasized his point. I believe what he undoubtedly had in mind was that, to make guerrilla warfare successful, the soldier had to depend on his own resourcefulness; extreme decentralization of mobility and firepower were essential. This idea was reflected in the two-man team of the British commandos.

The special action report of the 3d Marine Division for the Bougainville operation (1 November–28 December 1943), submitted to the Commandant of the Marine Corps on 21 March 1944, contains as Enclosure F the special action report of the 3d Marine Regiment, which reads: "The basis of all small patrols was generally the 'Four-Man Fire Team' (three riflemen and one automatic rifleman) in either the wedge or the box formation. For example, a reconnaissance patrol might form a wedge or box of wedges of four men each, with the leader of each team in the center. In combat, when contact was made by one of these teams with the enemy, the idea was that the automatic rifleman could cover the target. One rifleman would cover the automatic rifleman and the other two move in immediately to flank the target; the speed of reaction of the team generally measured the degree of success of the attack. Another important feature of the attack which was carefully observed was that the pair of flankers moved inboard of their formations so that their line of fire would be away from other fire teams in the formation."

From the first, the basic question was whether there should be three or four

men in the fire team. Both systems could be used in the nine- or twelve-man squad. After many discussions, compromises, and criticisms, the four-man team was finally decided upon as a superior fire unit because it provided a little more flexibility. In the three-man team, if one man became a casualty, the offensive action of the team was seriously endangered and the automatic rifleman was inadequately supplied with ammunition. Also, the three-man team provided no equal division of forces. Either the automatic rifleman had to stay behind and allow the other two men to make the flanking movement, or he had to hold one man with him as assistant ammunition bearer and replacement in case he himself became a casualty.

The question of armament also received a great deal of attention. It was early agreed that the BAR was necessary as a base of fire. It was also decided to arm the assistant automatic rifleman with an M1 rifle. Thus, all members of the team would use the same ammunition, with the result that there would be a common pool, and confusion would be cut to the minimum.

However, subsequent discussions provided two reasons against the use of the M1: (1) with all men armed with the M1s, the automatic rifleman might be left without an ammunition bearer in a fierce fight, and (2) the carbine was much lighter than the M1, and the ammunition bearer could carry just that much more ammunition for the BAR. Thus, Division of Plans and Policies recommended that the assistant automatic rifleman be armed with a carbine.

The significant feature of the new rifle company T/O was the fact that it broke down the squad into subgroups, thus displacing the squad as the smallest integral unit of combat. The primary innovation was a shift from the twelve-man to the thirteen-man squad and the division of the squad into three fire teams of four men each. One sergeant, the squad leader, was armed with a carbine. A corporal, armed with a M1 rifle, bayonet, and grenade launcher, was put in charge of each fire team and designated the fire team leader. The members of the fire team consisted of one rifleman armed with the M1, the bayonet, and launcher; one automatic rifleman armed with the BAR; and one assistant automatic rifleman armed with a carbine. The new change left intact the triangular formation of three squads to a platoon and three platoons to a company.

In summarizing their actions on Saipan (1944), divisional reports stated that the use of the fire team had definitely met and surpassed all expectations. Thus, from its official date of establishment to the present time, the four-man fire team, with the exception of a few changes in armament, proved beyond a doubt its place as an important unit in the Marine rifle squad. In all the battles since its establishment, this Marine Corps team formation had functioned smoothly and efficiently.

This, then, is the story of the four-man fire team and how it came about. Its validity has been battle tested.

MONITORING THE BUDGETARY PLAN

After an officer has instituted a program, he must establish a review mechanism that will allow him to step aside and critically review how well his goals are being met. An officer must avoid taking it for granted that a carefully designed program is going as planned. Seldom is this the case. A plan that is not critically reviewed usually is not carried out.

An officer must be particularly alert after the turnover of key personnel. Many tasks that formerly have been completed automatically can come to a full stop as a result of an incomplete or misunderstood passdown. An officer should also remember that a unit goes through a life of its own, and that his plans must take into account the pace and assignment of the unit. The amount of monitoring that is required varies considerably, depending on whether a unit is undergoing a post-deployment leave and upkeep period or making an overseas working port visit. Naval officers who periodically review their budgets and plans for funds, equipment, and personnel through personal monitoring are likely to use all of their resources to best advantage. It must be remembered that, throughout history, taxpayers have watched the Navy as well as the other services in their effective management of material. The public has always insisted on maximum utilization, because each one of them has a small investment in every purchase the Navy makes.[55-204]

MCPON Sanders: *While the officer must seek to economize on the use of personnel, material, and money, I should like to emphasize a concern dealing with volunteering to get a job done or volunteering your division for work elsewhere. In the first place, you must be there to help if the work to be undertaken is beyond what they normally are supposed to do. It is easy to overwork your crew if you are not aware of other assignments and jobs they will have to do. It is suggested that the officer be very careful about volunteering his division, at least until he has had a chance to talk with his leading enlisted and is aware of all commitments the division is responsible for now and in the immediate future.*

29. Logistics

Hannibal astounded the world by his foresight in his trek across the Alps; everything that was necessary to conduct a long and demanding march and military campaign was carried on the backs of his men and elephants. Hannibal never attended a service academy, a school of command and staff, a war college. No less astounding were the ill-fated expeditions of Napoleon's army and Hitler's divisions into Russia; the overly long logistics support lines employed in these expeditions reaffirmed the obvious lessons learned by their senior staff officers, most of whom had attended the finest of schools: it is unwise to launch an endeavor without sufficient equipment to see it through to conclusion.

LOGISTICS PLANNING

Few junior officers will participate in planning for evolutions on the scale of Hannibal's march or the French and German winter campaigns, but all junior officers will be required to plan and execute on a smaller, but no less important, scale. During deployments or exercises, poor logistics planning will become painfully obvious, whereas sound preparations and planning will serve the officer well. Why, then, do some young naval officers (who painstakingly inventory the equipment they plan to carry on a mountain backpacking outing or the supplies they will need to host a gala New Year's Eve party) overlook so many things when readying their division or platoon for a six-month deployment? One explanation is that backpackers and party hosts do not have a supply officer to depend on.

There is a tendency of officers yet unburdened by the mistakes of the past to assume the supply officer or the supply system will anticipate all their needs and be prepared to respond to all of their requirements long after the ship or the unit has left its home port or base. Not so. The supply officer, no matter how personally capable, is not as qualified as the element leaders are to predict the needs of the command elements. He has no crystal ball, and he has his own department or division to prepare. Just as each officer must always be a safety officer, a morale officer, and a public affairs officer for his segment of the command, he must also always consider himself a supply officer, anticipating and planning for the requirements of the deployment, the exercise, or the war.

MATERIAL ACCOUNTABILITY

Secretary Webb reminds us that the officer must conduct himself with impeccable integrity in handling equipment, as he does in all other areas of service. To act otherwise makes him vulnerable and weakens his credibility. One officer developed a friendship with a soldier in the supply corps, and at the end of the OCS program the kid gave the officer a field jacket that he had taken out of supplies, saying, "You know, basically I swiped this." Of course the officer returned the jacket, and he told his friend that he had violated a fundamental precept for the sake of a field jacket. Credibility with respect to equipment is no different than credibility anywhere else, and the officer who wrongfully takes something can expect his people to do the same, because the officer is the example.

In the field, accountability for equipment is, ultimately, an officer's responsibility. When the equipment sergeant brings his equipment inventory forms to sign, the officer should request to see all of the equipment he is signing for. If he signs the forms and the equipment has been lost, stolen, or transferred, or has never existed, that officer or an officer sometime in the future is going to be held responsible for holding the bag for a bunch of stuff that may have disappeared years earlier.

Protecting the equipment and supplies entrusted to him is a multifaceted responsibility of the officer. Adequate security and accountability procedures must be planned for and implemented to ensure that equipment and supplies are not pilfered or maliciously damaged at home, abroad, or even at sea. On board a ship, security watches are generally set up while the ship is in port, as this is when the ship is the most vulnerable to an external breach of security. The officer must ensure that security watch standers know the limits of their post as well as the steps that are to be taken in various emergency situations and security breeches.[19-53]

Many ships or aircraft have been launched with improperly stowed equipment. The results include material damage, personnel injury, fiscal loss, reduced readiness, and even loss of ship stability and aircraft controllability. Damaged equipment is of no value. Heavy-weather tie-downs and properly charged integrity watches or prelaunch inspections are a must. Admiral Itaya states that

> the conservation and maintenance of equipment is the responsibility of the officer in charge. He should inspect daily, or, when he does not inspect, he should have subordinates inspect. He should obtain their reports and confirm them. Equipment that is old or unserviceable should be exchanged immediately for new equipment so that it is ready for immediate use. In days of old, the samurai of Japan had his sword. It was said that the sword was the soul of the samurai. A tarnish on the sword was a tarnish on his soul.

Similar attention should be paid to conserving equipment on hand to ensure its availability. It would be ludicrous to expend all of the ordnance on a ship in live firing drills and be left without any when the war zone was reached. It is no less ludicrous to reach the middle of a deployment and have all of the systems unserviceable because a preventive maintenance system had not been established or implemented, because the only technician trained to trouble-shoot the system is on emergency leave, or because insufficient spares, technical manuals, or test program software is available. The Planned Maintenance Schedule system provides for the periodic testing, servicing, and repair of all machinery and equipment throughout the ship.[19-273] Each need should be anticipated and planned for. Cross-training, predeployment fast cruises (in-port simulation of underway exercises), discussions with personnel who have had similar experiences, and common sense with regard to the future all provide attractive alternatives to mid-deployment failure. A leader must train personnel to compensate for known deficiencies or potential requirements. A leader should not waste his time or that of his personnel with popular or readily available, but unneeded, training sessions.

Today's equipment and supplies are expensive, and tomorrow's will be more so. Waste through abuse or inopportune use cannot be tolerated by any officer. Far too often a ship system is down because it lacks a part; adequate stock of the part was on hand, but the stock was exhausted because of a lack of foresight in the use of assets. One destroyer CO reported with dismay during a Mediterranean cruise that spare electronic components intended for his unserviceable radar had been expended repairing recreational TV sets. Priorities have to be established, understood, and followed. Admiral Holloway points out that

> the commander who is wasteful in the use of, say, his aviation fuel, who lets his people go up and joy ride instead of making every gallon of aviation fuel count, instead of using it for training, is simply not doing his job to the best of his ability. He is not getting the most out of his squadron, and it is not going to be as ready at the end of the training cycle as it would have been had he used those flight hours in a carefully controlled and planned fashion. The officer who has planned ahead and is committed to following his plan will not succumb to the request of a young man who wants to use an aircraft to fly what he would call "training cross country" (and he is actually going out to California to see his girlfriend).

Proper equipment use and maintenance also affect an officer more directly. Wasting equipment creates a very bad impression, and those who observe an officer

190

doing so will consider the waste a flaw in the integrity of the officer. An officer who has little respect for things that he has been put in charge of, who wastes them or does not care about them, will lose the respect of his subordinates, and when he loses their respect, his ability to lead or command is also lost. Most sailors and noncommissioned officers are very bright, very observant people who are highly moral, and they react strongly to someone who wastes or misuses material.

MATERIAL DISPOSAL

Disposal of excess material and supplies is also a challenge. Ships and deployment storage are crowded. Everyone wants more room to store more things to remain ready more of the time. Thus, space used for items in excess of reasonably determined requirements is space denied to items of genuine requirement. Prior to deployment, a tough-minded appraisal of need and spaces or outfitting allowances is in order, and accumulated excesses must be disposed of in strict compliance with established procedures. Admiral Holloway says that

> everyone in the command—both the commanders and the subordinates—must dispose of older equipment properly. Usually the Navy can sell old equipment and use the money it brings to acquire new equipment. Old equipment should not be turned over to personnel unless that method of disposal has been agreed on beforehand.

A good working relationship between officers of similar commands in the home port often results in offloads of material from a command with an excess to one with a critical need for the same item. Cumshaw and midnight requisition have no place in the process, as expensive property of the Navy and Marine Corps is not to be trifled with, and encouraging extralegal transfer of accountability for equipment and supplies serves only to encourage sloppy material management

and, in extreme cases, criminal acts. General Wilson comments:

> Protecting equipment and supplies is something that the young American is not wont to do. He is profligate and careless and he lacks concern about his equipment because he thinks there's a never-ending supply, and this is one of the problems most commanders have to face. Troops will throw away their equipment or they won't have it repaired, because they think they can always turn it in and get another one. This happens in combat and this has happened since my days in the service, since 1941. I don't know whether it came about as a result of the enormous supplies that we had in World War II as the great American war machine began to come up with unlimited supplies—"Nothing's too good for our boys." Any time there is too much of anything it's not good.
>
> Now I know that there are people who will dock the pay of troops for failing to take care of their equipment, but they are in the minority. Troops must be made to be responsible for the things they have, and moralizing to them generally serves no purpose, except maybe once. After that they've got to be hit where it hurts— in their pocketbook. If they throw away things and deliberately do not take care of them, they've got to pay for them.
>
> Bulldozers were driven off cliffs on Guam and Saipan, and road machinery was buried in places, and this had a high visibility. People young and old reported to the newspapers the carelessness with which commanders treated American property. The fact is that, in most instances, it would have been much more expensive to ship back the equipment that had been used and for the most part had very little life left in it, to ship it back only to have it reconditioned and sold at bargain basement prices, than it would be

to destroy it. But this has such a high visibility that commanders now are afraid to do it, so they are willing to incur great expense to the government because they don't want to be accused of being profligate with American property. It's not the commander's job, however, to bring everything back here because he doesn't want to get criticized.

Deciding how to dispose of equipment is the commander's responsibility. It is a decision a commander has to make and live with. This is hard work. Any decision he makes he should completely justify and be sure it is kept as a matter of record, and he should be prepared to defend it when he is called upon to do so. He may not be able to defend it to the American people, and it could be that he loses his job over it; but those are the hazards of command, that's what a commander is paid for doing.

"Upon the strength of each link of the cable dependeth the might of the chain." It can be called the weak link, the long pole in the tent, or the critical path of a PERT network (Program Evaluation Review Technique). Proper planning for material support contingencies is one of the most important aspects of an officer's responsibility. The success of any important evolution will depend on it, and the junior officer who learns early that no one can predict or take care of his needs better than he can, has learned a valuable lesson.

30. Safety and the Minimization of Accidents

The young naval officer should acquaint himself with the following terms, which are used in discussions of safe material and personnel management. It is important to note that the U.S. Navy is no different from major industries. Safety first, especially safety at sea, has always been a prime concern of the Navy, and it will always be.[38-1313]

HAZARD. An existing or potential condition that can result in a mishap.

HAZARD PROBABILITY. The likelihood, expressed in quantitative or qualitative terms, that a hazard exists.

HAZARD SEVERITY. A qualitative assessment of the worst potential consequences, defined by the degree of injury, occupational illness, property damage, or equipment damage that could ultimately occur.

MISHAP. An unplanned event or series of events that results in human death, injury, or occupational illness, or equipment property damage or loss. One such example would be the USS *Forrestal*. On 29 July 1967, a rocket accidentally triggered while on the flight deck hit an A-4 Skyhawk. The ensuing fire caused more explosions and even more deaths. The total fatality rate was 134 dead or missing, while the ship, excluding aircraft, had seventy-two million dollars of damage done to her.[18]

RISK. An expression of possible loss in terms of hazard severity and hazard probability.

RISK ASSESSMENT. The identification and orderly arrangement of hazards to establish priorities for corrective action. Priorities are based on an assessment of hazard severity and hazard probability.

RISK MANAGEMENT. An element of safety management that evaluates the effects of potential hazards should they become actual hazards, and recommends acceptance, control, or elimination of such hazards based on availability of funds.

SAFETY. Freedom from conditions that can cause human death, injury, or occupational illness, or equipment or property damage or loss.

SYSTEM SAFETY. The acceptable degree of safety attained through specific application of system safety management and system safety engineering principles, whereby hazards are identified and risk is minimized throughout all phases of the system life cycle.

SYSTEM SAFETY ENGINEERING. An element of system engineering requiring specialized professional knowledge and skills in applying scientific and engineering principles, criteria, and techniques to identify, eliminate, or control system hazards.

SYSTEM SAFETY MANAGEMENT. An element of management that establishes the system safety program requirements and ensures the planning, implementation, and accomplishment of tasks and activities to achieve system safety consistent with the overall program requirements.

While *mishap* is included in this list, *accident* is not. This is because very few events occur accidentally. Rather, they are caused by one or more factors. These factors are sequentially linked in a serial or parallel manner and result in a mishap. If the mishap is dependent only on a serial-linked sequence of causal factors, then removing one of those factors may prevent the mishap. But if the mishap is dependent on a parallel-linked sequence of casual factors, then all of the factors may have to be removed to prevent a mishap.

IDENTIFYING AND REDUCING HAZARDS

Real-world situations that contain a potential for mishap include causal factors that are both serial and parallel linked. Which causal factor is the most crucial depends on the nature of the causal factors as well as available resources. Figure 3.3 depicts three possible causal factor arrangements.

Each causal factor may represent any identifiable hazard, such as:

—Lack of education
—Lack of training
—Fatigue (physical or mental)
—Improper procedure*
—Obsolete technical manual

*For example, as Admiral Carney notes, while formal safety engineering began in the twentieth century, before that, seamanship required that, if the weather was bad, lifelines had to be rigged on deck and people were latched or hooked to the lifeline, or even to a mast on a tether. Seamanship was a safety engineering project in the beginning.

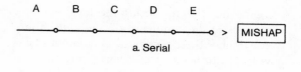

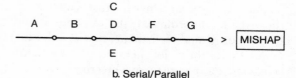

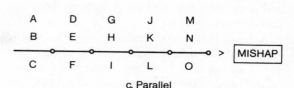

Figure 3.3   Causal Factor Arrangements

—Equipment operated outside design limits
—Thermal stress
—Lack of protective equipment
—Weather that does not develop as forecasted
—Unsuitable tempo of operations
—Inattentive operator
—Excessive noise
—Improper tool
—Task saturation
—Distraction
—Illness
—Design error

The factors involved and the relationship between them are linked to the mishap they may cause. A task that easily causes fatigue may be accomplished safely by replacing the human operator frequently or by having him rest periodically. However, not having the proper tools for a job is hazardous whether or not the operator of those tools is fatigued.

The leader must manage the manning, training, education, operational tempo, and drills/exercises of the unit to produce the highest possible level of readiness, a level that is consistent with the hazards inherent to the mission. He accomplishes this by raising the level of safety awareness of the command through education, which teaches those employed in hazardous tasks how to perform safely in a hazardous environment. Admiral Uchida notes that the Imperial Japanese Navy had a maxim that said: "First, show them [subordinates] the example of how to handle; second, tell them what are the key points to do; third, let them practice by themselves and encourage them when they succeed." He believes that this maxim remains valid in reducing accidents and improving methods for maintaining equipment.

A hazardous environment automatically heightens the operators' awareness of the dangers and risk associated with their task. On the other hand, infrequent incidents/mishaps can anesthetize operators, encourage management complacency, and divert attention away from safety matters. A timely, aggressive safety program and the availability of people and funds to investigate and incorporate necessary changes will focus the leadership's attention and action on safety issues. Concurrently, vigilance, a product of dedication and training, will preclude operator complacency. It is incumbent on the leader to ensure that safety awareness and hazard solution are customary activities in this program.

Admiral Hayward says that

> proper maintenance of equipment results when individuals progress beyond the "hardware" aspects of the machinery. The concept I like is the one of ownership. This sense of ownership is imperative if you're going to have a really ready ship, so that when a piece of equipment is not operating, it's almost a voluntary reaction you get from those responsible for that piece of equipment to get it back in shape as quickly as they can because it's theirs. I've watched them so many times, and the most successful units, whether they're aviation squadrons, ships, or the like, the standout "E" winners, are those who developed that sense of ownership.

> You can be in a shop or division or whatever, but the belief that the pump over there is yours is important, so that when it has to go through phase maintenance it's done right the first time, it doesn't have to be done over again, or if it breaks down, why, you're "Johnny on the Spot" to get it back into shape. My point is that if you want to have a ready ship and if you're going to win the "E," you want to develop the attitude that it's my ship, and that's my piece of gear, and it's going to be the best piece of gear on this ship, and it's going to be working all the time, and when it's not we're going to get it fixed as fast as possible. It's part of the team effort, that sense of ownership I'm trying to stress.

The objective of any safety program is to identify hazards and either reduce them to an acceptable risk or eliminate them entirely. Many leaders fail to recognize that a safety program that is working effectively is a natural part of leadership operational efforts at all levels of the command structure. They tend to view safety as a separate entity that is to be treated in a sterile and unrealistic manner. This mind set is wrong. Safety is as much a part of the infrastructure of sound leadership techniques as are defining problems, determining assets and requirements, setting goals, or fixing milestones.

Admiral de Cazanove suggests that

> the simplest way to reduce accidents is to use a checklist, with everyone in the unit assigned a task that will promote accident reduction. Drill and training are concurrent approaches to accident reduction, for they develop the teamwork necessary for all hands to react quickly to an incident or know when to take action to avoid something going wrong. It is sometimes difficult in these sophisticated days to break down completely who is responsible for what; however, the officer might want to adapt something we did on the PT boat,

where all 15 of my men were able to do all jobs on the ship, so that if someone were injured or killed, someone else was able to take over. While this may be easier on a smaller ship with its lesser degree of sophistication, those on larger ships can approximate this condition and make the duty of all hands even more interesting as they learn to do more things.

OPERATIONAL EFFICIENCY AND SAFETY

Operational efficiency may be measured via any number of indicators, such as:

—Rounds on target
—Cargo transferred
—Sorties/hours flown
—Training accomplished
—Persons reenlisted/augmented
—Persons promoted
—Workdays lost
—Inspection grades earned
—Mishap rate

Incidents or mishaps can negatively affect all of these indicators of efficiency. The leader who regularly examines such indicators and acts accordingly to make them positive, rather than negative, indicators is effective and safety conscious.

Each leader must strive to create and maintain a climate in his command or unit in which all hands understand that the only acceptable standard of performance for mission accomplishment is via the safest means possible. The following list is a summary of necessary ingredients that should be a part of every leader's operations management effort.

Objective
—Enhance readiness by preserving personnel and material resources

Methods
—Reduce personnel and material losses through hazard identification and elimination

Means
—Establish and support command safety programs through policy and example
—Ensure compliance with all existing safety directives
—Establish and support a command safety training program
—Establish a formal written program with specific goals, such as:
    Hazard awareness
    Hazard detection
    Hazard elimination/minimization
—Integrate each person into the processes of mishap prevention and hazard elimination as follows:
    Train and educate all hands
    Command-wide participation
    Motivate by example
    Offer personal incentives for safety performance
—Establish informal and formal communications methods by providing:
    Openness (admit there is a problem, even when the command image may suffer)
    Exemptions from disciplinary action
    Direct access to all levels of command structure
—Instructions for equipment operation and maintenance must be
    Clear, simple, straightforward, and reasonable
    Easily and quickly changed
    Evaluated continually via quality assurance methods to ensure proper use of instructions and currency of publications
    Used on the job as required
—Evaluate present programs, publications, procedures, and communications; constantly look for ways to make improvements
—Openly identify all types of potential hazards, including those caused by training deficiencies up and down the chain of command

It has been learned, through prior experience, that five major objectives to strive for in order to improve maintenance are:

1. Strengthening command attention and knowledge
2. Strengthening maintenance operations
3. Improving maintenance training for all personnel
4. Improving maintenance personnel management
5. Improving publications, tools, and repair parts support[45-8]

We must keep in mind that accidents in our ever-more-complex modern Navy are becoming increasingly expensive. Even more important is the fact that, with each new accident, there is a reduced readiness to cope with the demands of our mission.[39-60]

Admiral Larson thinks that

a two-pronged attack is called for to reduce accidents and make sure your equipment is properly cared for. The two-pronged attack is training and maintenance. Let me take training first. It's important that you review the safety bulletins, you look for past problems that other people have had, you incorporate lessons learned into your lectures, into your training with your troops, into your hands-on operation of the systems, into your qualification program, so that your people are trained and ready to operate that equipment, they're aware of potential problems, and they know what to do or what action to take if something does malfunction.

On the maintenance side, we need to put a lot of faith and emphasis into our planned maintenance system. We've had many years now in perfecting that system and making it operate in a way that is very effective and very efficient. We can't pay lip service to it, and you, as the division officer or the commanding officer, have to be the one on the scene to show your support for that system. Now I think one of the nice ways to double-check the

PMS (Planned Maintenance System), to see if the troops are actually carrying it out properly, is to show your interest in what they're doing, go around the ship, spot check, have someone help you go through those different steps, and watch them go through the steps. Not only will you learn a lot about your people and your equipment, but it's a nice spot check to make sure that they're doing these things properly. They won't resent you, they won't think you're peering over their shoulder or spying on them, as long as you're using that as a learning mechanism for yourself and you're honestly involved there, just trying to learn more about your equipment and trying to be involved as a good division officer.

I think we need never to lose sight of the fact that we are an equipment-oriented service. It's a technical Navy out there: propulsion systems, communications systems, and weapons systems are highly technical. We need to understand those systems, we need to work hard to get them on line, and that's where the rubber meets the road. If you're the greatest strategist in the world and you can't make your ship run out there, you're not going to be worth much to the Navy. So the people who really contribute are the ones who make that ship operate, operate efficiently, have good backup systems, good damage control, and at that point you can become a strategist and a warrior.

MCPON Sanders: *In the area of reducing accidents, we must do much better. The officer must know what caused the accident, why it happened, whether it happened because of overworked personnel or shortages or taking shortcuts. Each accident must be analyzed, not covered up, even though you may be at a loss to determine whether there is a human error, equipment malfunction, or some other problem. Information must be presented to the commanding officer so that perhaps the rest of the organization will benefit by knowing what has happened. Considering dollar shortages in the future, this will be particularly appropriate in developing methods for improving the care of equipment. If we do not properly care for our equipment, we are not going to make a difference on the world scene, and certainly with today's budget, we're not going to be able to just buy, carte blanche, everything we would like to have.*

31. Obtaining Optimal Performance in Sub-Optimal Conditions

Every organization by necessity contains jobs that have facets that may sometimes be physically dangerous, boring, demeaning, highly stressful, distasteful, or personally distressing, and the Naval Service is no exception. No naval officer can avoid encountering such jobs, and therefore every officer should remember that optimal performance in sub-optimal circumstances is one of the hallmarks of a leader. Admiral Fran McKee points out that

> officers have to set the pace by showing that, although there may be undesirable jobs to do in the Naval Service and super jobs, as well, it takes an accomplishment of all jobs to make the engine work. Generally an assignment, desirable or undesirable, should go to the level that normally would best accomplish it. If the division officer is the person who should handle it, it should not be passed on as the easy way out. I don't believe in passing the buck, and I don't think you should ask people to do things you wouldn't do yourself.

Duty Involving Physical Danger

Physical danger, invigorating as it is for some, will rank high on any list of undesirable job char-

acteristics. But naval officers go in harm's way; that is a fact of service. The officer who clearly displays fortitude in the face of danger will find that his subordinates are willing to follow his example and achieve his objectives. General Rice suggests that

> a naval officer very often will volunteer for a job, even a dangerous job, because he knows he is the best-equipped person to do it. That's where heroes come from. No one goes into the battlefield or into a crisis situation saying, "I'm going to be a hero." It is just that something within that individual drives him to take a heroic action.

> Marines on many occasions have not hesitated to risk their lives to bring back the dead body of a fellow Marine, and Navy corpsmen also go out to bring bodies back. No one tells them to do it, they just do it. You don't train to be a hero, you train to survive, and somehow something in us makes us react in times of danger to do what is right or what we think is right, or what we think may help the individual or the individuals.

Other Duties

Other duties are made undesirable largely by the personal judgment of the individual. What is boring for one may be pleasant for another. What is stressful for one may relax another. In the end, each task takes on the character given to it by the officer's attitude.

Officers must have pride in their role as military leaders in order to achieve success, but that pride should not be allowed to reach such proportions that required tasks are perceived to be "beneath" an officer's dignity or to be undesirable because they appear to have no direct career-enhancing value. If an officer develops this attitude, the mission will undoubtedly suffer, and the officer will inevitably lose the stature he covets.

Perhaps the most distressing of all possible

duties is making a negative appraisal of another's performance. Candor carries with it the risk of personal animosity, and most leaders would prefer to be on good terms with their peers and subordinates. In fact, however, an honest assessment of strengths and weaknesses will provide great assistance to someone who truly has the desire to reach his unmet potential. On the other hand, making an honest and frank acknowledgment of a lack of improvement, even though difficult, will go far to avoid institutionalizing mediocrity.

The duty of providing honest but critical input to a senior is often very stressful. If a leader is to avoid the fate of the emperor with new clothes, however, individuals in advisory or staff positions must exercise their moral courage and present dissenting opinions when necessary. To remain silent or, worse, to be a "yes man" can, in the long run, be the most damaging form of shirking one's duty. Admiral Nakamura thinks that an officer should

> carry out his duty even if he considers it undesirable, unless it involves clear illegality. In other words, when the legal superior gives the order to perform a mission, all subordinates given that order should assume that the superior is indicating how to attain his objectives from views broader than those of the subordinates, and therefore they should execute the order with sincerity and enthusiasm except in the case of a clearly illegal order.

> If an officer cannot agree to the order or instruction from his superior, he should offer his opinion directly and as early as he can. But if this opinion is rejected by his superior, he should make every effort to complete his given duty unless it is clearly illegal.

> There is no room for personal likes and dislikes or personal views in the military, which has to conduct its mission on the battlefield. Therefore, a commander is

required to evaluate the situation based on his mission, to base his orders on strong beliefs and firm grounds, and to take every responsibility for his orders to the end.

Physical courage, moral courage, and a positive attitude are high on the list of elements critical to success as a naval leader, and every officer worthy of the name possesses them to some degree. However, these elements must be tested and strengthened. Performing undesirable tasks is one way to develop them to the point of excellence. Admiral Burke believes that

> individuals should volunteer to improve themselves professionally, not personally, and they should only volunteer others when doing so is in the interest of the Naval Service, not in their own interest. Self-interest can become very evident, and it becomes evident that some officers and some people want to be good, there's no doubt about that, but they want to do it for a personal reason. They want the recognition. A little bit of that is all right and natural, but it can be an obsession, and that goes against the grain of everyone with them. In a ship, if a captain volunteers his ship to do things, you can't say whether he should or should not, because it depends upon what his motive is and what the crew thinks his motive is—not necessarily what it really is, but what they think it is—and if it's for his personal grandiosity, then it won't work. If they think it's for the good of the ship or for the good of the Navy or something like that, it will work nine times out of ten.

> I volunteered my outfit for combat all the time. If your crew, your outfit, knows they're going on the line, they're going to be pretty good. My squadron had a reunion, and a thousand people came back from the squadron 40 years after a battle. The thing that they talked about, that

they told my wife about, was that they didn't mind working, because I used to hold a battle practice after we'd had a battle, all the way home. Why? To tighten them up, to make sure that they got back to their accuracy, because you get careless in battle. You want their guns to shoot fast, and a little carelessness is a natural thing to do, to slip a little bit.

When I was skipper of the *Mumford*, we won a gunnery "E" on every gun, we made a hit with every shot we had fired in a short-range battle. It was phenomenal. I don't think it has ever been done since, and it never had been before. We stood high in engineering, but we didn't stand too well in communications, but one day a staff of COMDESPAC (we were in San Diego) came over to see me and said, "Somebody on the staff said your chief of communications, chief radioman, volunteered your ship for communication exercises and drill, and he stated that your ship is the best ship in the fleet in communications." And I said, "Well, it isn't the best ship in the fleet, but he's volunteered it, so we'll do it." We were supposed to be in port for a week, and I called him up and he said, "Yes, Sir, I did. I'm sorry about it." "That's all right, we'll go ahead and do it," I said, "But you take the rap." So I told the crew exactly what happened, that we were going out to sea, that this chief had promised we were the best ship in the fleet, and he's going to have to prove it. They did well. They didn't stand number one, but they did very well.

Now that chief had too much to drink when he volunteered the ship, but, still, that did more for the crew than anything I could ever have done, and they did do well. That ship was very good, so good— and I can't prove this—so good that something like 60 percent of the crew

became officers. In those days they had a lot of college people as enlisted men, but even so, that was a very outstanding thing.

32. Persistence in the Performance of Duty

Admiral Larson believes that
the Naval Service is not an eight-hour-a-day job, so you may be working more than eight hours or considerable hours just doing your basic requirements before you volunteer for any extra service. But it's also important for young people to understand, for junior officers to understand, that there are very few, if any, upwardly mobile professions that involve eight-hour-a-day jobs. In other words, regardless of where you are out there in the world, if you're going to be a leader, if you're going to move up, if you're going to be a person who makes things happen, you're not going to work eight hours a day. We accept that because it's very challenging out there, and it's very rewarding. So I think that there is a place for that extra work, I think there are great psychic rewards in understanding that you have something extra to offer. By taking on additional details or additional assignments from your commanding officer, you become a more valuable person to your ship, you learn from that, you grow from that experience, and I think that feeling of contributing is a very important one. One of the things I always felt when I reported to a new command was, the sooner I could get on that watch bill, the better I felt, because I was a part of that team. I think of volunteering for extra duty in the same way; the bigger contribution you can make, the more your reputation is going to grow within your community. And that should be your goal; to be the best fighter

pilot, the best submariner, the best surface warfare officer, and to have the respect of your contemporaries. You gain that respect by working hard, by being good at what you do, but also by looking at your output. I don't like to see junior officers who work hard but just spin their wheels, so junior officers should look at their output and their contribution to that command. If you're contributing extra, you're going to have that service reputation, you're going to have that self-satisfaction of a job well done, and you're going to develop yourself for future leadership.

Navy and Marine Corps personnel are repeatedly told that "accomplishment of the mission is of paramount importance, and that people and all other supporting elements are ancillary in nature." What does this mean? In the Naval Service, goals and mission are closely aligned; in other words, in the military, context goals are usually sub-elements that lead to mission accomplishment. For example, a skipper of a destroyer has a mission to steam from Norfolk, Virginia, to Barcelona, Spain, in ten days. The skipper may break down the total trip into a specific number of nautical miles per day: these daily miles are his goals. Or a Marine rifle company has a mission to seize and defend objective A, and as goals, the commander sees the necessity of taking certain intermediate objectives that will ensure the enemy's defeat at objective A.

Goals are an interesting part of every individual's life. Without them, humans have little direction and tend to drift aimlessly. The Naval Service can ill afford to have leaders who have no goals. Fortunately, a system is in place that all but eliminates aimless individuals from advancing to significant positions of authority. This system, although it is not perfect in design, is adequate and has been recently revised by both the Navy and the Marine Corps. Known as the fitness report system, it truly is a competitive system. In order to be competitive, Navy and Marine Corps officers must be organized

and be able to achieve goals and accomplish the mission at hand, whether in combat or in a peacetime environment. The division officer is at the critical point of the chain of command, in that he must perform "his duties on a level where he gets immediate results."[44-6] Admiral Ramage says that, "while every officer is expected to see his work through to successful completion, if this is not possible within the limits of time, endurance, or other reasons, he should not hesitate to ask for assistance."

Even the best laid plans at times go astray, but the effective leader is persistent and has "stick-to-itiveness," meaning the desire to see a project through to its completion. An officer who lacks this attribute may find his goals difficult or even impossible to accomplish. Causes for changes in plans are many. The officer's expectations and estimates of time and know-how may have been short-sighted; obstacles may appear that he did not anticipate; or the commanding officer may advance the schedule on a particular mission or assignment. Of course, these developments cause much consternation and sometimes even momentary panic in the young officer, but he soon learns to deal with them and continues to work toward the assigned goal or mission. In the estimation of many great leaders, this is a good test to determine an officer's mettle. It sometimes distinguishes the mediocre officer from the better officer, for "understanding, ability, and enthusiasm either produce smart, able, and efficient crews, or his lack of these qualities results in sloppy, poorly disciplined units."[44-7]

In addition to being persistent, officers must have a feeling of duty, honor, and country. Being an officer in the Naval Service is much more than having a job or even an adventure. There is no time card to punch, and if there is work to be done or deadlines to meet, the officer works or supervises as long as necessary or as long as schedules will allow to accomplish the mission, objective, or goal. At times this will require extra effort and time spent beyond "normal working hours." In fact, this is the norm, not the exception. If the officer is new and relatively inexperienced, he has to work hard to stay ahead of the problem and maintain credibility as a bonafide leader. If he is more experienced, he can spend more time sharpening his leadership skills and working on areas where he may feel a little weak, and this may require burning some midnight oil.[32-29]

Today more than ever before, it is imperative that spouses have a thorough understanding of the Naval Service and the operational commitments required of naval officers. The spouse who understands the inner working of the Naval Service is more likely to support the officer wholeheartedly. Spouses should never be kept uninformed or be made to feel unimportant.

The question of commitment is more than just putting in time. Everything done in the Naval Service affects something else. Even though the officer may be committed, poor organizational skills, lack of knowledge about his military specialty, or inadequate time management can result in the officer placing undue burdens on enlisted personnel. There have been times when naval officers have been "pulled out of the fire" by a united team effort. A leader who is considered to be superior by his subordinates will be able to depend on them, for they will respond immediately and without question to his call for help. If fire fighting becomes a daily occurrence, however, the officer will lose the respect as well as the support of his subordinates.

The good leader will be more than willing to perform additional work voluntarily for both seniors and juniors. There is nothing more rewarding than helping subordinates up the ladder of success, and even if the effort to do so bites into "after-duty" hours, the officer will find that the psychic rewards he gets from helping other members of the team are incalculable. Admiral McDonald notes that, "as we become more technical, the longer it takes to train the people the way they should be." Admiral Long points out that

Naval Officers can expect to work more

than eight hours a day. I think it's important to remind all of us that being a military officer is not an eight-hour job. Anyone who is interested in working from eight to five and is unwilling to work beyond that should seek employment elsewhere. There will be times, certainly in the fleet and also ashore, where it will be necessary to work beyond eight hours a day, and my observation has been that the more senior one becomes, the greater the responsibilities and the longer the working hours. I would quickly point out, however, that in other communities— such as business, law, and medicine—and in other professional fields where people aspire to achieve, the road to success is normally based in part on hard work.

I think an individual going to the fleet as a young Navy or Marine officer should understand that certainly at sea he is essentially on duty twenty-four hours a day. My observation has been that many times ships at sea do not do enough of the things there in order to alleviate the burden of doing things in port. Ideally, when you are at sea you work your people hard, and then when they come in to port, they will have more time to spend with their families or friends or in other pursuits. I think a ship that is managed well can do much to reduce the burden of in-port working hours. This takes some planning on the part of not only the commanding officer but also the division officer and the senior enlisted people. In order to maintain a high state of readiness, it is necessary to work long hours, and this should be understood not only by the officers and enlisted people involved, but also by their families.

A career in the Naval Service, then, is not an eight-to-five job with an hour off for lunch. It is a commitment to the Navy, the Marine Corps, and the country. It sometimes requires long hours, and it always requires achieving the assigned goals and mission. The effective leader will accept this responsibility willingly, and if at times it causes momentary panic, he will bounce right back, grab the bull by the horns, and accomplish the mission. Stick-to-itiveness can take an individual far toward a goal. Quitters are automatic losers, but winners continue, no matter how great the odds are against them, and see the mission through to its successful conclusion.

MCPON Sanders: *The officer must perform additional work voluntarily when necessary to meet deadlines or avoid delay. You will find that your subordinates will understand when there is a reasonable deadline, and they have to do something extra. For you and the troops it is a matter of personal integrity.*

33. Initiative, Decisiveness, and Strength of Character

All commissioned officers pledge their honor in the dispatch of their duty. Thus, every proper assignment constitutes a pledge of honor, and an officer is bound to devote full energy and capacity to its accomplishment. An officer who has been given an assignment should need no further orders to make him energetically pursue its accomplishment. The motivation to do so should spring from a sense of both honor and duty. This is not to say that if advice or guidance is required, he should not seek it.

Duty dictates that, in the absence of both orders and seniors, an officer is driven to search out, identify, and effect the accomplishment of mission-inherent tasks or unforeseen requirements. Admiral Hunt points out that, "when I am away, my deputy should act as if he were me, and he should pursue those actions which are required of him in the way he thinks that I would want them to be pursued."

Frequently in the naval environment, partic-

ularly in war, officers must make decisions quickly and without recourse to guidance from seniors. In these instances, the officer must evince initiative and decisiveness. General Wilson says:

I think it's good training for young officers to make decisions on their own, and everyone should be put in that position at one time or another. If he's going to have to ask for guidance every time he is confronted with a decision, he'll be in trouble. At some point his communications are going to be cut off, and if he's so frustrated, so afraid of making a mistake, that he is unwilling to carry his mission out, then he has reached his terminal rank.

I'm reminded of the young officer who was officer of the deck, when all the people were killed on ships in Pearl Harbor. He chose to take his ship out as best he could out of the line of fire. This is an example of an officer who took the initiative. Now, this had high visibility, but decisions have been made by many other people over the years that have been successful and unsuccessful. But it shows the initiative on the part of an individual who, after weighing all the facts, makes a decision and implements it. It is very difficult to criticize an officer who does this. I cannot think of an instance in my experience when an officer has been given this opportunity—I say it is an opportunity—and made a decision and carried it out, has taken initiative, and has lost anything in this profession.

INITIATIVE

Our initiative will restrict the independent will of the enemy and springs from our ambition, from the desire to "outdo others." This desire indicates the presence of leadership qualities. For the naval officer, this must represent "constructive ambition," a desire to excel in an enterprise aimed at the success of cause and country. Powerful personal ambition, although it is the wellspring of initiative, often must be repressed for the common good.

There has never been a superior performer who was without ambition; in fact, it is not possible to conceive of an ambitionless performer. Troops know instinctively that a leader's personal ambition is derived from a basic concern for them, since nothing can be achieved without their competent cooperation. Personal ambition is intellectual and subjective. Junior officers and enlisted personnel readily identify personal ambition that is also self-seeking, and their response to it is invariably negative. If, however, an officer's concern for his personnel is objective, and represents a genuine concern for their overall welfare, it is quickly recognized that personal ambition has been tempered and its compass broadened. This "constructive ambition" serves to forge bonds of loyalty between senior and junior which even the tumult of battle cannot weaken.

DECISIVENESS

Decisiveness is tied to initiative, since initiative without decisiveness invites chaos. Decisiveness springs from ambition but, particularly in the exercise of command, it remains set apart. In war, the struggle to make a decision is the most difficult part of command. Essentially, making a decision involves doing battle with fear—fear of making a decision that will prove unnecessarily costly in lives and material. This struggle to decide requires strength of character, and this strength will be manifested as courage and determination. Moreover, making sound decisions demands intelligence. Abraham Lincoln once said: "The dogmas of the quiet past are inadequate to the stormy present. The occasion is piled high with difficulty, and we must rise with the occasion. As our case is new, so must we think anew and act anew."[14-22]

War requires the best thinking a person is capable of, but it does not necessarily require intellectualism. Intellectuals by nature are usually incapable of making an immediate decision in complicated affairs, because their perception and their courage may operate separately and cannot readily be brought together to produce a decision. They want to know *all* the facts and to explore every possible course of action. Since the essence of war is uncertainty, the commander cannot hope to have complete information. Decisions must be reached rapidly based on what is known. However, intellectual power makes up a great part of naval "genius," and an officer training for command in war must develop reasoning power through a constant, critical examination of the past and the present.

STRENGTH OF CHARACTER

Strength of character displays itself as courage and determination. Intellectual courage produces the decision, and determination ensures that the decision is carried out. Determination uses the fear of vacillation and hesitation to overcome all other fears. Courage displayed in a specific case becomes a character trait only if courage becomes a mental habit.

Thus, an officer requires the strength of character to furnish the determination to fend off the host of doubts which will evolve once the order has been given and facts, circumstances, and conditions begin to change. Strength of character emerges as an unwavering adherence to one's convictions, whether they be classed as principles, opinions, decisions, or aspirations of the moment.

INSTILLING INITIATIVE, DECISIVENESS, AND STRENGTH OF CHARACTER IN SUBORDINATES

Today, as always, an officer must recognize that success in war depends ultimately on the proper development of the military personalities of all officers and personnel, for the capabilities of people rather than of weapons will bring success. Therefore, it is the responsibility of an officer to encourage initiative and decisiveness in subordinates and create an environment that fosters courage, self-confidence, and ambition. "The essence of responsibility is, then, obligation."[33-65]

The development of constructive ambition must be encouraged through personal example and by accepting mistakes of subordinates as a price that must be paid for professional development. While being firm or even stern in correction, an officer must remain patient and objective, despite the aggravation produced by energetic error. Moreover, an officer must never permit a senior outside the unit to correct subordinates without making a concerted effort to absorb the wrath of that senior. Subordinates must continuously be placed in situations requiring independent action, and they must know that proper and energetic exercise of initiative and decision is expected. The more demands routinely placed on subordinates, the more likely it is that they will respond appropriately in a time of crisis. During peace, leaders must keep the eyes of their subordinates fixed on the requirements for war.

In fostering an atmosphere that facilitates the growth of the constructive ambition that leads to sound, independent initiative and decisiveness, an officer fulfills a fundamental responsibility of developing the military personalities of subordinates. In addressing this point, Admiral Holloway observes that

> someone must always be in charge in a military organization, and if no one else does it, the person who has the spunk to stand up and take charge should do it, but he should always relinquish that responsibility when someone in proper authority

speaks up and takes control. In a time of crisis or emergency, the individual who speaks up and takes charge until he is properly relieved by someone senior to him is to be commended. When a boat carrying many sailors and officers is swamped coming back late at night in a strange harbor under high winds and rough seas, for example, someone must take charge. Someone—a second-class petty officer, maybe—must say, "Everybody stay in the boat. Don't strike out. The boat won't sink. You're safe as long as you're here." Perhaps the officers aboard are dazed by the suddenness of the situation or by the cold water and are unable to take command. And that person must continue to take charge until his senior takes over.

No subordinate can reduce his responsibility by delegating to another the authority to perform a duty.[33-66]

MCPON Sanders: *The officer must take responsibility for the completion of necessary assignments, even though his senior is not there to observe. Even if the job is not critical and is not going to impact everyone, go ahead and get it done rather than putting it off with the hope that the senior will forget what was supposed to be done. If you do put it off, the matter will come back to haunt you.*

Chapter 3 Bibliography

1. Adams, Gerald C., and Yoshpe, Harry B. *Supply Management*. Washington, D.C.: Industrial College of the Armed Forces, 1965.
2. Adcock, F. E. *The Greek and Macedonian Art of War*. Berkeley and Los Angeles: University of California Press, 1957.
3. "Adjustments to SWO Career Path." *Surface Warfare*, Nov.–Dec. 1983, pp. 2–6.
4. Alexander, Denise M., and Sprayberry, Sharon A. "Training Junior Officers." *Proceedings*, Oct. 1983, pp. 95–100.
5. Basil, Douglas C. *Leadership Skills for Executive Action*. New York: American Management Association, 1971.
6. Beardon, William, and Wedertz, Bill. *The Bluejacket's Manual*. 20th ed. Annapolis: Naval Institute Press, 1978.
7. Beaumont, Roger A. "Contingency Planning: A

New Perspective." *Proceedings*, Nov. 1968, pp. 26–37.

8. Becker, Lawrence J. "Joint Effect of Feedback on Goal Setting and Performance: A Field Study of Residential Energy Consumption." *Journal of Applied Psychology*, Aug. 1978, pp. 428–33.

9. Bellows, Roger; Gilson, Thomas; and Odiorne, George. *Executive Skills: Their Dynamics and Development*. Englewood Cliffs, N.J.: Prentice-Hall, 1962.

10. Bowers, Richard H. "No Substitute for Manpower." *Proceedings*, Feb. 1963, p. 70.

11. Bursk, Chapman. *New Decision-Making Tools for Managers*. New York: Mentor, 1963.

12. Cambell, Dennis. "Techniques for Effective Management." *Army Logistician*, Sept.–Oct. 1983.

13. *Challenge in Leadership*. Quantico, Va.: Marine Corps Development and Education Command, 1974.

14. *Challenge to Leadership*. New York: Free Press, 1973.

15. Codilla, L. R. "Keys to Self-Motivation." *Cost and Management*, July–Aug. 1968, pp. 48–52.

16. Denny, Richard F., and Stranger, Daniel. "The Underlying Theory of Incentive Contracting." *Defense Management Journal*, first quarter 1981, pp. 42–51.

17. Department of Defense, Armed Forces Information Service. *The Armed Forces Officer*. Washington, D.C.: U.S. Government Printing Office, 1975.

18. Department of the Navy. "Learn or Burn: Trial by Fire." Videotape. 1967.

19. Dodge, David O., and Kyriss, Stephen E. *Seamanship: Fundamentals for the Deck Officer*. Annapolis: Naval Institute Press, 1981.

20. Doran, George T. "There's a Smart Way to Write Management Goals and Objectives." *Management Review*, Nov. 1981, pp. 35–36.

21. Doughty, Leonard. "Mistaken Attacks in the World War." *Proceedings*, Dec. 1934, pp. 1729–34.

22. Downey, J. C. T. *Management in the Armed Forces*. New York: McGraw-Hill, 1977.

23. Fingarett, Herbert. *On Responsibility*. New York: Basic Books, 1967.

24. Flanagan, Edward M. "The Military Mind." *Army*, Feb. 1984, pp. 29–36.

25. Gibson, James L.; Ivancevich, John M.; and Donnelly, James H., Jr. *Organizations*. 4th ed. Plano, Tex.: Business Publications, 1982.

26. Goble, Frank. *Excellence in Leadership*. New York: American Management Association, 1972.

27. Harris, Lorenzo D. "The Sharp Edge of Leadership." *Airman*, Sept. 1983, pp. 8–12.

28. Hughes, David R. "Contingency Planning: A New Perspective." *Proceedings*, Nov. 1968, pp. 26–37.

29. Jacobsen, K. C. *Watch Officer's Guide*. 11th ed. Annapolis: Naval Institute Press, 1979.

30. Janowitz, Morris. *The Professional Soldier: A Social and Political Portrait*. New York: Free Press, 1971.

31. Johnson, Spencer, and Blanchard, Kenneth. *The One Minute Manager*. New York: William Morrow, 1982.

32. Kelly, J. M.; Patton, G. D.; Downs, J. F.; and Corini, G. J., eds. *Leadership and Law Department NL 303 Book of Readings*. Annapolis: U.S. Naval Academy, academic year 1983–84.

33. Koontz, Harold. *Principles of Management*. New York: McGraw-Hill, 1968.

34. Kuhlwan, Norman H. C. *Supply Management*. Washington, D.C.: Industrial College of the Armed Forces, 1969.

35. Latham, Gary P., and Locke, Edwin A. "Goal Setting: A Motivational Technique That Works." *Organizational Dynamics*, Autumn 1979.

36. Leaf, Howard W. "Mishap Prevention." *TIG Brief* 10 (1981): 1–2.

37. Locke, Edwin A.; Shaw, Karyll N.; Saari, Lise M.; and Plathaw, Gary. "Goal Setting and Task Performance, 1969–1980." Technical Report GS-1. Washinton, D.C.: Office of Naval Research, June 1980.

38. McDaniel, Irving B. "Industrial Accident Prevention." *Proceedings*, Oct. 1931, pp. 1313–17.

39. McGinley, Edward S. "Preventing the Preventable." *Proceedings*, June 1973, pp. 58–60.

40. Mack, William P. "Education and Professionalism." *Proceedings*, Oct. 1983, pp. 40–47.

41. Martin, Charles C. *Project Management*. New York: AMACOM, Division of the American Management Association, 1976.

42. *Medal of Honor*. Annapolis: Bureau of U.S. Naval Personnel, 1949.

43. NL 102 Course Committee. *Fundamentals of Naval Leadership*. Annapolis: U.S. Naval Academy, Dec. 1980.

44. Noel, John V., Jr., and Bassett, Frank E. *Division Officer's Guide*. 7th ed. Annapolis: Naval Institute Press, 1977.

45. O'Donnell, Robert M. "Maintenance Management Improvement Program." *Army Logistician*, 1981.

46. Peters, Thomas J. *In Search of Excellence: Lessons from America's Best-Run Companies*. New York: Harper and Row, 1982.

47. Petinak, Marko J. *Philosophy of Leadership*. Los Angeles: Petinak, 1937.

48. Prange, Gordon W. *Miracle at Midway*. New York: McGraw-Hill, 1982.

49. Presented to Parliament by the Secretary for Defense by Command of Her Majesty. *The Falklands Campaign*. London: Her Majesty's Stationery Office, Dec. 1982.

50. Ross, W. D. *The Right and the Good*. Oxford: Clarendon Press, 1930.

51. Schofield, Frank H. *Leadership Military Character*. Washington, D.C.: U.S. Government Press, 1931.

52. Tarbuck, Ray. "As I Recall . . . Duty at Berkeley." *Proceedings*, Oct. 1983, p. 94.

53. Thorpe, George C. *Pure Logistics*. Kansas City: Franklin Hudson, 1917.

54. *United States Navy Manual of Safety Equipment*. Washington, D.C.: Department of the Navy, 1954.

55. VanCreveld, Martin. *Supplying War*. Cambridge: Cambridge University Press, 1983.

56. Vernon, H. M. *Accidents and Their Prevention*. New York: Macmillan, 1936.

57. Von Wright, Georg Henrik. *Acta Philosophica Fennica*. Amsterdam: North Holland, 1968.

58. Vroom, Victor H., and Deci, Edward L., eds. *Management and Motivation*. Kingsport, Tenn.: Kingsport Press, 1978.

59. Williamson, Porter B. *Patton's Principles*. Tucson: Management and Systems Consultants, 1979.

60. Yukl, Gary A., and Latham, Gary P. "A Review of Research on the Application of Goal Setting in Organizations." *Academy of Management Journal*, Dec. 1975.

4

Organizing for Mission Accomplishment

Introduction

The Ten Most Wanted

The F.B.I. has its well-known list of "wanted" men; perhaps industry should, too. If I were to name them, they would be: (1) *The man who is skilled*, who stays abreast of his field, however rapidly it changes; (2) *The man who can think*, who can use his head to solve a problem for which there is no precedent; (3) *The man who can delegate authority*, both to create time for himself and to help his subordinates in their growth; (4) *The man who motivates people*, who helps them to formulate goals and to achieve them; (5) *The man who inspires confidence*, not only in himself but in those who work for him; (6) *The man who accepts change*, who sees change as opportunity, not as a threat to the status quo; (7) *The man who can be trusted*, who is as careful with company funds as he is with his own; (8) *The man who is loyal*, who sees his own goals and those of the company as one; (9) *The man who has drive*, who does not balk at extra hours nor shy away from problems; (10) *The man who is optimistic*, who meets the challenge of life with gusto and humor.

Keith M. Flake, *Vital Speeches*

Who Is the "Ideal" Manager?

What are the characteristics of the ideal manager? Assuming that he already possesses the qualities of emotional stability and intelligence, . . . (1) He is other-people oriented. He is aware of, and understanding of, the behavior of others, without being emotionally involved; (2) He adjusts his own behavior to the personal needs of his people so that they will more effectively serve the needs of the organization; (3) He is committed to his job, so that the process of accomplishing company goals is *intrinsically* rewarding to him; (4) He basically respects people, regardless of rank, so that people feel free and unafraid to communicate with him even on an emotional level; (5) He is an expert at analyzing the emotional makeup of his people and of using this knowledge so that it serves both his people and the company; (6) Knowing what is rewarding to each employee and what provokes anxiety, he does his best to maximize reward situations and to minimize anxiety situations; (7) Finally, the ideal manager recognizes the fact that the environment in which he lives and works is constantly changing. He is prepared not only to change himself, but to initiate change and to help others adjust to change.

David W. Thompson,
Personnel Administrator

How Do You Pick a Winner?

Why does one man make it in the world of management while another, with comparable experience, intelligence, and ability, does not? Certainly a man's own innate personality traits contribute to his success; in other words, *he is psychologically fit to be a winner*.

Most successful executives possess in common a number of these marks of personality: (1) They *want* to succeed. Ambition doesn't fade with frustration or accomplishment. It is not dulled by the facts of corporate life: constant change, insecurity, limited family life, ephemeral relationships. (2) They have a clear idea of their strengths and weaknesses, plus the ability to set themselves realistic goals, not too high, not too low. This enables them to plan realistically the intermediate steps required to reach long-range objectives. (3) They have the capacity to attract and to work successfully with top-notch subordinates, to win their loyalty and to motivate them to produce their best. (4) Top executives are not afraid to take risks, to make important decisions, even when the odds are against them. As a result, the successful executive tends to be assertive and, to some extent, dominant. He has faith in

himself and the energy, experience, and determination to express this faith.

Susan Margetts, *Dun's Review*

34. Motivational Leadership

Perhaps the most critical element in motivational leadership is the leader's ability to help his subordinates become aware of the importance of their contribution to the achievement of stated unit and naval goals. There are many techniques for increasing motivation, such as offering advancement, pay increases, adventure, camaraderie, and recognition. But none of these motivators is as effective in the long term as the simple act of informing subordinates about their responsibility. They need to know in what way their contribution is necessary for the achievement of unit or naval goals, as well as the possible consequences for these goals if they fail to perform. Admiral Burke notes that

a leader can obtain the cooperation of his people by developing their trust in him and showing them that their goals are goals that will benefit the organization and the country, not just the leader. I was able to work my people hard because they knew that they were working to achieve unselfish goals. The first thing you have to do in an organization, whether it's a ship or a division or a marriage, no matter what, is build up trust and confidence in yourself and your judgment. Not that they trust you all the way, but they have to know you, they have to know what your purpose is. So the most important thing, I think, in any organization is for the organization to know where it's going, what it's going to try to do.

I worked the daylight out of all enlisted people I ever had with me, I mean from the time I was a kid, because I had the daylight worked out of me. I inherited that from some of my predecessors, and I worked people very hard. I had to learn soon what it took to do that, and what it takes is to have a cause that is greater than yourself. You can't get them to "do this for me." That's your own business, that's not going to work. They don't care about doing anything for their boss if that's the reason. They might do it, but it might be for a different reason. People will do anything, they will work their heads off even for the thing they don't believe in, if they believe that their boss is really sincere and they like what he does generally. They will do it because they have trust in the boss's judgment; they will override their own opinion sometimes if they trust his judgment enough. They will put up with an awful lot, even doing things they believe to be wrong, providing they think that his judgment has been pretty good, that he's trying to do what he thinks is best for the United States. Some troubles in this country are from activists who have one cause and to hell with society, all other causes, or anything else. It isn't necessarily that there's anything wrong with the cause itself, but one has to consider not only an individual cause, but also how it impacts other causes that may also be important.

Nowhere is this element of leadership more critical than with the most junior people or those assigned to what appear to be the most onerous tasks. The typical distribution of responsibility in naval organizations results in the most junior personnel being assigned the menial tasks, such as mess cooking and compartment cleaning; for this reason, it is doubly important that these individuals be made aware of the importance of their contribution. To get all of the members of an organization to work for its objectives, Admiral Fran McKee points out,

> everyone has to understand what the job is, the importance of getting the job done,

and then the necessary training must be provided. Generally, if these essentials are met, the job gets done, but if any of these elements is missing, there will be a problem. Each echelon should be held responsible for the training and guidance of its own people.

Virtually all of the young men and women who join the Naval Service arrive highly motivated and have a positive attitude about serving their country. This attitude is strongly reinforced by naval training centers, so that these individuals begin work with an exuberant belief in themselves and the U.S. Navy or Marine Corps. Regretfully, their attitude often reverses very quickly when they are given an unpleasant assignment, such as cleaning heads or chipping paint, especially if the importance of the task has not been explained. General Rice makes the point that

> every person in a command should know that his job is important. The person who carries two ammo cans is as important as the machine gunner, because if that machine gunner gets to battle and he has no ammo, he is useless. The guy on mess duty is as important as everyone else in the battalion, because if the troops are not fed, they cannot function.

Officers at all levels need to make people feel important. They can do this in a variety of ways, from a pat on the back to visiting the unit. Officers should never be too busy to get out and see what is going on. The amount of paper work in today's Naval Service sometimes makes it difficult to get out of the office, to get into the field and make contact with the troops, talk to the troops, and make them feel that they are wanted and important and part of that command, but doing so is a vital part of being a successful leader.

Once a negative attitude has been created by poor leadership, it is quite difficult to turn it around. Good leaders help subordinates through this difficult part of their service. By continually offering positive counseling, effective leaders ensure that today's young service people become tomorrow's dedicated and patriotic petty officers and sergeants.

The following quote, from a book published in 1920, provides the reader with an example of the permanence of appropriate military thought.

> Knowing the Purpose. Human nature demands that before men can put their best efforts into work they must know the object of it. Purpose is the guiding motive in all life; and we are so made that we seek for the purpose in all our efforts, and finding it and believing in it, we naturally give it our endeavors. To win this added influence the leader makes sure that each man understands whatever part he directs him to play, its object and importance in the general plan, and what the plan is.[1-114]

Positive attitudes and job satisfaction can only be obtained when sailors and Marines understand that each task achieved is a necessary and important part of the whole, no matter how insignificant it may seem. It is important for the naval officer to know that his troops have changing needs and problems; to know that his unit has many maintenance requirements which must always be met. The leader must understand how technological and social changes can bear on the very nature of his unit's mission and the caliber of the people who work with him.[63-68] Lastly, the troops should perform the job to the best of their ability, not only for self-satisfaction, but also because they respect their leaders, trust their judgment, and know that, ultimately, "what we practice in peacetime directly relates to our attitude and capabilities in war."

MCPON Sanders: *I think it is critical for the naval officer to help everyone in the command to understand the relationship between the humblest chore and the unit's overall objective. This is certainly important with respect to the lowest-ranked individuals in your organization, so that they will understand how they fit into the total*

mission of their command and know that their work is important. It is also important for seniors in the chain of command to understand the contributions being made, as there is a tendency to overlook the contribution of the lowest-ranked individuals, even though they are a part of making the overall mission happen.

35. Scheduling

There are only 24 hours in a day, and there are more than enough fleas nipping away at the precious resource of time. The demands of time have no respect for rank. Effective officers manage their time. "The commander's efforts should be directed at marshalling his resources in such a way that all of the efforts within the unit are focused on accomplishing the goal."[49-49] Because time management is so important, over the years generally accepted techniques for managing time have evolved. These involve goal setting, delegation, communication, meetings, and personal time management. Secretary Webb notes that

> personnel in a combat unit receive orders for many, many missions, and often this causes them to lose their mental alertness, to become less conscious of what they are doing. They tend to get careless. One of the important things that the leader in a combat situation must do is continually rehabilitate his people's attitude about what they are doing. He must keep both short-term and long-term goals in front of them by laying out what he expects of them on a daily basis. In a continuous operational environment, a daily attitude check is essential.

Readiness in training is a serious issue. The Naval Services have compacted the amount of time available for their guard and reserve units to train before being mobilized. In World War II, the services mobilized in September 1939, which was two years before Pearl Harbor; in Korea, with the exception of the 1st Marine Division, which contained many reservists, reserve units had nine months to one year to train before going into combat; in Vietnam, the few reserve units that were mobilized had four to seven months; and now reserve units have a maximum of 60 days, with some reserve units shipping out well before the active units.

GOAL SETTING

The key to using time effectively is goal setting. Time cannot be assigned to tasks until the tasks are identified. Goals can be identified by simply drawing up a "list of things to do today" or by using the more sophisticated system of management by objectives (MBO), which has been popular in private industry for several years.

Goals can be organized in a number of ways. One way is by *type of goals*—for example, an officer's personal life goals or professional goals within the Navy and Marine Corps. Personal life goals might include spiritual, social, intellectual, cultural, physical, recreational, and financial goals. Professional goals would be subsets of the overall goals (mission) of the Naval Service or a specific command and should include an individual's career aspirations.

Another way of organizing goals is by *time frame* for accomplishment. Immediate goals are things that need to be done today. Intermediate goals require attention this week or this month, and long-range goals, this year, this tour of duty, or in five years. Lifetime goals are things an individual hopes to accomplish during his life. Goal planning and continuity are necessary here, as the short-term goals should support the accomplishment of an individual's long-term goals. Admiral Moorer explained that,

> when an officer makes a schedule, he must establish what can be called milestones. He has a job that must be completed by, say, June, but he must consider what part of the job must be

completed in May in order to meet the deadline, and that milepost should be part of his timetable or schedule. Every schedule ought to have mileposts in it.

The members of every ship and every unit should have frequent meetings attended by the commanding officer, to coordinate their schedules and the availability of personnel and material. Coordination revolves around the personnel, coming and going, and the degree of training they have, and the availability of material, and it is important for the various departments to get together and discuss the elements of the work load. If an officer reports that he cannot finish on schedule because the supply officer has failed to get him a spare part, the supply officer can explain that he ordered the part but the manufacturer failed to ship it. Then they can both take steps to remedy the situation, on the one hand, or adjust the schedule, on the other. Sometimes it is necessary for a commander to issue a memo to an officer who is falling behind for no apparent reason.

Admiral Moorer explained why the commander or captain must be a part of these discussions.

> I had captains who shut themselves up in their cabins and didn't talk to anyone. They thought that if they talked to people, the people became more familiar and wouldn't do what they were told to, which I think is a seriously flawed outlook. The more you talk to others and the more they understand what you're trying to do, the more they realize that you'll help them in every way you can and the more apt they are to do a good job. If the captain closes himself in, and they don't know how to deal with him and are uncertain as to what he's going to do next, it's not a very good organization.

Goals should also be organized *according to*

importance, ranging from things that must be done or should be done, to things that can be done if time permits. An officer must prioritize his goals! By some easy to use system (for example, Al, A2, . . . C3, C4), an officer needs to indicate the importance of all his goals, whether they are daily or long range. The following questions are helpful in assigning priorities: Which goals give the greatest payoff to the Navy and Marine Corps (the organization) or to me? Which goals must be met in order to avoid unacceptable consequences? What are the highest priority goals to my boss?

As John Paul Jones so appropriately said, "He who will not risk cannot win." But, by the same token, the risks a leader takes regarding human lives should not be foolhardy.

> The Hammelburg rescue attempt in March of 1945 is an example of a mission in which the safety factor was underemphasized in light of the significance of the mission. A small task force of approximately 300 officers and men from the 4th Armored Division was sent under great odds to rescue American prisoners from a prisoner-of-war camp at Hammelburg. Not only was the camp 35 miles beyond the American forward elements, but the small American force was setting out against unknown enemy forces, which proved to be far superior in numbers and capabilities. Only fifteen members of the task force returned to their unit. Not one of the prisoners was rescued. In execution, the risk proved too great. [16-6]

Good goal setting requires taking a few minutes at the end of each day to list the goals for the next day and devoting some time on Sunday (or Friday evening) to list the next week's goals. Prioritizing these goals comes next. It is important to distinguish between items that are urgent (but not necessarily important) and items that will truly move the individual toward his objectives. Determining what actions will accomplish his highest goals and doing those first is vital. It is better to complete one important objective during a day than to finish numerous minor tasks

that, although they may give a person a sense of accomplishment, do little to help him attain his important goals. A quarterback can run plays for four quarters, but he has got to put points on the board to win! By setting goals and assigning correct priorities, an officer will motivate himself to action and ensure that the action he takes in the limited time he has will maximize his efforts in achieving his highest objectives. The enthusiasm and interest of the officers, becoming contagious, will pervade their units, creating an excellent team spirit. [14-29]

The priorities that the officer sets up before an operation begins are subject to change as events unfold. The officer will have to change his priorities in many cases. Admiral Moorer provided this example of how network news people alter their priorities as the day progresses:

> Walter Cronkite was telling me how they set up these evening news programs. They have a list of news events according to priority, and then right in the middle of the day somebody shoots at the President, so that becomes number one all of a sudden, and you didn't know that when you first set up.
>
> An officer can expect to run into the same kind of unpredictable occurrences in combat operations. For instance, if he succeeds in destroying a certain part of the enemy force, the priority and the timing would then change. Once the operation starts, there is a "fluid" state of changing priorities.
>
> Before any operation, combat or otherwise, begins, then, the officer should in his own mind set up priorities based on what he would like to see, how the sequence of events should flow in order to capitalize to the maximum on the capabilities of his people. He also must consider his other commitments or involvement. In joint operations, for example, he will take the Army's plan into consideration as he develops his own. After he has set up a

list of priorities assuming the plan is going to work just as he has written it up, and the plan begins to change because of circumstances beyond his control, he may have to readjust his priorities.

Another consideration is that most officers are working out a plan that is based on another plan from his senior officer. He may give the officer a specific goal with a time limit, so that has to remain number-one priority, but within the area that the officer is controlling, he sets his own priorities. He has to take into consideration the length of time required to reach the goals established by his seniors. If something happens that demands his attention and that has an earlier time limit, he might let some of the other priorities slip a little, but he should always meet the deadline established by the senior officer.

It is not difficult to set up priorities before anything happens at all, but once the Go signal is given, an officer has to consider changing priorities. There have been many battles where the priorities were changed because the circumstances changed or because the intelligence was incorrect or because the power of the other side was under- or overestimated. At the outset of battle, therefore, the leader makes certain assumptions as to what the other side will do under the circumstances, and he sets up a list of priorities based on that, but the minute his intelligence indicates there has been a change, then he has to examine his priorities to see whether *they* should be changed.

DELEGATION

An officer's effectiveness can be greatly enhanced through the actions of subordinates. An officer can only do so much work by himself, but with proper guidance and motivation, his

subordinates can significantly increase the total output. As the day's list of goals is developed, an officer must ask himself what he can delegate. Getting things done through people is basic and vital. An officer who does not have enough time has not learned to delegate properly. Delegating requires, on the part of the officer, trust, courage, and patience and, sometimes, appropriate training for the subordinate. Admiral Ramage makes the point that

> the officer has to see that all requirements are properly assigned to those capable of taking appropriate action and be sure to follow up on the progress being made until completion. In other words, it's up to you to see that people know what they're doing, they're doing it properly, and that you're getting the results desired.

An officer should consider delegating work to his subordinates in the afternoon so as to encourage them to plan their next day's work. Tasking people in a haphazard, "knee-jerk" manner keeps them off-balance, confuses their priorities, and discourages planned, thoughtful, quality work. Eventually, it destroys their incentive. Successful leaders in the Korean War, for example, were very aware of their mission, but they also had a paternal-like concern for their men's well-being. Compassion for the wounded, a deep, sincere understanding of the individual soldier's problem, and a never-ending attempt to improve the lot of their troops under the worst combat conditions earned the respect of their charges and undoubtedly left an indelible impression on their own conscience.[14-29]

As he delegates jobs, the officer should try to take the time to explain how the accomplishment of these assignments fits into the achievement of higher goals. This might be difficult to do for each and every assignment given a subordinate, but an officer should, at least periodically, give the people who work for him information on how the jobs they are doing tie into the overall objectives of the organization.

Their work goals should be integrated with the officer's work goals and the organization's mission. If the subordinates' assigned tasks, the officer's work goals, and the organization's goals do not fit together, the officer needs to reexamine both his work goals and his delegation to subordinates.

Guidelines for proper delegation include:

1. Select the people who have the ability to do the job, and train those who do not.
2. Clearly explain what is expected of them.
3. Set a deadline for completion of the task.
4. Provide latitude for them to use their own imagination and initiative. Let them know you will be following up, and then follow up.
5. Reward them appropriately for the results they obtain.
6. Do not do the job for them.

Remember, delegation is supposed to save an officer's personal time and multiply his effectiveness.

COMMUNICATION

Volumes have been written regarding the communication process among people. Each individual involved in communication must assume 100 percent of the responsibility for receiving and sending the message. Remember, too, that listening is part of the process. Most individuals will listen to their bosses, but how well do they listen when their subordinates are trying to communicate with them?

Valuable time is wasted every day because of things not said, not heard, or misunderstood. Time wasted because of poor communication expands exponentially: the communication process must be repeated; the project may have to be redone; communication failures up the line impact on others' work; and so on.

If an officer takes the time to communicate effectively, both in writing and orally, one on one or in front of large groups, he will gain time to accomplish more things. An officer can learn to speak well by becoming a member of a speaking group such as a toastmasters club. As he moves higher up the ladder of success in the Navy or Marine Corps, an officer will find that the ability to communicate effectively to a large number of people becomes increasingly important. Speaking well is an extremely valuable personal attribute that greatly increases an officer's overall effectiveness. An officer should take the time to learn how to speak, to think through what has to be done and what has to be said, to get the other person's undivided attention, and to make certain the message got through.

MEETINGS

Holding meetings can be a very effective way for an officer to communicate with his people. Meetings can be regularly held to, for example, put the word out at quarters or morning formation at the start of each day. Meetings can also be scheduled in advance to discuss specified agenda items or called on an ad hoc basis to solve immediate problems. An officer can use them effectively to discuss or set goals with, to delegate work to, to inform, and to motivate his subordinates.

However, meetings can also be time wasters. Meetings have a very real cost in dollars and cents. The officer must be certain that the benefits from the meeting outweigh its cost. Ad hoc meetings can be disruptive to subordinates and their effective use of time, so ad hoc meetings should be kept to a minimum. Other types of meetings can also disrupt work, but they are not as disruptive, because they are planned for in advance.

An officer may spend a large portion of his day in meetings called by others. He must try to prioritize his attendance and only attend those meetings that require his personal participation; he can send a subordinate to represent him at the others. If he is calling the meeting, the officer should formulate the agenda and promulgate it in advance to allow attendees to prepare to contribute. When possible, a written agenda should be drafted and routed to the participants.

Meetings should begin and end on time. This encourages people to show up on time, allows the officer more control over his own time, and does not waste the time of others. Meetings that threaten to get out of control and run overtime could be set to begin an hour or so before lunch or quitting time. However, the true responsibility for control of any meeting rests with the chairman. The successful chairman takes time to plan the meeting carefully.

MANAGEMENT OF PERSONAL TIME

The development of sound personal time-management habits is a necessity for effective time management. A few of these time-management techniques are enhanced by the assistance of a secretary, a yeoman, or a clerk. Effective personal management techniques include the following:

1. Attend a time-management course or seminar or take instruction through a video or audio cassette program.

2. Always carry a pocket calendar. Use it to schedule tomorrow's meetings and appointments and list goals, things to do, and reminders. Doing so will reduce schedule conflicts and increase efficiency.

3. Use waiting time at the barber, the hairdresser, sick call, etc., to catch up on office reading.

4. Use your yeoman, secretary, or clerk to screen visitors. If necessary, ask unscheduled visitors to make an appointment. This allows you time to prepare and will make the meeting with that person more useful.

An open-door policy is fine, but it should be controlled. "Open door" does not mean your time can be interrupted by anyone, any time, on any subject.

Keep in mind that the boss's secretary, yeoman, or clerk controls the boss's schedule and time. If possible, get to know this person; doing so may allow you to see your senior when you need to.

5. Discipline yourself not to interrupt meetings or thoughtful work to take phone calls. Have your secretary, yeoman, or clerk get the caller's name and the subject of the call. Knowing the subject is vital in preventing a second, wasted, call back. If you don't have someone to answer your phone, simply and politely tell the caller you are busy and will call them back. Ask for the subject. Let the phone calls stack up, and return all calls during one or two periods during the day. Don't let the telephone control you —manage it!

6. Use a time log occasionally to find out where your time goes. You will be surprised at the various ways you waste your time.

7. Handle papers only once.

8. Instead of inviting others in the organization to your office for a quick meeting, go to their offices. That way you can leave when you are ready.

9. Train your secretary, yeoman, or clerk to screen your mail. He can dispose of the junk mail and prioritize the correspondence you should see or act on. If you do not have anyone to screen your mail, you can do it yourself by quickly going through the incoming stack and discarding some of it and placing the rest in an action priority sequence.

10. Endeavor to plan and coordinate your schedule regularly with the schedules of the people who directly influence what you do with your time. This includes your secretary, yeoman, clerk, spouse, immediate superior, and the senior subordinates in your organization. Doing so will enhance the more efficient use of both their time and yours.

11. If a meeting must be short, announce that fact before or at the start of the meeting.

12. Learn to read more in less time. Use the table of contents as a menu. Take a reading improvement course.

13. Learn to dictate to a secretary, yeoman,

or clerk, or use a tape recorder. This will save you considerable time in preparing correspondence, reports, memos, etc.

14. Listen to audio cassettes while driving to and from work. This is a great way to obtain information or training during what is normally dead time. Don't forget to keep your eyes on the road!

The effective management of time is an important aspect of achieving professional and personal life goals. The officer is urged to augment the preceding paragraphs with more extensive reading or training in the area of time management. A good leader schedules work and allocates his own time and that of subordinates after carefully coordinating all efforts toward the common goal.

> He must inspire, persuade or cajole men to make a sacrifice for what they must be convinced is a higher good; a sacrifice which may be of remitting application to some Herculean task to the point of exhaustion or of physical or mental pain to the point where life itself is poured out. This, in the final analysis, sets the leader on a different plane from the manager. No matter how many other qualities they may have in common, this vital spark in the leader is quite different from even the most humane, sympathetic or understanding characteristic of the good manager. This spark is the authoritative essence of leadership, which those who have experienced it in action perceive with a clarity which confounds the theorizing of armchair analysts and sceptics.[41-71]

MCPON Sanders: *While meeting mission requirements is important, it must be remembered that we cannot burn the candle at both ends. The officer must ensure that he doesn't exceed the total work capability of his unit. I would caution against starting a job unless you know that you are going to have all of the people and materials needed to complete the assignment. If a job is undertaken which can't be fin-*

ished, the officer will find that he has lost total control.

36. Making Job Assignments: Assessment and Monitoring of Personnel

Sooner or later every naval officer will have a direct hand in the placement of personnel. Unfortunately, a textbook cannot fully prepare a naval officer for that responsibility; nor can an officer sit down with a great leader and learn all he needs to know about personnel placement. Every circumstance presents a new and different challenge. Therefore, an officer must begin by learning all he can about the technical aspects of placement, while at the same time developing his own natural faculties by concentrating on the sound principles set forth by the leaders who have preceded him. An officer should keep these principles in mind, and let his common sense prevail in his actions. He must anticipate making mistakes along the way, but he should never lose sight of this axiom: "Optimum overall results do not come from the care exercised in seeing that every man is placed in exactly the right job, but from the concern taken that, in whatever job he fills, he will feel that he is supported and that his efforts are appreciated."[18-227]

ASSESSING THE CAPABILITIES OF SUBORDINATES

Accurately assessing an individual's capabilities and experience and identifying his strengths and weaknesses help the officer to place the individual in the proper jobs. The officer can begin the placement process by searching for data on the individual; then he should sit down with the individual and get him to open up and talk freely about himself, what he has done, what he would like to do with his life, and why. The officer should balance all the information he gathers against his own impression of the individual—

not just what he says, but how he talks, how attentive he is, what his bearing is, how much self-control he has. The decision he makes should be based on all these factors. General Wilson suggests that,

> in making assignments, a leader should take into account, first, the scope of the subordinate's job. An individual should not be given a job that is not within the scope of what he has been assigned to do (unless he is coming in for a special mission), because that is not fair to him.

> When giving an assignment, the leader should also take into consideration the subordinate's background, his education, and his experience. These are things that a commander should know about his officers, and that an officer should know about his people. An officer who came up through the ranks, for example, would not be commissioned to write a philosophical discussion on a specific subject, and an officer who just finished the Naval Academy, without having ever been on a rifle range, would not be assigned to conduct a rifle drill. The leader should make it clear what he expects of the person receiving the assignment.

Admiral de Cazanove believes that

> what considerations you should take into account when assigning someone to a job will vary depending on the level of position you are talking about. However, in general, I would say that the first thing is to know them. Know what they are able to do. It is not enough to fill in an organization chart, to put a certain name in a certain place just to be sure all the spaces are taken. You must put the right person in the right place, and for this you need to know the capabilities of all of the people who could be given a particular assignment. This is part of officer training, to think ahead as to what he would do under varying situations of personnel

need. And once you have been with a unit a while and learned the capabilities of your people, you should follow your own dictates, after talking with your senior enlisted, as to who should do what— keeping in mind the requirements of all positions and not just thinking of one out of relationship with all others.

An officer should remember to compare past performances of one individual with past performances of others. Attention to past behaviors may prove to be a very helpful tool in the selection of people for certain tasks. However, there is a tendency to use past performance as the only indicator of an individual's capabilities. All too often, poor performers' capabilities, as well as the weaknesses of stellar performers, are overlooked. This often results in overload and frustration for dedicated individuals, while poor performers are rewarded with more time off. By the same token, an officer should not spend 90 percent of his time on problem cases and disregard the needs of people who are doing a good job.

An individual's estimation of his own capabilities is always pertinent, but it is by no means definitive. Many people oversell themselves on things they like to do, and very few fully know their own capabilities. Many people resist doing things they do not know how to do well, because they are afraid of failing.

An officer must have knowledge of an individual's experience in order to nurture the individual's professional development. For example, an individual who has administrative experience may well serve the unit's particular needs, but will assignment to that unit stifle his growth? Is someone else available who is capable and needs to round out his career with administrative experience? The needs of both the Naval Service and the individual must be weighed in the decision-making process. An individual should not be left to stagnate in a job simply because the officer is comfortable having him there. He will do better in a job that forces him to grow. Producing future leaders is an officer's most important peacetime job—normally more important than carrying out the peacetime mission. Of course, carrying out the mission with excellence is the best way to train subordinates.

MAKING SURE THE JOB GETS DONE

Considering the capabilities and experiences of his personnel is only part of the officer's task of fitting his people into the proper jobs. Other important duties remain undone. These are discussed fully elsewhere in the text, but they are worthy of mention here.

1. Plan detailed procedures necessary to accomplish tasks (section 24).
2. Set high standards of accomplishment and provide a system of supervision and checks to ensure that the standards (time, effort, cost, and quality) are adhered to (section 52).
3. State orders clearly to ensure understanding. Make sure the task is understood, supervised, and accomplished (section 42).
4. Delegate the authority necessary to carry out the task (section 38).

The naval officer should act decisively, ensuring that each individual has the necessary tools, training, and abilities to carry out the task set before him. The officer should set measurable standards for accomplishment, and he should monitor progress. He should require that reports be made, and he should observe his personnel himself.

The officer should remember that not all of his people will be the best, and he should distribute talent where it will be most effective, compensating for a weak leader with a strong assistant, and vice versa. He should not hesitate to make adjustments early. If his pool of talent warrants it, he can change job descriptions to fit individuals. Furthermore, he should give constructive criticism, as well as praise, frequently. In criticizing, the officer needs to be candid and sometimes blunt, because people do not always

realize they are being counseled. Finally, the naval officer must not forget the importance of unit readiness; if they have been given sufficient counseling, the necessary tools, and adequate time to improve, poor performers who still fail to meet standards must be removed or reassigned. Admiral Holloway described the order of succession:

The military hierarchy provides a plan for succession, and in an emergency situation, such as when the leader is killed, the order of succession allows the smooth transference of authority to the next in command. But sometimes the next in line for the position of responsibility is not the best person for it, and under controlled circumstances he may be passed over in favor of someone who is more capable but less senior. Sometimes it is necessary to do what is right for the overall mission, even if one person's feelings get hurt.

When I was the commanding officer of a squadron in combat, I lost my operations officer, and I had to make a difficult decision. The next man in line was not a strong officer, he was not a good leader, he was not aggressive, but he was a lieutenant commander. The next senior guy was a lieutenant, and I picked a lieutenant to be the operations officer because he had the guts and the ability. He was a very strong leader, had very good savvy, and I wanted him in there. Well, the lieutenant commander came to me and said, "Skipper, you know that really wasn't fair. I should have had that job, and you didn't give it to me." And I said, "There are two kinds of fairness. Perhaps it wasn't fair to you when I didn't give you the job as operations officer, but it would have been very unfair to the squadron if you were ops officer, because you don't have what it takes, and I could not have this unit with you in that position just having lost your predecessor. It wouldn't have been *fair* to them, if that's the word you want to use. What's more important to me, our combat capability would have been impaired, because the lieutenant was the better man for the job."

I still think I was right under those circumstances. I don't think I would have reached down and grabbed an ensign for the job, and I did find a bureaucratic way of taking care of the lieutenant commander so it didn't look as if he had been passed over for that spot, but there are times when we want to take advantage of the experience and the ability of individuals who are not in the hierarchy but are ready for the assignment.

There is one last point. No officer can make progress in fitting personnel to jobs unless he is well informed about job requirements, including the training required for someone to perform the job capably. This is an essential part of an officer's education.

There are no wizards on the subject of placement, there are only individuals who know more about human nature than others because they have reached out and built their own text from what they have seen and heard from other leaders, both good and bad. Today's leaders must be good appraisers of their troops and the demand of the tasks to be undertaken. The officer must be able to take the needs of both the people and the jobs and try to find the best combinations of the two. Chap. 1:36-438

MCPON Sanders: *The officer must consider capability and experience rather than availability when making job assignments. However, due to the ever-increasing technical complexity of our Navy, the officer will have to make a special effort to see that there are enough people trained to meet mission requirements. If advance consideration of this point is not made by the officer, then he will find himself overworking some people and having others standing around unable to make a contribution, which is bad for them*

as individuals as well as for the Navy operationally.

37. Using Committees

There are no rules that dictate when a committee approach to decision making should be taken. Nor is the composition of a committee predetermined, although it is considered best to include representatives from every organizational element that may be affected by the recommendations of the committee. Secretary Webb suggests that

the young officer needs to interact with people, and the military is a great coming together of all segments of society. The young officer should test himself against people by getting in the operating environment.

An officer who has already gained experience in the operating Navy or Marine Corps may be in a position where much of his work is done in committee. Generally the process of deciding by committee begins with the action officer on the issue, who reaches the point of contact in all the appropriate offices. These contacts form a de facto committee that works for hours, making visits, working through the problem, constantly reporting back to their seniors, who often can only see them briefly.

These committees and their meetings must be run properly. Otherwise they are a waste of time, and the person who steals time is the greatest thief of all. It is essential for meetings to have a point-by-point agenda and a set time to end.

The foregoing is not meant to imply that getting through the agenda is more important than adequately covering the items discussed; an additional meeting may be necessary to cover items for which there was not enough time in the original meeting.

COMPOSITION OF THE COMMITTEE

If possible, the members of the committee should have relatively the same rank and experience, so that they may better build on their shared knowledge, but because the purpose of a committee is to provide a wider variety of thought than any one individual has, the best committees are composed of individuals who do not think problems through the same way. Nor should committee members have the same opinion on most matters that are to be discussed. The most productive committees are made up of individuals who do not work for one another and are unable to be "politically" influenced by other members of the committee. Otherwise, decision making by committee is a sham: it gives the impression that numbers are making the decision, but, in fact, the outcome may well be the decision of just a few influential members of the group.

Of course, the end result of any decision-making process must be usable and be the best application of resources. Therefore, a skilled individual will probably make a better decision than a committee that is influenced markedly by one or more overly aggressive, incompetent, or uninformed persons. The concept of the chain being no stronger than its weakest link is applicable to the utility and operation of a committee. One individual can make a mockery of the entire process, and for this reason, committee members must be carefully selected. Assigning to a committee the most junior individuals available just because they are junior is not a good practice.

Because the members of the committee will not all think alike, a certain amount of "get acquainted" time will be required at the start of the first few meetings, and this time should be considered in the planning stage. There is usually some tension and nervousness that must be dissipated, and this also requires time. Therefore, the first few meetings of any committee should be long enough to allow for a team to be built, for teamwork is required in committees. When a committee will only meet once, it is especially important that the first 30 to 45 minutes be considered warm-up time, and that the person running the meeting allow this preliminary phase to be completed, after which everyone can get down to business.

To say that a committee represents a group's thinking effort is not to say that a committee should or can operate without a leader. Committee members must have an agreement that one person (chosen either by the person who formed the committee or by committee members early in the committee's existence) will act as moderator. The moderator or someone else will act as secretary to record the thinking and recommendations of the committee. No meeting of a committee should be concluded until the date and time for the next meeting has been established with everyone present. This is a simple matter of coordination, for a delay in deciding on a future date only complicates that decision, because members will scatter at the conclusion of any meeting.

WHEN—AND WHEN NOT—TO USE A COMMITTEE

There are a number of reasons for using a committee, including the superiority that integrated group judgment usually has over the judgment of a single individual. Second, because those involved in the recommendation and decision-making process come from the affected groups, coordinating actions between and within groups is greatly enhanced. Groups that have been represented in the committee will not feel they are being dictated to. In echoing this point, Admiral McDonald notes that "committees are most important when coordination between units is involved, provided competent people are available to work on the committee. But views from incompetent committee members will not justify later incompetent actions." Third, the committee process produces the important by-product of training and experience for those who are members. It is interesting to note that Cecil Rhodes established his scholarships with the thought that future leaders of the world would get to know each other during their college days and thus, several decades later, would be better equipped to negotiate and work out the problems of the world.

While the use of a committee may, theoretically, be preferable in making most decisions, there are practical limitations that must be considered. These help determine when a committee approach should not be used. Of greatest concern to a military operation is making the best decision, considering the inputs available at the time of the decision, in the shortest time possible. Decision quality may be sacrificed if the early announcement of plans will allow units to get started and still provide time for corrections if they should be necessary. In other words, if a decision is made quickly enough, the result of the decision will often become clear, and a "correction in course" can be made that will have a better outcome than if the decision had been delayed.

Personnel time is an important resource, and thus the less important the areas affected by a decision, the less necessary a committee becomes. Allowing individuals to make decisions that, if proven incorrect, will not catastrophically affect other individuals or units can provide those individuals experience and training that may be significant in their long-range development. In this way the Naval Service benefits, because its members have been given every opportunity to make increasingly difficult decisions. It is also true that those who have had opportunities to be responsible for making decisions may be more tolerant of the committee process, for they will realize how difficult making a decision is at the individual level, and thus they will recognize that adding more individuals to the decision-making process makes that process even more complex.

Finally, a committee should not be used when the problem is one of execution rather than of decision. In the United States, military decisions are made by the President on the recommendations of the Secretary of Defense and the Joint Chiefs of Staff. However, the implementation— the execution—of those decisions has to be orchestrated by the authority of a single individual in order for all hands to know exactly what is to be done when, and how it is to be done. This does not mean that a theater commander or the captain of a ship or the colonel in charge of a Marine regiment cannot assign staff members to write the execution order. Rather, whether an individual or a committee makes the recommendations for a decision, the various members of a committee should not try to direct an operation. Command is a singular matter rather than one of committee action, a point that has not been fully understood by all nations of the world.

Admiral Long points out that committees and panels are not just the product of the military.

They are used in government as well as in business and academia. Committees and panels are properly utilized when an issue cuts across several different lines of responsibility. In this case, reaching a decision or making a judgment requires the viewpoint of several different groups, factions, and communities. A committee convened to discuss electronic warfare might be composed of someone involved in the communication side of the Navy, plus representatives from the group that is in charge of surface warfare and from material commands. Many times convening committees and panels is the most expeditious way of solving a problem that the Chief of Naval Operations is faced with.

I recently was asked to chair a committee looking at the introduction of the Tomahawk cruise missile into the fleet. On this particular committee, we brought in representatives of the technical community, surface warfare, submarine warfare,

221

air warfare, and they all brought their expertise to bear. Hopefully the recommendations that this committee gave to the Chief of Naval Operations were of value, and I'm pleased to say that those recommendations are in fact being carried out.

A committee, then, should be used when greater depth of thought is required and when time permits. Committees are more awkward than individuals in their operation, and the formation of committees with fully qualified individuals is sometimes a difficult task. However, a committee decision is easiest to sell to units that have been involved in the decision-making process, and this argues for committee use when "command presence" motivation is not required.

MCPON Sanders: *While good leaders will secure inputs from subordinates as to their recommendations, and seek out information so as to be ready when a decision is needed, the officer must realize that he is the one who has to make the decision. He should not rely on a committee to do it for him. Decisions in the military are not arrived at by a democratic voting process.*

38. Delegating Authority, Assigning Responsibility

With few exceptions, people join the Naval Service because it offers an opportunity to take on added responsibilities. While monetary income is an extrinsic motivator, service personnel receive their most valuable payment in a form known as psychic income. This provides intrinsic motivation and results in individuals wanting to do their jobs and receiving satisfaction from doing them.

In the first few weeks of boot camp and basic training, the individual's ability to accept responsibility for his own performance is severely tested by locker and uniform inspections and physical fitness and academic examinations. As the training and education progress, testing is expanded to measure the individual's ability to accept organizational responsibilities via platoon and company competition.

The midshipman or officer must clearly understand that responsibility cannot be delegated. The commander alone assumes responsibility for his unit, and he receives both the praise and the scorn for its performance. This is not to say that the commander will not assign tasks, for he must. Nor does it mean that, once the leader has issued an assignment, the subordinate does not assume certain responsibilities for that assignment—again, he must! In issuing assignments, the officer must exercise the authority that goes with his commission and billet wisely. With responsibility, the midshipman or officer also acquires the accountability that is inherent in the leadership position. Admiral Moorer points out that

delegation of authority is one of the most important functions of a leader, and he should delegate authority to the maximum degree possible with regard to the capabilities of his people. Once he has established policy, goals, and priorities, the leader accomplishes his objectives by pushing authority down right to the bottom. Doing so trains people to use their initiative; not doing so stifles creativity and lowers morale.

This is true in the corporate world as well as in the military. I have seen the chairman of the board of a tremendous corporation change one man to relieve another one, and the new man immediately delegates authority down, whereas before the authority was grouped at the corporate headquarters. The transformation of the organization was almost magic in terms of the morale of the people, the way they put their shoulder to the wheel to get the job done. The same thing will be true enough when you're captain of a ship and you turn the ship over to a new officer of the deck. I think that makes every captain a little nervous, but nevertheless, if you don't do that in the first place, you'll never have an officer with self-confidence. That's part of their training, and it makes the overall organization much stronger, because then, if somebody in combat gets killed or in peace gets sick or something like that, you have people who can keep the thing going, but if you force them to rely on you for every judgment, then they will quit thinking and exercising their imagination and so on, and they won't have an opportunity to enjoy exercising the responsibility they seek. . . . I believe in delegating authority and having your people get just as little permission as possible, because if you start having to ask permission every time you make a move, you're not going to do anything.

Initial training usually weeds out those who cannot accept responsibility. Individuals who do not have the capacity to be accountable to either themselves or their organization are, despite their wishes, removed from military service. The few who are not responsible but make it through despite that initial screening are the exceptions, and they usually find their way to administrative or disciplinary separation early in their first tour.

Service people thrive on responsibility, but some individuals in the military occasionally shirk responsibility when the effort or risk of failure outweighs the psychic income they expect to receive from carrying out their duties. Intrinsic motivation, which allows an individual to carry out duties in the absence of external rewards, is particularly important in the training programs of the Naval Service, and when such programs fail or positions of responsibility are improperly assigned, the service and its people suffer.

Delegating and Accepting Authority

It is far more difficult to assign personnel to positions of responsibility properly than it is for individuals to accept it, just as it is much easier to do a job than to supervise it, and that is why supervisors receive greater recognition and are paid more. To delegate authority properly, the commander has to know

- the full complexity and scope of the authority;
- the capabilities and capacity of the individual to whom the authority is to be delegated;
- what tools the individual will need to enable him to complete the project;
- the degree of risk the senior is willing to accept if the subordinate fails in carrying out the authority; and
- what method of monitoring project performance can be accomplished without interfering with or diluting the individual's authority.

Thus, a training program for seniors and subordinates in how to delegate and accept authority is necessary to prevent embarrassment to both. Without training, a subordinate can be expected to shirk responsibility. If proper training is provided, confidence is created, leadership is improved, and the subordinate will feel a strong moral obligation to support the senior and the organization.

While experiencing various degrees of difficulty in assuming responsibility, the officer will in time develop the expertise needed to exercise command successfully at all levels. This command growth is acquired on watch, during inspection, and in the day-to-day work routine. When his own experience is limited, the officer should call on the expertise of others, and, while what he learns from someone else will not take the place of personal experience, it will give him an appreciation for the difficulties and uncertainties that responsibility entails.

While an individual's service record and rank are indicators of capability and capacity, they should not be the sole basis for the delegation of authority. A senior enlisted may never have served in a billet that required leading a large group of juniors. To delegate to such an individual extensive leadership authority would be wrong. On the other hand, a junior enlisted may have acquired leadership experience through supervisory experience over individuals less qualified than he, and thus may be suitable for positions of increased responsibility. A leader should put the right person in the right job and cross-train to allow for understaffing, ensuring that someone is assigned to take over in the absence of the person normally in charge.

Eagerness is a quality that an individual to whom an officer grants special authority should have in abundance. An individual may be much less talented than other individuals whom the officer could use, but if that individual is eager and enthusiastic, he will be the most successful choice.[50-112] The officer will have the experience of observing subordinates acquire and hone new skills. The officer will also learn new ways to do things and learn from the fresh ideas and experience of others.

It is best to ease people into ever-increasing levels of responsibility through assignments that are clearly within their capabilities. During these assignments they should be given a chance to learn how to conduct business; this will build their confidence in themselves and their organization. Developing individuals gradually also provides the senior with a measure of what can be expected of them in the future, and as they are given ever-increasing responsibility, their potential will be evident, as will be any need for formal training or additional experience. It is well to point out that all assignments must stem from positive expectations, for the assignment of responsibility without such confidence is probably predictive of a doomed undertaking—failure.

Admiral Taylor believes there are two approaches toward delegating authority and turning things over to subordinates.

The first one, the one I lean more toward when I take over a job, is: I have

100 percent trust and confidence in the people who work for me. I think the people in Washington do a great job, I always assume they must have done a good job in assigning people to work for me. Then I watch very carefully with a trained eye, and I'll recognize where the not-so-smart and the not-so-industrious people are in the organization, who have 85 percent of my confidence. They'll take a little instruction and I'll keep pumping them up, but I will delegate to the extent that they're able to handle it.

Now I know others who say, when they check in, "I have zero confidence and trust until you earn it, thus, you have to work your way up." An intermediate position would be to check in and say, "I delegate at the level of 85 percent trust and confidence." Then you watch for a little while, knowing that before something gets out of hand you'll step in and fortify it, get it going in the right direction before some kind of disaster happens. In order to develop people with fighting spirit and a level of courage that a winning organization needs, you've got to delegate things to them so that they can achieve, and you can stroke them, and then they feel good about themselves and develop self-esteem, self-respect, and self-discipline. As George Patton said, confidence is the product of self-discipline and habit. So you have to have an organization where people are willing to get in and take these responsibilities, get strokes day after day, and you get that courage and fighting spirit that's the product of our business.

Many factors determine the degree of risk a leader will be willing to accept in delegating authority. The most important aspects of the delegating are personnel safety and effect on mission readiness. The least important, but sometimes the driving factor, is fear of personal embarrassment. The leader should arrange his priorities so that organizational needs rather than personal risk form the basis for a decision. This approach will result in major gains in readiness as well as an exponential increase in organizational confidence.

ENABLING THOSE WITH AUTHORITY TO CARRY OUT THE TASK

In allotting tools to an individual who is to carry out authority, the officer should be generous. To be less than generous is to provide an excuse for failure, deprive the person of the opportunity to develop new skills, and deny the senior the opportunity to evaluate the effectiveness of the subordinate's use of the tools. The leader must guard against being too stingy in granting tools—especially the tool of latitude. A classic example of someone who was not given the right tools is the division officer who is responsible for seeing that work gets done but is not allowed to control special liberty.

Monitoring the fruits of his labor is the fun part for the leader, but it is also the toughest. It is fun because it provides the opportunity to teach and recognize achievement. It is the toughest part because the leader must not meddle; he must accept a way of doing business that is different from the way he does it, and he must recognize subtle indicators as to how well things are going. It is poor policy to give an order and then explain to your subordinate in detail how it is to be done. What you want is the result; the method employed, except on rare occasions, should be of no concern to you.[17-103] The officer must also maintain surveillance to guide things back on track when adverse conditions are encountered or catastrophic mistakes are made. While looking for achievement, it is also necessary for the leader to recognize frustration that may result from someone being assigned more than he can handle. Providing more tools and allowing the individual to work his way out when he is in over his head will pay off more in the long run than stepping in with a heroic rescue effort. The leader must be prepared to exercise

all of his technical, leadership, and communication skills in the monitoring process. However, as Admiral McDonald points out,

> beware of reorganizations. Generally, one must work oneself out of problems rather than trying to reorganize one's way out. Before changing things, it is always best to look back and see just why you got to where you are. Often some dreamed-up reorganization will take you back to just where you came from.

Petronius Arbiter made the following statement in 210 B.C.

> We trained hard . . . but it seemed that every time we were beginning to form up into teams, we would be reorganized. I was to learn later in life that we tend to meet any new situation by reorganizing; and a wonderful method it can be for creating the illusion of progress while producing confusion, inefficiency and demoralization.

When the ground rules of delegating authority are understood, the method for implementation becomes more apparent. After choosing the most suitable persons and ensuring they understand both their authority and any uncertainties that may exist, the officer must make sure that other individuals know what has been assigned to whom and what authority those individuals have been given to complete their assignments. The officer should promulgate the word at quarters, in the plan of the day, in the organization manual, and through all other appropriate media. Only one person should have the responsibility that goes with any one assignment, and through the clear delegation of authority and specific detailing of assignment, dual subordination (the conflicting responsibility of two people performing the same mission) can usually be avoided. Assigning two individuals the same mission is worse than having no one assigned at all, for in any well-run organization it is probable that someone will take a leadership role in the absence of instructions to the contrary. If enough time is taken to make the assignment right in the first place, additional time will not be lost in reassignment.

The leader who delegates authority clearly and provides the tools necessary to complete the assignment is announcing to all concerned that he is a leader who has set the tone of the action, and that a challenge to this delegated authority will be seen as a challenge to the leader as well as to the subordinate to whom the assignment was made.

THE COMPOSITE WARFARE COMMANDER DOCTRINE

It is well that the Naval Service has always championed the concept of delegation of authority. The pace and complexity of modern naval warfare make it manifestly inappropriate to concentrate all decision-making authority in one commander. War games, formal and informal analyses, and experience at sea all testify to the necessity of distributing functional war-fighting authority among subordinate commanders within a Navy Battle Group or Battle Force. The Navy has responded to this evidence with a tactical command plan that is consistent with the principles of delegation of authority.

Identified as the Composite Warfare Commander (CWC) doctrine, this plan allows the overall group or force commander to concentrate his decision calculus on his main objective—typically, strikes on enemy targets. Meanwhile, each of the carefully chosen subordinates within the group or force assumes authority over one of several of the war-fighting functions (e.g., AAW, ASW, ASUW, EW). This arrangement facilitates the efficient employment of all the war-fighting resources in the combined arms team that constitutes the group or force.

Consistent with the principle that responsibility cannot be delegated along with authority, the overall commander remains in charge of the conduct of operations, but in practice he intervenes in the activities of his subordinates only to resolve conflicting demands for resources or to overrule a course of action that he judges to be unsound or counterproductive. The authority to react to threats as they develop resides with his subordinates, the warfare commanders.

The CWC doctrine is still being evaluated; however, it promises to permit the responsiveness and flexibility necessary to meet the demands of modern naval combat, and it illustrates how, ideally, delegation of authority works. The success of the concept will depend on the willingness of the commander to delegate the required authority and the capability of the subordinate to execute. In modern warfare, it is imperative that the Naval Service pass this challenge to leadership.

Great leaders of the past obtained their prestige by being ready for the moment. Robert E. Lee wrote that he had never read of a man who had distinguished himself in supreme command against an enemy who had not fitted himself for the test to which he was put by both long study and varied experience.[50-42]

MCPON Sanders: *While the theory of delegating sufficient authority along with the assigning of responsibility to get the job done is well known, the officer also has to remind himself to let go of some of that authority so that others further down the chain of command will have enough authority to get the job done at their level. Experience has shown that sometimes the job suffers because seniors in the organization, for some reason, are not ready to let go of enough authority for the junior to proceed adequately.*

39. Making Job Assignments: Selection and Cross-Training of Personnel

MATCHING PERSONNEL AND JOBS

One of the critical tests of a naval leader's judgment is his ability to choose the qualified subordinate of each key billet under his control. The task of matching sailors or Marines with assignments challenges the leader in two ways: he must know the strengths and limitations of subordinates, and he must understand the nature and requirements of the billets. To make a successful match, the naval officer must have experience in working with people as well as first-hand knowledge of the billets involved. Admiral Zumwalt suggests that

> an officer must develop a long-term outlook. He has to look at things in terms of time. He might prefer to have something happen immediately, but, thinking in terms of the life of the Navy and the country, if something does happen in ten years, that is better than if it does not happen at all.

An officer can never be certain that he is thinking with the same degree of insight that his senior is, so when he disagrees, he must proceed cautiously. If he engages in a battle over a decision, he may not accomplish anything other than alienating people. Perhaps, if he bides his time, he will be in a position to effect change to reflect his beliefs.

In selecting officers for command assignments, the first and most important consideration is to pick someone who has had the requisite operating experience. A bright and capable person who has insufficient operating experience appears ignorant or incompetent if he is put in a position for which he is unqualified. From within that rather large subset that has had sufficient operating experience in the various departments, it is important to look for someone who is the leader by example rather than the martinet and who is able, under the heat of operating exigencies or battle, to make quick, sensible, and rational decisions.

It is often easier to identify the martinet than it is to identify the person who is going to react improperly under extreme pressure. It is very difficult for the record to reflect in any meaningful way how an individual reacts under stress, so the offi-

cer must use his judgment as best he can. Sometimes an officer can test the reactions of the subordinate commanding officers by giving them an unexpected problem, handing them a slip of paper that says "The following has just occurred . . ." and have them take the necessary actions or identify the actions they would have taken.

Naval history is rich with examples of commanders made successful through the combined efforts of brilliant and carefully chosen subordinates. While everyone concerned was entitled to share credit, it was most often the wisdom of the leader, who painstakingly matched subordinates to their assignments, which ensured success.

On occasion, leaders must match sailors with assignments for which they are not prepared by experience or training. This takes place in even the most carefully managed commands and organizations, and it presents another leadership challenge. Leaders must also be teachers and trainers, and they should welcome opportunities to prepare subordinates for new and broader responsibilities. In selecting an individual for a job he is not fully prepared to hold, an officer must take into consideration that subordinate's potential for growth. Meeting this challenge successfully (and prudently) requires additional time and energy from the leader, because inexperienced subordinates who do not receive adequate guidance are prone to make costly mistakes. When a leader accurately gauges a subordinate's potential, the time and energy spent in training that subordinate is never wasted. In choosing staff members, Admiral Fran McKee looks for

> basic intelligence, desire to do well, energy, good health, loyalty to the Navy, to their seniors, and to their subordinates, and a desire to accomplish the job.

Naval leaders must always be mindful of the unique characteristics of Navy and Marine Corps combat. In naval combat, there are no replacements near the scene of action. Casualties on board ships, for example, cannot be replaced during a battle; nor can Marines be replaced in the middle of an opposed landing.

CROSS-TRAINING

Clearly, it is neither possible nor desirable for the leader of a large command or organization to attend personally to every billet assignment. Rather, each key subordinate must fill billets within his own span of control, and exercise care in the selection of these persons. A leader puts the right person in the right job and cross-trains to allow for understaffing, ensuring that someone is assigned to take over in the absence of the person normally in charge.[36-256]

Admiral McDonald makes the point that "the leader should ALWAYS have a number two; i.e., there should be no doubt in anyone's mind about who will assume your responsibilities should you suddenly disappear." This makes cross-training essential throughout the Naval Service. Cross-training prepares individuals to take on other than their primary tasks if the need arises, and "when a man knows he can handle just about any task put before him because of excellent training, his confidence level will undoubtedly rise."[15-103]

Cross-training involves the same leadership factors discussed in relation to assigning persons to billets for which they are untrained: judging potential for growth and expending a great deal of time and energy. In peacetime, leaders should exercise every opportunity to cross-train their subordinates, not only as prudent preparation for combat, but also to satisfy the needs of subordinates for professional development. Admiral Hunt comments:

> The important jobs should go to people who are independent minded, imaginative, and determined. I absolutely do not want "yes men" in my organization, and I absolutely do want natural rebels, buccaneers, and people who are prepared to challenge the system. Obviously an

assignment which needs an officer with particularly advanced or specialist training must be filled by someone with the necessary qualifications.

All naval units should be organized "in width" as well as "in depth." This means that subordinates should be encouraged to learn not only the skills required of their seniors, so that they may advance, but also the skills required of their contemporaries, so that all essential functions of the command or organization may continue despite the loss or absence of personnel. In his book *The Green Berets*, Robin Moore stresses the value of intense training methods: "Every man on an 'A' team . . . is cross-trained in at least two other basic team skills. A medic, say, can not only efficiently patch up the wounded and care for the sick, but knows how to lay down a deadly accurate mortar barrage and blow up the enemy's rail lines and bridges."[42-10] In this regard, organization charts guide training along the most efficient levels, because they illustrate the relationships between functional areas and levels of authority.

THE CHALLENGE OF PEACETIME LEADERSHIP

Admiral Hayward discussed the difference between wartime leadership and leadership in times of peace.

> Surprisingly—at least it was surprising to me—leading in wartime is generally considerably easier for the junior officer. There is such a high sense of motivation among individuals to accomplish what it is they are in uniform for, which in this sense is to win the battle, win the war, and there is a national purpose that is understood. Some of that was eroded seriously during Vietnam, and where that erosion took place, leadership was very difficult, with the whole country letting itself down, not having the stamina to stick with the task.
>
> But, in general, where you have that

very high sense of motivation, the quality of leadership can be sloppier and still get the job done very well. That's not to say leadership isn't critically important in combat. It is terribly important. I'm just saying that people will pull together better, and some of your worst people turn out to be your best in a combat environment.

In peacetime, leadership becomes more of a challenge, a serious challenge for a young officer, especially the longer the country is at peace. If there is no national purpose, then you have to create goals and objectives that are very visible to substitute for this national goal and objective. And one can do that, it's not hard to do, but it is a challenge. You've got to keep aware of it and use the circumstances and establish goals and objectives that may affect just a few people or may affect the whole ship or the unit.

When you're in a crisis, whether you succeed or not is going to depend upon how well you've trained beforehand and how experienced your people are while dealing with emergencies, and then people are going to pull hard together. In peacetime when you take on a challenge, everyone has to be motivated over and over again, and I suggest that you establish very high, tough goals to achieve as a way around this problem of generating motivation. Don't establish goals that are a piece of cake. Make them very difficult goals—achievable, however. You can't have an organization that never accomplishes what it set out to do, but make the challenge tough and push your people hard. People like to be worked hard, they want it to be tough, they don't want it to be easy. That might even suggest devising innovative ways to change the work schedule from time to time, things of that sort, where everyone has to stay for 12

hours in a row or put two whole days in a row to get something very specific accomplished, with compensation or recognition for it afterward so that the people who did especially well know that they did and that it is acknowledged by the command. I'm suggesting peacetime leadership is a challenge that is sometimes more difficult than combat leadership.

MCPON Sanders: *Cross-training is important. Everyone should know something about what's going on within a work center and be able to perform tasks not within their field of expertise. We must be careful with a criteria that always requires putting the right person in the right job, for it may end up that some people will never get a chance to learn on the job. On the other hand, we also have to guard against promoting people into a position because they can't handle the work originally assigned. We must not move people just because they can't do a job. We must hold them responsible and give them training so that they can learn to do what is expected and required. This does not mean that the officer shouldn't have some flexibility in how he assigns people within his unit. Additionally, it doesn't mean that everyone is trainable. If all efforts at training fail, then reassignment may be necessary, but first a good effort should be made to help the person learn.*

40. The Design and Purpose of Organization Charts

In 1913, Lieutenant Commander A. M. Proctor, USN, wrote an article on the need for better organization in the Navy and proposed an organization chart for the *Connecticut*-class battleship. Proctor said that the Navy had many examples of successful administration, but that analysis of conditions that existed on board the modern ship revealed that there was nothing that could be called an organization.

In a proper organization we find a grouping of personnel into units under appropriate leaders, and the establishment of lines of authority by which the head can control the personnel as a whole by dealing with appropriate subordinates. In the organization of our ships, we find an accidental grouping into units of various sizes, but when we attempt to trace the lines of authority through the various elements, we are involved in hopeless confusion. The present organization cannot be diagrammed.[48-551]

Admiral Larson observes that organizational charts are very important to define your chain of command, to define your supervisory authority, to allow people from other units to know where to tap into your particular organization, either for information or for interface. It's important for the troops to understand their chain of command, because it's important for them to work within their chain of command and up the chain of command, because that chain is responsible for their health, their welfare, their training, and their well-being. So charts are very important. Above and beyond the charts, though, I think we all realize that, regardless of what the chart says, there are going to be some personalities who may be more persuasive, who may be respected in a way that they will have influence that goes above and beyond their position on that chart. There may be people who have responsibilities outside that chart just because of these capabilities. One good example here at the Naval Academy is Rear Admiral Bob McNitt, who worked for me as my Dean of Admissions. If you looked at our wiring diagram and you looked at what Bob did for me, you would see that he ventured far beyond his responsibilities because of his experience and his wisdom and his corporate memory.

But the organization chart is an important one to start with, it's an important one to work with, and it's an important one for the unit to look at every now and then to ensure that they are functioning properly. If they do not like the way the organization chart functions, then they should reorganize. I've done a little bit of that in several areas here at the Naval Academy, to make that chart represent the way we really function on a day-to-day basis. I would also encourage people to remember, as they look at an organization chart, that that chain of command, that commanding officer, that division officer, that department head, is the person who is responsible for you; he is fair and he does care, and if you have a problem, air that problem up the chain of command before you go external to your command. You owe that to them as far as loyalty up, and they owe you loyalty down to ensure that you are well taken care of and that you are treated fairly and with dignity.

THE DESIGN OF THE ORGANIZATION CHART

An organization chart is a pictorial representation of elements comprising one or more organizations. The development of good structure for organizations has been a concern for managers and leaders throughout history. For example, Lieutenant Ernest J. King, USN, wrote in his 1909 essay "Some Ideas about Organization on Board Ship" that "good organization is vital to efficiency; efficiency is vital to success.[35-1]

Within the Navy, organization charts can show operational task organizations and/or administrative and logistics organizations. They may be personnel related, as in the case of a division or a command, or they may indicate functional relationships, as in the case of a task group or a battle group organization. It will be apparent from the following discussion that the running of large military organizations is a complex operation, which helps to explain why career naval officers are sought after retirement to run industry's large corporations. The experience gained by an officer during 20 to 30 years or more of service is directly transferable from military to civilian life. As the human life expectancy approaches 100 years, more and more individuals will prepare themselves for multiple careers. The Naval Service will provide an exciting and rewarding first career, and government and industry will provide second and third careers.

All organizations have both structure and process. The structure refers to the formal organization and the plans, schedules, and procedures that hold it together. Structure is the instrument by which people formally organize themselves to carry out a task. Process represents what actually goes on: what is done, how it is done, and the way individuals or groups behave and carry out their perceptions of the assigned tasks. Lieutenant King wrote: "The entire theory of organization rests upon the principle of division of labor."[35-2] The structure can be seen as the anatomy of an organization, and the process as the organization's physiology.

Structure is represented by the "wiring" diagram referred to as an organization chart. An organization chart summarizes an organization's structure. There are many different types of organization charts. NWP2, *Organization of the Navy*, contains numerous examples of Navy organization charts. Admiral Fran McKee believes that

> organization charts are very useful, but people should not use them to limit their responsibility. I recall many new assignments I've had where the first thing I did was to carefully study the organization charts to get a clear understanding of just how I fit into the new command. Most indoctrination booklets that you receive at any command have a detailed organization chart, and they are most informative to the newcomer. It has always been impor-

tant to me to have a clear understanding of the various areas of responsibility and how they interrelate.

> While it is not the usual case, a few people may have the tendency to get locked in their box of responsibility and become inflexible, and this may be detrimental to command effectiveness. We are all still on a team, and we are frequently called upon to cooperate with other people on the organization chart. The lines of responsibility may become somewhat blurred in solving a common problem, but they should always support the chain of command.

The seven key aspects of an organization chart are as follows.

1. *Division of work.* A large or complex organization must divide organizational functions among work units, and it must inform individuals and groups what tasks they are responsible for performing. By referring to an organization chart, each person in the organization can determine what his responsibilities are. Because of this, the organization functions more efficiently.

2. *Line of authority.* In the traditional organizational structure, authority is vested in the formal position held by a senior, and it is the duty of each subordinate to carry out the commands given by a senior holding that position. Therefore, an organization chart is characterized by a rigid, formal structure of authority relationships in which the authority and the responsibility for performing each specialized task in the organization are legitimized. Authority is impersonal, since it is vested in the position rather than in the individual holding that position, and this is reflected in an organization chart. Although most large organizations still define authority in the traditional way, the concept of exercising authority has been broadened in recent years to include a personal, as well as a formal, basis. This has had a significant impact on the design of modern organization charts. On the impor-

tance of good organization to battle effectiveness, DuPicq, in his *Battle Studies*, wrote: "The determining factor, leaving aside generals of genius, and luck, is the quality of troops, that is, the organization that best assures their esprit, their confidence, their unity."[26-145]

3. *Flow of authority.* On an organization chart, authority flows from top to bottom. This "downward" concept of authority defines the vertical, or hierarchical, structure of the organization. It emphasizes vertical senior-subordinate relationships, in which each subordinate has an identified senior. This is referred to as unity of command, and it accounts for the pyramidal shape of most organization charts.

Unity of command is evident in many organizations today, but a new, upward, concept of authority has altered this principle considerably. In the upward authority concept, authority is granted to a senior by the willingness of his subordinates to accept his orders. This reverse view of authority has the effect of counteracting the downward principle and thereby altering the traditional pyramidal structure of organizations somewhat.

4. *Span of control.* The span of control concept of organization structure refers to the number of subordinates who can effectively be directed and coordinated by one senior. As the number of subordinates in each echelon increases, the shape of the organization chart changes from a tall pyramid to a flatter one.

Traditionally, it has been thought that a narrow span of control is the most effective; it produces an organization chart that is tall and has many levels. In this type of structure, only formal, vertical relationships between seniors and subordinates are utilized in carrying out assigned tasks.

More recently, a wider span of control has been found to be effective in certain situations, especially where subordinates are self-motivated and require less individual direction by their seniors. In these situations, activities are coordinated through mutual horizontal relationships that involve less layering among the subordinates, rather than through the efforts of the senior.

5. *Delegation and decentralization.* These are structural concepts that are closely related to the span of control. Delegation is the assignment of responsibility and the transfer of authority for directing and coordinating task performance to one or more subordinates by a senior. When this is done, authority is in effect decentralized, or removed from the single central position it once occupied. Continued decentralization has the effect of transferring authority and responsibility relationships to successively lower levels of the organization, widening the span of control at the higher levels. Conversely, as an organization becomes increasingly centralized, authority of subordinates is subsumed by seniors, and the span of control is effectively narrowed at the higher levels. The ideal amount of delegation and centralization (or decentralization) of authority has been the subject of much debate. The nature of activities performed in an organization, as well as the level of organizational expertise and personal relations, has a marked impact on the optimum degree of delegation or centralization in a given situation.

6. *Departmentalization.* This is a natural consequence of specialization and division of labor. As specialization increases, division of labor naturally results in the formation of organizational segments, usually referred to as departments. Navy organization "departmentalization" may be based on (1) function, (2) mission, or (3) task force designation. Departmentalization by function involves categorizing activities according to the traditional functions, such as Operations, Engineering, Weapons, First Lieutenant, Supply, and Administration. Departmentalization by mission involves dividing responsibilities and assigning them to persons such as the Anti-Air Warfare Coordinator, the Anti-Surface Warfare Coordinator, the Anti-Submarine Warfare Coordinator, and the composite Warfare Coordinator. Departmentalization by task force designation

involves dividing the forces of the total group into several elements, such as in Task Force 75, Task Group 75.1, Task Unit 75.1.2, and Task Element 75.1.2.1.

The larger an organization becomes, the more departmentalization it requires to facilitate the specialization of activities. In very large organizations, the basis for departmentalization may vary at different levels. For example, departmentalization by function may exist at the highest levels, while departmentalization by mission may be employed at the middle levels, and by task force or specific assignments at the lower levels. Departmentalization is necessary in every organization to provide specialization, but it usually poses problems in coordinating activities.

7. *Line and staff relationships.* Traditionally, the line segment of an organization chart refers to individuals in the primary positions of authority who have direct vertical authority over others and perform assigned functions of the organization, whereas the staff segment advises and performs supporting functions for the line segments. Staff units become necessary as an organization becomes so large and complex that the individuals responsible for directing and coordinating activities require specialized knowledge and assistance to perform their functions. Staff groups complicate the structural concepts of authority, the "top down" principle, and span of control, especially to the extent that these groups perform line functions. The traditional line and staff concept of structure has certain limitations in the highly complex organizations of today, and the roles of both line and staff groups appear to be more diffuse than they were in the past.

THE PURPOSE OF THE ORGANIZATION CHART

The purpose of an organization chart is to depict the skeletal structure of the organization, including, usually, the functional relationships between, among, and within specific elements. An organization chart for a functioning organization provides a point of reference, or a point for comparison, similar to the function of True North on a navigational chart. Use of organization charts by individuals assigned to the organization

- decreases overlap and duplication of work, which usually wastes time and money;
- improves the flow and direction of communications;
- supports the chain of command;
- allows people to see how they fit in the big picture;
- improves understanding of the functions of each element of the organization;
- increases efficiency of flow of materials and paper work;
- maintains a balance in the organization;
- facilitates setting up work schedules, work shifts, vacation schedules, etc.;
- identifies key internal organization interfaces among elements of the organization;
- indicates individual responsibility in the case of someone's absence;
- binds individuals to an organization preference scale; and
- reduces the opportunity for individuals to make decisions outside the sphere of their assignments.

Admiral McDonald believes that organization charts are very useful in the Navy, and because they generally have been deliberated for some time before coming into use, they are long lived. Sometimes people believe that changing a few lines on a chart will solve a problem, but changes should be made only after careful consideration. When an officer assumes a new command, he should very seldom make radical changes. Admiral McDonald discussed the reasons for this.

If I took a job and I started to change from what my predecessor did and I went 180 degrees, the person who came along behind me might think the way my predecessor did, and he would have to go 180

233

degrees the other way. Because we do change bosses, commanding officers, commanders in chief, periodically, it has always been my view that in making changes in the military, the change should be made gradually. Then if during my time on the watch these changes have proven to be fine, the next man can come and make a few more gradual changes, but in the same direction. If, on the other hand, these changes that we thought would be good really aren't, the next man can bring it right back without really upsetting the apple cart. This thing of going in and saying, "Look, I'm going to turn this thing upside down so my name will be in the history book"—I don't like that.

Remember that it is not considered proper to change the set of the sails within 30 minutes of taking command. Continuity is also important in an emergency situation. For example, after the Pearl Harbor attack, Admiral Nimitz retained almost the entire staff, and then he made some redirections. But he did not destroy everyone's confidence by throwing them all out.

Admiral de Cazanove remarks that, while he realizes organization charts have their place,

they should not overly influence the operation of a unit. They do serve a purpose in providing a reminder as to what billets have to be filled, and they furnish a visual display of how you have assigned your people. However, relying on the chart as a guide to control of the organization will probably result in trouble in time. You must feel free to make changes in personnel assignments as needed, and it is convenient to have a graphic means of explaining to others, as well as to yourself, how the overall unit works together. As with computers, organization charts have their place—but the leader must remain in charge and not let an administrative

tool dictate his method and approach to operations.

Admiral Hunt cautions that

an organization chart must make it quite clear who is responsible at each level. There must be no doubt at all where responsibility lies for anything that goes wrong, and where praise should be directed for the successes. That is the most important consideration.

The second is the minimum use of people. It is too easy for organizations to become unnecessarily large, over-burdened with bureaucracy, and therefore inefficient. They must be lean, simple, and easily understood.

The following experience, recalled by Admiral Zumwalt, illustrates how important administrative matters can be to the operation of the Naval Service.

I was ordered, as a commander, to my second command, the World War II destroyer the USS *Arnold J. Isbell* (DD-869). It was serving in a squadron of eight ships, and it had just finished standing number eight in the squadron. One of the things that I discovered upon taking over was that in my division of four destroyers, the voice radio calls of the other three ships were Fireball, Airtight, and Viper—all rather macho voice calls—and the voice call of the *Arnold J. Isbell* was Sapworth. The favorite custom within the division was for a radioman or a skipper to call up and say "Saphead, I mean Sapworth, this is Viper," and the crew were all being referred to as Sapheads.

I sat down and wrote a letter to the Chief of Naval Operations via the chain of command describing that, and saying that is was definitely not in keeping with the tradition of 31-knot Burke (Admiral Burke then being CNO) to have a voice call of Sapworth, and I requested it changed.

The division commander, a rather cautious man, endorsed it forwarded. The squadron commander, a courageous man, endorsed it forwarded, strongly recommending approval; the type commander, being a bureaucratic staff, said forwarded, strongly recommending approval provided it was not in violation of the policies of the Joint Committee on Electronics; and the Commander in Chief of the Pacific said forwarded, adding that it is a well-known fact that there are insufficient words in the English language to provide a voice call of the type described as necessary by the commanding officer, however, within that general caveat, no objection stated. It got to the CNO and waited for many weeks of study by his staff.

The Director of Naval Communications and former skipper of mine, and this speaks to the continuation of loyalty, Admiral Bruton, was responsible for the changing of voice call designations. I wrote him a personal letter saying what my problem was and asked him to give me the voice call of Hellcat. The correspondence shows that it was turned down three times by his staff and that he finally had written a note on it, "For God sakes, answer this, and if you can't give him Hellcat, give him something else." We got the name Hellcat and morale mushroomed, the symbol was a black cat with the flames of hell and a devil's tail, and, needless to say, with that and a few other things, we won the Battle Efficiency two years later.

41. The Staff Officer

"No commander can be successful whose time is occupied with administrative details," wrote E. A. Anderson in criticism of Napoleon. But if a single commander cannot make all decisions or insights for himself, who should he choose to help him in these matters? The answer to this question seems to be the staff assistant.[21-1305] "The staff of a unit consists of the officers who assist the commander in his exercise of command."[53-821]

Admiral de Cazanove points out that the first requirement for staff officers is to establish their loyalty to their boss, and if they do not have this capacity, then they should say so right away. They may try to improve, and can so dictate to their senior their intention, and while it is not very easy to be so honest, they must be honest enough to say it. I've seen many mistakes come from people who believed they understood what was wrong but didn't; thus, it is extremely important that the staff officers ask questions and provide feedback to the senior so that both can be assured that they are working from the same point of view. A staff officer must be able to defend his personal ideas but remember that his duty is to provide inputs and help a decision to be formed. While it is easier for the staff officer to offer up ideas he knows are those of his senior, this is a matter of honor and requires the staff officer to say what he really thinks. When the decision is made, but before the final orders are given—the staff officer must know how to say "No, Sir" one last time—but when the orders are given, then strict obedience is required, and no matter how he felt before, the officer must now act as if the order by the boss was his own point of view. This is what I would call an intellectual necessity which is fundamental to the operation of a command and its staff.

Admiral Clausen described the importance of one of his staff officers.

I think most misunderstandings of

orders stem from two sources: (1) a lack of purity of language, which leads to a wrong interpretation of orders, and (2) excessive rapidity in conveying orders to gain time, which produces a lack of concentration and flightiness.

There is probably only one efficient means of avoiding misunderstandings: counter-control of an order when drafting, and even during transmission, in view of continued development of the situation. When an officer is drafting an order for a mission, I think, according to my experience, that he should give this draft to another officer, and he could make very short checks to see whether this order draft is understandable and to the point concerning the idea behind it. When I was a squadron commander it was a normal practice, ordered by me, and therefore at the same time a routine that my "Obersteuermann" (a specialist in navigation of the rank of a CPO) had to check and reexamine all my activities which came in contact with questions, measures, and orders in the navigational scope. This worked very well and prevented me from possibly making mistakes as a squadron commander. The status as his superior did never suffer from this special task assigned to him.

Preparing for Assignment as a Staff Officer

Preparation for assuming the duties of a principal staff officer is a dynamic undertaking that begins early in an officer's career. With nothing more than perfect attendance as his career matures, an officer can compile a history of both positive and negative staff experience. Admiral Carney reminds us that,

> since officers move back and forth
> between line and staff assignments, they

should constantly expand their knowledge of factors affecting both groups and certainly seek out any and all information that would affect their own job and their ability to support those for whom and with whom they work.

Not all staff activities place individuals in harm's way, and certainly few are as exciting or stimulating as duty with the troops for Marine officers or the deck of a ship for Navy officers. However, if the organization structure is properly designed, each staff function will be a challenge and contribute to a significant mission. As General Rice points out,

> a good staff officer is knowledgeable,
> shows initiative, is dedicated, and is loyal.
> Everything that makes someone a good
> combat leader also makes him a good staff
> officer. A staff officer must learn to write.
> Because the Naval Service is an organiza-
> tion full of paper work, whether officers
> like it or not, the individual does not go
> up through the chain, the paper goes up
> through the chain. Part of the education
> of being a staff officer is to learn to write
> and to be able to put thoughts down in
> clear, concise statements. There is not a
> great deal of difference between staff
> assignments and field assignments. The
> officer is just serving the country in a dif-
> ferent manner.

The procedures for any staff section are, of necessity, scenario driven. They often depend on the requirements of a functional action in a higher headquarters or operational events that support the fleet. To meet these requirements, the staff officer must consider the basics of accuracy, speed of response, initiative, and knowledge. These basics can be captured in one word: *credibility*. Admiral Fran McKee comments:

> I'm a great believer in teamwork. The
> Navy has succeeded over the years with
> the understanding of that basic concept by
> its people. It is very important to learn to

be a team player. While there may be times that this may be difficult, especially if you think you have a better idea than the other guy, teamwork doesn't keep you from expressing another viewpoint if done properly and within the chain of command. In the process of selecting new staff members, I would look for people with the best intellect and adaptability who had skills in the areas that I needed assistance in. I would then invite their comments when discussing various issues, especially those least familiar to me. I assure you that none of us knows everything. It's necessary to set the pace and create an atmosphere to encourage free exchange where staff members are not reluctant to voice opinions. I value a member of the team who can comment intelligently on a particular subject, including any impact on other divisions or departments. This will help avoid problems and greatly assist in accomplishing the mission in the most productive manner.

Admiral Clausen suggests that
qualified naval officers should be selected for staff duties; that is to say, experienced officers who display intellectual mobility and agility. Although these qualifications should exist, to my mind it would be a mistake to employ in staff duties intellectual theorists who have insufficient experience in practice. A staff officer must be a naval officer experienced in the fleet who disposes of matters through knowledge and experience in the circumstances of reality and, at the same time, uses intellectual power. I can recommend only that these officers maintain their qualifications in practice, theory, techniques, and staff work by means of continuing studies, exercise, and diligence. The most important qualification for a staff officer in my

opinion is that he has to be able to put himself into the realities of each situation.

STAFF WORK

Staff procedures are more easily defined if staff work is divided into two categories, one that impacts directly on operational events in the fleet, and one that is purely administrative in nature. The impact of extending time lines and due dates differs widely in these two categories. The scenario and mission importance dictate priorities. Constants in this matrix remain the skill of the staff officer and the relationship the officer establishes with other members of the staff.

Duties assigned to a staff assistant may include the following; they are to be accomplished in a timely manner:

—Assembling facts.
—Recommending courses of action. The first responsibility of the staff officer is to be in a position to know what the seniors' opinions are on different subjects.[45-205]
—Discussing proposed plans with various other officers, and obtaining their concurrence or reasons for objection. When the staff officer has the knowledge or experience in the areas that the line or functional officer has, he is respected by these line officers, and his propositions are "sold" to them. Because the staff member has no functional authority, his ideas should win voluntary acceptance from the line officers.[35-12]
—Preparing written orders and other documents necessary to put a plan into action. The assistant must keep in mind that the commander's final test before signing any of the orders or documents is to ask himself, "Can I sign this paper and stake my professional reputation on its being right?"[23-123] If the assistant has done his job well, the commander will need only to affix his signature to the paper.
—Explaining and interpreting orders that have been issued. In a sense, staff assistants act as an extension of the executive's personality.[45-199]

—Watching actual operations to ascertain if the orders issued are achieving the desired results.
—On the basis of operating experience and anticipated conditions, initiating new plans.
—Promoting an exchange of information among operating officials to increase voluntary coordination.
—Developing enthusiasm among operating people for established policies and programs.
—Providing information and advice to operating people regarding performance of duties that have been delegated to them.

Most officers will take their accumulated staff skills to billets that are already established. In that case, an examination of the billet is in order. The staff officer must know the details of the billet responsibilities as they currently exist. With this information, he can produce an organization diagram that will establish who the staff officer reports to and who is responsible to the staff officer, as well as lateral coordination requirements. Now, knowing what the billet responsibilities entail and who reports to whom, the officer can conduct a constructive challenge of the system.

Every officer taking a staff billet should question what the job entails. What is this job? What should this job be? What am I capable of making it? Perhaps the responsibilities are on track, but the officer should rely on his examination to determine if this is the case. He should not accept the phrase "We've always done it that way." The stimulating effort is the officer's constructive challenge of the billet responsibilities.

The aggressive staff officer is interested in how he can shape billet responsibilities. What can be done with them? When this questioning takes place, the entire organization is strengthened by the imagination and initiative of the members. New ideas and directions are developed, and the commander is supported by a dynamic staff. However, these ideas and directions may be tempered by the personal limitations of the staff officer.

Unfortunately, the answer to "What should this job be?" may be a goal that is not attainable. The physical assets provided the staff officer or the skill of the officer may make it impossible to accomplish the goal. A sensible compromise can be struck between the "now" of the responsibilities and the "vision" of what the responsibilities could be. With the parameters and direction of the staff billet confirmed, the officer is ready to bring personal attributes and skills to bear.

All officers trade heavily on their professional reputations, on their credibility. The confidence of seniors and juniors must be earned with each new job. Knowing well the things the officer is charged with in the staff billet is primary. After that, the individual's personal skills and talents come into play. Given a sound base of knowledge, then, accuracy, initiative, speed of response, and staff work establish the stature of an officer's credibility. Bosses by their nature are impatient. They want the answer yesterday and they want it right the first time.

In short, then, knowing his job, who reports to him, and who he reports to allows an officer to follow the SOP to provide appropriate staff support. No staff section functions in a vacuum, and the officer's ability to perform as a member of the team impacts directly on the effectiveness of the officer's staff support. Effective staff officers learn early the difference between constructive and destructive staff conflict. It must be recognized that some officers may more effectively serve as staff officers than line commanders, and in order for that officer to best serve his commander, he probably will possess certain qualities, which were best summed up by Leonard D. White:

> The qualities of a successful staff officer are ability to negotiate rather than a highly developed ability to command; the possession of a broad range of practical knowledge rather than specialized expertness in one field; patience and persistence rather than a tendency toward quick and fixed decisions; a willingness to remain in

the background, rather than a desire for personal prominence; loyalty toward the policies and views of seniors, rather than insistence on one's conclusions or recommendations. Such men can be found; and in the conduct of administration they are invaluable.[45-208]

Battles over "turf" are an everyday part of life in a staff, and an officer's survival on this battlefield requires the quiet confidence that comes from knowing his responsibilities and being able to articulate them well. The power to resolve conflicts rests with the chief staff officer. His personal style of leadership will establish the method of resolution, including deciding whether something is a matter for command attention. Major General Orland, USA, stated in 1934 that "a yes man is a menace to the commanding officer. One with the courage to express his convictions is an asset."[39-239] Admiral Hunt asserts:

A staff officer has an extremely important position in an organization such as mine. I must rely on him entirely to do his work and cover his ground. At the same time it is essential that a staff officer and his boss take every opportunity to establish a personal relationship which allows the former to oppose the latter's views robustly and honestly when he thinks it necessary. I like to have around my table the maximum opposition, regardless of relative hierarchical positions, to allow a completely free debate. Then, once the discussion is over, the boss should make his decision and be supported, even if that decision conflicts with all the advice he has been given at the table. An example of what I mean is the way business is done in our national Cabinet in the UK. There was a celebrated occasion when one Prime Minister took a vote around the Cabinet table—an unusual step. He went from member to member saying "Are you for it?"; each time the answer was "Aye." Finally the vote rested again with the Prime Minister who said,

"No. The no's have it." From that moment he received the Cabinet's full support. That is how an organization should be run; I am against consensus.

THE SUCCESSFUL STAFF OFFICER

Being successful in a staff responsibility requires applying leadership skills to the challenge of everyday staff life, which can be bothersome at times. After establishing credibility, the parameters of his billet, and the procedures to follow, the officer should look at the work group dynamics. Successful staff support requires the productive input of individuals the officer controls and, often, input from other staff sections. The staff officer's style of leadership influences the behavior of those in the work group and the ultimate product, staff support.

The duties of a staff assistant should build experience and develop skills useful for command positions yet to come. It is plain to see that a staff assistant with no knowledge of battle procedures could not easily draft a plan for battle that a commander could agree with, even if the assistant thought he understood the commander's views. An example of this in history is the case where Frederick the Great's aide, Finck, was called upon to cut off the retreat of the Austrian army. Although Finck was Frederick's most able assistant, he had never been trained in such operations. He knew how to lead a division under direct orders of the king, but in such a case as this, he had no idea what to do. Instead of following Frederick's spirit, which was indeed liberal enough to allow changes, he followed strictly to the letter orders given, and his entire force was destroyed by overwhelming numbers. Had Frederick required that his staff not only be able administrators, but also possess operational knowledge or experience, this loss may have been avoided.[21-1333]

A unique characteristic of successful individuals in the Naval Service is a desire for increased responsibility. When he is assigned as a staff officer, remembering the importance of accuracy, speed, initiative, and knowledge will help the officer perform effectively and prepare him for increased levels of responsibilities. Some final words on the successful staff officer: Generally he holds himself in the background as one who is merely assisting others to do a good job. A staff officer must be humble in this case. He should allow the operational officers to take credit for new ideas, letting facts speak for themselves.[45-208] By doing this, the staff officer shows his commander respect and support.

Chapter 4 Bibliography

1. Andrews, Lincoln C. *Military Manpower*. New York: E. P. Dutton, 1920.
2. Appley, Lawrence A. *Management in Action*. New York: American Management Association, 1956.
3. Argyris, Christopher. *Interpersonal Competence and Organizational Effectiveness*. Homewood, Ill.: Dorsey Press, 1962.
4. Bain, David. *The Productivity Prescription*. New York: McGraw-Hill, 1982.
5. Ballou, Paul O. "Management Approach to the Eighties." *Concepts*, Autumn 1980, pp. 102–12.
6. Bass, Bernard M. *Stogdill's Handbook of Leadership*. New York: Free Press, 1981.
7. Beal, George; Bohlen, J.; and Radabaugh, Neil. *Leadership and Dynamic Group Action*. Ames: Iowa State University Press, 1962.
8. Berne, Eric. *The Structure and Dynamics of Organizations and Groups*. New York: Random House, 1966.
9. Blake, Robert R.; Bryson, Dale E.; and Maurton, Jane S. "The Military Leadership Grid." *Military Review*, July 1980.
10. Bradford, Leland P., ed. *Group Development*. Selected Readings Series. Washington, D.C.: National Education Association, 1961.
11. Buck, James H., and Korb, Lawrence J., eds. *Military Leadership*. Vol. 10. Beverly Hills: Sage Publications, 1981.
12. Burke, Arleigh A. "Integrity." *Proceedings*, Oct. 1985, p. 116.
13. Caplow, Theodore. *Principles of Organization*. New York: Harcourt, Brace, and World, 1964.
14. Carthners, J. H. "The Combat Leader Needs Managerial Know-How." *Armed Forces Management*, Nov. 1954.
15. Cebulash, Mel. *The Man in the Green Beret*. New York: Scholastic, 1969.
16. Clark, Bruce C. "Leadership, Commandership, Planning, and Success." *Army Logistician*, May–June 1981.
17. Cope, Harley. *Command at Sea*. New York: W. W. Norton, 1943.
18. Department of Defense, Office of Armed Forces Information and Education. *The Armed Forces Officer's Guide*. Washington, D.C.: U.S. Government Printing Office, 1960.
19. Deutermann, Peter T. *The Ops Officer's Manual*. Annapolis: Naval Institute Press, 1980.
20. Fraser, Ronald. "Taking a Cue from Q-Charts." *Proceedings*, Feb. 1982, pp. 96–97.
21. Frost, Holloway H. "Letters on Staff Duty." *Proceedings*, Aug. 1919, pp. 1305–42.
22. Gabriel, Richard A., and Savage, Paul L. "Turning Away from Managerialism: The Environment of Military Leadership." *Military Review*, July 1980.
23. Garrison, Lloyd W. "Completed Staff Work." *Proceedings*, July 1961, pp. 122–23.
24. Gibson, James L.; Ivancevich, John M.; and Donnelly, James H., Jr. *Organizations*. 4th ed. Plano, Tex.: Business Publications, 1982.
25. Gulliver, Victor S. "Up and Down the Organization." *Proceedings*, Aug. 1978, pp. 103–6.
26. Hittle, Sue, ed. *Reef Points*. Annapolis: U.S. Naval Academy, 1982.
27. Horsfield, John. *The Art of Leadership in War: The Royal Navy from the Age of Nelson through World War II as a Case History*. Westport, Conn.: Greenwood Press, 1980.
28. Indik, Bernard F., and Berrien, Kenneth, eds. *People, Groups, and Organizations*. New York: Teacher's College Press, 1968.
29. Jacobsen, K. C. *Watch Officer's Guide*. 11th ed. Annapolis: Naval Institute Press, 1979.
30. Jacobus, Guilbert C. "What Management Means to Me." *Armed Forces Management*, Jan. 1956.

31. Janowitz, Morris. *The Professional Soldier: A Social and Political Portrait*. New York: Free Press, 1971.

32. Johnson, Jack O. "One Staff Too Many?" *Proceedings*, May 1964, pp. 114–15.

33. Jucius, Michael J. *Personnel Management*. 5th ed. Homewood, Ill.: Richard D. Irwin, 1963.

34. Kimmel, Husband E. *Admiral Kimmel's Story*. Chicago: Henry Regnery, 1955.

35. King, Ernest J. "Some Ideas about Organization on Board Ship." *Proceedings*, Mar. 1909, pp. 1–35.

36. Loper, Marvin, and Reeser, Clayton. *Management*. Dallas: Scott-Foresman, 1978.

37. McDonough, James. *The Platoon Leader*. Novato, Calif.: Presidio Press, 1985.

38. McGruther, Kenneth R., and Morse, John P. "Setting Shipboard Priorities." *Proceedings*, Feb. 1979.

39. Mack, William P., and Konetzni, Albert H., Jr. *Command at Sea*. 4th ed. Annapolis: Naval Institute Press, 1982.

40. Mack, William P., and Paulsen, Thomas D. *The Naval Officer's Guide*. 9th ed. Annapolis: Naval Institute Press, 1983.

41. "The Military Man as a Leader and Manager." *Royal Air Force Quarterly*, Spring 1978.

42. Morre, Robin. *The Green Berets*. New York: Ballantine, 1965.

43. Mumford, Robert E., Jr. "Get Off My Back, Sir." *Proceedings*, Aug. 1977, pp. 18–23.

44. Nevis, Edward C. "What Management Means to Me." *Armed Forces Management*, Oct. 1955.

45. Newman, William H. *Administrative Action*. 2d ed. Englewood Cliffs, N.J.: Prentice-Hall, 1963.

46. Perry, Marvin. *Western Civilization: Ideas, Politics, and Society*. Dallas: Houghton Mifflin, 1985.

47. Presthus, Robert. *The Organizational Society*. New York: Random House, 1962.

48. Proctor, A. M. "Organization of the Ship." *Proceedings*, June 1913, pp. 551–74.

49. Reck, Franklin M. *Beyond the Call of Duty*. New York: Thomas Y. Crowell, 1945.

50. Richmond, Herbert W. *Command and Discipline*. London: E. Stanford, 1927.

51. Roberts, E. L. "Managing Soldiers: A Personal Philosophy of Management." *Military Review*, July 1980.

52. Russell, Bertrand. *Authority and the Individual*. New York: AMS Press, 1968.

53. Shaw, S. R. "A General Staff System for the Navy?" *Proceedings*, Aug. 1951, pp. 821–27.

54. *Ship Organization and Personnel*. Annapolis: Naval Institute Press, 1972.

55. Sloan, Stephen B. "The Management of Time." *Proceedings*, Feb. 1978.

56. Spark, Michael. "Marines, Guerrillas, and Small Wars." In *The Guerrilla*. New York: Praeger, 1962.

57. Spencer, John W. *The Truman-MacArthur Controversy*. Cambridge: Belknap Press of Harvard University, 1959.

58. Stanley, E. D., Jr. "Basic Principles Underlying Staff Organization." *Proceedings*, May 1950, pp. 88–89.

59. Taussig, J. K. "An Organization for the Navy Department." *Proceedings*, Jan. 1940, pp. 52–57.

60. Urwick, Lyndall F. *Sixteen Questions about the Selection and Training of Managers*. Hobart Place, London: Urwick, Orr and Partners, 1964.

61. Wall, William C., Jr. "The Two-Tier Matrix Organization in Project Management." *Defense Systems Management Review*, Jan. 1978, pp. 37–46.

62. Walmer, Max. *Modern Elite Forces*. New York: Arco Publishing, 1984.

63. Zumwalt, E. R. *The Navy N: Integration of Men and Mission*. Washington, D.C.: U.S. Government Printing Office, 1972.

5

Directing and Coordinating Operations

Introduction

The military, particularly the Naval Service, is neither organized nor operated the way most businesses are. In general, the Naval Service's "top executives" have more authority, and the Naval Service's junior personnel are given more responsibility earlier in their careers, than their industry counterparts. The Navy has a more readily apparent set of goals and objectives, and its successes and failures are measured in a much more dramatic fashion than successes and failures in the business world are. The Navy's commanding officers are charged with total responsibility for the readiness, the performance, and the safety of their ships and crews. These commanding officers enjoy authority commensurate with their responsibility, and they are, in every sense, accountable for their every action. Nowhere else—not in business or in industry—is this degree of responsibility, authority, and accountability found. We can find a common ground between the military and industry if we agree that both the military and more traditional business organizations contain a common indispensable asset: people.

When viewed in the context of motivating people to get a job done, the military and business organizations have many similarities. We may call the motivational factors by different names, and we may measure their effects by different criteria, but nonetheless, the principles applied in both organizations are virtually identical. Take, for example, the words *leadership* and *management*. Webster defines *leadership* as "the capacity to inspire others; a quality of personality which causes people to follow." The essence of leadership is successful resolution of problems. *Management*, on the other hand, is defined by Webster as "the executive function of planning, organizing, coordinating, directing, controlling, and supervising any industrial or

242

business project or activity with responsibility for results." In other words, the judicious use of means to accomplish an end.

The leader and the manager, thus, are both responsible for results. In most instances, the results are highly dependent on whether or not the people working on the project are properly motivated. The principles by which leaders and managers motivate are universal. We think of General Robert E. Lee and Admiral Chester Nimitz as great military leaders. Lee Iacocca, president of the Chrysler Corporation, is a giant among corporate managers. Perhaps these men shared management philosophies and perhaps they did not, but they all possessed certain qualities that caused people to get the job done: knowledge, vision, determination, personal example, and concern for their people, to name a few. There are certain motivational techniques that work, regardless of the setting. There is more common ground between the military and the corporate world than there may appear to be at first glance.

What is it that makes people want to do a good job? What makes a good leader? In explaining how we manage to run the large, complicated, very technical Navy of which we all are so very proud, it is easy to recite the textbook answers. In the Navy, we list these as knowing and taking care of your personnel, knowing your job, and setting the example. These are held up as the recipe for success and should be diligently applied at every echelon within our chain of command. But sometimes it is very difficult to translate these lofty principles into the practical day-to-day actions required of successful leaders. Occasionally we find a striking example that demonstrates how inspired leadership works, and examples help us make the translation.

Such an example involves Second Lieutenant David M. Shoupe, USMC. The Marine Corps prides itself on officer participation and equal treatment for all. During an amphibious landing on one of the Pacific islands during World War II, Lieutenant Shoupe's company had encoun-

tered heavy fire and suffered several casualties. After 20 hours on the front line, his company was moved to the rear. When he reached the support area, Lieutenant Shoupe immediately checked on the status of injured personnel. After being on his feet nearly 48 hours, Lieutenant Shoupe was nearly exhausted. He was returning to his bivouac area when he realized he had to pitch his tent and make his bed before he could rest. But when Lieutenant Shoupe reached his area, his tent and bedroll were ready for him to use. This was not customary, and it required extra effort from a group of men who had already given all they had. The lesson is a good one, then and now: take care of your people, and they will take care of you.

"Leadership," said Dwight Eisenhower, "is the art of getting someone else to do something that you want done because he wants to do it." A *good* leader inspires others with confidence in him, but a *great* leader inspires others with confidence in themselves. The following attributes are found in great leaders.

A leader should have strength. He should have the courage to risk making mistakes. He should have the courage to unsettle his staff by the clarity of his standards. He should have the courage to admit to others when he has gone too far, and he should have the courage to admit to himself when he has not gone far enough.

A leader should have imagination. He should be willing to go as far as he can see—with the exciting awareness that when he gets there, he will see even farther. He should look beyond the limits of custom and over the ruts of practice. He should do more than implement, he should also experiment.

A leader should have sensitivity. He should be attuned to the tempo of his followers. He should never forget that his first problem will always be the problem of winning over people to do what he wants because they want to do it. Carl Sandburg wrote about Lincoln as a man of "steel and velvet." A wonderful way to say a leader should be tender as well as tough.

A leader should have conviction. Especially in this age of disbelief, of skepticism—of a tendency to skim everything "once over lightly"—the person with conviction is the person others will respect. To stir the fires of change in people, to inspire them to work with conviction, the person who leads must be nothing less than convincing.

A leader should set the example to help others find value in their work and pride in their performance. The leader who directs this work must convey, by personal example, those qualities in his own approach that become the accepted standards for everyone else.

A leader should have the facts. The possession of facts is knowledge; the use of them, wisdom; the choice of them, education. To know the facts—and to know how to use the right facts—is a fundamental obligation of the leader.

Knowing the facts imposes the necessity for *study*—for continual study. Leadership, in many ways, is a process of self-discovery, because the more a leader learns about working with others through his professional skills, the more he learns about himself, and the more he sharpens his skills. In this process of self-discovery, he comes to realize that all people will always have much more to learn than any lifetime allows for. And unless he learns this, he has not learned anything.

A leader should have patience. He must arrive at the realization, early in his career, that people are not perfect, but that people can be inspired to pursue the ideal of perfection. He must be generous in attitude toward the imperfections of others, or he will come to expect too much, too soon, from too many.

A leader must demand accountability. He must instill in people the belief that they are personally responsible for doing a job right. The larger the organization, the more difficult this is. In response to complaints of a job poorly done, a leader often hears the excuse "I am not responsible." The person who says that is probably correct: he is irresponsible. No one involved in a job can shed himself of responsibility for its successful completion.

A leader must have determination and tenacity. Deciding what needs to be done is easy. Getting it done is more difficult. Good ideas are not always automatically adopted. They must be driven into practice. Once implemented, they can be easily overturned or subverted through apathy or lack of follow-up, so a continuous effort is required.

A leader must concern himself with detail. If he does not consider details important, neither will his subordinates. Sometimes it is monotonous to pay attention to seemingly minor matters, but once the details are overlooked, the project fails. It follows, then, that the boss must have a method of obtaining feedback or finding out what is going on. The method must be simple and direct so that valuable time is not wasted creating meaningless or useless reports and statistics. The majority of this feedback should be obtained via frequent visual inspection and one-on-one dialogue with subordinates.

A leader must set priorities. Because he will never accomplish everything there is to do, he must exert the self-discipline to focus energies where they are needed. Some things are more important than others. It is necessary to recognize what provides the greatest contribution to the overall effort and then to march off and make it happen. The corollary to this is that the leader must be prepared to justify his course of action and to defend his people when minor matters slip through the cracks.

A leader must be flexible. There are times when the leader's course of action is just plain wrong. In such cases it is often easy to accept the status quo or hope things will work out. It is much more difficult, but absolutely necessary, to admit a mistake and try again. Effective leaders understand the subtle differences between flexibility and determination.

The foregoing attributes are routinely displayed by people who run a successful operation. These characteristics of effective leaders are by no means exhaustive. Nor are they new. Generations before ours have recognized their value.

These attributes represent the common-sense approach to getting the job done. Some people develop these qualities early in life, and putting them into practice comes quite naturally. Some people have to learn the style by constant trial and error, as they try to adapt the principles of effective leadership to their own personality. But these principles do work; they motivate people, and people get the job done.

Human resource management certainly encompasses more than these principles. It includes the organizational structure that permits the successful leader or manager to function. We in the Navy believe there is great benefit in defining and assessing that structure, and we have devoted a great deal of effort to doing so. We have established human resources management schools, and we require that our officers and senior petty officers receive formal training. We subject each of our commands to annual assessments whereby, through a series of preplanned private and group interviews, we analyze the unit's planning and work environment at each management level. The trained facilitators use proven techniques from behavioral and management science to improve the process at each interface. The goals are improved communication and organizational maturity, which ultimately contribute to unit effectiveness and combat readiness.

Management organizations are important, but people get the job done. It is up to leaders and managers to create a positive atmosphere within which people can achieve their full potential.

A philosopher once observed, "You can buy a man's time, you can buy a man's physical presence at a given place, you can even buy a measured number of skilled muscular motions per hour. But you cannot buy enthusiasm, loyalty,

or the devotion of hearts, minds, and souls. You have to earn these things."

42. Introduction to Issuing Orders

A good order states *what* is to be done, *who* is to do it, and *when* it is to be done. The order also may specify *how* the task is to be performed, but an effective leader often allows the person to whom the order is given to determine how it may best be carried out. Secretary Webb notes that

> most seniors, by virtue of their mission responsibility, want to see the job done. Some will be especially demanding and others relatively easy to get along with. You can tell a lot about the leader by observing those under his immediate span of control, for those are the people he has chosen, and they will reflect his style of leadership. If the leader is comfortable with himself, so will be his subordinates, which will contribute to a reasonably relaxed environment, which will tend to help orders be understood and complied with.

Admiral Itaya remembers that,

> to know whether or not subordinates understand orders, one has only to look at the expression in their eyes. When an officer cannot observe directly, he should take measures to confirm that the orders are understood. One method is to have the recipient of the orders repeat them. Significant verbal orders should always be followed up later with written orders.

A typical order from an executive officer to an officer of the deck on the morning of getting underway might be "Have all boats hoisted by 0700." *What* is to be done is clear: Hoist all boats. *When* is equally clear: By 0700. *Who* is responsible is also evident: The OD. The executive officer assumes that the officer of the deck knows who under the OD's command should carry out the order as well as when, specifically, it should be executed in order to be completed by 0700. The XO also assumes that the OD and his personnel know how to execute the order. General Barrow notes that anyone given a task should

> never be embarrassed to ask questions of those who assigned that task. Most effective leaders, after they have finished issuing orders, particularly if the orders are oral or are given in combat, ask if there are any questions. The persons who have been given the orders should not hesitate to say, for example, "Yes, Sir, how many days' rations are we going to take? I didn't see that in the order." The usual response will be "Very good question. Where were rations covered in the order?" Two-way communications are very important in the assignment of tasks.

Thus, in the above typical order, the executive officer has given clear instructions. He has given specifics as necessary, but he has left the details of the task to the discretion of the person or persons designated to carry out the order. All of the essential parts of an order have been included, and no excess parts are present.

There is no reason for the executive officer in this case to expect that his order will not be understood and carried out correctly. However, a good officer not only gives orders, he also follows them up. The XO here might plan to pass through the area about 0645 to ensure that the boats have been or are being hoisted. McCracken opines that, whenever an order is improperly carried out, the failure is that the order was improperly given. He states, "Be as careful as possible in thinking and planning what you want, express it in phraseology precise and accurate, and then keep in mind the human frailty from which all human activities must expect to suffer, no matter how much you would like your own operations to be exempt."[34-53] For example, the USS *Liberty* was assigned to monitor the radio traffic of the Israelis and Egyptians in the Med-

iterranean in June 1967. The attack on the USS *Liberty* has been described as "a crisis that can be characterized as a main dish of poor communications, with a dash of a bad 'people' factor, and a pinch of unimaginative, sloppy staff work among the operational commands involved, all smothered in the sauce of failure-to-follow-through."[59-22]

When issuing orders, it is best to spell out *who, what,* and *when,* and to leave *how* to the initiative of the persons receiving the order. Admiral McDonald suggests providing, whenever practical, an explanation for orders of an unusual nature. On the subject of delegating authority, Admiral Long states that,

> even when he delegates a task, the officer retains responsibility for its proper completion, and staff work must reflect the views of the person who signs the document. In a military sense, responsibility of an officer in charge is absolute, and that means that even though he may delegate his authority, he cannot delegate his responsibility. A mistaken view in some quarters in the Navy, though fortunately not too often, is that if you give a subordinate something to do, then you are no longer responsible for that particular action; as a corollary, if you have given a subordinate something to do, not only are you no longer responsible for that action, but you should not look over your shoulder or check to see how he's doing. If you do such a thing as asking for reports as the action goes on or actually visit the area where the action is being carried out, then this is actually translated into a lack of trust for one's subordinate. But I do not subscribe to that view.
>
> I believe that it is the responsibility of an officer in charge not only to assign work and delegate authority but also to require follow-on reports. He should actually witness how things are going, and this action is essential, in my view,

because it permits the officer in charge to carry out his own responsibilities and to ensure that the actions he has ordered are being carried out the way he wants them to be.

One thing that is sometimes overlooked is that many times officers who are in charge actually have a knowledge of the subject that is superior to that of subordinates, and that's the way it should be. Possibly not in the technical details of overhauling a missile mount or replacing an engine on an aircraft, but there are many other aspects of work to which a senior can contribute. So I would urge that all young officers understand the meaning of responsibility, understand that requiring adequate follow-up action, adequate reports, adequate inspections, is an essential part of carrying out their responsibilities and is not a reflection on or a lack of trust in their subordinates.

Completed staff work, to some, means that an officer in charge assigns work and that the staff's work is completed without further consultation with the officer in charge: when he next sees it, it is to put his signature thereon. Here again I believe that an officer in charge needs to assign the work and then instruct the staff to issue progress reports to the officer in charge. The officer in charge then comments on the work and gives additional guidance, which produces the next iteration. In this way, at the conclusion, the staff's work will be truly reflective of the views of the officer in charge and not of someone down in the bowels of the organization who does not have the perspective or knowledge of the officer in charge. The product that we want should reflect, insofar as possible, the views of the person signing the document. This idea of interchange between CO and staff is really the most efficient way of doing business.

It's less work on the staff, and it turns out a product that is truly reflective of the officer in charge.

I would like to relate how we went about the work of the commission looking into the Beirut bombing on 23 October 1983. We had a real tragedy there when a truck bomb exploded at the Marine headquarters building and killed about 240 United States military personnel. The Secretary of Defense formed a commission and named me as the chairman, and we had four other members on the commission, including a three star Army general, a three star Marine general, and a three star Air Force officer, plus the former Under Secretary of the Navy, who was at that time a professor at Harvard University. We also had supporting the commission a very professional staff of about 25 people consisting of special warfare experts, intelligence officers, and specialists from Naval Intelligence, from Central Intelligence, and from Defense Intelligence. We also had experienced lawyers from the various services, as well as medical officers from the Army and Navy, with most of those officers having operational experience.

We interviewed well over a hundred people, we visited all the elements of the chain of command, we interviewed the Secretary of Defense, Secretary of State, the members of the Joint Chiefs of Staff, the Director of Central Intelligence, and the National Security Advisor to the President. We gained a tremendous amount of information, with the name of the job being to prepare a report for the Secretary of Defense.

The staff clearly had enough talent to prepare a report without any recourse to the members of the commission, but the members of the commission sat repeatedly with the staff and essentially reviewed drafts that the staff had submitted, gave the staff guidance. They in turn produced another iteration of the report, and I would expect that we went through in some form or another probably five iterations of the report before the members of the commission finally agreed unanimously that that was what they really believed. To me, that was a classic example of the way people in charge should go about important business, and that is to ensure that their views are being reflected. Otherwise we may as well get someone else in charge.

MCPON Sanders: *The most important thing that anyone who is in charge of other people can do is to make it clearly understood what he expects. If the orders issued are not understood, then the job will not be completed properly, simply because of the misunderstanding of orders. When dealing with enlisted personnel, make sure that the group understands the words being used. While fifty-cent words may be appropriate on a college campus, that is not the case with everyone in the work center, where there will be those who have less education. If you will make sure that the senior enlisted understand what is to be done, they can get the job done with a list of orders. Consult with the chief before issuing orders and/ or issue the orders through the chief or senior enlisted; they will make sure that the lowest educated person in that work center understands what they should be doing to complete that job.*

43. Approaches to Issuing Orders

All officers, to a greater or lesser extent, continually act to implement the directives of those having higher authority. This is particularly so in the case of junior officers. Thus, it is essential for an officer to be able to give orders effectively to subordinates. Admiral Uchida states that

an officer, when giving orders, should

examine if the orders are moral, legal, feasible, and within his subordinates' capacity, and also cover four conditions of when, who, where, and how. If an operation is part of a series, an officer should give subordinates a set of orders and help them understand their position in the whole operation. When the officer has a close communication network, he does not need to issue orders that are as detailed as orders issued within a less well defined communication network.

Giving an order requires (1) knowledge: knowing what needs to be done and how it is to be done; (2) clarity of expression: being able to articulate the directive clearly, so as to avoid ambiguity and the confusion resulting therefrom; and (3) self-confidence: the officer needs to develop a self-assured but not overbearing manner (some refer to this as "command presence"). Admiral Hunt remarks:

I think that the giving of orders must be an entirely personal affair. I've often met officers who give orders in a strong, authoritarian, forceful way, and they are clearly understood, and I also have met stacks of people who give orders who are completely different, who give them in a rather quiet and sometimes slightly uncertain way, who are also completely understood. So I personally don't think there should be a rule about the way you give orders. It must be a personal matter.

As far as I am concerned, I would much rather not use the authoritarian way, but I do think it's important from my own personal position to have up my sleeve enough steel to make sure that people understand that I really mean it. I like to give orders in the most friendly and constructive way that the people can understand that they're meant to be obeyed.

When giving an order, the officer must make the order his own. He may be carrying out the directives of his commanding officer, but he should not act as if he is simply relaying what someone else wants done. If he does, he will be implying a lack of commitment and a lack of conviction, and his order will not be effective. Even if a CO with many years experience finds that one particular approach has worked in every command he has had, he still must be open-minded about the style he will use at his next command. It has been pointed out that this type of situational leadership is especially difficult for the military officer. He must be able to adapt to two significantly different situations, wartime and peacetime.[43-76]

The officer must follow up with subordinates to ensure that the action he directed is being carried out properly and in a timely fashion. He should not do so in a way that suggests he does not trust his people or lacks confidence in their ability. He should simply let them know that he is interested in what they are doing to comply with his order and how well they are doing it. Secretary Webb says that

> every leader has the responsibility to establish his or her own expectations of subordinates. The format that should be used depends on many things, such as the size of the unit and the intricacy of the responsibilities involved. In some cases— for example, on a nuclear submarine, where the individual's tasks are very specific, down to the degree of turn— detailed instructions are necessary because small mistakes can cause great problems.
>
> Sometimes the best method is for the leader to talk personally to people when they report for duty. This is a very good way to set down all guidelines in a nonauthoritarian manner. Individuals respond well to receiving instructions from the person who is responsible for them. The leader can encourage his people to ask questions and in this way establish rapport with them, but also lay down the specifics of what he expects.

MCPON Sanders: *Consistency is one of the keys to good leadership. An officer may be demanding and not be personally popular, but if the troops see him as fair and predictable, that will help them know what is expected and thus they will meet set standards. It is very difficult to maintain order without this consistency, for the crew may constantly test the system to see what exceptions may be made or tolerated.*

44. Effective Communications in Issuing Orders

Methods of communicating effectively are discussed in detail in chapter 7, but because giving clear and complete instructions is the primary means the leader has of organizing for mission accomplishment, a brief discussion of communications is in order here.

Admiral de Cazanove suggests that

> the orders being understood is the prime requisite, and the person giving the orders is the one responsible for adjusting what is said so that it will be understood by the person addressed. While this is not possible in all chains of command, it is possible in your own chain of command. The manner of giving orders (and I am not speaking about straight orders like "Turn to starboard side") is of prime importance. In 1941, when the German battleship *Bismark* was in the Atlantic, the admiral in London gave the order "Sink the *Bismark*." This was a wonderful way of saying the order in the most simple of terms, leaving it up to the fleet to get the job done. As a cadet at Dartmouth at the time, I was horrified to see my friends assume that the job was all but done. But they were right, for confidence in your country and Navy are of utmost importance. I remember another time when the admiral in charge of the French Navy in Tunisia called back to General de

Gaulle and asked what he should do. And General de Gaulle said, "Do what is necessary"—without another word. The implication, though not actually said, was, "Don't bother me, for you are on the spot, and as your chief I tell you to do what is necessary and I will support you and your action." These, then, are two examples of orders that were short and the best possible. "Sink the *Bismark*," and "Do what is necessary."

The important principle of conveying information to individuals in language they understand requires the leader to prepare in advance of issuing written or verbal orders, as well as to follow up on orders to be certain they were understood. The "*clarity* and accuracy of communication affect the behavior and performance of followers."[19-234] When the time comes for the leader to direct the implementation of a battle plan, those receiving the instructions must understand the message in the context in which it was sent. Junior officers will find that their seniors expect them to use the right words and to use them in a context that everyone up the chain of command will understand. Officers are also expected to use the fewest words possible to convey the greatest amount of information, but to avoid using so few words that comprehension is impeded. An individual can rehearse his words effectively by recording himself on a cassette or video cassette recorder.[39-108]

When joining an organization, officers would do well to review the written files to learn the "language" of the unit and how it has been used by the commanding officer and others in the organization. After receiving an assignment to prepare a message or instruction, officers should write several drafts over a period of hours or days. In this way, they will have a chance to "digest" what they have written and attack each rewrite afresh, as if they had not written the earlier draft. Officers of the Naval Service have to be ready at all times to take command, no matter how lowly their station may be at the

outset of operations. This is one reason that great stress is placed on an officer's ability to write clearly and to cover the topic at hand completely.

Instructions must include all essential points, so if time permits, officers should have others check their messages to ensure that everything intended to be has been included. Again if time permits, officers can ask a subordinate or an associate, or even a senior, to read their instructions and describe what they think the instructions will accomplish. This will provide officers with valuable feedback. This approach assures officers that they have taken every action possible to avoid a communication breakdown. Admiral Fran McKee offers:

I think the form of the instruction depends on the complexity of the instruction. If it's a standing instruction and requires a great deal of explanation, it's probably best to have it written and not use a lot of jargon in it that people won't understand. We're all guilty of that, we have our own way of speaking in the Navy, and not everyone when they first come in understands it. If expediency is the order of the moment, then I think you can give verbal instructions and make them clear and short and concise, and most people will understand them. I guess that's why we invented "Aye, aye." That tells you that they do understand, and hopefully it's used for that purpose.

Since words have different meanings for different people, meanings that are affected by various circumstances, officers can further safeguard their communication by providing an explanation of what is intended, including, if necessary, illustrating the message visually. Officers can display charts and graphs listing current instructions or outlines of past operations side by side with the latest plan and a diagram of significant differences between the two.

While officers can assume some specific knowledge and experience on the part of those they send messages and instructions to, it is essential that they not overlook the obvious. Furthermore, it is better for them to err on the side of giving too much information than on the side of not giving enough. There is no apparent ambiguity in a directive to prepare a ship for sea, but crew members responsible for the task certainly need to know whether the evolution will last two months or six. Admiral Ramage suggests that "it is all important that the subordinates understand the reasons for actions taken or to be taken. Only in cases of strictest secrecy which would affect the command would the information be withheld."

It is equally important for verbal instructions and written instructions to be understood. Officers must take steps to ensure that there are no breakdowns in verbal communication. These can take place if people incorrectly believe they have received the message intended. This anonymous saying is applicable:

"I know you believe you understand what you think I said, but I am not sure you realize that what you heard is not what I meant."

Admiral Moorer reminds us that, in meeting with his people, a leader should always ask if there is anyone who does not understand what the group is trying to do. If they are given the opportunity to ask questions, if the leader has created an environment that encourages them to do this and does not make them think that if they ask a question the people will think they are stupid or the leader will think they have not been following the job, the fewer questions the people will ask, because they will be very responsive to the leader and his goals.

While "Aye aye, Sir" signifies that the receiver has heard something, the repetition of "Right standard rudder" assures the officer with the con that his instructions were understood.

It is general knowledge that people speak at different speeds—this can be discerned by simply listening to different people speak. But it is not as widely recognized that "listening speeds" vary for different people, too. Just as some people use fewer words to express an idea in writing, or, when speaking, use fewer words to convey their thoughts, so do some people require fewer—and some more—words to grasp a verbal or written message.

Some people hear one word and can imagine the paragraph that it stands for, while others need to hear a great many words to understand what the speaker means. To speak to individuals in terms they understand, officers must be aware of the language capabilities of the listeners. It is one thing for the captain of the ship to tell his XO what he wants and quite another for the XO to pass the message to the master-at-arms so that it will be both followed and implemented in the manner the captain intended. This is somewhat analogous to an individual talking one way to his younger sister, another way to his older sister, and another way to his father. Of course, relaying information to one's father will take one form, and relaying the same information to one's commanding officer will take another form.

Knowledge of the listening capabilities of subordinates, peers, and seniors, then, is very important. Thus, the point stressed elsewhere (especially in chapter 8), that officers must know the people they interact with, takes on greater meaning when considered from the practical standpoint that people you do not know and who do not know you are difficult to communicate with. The officer who learns the jargon of his people (the idioms of the unit) and the unit's operational and technical requirements is likely to give clear and complete instructions.

The final step in communications for the officer is to recheck his plans. Is what he wants his subordinates to accomplish or his peers and seniors to do for him possible? The achievement of an order or request may be difficult, but it must never be impossible. Therefore, officers must consider the constraints under which others operate and their own schedules and capabilities, as well as be aware that, just because an order is issued with the force of the commanding officer's signature, does not guarantee that it will be carried out. Misunderstanding and ambiguity can quickly lead to disaster; therefore, there must be no possibility of a command being misunderstood, and there need be no confusion if official terminology and phraseology are used. [26-150]

An officer seldom can spend weeks preparing instructions. Nevertheless, an officer can give clear and complete instructions by (1) being knowledgeable about the people who will act on the instructions, including their listening speed, (2) being knowledgeable about the unit's resources and other commitments, and (3) being certain that compliance with the instruction is possible, even though it may be difficult. General Rice makes the point that

> one way to determine whether an order is complete is to consider whether, if someone gave you that order, you would know what to do. If you would know exactly what to do, obviously, you have a clear, concise order, and your subordinates will react to it properly. As an example, what does "See me after breakfast" mean? It seems simple enough, but consider that, if you are a PFC, you eat breakfast at six o'clock in the morning; if you are a captain, you probably eat at seven o'clock; if you are a colonel, you probably don't eat breakfast at all, because you are worried about your weight; and a general may eat sometime after eight o'clock. Thus, the simple statement "See me after breakfast" means different things to different people; a better order would be "See me at 0800."

MCPON Sanders: *While instructions should be clear and concise, I would caution against giving too much detail in an attempt to ensure that the slowest listener understands everything. It's better to speak to the average level of the crew and leave it up to the crew leader* *to get the point over to the very slow learner. Keep in mind that listening speeds vary, and thus, during the process of passing instructions, you don't want to lose your brighter people out of boredom. By explaining to the chief or senior enlisted what you are trying to accomplish, and discussing with him the extra details, only that information which is needed by the crew will be passed down, and they will not be overloaded with information.*

45. Issuing Motivational Orders

A study of superior units indicated that, rather than just officers' call, they had officers'-LPOs' (leading petty officer) call. In this way, they were able to get more information to more people than they could in an officers' call. At divisional muster, this results in at least two individuals knowing the information, and they will convey that information, along with explanations of it, to others. During a stretch at sea, little things such as time to return to port, dates of mail pickup, and alterations in a ship's schedule all carry increased significance. It is suggested that the petty officers be informed first, so that their prestige and authority may be increased. The men will then be encouraged to come to them for information. [29-60] It is clear that, the more people who know what is happening and have the background information on a ship, the better the ship is.

People can be ordered to do things blindly, but experience has shown that, if an officer tells someone to do something because "I said to do it, and do it now," the likely response from the individual will be "Aye, aye, Sir" and a task undertaken without the self-motivation that is usually necessary to get a job done right. As an example,

> to merely tell the men of an air wing "You must keep more aircraft in commission" would probably accomplish little good. On the other hand, a great deal can be accomplished if the same

men are told, "A maximum sustained effort is going to be made during the next two weeks. The object is to destroy a major force of the enemy who have engaged our ground forces. The fate of the Army Units engaged depends upon the magnitude and success of the Air Force operations coming up. Everyone must work as fast as he can without being careless. Many lives will depend on us. Let's all have at it!"[30-147]

After such an explanation is offered as to the need for improved productivity, most, if not all, persons in the armed services will work with more zeal and motivation to increase production while actually exhibiting a positive attitude.

In the superior commands that were studied, explanations are given as to why a policy exists or why people are being asked to do something. Personnel are told what is coming up—inspections, evolutions, detachment—and what is involved and what needs to be done to prepare for it. Personnel in these commands not only know what their job is and the standard by which their performance is measured, they also know the "big picture." Walking about is a *planned* activity, not something squeezed in during spare moments. This shows the officer the big picture, and, at higher levels of commands, indicates to the entire crew that the officer is interested in all of the ship and not just in his specialty.

It must be kept in mind that every member of a unit, not just the commanding officer, wants to have a successful operation, and, as pointed out in chapter 7, two-way communication is an integral part of the success of any enterprise. It so happens that complaints are a service to the leader, in that they eliminate the necessity for the leader of surmising if and what is wrong. The leader should stress once again the importance of the function of the chain of command. He should make every effort to hear out and acknowledge the complaints or problems, and, within some reasonable time, take a definite position on them. If they can be rectified, fine; if not, it is vital that the troops be told why.[17-119] Even if the troops do not agree with or like the explanation, it is essential that the officer make sure the explanation is understood. Communication in this sense is the best preventative for poor morale. The worst situation will arise from lack of feedback and communication. Admiral Larson stresses that

good communications are essential. One of the important questions is how far you go in providing a detailed explanation of each of your actions. Let me tell you a little sea story, if I may here, on when I went to command of my submarine. In order to open up good communications with my crew, I met with the nonrated men privately in a group, then the third-class petty officers, then the second class, then the first class, then the chiefs, and then the officers. I did this on a one-time basis. I gave them about five minutes of my basic philosophy of how I interacted with my crew and what my goals and objectives were, and then I asked for their questions or complaints. I took it all aboard, and then I moved out that first week to try to change some of the things that bothered them with the ship's routine or the support from the base where we were home ported. Then I never met in a segregated fashion again. I did that the first time to open up free and honest communications, so the seamen would not be inhibited by the master chief, and then, once I did that, I started meeting weekly within my integrated crew, with the crew as a whole, and quite more frequently with the officers separately. So that established that open, honest, free communication, so people felt comfortable. From that point on I tried to describe our goals and objectives. Each week I talked about where we were going and what we were trying to do. But I think you have to be very careful that you don't take hat in hand and go and try to justify each action you take as a commanding officer or as a division officer, or be apologetic for things you do. If you do what is right and you're honest and you're out there supporting the ship's mission, you don't have to justify each and every action, so, rather than justifying your decisions, I would say talk about your goals and objectives, keep the crew well informed of where you're going, and then the individual actions will make sense within that framework and they will take care of themselves.

When subordinate members of the command know what is going on, their status is increased, as is the respect shown by their own subordinates when these subordinates realize that their seniors are "in the know." To believe that what they are doing is worthwhile, individuals must believe that their presence is important, that they make a contribution, and by keeping them informed, their seniors encourage them to believe this. The military services are dependent in their operation on a team spirit, and a team spirit is built when people know what is going on, when, and why. Admiral Long remarks:

I think the same philosophy has always applied in my case whether I had command of a ship or command of a theater. I go back to a basic view that I hold, and that is that a person in charge is responsible, and it is impossible for him to exercise his responsibilities unless he is informed, and so, as commanding officer of a ship or as commanding officer of a theater, I set procedures whereby I was kept informed of what was going on within the organization, and I insisted on being kept informed. In this regard, I would urge anyone who is in charge of a complex organization, particularly as he attains a more senior position, never to rely on only one channel of information.

With regard to a division officer, you should certainly require that your junior officers underneath you or your leading enlisted person keep you fully appraised

as they see the situation in the division. But I submit that they are not in a position to give you all of the information about that division, not because they don't want to, but because they just don't know. So there is some information that you must get elsewhere, and I would urge that any division officer supplement, you might say, the formal flow of information with other sources of information, and that would be primarily from walking your spaces and seeing for yourself and talking to your people. I would be quick to point out that information can come from a variety of sources and does not necessarily have to come up through the chain of command. However, orders or directives properly go down through the chain of command and do not bypass the chain of command.

Most individuals wish to improve their position in life, and it is the responsibility of the senior in any organization to make that possible. By keeping everyone on board advised as to what is going on, the senior makes it more likely that members of the team will be able to anticipate required actions and train themselves to attain higher positions. Thus, knowing what is going on and will go on provides personnel with opportunities for development in that they can anticipate what the fruits of their labor will be and then see what the fruits are.

All work areas have varying levels of difficulty, and the officer can promote the overall success of his unit by making the work as attractive as possible from the standpoint of the individual. Every position in the Naval Service has a reason for existing, and the officer who determines the rationale involved in each assignment and conveys it to the "worker" will find that both he and the worker benefit from this knowledge. A paint chipper who understands the reason for his activity is more likely to achieve satisfaction from his job than one who does not. There is a saying that, when two men ride a horse, only one can lead, and from that point of view, one person has to make the final decisions in any unit. However, people who believe that they have a voice in their own affairs are much more likely to expend the maximum effort possible in helping their senior achieve the objectives of the unit. Thus, an effective leader does everything necessary to obtain maximum performance from subordinates, and these things include keeping them informed and supervising them fairly and diligently. Admiral McDonald, however, cautions the leader to "beware of asking for advice unless you are prepared to take it; ask for views instead. It will make your response easier."

MCPON Sanders: *From the time the officer first arrives on duty he should make it clear to the crew that he will give them details of all operations whenever possible, and when time prohibits will provide a briefing after the fact. If you take every opportunity to tell the crew what's going on, then they will understand when the urgency of the situation did not make it possible. Remember that a primary incentive for people doing a good job is that they want to do the operation correctly. Where your expectations are not met, consider providing further training to the poorer performers, and this extra effort will bring their performance closer to that of your best performers.*

46. Records Management

Many naval officers want to "operate" instead of push paper, but most of them will discover that records management and "value added" paper work are generally a help rather than a hindrance in improving the quantity and quality of an officer's operational time. Admiral Holloway related this story:

> When I was taking over a squadron in 1956, it was an A-4 Skyhawk squadron under fairly controlled circumstances, and after the change of command, the execu-

tive officer I had inherited from my predecessor and I sat down in my office and he said, "Now, Skipper, are we going to be a flying outfit or a paper work outfit?" and I said, "What do you mean?" and he said, "Well, is the emphasis going to be on operations or administration?" and I said, "Both. One goes with the other. You can operate like mad, but unless you make records of what you did and you have a plan for what you're going to do, all of those good operations come to naught because you can't build on them unless you keep the proper records to know where to emphasize your future operations."

Records management can vary in complexity and priority from simple, relatively unimportant records (such as car mileage) to complicated, critical records (such as control files for classified material).

The Purpose of Keeping Records

The most important aspect of records management is accuracy. Adequate and accurate records are a hallmark of success. An officer can use records to insure that his men receive the training and qualifications they need for advancement in rate.[46-70] If an individual knows what goals (advancement, training, leave, etc.) he is working toward, he is going to have a higher motivation to do good work.[52-51] The officer who has a reliable tickler system (a dated calendar or accordian folder that reminds him of upcoming reports) is less likely to forget deadlines; an officer who can document his commitments and assets adequately and accurately can set priorities more simply; and when an officer's personnel advancement paper work is anticipatory (rather than done on a last-minute, "crisis" basis), his division, battalion, or unit advancement percentages will increase. (And increased advancement means increased retention.) Admiral Fran McKee adds that

> every organization has to have a procedure set up to review instructions and

keep them up to date. Most reviews are done by scheduling, reviewing at intervals to see if instructions are properly done. Financial records and things like that have to be done in a different manner. Audits have to be held, and people have to be held accountable. That responsibility should be watched very carefully, because we're all representing the public and we operate on public funding, and the fastest way to get in trouble is to mess that up.

It is also important for a naval officer to ensure that accurate, up-to-date records are maintained in order to exercise successful leadership. This is necessary for several reasons, not the least of which is that it is required by naval regulations.[39-67]

Further, the more aware the officer is of the personal details concerning his personnel, the better he can counsel them. Personal details are too numerous and too important to be trusted to memory; proper records keep them straight. As he improves his counseling, the officer will find that his personnel are less anxious about their individual roles in the command, and a widespread feeling of self-worth will result. The final result of improved self-worth is high morale and attendant high combat readiness.

Every officer is required at some point to maintain custody of classified material. While it is true today, as Thucydides once observed, that a collision at sea can ruin your whole day, make no mistake: hundreds more days have been ruined by lost classified material. The classified material control system is simple, but it demands that records be painstakingly kept. The penalty for a lapse is severe.

Without a doubt, useless records are kept and worthless paper work is shuffled. The officer should continually look for ways to streamline paper work, but he must be certain that files, reports, or records are truly obsolete before he eliminates them. Streamlining efforts must also be approved by an officer's senior to prevent the loss of something he has to have. A rule of thumb

from the old sailing navy was that the set of sails should not be changed in the first 30 minutes of the watch. Today, that advice is twice wise; an officer should not embarrass the officer he relieved by housecleaning too quickly, and he should be on station a few months before he believes himself capable of separating the "important" from the "trivial." In other words, if it works, don't fix it.

A characteristic of the Naval Service is frequent job changes, so naval officers must be masters of many trades. Sometimes, sadly, an officer must take over the position of a fellow officer who was killed or injured, allowing no opportunity for check-out on the job. Despite the tragedy, the mission remains. It is a much easier mission for the short-notice relief if the incumbent maintained a detailed, accurate division officer's/platoon commander's notebook.

TYPES OF RECORDS

These are some of the reasons for effective records management. Determining what records to keep is another part of the equation. First, the officer must set his own house in order. He must be certain to arrange his personal affairs so they do not impinge on his professional life. A poorly controlled home budgeting system—one that results in a bounced check at the Navy or Marine Corps Exchange or a forgotten payment—can also claim too much of an officer's attention and energy. An officer should update his record of emergency data prior to deployment and be sure that all insurance policies and financial accounts are centrally located and current. Concurrently, he should enjoin his personnel to do the same before deploying; the principle of leadership that says "Know your troops and look after their welfare" correlates to this effort.

The records the officer keeps within his command will vary with ship or squadron type and from billet to billet. (Some records, though, like preventive maintenance, training, classified material control, and division officer's personnel records, are nearly universal.) A thorough study of his billet section in the Ship's Organization and Regulation Manual (SORM) and the type commander's Training Readiness Evaluation (TRE) will give the officer a good indication of what needs control through record keeping. He can also quickly identify shortfalls by studying the results and recommendations of the last Board of Inspection and Survey (INSURV) inspection or of the last Operational Readiness Exercise (ORE). In the Marine Corps, the Command Evaluation Program (CEP) and Inspecting Generals (IG) inspections are important indicators of an effective or ineffective system. Frequently the grade sheets they produce contain recommendations for improving the administration or operational efficiency of the division. Unfortunately, although the young officer usually has the best intentions of acting on those recommendations, the exuberance that comes with completing the inspection or the exercise and the need to work out an imminent drill often push these recommendations out of sight and out of mind.

Of course, if the required actions are recorded on a calendar some weeks in the future, then the officer who regularly checks his tickler file will be reminded that pending action is due. No one makes mistakes on purpose. The majority of errors are due to forgetting a deadline that was not covered by a personal tickler file and a periodic review habit.

The officer should know himself and establish self-checking procedures. When he is given a task, he should write it down and record the due date on his calendar. Even better, though, is recording the task a few days prior to the due date, so he has a chance to catch up.

THE IMPORTANCE OF KEEPING RECORDS

Records management is very important, but it must be kept in perspective. An officer's ability to lead his personnel, to conn his ship, to fly his airplane, or to conduct whatever operational function he chooses—and his ability to prepare for, and, when necessary, perform in combat— are the benchmarks by which he is judged. His ability as an administrator is important (and frequently is the key to improving his abilities as an operator), but administration remains a support function: it is a means, not an end. However, the operational and leadership achievements of half a dozen competing junior officers are frequently so close that the CO has difficulty deciding who should be number one. In these photo finishes, the officer who is also an outstanding administrator will come out ahead. General Wilson tells us that,

in reviewing the use and importance of records, officers need to understand that records are important, and they can learn this by being assigned to keep a log that the commander reads. They should know that the commander will check it. A service record is an example of a record that is obviously very important to an individual, just like his name. His name should be pronounced properly and spelled properly, and his service record book should reflect the things that he has done, and reflect them accurately, because at the end lies his future in the service. The records of the organization, the records of operations, are just as important.

So many records these days are kept by computers, and I believe that computers are a way of life for us. I think that every potential commander and every officer should learn the basics of computers. How far he goes into them depends on his assignment, but certainly everyone should know the capabilities of computers, what they can do and how quickly that information can be retrieved. On the other hand, we all know they are no better than what's put into them, so what you put into a computer is important. You cannot be haphazard with that, because of the old garbage in, garbage out routine.

An individual can determine where he

stands within the Marine Corps through
the fitness reports, which are made out
every six months covering every day of his
service. There is also the so-called "truth
gullet," which requires that an officer be
marked according to where he stands with
his contemporaries in the same rank.
Therefore he knows by virtue of being
told his position—fifth of thirteen lieutenant colonels, for example—how he is progressing.

An officer should know whether he is
aware of and is meeting all the administrative and operational requirements and
regulations, because the commander
should tell him. If the commander does
not tell him, the commander is derelict in
his duty. Every commander should tell
his officers where their strengths are,
where their weaknesses are, and how they
can improve. He should let them know
what he is and what he is not pleased with.
The commander who fails to do that is perhaps being intimidated by his officers.

MCPON Sanders: *Many enlisted are either not
aware of or do not know how to go about getting
their records properly documented. The division
officer can be extremely helpful if he will discuss
the enlisted personnel records with the person
involved and explain what's in the record and
what is still needed. Sometimes service jackets
do not accurately reflect what the individual has
accomplished, the schools he has attended, or
his qualifications. Thus, the officer can make a
big contribution by taking the time with each of
his people to sit down with them and review their
experiences so that the record, if deficient, can
be brought up to date.*

47. Inspirational Leadership

An officer's ability to motivate people, in Admiral Long's view, is a
complex leadership ability that in most

cases depends on developing an individual
style. I can remember back to one commanding officer I had, and his style of
leadership on the ship was very physical.
He was a big, big man, he was a former
Naval Academy football star, he was a
rough-and-ready kind of a guy, and I can
remember the time when he stood the
crew up at quarters early on in his command and said that he was the commanding officer of that ship in every sense of
the word and anyone who doubted that
please step aft on the fan tail and they'd
take their coats off and settle it right
there. That was one form of leadership
that clearly I could not have taken if I
wanted to, since I'm about 155 pounds
wringing wet. Another form of motivation
or leadership I have seen is from officers
who use an element of fear or terrorism in
their ways. Other leaders, I think, have
done it really on the basis of true motivation, to make the individual feel that he is
contributing.

Admiral Ramage offers:
You have to find a way to relate to individuals as well as large groups. You must
find some common thread, be yourself,
don't lose your sense of humor. An officer can pretty well sense his limitations in this respect. You sense the
reaction of the group you're working with,
if they seem to be hostile or they don't
seem to be taking the right interpretation
of your remarks correctly, you've got
to change a little until you get your
point across in such a way that they will
accept it.

Admiral Long goes on to say:
The message I'm trying to get across is
that the way officers in charge motivate
people is a very complex thing. I would
suggest that everyone has his own style of
leadership, but that there are some basic
elements that I think are held in common.

One is, in my judgment, that a basic respect for the individual is essential today. I think anyone who treats his subordinates with contempt is going to be the loser in the long run. I think also that element of respect must flow both ways. An officer does not gain the respect of his subordinates by being a chum. An officer gains the respect of his subordinates primarily by knowing his job; by demonstrating that he has the courage to do what's right, to recognize the situation when the welfare of his people is at stake; and by being willing to stand up for the welfare of his people. The ability of that officer to establish high standards, reasonable standards, and insist that they be carried out also is a factor in respect. People like to work for a winner, and that means that they like to work for a person who they see is squared away, is on the ball, and is truly concerned with the welfare of the troops.

Admiral Taylor puts it this way:

It has been pointed out that we all have a heart, but some hearts are better than others. The recruiters have to go out and find the hearts that really have the capability of developing a fighting spirit, which marks those people who will not just be led, because leadership is getting people to accomplish a goal, by my definition. What you're really seeking to do is to get people who *want* to achieve that goal. That's called morale. They *want* to do what they *have* to do.

There are some magic steps in there, and they're spelled out. Some kids are basic wimps, they've been overprotected, they don't want to compete, maybe they're physically out of it, they don't have the stamina, maybe they aren't smart enough. What we do within our recruiting business is go get the basic resource, a good sharp he or she who is ready, who wants to compete and wants to be stroked, wants to achieve. You bring them and you take care of their basic needs, which is the responsibility of every officer first and foremost, to look out for the troops. Is what they're doing safe? Are they well taken care of? Psychologically are they balanced? Do you have a program that's going to enable them to free up their minds? Are the JOs, the chiefs, and the first class looking out for the troops? So you provide these basic needs on which now you develop something else. You get into good training programs that are repetitive, where you develop a self-discipline, and you give them little rewards and you give them a pat on the back and say, "Good job, seaman," and you just reach out and touch a few people, and now you've recognized them, and if they were puppy dogs, their tails would wag. You're starting to fire them up with self-respect and self-discipline and self-esteem, which are the very crucial feelings that exist in good outfits and do not in bad outfits.

Admiral McDonald suggests that leaders often have to assume the role of teacher, father confessor, etc. Thus, at appropriate times, the naval leader must explain that the appearance, the conduct, the efficiency, etc., of each and every individual in the Naval Service often determine the opinion that others have of the Navy in general and the type of support they will give it. This is most important.

Admiral Taylor refers to the fire rooms on the *Coral Sea*.

That upper level down in old Two Bravo, it's going to be 140 degrees, and you have to have people go down there and do that stuff day in, day out, six hours on, six hours off. How do you do that unless they want to do that? Well, if you're going to run a fighting ship, you have to have people who will do that kind of thing. You build their reservoir of confidence up so that they can go into that smoke because they've been into that smoke a bunch of times.

The first time you go to firefighting school, it looks like, "Hey, I can't do this," but after they do it a few times, guys or gals start to feel good about it and can do it. That's what it's going to be like when the shooting starts. If you train for that, you're going to have it. So how do you get that? It is with the JOs participating, the commanding officer finding ways to reward achievement, training the lazy and dumb to be smart people, and when you do that you have a crackerjack outfit.

Admiral de Cazanove believes that, to inspire others,

you set the example and be yourself. Never play a game. Your ship is not run by a committee, and you as leader should not be an actor. I remember when I was commander of the French Naval Academy and had occasion to deal with a senior petty officer whom I had previously known when he was on my staff. The night before he was to be elevated to the officer corps, he came to see me and asked my advice on how he should behave starting the next day, when he was commissioned. I simply told him: "My friend, be yourself and everything will be right." I believed then, as I do now, one has to be oneself and not play a game.

Colonel John Ripley, USMC, makes the following points:

The classical view of the battlefield leader is that of an officer in front of his troops, sword or pistol in the air, and moving against the enemy. His troops are behind and around him, rifles level, bayonets gleaming, shouting as they follow their leader into the shared peril. True

enough: this is a classical view. What it represents, however, is the culmination of effective leadership—or leadership in the extreme—and not the hours, days, and months of preparation for that one moment. The battlefield gives a great advantage to any leader, young or experienced, because on the battlefield, and particularly during the attack, there is a sense of great urgency and collective danger. The individual Marine feels that he alone is responsible for success, that his actions, or the failure to do them well, will directly affect the safety of his fellow Marines. He is *inspired* by the urgency of the moment, his sense of duty and care for his comrades who rely on him. He is also greatly influenced by a fear of failure in this ultimate test of his ability. In battle, most Marines or soldiers fear failure before their squad and platoon mates more than they fear the enemy.

In battle, then, much of a soldier's inspiration is self-inspired and is due partly to heightened anxieties and individual emotions. Leadership in a garrison environment, away from the battlefield, might be expected to be more difficult. It can be, and it usually is, but it does not have to be. The missing element, whose absence makes leadership tougher in this case, is the self-inspiration or motivation which a closeness to death brings.

In the Marine Corps, leadership style is based primarily on *inspiration*. For a Marine leader, it is not enough to stand in front of the troops and tell them what must be done, he must also inspire them. Then, and most importantly, he must lead them physically. The results are predictable. The troops follow him and their respect for him builds. The point at which respect becomes inspiration is difficult to perceive; indeed, most young Marines confuse the two and never realize that "their" lieutenant inspires them to do their duty. Generally, troops will begin an assigned task if the leader gives them a simple mission statement and a statement concerning their importance to the mission. The less said, the better; copious descriptions and explanations are generally unnecessary.

Colonel Ripley recalled the following incident, which illustrates this point. At the time of the incident, he was a captain and a company commander.

Returning from a three-week operation in the DMZ area of Vietnam where the whole battalion had been severely bloodied, my company settled into their former fighting holes in the line at a position we called "the Rockpile." The battalion and company commander were permitted to fly out to a hospital ship to visit the wounded while the troops read mail, cleaned up, cared for weapons, etc. This process usually lasted three or four days. Most rested, having returned exhausted—some even in mild shock.

When the helicopter dropped me back at the Rockpile after visiting the wounded, I was happy to see my men relaxing. Routine patrols, ambushes, and listening posts were assigned but would not be as demanding as the combat of the three previous weeks. Settling into my mail and a hot meal, I finally began to relax myself. It was already getting dark. In an hour or so I began a letter home, hoping to finish it before the warmth of the bunker forced me into a long-awaited full night's sleep. The letter, however, would not be finished, and sleep would not be the reason. Instead, a call from the operations bunker required that I come immediately. As I left, I was sure that my radio operator was the only one awake in the company bunker.

The news from operations was, as expected, not good. In a terse brief, I was told that another battalion in the area we had just left had been overrun and desperately needed reinforcing. My company was picked. Under the very best circumstances it would be two hours before we could reach them, putting us there not before midnight. The final comment from the operations officer attested to the urgency of the situation. "Get your company saddled up and on the road. We hope to have transport for you in 30 minutes. If not, you march." The distance was not excessive, approximately 15 miles, but the state of exhaustion of my company, and the night, gave me great concern.

Moving straight to my CP bunker in the blackout, I could see and hear that something was different. Indeed it was. Entering the bunker, I was shocked to encounter my entire staff—platoon commanders, gunnery sergeant, chief corpsman, XO, and radio operators—all in full battle dress. Orders had been issued to the platoons and they were assembling on the road—the activity I had heard when returning. Every Marine had been rearmed and reequipped. Rockets, grenades, link and ball ammunition, mortars, blood plasma, rations—all had been acquired and distributed. And all had been done in an incredibly short period of 30 to 45 minutes. It was a near-miracle for bone-weary Marines, at least half of whom had been asleep. Most importantly, all this had been done without so much as one word from me. As I looked into the gaunt eyes of my men, they must have seen in mine the shock, and enormous pride, at their accomplishment. My Company Gunnery Sergeant, his jutting chin pushing against his helmet chin strap, broke the silence with "Sir, the Company don't want you going nowhere without them. Where we off to this time, Skipper?"

This incident more than any other gave me an understanding of inspirational leadership. The Marines responded in this case because they knew they were needed, that the situation was serious, not because they were told to do it. There was no carping about whose turn it was— about the other companies—or "For how long this time?" The company saddled up and moved out because everyone saw the need and was inspired to act. As far as I know, they never received any orders or explanations apart from "stand by to move out." I had never been so proud.

Subordinate leaders are obviously an essential element in the leadership of any unit. Colonel Ripley recalled how, as a young officer, he found it nearly impossible to run a platoon correctly without a platoon sergeant:

Mine was absent a good deal for various reasons. Unlike my first two platoons, which had typical take-charge-type sergeants, this one did not; and he also managed to miss training, at least initially, for ill-defined reasons. We hobbled along for six months until it was obvious the man had to be replaced. What this incident did, however, was attune me to what I could expect from my subordinates—their strengths, and their limits.

There is an understandable tendency for the young officer to defer to the experience and leadership of senior enlisted: platoon sergeant, section chief, leading petty officer, etc. Overuse of this concept is a mistake, however. In most units, junior or new officers are reticent to a fault and would much prefer that handling of the troops— formation, drill, discipline, ceremonies, and related events—be the exclusive province of the senior enlisted person. Whereas this is correct in many cases, it is totally incorrect for the platoon sergeant always to direct the troops in out-front leadership events while the lieutenant is doing "admin and supply."

Furthermore, subordinates are limited in what

they can do, or are expected to do, compared to what the leader can do. They rarely have the same depth of understanding or knowledge of what is required as does their leader. Nor have they benefited from the guidance or the rapport that the officer gains from his leader, his commander. Simply stated, the platoon sergeant will not know as much, or be expected to accomplish as much, as the platoon commander. It is wrong, therefore, for the platoon commander to task him with the things the platoon commander should be doing. Colonel Ripley's description of an incident during the Vietnam conflict illustrates the point.

My company had spent the better part of a day moving through the jungle and then up a steep ridge, where we would establish a night defensive position. Conditions of heat and humidity were excruciating, and, together with heavy loads, began to produce heat casualties. Finally a machine gunner became a severe casualty from heat exhaustion, requiring immediate evacuation. The medivac helicopter arrived and began to attempt to lift out the casualty by basket litter, which was lowered into a stream bed with near-vertical jungle slopes on each side. Despite extraordinary airmanship, the pilot could not hold his altitude under the conditions. His aircraft began slowly settling, while the casualty dangled beneath, and then finally crashed into the large rocks of the stream. The company now had even more casualties and no hope of evacuating them.

Tactical conditions required immediate movement, as the enemy now had a perfect fix on our location and an even better idea of our predicament. What had been slow, difficult, exhaustive movement was now even more so with a load of casualties. I modified existing orders to my platoon commanders—the company must move with all dispatch. We could not

afford any time loss to the miserable conditions, the casualties, or to almost certain
enemy action. We had to reach our night
position, which was the only defensible
terrain we had any hope of making. To be
caught anywhere en route after last light
would have been tactically disastrous. The
signs of enemy activity were everywhere.
There was no question he was following
and stalking, waiting for the precise
moment when our exhaustion gave him
his best opportunity to pounce.

One platoon had more difficulty than
the others keeping up and continued to
fall back. The column continued its deliberate pace, however. To have slowed
down would have hazarded the entire
company. We would maintain contact
with the lagging platoon and then, on
reaching our position, they would continue moving until arriving at their pre-
designated segment of the company
defensive perimeter. During our climb
and advance, the platoon made continuous
position reports to me indicating they
were moving.

With less than five minutes daylight
remaining, we crested the ridge and then
immediately began a security sweep, followed by digging-in. Standing astride the
trail as the exhausted Marines moved into
the position, I strained in the darkness to
see the file connectors. These were men
positioned between the last two platoons
to maintain visual contact and column
security. They never showed up. Furthermore, no movement or any other noise
could be detected down the trail.

Raising the platoon by radio, we determined they had fallen behind considerably
for a variety of reasons, mostly exhaustion.
Because of darkness, however, the situation had changed radically. No longer was
it possible for them to push on. Night
movement under these conditions vir-

tually assured enemy ambush, and with
circumstances greatly favoring him. Had
the platoon been closer, we could have
attempted a night uncovering (meeting)—
difficult under the best of conditions, but
with the enemy hovering about and knowing precisely where both separated units
were, it would have been ripe for disaster. The platoon was ordered to form their
own perimeter, go to ground, and dig-in;
we would place defensive fires around
them.

I was trying to make sense of the radical departure in performance of this one
platoon when I remembered that its commander, relatively new, was on his first
operation. His platoon sergeant was just
recently the acting commander. He was a
strong, firm NCO with total control of his
men. The problems the platoon were having now became very apparent. Whereas I
had been in contact with the lieutenant
from the beginning—relaying orders,
encouraging movement, and in general
ensuring that he understood the urgency
of getting to our destination—he had
almost totally deferred control of the platoon to his sergeant. On the other hand,
the platoon sergeant had no sense of the
tactical urgency to push the men physically despite arduous conditions.

Results were obvious: troops reluctant
to move, as they were, in their opinion, at
the limit of their endurance, and a platoon
sergeant—who was not the actual leader
but definitely in control—equally reluctant to push his men. Also, and most
importantly, the lieutenant platoon commander had deferred his own judgment
(despite his commander's very clear
orders) and the control of his men to his
subordinate. He did not understand the
limitations of his subordinates, but then
neither did I. We were both victims of
bad assumptions. Mine had been to rely

totally on my new lieutenant, discounting the continued strong influence of the platoon sergeant. His had been to leave the business of *leading*—clearly the lieutenant's role—up to the platoon sergeant.

This entire affair was regrettable and preventable. Had I been more attentive to the leadership axiom "Know your men," in this case the new lieutenant, then none of it might have happened. As it was, the platoon overcame the exhaustive events of the day and moved into their night positions. Not surprisingly, the enemy made an effort to isolate and damage them during the night, but the Marines in the platoon were ready. They performed as they had in the past and ended up doing far more damage to the enemy than they received.

Several days later, while at our base camp, my new platoon commander and I agreed that perhaps one of the most important lessons of this operation was to be aware of the strengths and *limitations* of one's subordinates. Decisive and bold leaders will be successful in combat. There can never be any question of who is in charge, who is the leader.

MCPON Sanders: *My experience has been that I have been inspired by those officers who showed personal interest, had personal integrity, worked at planning and getting the job done, and showed me by their example what was required and expected.*

48. Efficient and Professional Conduct of Operations

Measuring efficiency is not a new concept. As Admiral Mahan pointed out long ago,

Naval administration is very clearly and sharply differentiated by the presence of an element.

. . . The military factor is to it not merely incidental but fundamental . . . [and] naval administration has failed unless it provides to the nation an efficient fighting body, directed by well-trained men, animated by a strong military spirit. . . . The business routine of even the most military department of a naval administration is in itself more akin to civil than to military life; but it by no means follows that those departments would be better administrated under men of civil habit of thought than by those of military training. The method exists for the result, and an efficient fighting body is not to be attained by weakening the appreciation of military necessities at the very fountain head of their supply in the administration.

Modern information systems have not changed the fundamentals of naval administration. Volumes of data can be passed in nanoseconds, but it is still difficult to determine the proper mix of forces to withstand or launch an assault.

Naval operations can seldom be quantified in terms that are subject to efficiency analysis. Obviously, the resources of the nation, the command, and the division should not be wasted. But what yardsticks can be applied to measure the efficiency of military efforts? If the mission was a success, and if that success was achieved with an appearance of professionalism, then perhaps operations are being conducted efficiently. But is the unit as effective as it could be? The inspection of division or platoon spaces and personnel by a senior officer is one activity with which every naval officer is familiar. A reasonable measure of effectiveness for an inspection would be whether every man successfully met the standards—that is, whether the division or platoon passed the inspection or not.

Indeed, a hallmark of any leader is getting his men to accept and achieve his goals. General Wilson points out that

the commander should let his subordinate commanders know that he expects them to run a fine organization and that he will stay out of their hair up to the point that they are successful and up to the point that they are doing their job, and in fact that he will back them up to his seniors if he believes they are doing the right job. On the other hand, he should let them know that he will not back them up just because they think he is going to back them up. They have to prove to him by thought, word, and deed that they are indeed carrying out the broad policy he outlined, and if they have any questions as to whether or not they are carrying out his policy, his telephone is available, his office door is always open, and he will tell them.

The measure of a professional is accomplishing goals with a minimum of resources. It is even more important for the leader to recognize and articulate worthy goals. For example, personnel inspections are conducted to build the team; they are not an end in themselves. The true goal of inspections is to enhance the Navy's and the Marine Corps's readiness to fight or conduct any naval operation that is assigned to them. Therefore, the way the officer approaches an inspection determines the efficiency or effectiveness of the inspection effort. Is the inspection a milestone or a building block? An inspection can be an opportunity to develop a sense of pride in personnel, a sense that they can do any job well. An inspection is also a chance for the leader to get to know his people better, and for all to participate in a team-building experience. Admiral Moorer suggests that it is vital for a senior officer to

> invite or welcome comments on a certain issue from everyone. Everyone on the staff or in the unit should know that they are entitled to give their views. The commander gets paid to make decisions, and the final decision is his, but he should listen to the thoughts and opinions of his people. This is good for him, because he receives input, and it is good for them, because they need to know that the senior officer will listen to what they have to say.

> I followed this policy throughout. "Tell me what you think, what your views are, and be absolutely free to say anything you like. Whatever you think is not going to be held against you. I want to be sure you have an opportunity to let me know what you think." And then I'd go around the table or wherever we are and then I would say, "Okay, I hear you and appreciate your comments and recommendations, and we're going to do it this way." Now once we went through that process, then if anyone disagrees and then by various and sundry means tries to indicate to my boss that he told me not to do that but I did it anyway, then I'd get rid of him.

In other words, the goal is not to present a sharp outfit to the commanding officer, but to sharpen the outfit. Using that perspective, the officer will determine how to handle the sad sack who does not measure up. Does he cull him out for a sudden dirty detail, or does he use the opportunity to bring that individual aboard and develop the leadership skills of his petty officers or noncommissioned officers? If how the unit looks is the measure of effectiveness, it would suffice to cull the sad sack out. Failure to optimize in a situation can happen in the military. When the emphasis is on achieving a surrogate measure of success, the natural result is to lose sight of the true objective.

The goals that the military seeks are often difficult to quantify into incremental units, which makes it difficult to measure progress or efficiency. In the Navy, if the captain wants a smart-looking ship that is ready to sail in harm's way, the crew knows that, but his approach in assessing them will affect how they cooperate. If the captain likes to see men shining brass, the men will spend a great deal of effort shining brass or to be seen shining brass. And if the captain puts more emphasis on the quarterdeck than on boiler water chemistry, he can expect the quarterdeck to receive a great deal of attention.

Sailors want to be responsive and do well. In

that simple fact lies the importance of measuring and being conscious of efficiency. Measuring efficiency requires making a statement of values, and when the leader begins to take the measurements, the organization begins to respond and maximize those values. The more emphasis officers place on this measurement and the acceptable standards, the more the organization will concentrate on achieving the standards.

The officer should expect to find what he is inspecting to be in good shape, but at the expense of an area he is not inspecting. It is for just this reason that judgment is so critical in the making of a professional naval officer. It is judgment that will determine whether the crew turns to doing things right, or doing the right things. Doing the right things requires a sense of values far beyond the frame of reference associated with carrying out orders. It requires integrity and character. Getting a crew to do the right things is the measure of an efficient manager and a professional leader.

The ultimate purpose of the Navy and the Marine Corps is to be ready to fight and win. But even in combat, officers have been known to fail to consider what they are trying to achieve, and their zeal for measuring their efficiency can become counterproductive. In Vietnam, the services measured bombs dropped and sorties flown per day. Since effectiveness was so difficult to measure, efficiency was defined in levels of effort that could be measured. It is much simpler to calculate the costs than to estimate the worth of an endeavor. Activity rather than success was measured, and that form of failing to optimize is the constant activity trap that must be avoided in naval operations.

In naval leadership, seeing and articulating the true goals is vital, but it must be balanced by a pragmatic awareness of the standards of the organization and the current problems. The professional approach to every problem, however, should emphasize meaningful goals rather than measures of efficiency. Efficiency comes from going in the right direction rather than

maximizing miles per gallon or minimizing fuel expended.

To many, the "direction" always seems to be above their rank or pay grade. Many would even say that "they" not only tell us where to go, but will also tell us how to get there. That kind of thinking puts people back in the activity trap; it is not professional, it does not lead to more efficient operations, and it certainly is not leadership. The Navy and the Marine Corps have indeed institutionalized many ways of doing things. "They" have given their officers a frame of reference that has worked for hundreds of years, and that tradition and experience provides an excellent point of departure for solving the problems of today.

Since it is normally that historical frame of reference that is used to develop measures of efficiency, the officer must always be wary, for history has also taught that change is the only certainty. The quest for efficiency will lead officers to do whatever they do better. It is even better yet to be doing the right thing. The right thing to do is more likely to require a new approach in the ever-changing world of military technology.

The individual who wants to be a professional naval officer must look to his own sense of values and recognize the constraints of the world and the inevitability of change, and then begin the long process of exciting his comrades with his own vision of the future.

Ultimately, every serviceman knows that he is always responsible to wage war when the need arises, and it is his duty to be prepared for that day and carry that duty out when called upon to do so. Even if it means his own demise. "Combat effectiveness hinges ultimately on leadership. Good leadership will result in good discipline; discipline is a result of good leadership but is never a substitute for leadership."[51-80] Concerning discipline, you must, most importantly, apply yourself with a more concentrated devotion to duty than you would expect from the troops responsible to you. Be visible. Be demanding of yourself. Discipline your actions and your spirit, and you will find the effect on your troops electrifying.[46-72]

Finally, an area that professionalism must encompass is preparedness: Think combat, think war. Distasteful as the proposal is in a nation dedicated to deterrence to forestall combat, you personally must be prepared right now to go to war. Know what is important to that end and what is not. Pick as your role models the senior officers who stress combat readiness, tactical preparedness, and warfare skill to the limits of the ship or aircraft.[46-72]

49. Developing Teamwork and Coordinating Operations

When Admiral Lord Nelson faced the challenge of coordinating his forces, comprising 27 ships, at the Battle of Trafalgar, his plan was relatively simple. He called his captains together, discussed how he would split his force into two columns, and laid out his plan to defeat the larger and more powerful Spanish and French force of 33 ships. Each captain was enjoined to do his utmost, and each was told that he could do no wrong if he laid his ship alongside the enemy. Nelson was supremely confident of his ships' fighting qualities and knew that it was most important that each ship get into the engagement. He wanted to ensure that none of his captains failed to engage the enemy in a decisive way. To every captain who went into battle, the objective and the method of achieving it were very clear.

Nelson had a large force, but the limitations of ship speed and maneuverability bound his options to a great degree. He was concerned with surface forces only, and they were generally within sight. Coordinating forces today can be very complex, involving the variables of great distances, speeds, and dimensions. Air, surface, and submarine forces, each with unique capabilities and limitations, must be coordinated to bring the most effective power to bear

on the enemy. Emotional inspiration and the leader's example and character are very important elements of leadership.[31-1890] Admiral Carney recalled how he obtained the cooperation of his personnel. He was friendly with them, and he took part in the ship's activities, but he also required his personnel to fulfill their obligations.

When I reported to my first ship, after graduation, it was the *New Hampshire*. When I reported on board I was assigned to the quarterdeck division, and my division officer was on leave, so I had the quarterdeck division.

I introduced myself to the turret captain, who was very tolerant, and he said, "All right, Sir, I'll tell you what. You bust it and I'll fix it." So that was my relation. It was scarcely a command relation, it was a cooperative relation. On the first admiral's inspection, I had a frocked coat, I wore a schooner-rigged hat, cocked hat, which didn't fit very well. When the division commander came onto the quarterdeck, I snapped my division to salute, eyes right, and I whipped around to salute him, and the hat just stayed there and I just sort of turned around under it. Even the division commander had to laugh at that one, because I looked more like Napoleon than I did a junior officer when I finished up. I had to depend on my petty officers in the division, and fortunately I didn't have any inhibitions about asking them questions, and apparently they liked that. But then I insisted on their haircuts and I insisted on this and insisted on that. If inspections were not right, I docked their liberty. As the head of a department, I was a gunnery officer on a cruiser. I interested myself in ship athletics and I ended up in a highly competitive position in the fleet, and I knew most of the people by name. But with the junior officers and the people under me, I still demanded the extra mile, and I had my own system of penalties. Hopefully these penalties didn't exceed what the Navy Regulations permitted, but they were effective.

Admiral de Cazanove points out, in relation to one's command, that

the first thing is to develop a sense of responsibility in the team, and a feeling of initiative in the individual members of the team. The more the members take initiative, the more efficient will be the team. One thing to bear in mind with respect to coordination within the team and the implementation of the ideas developed within the team is that the team will be proud of itself and consider itself to be one of the best. Thus, whether the idea is internally or externally developed, pride must be established and sustained, for men who are not proud of what they are doing will not do it properly.

Personnel must be shown that they are an integral part of any group effort. "Cooperation and teamwork are promoted by the knowledge that all must go up or go down together. Some may go farther than others, but all must share in the success or adversity of the team."[11-1312]

Regardless of whether a battle force, a four-ship division, a flight of aircraft, or a submarine element is being coordinated, the basic principles apply. "Every member of the team must understand where he and the employment of his weapons fit into the common effort of the unit."[54-194] The objective must be clearly understood, the forces must be directed in the most efficient manner possible in order to avoid unnecessary duplication of effort, and each element must thoroughly understand its part in the overall task.

The detailed coordination of operating elements is the basis for successful military operations. Admiral Fran McKee makes the observation that, frequently,

accomplishing the mission requires coordi-

nated efforts of more than one unit, and if the various groups can operate successfully as a team to accomplish a common goal, the job gets done. Most of us enjoy success, and if joint effort is put forth in the same direction, then the chance of successful mission accomplishment is greatly enhanced. I have always found that the majority of people want to get the job done successfully and to be on the winning team.

The leader has to build team spirit and to make the goal and each unit's part in it clear. The leader must know the strengths and weaknesses of his elements in order to match the right element with the right task. Subordinates must be allowed sufficient latitude to execute their portion of the task, thereby maximizing individual participation. Certainly Nelson allowed maximum latitude for others to take individual initiative, just as he always did. Authority to act must go with every assignment, and, of course, each element must be held accountable for its action. Finally, as in any task, the leader must monitor progress, provide positive reinforcement for performance, and follow up to ensure proper task completion.

Nowhere is the need for successful coordination of operating elements more graphically demonstrated and vital than in antisubmarine warfare. Searching out an enemy submarine is a difficult and complex task, under even the best of circumstances. It requires intricate coordination between surface, subsurface, and airborne platforms. Orders to the various operating elements must be precise. The areas of ASW prosecution, "on station" times, enemy submarine reporting criteria, rules of engagement, management and correlation of detection and tracking resources, and command and control responsibility must be coordinated through explicit orders. A single unit (i.e., destroyer or P-3 squadron) generally cannot cover the area or prosecute the threat alone, but a well-coordinated team of ASW platforms united in their efforts can provide the capabilities necessary to ensure overall operational success.

Admiral Holloway described how teamwork is built:

> Teamwork is built best through training. First the individual is trained to make sure he knows how to handle his skills; then the subunit is trained as a subunit, then the unit as a unit, and then the command as a whole. This is how people learn to work as a team, because they know that other people are doing the same thing they are. Training can be enhanced in many ways. When I was Commander of the Seventh Fleet, I believed it was important that throughout the fleet there be an understanding of what was being done by the Navy in that part of the world, so I sent officers from carrier squadrons to ride a destroyer for a week, I brought destroyer people over to the carrier to observe flight operations, I put a submariner in the back of a search aircraft for a couple of missions. You don't always have an opportunity to do those kinds of things, but teamwork, I believe, is built on constant training under realistic conditions that replicate the mission of the organization.

A leader must apply the principles of effective groupings of individuals to provide for the maximum teamwork of the unit. It is imperative that he convey to his troops that they are doing important work as part of an important team, and at the same time, he must set high standards of discipline in team training.[54-199]

Teamwork and coordination of forces were dramatically illustrated in the Battle of Surigao Strait in World War II. Taking part in the Leyte Gulf Campaign, Rear Admiral Jesse Oldendorf, Commander of the Bombardment and Support Group, was responsible for defending the narrow (twelve-mile-wide) Surigao Strait against the attacking Japanese southern force under Admiral Nishimura. Rear Admiral Oldendorf pre-

pared a meticulous battle plan that carefully assigned tasks to each element of his group, from PT boats to battleships. The battle plan, to be executed at night in the narrow confines of Surigao Strait, used PT boats in initial harassing attacks, then destroyers in coordinated multiple axis torpedo attacks, followed by heavy bombardment from two lines of cruisers and battleships, using the classic naval warfare maneuver of "crossing the T." The U.S. attack had to be carefully orchestrated, with detailed timing and execution by each element of Oldendorf's forces, to avoid firing on their own ships and to avoid "spooking" the Japanese into retreating before they got into range of the big guns of the American battleships.

The ensuing Battle of Surigao Strait, conducted entirely at night, was a perfectly executed series of increasingly severe attacks on the Japanese southern force. Although the initial PT boat attacks were ineffective destructively, they gave the Japanese a false sense of confidence and served to keep Rear Admiral Oldendorf informed of the location, size, and steaming direction of the Japanese ships. The well-coordinated destroyer torpedo attacks on either side of the strait crippled the Japanese and created confusion and chaos in the Japanese force. Minutes after the destroyers had withdrawn, the American battleships and cruisers opened fire, pouring thousands of rounds into the Japanese force and nearly destroying all of the enemy ships.

Personnel who are well led

> know the objective,
> know the enemy,
> have faith in their leaders,
> coordinate their efforts, and
> act as a team.

These are the people who will overcome the adversity, chaos, and destruction of combat and defeat the enemy in war. Not only must a unit commander know how to lead his troops and how to make correct decisions, but he also must be able to control his subordinates in the execution of the adopted plan of action. Through control and supervision, he achieves unity of effort.[54-765]

MCPON Sanders: *While divisions competing with each other for improved performance is healthy, it is important not to let it get out of hand. It's very good to have good morale within your particular area of responsibility, but it should not be at the expense of another area. It is important to develop teamwork so that the job gets done, and that includes teamwork with other divisions so that the entire organization meets its collective objectives.*

50. Displaying and Building Confidence in Subordinates

The mental set of individuals, their self-confidence, and their understanding of the facts greatly affect their performance. The outcomes of battles both physical and mental are often determined by the attitudes of those involved. "A man will do a surprising amount of work based on the perception that he is someone special doing a tremendously difficult job."[51-75]

Human beings go through a long socialization process, during which they must learn what is and what is not acceptable behavior and performance, and while most individuals have gone through this process and emerged with good self-esteem, not all of them have. Those who have a good self-image will tend to continue doing those things that others compliment them about, and to discontinue practices that are criticized. On the other hand, people who have matured with significant self-doubts believe that they are not as good as others, and, unfortunately, they will try to live up to that image; that is, they will act in a way that will cause others to think as poorly of them as they do of themselves. When these individuals do something right and that is pointed out to them, they will be determined not to make that "mistake" again, for, just as individuals with positive self-esteem want to maintain their self-image (in this case, positive), those with negative self-images will try to retain other people's negative view of them and thus will act in a way that others do not approve of. This is not a book about clinical psychological counseling; however, officers need to have an understanding of the dynamics involved so that when and if they are assigned someone who does not meet their requirements, they can recognize that they may need the help of a Navy psychologist.

Leaders of individuals at the lower enlisted and lower officer grades must meld their people into a working team despite being unable to select specific individuals for particular assignments, as flag rank officers are able to do. The junior officer can be assured that a great deal of screening has gone into the personnel selection process, and that those with whom work relationships are established will be able to meet the requirements of the Naval Service and do so in a manner that will lead to mission accomplishment. At the same time, this screening process allows the working relationships between individuals to be retained; these relationships are vital to a unit's ability to "fight" today and be prepared to "prevail in combat" tomorrow. No screening process can eliminate the need for an officer to bring individuals together in a team, just as a basketball team needs a coach to guide them.

It is difficult for individuals to continue to believe in themselves if they perceive that this is not the prevailing attitude of those with whom they work, and it is especially difficult if they do not think they have the confidence of their senior. Thus, it is particularly important for the leader to display confidence in the ability of subordinates to accomplish their assignments, for those who have the trust and approbation of their leaders will march "into the Valley of Death," should that become necessary. When the supervisor has given the subordinate the responsibility for the decision as well as the work, the leader can spend more time supervising and developing the subordinate than in frequent detailed inspections, where the only purpose is to see that the job has been performed adequately.[5-142] The military provides a comfortable living for its members and has a retirement program that is comparable to those in many large companies, but it should be clear to all that personnel do not work solely for the dollars they receive; their motivation is connected to the psychic income associated with protecting their country and working with their fellow service personnel.

THE BENEFITS OF DISPLAYING CONFIDENCE IN SUBORDINATES

Thus, there are two benefits from letting subordinates know that they are contributing to the overall mission of the Navy. First, the individuals will reap personal rewards from the knowledge that they have made a contribution, and this in turn will have a positive effect on retention rates as well as on the general feeling of well-being of the individuals and their families. Second, individuals who know that they are playing an important part on the team will try even harder to do a good job, improve their efficiency, and seek additional responsibilities so that they can pay themselves even greater psychic income as they increase their contribution to the organization.

METHODS OF DISPLAYING CONFIDENCE IN SUBORDINATES

An officer can indicate to his personnel in a variety of ways that he has confidence in their ability. The first is saying just that. Certainly words of praise about an individual's performance when spoken by an officer in front of that person's peers and subordinates will be well received. In writing or at social occasions, the officer can let the individual's family know what a good job the individual is doing. Offering praise in these ways will build a sense of teamwork that will pay benefits in the future. This is not to say that an officer should favor form over substance,

that is, "act" as if he is interested when he is not.

In addition to praising his personnel, the officer should make a point of letting subordinates know how they are doing, even offering criticism when that is appropriate, and later on congratulating the individual on improvements made. An officer who visits the working spaces of subordinates in the early-morning hours and congratulates them on their part in keeping the ship moving will convey his genuine interest in his subordinates. The senior will benefit from the realization that he is in charge of a successful team. As General Rice points out,

> supervision does not mean that a leader should do an assigned task for the individual who has been assigned to do it. It means, rather, that, after he has given an individual a task, the leader should check to see how the individual is doing. The leader should do so for two reasons. First, he can sometimes make a suggestion or give the individual an idea of how the task might be done better.
>
> Second, he can make sure the individual understood the assignment. If the individual has gone off in the wrong direction, he is wasting his own time, and he is wasting the leader's time. Everyone at some time has sat around a table and heard an individual speak and walked out with five different ideas of what that individual said. For this reason, if the leader does not go back and supervise the task he has given out, he may be wasting valuable time.

Another way to display confidence is to provide subordinates with new and additional opportunities to demonstrate their capabilities and/or ability to learn. Admiral McDonald advises to delegate whenever possible. But then, he says:

> do not take over just because work is not being done the way you would do it or as well as you would or could do it. Accept the acceptable rather than perfection if

you possibly can. Soon your juniors will be trying harder than ever, believing that you will accept their version and they do not want to embarrass you. If you keep changing their actions, they might soon reach the point of being careless because they know that you are going to kibitz their work anyway.

METHODS OF BUILDING CONFIDENCE IN SUBORDINATES

Cross-training of subordinates is important for the welfare of the ship and improving combat readiness, but it also affects the attitude of personnel. Anyone who is able to do more than he formerly could receives psychic income, which in turn will reward the senior, because his subordinates will be more willing to accept responsibility and more able to be trusted. Allowing a junior officer to bring a ship into port (assuming the officer has been OD qualified) is a significant way for the commanding officer to demonstrate confidence in the JO. Enlisted personnel who are provided with opportunities for on-the-job studying under more experienced chiefs not only will increase their own value to the service, they also will desire to undertake even more difficult assignments, thus maximizing their value to the organization. There are inherent dangers in being a senior—subordinates may and do make mistakes; however, the senior who takes the risk of giving subordinates more responsibility will be well rewarded (though the unit may suffer setbacks in the process). Admiral Nakamura suggests that

> it is usual for a sincere person who is shown that his leaders have confidence in him to try even more to respond with his best efforts.

Admiral Mitsumasa Yonai, who was the last Navy minister and led Japan to the termination of the war, consistently pursued the course of laying down his policy and the points of importance briefly and straightforwardly to his subordinates and

then delegating to them fully the execution of what needed to be done. He was quite strict when the subordinates did not follow his policy, but otherwise he never condemned the mistakes of the subordinates and took every responsibility himself. Accordingly, it was said that his subordinates could not help doing their jobs ever more seriously, and as a result they displayed their abilities to the utmost. Furthermore, it was said that every subordinate felt that he won the deepest confidence from Admiral Yonai. The fact that Admiral Yonai was quite fair, totally unselfish, and a man of sincerity also contributed to his success.

There may be times when a senior sees a subordinate in difficulty. If lives or the battle are at stake, it would be foolish to allow the subordinate to proceed unchecked, but in less than critical situations, it may be best in the long run to allow subordinates to work themselves out of their difficulties so that they both learn how to overcome their own mistakes and develop self-confidence in their ability to meet unexpected difficulties. Seniors must constantly keep in the back of their minds that they might have to be replaced by a subordinate, and thus senior officers must provide subordinates with occasions on which they can assume some of the senior's obligations. If that eventuality does come about, these subordinates will be ready to take over, for they have had both the experience and the challenge of working in the "shoes" of their senior.

Individuals who have the confidence of their seniors will both work hard to maintain that regard and look for ways to increase the confidence. We not only *say* that the military is an opportunity, we *mean* it, and it is the responsibility of officers to provide meaningful challenges to their subordinates so that they can accomplish the mission and maintain their spirit. Admiral Burke:

> A leader must train his people so that

he can have confidence in them and in their ability. Once he is confident they can perform, he must make sure they have enough self-confidence to do so. When I was CNO I kept a phone by my bed, and they usually called up half a dozen times during the night. One night I got called up between eleven and twelve o'clock, and a watch officer said, "Sir, we've got a dispatch from Cuba that Cuban rebels have captured two people in a U.S. plant." I asked the officer of the watch what U.S. ship was closest to Moa Bay, and he said an LPD, which is an old four-stack destroyer that's cut down, two boilers taken out. It was just going down to Guantanamo to be shaken down and go through its exercises; it had been in overhaul. I asked, "Is there another ship close by?" "No, Sir." I said, "Well send her in. Tell her to protect American lives properly and report time of arrival." I went back to sleep. After about another hour or so, I got a call that said, "We got a dispatch which says they're on their way, and they'll be there at seven-thirty tomorrow morning, at the end of the dispatch it says 'request further instructions.' " Of course, I blew my top. How could I know what further instruction to give to the ship? So I said, "Tell him his relief will have further instructions." After another hour I was called back again and told, "We got another dispatch from the ship. It said 'Cancel my last dispatch.' " I didn't know what the ship had, though I knew it was untrained. He had roughly thirteen rifles aboard, but he had no landing force. The CO made a landing force on the way in during the night. He put an ensign in charge of his landing force, and he practiced shooting in the dark, and they did everything they could. When he got in there in the morning, he debarked his landing force, went in and got those two

prisoners from Castro, and he reported about every fifteen or twenty minutes. We got more reports from him than anybody else I've ever seen, but that kid did a marvelous job, he was a lieutenant commander with a completely unprepared ship, he did a magnificent job, it was just wonderful. He was successful, and while his people were absolutely incompetent for a landing force, he was successful because he moved fast. He went in there, and when the Cubans learned the Americans were coming, they turned the prisoners loose. He never had any battle, but he got those people back.

Well, they thought he was wonderful, he was rated, as he should have been, he was wonderful, and his crew was rated. His name was Robinson, he was later killed in Vietnam. But that kid did a marvelous job. There's no way that he could know what would need to be done, he was completely up the creek. But what he didn't recognize was that no one else could know, either. He had all the information we had, which was nothing except two people had been captured. So how could he get further instructions? I could have given him further instructions, but I wouldn't have known any more about it than he did.

MCPON Sanders: *It's important to show confidence in the ability of your subordinates, as they need to be recognized for their good work, and doing so will continue their good habits. It is important not to say "Well done" if that praise isn't earned, and just as important to reserve your good comments for significant accomplishments. By that I mean don't dilute your praise by saying that everything they do is exceptional. My biggest point is that showing confidence in subordinates is not merely "Atta boy," but, rather, by showing your trust in them by giving important assignments for them to do. Diluting your praise by giving it for anything will cause the good people to feel that the level or quality of their performance isn't really that important, since poor performers are equally recognized.*

After making an assignment it is not necessary for you to continually look over the shoulders of your subordinates to see how things are coming along. Yes, you will want to closely inspect when the job is completed, but show your confidence in your troops by the fact that they realize you don't feel it is necessary to supervise them every step of the way.

51. Delegating and Supervising

Reluctance to delegate is occasionally justifiable. But the logical extension of reluctance to delegate—failure to delegate—always results in an inefficient use of human resources. In a unit whose leader fails to delegate, some members are overworked and others are underworked. As a consequence, failure to delegate degrades the capability of the unit to accomplish its mission; failure to delegate directly affects combat readiness. Since the persons most likely to be overworked are the seniors, the seniors' reluctance to delegate is puzzling. Admiral Zumwalt suggests that

> an officer's reluctance to delegate, in over 90 percent of the cases, indicates an absolute lack of self-confidence by the officer who does not delegate. In the other cases, it is the officer saying "I know so well what to do and nobody else knows nearly so well, that I'm going to try to do it all." Unfortunately, no one person has the time to do all his subordinates' jobs.

JUSTIFIABLE FAILURE TO DELEGATE

A leader may justifiably be reluctant to delegate under certain limited conditions. There are times when tasks that normally would be appropriate for a junior should not be delegated to him. Exceptions of this type are driven by

one or a combination of these three constraints: (1) mission criticality; (2) available time; (3) experience level of the subordinate. Under normal peacetime conditions, a senior should fail to delegate only rarely and only for these reasons. Admiral McDonald points out that,

> the higher an individual goes in the service, the more important his ability to delegate becomes. Many officers as lieutenants, lieutenant commanders, commanders, are outstanding, but as they go a little bit higher, their job performance suffers because they are either unable or unwilling to delegate.

> And when he delegates, the officer must be willing to accept a less-than-perfect performance from the individual doing the job. The lieutenant commander who, say, has always done the job perfectly, tells Ensign Smith to do it; but although he might be doing it satisfactorily, Smith is not doing it as well as the lieutenant commander thinks he himself can do it, so the lieutenant commander pitches in and does it. This ruins the confidence of Smith, to whom he delegated the authority; furthermore, the lieutenant commander can step in and do it himself just so many times. He must learn to accept performance that is short of perfection—although, of course, an unsatisfactory performance is not acceptable.

> One reason officers are reluctant to delegate is that they are afraid someone else's mistake will reflect badly on them. But juniors cannot learn unless they are given the opportunity to do things on their own. When I took command of the carrier *Coral Sea* after having the little *Mendora* for a year, people asked me whether I would practice putting the ship alongside a tanker. I said no, because when I was executive officer of the *Essex* during the war my skipper let me do practically all the refueling and all the

replenishing, so even though I hadn't done it with that particular type, I'd done it many times. Furthermore, the commanding officer must be willing to delegate various things like that. Otherwise, how are these fellows going to learn?

When he delegates, the officer should tell someone *what* to do, being careful most of the time not to tell him *how* to do it. There will be times when the officer must tell the individual how to do a job, and the officer should say, "I would prefer if you do it this way this time."

CULPABLE FAILURE TO DELEGATE

Culpable failure to delegate is rooted, in almost all cases, in a flaw or a bad habit in the senior's makeup. And in nearly all instances, the senior is the person upon whom the solution depends. Less frequently the junior is the cause of the problem. The leader must keep in mind that "delegation is not abdication or abandonment, dumping, or avoiding any decisions."[50-176]

When juniors cause the problem. Juniors sometimes lack technical proficiency, self-confidence, or the motivation to seek out and accept delegated tasks. The missing element or elements may surface before or after a task has been assigned. After the task has been assigned, the junior will give evidence of his shortcomings at one of three junctures: before starting the task, through his comments; during the task, through his obvious difficulty in carrying it out; or at the completion of the task, by turning in a clearly unacceptable performance. The fact is, seniors should be alert for problems at the time they assign tasks and should take actions to preclude an unacceptable result, as well as remembering that "different group 'personalities' pose different problems for the leaders."[32-65]

The senior who discovers that one of his subordinates is lacking must take corrective action— through counseling, critiquing, training, etc.— or he will be loath to delegate to this subordinate the next time around. Assuming that the junior's

lack of technical proficiency, weak self-confidence, or lack of motivation can be corrected, the senior can compensate for his previous pretask misperception by instilling the missing element in the junior prior to the next tasking.

What if the next time, in spite of an honest effort by the senior to correct the junior's shortcoming, the junior again produces an unacceptable result? Obviously the answer depends upon the degree of progress. If after the second tasking, or the third, the senior concludes that, notwithstanding his honest attempt to bring the junior along, the junior is not making acceptable progress, then the problem moves from delegation to another area of leadership.

In fact, however, juniors are almost always capable of handling delegated tasks. The culprit in the majority of cases of reluctance and failure to delegate is the senior. As Pogo is reputed to have said, "We have met the enemy and it is us."

The senior's foibles: a dozen wrong reasons. Why, then, do some seniors—probably all seniors at one time or another—culpably fail to delegate appropriate tasks to subordinates? Here are a dozen reasons (there undoubtedly are more):

1. He wants to do it himself; he likes that kind of project.
2. He is assigned a short due date by his senior; to complete the assignment on time, he must have the most experienced person—himself—tackle the task.
3. He is a zero-defects manager; the product must be perfect by his definition.
4. Ego compels him to emblazon his personal stamp on the final product.
5. He wants to bask in his senior's approval for having done the job so superlatively, or he is afraid that, if the subordinate fails, the failure will reflect badly on his own leadership.
6. He is a "long-suffering" soul who doesn't "mind" doing the project himself; this is closely related to number 7.

7. He wants to be "liked" by his subordinates; he thinks tasking them with nonroutine tasks and duties will cause them not to "like" him so much; this in turn, is very similar to number 8.

8. He is too timid or, to use an old-fashioned word, too lacking in "gumption" to assign the task to a subordinate.

9. He is uncertain of the scope of his authority; he has lost sight of his responsibility to get the total mission accomplished and the fact that he is provided with other human resources to get the job done.

10. He does not understand how to train, then supervise, subordinates in the accomplishment of appropriate tasks; or, if he does, then through poor planning or other factors he neglects to train, then supervise, on a timely basis.

11. He desires to avoid the interpersonal stress of rejecting an earnest subordinate's initial effort; this is related to number 12.

12. He expects a priori that the subordinate's initial effort will be wide of the mark or lacking in depth or insight; he prefers to do it himself rather than have to edit and stick with the subordinate's approach to the task, an approach that he personally would not have chosen.

None of the above reasons reflects well on the senior, and each of them is avoidable. They are derived, essentially, from human foibles. Even the most proficient officer has fallen prey to one or another of these foibles during his years of service. At any given time, one or more of these reasons may cause a senior to pass up yet another opportunity to task a subordinate with an appropriate project. Admiral Hayward notes that, while responsibility cannot be delegated, it is necessary at times for authority to be delegated to subordinates to ensure that a job is done in the absence of the senior or because the senior cannot possibly supervise everything himself. One of the first

signs of a truly strong leader is that he is comfortable delegating authority. The good leaders have developed the ability to permit others to make mistakes, to give people more leash than they would have expected to get, and to show confidence in those people, to let them know that they expect them to be able to perform. Most people will respond affirmatively to that authority, to that delegation. In almost all cases the individuals will be surprised at how much they enjoy having the authority, and they will do better than the leaders might have anticipated.

The errant leader is the one who is uncomfortable taking a chance with his troops because of how it might reflect on his or her performance. There are times when close supervision is essential—while a unit is developing its team approach, for example—but almost everyone has talent, and leaders need to recognize and use other people's talent.

When there is one junior in a squadron made up of senior officers, the skipper and the exec are offered a challenge. They must delegate down into the organization far enough to bring out the junior officer and make sure that he is identified and that his talents are not overlooked. Effective leaders build their team around the talented people.

The skipper can never give up his basic responsibility for the whole unit. Nor can a division officer delegate his responsibility for the conduct of anyone in his or her division or the quality of performance of that combat information team. But how can the leader develop a capability in his unit to deal with combat damage when his top supervisor is either dead or immobile? Someone must have the experience to step forward into that spot. The supervisor can only be replaced in an emergency if someone has been given the opportunity to perform some of his duties prior to the emergency.

Most people wait for the opportunity to take on a challenge, and the leader ought to let them try. After he has successfully delegated authority on several occasions, the leader will develop confidence in his people's ability and will be less concerned about them making a mistake. In any echelon in the chain of command, the supervisor must grant authority and delegate to the maximum, so that he knows that when the chips are down he has a team that can perform, he has more than one person who can carry the load.

SUPERVISION: THE KEY TO DELEGATING

The officer of several years' experience who is frequently guilty of failing to delegate simply must recognize his mistake and correct it. The degree to which he is successful is the degree to which he improves as a leader and helps his organization to function more efficiently. To avoid the mistake of failing to delegate, a senior must develop his supervisory skills.

The six troop-leading steps are:

1. Begin planning
2. Arrange for a reconnaissance
3. Make a reconnaissance
4. Complete the plan
5. Issue the order
6. Supervise

The sixth step—supervise—is the keystone. Supervision applies to all assigned tasks, not just to combat orders, to which the above steps refer. When an undertaking fails, it is usually not because there was no plan or because the leader failed to study the problem thoroughly or because a comprehensive yet specific order had not been issued. An undertaking usually fails because of a lack of proper supervision.

A CONCEPT OF SUPERVISION

The following concept of supervision may strike the experienced senior as simply a statement of common sense—the things an experienced leader does, almost without thinking, to ensure that the job is done right. And it is. But a concept of supervision has other salient benefits, even for the experienced leader. It tends to sort out three additional dilemmas faced by commanders: (1) How much authority should he turn over to a subordinate? (2) How can he ensure that he retains control? (3) How can he ensure that he is meeting the goals established by his senior? The answer to each of these dilemmas is situationally dependent—dependent upon the mission and on the proficiency, motivation, and effort of the principals involved. For the apprentice leader, a concept for supervision is a solid datum.

The ability to delegate tasks effectively is a learned skill. The key to learning this skill is understanding that, with rare exception, *every task delegated must be supervised* to one degree or another from the time the order is given to the time the project is completed. Determining when and how closely to supervise is an art. To make this determination, the officer must understand the task, assess the mission, and evaluate proficiency.

Understand the task. First, the senior must clearly understand the task. The task may have been assigned to the senior by his senior, or it may have been initiated by the senior himself. In either case, the senior must understand it in order to be able to communicate it clearly to the junior. After tasking the junior, the senior asks for feedback and then clarifies anything the junior did not understand.

Assess the mission. Second, the officer must know how critical the task or mission is.* A crit-

---

*A commander rarely has only one iron in the fire, and given the operating tempo of most Naval Service organizations, any commander worth his salt has many in the fire at any given time. He cannot supervise all missions or tasks to the same degree. He must decide which of them most needs his command attention and thus determine, in effect, his "priority of neglect." Subordinates in whom he has the greatest trust and confidence will probably be assigned the more important tasks and receive the least supervision. This problem is usually not as great for junior officers as it is for senior officers.

ical mission can be defined either negatively or positively. A negative definition would consider the severity of the consequences of failure on the first attempt, as well as whether the consequences would be irreversible. A positive definition would be based on the degree of importance of a completely successful execution on the first attempt.

Inherent in the idea of mission criticality is the allowable margin for error. Is the mission a training task, the purpose of which, in part, is for juniors to learn from errors and through successive iterations? If so, the consequences of error are negligible and mission criticality is low. Does the task involve the expenditure of highly restricted money or material? If so, the task is mission critical; the resources must be expended efficiently and effectively the first time. For pur-

poses of the concept of supervision, mission criticality is said to be high, medium, or low.

Mission criticality may be assessed by evaluating a task in terms of its operational characteristics. A list of operational characteristics can be simple or exhaustive, but it is easy to develop. Table 5.1 is one way of characterizing types of missions and assessing their criticality.

Evaluate proficiency. The third component in determining the appropriate degree of supervision involves evaluating proficiency. The officer must be knowledgeable of two individuals' proficiency in the skills required to complete the task: his own and the subordinate's to whom the task is assigned. This is not to say that an ensign assigned as Food Services Officer aboard ship must be a skilled cook. It is to suggest that the ensign should be able to evaluate a cook's pro-

Table 5.1 Mission characteristics and criticality

	Mortal Danger to Individuals	Important Milestone for Unit	Building Block for Unit	Garrison/at Sea Administration and Maintenance
Combat				
Contact with enemy	High[1]	High[2]		
No contact	Medium[3]	High[4]	Low[5]	Low[6]
Peacetime				
High visibility (externally assigned	High[7] (4%)	High[8] (10%)	Medium[9] (15%)	
Routine (internally assigned)	Medium[10] (6%)	Medium[11] (15%)	Low[12] (35%)	Low[13] (15%)

Key
[1]SEAL team operations
[2]Battalion attack
[3]Emplacement of antipersonnel mines
[4]PHIBRON transit to Amphibious Objective Area (AOA)
[5]Orientation of unit replacements in rear area
[6]Erection of barbed-wire entanglements around defensive position
[7]Live Fire Combined Arms Exercise at MCB Twenty-Nine Palms
[8]Force commander's annual inspection of unit
[9]Preparation of Operations Plan for unit deployment
[10]Flight operations at sea; small unit demolitions training
[11]Hail and Farewell Party for incoming/outgoing COs
[12]Response to congressional inquiry
[13]Inventory of battalion supply warehouse

NOTE: Percentages in parentheses indicate the hypothetical percentage of time spent on tasks of this type.

ficiency based on his own understanding of the cook's duties and his observations of the cook's performance. In the case of tasks that are not routine for either the officer or the subordinate, the number of times they each have executed the tasks or have observed the tasks being executed is a key consideration.

With respect to this third component, the officer must also determine how motivated the subordinate is to perform the task, as well as how much effort the officer can expect to see the subordinate put into his work. Proficiency, motivation, and effort can range from high to medium to low for purposes of the concept of supervision.

To summarize, any task must be understood by seniors and juniors. In addition, five criteria must be evaluated or analyzed to determine the appropriate level of supervision: mission criticality; senior's proficiency; and junior's proficiency, motivation, and expected level of effort. For simplicity's sake, the last three criteria are considered as one. Each criteria can be categorized as low, medium, and high.

INTENSITY OF SUPERVISION

The level of supervision must also be considered in degrees of intensity. Three degrees of intensity are discussed here: close, normal, and minimal.* Each level of supervision needs to be defined operationally within a general framework for the assigned tasks.

Close supervision. Generally, close supervision is appropriate for tasks with a high or medium mission criticality. The task could be preparation for a flag or a general officer's inspection of the unit, a demonstration for the public, a formal briefing for the senior's commanding officer on an important operational matter, or drafting a

---

*Two other degrees of supervision exist, but they are too extreme for consideration here. One is continuous supervision: the senior simply stays with the junior until the task is done. Continuous supervision of the junior in the presence of the junior's subordinates is justifiable only in the most unusual circumstances. The other extreme form is no supervision at all: the senior simply gives the order; he may or may not be present to see the final product.

letter to respond to an inquiry from a member of Congress. Six steps are required for *minimum* close supervision:

1. The order for the task is given to the subordinate. Feedback is elicited to ensure the task is understood. Unclear points are clarified. At this point the senior considers how much time remains until the project is to be completed or the event is to take place.

2. After one-fifth of the time has elapsed, the senior visits the site or summons the junior for a progress update.

The senior should be prepared for very little to have taken place, because at the time the order was given, the junior already had a list of things to do. By the one-fifth point, the junior no doubt is still coping with rearranged priorities, has just completed his plan, and has just given the order to his subordinates, but, with luck, the junior's subordinates may have actually organized for the task and commenced it. At this point the senior reviews the junior's plan and further clarifies the task as necessary.

3. At the halfway point, the senior repeats the visit or summons the junior for a progress update. By this time the junior and his unit are turning to on the task. The senior should be able to provide specific guidance if it is required. The senior reiterates that he expects the project to be ready for execution by the three-quarter point, thus allowing one-quarter of the total project time for changes, if necessary.

4. At the three-quarter point visit, the senior checks the final preparations. If the project involves a demonstration or a briefing or any activity related to movement or speech, rehearsals are conducted. The senior critiques. Depending upon the quality of the effort at this point, the senior must decide to take a greater or lesser role in the time remaining to actual execution.

5. Just prior to final execution, the senior makes one final spot check of the junior and his unit to square away the remaining loose ends. If possible, the senior is present for the execution.

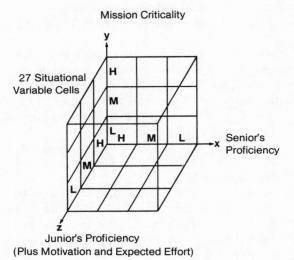

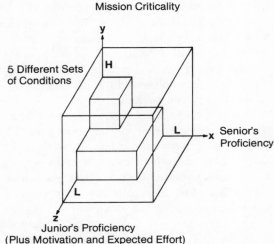

Key
H – High
M – Medium
L – Low
NOTE: The farther the situational variable cell is
from the point of origin, the more intense the
degree of supervision required.

Conditions		
Mission	*Senior*	*Junior*
Medium	High	High
Low	High	High
Low	High	Medium
Low	Medium	High
Low	Medium	Medium

Figure 5.1   Intensity of Supervision   **Figure 5.2**   Minimal Supervision

6. Finally, after the execution or final product, the senior evaluates the junior's performance and provides constructive criticism.

Normal supervision. Four steps are required: give the order, visit at the halfway point, make a final spot check, and critique the final product.

Minimal supervision. Three steps: give the order, visit at the three-quarter point or make a final spot check, and critique the final product.

A THREE-DIMENSIONAL PORTRAYAL OF SUPERVISION

The degree to which supervision should take place is dependent upon the degree to which the task is mission critical and the degree to which the senior and the junior are proficient in the task at hand. If each of these criteria is separated into three degrees, then there are 27 different combinations of criteria and degrees. Figure 5.1 shows the criteria laid out on a set

of X, Y, Z axes. The degrees of mission criticality are depicted on the Y axis. Degrees of proficiency are shown on the X and Z axes. Notice that the degrees of proficiency are in inverse order of magnitude with respect to the origin. The Z axis, "Junior's Proficiency," includes the junior's motivation to do a good job and the level of effort the senior can expect him to put into the project.

Figures 5.2, 5.3, and 5.4 suggest for the apprentice three combinations of conditions which can help him determine the degree of supervision he should put into the task. The columns of situational variables under the figures are represented by separate blocks within the figures.

Figure 5.2 suggests that minimal supervision is appropriate under five limited sets of conditions, or in less than one-fifth of the situations. Notice that minimal supervision is never appropriate if either the senior or the subordinate is

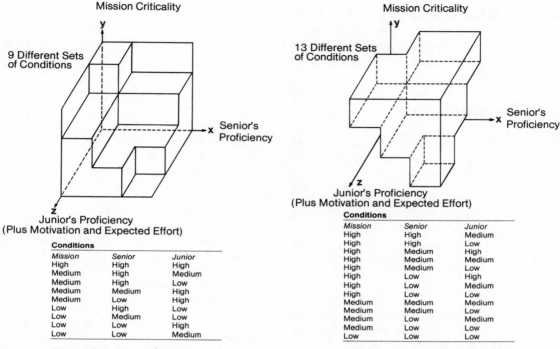

Figure 5.3   Normal Supervision

Conditions		
Mission	*Senior*	*Junior*
High	High	High
Medium	High	Medium
Medium	High	Low
Medium	Medium	High
Medium	Low	High
Low	High	Low
Low	Medium	Low
Low	Low	High
Low	Low	Medium

Figure 5.4   Close Supervision

Conditions		
Mission	*Senior*	*Junior*
High	High	Medium
High	High	Low
High	Medium	High
High	Medium	Medium
High	Medium	Low
High	Low	High
High	Low	Medium
High	Low	Low
Medium	Medium	Medium
Medium	Medium	Low
Medium	Low	Medium
Medium	Low	Low
Low	Low	Low

inexperienced in the task at hand. Similarly, minimal supervision is never appropriate in a mission-critical situation.

Close supervision is appropriate in 13 of the 27 situations, or almost half, while moderate (normal) supervision is called for in at least one-third of the situations.

SUPERVISION AND LEARNING

Why should an inexperienced senior closely supervise a medium or highly experienced junior in the execution of an assigned task? To learn. The inexperienced senior is not always going to have the luxury of working with experienced subordinates. Given the vagaries and vicissitudes of the personnel assignment process, the next time that particular task comes up, that inexperienced senior may be the most experienced person available, and he will have to teach his new subordinate, just as he learned from his old subordinate. Also, the inexperienced senior is responsible for the assigned task, and his instructions may not have been as clear as necessary. Without the inexperienced senior's participation, the effort could go awry, and the completed task may not be what the senior's superior wanted.

The object is for both senior and junior to become highly proficient in the shortest possible time. As depicted in the figures, the sooner they are both highly proficient, the sooner they become a team. Once senior and subordinate have formed a highly experienced team, only minimal supervision will be necessary to achieve highly satisfactory results in almost any foreseeable peacetime scenario, and normal supervision will be called for in mission-critical combat tasks. That team, in part, is what combat readiness is about, and it is what our peacetime efforts are attempting to achieve.

MCPON Sanders: *Knowing how much authority to delegate to subordinates is learned with experience. However, you might want to remember that, just as you welcome authority you consider* necessary to do the job, put trust in your chief and senior enlisted and they will try to help get the job done, as they will feel part of the team.

Chapter 5 Bibliography

1. Adorno, T. W.; Brunswick, E. F.; Levinson, D. J.; and Sanford, R. N. *The Authoritarian Personality*. New York: Harper and Brothers, 1951.
2. Ageton, Arthur A. *The Naval Officer's Guide*. Annapolis: Naval Institute Press, 1970.
3. *The Art of Leadership*. New York: Macmillan, 1960.
4. Atkinson, Rita L.; Atkinson, Richard C.; and Hilgard, Ernest R. *Introduction to Psychology*. 7th ed. New York: Harcourt Brace Jovanovich, 1979.
5. Beam, Henry H. "Leadership: A New Answer to an Old Problem." *Proceedings*, Dec. 1983, pp. 140–42.
6. Becvar, Raphael J. *Skills for Effective Communication: A Guide to Building Relationships*. New York: John Wiley and Sons, 1974.
7. Bender, James F. *How to Talk Well*. New York: McGraw-Hill, 1949.
8. Bieg, V. N. "Naval Men and Their Management." *Proceedings*, July–Aug. 1915, pp. 1171–83.
9. Boggess, William C. "Pass the Word—Well." *Proceedings*, Sept. 1970.
10. Bowling, Ronald A. "A Return to Military Smartness and Discipline." *Proceedings*, June 1981, pp. 46–50.
11. Brandt, George E. "Harmony." *Proceedings*, Aug. 1924, pp. 1311–14.
12. Dean, Bill C. "Authority: The Weakened Link." *Proceedings*, July 1971, pp. 48–52.
13. DeMarco, Anthony L. "Motivating DOD's Work Force to Be More Productive." *Defense Management Journal*, no. 3, 1983, pp. 26–31.
14. DeVito, Joseph A. *The Psychology of Speech and Language: An Introduction to Psycholinguistics*. New York: Random House, 1970.
15. Dyer, William. *The Sensitive Manipulator*. Provo, Utah: Brigham Young University Press, 1972.
16. Flanagan, James L. *Speech Analysis, Synthesis, and Perception*. 2d ed. New York: Springer-Verlag, 1972.
17. Gellerman, Saul W. *Managers and Subordinates*. Hinsdale, Ill.: Dryden Press, 1976.
18. "Getting the Best Results from Men." *Proceedings*, Sept. 1910, pp. 906–7.
19. Gibson, James L.; Ivancevich, John M.; and Donnelly, James H., Jr. *Organizations*. 4th ed. Plano, Tex.: Business Publications, 1982.
20. Gole, Henry G. "A Personal Reflection on Leadership." *Infantry*, Sept.–Oct. 1983, pp. 12–15.
21. Graves, Fielding L. "Speech and the Leader." *Proceedings*, Nov. 1969.
22. Halsey, William D. "General Douglas MacArthur." *Collier's Encyclopedia*. 1979.
23. ———. "Admiral Chester W. Nimitz." *Collier's Encyclopedia*. 1979.
24. Herzberg, Frederick. *The Managerial Choice*. Homewood, Ill.: Dow Jones–Irwin, 1976.
25. Hickling, Harold. *One Minute of Time*. Sydney: Halstead Press, 1965.
26. Jacobsen, K. C. *Watch Officer's Guide*. 11th ed. Annapolis: Naval Institute Press, 1979.
27. Jennings, Eugene Emerson. *An Anatomy of Leadership: Princes, Heroes, and Supermen*. New York: Harper and Brothers, 1960.
28. Kelly, J. F. "Command Authority and Professionalism." *Proceedings*, Aug. 1978, pp. 26–32.
29. Kelly, J. M.; Patton, G. D.; Downs, J. F.; and Corini, G. J., eds. *Leadership and Law Department NL 303 Book of Readings*. Annapolis: U.S. Naval Academy, academic year 1983–84.
30. Kinney, A. J., and Napier, John H. *The Air Force Officer's Guide*. 26th ed. Harrisburg, Pa.: Stackpole, 1983.
31. Knox, Dudley W. "The Elements of Leadership." *Proceedings*, Dec. 1920, pp. 1883–1902.
32. Laird, Donald A., and Laird, Eleanor C. *The Techniques of Delegating*. New York: McGraw-Hill, 1957.
33. Long, Gavin. *MacArthur as a Military Commander*. London: Clowes and Sons, 1969.

34. McCracken, A. M. "When Is an Order?" *Proceedings*, June 1949, pp. 653–57.
35. Magerison, Charles J. *Managerial Problem Solving*. New York: McGraw-Hill, 1974.
36. *Military Leadership*. Vol. 1, pt. 1, "A Concept of Leadership." West Point, N.Y.: U.S. Military Academy, 1962.
37. Mott, Paul E. *The Characteristics of the Effective Organization*. New York: Harper and Row, 1972.
38. Mumford, Robert E., Jr. "Get Off My Back, Sir." *Proceedings*, Aug. 1977, pp. 18–23.
39. Noel, John V., Jr., and Bassett, Frank E. *Division Officer's Guide*. 7th ed. Annapolis: Naval Institute Press, 1977.
40. Outerson, William. "Peacetime Admirals, Wartime Admirals." *Proceedings*, Apr. 1981, pp. 33–37.
41. Paulsen, Thomas D. "Change of Command." Videotape. Yokosuka, Japan, Jan. 1984.
42. Pedneault, H. R. "Take Care of Your Men." *Proceedings*, June 1964, p. 117.
43. Penergrast, James M. "Situational Leadership." *Proceedings*, June 1977, pp. 74–77.
44. Penfield, Wilder, and Lamar, Robert. *Speech and Brain Mechanisms*. Princeton, N.J.: Princeton University Press, 1959.
45. Pfiffner, John M. *The Supervision of Personnel*. Englewood Cliffs, N.J.: Prentice-Hall, 1960.
46. Pocalyko, Michael N. "The Fleet Nugget." *Proceedings*, July 1983, p. 72.
47. Postman, Neil. *Crazy Talk—Stupid Talk*. New York: Delacorte Press, 1976.
48. Potter, E. B., ed. *Sea Power: A Naval History*. 2d ed. Annapolis: Naval Institute Press, 1981.
49. Sanford, H. J. "Organizational Engineering: A Hidden Leadership Resource?" *Proceedings*, Apr. 1981, pp. 76–78.
50. Scanlon, Burt K. *Results Management in Action*. Cambridge: Management Center of Cambridge, 1969.
51. Stavridis, James. "War, Peace, and Leadership." *Proceedings*, Aug. 1983, pp. 78–80.
52. Student, Kurt R. "Back to Basics for Improved Human Resource Management." *Management Review*, Aug. 1978.
53. Swarztrauber, S. A. "Take Care of Your Men." *Proceedings*, Dec. 1963, p. 30.
54. Sweet, J. B., ed. *Essentials of Military Training*. Harrisburg, Pa.: Military Service Publishing, 1954.
55. Tarr, Curtis W. "Authority." *Air University Review*, May–June 1982, pp. 71–77.
56. Theobald, R. A. "Handling of Men." *Proceedings*, Sept.–Oct. 1915, pp. 1475–88.
57. Torgensen, Paul E. *A Concept of Organization*. New York: American Book, 1969.
58. Vaeth, J. Gordon. "Communications: A Lost Art?" *Proceedings*, Sept. 1976.
59. Ware, Hugh C. "New Tools for Crisis Management." *Proceedings*, Aug. 1974, pp. 21–22.
60. Webb, James. *A Country Such as This*. New York: Doubleday, 1983.
61. Webster, H. O. "A Crisis in Communications." *Proceedings*, Aug. 1959, pp. 27–32.
62. ———. "The Message Gap." *Proceedings*, May 1963, pp. 29–37.
63. Woodham-Smith, Cecil. *The Reason Why*. New York: E. P. Dutton, 1960.
64. Zveare, Dennis L. "Personal Commitment: Missing and Presumed Lost?" *Proceedings*, Jan. 1984, pp. 105–6.

6

The Controlling and Monitoring Components of Military Leadership

Introduction

"He's Great in a Crisis . . ." (But Why Is He Always *in* One?)

Ask most managers what gives them the greatest satisfaction in their jobs, and they will tell you that it's solving a crisis that demands fast thinking and decisive action. What is too often forgotten is that the executive who must constantly exercise his talent for handling emergencies is at the same time demonstrating his lack of talent in preventing emergencies. To be sure, crises cannot be eliminated completely, and poor handling can turn a minor problem into a disaster. But it is an essential part of every manager's job to forestall crises—by planning, organizing, and controlling his department. When it comes to measuring the performance of a manager, the criterion should not be the number of crises he handles successfully, but the number of crises that never—because of sound planning—arise at all.

Lyle A. Otterness, *Supervisory Management*

Planning to *Prevent* Problems

Everybody knows that it's easier to prevent a possible problem from becoming real than to try to solve it after it has happened. So if a manager is smart, he'll consider—ahead of time—all possible obstacles to his plans. He can be pretty sure of his success by getting the answers to these questions: (1) What could go wrong? (2) What is each problem? (3) How risky is each problem? (4) What are the possible causes of each problem? (5) How probable is each possible cause? (6) How can a possible cause be prevented or its effects minimized? (7) How can the most serious potential problems be minimized? A manager should remember that his plans are really a series of "shoulds"—performance points at which certain things are supposed to happen.

He should look for trouble: (1) where something new, complex, or unfamiliar is tried; (2) when deadlines are tight; (3) when a sequence is critical or has impact on others; (4) when an alternative is missing; (5) when things involve more than one function, person, or department; (6) when responsibility is hard to assign or is outside his area. He should set priority according to: (1) How serious will it be if it happens? (2) How probable is it that it might happen?

C. H. Kepner and B. J. Tregoe,
International Management

Correcting a Bad Decision

How can you "cut your losses" when you realize you've made a bad decision? Here are some suggestions:

(1) *Don't try to cover up*. If your main concern is covering up your original error, you'll be likely to make additional poor decisions. (2) *Remember your batting average*. Most of your decisions have been good ones. If you remember this, it'll be easier to acknowledge this one poor choice. (3) *Get advice*. Consult with the people who had a hand in the decision. Present the situation and hash it out. Or seek out someone who was not involved, whose advice you respect, who is not in the chain of command above you. (4) *Let your boss know*. Once you feel confident about your new plan of action, clear it with your boss. Be ready to justify your position, and don't be defensive. State your reasons for the reversal as simply as possible. (5) *Don't try to shift the blame*. Others were probably involved in the decision. But, ultimately, it was your responsibility. (6) *What are the future implications?* Are you setting a precedent? If so, spell it out. If you aren't, point that out too. (7) *Prepare your people for a change*. Have a well-thought-out phase-out period planned, and let your people contribute their ideas to it. Minimizing losses is just as much, and just as important, a function of management as milking opportunity.

Successful Supervisor

52. Setting Standards and Monitoring Subordinates' Adherence to Them

Time, cost, and quality are routine yardsticks against which the operations of organizations, public and private, are evaluated. Performance indexes come in varying forms and titles, but they can usually be grouped into one of these three categories. The financial troubles of Chrysler Corporation and its market share loss to the Japanese made front-page news in the early 1980s, and the causes were to be found in poor performance in these areas. The Naval Service also can be evaluated in terms of these three areas. The amount of emphasis placed on each area necessarily depends on the goals and missions of the individual organization, as well as on the focus of the organization's authority, whether it be corporate headquarters or the Department of the Navy. The exigency of specific situations, obviously, also influences the weight applied to each. Frequently there is conflict between time available, funds in hand, and quality standards that are to be met. Leaders must perform risk analyses to determine which factors to weigh most heavily in the execution of their assigned duties and responsibilities.

The effective leader clearly articulates his standards of performance and in the execution of his responsibilities, puts in place the structure that measures the time and cost of the input, as well as the quality of the output. Admiral Carney took the following approach to ensure that his orders and plans were being carried out:

When I was Chief of Naval Operations, I told my deputies, "If I'm assigning to you certain delegated responsibilities and you can't perform under the directive that I give you, it's for one of two reasons. Either you're incapable of initiative or my instructions have been inadequate." I said, "In either case, when I find out that what I want is not being carried out, I'm going to send for you and I want your frank answer: Did I give inadequate or insufficient guidance? In that case, I'm fully prepared to take the responsibility of correcting it. If I have, however, you had better be prepared to pack." In one case I actually moved a man. Without prejudice, I sent him someplace where I knew he could perform and perform well. He just wasn't up to what I needed in that particular responsibility.

A rigorous, highly structured monitoring system is not always necessary, but the leader must be prepared to assess the performance of his operation on a continuing basis. Seldom can a leader know everything that is going on, but he has the means to sense the pulse of the organization as a whole and, based on his confidence in his subordinates and the knowledge he has of the structure in place and the priorities of the work in hand, he can identify the soft spots in his unit that require direct action. The tone of command is set by the degree of rigidity with which this principle is applied. The leader who creates an environment of fear runs the strong risk of only hearing the "good news" and losing touch with what is actually going on.

Admiral Hayward believes that

first, circumstances, and second, level of rank, determine how much supervision an individual requires. I think the circumstances are probably more important than any other factor as to the level of oversight a senior gives to a subordinate. The objective is to arrive at that point where there is so much confidence in both directions as to what's expected, how to do that job, that the level of supervision takes its own natural path. There are some circumstances of urgency where it requires a great deal of supervision to get it done fast and well and out. There are many other times when you can afford to let an individual make a lot of mistakes and you can correct those mistakes because you have the time to correct them and the

end result isn't all that critical at the moment.

Let me suggest that it's the scenario that makes the issue rather than whether you're a first class, supervising the Navy staff, or supervising the fleet. You know, the CNO has perfectly logical expectations that if he puts a four star in charge of a fleet, that individual knows how to do the job and he's not going to do much supervision of that person. What you do find as people go up in rank, is that you have a natural expectation of their professional competence that goes with that rank. A Surface Warfare Officer's badge on your chest means something to everybody on board that ship. So the level of supervision for one who's not wearing that is obviously going to be quite a bit higher than the one who is, whatever their rank might be. So passing examinations and demonstrating watchstanding capabilities and that sort of thing are important to development of that level of confidence. You've got to achieve it. Until the crew of a P-3 is worked up as a team, you've got to put the supervision on the weak spots and build that up; the better it gets, the less supervision is required, and the better the team members know what to expect of one another.

The principles underlying the successful application of leadership at large commercial enterprises might appear to differ radically from the principles a naval officer at one of the Naval Service's many operational or industrial commands is expected to adhere to. Yet many of the basic characteristics of public and private successful organizations are remarkably similar. In a naval shipyard, which is similar in operations to a private-sector commercial enterprise, the commanding officer is faced with the challenge of molding as many as 14,000 civilian and military personnel to meet a common objective: the readiness of the fleet. In this regard, his task is not different from that of the commanding officer at the fleet operational level. The scope of the problems they face may differ, but the techniques they utilize to motivate and control are similar.

CHARACTERISTICS OF THE IDEAL ORGANIZATION

In 1982 the Naval Sea Systems Command convened a shipyard operations review group composed of senior civilians and military officers who were experienced in industrial operations. The group was to assess the effectiveness of each of the eight naval shipyards. As part of their extensive review, group members attempted to answer the question "What constitutes a good shipyard?" Their review reported a set of characteristics and features that should prevail in any successful organization. The review was not intended as a rigid set of instructions in shipyard operations; rather, it was a discussion model for examining individual operations and their impact on overall performance. The characteristics of this Ideal Shipyard, each influencing the other to some degree, have application in any organizational structure.

The Ideal Organization, therefore, should be *disciplined*, meaning orderly. This requires that operational processes and procedures be institutionalized and that they be well understood and effective. They do not have to be written. The people in the organization, from top to bottom, must understand that there are procedures, processes, and practices that apply to their work—the functions they carry out—and that they must comply with them. (*Compliance* could have been used in this discussion, but *discipline* was selected because it is a broader term.) In the Ideal Organization, discipline will be found. In those places where compliance is called for, compliance will be found, and in those places where there is an opportunity for judgment to be made, judgment will be found; however, discipline will be found throughout Ideal Organization operations.

The Blue Angels maintenance crew gets up very early every morning and starts a rigorous maintenance check on every airplane in the team. The supervisor of the maintenance crew makes sure that every standard set by him is adhered to and all work is checked against detailed lists to make sure that it is correct. The result is that the Blue Angels have never canceled an air show due to maintenance problems since their beginning in 1946.[1-40]

In the Ideal Organization, the ideal leader has injected a *bias to improve* into the discipline process. It is not enough for a leader to say "Do better." The bias to improve must be firmly fixed in the foundation of organizational operations. This means establishing processes and procedures, or enhancing the features of existing processes and procedures, to require the unit, in its day-to-day operation, automatically to achieve or strive for improvement.

Feedback is essential to attaining a bias to improve. If productive output is not closely scrutinized, much of the information and intelligence needed to achieve a bias for improvement will not be obtained. The Ideal Organization not only assesses itself when it fails to achieve a desired goal, it also assesses itself when it succeeds. It never fails to examine its performance. Numerous opportunities to look at important operations present themselves. In fact, the available data can be overwhelming. The will and the desire to understand that information (feedback), and the commitment to use it, are characteristic of Ideal Organizational management or leadership. An effective leader continually eliminates unclear or unnecessary data and seeks out meaningful information.

Another characteristic of the Ideal Organization is a commitment to *breakthrough*. Breakthrough is more than a "bias to improve." It is a conscious, deliberate attempt to grapple with the complexities of management or leadership and make changes that will result in improvement. Breakthrough usually involves major change, and it can result in the demise of an existing institutionalized process. Ideally, every organization should have an institutionalized approach to breakthrough. Every system, no matter how cherished or how well accepted, must be closely examined relative to the goals and objectives it was established to meet, and managers or leaders must make sure that their individual system objectives are supportive of the prevailing overall organizational objectives. Breakthrough also requires leaders to keep an open mind as they assess new processes or procedures that may initially appear to diverge from existing institutions. A disciplined, orderly, and focused approach to assessing existing and new processes or procedures is required to achieve significant breakthroughs.

The last characteristic is *Pareto*. The Pareto concept refers to the ordering of priorities by separating the (typically) few important issues from the numerous trivial issues surrounding most problems or decisions. The Pareto concept is most commonly thought of in the quality assurance department, though it is used in other places, as well. Its main importance is to serve as a reminder that priorities change. In the Ideal Organization, changing priorities are recognized. The key to wise and prudent allocation of resources is setting priorities that maximize what can be accomplished with the limited resources available. The Ideal Organization constantly examines its balance between resources and work requirements to establish an expenditure priority that ensures the maximum return on invested resources.

These, then, are the five characteristics of the Ideal Organization. There are several other basic features that prevail within any effective organization and that set the tone for the total operation.

At the top of the list is *get the job done*. This feature applies to whatever job the unit has been directed to do. That job could be overhauling and repairing ships, aircraft, or amphibious vehicles, or it could be closing with and destroying the enemy. Whatever the assigned job, the Ideal Organization will accomplish it to the specified requirements (time, cost, quality, loss ratio, etc.). Admiral Taylor makes the point that,

> if you don't set a plan with milestones and have a goal, you're going to wander around and you're not going to get there. A lot of people will take a long time coming up with a plan because they want to get it right the first time. Suggestion: Get it roughly right. A good plan tomorrow is not as good as a good plan today. Get a plan from which to deviate and you'll start out in the right direction, and then keep people working on that. Stroke them for achieving those little milestones, and you'll start moving.

> I have a favorite saying, and it works throughout life: Eat the elephant one bite at a time. There are a lot of people getting ready to chew the thing all at one time, but they never get off the dime, they never get started. So to me, in making something work, get started. Get the best minds around you, the people who are hired to help you, get them in, come up with a plan. Get your best writer to put down what the group has said. You've blessed this thing, and now your planning is over, you've got it organized and you've delegated authority, you've mapped out all the basic principles, so now you supervise, give a little encouragement here and there, go down and get with the troops and keep things working, report to the seniors all the good things, ask for help on the problems, and you're going to execute a plan that's going to be successful.

As a rule, general supervision and high output have been found to go together at a level much too high to be accounted for by chance.[5-212]

The second item is *time is managed*, which is not to say "time management." Time *is* managed includes time management, insofar as managers or leaders account for their own time and that of their subordinates, but it also includes a recognition that time is one of the most important things managers or leaders can manipulate. It means that members of the unit understand that there is very little they can do about anything except tomorrow's job. Nothing can be done to change yesterday (one can only learn from it). Other than in combat, today's job cannot be substantially changed either, because it was mostly determined yesterday, However, tomorrow's job can be changed by taking action today.

In the Ideal Organization, a recognition and understanding of this aspect of time will be apparent throughout the chain of command, but particularly among the managers or leaders. Additionally, leaders in the Ideal Organization exercise restraint and consideration in placing demands on the time of their subordinates, and vice versa. Meetings and other activities that consume time are well thought out and carefully constructed. Managers and leaders always attempt to obtain more mileage out of time available in predeveloped schedules before seeking additional time.

The Ideal Organization has a *constructive atmosphere*. This does not mean that everyone in the organization is happy and content. It means that the work atmosphere is professional. It means that personnel feel that they belong to a solid, important, and successful organization and that they will be listened to and heard. Difficult problems will not be avoided, they will be addressed, and actions precipitating reasonable improvement will be taken.

In the Ideal Organization, *important operations are institutionalized*. This, of course, includes any process that affects the foundation of the organization. *Institutionalized* normally equals *documented*, but not always. However, because personnel move frequently and rapidly in today's world, it is dangerous indeed to omit documentation of operational systems. Personnel must readily be able to ascertain the respon-

sibilities and appropriate procedures associated with their work. This is particularly important for new personnel, who must be able to find out what should be accomplished, how, when, and by whom. If this capability (currently and in the future) requires documentation for a given system, the Ideal Organization will have the appropriate documentation. Every important operational system in the Ideal Organization will be institutionalized in a way that limits the adverse impact of personnel transitions on operational efficiency and effectiveness.

Solid infrastructure refers to a multiplicity of aspects of an Ideal Organization. It requires that personnel administration be reasonable and sensible; that the industrial relations office function as an unbiased proponent, rather than opponent, in resolving organizational problems between different groups; that the military police or the security office maintain security yet be understanding of individual problems and assist in rectifying them. Every section, department, or office, whenever possible, must, in addition to striving to accomplish their own work, support other organizational sections,, departments, or offices in their efforts to meet individual work objectives. Clear and open channels of communications are maintained between Ideal Organizational departments. In total, *solid infrastructure* means that all parts of the organization understand that they are a part of a much larger entity and that parochial interests or efficiencies sometimes must be sacrificed for the success of overall operations.

As previously mentioned, another feature that should be found in the Ideal Organization is *wise and prudent use of meetings*. This requires recognition of the uses and limitations of meetings. Meetings can be magnificent when they are properly used; they can give visibility to and provide understanding of the problems at hand. Conversely, meetings can be difficult forums in which to make decisions. The interpretation of "facts" and other information can be as varied as the people attending a meeting. Individual interpretations or opinions are necessarily biased by an individual's work responsibilities and limited understanding of overall organizational requirements.

Only the commander and a few of his senior officers have the experience, knowledge, and perspective to evaluate each activity relative to the other activities in meeting overall goals. Only the commander has this as his responsibility. This is not to say that the commander is an all-knowing or omnipotent being, since he clearly must rely on information and advice provided by his subordinates. However, the final decision on significant issues must come from the commander.

Meetings must facilitate the decision-making process, not hinder it with burdensome details and excessive debate. Meeting topics should include only those issues that have a high priority, clearly impact on overall operations, and cannot be resolved at a lower level. The commander must set parameters and priorities that support this philosophy and impart this approach to everyone responsible for conducting meetings throughout the organization. If it becomes apparent that responsible individuals have lost sight of this concept, ameliorative steps must be taken to safeguard operations.

Related to feedback and a bias for improvement in the Ideal Organization is an *institutionalized self-assessment* system that is well structured, well understood, and routinely practiced. Typically, the self-assessment process is left to last, and often it is omitted entirely, but in some parts of a unit's operations, self-assessment can be very successful. After reasonable expectations for an organization's operational assessment have been determined, what can be done to remedy shortcomings?

Outside review agencies provide only a partial answer. It is clear that each manager or leader must conduct self-assessments on a regular basis. This includes assessing whatever portion of the total operation impacts on his operation. This is not to say that managers or leaders should necessarily assess operations outside of their areas of responsibility, but they should examine their interface with other operations, the health of that relationship, and the impact of other operations on their work and vice versa. Managers and leaders should ask themselves questions such as "How do I know that my subordinates are doing what I told them to do?" Answers such as "Well, I raised him from a pup," "He was my apprentice," or "I know I can trust him" are not good enough. Managers and leaders should follow a system of institutionalized self-assessment that requires a close examination of operations, makes visible hidden assumptions, and evaluates assumptions and procedures as warranted. In summary, the system must be in place that allows the leader the means to assess the performance at the *interface* between elements of the organization for which he is responsible.

Effective communication is the next feature. Military command, obviously, is a faithful adherent to the chain of command; however, the chain of command can be an ineffective system for communication. At times, communications undergo unnecessary and burdensome changes as they make their way down the chain of command. By the time they reach the seaman or the private, they may not reflect the intent of the commander. If a leader depended solely on an accurate translation of verbal instructions through his department or office, all the way down to the bottom of the organization, he would constantly be frustrated in his communication.

The leader does not have to put everything in writing or avoid passing decisions through subordinates down the chain of command. Rather, he must ensure effective communications, which means communications that are not misunderstood and that do not go astray. The organizational hierarchy has to make reasonable adjustments to the imperfections inherent in any communication technique. Some communications should be written, some should be oral; some communications should follow the chain of command, others should not. In every case, paper work is kept to a minimum and personnel requiring the information are quickly and clearly informed.

Peters and Austin, in their book *A Passion for Excellence,* stress the importance of leadership visibility. The effective leader stays in touch with what is going on within his organization, and one way he can do this is by using their technique, called MBWA (Managing By Wandering Around). Properly utilized, it allows leaders to apply a different but more direct communication vehicle, and in the process they demonstrate interest in and concern with the day-to-day obstacles encountered by their personnel.

The Ideal Organization has *clear and stable direction.* Starting in the commander's office, the organization provides clear and consistent direction that does not frequently change. An understanding of this direction should be evident throughout the chain of command, all the way down to the bottom. First-line supervisors (POs or NCOs) should know exactly what they are expected to do and that these expectations will not change from day to day. A reasonable and sensible reaction to the broad spectrum of actions and changing priorities with which managers and leaders must contend is to be expected; but leaders and managers must always provide clear and stable direction. Changes are to be made in a sane, sensible, and controlled fashion, and the reasons for these changes are to be well understood (though not everyone may agree on the changes, everyone must support them).

Effective delegation of authority is not easily accomplished, but it is a feature of the Ideal Organization. Most people have a general understanding of what is meant by delegation of authority, but some are not aware of how to delegate *effectively. Effective delegation* means that the commanding officer is not assuming the ship engineer officer's responsibilities. Similarly, a platoon commander is not operating as if he were a squad leader. In the Ideal Organization, management and leadership decisions and actions are initiated at the lowest possible level that will ensure a knowledgeable, effective, and timely response to work situations. Senior leaders and managers nurture the decision-making process in juniors through communication and interpretation of policy and procedures, and they avoid making decisions for subordinates. Workers like to work for a manager who has enough confidence in himself and in them to relax, at least to a reasonable degree.[5-213]

The foregoing discussion concerns supervisory responsibilities and administrative approaches of leaders. The following section provides a reminder that, in the final analysis, we are also very much concerned with how the leader proceeds.

EXAMPLES OF NEGATIVE LEADERSHIP

In discussing leadership traits, characteristics, and principles, examples of good leadership are frequently provided, wherein an officer excelled in his performance based on his exceptional leadership. General Barrow believes that it also

> would be helpful to those studying leadership and beneficial to them after they have been put in a leadership position to be able to ferret out what I would characterize as negative examples of leadership. This is more than a fellow not doing his best, a fellow who is a weak leader, not as effective as he ought to be, just doesn't quite have it. This is a fellow who is doing something wrong, but it's so bad that it goes beyond just being short of good leadership, it is totally in the opposite direction. The worst kind of negative leadership is worse than not having any leader at all, because if there is no leader, someone will emerge as a leader.

> What kind of people are we talking about when we say practicing negative leadership? I'll just give you four examples, and there are probably many more. There is a fellow who believes that he is an effective leader if he does everything

in a loud, grand, overbearing, overpowering sort of way. When someone told him that effective speaking and forcefulness were an important part of being a leader, he got it all distorted, and he believes that loudness, etc., is the way of asserting your personality, you know, you're just super. The fact is, the troops probably disrespect that as much as any other thing I can think of. The person may be well read and knowledgeable of his job, and his military bearing may be impeccable, but he misunderstood what that business of demeanor, speaking assertively, is all about.

Close kin to him is number two, the fellow who thinks he is projecting himself as a leader through rough language. "I'm demonstrating to the troops that I'm kind of one of them. We are all brothers under the skin," and so every other word is a vulgar four-letter word, which shouldn't be used, in my judgment, anywhere, anytime, not even in the company in your BOQ (Bachelor Officer Quarters) with your peers. There's nothing worse than verbally abusing troops, whether it's directed to an individual or just fussing at them about something and lacing your words with vulgarity. They can't come back at you, and it's demeaning, not only of them, but of the person who does it. Its effect is just the opposite of what he thinks it is.

Number three, the fellow who believes that if he can just get close to the troops, he can be a good leader. Nothing suits him better than company picnics, beer busts, boss's night, all of which I disapprove of totally, and he likes to call the enlisted people closest to him by their first name, not their rank or last name. He thinks that if he can just be one of the boys that everybody will love him and therefore whatever he asks them to do,

they'll do it because he's one of the boys. Most of the troops don't like that. They want a leader to act like a leader.

Then you have a very unusual fellow, number four. Mr Super Macho. We've got some of those around. He reckons that if he alone, or he compelling his command, can run farther than anybody else, chew more tobacco, shoot more wild game, drive four-wheel vehicles deeper in the mud, then he's a good leader. His whole image is "I'm physically overpowering. There isn't anything I can't do. I like to go around with a chain saw in one hand and a shotgun in the other, ready to take on whatever moves, and my favorite thing to do is get up and run. More favorite than that is to make everyone who is under me run, too." He substitutes physical prowess, physical achievement, physical fitness, often, for brains and command presence, proper persuasiveness.

Now, I'm telling you all of this because it might make someone think, "Well, I shouldn't do that. Somebody told me that, and I'll be careful of how I project myself in these areas." More importantly, it ought to tell those in leadership positions that if they are on the ball, they can go out there and they can find these guys. It only takes one here and there to spread a bad influence far beyond what you might think.

53. Record Keeping

If someone were to survey a group of randomly selected officers regarding the ultimate goal of any command, the most frequent response would undoubtedly be mission accomplishment. Leaders are in the business of getting tasks done as effectively and efficiently as possible. As one source puts it, "The naval officer is a leader. His primary functions are to organize, plan, and supervise such tasks necessary to accomplish the mission given him."[59-1] There can be no argument about what officers in the Navy are striving for.

Mission accomplishment is the goal, then, but how is the goal best achieved? Unfortunately, this is a complex problem and cannot be solved with any standard formula. In reality, there are many steps necessary for mission accomplishment.

One naval publication says that the mission-oriented leader always "identifies the problem facing his unit. He does this on the basis of hard data—daily, weekly, and monthly reports on the status of supply, maintenance, and operations."[76-20] Simply put, the effective leader keeps accurate and up-to-date records. In principle this seems easy enough, but record keeping is not always carried out as well as it should be. In the fleet, an officer may scoff at the thought of paper work. The only answer to this is that all officers are also administrators and must learn to become proficient in that capacity. Admiral Itaya tells us that

> accurate administrative and operational records are absolutely essential when preparing reports or when after-action research or instruction is required.
> I had the exceedingly difficult experience of reconstructing exercises, tactical movements, and actual scenes of combat. I learned firsthand that accurate and complete records are a necessity.

Keeping records contributes in many ways to mission accomplishment. First, records allow the leader to judge whether his unit is combat ready, showing whether all systems are operational and personnel are prepared to use them. Next, keeping records can keep the operation running smoothly by improving efficiency, security, and safety. Finally, operational reports are an aid in battle because they provide guidance and vital information at a glance. Consequently, keeping records is a major factor in getting the job done correctly the first time.

Admiral de Cazanove believes that

records must in fact be up to date, and it must be remembered that it is extremely dangerous for a commander to be working from records that are not up to date. One must remember that records are also important to let others know the status of things if the officer is wounded or killed and someone else has to take over. By having up-to-date records, the person taking over will be able to perform a quick and simple review and best evaluate how to proceed. This approach turned out to be very important one time when I was called back from China to return to France and I had to leave the day my relief was to take over. Because my records were up to date, he was able to take over on this short notice. A month later, when back in France, I received a letter from the officer who relieved me, saying: "Well, I found the records up to date and so clear that everything was made simple for me." So, while records are indeed necessary, you can only rely on them when they have been carefully kept and are up to date; otherwise they are of no use.

PAYING ATTENTION TO DETAIL

The rationale for keeping accurate records is partly seen in a phrase that is often heard during precommissioning education and training. That phrase is "attention to detail." It means receiving a 4.0 on a room inspection because people took the time to clean spaces that they knew probably would not be checked. This same attention to detail must remain with the officer as he enters the fleet. Out there it means saving lives and winning battles because every person and every system has been checked. It is that important. Admiral Taylor:

> Records are important; if you're going to get the lessons learned from the past and put them to work in the future, you have to have records. The question, then,

is, How do you make them accurate? and that's just attention to detail. We'd all like to be roughly right, but that isn't going to work all the time. So a very important attribute for an officer is paying attention to detail, and I think probably that's the crux of record keeping.

The only way for the officer to make the required checks on systems and personnel is to keep records. The leader must be assured of his unit's combat readiness at all times. To do this, he needs a follow-up system to be sure that nothing has been forgotten or left out. By keeping records, the leader can ensure that his people have sufficient training to use them to their full potential. This represents a tough leadership problem. However, there is generally a two-part solution to any problem. The first part comes from subjective inputs from the officer, and the second and most important part comes from objective inputs from other sources (data files, reports, and records).[59-4]

The Utility of Operational Records

When should records be kept? As often as possible. On the other hand, according to Army guidelines, "the officer should not become chart happy, covering his walls with useless charts that are impressive to see but require major effort to prepare and maintain."[22-268] Therefore, the information that is gathered must serve a purpose and be understood by all.

How, then, are accurate records used in the daily running of a ship? A good place to start would be in the engineering department. The fact of the matter is that battles cannot be fought by a ship that is unable to get to the front. Down in the engine room, records take the form of a log book, and in no other area is it more important to keep records up to date. There are literally hundreds of gauges in the modern boiler plant or nuclear power plant, and each one must be carefully checked on the hour. By evaluating these reports, the competent chief engineer can predict when a turbine will overheat or a pump

will lose sufficient pressure and can intervene before that point is reached. PMS or preventive maintenance should also be logged. With this done, the leader can assure himself that his engineering department is combat ready.

Damage control is very important in the engineering department. A ship is useless if it cannot sustain damage during battle. Sometimes people on board are not as conscientious as they should be, so it is up to the leader to keep detailed information on all emergency equipment in his division's spaces. It goes without saying that he should keep records assuring that the equipment has been checked and is working properly. The leader can be sure of the ability of his people to carry out the mission because he has checked the equipment and their ability to operate it.

The supply department on board is almost synonymous with paper work. One effective control method is to conduct a SEAS (Supply Edit Audit System).[56-221] This monitoring system compares total requisitions against consumption rates. If the officers involved keep accurate records, waste can be eliminated by measuring the ship's needs and expenditures. There are few things worse than having an extra thousand cans of boiled broccoli but no meat.

Another important consideration for the supply officer is spare parts. Today's Navy is too advanced technically to make it feasible for parts to be manufactured aboard ship, so officers need to keep records of what they have and what they are going to need. When this data is assembled during a deployment and then returned to higher commands, Navywide usage records can be established so that the fleet can better determine its supply needs.[17-49]

Perhaps the worst nightmare of naval officers is a collision at sea. Nothing can end a promising career faster. Collisions can be avoided, however, if the proper precautions are taken. The bible for commanding officers, *Command at Sea*, compiled a list of mistakes that can lead to a collision or running aground. Many of these mistakes can be eliminated by accurate record keeping. Keeping track of gyro errors, soundings, and wind and tide information is a small effort to expend to avoid disaster. The officer of the deck should also keep abreast of contact reports, have the combat information center keep a dead-reckoning plot, and demand updated maneuvering board solutions.[48-244]

If there is one thing that must never be compromised in the Naval Service, it is safety. Everyone expects a civilian nuclear power plant to keep records of its radiation emissions, and this same attention to detail should be practiced in the military. The highest safety standards must be observed, and keeping records is a good way to improve safety and avoid accidents.

It is also important to keep "records on records." Potential enemy intelligence gathering is a large problem in itself, and it is imperative that officers protect confidential material. Records must be kept on what documents are present and who has the authority to view them. Periodically, the destruction of records is necessary, and the completion of this task should be reported. Security is an essential part of any operation, and it, too, deserves to be accounted for.

Keeping precombat engineering and supply department records, as well as safety records, is essential. In the operational and combat environment, documenting information is equally important. In battle, the heart of the ship is the combat information center. Here the vast majority of decisions are made. Because of the varied threats in modern warfare, the officer must be acquainted with hundreds of different procedures. The CIC can keep an emergency action folder, which outlines all of the necessary actions required for any number of situations. There should be a checklist for appropriate weapons use, electronic support measures, and communications. Along these lines, reports should also be kept on all of the electronic equipment, detailing location, operating parameters, and emergency procedures.[27-132] These records can be critical, as quick decisions and action can mean

the difference between winning and losing an engagement.

Despite all of these examples on how keeping records can improve a leader's capabilities, there may still be some doubters. These people may be convinced by the many historical cases of intelligent leaders who benefited from their attention to detail. In early 1917, the British Admiralty was clinging adamantly to the old merchant shipping methods, even though merchant ships were being sunk by German U-boats. Young Commander Henderson, RN, pleaded in defense of the convoy system, but to no avail. Thereafter, he began a private study and kept daily records of English versus French shipping (the French often used the convoy system) in certain common sea routes. He showed the Admiralty that the French experienced a .2 percent loss rate, compared to the 25 percent rate of the British, and the Admiralty had no choice but to change strategies.[63-227] Because of Henderson's figure keeping, losses dropped twentyfold, and the Allies could get on with winning the war.

Twenty-five years later, the British immediately adopted the convoy system in World War II with excellent success. However, this time it was the German Navy which gained from record keeping. As head of the U-boat force, Admiral Karl Donitz began examining certain trends. He plotted on maps the locations of his most successful hunting and where his subs were being sunk. From these records, he pinpointed an area called the Black Pit in the North Atlantic, which Allied air cover could not reach and his wolfpack tactics could best be utilized.[67-259] Over the course of the next several months, Donitz's forces sunk 217 merchant vessels and lost only six U-boats.

THE UTILITY OF PERSONNEL RECORDS

In addition to operational records, other types of information should be documented, such as information on personnel. Leaders should know their people inside and out, because this helps them to discern how their people will react and what will motivate them. An officer must not be too busy to know his people; hoping that his people will do a good enough job if left to themselves is not sufficient.

There are many ways for an officer to come to understand his personnel. Admiral Clexton, at one time commanding officer of the USS *Eisenhower*, suggested a device known as the division officer's notebook. This should be used to record any information that might prove useful in improving performance. The leader should hold frequent interviews to find out how each individual is doing and to discover any personal problems that are being experienced which could affect output. This valuable tool should be constantly updated and passed on to a leader's relief. Not only does the officer gain a better understanding of personnel, but morale is improved, because the troops feel that they are being looked after with concern.

Another reason the officer should follow the progress of his personnel is for performance evaluations. The military depends on good soldiers and sailors who can get the job done. This is why evaluations are extremely important. An officer should see evaluations as an opportunity to recognize the performance of subordinates. A hastily written report is useless, whether the subordinate deserves praise or reprimand, especially if areas for improvement are not identified. The division officer's notebook is useful here, and in it should be recorded what jobs each person performs and how well he does them, along with collateral duties, educational achievements, or awards received.[48-186] Another indicator to monitor is personnel status in relation to Personnel Qualification Standards (PQS). By keeping these and other types of records, the leader can be assured that individuals are receiving the evaluation they deserve and that the Navy will be able to make an informed decision in assigning personnel. Secretary Webb:

> Individual record keeping is important for the officer, because he or she may need to produce documentation on an action in order to defend it. But unit record keeping is important also, for that reason and to develop unit pride, to form a sense of history about what the unit is doing. The Navy's traditional ship's log and its special entries—the entry made on New Year's Eve, for example, to record the officer of the deck as the New Year is turned over—have become cherished commodities.

> In addition, an officer should keep records on his personnel, people who, 15 years down the road, may want a letter of recommendation or need help. My written report on one special individual proved invaluable. I had recommended a fellow for a Silver Star for gallantry, and two months later he had been blown up and he became a triple amputee. I had lost track of him, and his award had lost track of him, too, and I was able to go to the Marine Corps on this because I had been so impressed by what he did that night that I wrote a spot report, which is sort of unusual in combat, about what had happened. The Marine Corps was able to go into our battalion journal, pull the incident out—it was a matter of history—and reconstruct the award, and the Chief of Staff for Manpower went down and pinned it on the kid in his hometown in North Carolina.

Admiral Carney notes that,

> when officers are required to keep a journal, they should make periodic contributions to it that incorporate experience and familiarity with the equipment and duties for which they are responsible, and, in addition, preparation for competence in the next grade up the ladder.

Admiral Carney provided this story about the value of concise and literate writing.

> In 1941, a friend of mine who was on the faculty at the War College brought a draft of a publication to me and asked me

to look at it. He asked what I thought, and my response was not favorably received at the War College. I said that everything that they had said at great length had been said more precisely in the two publications which had preceded it. The publication finally came out, and one day during the war I was going up to Pearl Harbor for a conference or something and I was having lunch with Admiral Spruance and the subject came up about this book. He asked me if I was familiar with it, and I said that I had read a draft of it but I hadn't gone any further. He said, "But what did you think of it?" I said I thought it was verbose and had too much explanation of the obvious. Spruance perfectly straight-faced said, "Well, I don't think it's all that bad. All they needed to do was change the title." And I bit and said, "Yes, Sir. What do you think the title should have been?" He said, "Common Sense Made Hard." There is a point beyond which further explanation either doesn't accomplish anything or might even have a negative effect.

Finally, officers should keep a file on themselves. Through these personal records, an officer can keep a clean house, and he should have his own matters in order before he leads others. All material concerning financial matters should be closely monitored (e.g., pay slips, bills, credit card reports, and loan payments), and documents such as car and real estate titles, medical and insurance reports, and education certificates should be kept in a file. An officer can save a great deal of time by keeping good records.[50-14]

These, then, are some of the sound reasons for the leader to keep accurate and up-to-date records. There must be some way for him to know where he and his unit stand. For instance, it would be madness to follow a Marine lieutenant on a night patrol if he did not know how much ammunition his people had, where the enemy strongholds were, or what frequencies to

communicate on. Competence involves attention to detail, knowing everything that there is to know about the working environment. To be effective, a leader must keep pertinent records that allow him to know these details.

54. The System of Checks

Officers are the key to everything that happens in the military service, and therefore they must have built-in checks to ensure their ability to give their best performance. To ensure that the actions they take or direct others to take are in tune with the actualities and the requirements of their own unit as well as the requirements of other units, officers must develop a system of self-checks. If, through negligence or oversight, an officer fails to inform other units of plans or occurrences that may affect them, he has not fulfilled his responsibility to them. Furthermore, not knowing something that was his responsibility to know is not a viable excuse for an officer.

Certainly in multi-ship and multi-unit operations, officers have to rely on information supplied to them by others, and even in squad and small ship operations, it is impossible for leaders to come by all information firsthand. Thus, officers must apply a system of checks to information from other sources. An officer cannot check all the work of his subordinates, yet he is responsible for all the work they do; this is why officers must establish a procedure to verify that subordinates' actions, as well as their own, have been correctly taken. Self-confidence results from, first, exact knowledge; second, the ability to impart that knowledge; and third, the feeling of superiority that follows. Troops will not have confidence in an officer unless he knows his business, and he must know it from the ground up.[4-44]

There are four parts to an officer's system of checks. First, he asks his peers and subordinates their opinion of actions he plans to take. By doing this, the officer is not admitting incompetency; he is, rather, making it known that he is interested in using all of the information sources available to him. A second check on actions to be taken can be made by asking lateral units whether the action will support, interfere with, or have no effect on their operations. Discussing actions to be taken with seniors is the third part of the system. This enables the officer to incorporate the seniors' greater knowledge and scope of information into his own plans, thus improving them. In the final step, the officer conducts a critique meeting, usually after an operation has been concluded, but sometimes while the operation is being conducted. Regardless of how well the operation went, participants usually have ideas as to how things could be done better in the future.

The fourth part of the system, the critique, is not an admission of poor planning, but, rather, a recognition that every organization is planning for the future, even during current operations. Further, it shows everyone concerned that the officer is not afraid of criticism, and that doing the job right is his goal. Senior officers do not have problems with juniors who ask for help or bring mistakes to the attention of their seniors. It is the junior who will not admit a shortcoming or a lack of understanding—which results in a senior officer hearing from his senior that something went wrong—who causes anguish.

PROFESSIONAL KNOWLEDGE: THE KEY TO THE SYSTEM OF CHECKS

The key to establishing a system of checks is the professional knowledge of the officer. An officer cannot determine whether something has been done correctly if he lacks the ability to analyze results and compare them against standards. Thus, the officer who is proficient in all aspects of his position, including personnel, money, and materials, is better able to evaluate work.

One way an officer evaluates the information provided by others and the work of others is to keep mental or written records. Every officer can keep such records, and he will find that

writing down his problem and his solution and its results is a very stimulating and suggestive procedure.[23-598] Every officer is responsible for preparing evaluations of others in the unit. Keeping a record of day-to-day operations allows the officer to review exactly what took place at a particular time, and will help him evaluate the competence of his personnel. Without these background notes, the officer will find it difficult to counsel enlisted regarding their performance and need for improvement, for it is impossible for an officer to remember everything that every one of his subordinates has done. Professional competence is a factor in an officer's ability to evaluate information received from others and the performance of subordinates. People hear in terms they understand, so it is very important for an officer to know as much as he can about the work of subordinates, though of course he is not required to know everything or to be able to do everything with which the subordinate is charged.

While a good memory is an important tool for officers, when they receive new information, they need to be able to compare it against what they already know and thus check its accuracy. Consider the following example:

	(1)	(2)	(3)	Y Total
A	5	7	9	21
B	4	9	12	25
C	8	3	2	13
X Total	17	19	22	58/59

If someone were to add the numbers only vertically, he might miss the error in column 3, but by adding numbers both vertically and horizontally, he would discover the difference in the total values of X and Y, which should be the same, and recheck his work. The officer who has multiple sources of information and feedback can determine whether what he receives is correct.

An officer has to become accustomed to storing great amounts of information, not unlike doing a puzzle and keeping in mind many shapes and colors while waiting for connecting pieces to place the "lone" parts in perspective. By storing knowledge, the officer will be able to evaluate new information against other data received and decide that it is in basic agreement with what he already knows or that it requires further thought or action. For example: because he has a rough idea of the mean time required to repair a number of kinds of equipment, the officer, when he is advised of the downtime of a motor generator, can determine whether the repair time projected is realistic. An officer who knows how much time it takes to enter data into a computer and process it can plan for delays in data availability or, better still, request the data in advance, so that delays are minimized.

At times it will be useful or necessary for the officer to ask additional questions. If he does not understand what is being presented or suspects that there may be things he does not know which might influence his judgment, the officer should seek more information. Asking subordinates to explain their recommendations and to expound on what it was that led them to their conclusions is another effective way for the officer to ensure that what he is going to do is the best possible action given the information known and the time available for making a decision. Admiral Taylor sees as part of leadership

> the ability to ask the hard question. This is what separates, quite frankly, the successful from the unsuccessful. How tough-minded are you? Are you easy? Do you sign everything and just accept it, or do you have the knowledge, the exerience, to zero in on a couple of things that your subordinates give you and ask them the hard question? So what you're doing is asking a question so that (a) you'll let them know that you know something about the business, and (b) when they give you the answer you can stroke them, say, "That's a good point. I think you've got a great piece of paper here." It's essential in leadership that you under-

stand the necessity to ask the hard question, the tough question. Don't assume anything is okay all the time. Get back to people, put a little feedback in the process. It will fire them up to give you a better piece of paper.

> I have worked for bosses who just said, "That's a good job." Gone. Others have said, "That's a good start," and you say, "Boy, which way do I run? Do I go back and write this paper?" You go back and you rewrite it, and he says, "Ah, you're getting closer." Back again. Then, about the fourth time, he says, "Well, that's about right." Boy, you worked real hard for that kind of an admiral. In this case, after he was relieved, a second three star came in, and he had a different management style. He read the paper and said, "Good job," and away it went, but then when it got back to my desk I said, "Gee, that was too easy. I've always been bounced around about three or four times before I got this message out. Now I'd better read it over again, because he has such trust and confidence in me I might get him in trouble." They are just two interesting, different styles, but I quite frankly go to the guy who asks the hard question. He keeps you honest, he's a participating player.

THE PRINCIPLE OF MANAGEMENT BY EXCEPTION

In all probability, there will not be enough time to acquire and analyze all the information concerning a particular situation. Thus, a priority system must be established; this will make it likely that if certain matters are taken care of, the rest will follow. For example, consider the case of monitoring the grades of those in officer accession programs: there are probably too many people taking courses for the progress of every individual in every course to be followed individually. The principle of management by exception states that the standard is determined and that only information outside the standard is examined. If the standard is set at a 2.00 grade point average, with no grade lower than a D, then the computer can be instructed to eliminate all those who exceed the standard, saving data analysis time for considering only those who do not meet the standard. On a more complex level, consider the status of a squadron of ships preparing for deployment, with each ship having hundreds of activities to complete. Each ship can report its progress on each of its activities, and a computer can be programmed in such a way that the officer who is monitoring the progress receives notice only of the exceptions to the schedule, and thus he can apply his management and leadership skills to known problems rather than spending a great deal of time sifting through available data.

The officer can delegate authority for data acquisition and analysis with good results. Subordinates should be instructed to advise the officer only about trouble areas, because those meeting standards should be of little concern to the officer. However, it is well to keep in mind that from time to time those who do meet standards should be thanked and commended for their part, both to recognize their achievement and to show that the senior is informed about what is going on.

It goes without saying that when the officer discovers instances of misinformation or inappropriate action in himself or in others, he must take action. First, he should review what went wrong, and then, in consultation with others, he should expand the area of investigation, not only to establish causes, but also to enable steps to be taken to prevent a repetition. When subordinates are thought to have made a mistake or provided inadequate information, the officer should first look to himself to make sure he did not fail to supply enough or the correct information. He should also consider whether he obtained sufficient feedback when he passed the information on to ensure that the persons receiving it fully understood it. A person usually "does not know what he does not know," so asking whether anyone has any questions does not provide a very good check on understanding. It would be better to ask what action will be taken regarding the information and what problems are foreseen in the undertaking. This often provides a warning as to what might go wrong or what information may have been incorrectly or inadequately passed.

The officer still must be able to trust each man fully in his specific department, and at the same time hold him responsible for it. He who has full power to do right cannot complain that he is censured or punished when he does wrong; but where that power is limited or restrained, he is not responsible at all, for, while the subordinate can sometimes be excused on the grounds that his discretion was taken away from him, the superior will never be allowed this.[26-42]

MCPON Sanders: *I strongly endorse the principle of management by exception. Not only is it a time saver, but it creates good will by showing your confidence in the work being done by individuals, as opposed to checking them constantly every step of the way as to the progress of their work.*

55. Avoiding Problems

Douglas MacGregor sums up the task of management best when he states: Management consists of getting things done through other people.[47-5] A leader should have positive, enthusiastic, and supportive interactions with his subordinates. Every person should approach every task as "a chance to excel," and every member of a unit should feel that he is a part of the team effort. In this following passage, Vince Lombardi speaks of how he idealized his subordinates and how he apparently coached them:

> And in truth, I've never known a man worth his salt who in the long run, deep down in his

heart, didn't appreciate the grind, the discipline. There is something in good men that really yearns for, needs, discipline and the harsh reality of head-to-head combat. . . . I believe that any man's finest hour—his greatest fulfillment to all he holds dear—is that moment when he has worked his heart out in a good cause and lies exhausted on the field of battle—victorious.[57-116]

When a task is assigned to an officer, he should think it through on his own and outline specific tasking, time limits, quality standards, and other constraints. Then he should call a meeting of his senior enlisted personnel and/or front-line supervisors to discuss tasking and to receive their feedback and recommendations. He can then prepare a plan of action, outlining organizational responsibilities, who does what, and deadlines. The following passage tells of how General Eisenhower devoted himself to meeting with subordinates to monitor current and potential problems of the Allied offensive in the European theater:

> He (Ike) once left his headquarters at 3:00 P.M. and arranged to meet various commanders along the way, working until midnight. Then he lay down for three hours of sleep and began again until he returned at noon the following day to headquarters. There he held conferences until dinnertime, and then set about studying maps and plans until 11:00 P.M.[53-228]

As as example of how an officer can best approach a task, consider the preparations required for an upcoming inspection. Several months before the inspection, the officer should obtain copies of the inspection guide of standards and the discrepancy reports from the last few inspections. He should become familiar with these and give copies of them to his senior enlisted personnel. At the supervisors' meeting, the officer needs to discuss the guidelines and timetable, and to assign areas of responsibility. He should make sure that he receives periodic status reports. The officer and his senior enlisted members should go through the inspection guide,

item by item, to ascertain compliance. It may also be useful for the officer to ask his department head or executive officer to go through the guide with him, so that he can benefit from the senior's experience.

MONITORING THE PROGRESS BEING MADE BY OTHERS

After planning, the officer's job becomes one of following through to ensure that the task is being done efficiently and effectively. He can do this informally by touring his spaces and chatting with members on project status. The officer should perform these "spot-checks" in a friendly manner; he should show his interest and encourage subordinates to give him feedback on current and potential problems. Admiral Hayward cautions that

> an officer must guard against over-supervising. His ability to judge what constitutes too much supervision will generally be determined by his experience. A junior officer can expect to be supervised quite a bit, and from that he can learn lessons as to what the right style of supervision is.
>
> Some people are born with the natural ability to supervise others, but most people have to acquire the ability through experience and education. Leadership talent can be acquired through studying books and observing others. Constructive lessons—in how to and how not to supervise others—are going on all the time. After observing, an officer can simply try a style of supervision on "for size." Most new officers can expect to make at least one big mistake. For example, I was a maintenance officer of a squadron as a lieutenant, and we had quite a number of different types of airplanes in this squadron; it was a unique type of development squadron. The airplanes were all relatively new to the fleet, and we had the first models. I can recall one day we were having a particularly complex problem with

an airplane and we just couldn't find out what was wrong with it, and I had four or five of my chiefs around. We were debating, and I said "Let's get ahold of Mr. So and So of Such and Such Company. Let's call in the experts." Well, let me tell you, the chiefs didn't like that comment one bit, they had every right in the world to believe that they *were* the experts. So whereas in fact we all needed some outside advice, the style of leadership exerted at that moment wasn't exemplary.

Periodically, the officer needs to hold meetings with his supervisors to ascertain the status of assignments more formally. As problems arise, he can brainstorm with the group, offering constructive feedback on how to resolve problems and evaluating the availability of additional resources. The officer must keep to the designated timetable so that all players continue to know what is expected of them. The Ford Motor Company has used research from Herzberg to set up guidelines for the manager to follow to improve job attractiveness for employees; these guidelines are directly applicable to the military and provide a challenge for the officer corps:

1. Once an employee has earned the right, let him really run his job.
2. Develop ways for giving employees direct, individual feedback on their own performance.
3. Invent ways of letting the job expand so that the employee can grow psychologically.[30-188]

The officer is also the "resource person," and he should be communicating with the chain of command and lateral units, keeping others apprised of current and potential problems. He should be prepared to recommend options and additional resources, and to evaluate current timetables and goals. When he reports the results of these discussions to his subordinate supervisors, he should maintain a positive attitude and continue to display enthusiasm for the task. All officers have the opportunity to excel, as did the famous "Chesty," who, although he preferred the action of battle, demonstrated enough interest in the development of young Marines to receive comments from officers who received his trainees, such as: "I can always tell when we get a Puller-trained Marine. He's ready to go."[24-233]

In all areas, the officer should challenge his people to think creatively, to offer their ideas and suggestions, and to accept his decisions with a cheery "Aye aye." All levels of the unit should feel involved with the project, whether they are working on it directly or "picking up the slack" and doing routine work. The officer needs to encourage his subordinate supervisors to spot-check their subordinates' work, and he should let them know that he will be doing the same. A subordinate should never be put in a position where he has to go out of his way to gain recognition from his senior; and, as Vince Lombardi states: "Don't tell me how good you are—let me find it out."[57-93] When making formal or informal spot-checks, the officer should provide encouragement and praise where indicated and constructive feedback in problem areas. As we in the military know very well, and as MacGregor states from his own experience:

A leader cannot avoid the exercise of authority any more than he can avoid responsibility for what happens to his organization. In fact, it is a major function of the [leader] to take on his own shoulders the responsibility for resolving the uncertainties that are always involved in important decisions. Moreover, since no important decision ever pleases everyone in the organization, he must also absorb the displeasure, and sometimes severe hostility, of those who would have taken a different course.[47-67]

Problem areas are best discussed in private, with the senior enlisted supervisor and/or front-line supervisor. If they are addressed in a group meeting, problems should be addressed in general, task-oriented terms.

Senior enlisted personnel and supervisors must be given the authority to carry out the tasks assigned to them, and they must be held accountable for task performance. The officer should keep close track of problems, conflicts, and other factors so as to maintain realistic expectations of the unit's capabilities. Ultimately, the officer will be held accountable for the performance of the task, so he must stay involved, keeping the chain of command informed (both up and down), and providing his subordinates his attention and showing them his confidence in their abilities. Admiral Zumwalt points out that,

> for work to be completed in a timely and efficient manner, everyone involved must understand what the mission is for that day, that week, and that month, and how the specific assignment that is being passed out at any given time fits into it. Further, the assignment must be clearly expressed and understandable. General Taylor used to comment about the famous fitness report that reads, "This officer has a tendency to become confused when given conflicting directives." It is very important that the directive not be confusing.

The follow-through is a key part of any job, whether it be operational or managerial. The successful leader keeps a written log of the assignments that he has been given and the assignments that he has passed out. Each assignment made should be followed by a notation of a date for checking on it.

Admiral Zumwalt used the following standard for checking someone's progress:

> If I gave a job to a petty officer or a subordinate officer that I knew he could do and I knew was a kind of standard job, I made a note to check on him once before the deadline that I had in mind and then again at the deadline. But if it was a job that had some appreciable complexity or involved enough analytical composition that there would be some uncertainty that when it came back I

would be satisfied with it, or that it really matched what I thought I had asked for, I would make it a point to check at about the 15 percent point and about the 30 percent point, to avoid the need to have the individual given the assignment completely rework something. I found it was good to wade into it with him a couple of times early in the assignment.

So the officer should periodically check on his subordinates when they are working on an assignment for him. Conversely, when he has been given a fairly complex assignment, the officer should check with his boss early on to make sure he is proceeding in the right direction.

THE ZERO-DEFECTS PROGRAM

As previously discussed (in chapter 1), it is not possible to achieve perfection in all operations and assignments. However, the officer who attempts to run a zero-defects program (analogous to that in equipment design and development) is proceeding in the right direction, because he is trying to do the very best with the personnel and material resources at his command. It is not enough to solve problems as they arise; the officer must mentally contemplate an operation and consider what might go wrong and take preventive action to avoid problems in the first place. Many operations can be thought out ahead of time, and brainstorming sessions are particularly effective in this regard. Furthermore, almost all military operations have at some time or another been rehearsed prior to combat; confronting people with deviations in training plans and asking them to try to solve difficult problems prepares them to adapt to changes in procedure during a wartime operation. Participative management is not a specific technique but is, rather, a concept of applied management that involves employee participation in developing and implementing decisions that directly affect their jobs.[31-97]

Although a zero-defects program may not be attainable, experience has shown that those units which try to have no errors, and implement programs and procedures to support this effort, usually do far better than those who only after events take place try to determine what went wrong and how the error might be avoided in the future. In the military we must try to avoid problems, where possible, rather than trying to solve them after they have had their effect. Admiral Moorer makes the point that

> recognizing the symptom of a problem is the first step in removing the problem, because it is an indication of a harmful trend. If that trend is allowed to continue, there will be a major problem instead of one that is solvable. Since a symptom is indicative of a problem, a leader should look for symptoms so he can intervene as early as possible to remedy the problem. Frequently in the case of an individual you can sense a problem by his attitude. He may become withdrawn, he doesn't enter into the activities, be they social or otherwise, with the vim and vigor that he demonstrated previously. This means not that he doesn't like to participate in the activities, but that he's got something that's really troubling him. You have to observe what is unusual behavior or different behavior than the patterns established before by the individual. Something is bothering him, so you've got to endeavor to try to find it and see if you can help him. It may be a family problem, or he may feel that his senior is being unreasonable with him, or something like that. You've got to talk with him and find out.

> One thing that the commander or the officer in charge has to do, in my view, is maintain an open house for people who want to come up and talk to him about their problem. I've had situations, for instance, where you could see that the youngster was depressed or whatever and it was something at home. We let him

have ten days leave, and he straightened it out and came back as a new man.

MCPON Sanders: *While officers need to offer constructive suggestions for improvement of work, I strongly encourage them to do so through their chief, or, if none is available, the officer should speak to the senior enlisted and discuss with him the problem and suggestions for improvement. Going directly to the individual worker may detract from the authority of the senior enlisted, and this is authority that you want the senior enlisted to have so that he can accomplish other assignments you give him.*

56. Decision Making

In peacetime as well as during armed conflict, an officer who is responsible for taking action must make decisions promptly. It is especially crucial for officers to make clear-cut, timely, and unequivocal decisions in combat. Several factors can make this an extremely difficult task, so young officers must prepare themselves for it. Knowledge, skill, experience, intuition, and creativity are all resources for a decision maker. In addition, there are many techniques that have been developed for effective decision making. "Decisions should be thought of as a means rather than ends. They are the organizational mechanisms through which an attempt is made to achieve a desired state. They are, in effect, a response to a problem."[31-420]

Often, not all of the facts that the officer needs to make a sound decision are available to him. The enemy may strike from an entirely unexpected direction with a force of unknown size. The first officer to discover the attack, often, is a unit commander. He must make a decision of some sort—in fact, several of them—without delay. He must evaluate the situation, aggressively direct the counterattack, ensure communication with the remainder of the friendly force, and implement defensive measures to secure his position in the event of a second attack.

Sometimes an officer must make a decision on his own because he is unable to contact his senior. A young lieutenant, for example, may, while he is carrying out orders, encounter conditions that he believes were not known to his senior officer when the senior issued the orders. The lieutenant may believe that to comply literally would not be proper under the circumstances and would, in fact, contravene the intent of the original orders. When further communication with the senior is not possible, and the situation is crucial, the lieutenant must use his initiative to make a decision and carry it out.

Decisions, once made, should be vigorously followed up with positive, aggressive action. During combat, there is no time for hesitation or indecisiveness. This was illustrated during the 1968 battle for Hue City in Vietnam. Elements of the 1st Battalion, 5th Marine Regiment, became separated from the main body, but they were still highly successful in clearing a well-fortified area of the citadel because they took decisive action on their own.

PREPARATION FOR DECISION MAKING

Because making decisions without complete information, without the assistance of seniors, and under stressful conditions is so difficult, young officers must train and study to develop the ability to make timely decisions and to issue appropriate orders automatically. As part of this training, officers need to cultivate imagination, initiative, and alertness, all of which will help them to make decisions. "The quality of the decisions officers reach is the yardstick of their effectiveness."[31-418]

Officers can develop these traits in part by serving in peacetime billets that challenge them and require them to plan for combat. They should also participate as frequently as possible in graded exercises conducted under conditions approximating actual combat. While the officer cannot expect to encounter identical situations in combat, he will be better prepared to develop responses to analogous situations by taking part in these training exercises.

Training in actual decision making, however, is the most valuable kind of training in this area. Being timed on decision making as part of graded exercises enables an officer to judge his ability to make decisions under stress. General Rice suggests that

an officer can prepare himself to make decisions promptly in several ways. He can practice making decisions in his mind, decisions that are not his to make, but someday may be his to make. He can also read, particularly history, for there is much to be learned about life and decision making by reading what people have done in the past. A young officer can also read about current events, to learn from politicians and others. A good military officer is not oriented solely toward military history; he also has a grasp of world events and issues. He can learn from reading, and he can practice making decisions, and then experience and time will play a part in his decision-making ability.

Sometimes, of course, a young officer is forced to make a major decision early in his career. He may be the officer of the deck and suddenly the ship is off course and the rocks are ahead, and he has to make a decision very quickly. Or he is a lieutenant and a tank is moving down the trail and around the curve, and he has to make a decision. These incidents and the decisions made in them can be filed in the memory bank and drawn on as the officer gets older and wiser. Finally, an officer can anticipate what he would do in a variety of situations. An individual need not have a hundred different experiences in order to think about them. If he has given thought to some possibilities, he will be prepared when one of them comes along.

All decision-making training is designed to

support the premise that almost any plan of action, vigorously pursued, is better than no action at all. It is human nature to hesitate in an unfamiliar situation, but training should counteract this tendency. As Admiral Ramage points out, "most cases of failure are due to an individual's failure to make decisions promptly, or making a poor decision. You've got to be positive in your action; if you falter or hesitate, then the case is lost." Admiral Long notes that

> most complex decisions involve many factors. If it is a particularly complex decision, the officer will find that many of the critical factors are judgmental in nature. He may also find that he can collect facts and information forever and never arrive at a decision. Therefore, he collects the facts and the information and the judgments of other people up to a certain point, but then, at that point, he must make a decision or recommend a decision.
>
> In an operational situation—when the officer is flying an aircraft or driving a ship—the time available for decision making is sometimes just a matter of a second or two, and in those situations the decision he makes is based on his training and on his past experience and knowledge.
>
> You will find as you go through your life, as I have found, that some decisions or some judgments that have been made are poor. I would suggest that if you give it your best shot and you make a poor decision, particularly when you're in a position of command, you cannot dwell forever on those poor decisions. You make the decision and go on, and hopefully you will learn, if it is a poor decision, to make the right one the next time.

MAKING TIMELY DECISIONS

General Barrow believes that,
> while deliberation is called for in some cases, oftentimes quick decisions are best.

If you feel strongly about something, for God's sake don't study it to death. Where does your gut feeling come from? It comes out of your background, experience, knowledge—all of these things that you have been developing over the years. By the time you get to be, say, Commandant of the Marine Corps, or Commanding General of a Marine aircraft wing or division, you are very capable, in terms of knowledge, experience, and all of the other things, to say, from time to time, "We're going to do this," and it comes right out of your brain with a minimum of gyrations, as opposed to saying, "Well, you know, maybe we ought to take a look at, . . ." and you're looking at it six months later. Now there are some things we need to do that to, but I made a number of "gut decisions" while I was the Commandant. The maritime prepositioning ship concept was one. The Navy had been so great in building these roll-on and roll-off container ships to put Marine supplies and equipment out there for Marine amphibious brigades up to sixteen thousand men, and it made a proposition, and we did one that went to Diego Garcia in an early up-front exercise until we got the others really built.

Well, when that idea was first broached by the Secretary of Defense, we didn't have time to study it and I didn't feel I needed to. General Kelley, incidentally, was head of programs down in Headquarters, Marine Corps, and he was on board with the idea, though I felt that there were other people who would have resisted it in the Marine Corps, and while we probably didn't have the time to study it, even if we did have the time, it would not be the wise thing to do because it would get bogged down in disagreement with those who said, "This is going to destroy the amphibious part of the Marine Corps by putting out these mass MPS" and a thousand and one arguments.

So how did I get to be Commandant of the Marine Corps? I got the authority and the responsibility because someone thought I had the smarts and the capabilities to discharge those responsibilities, including making quick decisions based on broad experience, knowledge, etc. Otherwise, they can hire anyone to go up there, and every time a problem emerges say, "All right, I will convey that to the staff and ask them to give me a study, and based on that study I will then give you the answer that they gave me." So, back to the maritime prepositioning ship, we went to a JCS meeting where the Army and the Marine Corps were both vying for this, and I made a somewhat passionate recommendation that it be the Marine Corps, and the Air Force and the Navy agreed with me, and that's why the Marine Corps is involved. If I had been Mr. Mamby Pamby and agonized and said, "You know a lot of my generals are not going to like this," the Army would have had it, and then the Army would have been significantly involved in this maritime mission. So it's going to be done anyway. Who can do it better? We can, because it is in a rough way akin to amphibious operations in that you move from these shores to another shore.

Orders, of course, must also be timely, but they must be clear and distinct, and they must express the will of the leader, as well. It is essential that confusion resulting from the stress of battle not be increased by vague, delayed, or ambiguous instructions. A commanding officer should word orders meticulously so that the possibility of confusion is reduced to the absolute minimum. Orders should be as brief as possible and should define the mission. An important

consideration is that, whenever possible, orders should be issued in time to permit subordinates to make necessary arrangements before executing them. Simplicity, however, is still the key, as time constraints often may not allow for elaborate arrangements and coordination.

MCPON Sanders: *I strongly endorse the concept that the leader must make decisions promptly when responsible for action. Any time you delay a decision, especially in today's Navy, your delaying action will compress things at the end of the time availability for decision making to the point where life will become very difficult.*

57. Decision Making: Following Through

In most organizations, decisions are time sensitive, and this is particularly true in the military services. A delay in carrying out an order, or implementing it too soon, can have disastrous effects on personnel, equipment, or an entire operation. Admiral Burke suggests that "quick, decisive action is called for in many circumstances. I think Grenada was a good example of something that was done fast, done well, and people accepted it." Failure is a damper on initiative. While there are a few exceptions, most operations are carried out by several units. Thus, the leader of one unit must not start an action ahead of schedule, because other units may not be in position or be ready to provide the necessary support. Another reason for not starting the battle early is that those planning the operation may have taken into account specific conditions that would be true at a particular point in time, and not earlier or later than that time.

The major concern here is that the officer understand the importance of following through on decisions precisely on schedule. This is true for all actions required in the Naval Service, not just those associated with combat operations. As noted, almost all operations the officer will be involved in require the cooperation of several groups. Even the so-called "independent operations" of special units require both planning and action by other entities, and thus even the so-called "independent unit" must precisely carry out its mission. Since no unit truly operates independently of all others, the performance of every unit will be monitored to see that it is carrying out its particular functions properly, so that other parts of the master plan can continue as scheduled. When a unit falls behind, its slippage usually makes it necessary to adjust the schedules of many other groups who depended on the information or the action that was scheduled to be conveyed or completed at a particular time. The slippage frequently affects even those in a tertiary position, those who were waiting for the first unit's action to start a second unit's action, which in turn determined when they could become involved.

Headquarters is responsible not only for monitoring the action of all subordinate units, but also for seeing that plans are changed across the board if one of the units falls behind. Of course, if a unit overcomes resistance faster than expected or completes its administrative assignment much sooner than expected, then the higher headquarters will, if possible and advisable, adjust the schedules of other groups to take advantage of the good fortune. For example, if, while several units are landing on a wide front, one unit gets far ahead of those on either side, thus possibly presenting an opportunity for the enemy to come in behind it and attack a lateral unit, headquarters must adjust the landing pace of the lagging units. This is an example of the overall coordination that is required in the military, and it further illustrates the necessity of units not only moving on time, but also not moving too fast without receiving coordinating direction from higher headquarters. General Barrow discussed decision making in combat:

That's what they pay you for, to make

decisions, and where the payoff really occurs is in combat. You don't make these quick decisions in a way that's like the flip of a coin. There's going to be risk involved. You didn't call it right this time so a bunch of people got killed. You make decisions based on your experience, and even on something that might be called intuition and instinct. There's a feeling that takes over and says, "This is what we should do," and that comes out of knowledge and confidence—confidence in yourself, confidence in those you are asking to do it—and those intangible things you can't put your finger on. One of my favorite leadership characteristics—it ought to be almost a principle of war—is audacity. Do the unexpected, the unusual, move quicker than the enemy or anyone else thought you could, and that may be the difference between winning and losing, saving lots of lives or losing lots of lives.

So the whole business of decision making is not a laborious project. Now I can be patient and methodical as the best of them if the subject is not of great importance or it is of importance but the need to come to a decision quickly is not important. So we'll study it, we've got someone at Headquarters, Marine Corps, who probably has been studying it almost to death. Maybe these decisions need this treatment because the subject warrants it, and maybe the decisions have been put in that category because no one really wants to see a decision made, either because it's of no consequence or because the answer is likely to be one that no one wants to have.

In the case of administrative actions, an excessive concern about completing assignments early is unnecessary, *provided* that every effort has been made to produce a quality product. When an officer sees that work has been completed far sooner than expected, his first concern should be whether all required aspects of the work have been completed; only when quality of product has been assured can the officer relax. At that point the officer can consider one of two alternatives, or a combination of both. The officer should first look at his overall schedule and determine whether other activities can be started sooner or given greater emphasis to ensure their timely completion, for rarely are all aspects of an operation completed on time, and, while some may be finished ahead of time, others may require extra effort to be completed on schedule. The importance of cross-training within a unit, so that members may help each other when someone falls behind, is illustrated in this alternative.

As a second alternative, the leader may consider giving extra time off as a reward for outstanding work on the part of all hands. This is generally a good practice when all operations of the group are ahead of schedule. The officer should exercise caution in awarding such time off, because often "pride goeth before a fall"—practically speaking, when a unit has built up momentum, care should be taken not to let the momentum die. In combat operations, when a unit has the advantage, it does not let up, it presses the advantage. However, in the case of peacetime operations, building the morale of personnel is very important (so that there are people in the organization when they are needed to fight wars), and additional liberty can and should be considered so that personnel understand that their work is appreciated and recognized. Additional liberty for timely completion of tasks must be awarded judiciously, because high performance is what the Naval Service expects of its people, and because indiscriminate awarding of liberty for ahead-of-schedule completion may affect the quality of work, as liberty becomes the objective of finishing work, and quality of performance takes a back seat to speed.

When the leader is advised of the decision for action by senior units, he should check, before taking action, whether what is being required is the same as what was planned. Normally, higher headquarters will direct an action based on inputs from subordinate units; however, since inputs from many subordinate units go into the final decision, it is possible that some approaches proposed by the subordinate units may be changed to provide for the best overall plan. Often such changes are conveyed to affected units during the planning phase; nevertheless, when a directive is received, the leader should recheck the unit's plan to see that current plans are in conformance with previous plans and that changes in plans have been made where appropriate. Once the plan of operation has been confirmed (or modified where necessary), the leader must monitor his unit's actions and the overall progress of the operation to ensure that everything remains on track and that corrective action is taken if necessary.

It is not enough for the leader to have been involved in planning, organizing, and directing actions, to have monitored progress and exercised control to keep the operation running in accordance with plan, and to have provided for changes as required by changing circumstances. When the leader finally decides which alternative is most favorable, it is his responsibility to implement and monitor its results, for it is this decision that he is held personally accountable for.[31-422] Officers are educated and trained to provide leadership that is capable of reacting quickly to changes. In the Naval Service—whose business is to defend the country and prevail in combat—it is impossible to plan for every eventuality and action by an enemy. It has even been suggested that a peacetime operation that operates perfectly does not necessarily prepare personnel for what will be required of them when the shooting starts. Therefore, the ability of an officer to react to the unexpected cannot be overrated. Thus, in peacetime, officers should see difficulties not only as matters to overcome, but also as training opportunities for all hands, to ready them for combat operations, both defensive and offensive. A pessimist, remember, is an individual who sees the difficulty in every opportunity, while an optimist is an individual who sees the opportunity in every difficulty. Admiral Larson believes that

> following up on orders should be done with sensitivity. First of all, the leader has a responsibility to ensure that the orders are properly understood, and then that the work is being properly done. He also needs to have some confidence that we're meeting schedule as far as timeliness, as far as cost, and as far as utilization of personnel. So how do you follow-up on all of that without making the troops think that you don't trust them or you're spying on them or you're peering over their shoulder or you're trying to micro-manage their affairs. I think the best way to do that is through spot-checks. First of all, you should have a sincere interest in what they're doing, in the equipment, in maintenance, and in learning. If you go around and talk to people on the job, ask some questions, tell them you want to learn, you want to understand the procedure they're going through, not only will you become more knowledgeable about the ship, but you'll soon find out whether the troops have understood your orders, whether they're carrying them out properly, and whether they're achieving your goals. And then, when you interface with the senior petty officers, you can do the same type of spot-check on a higher plane, looking more at schedules, more at costs, more at utilization of personnel. If you're the type of person who has that frequent interface with your troops and you're visible around the ship and you're talking to them, it won't appear as if you're spying on them. But you do have a responsibility to satisfy yourself in your

own mind that those things are being done properly. There may be a rare occasion—and I can't think of any that I've run into in my career—but there may be a rare occasion when someone decides that perhaps he doesn't want to follow your directions as given because he knows a better way to do it. This will also help you detect that, and if you do, that has to be put to bed very quickly. They have to understand who's the boss and how things are going to be done. It can be done in a very pleasant way, and you can get to know your troops better and educate yourself as you do it.

In the Naval Service, people are directly responsible for others' lives, for even in peacetime the deck of the carrier moves up and down and requires expertise on the part of the pilot, especially for night carrier landings; submarines on patrol require the same excellent handling whether this country is at war or not; and operations of other service activities require expertise on the part of service personnel. Those in the service are involved either in mission accomplishment during war or in preparing themselves to prevail if war comes. In athletic contests, it is the pregame preparation by players that leads to success, and the same is true of operations in the Naval Service: they must always be conducted as if they were battle related, so that when action comes, naval personnel are ready. Naval personnel must be prepared at all times, even if that means a lifetime of waiting, which is something all military people should hope for.

MCPON Sanders: *The leader must follow through on decisions promptly and precisely. Where the job had sufficient amount of time to get it done before, a delay will cut the period of performance and impact on your ability not only to do the first job, but also to get subsequent jobs done. You have to do a job as soon as possible, even if there isn't another job on the horizon, for we are in a business where things change very quickly and we must always be ready for the next job and not be slowed down because we haven't finished previously assigned work.*

58. Planning for the Unexpected

A senior ship or command CO and a junior officer managing his first division or platoon will both follow the same process when preparing for unexpected problems. The steps in the process are discussed in this section.

ESTABLISH A LONG-RANGE PLAN

Before an unexpected problem arises, the officer should establish a long-range plan that is consistent with the needs of higher authority, will be complementary to requirements of support units, and will meet the operational goals of the officer's own unit. This plan must be comprehensive, detailed, and anticipatory of problems that might arise. It should be understandable to all who depend on it for guidance and, in most cases, should be discussed with others who are involved before being formally released. While the officer will want to make it his plan, since he is responsible for its operation and success, he must take the time to determine the long-range plans of his seniors so that his plan will mesh with theirs in terms of long-range outcomes.

While the plan must be based on known requirements, it is wise to receive inputs from others whose experience and thinking may lead to areas of consideration and planning that might not otherwise have been thought of. Planning for the unknown can be most successful for the officer who has spent time considering and reviewing past activities and battles. This additional effort will make it clear to him that most problems have happened before, and past solutions may be partially applicable to new situations that might arise.

FOLLOW A SHORT-RANGE PLAN

Of immediate interest to the officer and his subordinates, as well as to parallel operational units, will be the short-range plans that are devised for the day-to-day operation. It is, of course, important for the short-range plan to be built on the requirements of the long-range plan and constructed in such a way that many modifications can be made in it without affecting the long-range plan. Since the short-range plan is designed to meet immediate requirements, it follows that those within the organization, and those in other organizations, as well, must be aware of the goals of both long-range and short-range plans. This will ensure that events impacting important areas are brought to the officer's attention, permitting modification of the short-range plan without requiring changes in the long-range plan. This also makes it unnecessary for headquarters and adjacent units to change all of their short- and long-range plans.

Anticipating changes in short-range plans and projecting possible courses of action and training for them will help all hands get used to the idea that change is the only sure thing in life, and thus adjust to change with a minimum of lethargy and disagreement. Personnel who are prepared in their thinking to be dynamic and who can shift when necessary will be far better able to devise countermeasures for problems than those who have been allowed to think that they will always do it as they have in the past and to stipulate that if it was not invented here, they don't want to hear about it. Admiral Burke suggests that

the officer who has spent time visualizing possible future situations will be prepared for those situations. But in combat, events rarely unfold as the officer has imagined they would. For this reason, an officer must be able to make immediate decisions as a situation develops and then make changes.

In the Battle of Augusta Bay, we knew we were going to have to fight that night, and I went down to refuel and I came up at a very high speed to get in position before dark, before the action started. I persuaded Admiral Marshall to let me attack as soon as we sighted the enemy. That was the first time that had been done in that war. So I wanted to be there, and I wanted to slow down a little bit because we were pushing through the formations of other ships just to get there, but we finally made it all right. Well, I was up on the port bow of the cruiser line when we got a radar contact. We knew that the Japanese were planning on driving us away from Augusta Bay and destroying our amphibious force and that it was our job to stop it. Well I got there, and as soon as I got the bearing, I headed off and said, "I'm on my way toward the enemy."

On the way into the attack I could see that there were three columns, three groups somehow, and I had intended attacking on their port side. Well, it looked partway as if I wasn't going to be able to get over there, and I had a choice then of going down between two columns, which is not a good thing to do, or maybe getting ahead and then turning. I decided I might go down between the two columns, but if I still tried to ease over to the right a little bit, I could make it. What happened was that before we got to the position where I had to make that decision, the enemy turned to starboard and I had fired torpedos just after the enemy had turned and without knowing that they had turned, so our torpedos missed. We had failed in a torpedo attack, failed in making a killing. It was an absolute disaster.

Of course after I made the torpedo attack I turned away, according to doc-

trine, and headed away. What I didn't do was recognize how fast you could open on ships when you're making high speed, and suddenly I found out. Maybe after five minutes, I found out I was a long ways from the bow and I had to go back. It's a horrible thing to think "I just wasted a half-hour by misusing five minutes." We went back and finished the battle, they were routed, but we had not done well.

Using forethought, the officer can assure that changes in short-term plans assist in the accomplishment of long-range plans. Even though short-range plans have been carefully worked out and are the basis of knowledge for his unit's activity in the minds of higher commands, the officer should continually review what he has proposed and is doing, so that if a change that will improve everyone's chances of success is required, this change is forwarded and can be discussed. The contemplation of change before it is necessary provides for a far more orderly change than a change that takes place in a time of crisis.

BE FLEXIBLE AND ENCOURAGE SUBORDINATES TO BE FLEXIBLE

It is apparent from the foregoing that flexibility in thinking, planning, and action is one key to the ultimate success of a military operation. Everyone in the Naval Service must be prepared for an instant transition from peace to war, and many training activities require preciseness regardless of whether the nation is at war or not. It does not make much difference to the pilot landing on a carrier far out at sea whether he is successfully returning from an operational or a training bombing mission—the deck is moving in both cases.

Only that which already exists can be changed, so preparing detailed and comprehensive plans is important. If requirements are stated in the plan in ten words and the mission changes, all ten words will probably have to change. However, if every aspect of the operation is neatly spelled out to the understanding of all hands, then individual changes that only affect a part of the organization can be made without disrupting the training or thinking of everyone. Admiral Burke:

> Training, teaching people how to do something, is always good, and it ought to include training on mind management. The largest error that is in military operations is the delay in making the decision. When a leader is confronted with a situation, he should handle it and be confident in his ability.
>
> One way an individual can prepare himself is to think of what he would do under various circumstances by daydreaming a little. When he is trying to go to sleep, particularly in a war situation, he should ask himself what he is going to do tomorrow, what might come up. The leader who has asked himself what situations might confront him tomorrow and how he might respond will be at least partially prepared for most situations that arise.

Admiral Burke recalled an exercise that prepared new officers mentally for various situations that arise on board ship.

> Before we took the deck of a ship when I was a kid, and I guess it's still true now, particularly for junior officers, we went through a certain routine: man overboard starboard side, what do you do? He knows where the wind is coming from, he knows the speed the ship is making, and then he sights a ship broad on the starboard bow, it has a green light. We went through normal situations of collision sightings, man overboard, normal situations that might confront an officer when he first takes over, and he was always asked those questions. Whether it did much good or not, it did make him think about what he had to know when he had to take over the deck. He knew where the wind was from and the speed you were making and where the other ships were.

Leadership is partly being able to judge other people. A leader needs to be able to predict what the situation is going to be sometime in the future, and the situation is usually caused by a combination of what his own people are going to do, what the people he is associated with on his side are going to do, and what people opposing his side are going to do. The individual who has good judgment concerning people, therefore, is usually better prepared than someone who just waits until something happens and then tries to cope with it. Seldom can people make a proper judgment without some study, and it is always better to study before a situation occurs.

In any team operation, whether it be a sport or a military evolution, the concept is to go with a plan that can be quickly modified as needed, not to have a plan that is affected by every change in the wind. The primary objective is to be ready for a short-notice change that may take place. This means that all hands must understand mission objectives and have advanced links of communication established so that if and when a change is needed, it can be not only planned but also communicated quickly to those having need of the information. When making a change it is better to communicate that change to too many than to too few, assuming the change is not also communicated to a potential or real enemy.

FOLLOW-UP

Another part of preparing for unexpected changes is follow-up. The CO and all officers, as well as leading petty officers or staff noncommissioned officers, need to review plans, goals, and objectives to ensure that they are being met. More important than being ready to change plans is being sure that the existing plan is being followed in the manner intended. If the plan is completed in some manner other than the addressees were led to expect, be sure to let them know of the difference in approach, for it may have some effect on their operation. This is especially important with respect to supporting higher units. This will allow them to adjust their own plans if necessary. By doing so, they may be able to provide additional support to ensure that operations in the future will not have to be changed when a problem arises, or to make it easier for changes to be made. In the long run, this may preserve mission accomplishment for all units.

The officer must not lose sight of the long-range objectives while coping with the short-term changes that occur. An officer cannot be considered successful if the unit or ship has not been equally successful. All officers are part of a larger organization, and as with the weakest link in the chain, no officer will be truly successful if one of the supporting units in the operation is in trouble or fails. It is natural for an officer to want to succeed and get ahead and not tell others about his problems; however, the officer must remember that everyone in the Naval Service is important, every action is important, and if and when he is having problems, he should go to his senior and ask for help. He will usually find that the senior's greater experience will provide solutions to problems that are particularly vexing to the junior officer.

ENCOURAGE STABILITY AND PREDICTABILITY

Another phase of preparing for unforeseen problems has to do with the need for stability, which is vital for success. As in any team effort, mutual dependability is essential (but flexibility is also necessary, because of emergency changes that may be required). When all hands follow a somewhat predictable approach to their jobs, others will know what to expect and be able to plan and depend on that stability. (Nothing said herein is intended to suggest that the Naval Service will always do things a particular way just because they have always been done that way. But, where possible, an officer should act in a predictable way, though being

unpredictable to confuse an enemy is also proper if it doesn't hurt other forces you are working with.)

It is extremely important for the leader not to change for the sake of changing. As the old mariner's expression goes, "It is not proper to change the set of the sails within 30 minutes of taking the helm." The point of this axiom is that careful thought should be given to making a change. The effect it will have on everyone, including those external to an individual's organization, is an important consideration. Sometimes, and this is a matter of command or leadership judgment, it is best to go with an existing plan on which everyone has been briefed and is prepared to act on, a plan that requires only execution, than to go to a new plan that requires a major change in the training of all concerned. This is not an easy decision, but that is what being in command is all about. Previous experience and knowledge will enable the officer to make the right decision at the right time, if he is prepared. For an officer, that means attention to detail and a great deal of personal and professional preparation. Much can be learned from history, in this case, from studying the Roman Republic and Hannibal, who seems to have created a key factor in solving the problem of unexpected situations. He endeavored to initiate them, rather than react to them. In other words, Hannibal studied the enemy to find their strengths and weaknesses and proceeded to make tactical innovations to compensate for them. The Battle of Cannae is a prime example of this.[62-110]

BE ENTHUSIASTIC AND SOLICIT COMMENTARY

The officer must be aggressive in following the plan. He should give it his all, and require and encourage all subordinates by his own example. He should show enthusiasm for the plan by his actions and encourage leading petty officers, staff noncommissioned officers, and junior officers to ask questions so that he can better prepare them for the questions of their subordinates. It is true that the final decision as to what to do or change will be his, but no one person has a lock on knowledge. By encouraging subordinates to speak up, the officer will find that there are times when they will assist him and his staff in achieving mission accomplishment. Admiral Larson suggests that

> in your training, in preparation for missions assigned, in equipment maintenance and operation, you should always ask yourself these questions: What could go wrong here? What would be the worst thing that could happen here? And if that occurs, what am I going to do about it? What are my contingencies? Who do I want to consult if I have a problem in this area? On board ship, you develop confidence by knowing who the people are on that ship who are experts in each area, who have the background to help. I used to have meetings in the wardroom when things would go wrong with equipment, or even contingency planning for missions, where I would bring in certain officers and senior petty officers, and we would do a seminar about a particular problem, and I would make the final decision after getting input from a variety of people. So you need to know who you would call in. You need to know who in higher authority you would consult. It's important for you to know how your boss thinks in the chain of command, so that if something goes wrong you can anticipate what his reaction might be, and so that you can operate in a way or anticipate so that you can minimize any effects on the mission assigned.
>
> But I think the very important thing in all your training and preparation is to think through contingencies. During training, have your crew think through contingencies, because when the time comes you may have only seconds to act, and in those seconds you need to make well-founded decisions, and if you've thought

them through in advance, then chances are you're going to be ready, you're going to be prepared, and you'll do the right thing. This also develops a lot of confidence in the crew. If they see you thinking these things through, then they will know that here's a commanding officer (or here's a division officer or here's a department head) who really has his act together, because he thinks things out in advance, and I've got confidence that, if something goes wrong, he'll be there to back us up and he will be part of the solution rather than part of the problem.

CONTROL THE SYSTEM

A well-known expression says "The officer must manage the system and not let the system manage the officer." In effect, this means that planning and follow-up must always be under the control of the officer. During flight planning, additional fuel allowances are made for possible weather problems. Flying 1,000 miles with only enough fuel to get there in perfect weather is asking for trouble. The pilot who has not planned properly will find that the system (the fuel tank) is managing him, and all his knowledge and experience will be to no avail because he will not be in control.

At all times the leader must be in charge, whether of personnel or equipment. In the latter case the need for repairs must be anticipated, and in the case of personnel the leader must constantly be in touch with the pulse of the operation so that when instability starts to set in, he can take action before a major problem develops. The officer who does not know subordinates as individuals or how they interact as a group will be managed by the personnel subsystem rather than be in control of it. Not all losses of personnel control result in mutiny, but when control is lost, individual members of the team are no longer thinking of the best interests of the team, they are thinking of their own best interests. Therefore, the ticket is not to lose control in the first place. Problems arising in a well-developed plan can be more efficiently taken care of and, most importantly, the system (the crew) will be looking after the officer as he is looking after them.

SUMMARY

The officer should not forget that plans are subject to change; otherwise, change will plan for him. If there is no plan and something comes up that was not expected during the officer's last conversation with his staff or subordinates, no one will know what to do, and though they will try to do something, there will be no assurance that what they do will mesh properly with what adjacent, subordinate, and higher units are doing. The leader must take appropriate steps to solve unexpected problems that arise, including revising original plans as necessary and as approved by higher authority. During the attack of 7 December 1941 on Pearl Harbor, Lieutenant Commander Francis J. Thomas, as the Command Duty Officer of the USS *Nevada*, got the battleship underway while the Japanese attack began. Under fire, the *Nevada* got underway and began steaming toward open water. Misfortune struck the *Nevada* when it was hit by bombs and a Japanese torpedo. With this change in circumstances—the ship was now in jeopardy of sinking—Thomas reacted quickly to steer the ship out of the channel and thus avoided blocking the entrance to Pearl Harbor.[81-134,148] This example is indicative of the challenges that a military leader must be prepared to meet during his career. It is an excellent lesson, in that Thomas's plans changed more than once during the course of the event. He reacted correctly at first by getting underway—not all battleships were able to do so. Then, when his original plans had been carried out, more complications arose, forcing Thomas to revise his plan again and purposefully ground the ship. Thus, it becomes clear that a leader's environment is always changing, and he must be able to adapt to the changes.

59. Teamwork in Action: Helping Others to Meet Deadlines

Officers clearly have a duty to provide assistance when important deadlines are in jeopardy. Like many leadership roles and responsibilities, helping out in an emergency is an instinctual response of good officers. Admiral Fran McKee remarks:

I think if two organizations are involved in accomplishing the same mission, you should assist the people in the other organization to the greatest extent possible, as long as it does not prove detrimental to you doing your own job (unless your senior acknowledges the risk and still asks you to pitch in). They may have a problem and they call on you to assist them, and you're balancing two balls instead of one. It surprises us, sometimes, what we can accomplish when we stretch ourselves a little bit, and that happens a lot.

Officers help others to meet deadlines primarily for four reasons. First, providing assistance in such circumstances exemplifies teamwork. When one member of an organization is facing a difficult deadline, there is usually a critical period during which other individuals make a decision about their involvement. Will they follow the inclination to pitch in and get the job done? Or will they yield to another side of human nature and avoid the extra work? The answer is often decided through leadership. If officers take the initiative, "roll up their sleeves," and lend a hand, other individuals will usually follow their example.

When a task is completed on schedule, those involved in meeting the deadline have a sense of accomplishment. Few efforts are as rewarding as being part of a team that works hard together to meet a challenge. This is a primary source of esprit de corps. As an added benefit, individuals will find that this type of assistance is frequently reciprocated. By helping other members of the team, individuals are much more likely to be helped when they face a similar situation.

Second, an officer's first priority is always to accomplish the assigned task or to further the organization's mission. There is a natural (and healthy) tendency to question why a project has fallen behind schedule or is under such a stringent deadline, but this issue should be set aside until the task has been completed. There will be time later to examine the administrative or organizational problems that created the situation. Time-consuming discussions and divisive finger-pointing will only further delay the effort. The first responsibility is to complete the project.

The officer can play an important role here by establishing priorities and assuring others that organizational issues will be considered at a more appropriate time. By lending assistance to meet the deadline, the officer demonstrates by his actions where the immediate emphasis should be placed.

Third, failure to render assistance could have adverse consequences. More than likely, without the officer's assistance, the appointed deadline will not be met and the project will suffer. In addition, there likely will be a spillover effect into other projects. Delays and schedule problems have a cumulative effect, and failure to meet one deadline can cause a chain of problems as schedules for succeeding tasks slip further and further back.

Officers recognize that delays reflect poorly on the entire organization. If one unit misses a deadline, other units may be hindered in their work. If delays become endemic, they can hurt an organization's reputation and, consequently, its morale.

Fourth, assisting others when necessary is consistent with the officer's overall leadership role and high standards of responsibility. It sets a worthy example for subordinates, who will be sure to notice the officer's willingness to jump into the breach when doing so is in the best interests of the organization. Also, since deadlines are normally set by higher officials, the officer's participation demonstrates to others a

respect for authority and an acceptance of responsibility.

Meeting deadlines—no matter how routine the task—establishes a pattern of responsiveness and professionalism that will naturally carry over into more critical situations, including battle. General Rice remarks that

naval officers cannot work in a vacuum, and for this reason if for no other, teamwork is essential. There are no successful loners in the Naval Service. For example, the company commander cannot perform alone; he has someone on his left, someone on his right, and someone behind him. Anyone who tries to go it alone and work in a vacuum is bound to be a loser.

Naval officers should not consider whether they look better than someone else because they made a deadline; they should consider the success of the unit and the organization, and they should share and work together. Paramount to being a good officer and a good leader is willingness to share credit, knowledge, experience, and anything else that is needed by seniors, subordinates, and officers of the same rank. An officer who makes his deadline but is not concerned if someone else does not make his does not have the attitude that most benefits the Naval Service.

By doing their best to see that deadlines are met, officers demonstrate their awareness of the larger picture rather than a preoccupation with carefully drawn lines of responsibility. Admiral Long emphasized that

officers should encourage all personnel to think of the ship as their "own" and should make sure they understand that their contribution to it is significant. When I was a younger officer, a lieutenant, I was assigned to be the executive officer of a submarine, and this submarine had a history for the year before I reported aboard of being fouled up. In the course of the year they had gone through three skippers, two executive officers, it had had a collision, they had a very embarrassing situation where a large load of illegal whiskey was found aboard, the morale was down around their shoetops—it was a sick situation. I reported aboard as the new executive officer, and the new skipper was a very dynamic, hard-charging officer, and I soon found myself in a position of finding not only the crew unhappy but the wardroom unhappy. They worked very long hours, and it became obvious to me that it was a case of various factions aboard the submarine and they were, as I say, working hard, and in general doing their job, but it was not an outstanding ship. One of the messages that I tried to get across and eventually did get across was a very simple fact, and that was that that ship did not belong solely to the commanding officer, it did not belong solely to the officers in the wardroom, but the ship was really the responsibility of every man aboard, and if the ship was not run properly then the first question a person who was a member of that crew should have asked was, "What am I doing to make this ship better?" And eventually, over a period of a couple of months and a few ship's parties and beer ballgames and the enforcing of high standards and a genuine reflection of concern for the people on there, all hands turned around, including the wardroom, the commanding officer, the chiefs, and the rest of the crew, so that there was a very high esprit de corps. Obviously, just the desire to make a ship the top ship in the squadron, that is not the only solution. Proper material condition, support, repair parts, maintenance, professional standards—all of those things factor in, but I can assure you you'll never have a

good ship or squadron if the ship's company or crew do not feel that they're on a good team.

MCPON Sanders: *During my tour as Master Chief Petty Officer of the Navy, I visited many ships, and any time I walked into a chief's mess I could basically tell how that ship was running just by seeing how the chiefs interacted with each other. If we had a group of people who were actively talking together and helping each other, I could tell that the ship was going to be basically a happy ship, with the job getting done, and morale high; invariably it worked out in the inspection throughout the ship that everything was being done right. I want to emphasize that it seems to be true that any time we have a ship that's getting the job done, it's because the people are working together and not just for themselves to meet their own ends.*

60. Providing Feedback

If an officer does not provide adequate feedback information to his seniors, his peers, and his subordinates, they will compensate by filling in with information obtained from someone else, their own imagination, or rumors. Clearly it is preferable to have those concerned obtain information from the officer who is responsible rather than from another source.

A good deal of judgment is required to determine how often and how extensive to make feedback. In general, a junior needs to provide his senior with only enough feedback to make him confident that the junior is in charge and that things are on track. Peers need to receive enough to be confident that their areas of responsibility are not being interfered with. The leader's subordinates need to know whether things are going well or poorly, and the leader should give them a course correction promptly when one is needed.

It is very easy to overdo feedback to a senior.

He is more interested in having the junior solve problems and get things done than he is in solving the junior's problems for him. Too much feedback can easily indicate to a senior that the junior is unsure of himself or that the junior needs more personal direction from him than the junior actually does. Admiral Holloway suggests:

> The first rule in reporting to a senior is to tell him everything he asked to be told. Some seniors are explicit and tell the officer just what they want to know. Other seniors are not, and in that case it is incumbent on the officer or the commander to put himself in the senior's position and decide what he needs to know and what he wants to know.
>
> An officer should never give a senior more information than he thinks the senior needs, because doing so wastes his time and the officer's time. The officer must make a judgment concerning what his senior needs to know to properly do his job.
>
> In addition, the officer should evaluate his senior. Is he the kind of person who wants to know all the details? If so, give him a little bit more detail. Or is he the sort who is going to let the officer carry the ball on his own? Then the officer should not fill him in on all the details, because he does not want to be bothered with them.

Providing too much feedback to peers will brand an officer as a "worrywart" or a "pain in the tail." Providing too much feedback to subordinates can make a leader appear not to know what he is doing. On the subject of providing subordinates with feedback on overall operations, Admiral Hunt suggests that

> this must depend upon the sensitivity of the mission, but the general rule should be: Brief as many people as possible. I am sure it is right—as Montgomery among others showed—to brief the fullest information to the lowest feasible level. It is very common in ships—and I applaud this—for the captain to tell the ship's company practically everything.
>
> It is no good, as we've seen to our cost, trying to conceal from people the secrets of an important mission, because it's only when they know how important and how sensitive the mission is that they will put in all the effort necessary to make sure it's successful. If they don't think it's that important, the chances are you will have failures in personal equipment which you otherwise wouldn't have to have. It is also, I think, important for morale that you should have the contact with everyone and that they should know that when there is danger or things of great interest or importance to them, or family problems, that when those sorts of things are relevant, you will talk to them about it. So my view is for a mission, brief down as far as you possibly can, taking into account only the most vital security that you need.

An officer's style of communication through feedback depends on his personal style, which is based on self-confidence. "Remember that with every report you write to your senior, colleague, or subordinate, you demonstrate the way you think, your vocabulary, and the way that you organize your ideas. The memo that goes out with your name is as revealing as the clothes you wear or the quality of your handwriting."[77-9] A prerequisite to effective leadership is self-confidence, and with self-confidence comes the ability to gauge just how much feedback is effective and appropriate. Generally, however, the more clear-cut and straightforward an officer's plans and directions at the outset of an effort requiring his leadership, the less feedback he needs to issue along the way to provide assurances to others. General Wilson comments:

I think the commander should explain to his subordinate commanders what he expects, but when the commander goes out and talks to the troops, he should talk in generalities. Certainly he should not tell every subordinate commander to the lowest subordinate commander the details as to what he expects, because this does not leave leeway for the intermediate subordinates.

The more people he gives specifics to, the more people will try to interpret what he says. The English language is subject to misinterpretation, and if he is too specific, there will be more opportunity for misunderstanding. He can be as specific as he likes to his immediate subordinates, but he should keep his plan and his policy broad when he talks to other troops, because otherwise he may undermine what his commanders are saying to the troops.

MCPON Sanders: *You must keep both seniors and subordinates informed about what is going on. Remember that your supervisors/seniors not only are concerned with your job, but also have many other projects on which they have to report to their boss, so it's important to keep the chain of command up to date on what is happening. As for your subordinates, you don't have to give them a running commentary on what is going on, but if you will keep in mind that everyone is interested in what affects their unit, you will give them as much information as possible and have a much better work crew.*

61. Honesty in Communications

KEEPING SENIORS INFORMED

The 9 June 1985 edition of the *New York Times* contained a short item that illustrates how important it is for a naval officer to present complete information, whether or not that information is favorable to the situation, to others, and to himself. A Reuters wire story said:

Soviet Air Bungle Almost Costs a Ship

A Soviet Air Force pilot on a bombing test almost sank the ship monitoring his performance because of an air traffic control error, the Soviet aviation journal *Aviatsiya i Kosmonavtika* said today.

Ground control officers were to blame in the case, the journal said, because they failed to tell the pilot he had gone off course, and he released his bombs in the test sector where the monitoring vessel was patrolling.

The article criticized the overall standard of military air traffic controllers, saying they often gave imprecise instructions and failed to tell pilots about navigation errors.

The journal said the worst instances occurred when a high-ranking official was at the controls of a plane and ground controllers were afraid to tell him he had made an error because he was their boss.

That certainly is not the way we should do it. We live in an open society in which fear should not be a factor. Our leaders should be willing to hear bad news. If they are not aware of problems, they are not able to function—they cannot solve them. In short, they cannot lead.

A platoon leader who reports that his squads have scouted their sectors and then discovers that one of the squads went out a few hundred meters and then doped off, waiting until it was time to return, and thus did not cover the area, is bound immediately to report the fact to his company commander. That such a report might reflect adversely on the platoon leader's leadership is not germane. Certainly do not fear non-promotion, for, as Admiral McDonald points out, "you can always make it in civilian life." The company commander must be informed that part of his sector was unsearched and therefore may be vulnerable. He can then govern his tactical dispositions accordingly. He will also realize that the platoon leader learned a valuable lesson in human nature. The company commander will no doubt observe closely the platoon leader's subsequent actions with that squad.

Admiral Larson points out that

it's critically important for an officer to have the respect and the trust and the confidence of those who work for him, of those who work with him, and of his seniors. And so, in that environment of openness and honesty, you must report both the good and the bad. Any officer who is seen to be hiding problems to make himself look good will soon lose the respect of his troops, and it'll be extremely difficult, if not impossible, to lead in that way, because they will see that person as self-serving and they will see him more for self than for unit or for ship or for country. So it's important to be open and honest. Now, in doing that, it's also critically important that you do not shift the blame. If something goes wrong on your ship, don't report in detail what your subordinates did wrong or where your subordinates made a mistake, just report what went wrong, accept responsibility yourself, and explain how you're going to fix that. Accept that responsibility and then work with those troops to ensure that they don't make that same mistake twice. When something goes wrong and you identify a problem, also identify a solution. There's nothing more frustrating to a senior person or a person in command than to have a number of subordinates who are always turning up problems but never have an idea about what to do about them, so when you come forward with a problem, come forward with a solution. The best thing you can do if you're a sharp commanding officer or a sharp division officer is say "Here's the problem and I'm already working on the solution and I'll have it fixed at such and such a time."

I think that open and honest appraisal has to be there; without that, your organization is not going to be solidly behind you.

KEEPING SUBORDINATES INFORMED

Likewise, a leader should not be reluctant to share bad news with his subordinates. They look to him with trust and confidence. He should not betray that trust and confidence by withholding unfavorable facts that may affect the lives of those he leads. Some leaders adopt a paternalistic approach; they rationalize that, by shielding subordinates from grim facts, they are protecting them from fright and worry. But that is not an acceptable approach to leadership. Officers who level with their subordinates will find that their subordinates level with them. Once caught in the act of withholding information that should be revealed to the crew or troops, the leader loses his credibility, possibly forever.

Imagine the skipper of a submarine poised at his periscope as a group of Japanese destroyers home in for a depth-charge attack. Does he say, "Rig for depth-charge—but don't worry, it's only a small patrol boat and of no consequence"? Or does he give them the straight scoop: "Rig for depth-charge and prepare for a long siege. There are six big destroyers up there, and I think that they spotted our periscope before we went deep"? If the former, you can bet that after several hours of sitting on the bottom shaking under depth bomb shocks, that crew will never trust that skipper again. They will either question his ability to distinguish six destroyers from one patrol boat or determine that his word is unreliable. In either case, his effectiveness as a leader and skipper of that crew will have been destroyed. On the other hand, the skipper who tells the crew to expect the worst shows he is willing to share with them not only the danger, but also his knowledge of it. Such leaders command happy ships.

In the realm of combat, there are too many variables to provide for anything more than probabilities and an occasional long-shot possi-

321

bility. Commanders may assign subordinates a mission in several ways, but the most effective commanders generally provide subordinates with all the information they need. If the commander advises the subordinate of the expected difficulty and the chances of success, he is providing the subordinate with the facts the latter needs, as well as informing him that the level of difficulty is fully understood but that the mission must be attempted at all costs. A leader can direct his troops in the *what* of a situation and obtain satisfactory results. The leader who shares with them the *why* of a situation can expect outstanding results, even if he is not around to see them. Such an approach inspires respect.

If a subordinate receives orders to carry out a mission that he believes his unit would be unable to accomplish due to the current status of its personnel or equipment or due to any number of fortunes of war, he has a duty to make that belief and the reasons for it known to the senior. Not to do so may endanger the operation. The senior must then reassess the situation and determine the course of action.

ADMITTING MISTAKES

Finally, there is the example of the subordinate leader who has been guilty of an omission. This happens to everyone, inasmuch as human nature is fragile. Overwork, interruptions, and any number of other things can cause oversights. They become more than oversights when they are not remedied promptly and are ignored or, worse, covered up. When a naval officer "blows it"—and every one of them will, sometime in his career—he must let the leader who has the responsibility know what has happened as well as any results he can foresee. The leader should be in a better position to determine what effect the oversight will have on the ship, aircraft, or mission. He will be knowledgeable about what action he should take. And he will respect the naval officer's integrity. Admiral Long concurs, and adds that,

when an officer discovers that he has

made a mistake, by some action or inaction, either operationally or in judgment, the best thing he can do is step forward and tell his boss that he has made a mistake. When he approaches his boss and says, "This is what happened. I've made a mistake. I'm sorry, and I will try not to let it happen again," the officer is reassuring his boss, because the primary interest of a senior is to find out about a problem as soon as possible after it has occurred and to have some assurance that the problem will not be repeated. So when an officer steps forward and in a very straightforward way admits his error and indicates that he intends to take steps so that it does not happen again, he has solved most of the problem.

In ancient times, legend has it, aides-de-camp wore the aiguillette (now often referred to as loafer's loops) as their own noose, ready for the general to hang them when they brought bad news. That concept may still exist in the armed forces of primitive societies, but the Armed Forces of the United States are above that. Naval leaders should be well aware that honesty in all dealings is still the policy of the American officer. It could never be otherwise. This concept is echoed by Admiral Ramage, who adds:

I never hesitate to make favorable comments to either seniors or subordinates if appropriate, and I wouldn't hesitate to advise seniors of unfavorable information on an officer if it would otherwise affect the well-being or security of the command.

Admiral de Cazanove suggests that the key in dealing with others is frankness, which also implies knowing one's personal limitations and being able to state them to others. There should be no hesitation about presenting negative as well as positive information about oneself, for the boss must be told everything, not just what he may want to hear. I remember when I was advisor to the Prime Minister and told him that it was much easier to say "Yes, Mr. Prime Minister" than "No, Mr. Prime Minister," and he told me that it was because I was able to say "*No*, Mr. Prime Minister" that he had asked me to work with him. This allowed me to work with great confidence in the months ahead. Of course, when you are a young officer it is easier to say no to others, for you aren't sure of the limits of your responsibility and authority. But when you become more senior it becomes more difficult to say no, and this is precisely the time when it is most important to say no and to tell the senior that you do not recommend doing so-and-so. By saying no, the officer is thus presenting unfavorable information about himself, in the sense that his thinking is different from his boss—but such a declaration must be made so that the boss will best understand how his subordinate thinks.

MCPON Sanders: *While there is a tendency for some to withhold complete information about themselves when they have made a mistake, I would offer that, if they can present complete information, both favorable and unfavorable, to a situation and/or themselves, they are on their way to being not only a naval leader, but a leader in general. When we cover things up we usually make the situation a little bit worse, and quite often you harm other individuals, because sometimes when you are covering up a situation that you know about, and perhaps caused, you are also hurting your shipmates and your command. It never gets better, it always gets worse.*

Chapter 6 Bibliography

1. "All Hands." Dec. 1983.
2. Allison, Graham T. *Conceptual Models and the Cuban Missile Crisis: Rational Policy, Organizational Process, and Bureaucratic Politics*. Santa Monica, Calif.: Rand Corporation, 1968.
3. Argyris, Christopher. *Increasing Leadership Effectiveness*. New York: John Wiley and Sons, 1976.
4. Bach, C. A. "Know Your Men, Know Your Business, Know Yourself." *Proceedings*, Apr. 1974, pp. 42–46.
5. Baker, Alton, and Sartain, Aaron. *The Supervisor and His Job*. New York: McGraw-Hill, 1965.
6. Baker, Leonard. *The Johnson Eclipse*. New York: Macmillan, 1966.
7. Barnes, H. E. *Pearl Harbor*. New York: Arno Press, 1972.
8. Bates, L. F. "The Coordination of Maintenance Activities in Bomber Wings: Synchronization and Performance." Chapel Hill: Institute for Research in Social Sciences, University of North Carolina, 1953.
9. Berg, Charles J., and Grillo, Elmer V. *Work Measurement in the Office*. New York: McGraw-Hill, 1959.
10. Bernstein, Barton J. *Politics and Policies of the Truman Administration*. Chicago: Quadrangle Books, 1970.
11. Bittel, Lester R. *What Every Supervisor Should Know*. New York: McGraw-Hill, 1974.
12. Brainerd, George E. "So Much to Do, So Little Time." *Proceedings*, Sept. 1972, p. 62.
13. Brandt, Edward. *The Last Voyage of USS Pueblo*. New York: W. W. Norton, 1969.
14. Brigade of Midshipmen Honor Education Training Manual. Annapolis: U.S. Naval Academy, Office of the Commandant.
15. Browning, D. C., ed. *Dictionary of Quotations and Proverbs*. London: Octopus Books, 1982.
16. Buck, James H., and Korb, Lawrence J., eds. *Military Leadership*. Beverly Hills: Sage Publications, 1981.
17. Calvert, James. *The Naval Profession*. New York: McGraw-Hill, 1971.
18. Catton, Bruce. *Never Call Retreat*. New York: Doubleday, 1965.
19. Chayes, Abram. *The Cuban Missile Crisis: International Crisis and the Role of Law*. New York: Oxford University Press, 1974.

20. Clausewitz, Karl Von. *On War.* Trans. Michael Howard and Peter Paret. Princeton, N.J.: Princeton University Press, 1976.

21. Clexton, E. W., Jr. "Thoughts on the Mechanics of Leadership." Commanding Officer's Memorandum no. 11, USS *Dwight D. Eisenhower* (CVN 69), 15 Nov. 1981.

22. Crocker, Lawrence, ed. *The Army Officer's Guide.* 40th ed. Harrisburg, Pa.: Stackpole, 1979.

23. Cummings, D. E. "Personnel Management in the Navy." *Proceedings,* Apr. 1924, pp. 596–99.

24. Davis, Burke. *Marine! The Life of Lieutenant General Lewis B. (Chesty) Puller.* Boston: Little, Brown, 1962.

25. Dayton, Eldorous L. *Give 'em Hell, Harry.* New York: Devin-Adair, 1956.

26. Dean, Bill C. "Accountability: Crumbling Keystone." *Proceedings,* June 1973, pp. 40–44.

27. Deutermann, Peter T. *The Ops Officer's Manual.* Annapolis: Naval Institute Press, 1980.

28. DeVito, Joseph A. *The International Communications Book.* New York: Harper and Row, 1980.

29. Dougherty, J. J. "Personnel Management: Which Way Is Up?" *Proceedings,* Dec. 1967, pp. 76–80.

30. Ford, Robert N. *Motivation through the Work Itself.* New York: American Management Association, 1969, pp. 97–99, 188–92.

31. Gibson, James L.; Ivancevich, John M.; and Donnelly, James H., Jr. *Organizations.* 4th ed. Plano, Tex.: Business Publications, 1982.

32. Gonzalez, Rene E., Jr. "Too Much Management, Too Little Leadership." *Proceedings,* Feb. 1985, p. 86.

33. Graham, Loren. "The Soviet Union Is Missing Out on the Computer Revolution." *Washington Post,* 11 Mar. 1984.

34. Griffith, Dewitt J. "Principles of Command, Guidelines of Conduct." *Sea Power,* Feb. 1976, pp. 31–36.

35. Hastings, Max, and Simon, Jenkins. *Battle for the Falklands.* New York: W. W. Norton, 1983.

36. Heinl, Robert Debs. *Dictionary of Military and Naval Quotations.* Annapolis: Naval Institute Press, 1966.

37. Hellriegal, Don, and Slocum, John W., Jr. "Decision-Making Concepts and Contingencies." In *Management.* 3d ed. Reading, Mass.: Addison-Wesley, 1982.

38. Hoagland, Steven W. *Operational Codes and International Crisis: The Berlin Wall and the Cuban Missile Crisis.* Ann Arbor, Mich.: University Microfilms International, 1978.

39. Iacocca, Lee, with Nevak, William. *Iacocca: An Autobiography.* New York: Bantam Books, 1984.

40. Jacobs, Arturo A. "Performance Evaluation Programs." *Supervisory Management,* July 1977, pp. 10–14.

41. Jacobs, T. O. *Leadership and Exchange in Formal Organizations.* Alexandria, Va.: Human Resources Research Organization, 1970.

42. Kennedy, Robert F. *Thirteen Days: A Memoir of the Cuban Missile Crisis.* New York: W. W. Norton, 1969.

43. Laird, Donald A., and Laird, Eleanor C. *The New Psychology for Leadership.* New York: McGraw-Hill, 1965.

44. Lawrence, W. P. "Common Qualities of Good Leaders." *Proceedings,* Jan. 1985, p. 86.

45. Lesikar, Raymond V. *How to Write a Report Your Boss Will Read and Remember.* Homewood Ill.: Dow Jones–Irwin, 1974.

46. *Life Goes to War.* Time-Life. New York: Wallaby Book, 1977.

47. MacGregor, Douglas. *Leadership and Motivation.* Cambridge: MIT Press, 1966, pp. 5–8, 67–69.

48. Mack, William P., and Konetzni, Albert H., Jr. *Command at Sea.* 4th ed. Annapolis: Naval Institute Press, 1982.

49. McKim, John D. "Aegis Weapons System." Class Notes, Course no. ES 300. Annapolis: U.S. Naval Academy, Naval Weapons System Department, 1983.

50. "Managing Your Money." *All Hands,* Aug. 1985, pp. 39–41.

51. Marshall, S. L. A. "Men against Fire." In *Infantry Journal.* New York: William Morrow, 1949.

52. Menning, J. H., and Wilkinson, C. W. *Communicating through Letters and Reports.* Homewood, Ill.: Richard D. Irwin, 1967.

53. Miller, Francis. *Eisenhower: Man and Soldier.* Philadelphia: John C. Winston, 1944, pp. 170–75, 228–33.

54. Miller, Merle. *Plain Speaking: An Oral Biography of Harry S Truman.* New York: Berkley, 1977.

55. Miller, Nathan. *The U.S. Navy: An Illustrated History.* New York: American Heritage, 1977.

56. Newman, William H. *Administrative Action*. 2d ed. Englewood Cliffs, N.J.: Prentice-Hall, 1963.

57. Newton, Joe. *Motivation: The Name of the Game*. Oak Brook, Ill.: All American Publishing, 1975, pp. 92–93, 116–17.

58. Niles, Henry; Niles, Mary; and Stephens, James. *The Office Supervisor*. New York: John Wiley and Sons, 1959.

59. Operations Analysis Study Group. *Naval Operations Analysis*. Annapolis: Naval Institute Press, 1977.

60. Orr, George E. *Combat Operations C³I: Fundamentals and Interactions*. Alabama: Air University Press, Maxwell AFB, July 1983.

61. Pierce, Terry C. "The Critical Link: Junior Officers and Strategic Thought." *Proceedings*, Sept. 1983.

62. Polybius. *The Rise of the Roman Empire*. Trans. Ian Scott-Kilvert. Harmondsworth-Middlesex, England: Penguin Books, 1979.

63. Potter, E. B., ed. *Sea Power: A Naval History*. 2d ed. Annapolis: Naval Institute Press, 1981.

64. *Principles of Naval Weapons System*. 7th ed. Annapolis: U.S. Naval Academy, Weapons and Systems Engineering Department, 1982.

65. Saur, Joseph M. "Leadership in the Computer Age." *Proceedings*, Nov. 1983, pp. 140–43.

66. Shelby, Larry W. "Bridging the Leadership and Management Gap." *Military Review*, Jan. 1982, pp. 52–59.

67. Sorensen, Theodore C. *The Kennedy Legacy*. New York: Macmillan, 1969.

68. ———. *Decision Making in the White House: The Olive Branch or the Arrow?* New York: Columbia University Press, 1969.

69. Stogdill, Ralph M. *Stogdill's Handbook of Leadership: A Survey of Theory and Research*. New York: Macmillan, 1974, pp. 26–33.

70. Tannenbaum, Arnold S. *Social Psychology of the Work Organization*. Belmont, Calif.: Wadsworth, 1966, pp. 26–33.

71. Taylor, Maxwell D. *Responsibility and Response*. New York: Harper and Row, 1967.

72. Torrance, E. P. "The Behavior of Small Groups under the Stress Conditions of Survival." *American Sociological Review*, 1954.

73. Truman, Harry S. *Mr. Citizen*. New York: Bernard Beiss, 1960.

74. ———. *Memoirs*. Garden City, N.Y.: Doubleday, 1955.

75. United States Congress. Senate. *Report of the Joint Committee on the Investigation of the Pearl Harbor Attack*. 79th Cong., 2d sess. Washington, D.C.: U.S. Government Printing Office, 1946.

76. United States Navy. *The Navy N: Integration of Men and Mission*. Washington, D.C.: U.S. Government Printing Office, 1972.

77. Uris, Auren. *Memos for Managers*. New York: Thomas Y. Crowell, 1975.

78. "A View from the Balcony." *Proceedings*, Aug. 1984.

79. Waggener, John G. "Scientific Military Decision Making." *Military Review*, Oct. 1969, pp. 60–67.

80. Wainhouse, David W. *Alternative Methods for Dealing with Breaches of Arms Control Agreements*. Vol. 5. Baltimore, Md.: Johns Hopkins University Press, 1968.

81. Wallin, Homer N. "The Raising and Salvaging of the *Nevada*." In *Air Raid: Pearl Harbor*. Annapolis: Naval Institute Press, 1972.

82. *War in the Falklands: The Full Story*. Sunday *Times* of London Insight Team. New York: Harper and Row, 1982.

83. Williams, Andrew T. "Multiplan Meets the Mac." *Macworld*, Feb. 1984, p. 72.

84. Williams, John D. "Tactical Training, Tactical Testing." *Proceedings*, Oct. 1983, p. 126.

85. Zaleznik, Christenson, and Zaleznik, Roethlisberger. *The Motivation, Productivity, and Satisfaction of Workers*. Boston: Plimpton Press, 1958, pp. 34–40.

86. Zenophon. *Anabasis*. Cambridge: Harvard University Press, 1961.

87. Zveare, Dennis L. "Personal Commitment: Missing and Presumed Lost?" *Proceedings*, Jan. 1984, pp. 105–6.

7

Achieving Effective Communications

Introduction

An effective officer is an effective communicator. He expresses himself well both orally and in writing. Further, he projects an image of positiveness; of professional knowledge commensurate with his age, rank, and assignment; of self-assurance; and of understanding. These attributes are continuously communicated by his actions and demeanor.

Since integrity is one of the most important attributes of leadership, all of an officer's communications, direct and implied, must be sincere. Use of "lip service" and a facade of seeming to do the "right thing" is soon discovered by seniors and subordinates alike.

The effective officer should concentrate on the positive aspects of good communications, but he should be aware that there is also a negative side of communications. The individual who always has an alibi for his actions is communicating; he is sending the message that his paramount concerns are self-interest and dodging responsibility. The officer who chronically uses excuses—"Not on my watch," "Mr. Gish's division was supposed to do that," "According to regulations, ..." "The widgits weren't delivered to me on time"—is not a leader. He lacks a sense of responsibility, displays no initiative, and is lacking courage.

A leader must also communicate an aura of approachability. If he does not, his subordinates will be reluctant to tell him of potentially dangerous situations because of their fear of harsh rebuke or excessive punishment. This reluctance can lead the fearful subordinate to attempt to remedy the situation on his own. The CO must always be kept apprised of what goes on in his command; if he is not, events can occur that are detrimental to the unknowing senior, who has the ultimate responsibility. Likewise, an officer must never hesitate to inform the CO of when, where, and how he (the officer) goofed.

Colonel James W. Hammond, Jr., USMC (Ret.), provided this example of an officer who projected an image of both being willing to listen and tolerating no nonsense.

As a Plebe, I put in a dining-out chit for Sunday dinner with a family in Annapolis. Regulations allowed Sunday dining out with parents, roommates' parents, and commissioned officers. (The current sponsor program did not then exist.) The head of the family was a St. John's graduate (in the days when it was a military school) and had a reserve commission in the Army. On my chit I identified him as a lieutenant colonel. The midshipman company commander forwarded the chit and recommended approval. The company officer, Lieutenant Commander G., was suspicious. I was invited to his office for questioning:

Lt. Comdr. G.: "Tell me about this officer."

Midn. H.: "He's an Army officer, sir."

Lt. Comdr. G.: "Does he wear a uniform?"

Midn. H.: "Well . . . ahem . . . ah . . ."

Lt. Comdr. G.: "Mister, you're trying to *big deal* me!" [or words to that effect].

Midn. H.: "Yes, sir!"

Lt. Comdr. G.: "Request approved. Any other answer and I would have denied it. Dismissed!"

Colonel Hammond had put himself in the soup, and the best he could hope for was a well-deserved chewing out for a frivolous request. Instead, he received a lesson in leadership that he no doubt had occasion to apply several times over the years.

Colonel Hammond related an incident in which a division logistics officer did not communicate his requirements to those who could have helped him remedy a bad situation. Instead, he tried to please the chief by doing everything himself.

In the late 1950s, the 3d Marine Division was making an orderly redeployment from the Japanese main islands to Okinawa. The Marines were to construct new camps and facilities while initially living under canvas. Suddenly, for political reasons, the movement was expedited. It became an aggravated rush with the consequent confusion.

One of the worst problems was accounting for the vast amount of supplies. There is a difference between having supplies on hand and knowing what is where. The logistical records showed that the division had ample supplies—but they couldn't be identified for issue.

The G-4 (division logistics officer) was thoroughly perplexed as he tried to sort out the mess. He wasn't helped by the constant badgering of a fellow colonel, the chief of staff. The latter's impatience was accelerated by the fact that he was in the zone for selection to brigadier general. The more the chief demanded of the logistics section, the less the G-4 delegated authority to his subordinates. Just then a typhoon hit, and even the canvas was blown away. A month later, a new commanding general arrived and immediately ordered all the principal staff officers (chief, G-1, 2, 3, 4, division engineer, etc.) to Kyoto on a fool's errand designed as relaxation. They were to meet him later in Yokosuka for the Seventh Fleet Conference.

The first night in Yokosuka, the commanding general assembled his staff at dinner. After dinner he spoke. "Gentlemen, you have been gone a week, and I am pleased to report that the 3d Marine Division is alive and well, despite your absence. No man is indispensable. You must communicate your desires to those who can take care of them and not try to do everything yourselves." (Incidentally, the new CG brought his own chief of staff, who had a better feel for communicating the general's wishes, and the former chief was not selected for brigadier general.)

Colonel Hammond related that, when he was plans officer in Fleet Marine Force Pacific, he had 15 action officers under him, and he suggested that they avail themselves of a "Ropeyarn Sunday" or afternoon off each week to relax.

> The work load wasn't heavy and most of them had already spent two tours in Vietnam. (And, after all, everyone already thought we spent all our time on the beach.) Evidently, they didn't take me seriously or were afraid to leave their desks. I had to find a way of communicating, but I couldn't use the general's old ploy of sending them to Japan. I needed another way to communicate. At the next cocktail party, I asked each lady why her husband wasn't taking advantage of a weekly afternoon off in Hawaii. The message got through; afternoons off were arranged among the 15 officers and, not surprisingly, the quality of work improved.

In an organization as complex as the Naval Service, it is impossible for anyone to know everything, particularly concerning areas outside his immediate assignment. Therefore, the officer should not try to be the expert in someone else's job, and he does not have to answer a question just because one is put to him. One of the first things a plebe learns is to say "I'll find out, Sir!"—not "I don't know." Even the latter answer, however, is preferable to giving one that is inaccurate.

In addition to being able to reply "I'll find out, Sir!" the officer must be able to accept that same answer from a subordinate. If, on the other hand, a subordinate supplies quick but inaccurate answers just to appear to know everything, the officer should confront him the first time he

catches him at it. It will be cheap tuition for the subordinate to learn the lesson early, before the automatic response becomes a habit and he is caught in a more serious situation.

One hallmark of an effective leader, in both command and staff assignments, is the ability to write clearly and concisely. There is no place for ambiguity in military service. Staff papers should be models of brevity and clarity. There should not be one unnecessary word or any stilted language. The organization and syntax should convey the message. The reader should have no doubts about what is expected or described. A staff paper should spell out for an action addressee WHAT, WHEN, and WHERE. He should be allowed to determine HOW.

Effective communication is also important because a large portion of a leader's time is spent communicating with others. A leader's day is filled with face-to-face communications with seniors, peers, and subordinates. When not speaking directly, the leader may be communicating through other means, such as memos, letters, and reports (which will be discussed later). Chap. 2:57-560

Colonel Hammond described a singularly effective communication.

> During the heavy fighting in the late 1960s around Con Thien, south of the DMZ in Vietnam, a Marine infantry battalion was fighting head-to-head with a NVA regiment. The latter was trying to flank the Marines and isolate them by seizing a bridge to the rear of their position. The battalion commander picked up his radio and in the clear gave instructions to one of his company commanders, "Art, there's a NVA column heading toward the bridge. If it gets there before you do, I'll have your ass!" The Marines held the bridge.

The officer who writes professionally and submits his work to one of the several professional military and naval journals is enhancing both his career and his communications skills. Every time an officer sits down to write, he becomes better at it. Writing is especially rewarding if the work is published. The officer is identified as one who is willing to offer ideas to the scrutiny of seniors and juniors alike and to accept the criticism of his contemporaries. Writing professionally builds an officer's "service reputation."

Colonel Hammond provided this example, which illustrates where effective communication leads:

> Years ago, a Marine major general had a young captain as his aide. The aide was tasked with writing the general's memoranda, letters, and speeches. Almost all of the captain's writing was rewritten by the general and was hardly recognizable to the captain in its final form. One day after the general had given an outstanding speech, the aide quite guilelessly said, "Gosh, general, I wish I had written it like that."
>
> The general replied with a smile,"If you had written it like that, then you would be the general and I would be the aide!" The bottom line is that the major general became the Commandant of the Marine Corps.

62. The Basics of Effective Communications

People cannot be led, save on the end of a rope, if they cannot understand what the leader says, means, or expects. Clear direction is a critical dimension of organizational climate. When people understand the mission, values, standards, and expectations of the organization, they can do what needs to be done. Lack of such understanding leads to false starts, ineptness, and discontent. Admiral Holloway suggests that,

> in communicating with seniors, the officer should try to let them know what his plans are, but only up to the point where his plans are relatively firm. The officer should not continue into an area where he

is not on firm ground, because conjecture is not helpful to the leadership. If he does discuss the distant future, where conjecture comes into play, the officer should offer rational appraisals of what his probable future course of action will be.

An officer should tell his subordinates what the missions of the organization and his particular group are and, in general, how the officer plans to accomplish them. Subordinates usually are very bright, concerned, and interested, and they should be kept informed.

Generally speaking, however, in communications, the further down the chain of command, the closer to the front line, and the more the troops are involved, the less security a message has. First, the communication systems that are used in front-line units tend to be more vulnerable to code breaking and listening-in by the enemy. Second, junior people tend to talk more than senior people because they do not understand as well the need for security. So, in deciding what to pass down the line, the officer should remember to tell people what they need to know to do the job and what is important for their morale purposes, but he should avoid providing information that, if it got outside the command, could impair his ability or be a detriment to his plans or do harm to his country.

The officer should not communicate his plans for the future laterally to anyone except those individuals who must know. How guarded he must be depends on the officer's assignment. For example, the leader on a mine sweeper must be more guarded in communicating to those in charge of other mine sweepers than a task force commander at headquarters who is communicating to other headquartered task force commanders.

There are many kinds of communications, but the same rules do not necessarily apply in electronic communications and in person-to-person communications. The officer who is talking to his troops at quarters for muster and sort of pumping them up and telling them what a great bunch they are can be more wordy and innovative than a strike leader who is calling back to say that five SAMs have just lifted off. In the first case the officer can afford to use a better rhetoric; in the second case he just wants to get that message out quickly. The same idea applies when a four-star admiral writes a message to the Chief of Naval Operations or the Joint Chiefs of Staff. His communication will be more philosophical than the message of a destroyer skipper to his task group commander telling him what he is and is not going to be able to do in the projected operations over the next 48 hours because of a problem with his number-one fuel pump. The number of people in the chain of command for communication should be reduced to its absolute minimum, but not one less than the absolute minimum. Arbitrarily saying that there can be no more than five people in the chain of command, for example, is not sound policy, because the number of people in the chain of command has to be based on the circumstances. For example, if only five people were allowed in the chain of command, the individual who has the helicopter air-sea rescue unit and may be called into play at any minute to extricate people might be left out.

There should not be anyone unnecessarily included in the chain of command, however. Because someone is a nice person and is interested does not mean he needs to know. He should not be in the chain just for that reason.

Many basics are involved in effective communication, among them audibility, articula-

tion, spelling, and grammar. A longstanding naval tradition is for officers to exceed minimum requirements. Refinement is expected. The way an officer speaks, writes, and thinks should convey an image of an "educated person." Much of this striving for excellence stems from a concern for image and credibility, and it is an entirely practical and fine tradition, alive and well among outstanding officers.

EXPLAINING DECISIONS AND SHARING INFORMATION

When power is effectively used, people do not feel like pawns. Rather, they understand and subscribe to the goals and values of the organization and feel empowered, not dominated. When the reasons for orders are not apparent, the likelihood of the orders being disregarded increases. A steady diet of such orders breeds resentment.

Emergencies, when there is no time for explanations and officers must rely on trust, do arise. Trust is usually built through people's discovery over time that officers have good reasons for what they require. For example, there are compelling reasons for the insistence on obedience, respect for the chain of command, cleanliness, and order. These are not arbitrary personal preferences, but if these requirements are viewed as such, personnel will be little concerned about slip-ups as long as they avoid being caught. When the standards are seen as being vital to the health and survival of the organization, people will work at upholding them without constant prodding. Outstanding officers seem to understand the principle of providing reasons for orders quite well, as the following example of communications illustrates:

"Okay, the ship is going to sail over the horizon with twelve airplanes on it. The only defense that ship has in its battle group, in its cruisers, in its destroyers, are the F-14s. So if we're ready, we can protect that battle group. If we're not ready, then the battle group might as well just go back to port and tie up. Now, the Chief of Naval Operations won't hear tell of that. The President, the Joint Chiefs of Staff, nobody would allow that to happen. So it comes down to you. You've got to be on your toes. You've got to be ready."

And they got ready because they understood the mission's importance.

Officers can share information with department heads through regularly scheduled meetings. They can inform their personnel of upcoming events so people can plan ahead. COs and XOs can also make certain that the crew is briefed on what to expect during special evolutions. Even trivial rumors must be squelched, as the transmission of *accurate* information is vital.

Sometimes COs personally brief the crew at quarters in preparation for inspections. Members of the crew are told what is going to happen and how they are expected to behave, generally in words similar to these: "No need for you to be nervous. The house is in order. You are well prepared for this inspection. Try to relax and give honest answers to any questions the inspectors have."

MAKING SURE PEOPLE ABSORB WHAT IS COMMUNICATED TO THEM

When they talk to people, outstanding officers watch the expressions of those in the audience to be sure they are taking in what is being said. Where there is any doubt, officers ensure understanding by making a clearer restatement or requesting that an individual repeat the message in his own words. Important oral communications are sometimes followed up in writing, or vice versa, all to ensure uptake and understanding.

The importance of making sure that oral communications are understood is illustrated by the example of an air squadron that was out for muster in a noisy open hangar at the airfield. To make sure that everyone in the squadron could hear him, the commanding officer pulled everyone in close around him, in football-huddle fashion, instead of leaving them spread out and neatly lined up.

TAILORING COMMUNICATIONS TO THE AUDIENCE'S LEVEL OF UNDERSTANDING

Many factors are involved in tailoring communications to people's level of understanding, an advanced skill of leaders and teachers. If he wishes to have people understand a message fully, a leader must think about what they need to have in order to do so. A few techniques related to tailoring communications to people's level of understanding for solving communications problems are listed below.

1. Problem: Insufficient background information.
   Solution: Provision of background information.
   He [DH] was new to the ship. He launched into the Supply DH about the way he was handling configuration management. He didn't understand the logic of the procedures and wasn't listening to the senior officer. The CO decided to intervene and take him aside and tell him some sea stories about fiascos that led to the SupO's current procedures. Once he understood the background, the DH saw the procedures' merit.
2. Problem: Idea too abstract or too theoretical to grasp.
   Solution: Provision of a concrete example that connects with the person's experience.
   In high-stress conditions, people regress [theory]. Take Steven and Tom, for example. They are rocks of Gibraltar. Ordinarily, they wouldn't dream of blaming their mistakes on anyone else. But here was pressure like they'd never seen, and they babbled incessantly about how stupid the other one and everyone else was but themselves. They were behaving like kids [concrete example].
3. Problem: Idea too strange or too complex to grasp, or too pedestrian and commonplace to remember.
   Solution: Use of a metaphor or an analogy.
   The lady [the ship] [metaphor] is suffering the usual maladies of middle age. She requires an extra dose of tender, loving care [analogy].
4. Problem: Vocabulary and phraseology too exalted.
   Solution: Assistance of an editor.

5. Problem: Vocabulary strange.
Solution: Avoidance of the use of Navy or Marine Corps jargon with non-Navy or -Marine Corps audiences.

In summary, outstanding officers make sure that people "hear" them, understand the message, and understand its import. In doing so, they uphold a longstanding naval tradition.

MAKING SURE PERSONNEL ARE CONTINUOUSLY INFORMED

In superior units, plans of the day (POD) are viewed as a major vehicle of communication. They are always thorough, and they include the long-range view. Through plans of the day, personnel are alerted to upcoming events and to what they are expected to do. Their attention is drawn to important issues. One plan of the day reported that a man had fallen down and broken his leg because a hatch had not been properly secured. The POD did not point out where the accident had happened, so that all hands would be careful.

Another aspect of keeping the troops informed is the indoctrination program for new troops. All units must have these programs, and the effort and time put forth to make them effective is worthwhile. In an effective indoctrination program, commanding and executive officers get directly involved and talk to all new personnel, individually and as a group. Indoctrination programs must be timely; only in average units does the indoctrination program take place three or four months late. In one poorly organized program, the instructor had to ask people in the room for the latest information, and the commanding officer who was supposed to attend had gone flying instead.

CROSS-COMPARTMENTAL COMMUNICATION

Cross-compartmental communication is essential. Operations officers must talk to maintenance people; the engineering department head must coordinate with the other heads of departments; Marine Corps battalion staff members must coordinate effectively with company commanders. Without telling anyone, one engineering department head arbitrarily cut off a communications line to the commanding officer. After considerable inconvenience to the commanding officer, the operations officer finally tracked down the problem and restored the cross-compartmental communications.

MAINTAINING CONTACT WITH PERSONNEL

As part of their emphasis on communication up and down the chain of command, leaders should regularly walk around their units to learn what is going on. This is a *planned* activity, not something that is squeezed in during spare moments. In this way, leaders gain a sense of their unit as a whole, instead of focusing excessively on details. An officer on a ship who spends too much time below deck, focusing on individual activities such as the installation of a pump (which will only make the crew nervous and impede progress), is missing the opportunity to monitor all activities in an unobtrusive way.

Officers should emphasize the importance of communication up the chain of command. During tours of the unit or spaces, officers are alert to working conditions, individual performance, and opportunities for individuals to say how they think things are going. This approach is not an invitation for circumvention of the chain of command or confrontation; rather, it allows individuals to communicate directly, and it also provides a chance for officers to express their interest in the welfare of their troops.

REMAINING AVAILABLE AND VISIBLE

Outstanding officers "manage by walking about." Yet they do this only partly to keep informed and monitor what is happening. Another very important part of walking about is to show interest, concern, or appreciation. Many senior officers make an effort to get to know people's names and something about them. On their rounds, these officers can make statements such as: "Seaman Jones, how's your mom doing? Has she recovered from her operation?" or "Private Smith, I hear you're getting ready to ace the essential subjects test." Overall, the walking about is upbeat; it is not a fault-finding mission.

Officers can show interest by sitting in on training, observing drills, and stopping on a stroll to watch an evolution: "Carry on; I'm just watching. Never saw it done quite like that before." During pre-inspection drills, one ship's CO stood up on the bridge spotting people putting out extra effort or doing an especially good job. The CO would get on the speaker and single them out: "Nice job, John Smith. . . . Can't see Tommy Jones, he's moving so fast. . . ." Several officers noted that they genuinely enjoyed these strolls and that the strolls paid off considerably.

MCPON Sanders: *When communicating with the crew, I would first recommend that the officer discuss what is going to be said with the senior enlisted, and let that individual provide some of his own thinking and arrange the meeting with the troops. In this way you will know that what is being communicated is consistent with the ideas of the senior enlisted, or, if there is disagreement, that can be worked out ahead of time so that you provide a unified front to your unit. Going through the chief serves several purposes. First of all, it gets his confidence; he understands that you are working through him, and it builds him up a little bit; second, if you just walk into an area and call all hands up to let them know what you want to talk about, you may be disrupting previously scheduled work. Thus, it's a lot easier to go through that senior enlisted and then speak directly to the crew.*

63. Producing Effective Oral and Written Communications

People communicate to let other people know their thoughts. In the military, effective communication is particularly important, because mission accomplishment usually depends on everyone acting with the same knowledge. Effective communication is based on five basic principles. These are knowing what to say, whom to say it to, when to say it, and how to say it, and having the responsibility to improve the communication network.[23-344] Therefore, it is advisable for an officer to determine in advance whether people are likely to understand what he has to say as he meant it to be understood. This saying, introduced in chapter 5, makes the point well:

> "I know you believe you understand what you think I said, but I am not sure you realize that what you heard is not what I meant."

People learn through experience to evaluate how well they have communicated what they intended to communicate. By a lack of response or a failure to act, the people receiving the message indicate that the sender did something wrong. The effects of the feedback will cause the sender either to continue with his style of communication, when the feedback is positive, or to change it, on receipt of negative feedback. The feedback is intended to help the process and must be specific and well timed in order not to overwhelm the receiver. [Chap. 2:57-560]

An important lesson in communicating, then, is that the sender of the message has the responsibility of ensuring that he says what he says in terms the receiver will understand. In the Battle of Dogger Bank, faulty messages were given, or messages that were sent were never received. A flotilla of ships failed to carry out its mission due to ineffective communication.[9-90] It is, therefore, prudent for an officer to check with someone in advance of communicating, if there is time, to determine whether the message is likely to be understood by others. Both officers and enlisted with whom the officer is associated are appropriate persons to review the message, for in many cases individuals in both groups will have to act on the information. On the other hand, if comprehension of the message requires a specialized background, it is appropriate to have the communication checked by someone with the appropriate specialized knowledge. Consulting the various experts in each separate field can give a person a greater understanding of how to communicate better. Also, availability and cost can be taken into account.[44-2]

Before having the material reviewed by others, an officer should write a draft, keeping in mind the receivers' knowledge and interests. He should revise ruthlessly and ask himself whether he has been clear and accurate. He should try to find fault with his work by quarreling with the need for every paragraph, every sentence, and every word. He can avoid using terms others may not understand by testing his language through assuming the role of the receiver. "Just Plain English," written in the Office of the Chief of Naval Operations (OP-09BR, Washington, D.C. 20350), is a valuable aide. As an example of the changes in communication style over the years, consider the old and new preambles to Executive Orders.

> *Old:* By virtue of the authority vested in me by the Constitution of the United States of America, and as President of the United States of America, it is hereby ordered as follows . . .
>
> *New:* As President of the United States, I direct . .

Once he has written a draft, the officer should read it aloud. He should not say anything by mail that he would not say in person. For most people, good writing means good rewriting. Revision is worth the effort. A single naval letter is likely to be read by many people as it goes up for signature in one activity and down for action in another. The officer should work to help the many people who must read his writing. If he does not sweat, his readers will.

When he consults with others regarding his communication, the officer will find that they will probably be able to help him by: checking to see whether he gets quickly to the point, has enough but not too many references, states rules before exceptions, says who does what, gives examples for difficult ideas, and answers likely questions. Until Murphy's law is repealed, an officer must write so he cannot be misunderstood.

To be effective as a leader in today's Naval Service, an officer must become an accomplished speaker. He has to be able to present facts clearly and concisely to individuals and to groups of varying sizes in both off-the-cuff and formal situations. By practicing his delivery in front of others, the officer will get feedback that will enable him to determine whether he has the following traits of a good speaker:

1. Has knowledge of the subject
2. Is adequately prepared
3. Is up-to-date professionally
4. Is poised and self-confident when speaking
5. Has a natural delivery style

The foregoing is only an introduction to effective oral and written communications. Naval officers are encouraged to seek out methods of improving their delivery of information. Writing for publication and speaking to civilian groups are effective means of improving communication style and ability, and by consulting others during the planning phase of his communications effort, the officer will find that he is better understood, that things go better, and that others look forward to receiving his messages. Admiral Holloway makes the point that

> juniors should be asked for inputs in areas where they are qualified to give them. The officer can talk to a young pilot, for example, and ask him if there is anything that would speed up his check-in procedures coming back from the beach. The pilot might ask why he has to check in with the Tom Cat, and maybe that could be changed. The point is that the officer is asking the pilot for advice in an area where he is competent to respond. Giving people the opportunity to comment in

areas where clearly they are not competent is almost always a waste of time.

In writing for publication, an officer should address subjects on which he has some expertise. Rather than outline his ideas on how the Pacific Fleet should be run, he should write on a subject he knows from first-hand experience. He will in this way be making a valuable contribution.

64. Determining the Purpose and the Audience for the Message

An effective officer continually works to develop good communication skills, for lack of clarity in communication is a problem even the most effective military leaders must struggle with. For example, General of the Army Dwight D. Eisenhower stated, "All my life I have been an incorrigible reviser of written material. Whether I dictate a draft, or a draft has been prepared for my signature, I find that I have almost never said exactly what I wanted to say, in the way I hoped to say it."[21-323]

Effective communication up and down the military chain of command is essential to mission accomplishment. Admiral McDonald points out that, "if orders are misunderstood, it may be that someone along the line didn't know how to communicate, and that the senior in the chain hasn't put enough emphasis on transmitting orders." Communication is a key link in execution and integration of effort. Before a leader can issue a crisp and clear oral or written order, he must be clear in his own mind exactly what the goal of the mission is, and what he needs to communicate to whom in order to accomplish that objective.

Once the purpose of the communication is clear, the leader must consider who will be receiving the communication.[Chap. 2:12-167] Seniors receiving the communication will usually voice any confusion they have, especially if the situation as described in the message is different from the receiver's assessment of the situation. It must be emphasized that communication is not just a downward process. It goes both up and down. We must communicate with our seniors just as often as with our juniors, and they must communicate with us. Put simply,

> Communication occurs if Joe is talking to Tom when Tom is listening to and understanding what Joe has said. Two-way communication occurs when Joe stops talking long enough to listen to what Tom has to say and Tom may also talk. If Tom may only listen to Joe, then the communication is said to be one-way. But if Tom is allowed to talk freely as well as listen, the communication is said to be two-way.[40-28]

Subordinates are less likely to indicate confusion or disagreement, so the leader must take steps to ensure that they understand his message. Secretary Webb states that

> a leader must be able to communicate to his or her people with a sense of presence and self-confidence. The form that communication takes depends on several factors, including the setting and the leader's personality. Communication can be written, verbal, or physical—such as posture or standing up in combat. But the leader who understands, yet cannot communicate to his troops on a level they will appreciate, is probably doomed to fail.

"Mobilization of minds" is a phrase that, in modern warfare, suggests that wars are fought with words as well as with weapons. An order must be understood by the lowest command level tasked with carrying out the mission or objective. The military leader, then, must know the capabilities of his followers before he issues an order. The added stress in the heat of battle or in a crisis demands that words be carefully chosen to avoid confusion. In battle, a missed, ignored, or misunderstood communication can result in poor transmission of ideas, thoughts, orders, etc. With respect to writing, many supervisors or seniors believe they can communicate effectively via messages, command letters, bulletins, memos, and other means exclusively.

> Even if the message, by whatever medium it is transmitted, is clear and concise, it may very well not be understood despite the writer's good intentions. Obviously, if the message is misunderstood by its recipients, it will fail in its mission. As leaders, we often overestimate the true effectiveness of dealing with seniors via messages. We put the word out, but who, if anybody, is receiving, or heeding it?[62-21]

In the World War II Battle of Leyte Gulf, one of the main U.S. Navy leadership problems was the lack of timely and clear communications between the Commander Third Fleet (Admiral Halsey) and Commander Seventh Fleet (Vice Admiral Kinkaid). "The communication problem compounded by messages obscurely worded, misinterpreted and, in one instance, accidently corrupted resulted in Halsey and Kinkaid basing several decisions on misinformation."[59-290] Misinformation is an even more important factor today, as the enemies of the United States actively try to confuse and disrupt military communications efforts in times of crisis. Again, getting "back to basics" helps avoid "slips of the tongue."

In war, self-distraction and miscommunication can quickly defeat an officer. Admiral Chester W. Nimitz, USN, Commander in Chief Pacific, wrote a letter to his commanders in World War II saying,

> There are certain psychological factors which have fully as much to do with safety at sea as any of the more strictly technical ones. A large proportion of the disasters in tactics and maneuvers comes from concentrating too much on one objective or urgency, at the cost of not being sufficiently alert for others. . . . No officer, whatever his rank and experience, should flatter himself that he is immune to the inexplicable lapses in judgment, calculation, and memory, or to the *slips of the tongue in giving orders*, which throughout seagoing history have

so often brought disaster to men of the highest reputation and ability.[57-139]

MCPON Sanders: *If an officer does not clarify his own thinking on something that he is going to pass down, the orders will become very fuzzy and not understood. The end result will be problems within the command, department, or work force. It is important for an officer to know what he wants to say in advance, formulating his ideas and using the correct words, remembering that what you say should be said in terms appropriate to the audience being addressed.*

65. Getting the Message Across

A successful communicator understands that people are different and that people respond not only to the carrot and stick methodology, but also to ambition, patriotism, self-doubt, and a host of other emotions. General Rice suggests that

> one way an officer can ensure that his intended message has been received is to look at the results. If he has given his orders correctly, if people understand him and know what he wants, they will provide feedback indicating that. When an officer has given guidance, and the paper he gets back indicates that the staff has achieved nowhere what he wanted them to achieve, then obviously something is wrong: either they did not understand or the officer's guidance was poor. In this case, the officer should rethink the way he communicates.
>
> Setting the example is a basic way to communicate. If the officer expects people to look sharp and be sharp, he has to look sharp and be sharp, and he will readily be able to tell whether people have received his message.
>
> An officer must know his job before he can expect someone else to know theirs.

That does not mean a unit commander has to be a mechanic or has to know everything there is to know about an engine, but he should know some basic things about the engine. The mechanic gets paid to do the detailed work, but the officer should have general knowledge of what the mechanic is supposed to do, because otherwise he will be unable to supervise his subordinates and check what they are doing. The machine gunner may not know the tactics involved, but he knows that machine gun; the officer has to know how that machine gun should operate and where it should be placed to provide the most effective fire. So an officer needs to have a general knowledge about many things.

After every briefing it is a good habit to ask if there are any questions. There are many ways to do this, but it is important to do it in a way that lets the troops know they are free to ask questions. Many people are afraid to ask questions because of the reaction that sometimes elicits, so the officer must establish a reputation as someone who genuinely wants people to ask questions or to ask for a clarification.

Achieving effective communication in the military presents special problems. Because service personnel face extreme risk, injury, or death and therefore may have to be replaced, sometimes continually, there are important reasons for treating them uniformly and, at times, mechanically. Each person's responsibilities and duties must be delineated clearly and understood both up and down the chain of command. Admiral Hayward notes that,

in communicating, an officer uses the chain of command, transmits as clearly as he possibly can, and meets frequently with his senior officers. He develops policies with their advice so that when the policy is ultimately distributed to the chain of command, he knows that it is

starting out understood. An officer can only hope that the chain of command will keep transmitting the policy clearly. The chain of command is the right way to get the word out, from any size unit on up. Good communication is a requirement of good leadership. Some people are naturally very effective at it and some simply are not, but it is one of those skills that a leader must acquire. He must learn to write and to speak with sincerity and objectivity. Eyeball-to-eyeball contact is part of effective verbal communications.

Admiral Hayward explained how his action with regard to drug use was an aid to, not a sidestepping of, the chain of command.

I've stressed the importance of communicating through the chain of command as a traditional, proper way for the Navy to get things done, and let me suggest that even in this instance the chain of command was employed. I used the television two or three times in four years, in each case for circumstances I thought were out of the ordinary by a long measure, and therefore in order to address the issue we went at it with several techniques, of which the television communication device [video] was one.

In this instance we were talking about the drug issue. After two years of looking upon it very hard I saw no results and I finally got to the point where as the Chief of Naval Operations, with the responsibility to the nation for fixing this problem that couldn't be fixed without taking extraordinary measures, I had to take those measures. Those other individuals in the Navy responsible for helping the CNO develop a policy worked together, and we spent about six months putting into place each piece of the pattern. We met with the master chiefs of the Navy, we developed a program with their support, we got the fleets involved, and finally all the three and four stars. My message to the fleet, while it was transmitted obviously in a personal sense from the CNO to every individual in the Navy, was literally handed down by the Chief of Naval Information to each command, and it was up to each command to use it as they saw fit. They didn't have to show that film if they didn't want to, or they could use it if they thought it was an important tool, and they used it very effectively. So it certainly wasn't a device to subvert the chain of command, it was a device to assist the chain of command grapple with a very difficult problem. I thought it was very encouraging and one of the finest things that the Navy has done for our country.

BARRIERS TO COMMUNICATING EFFECTIVELY

Effective communication is essential if plans and programs are to be successfully translated into action. The fundamental difficulties in communication arise from two assumptions. First, on the part of the speaker or writer, that others understand what he states as he intends it to be understood. Second, on the part of the listener or reader, that he understands what has been said as it was intended to be understood. Because we rarely test these assumptions, we are rarely sure that we are truly communicating. Descartes left us with his rules of logic of speaking, which state:

1. Discard everything except that which you know to be true.
2. Break the subject down into as many parts as possible.
3. Start with the easier parts and progress to the hardest to understand.
4. Summarize.[73-130]

In other words, you are trying to persuade the person to think like you on an issue, and that is where the true work will begin, when speaking to people; or, to put it in the words of A. H. Leighton, "Man acts in terms of what he perceives, and what he perceives must pass not only through his eyes, ears and other special senses to reach his consciousness, but also through the dark and iridescent waters of his belief."[45-288]

The higher officers go in management and leadership positions and the more authority they wield, the less they are forced to listen to others. As individuals gain authority, they sometimes develop a lack of patience in listening to subordinates, yet their need to listen is greater than ever. A deaf ear may be the "first symptom of a closed mind."

The farther officers get from the firing line, the more they have to depend on others for correct information. If the officer corps has not formed the habit of listening—carefully and intelligently—officers are not going to get the facts they need. The ability to listen is also an important ingredient in successfully transmitting the message. Lessons in delivering orders can also be found in the historical practices of old warriors like Napoleon and Marshal Foch: It is recorded of Napoleon, the most autocratic of men, that he never gave an order without explaining its purpose, and making sure that this purpose was understood. He knew that blind obedience could never ensure the intelligent execution of any order. Marshal Foch, in his Principles of War, makes the same point in his distinction between passive and active obedience. "Command," he says, "never yet meant obscurity." Active obedience implies initiative, and intelligence in the exercise of this initiative requires a knowledge of how the specific objective fits into the general plan.[54-131]

THE EFFECT OF OVERTONES

In both written and verbal communication, it is important to be mindful of the overtones of the message. In verbal communication, the implication of "body language," the sending of additional signals to the receiver through gestures or posture, is well recognized. Additionally, the tone of voice, manner, and pace in which words are spoken can sometimes convey a message to the listener far different from that intended, and far different from the words spoken. Conversely, officers may intentionally use this technique to color the message; however, it is more professional and honest to communicate thoughts clearly and directly, without ambiguity, than to risk miscommunication.

"An effective speech is perhaps one-fourth or one-third what your listeners see. They see you: how you stand, the look on your face, how you walk, what you do with your hands—what you are. They size you up, curiously and candidly, favorably or unfavorably. They will decide, without knowing it, whether they are going to like you and whether they are going to accept what you say."[69-122] "However important physical appearance is, it will not take the place of the right attitude. In fact, as the speaker gets into his talk, he may cause his listeners to forget his appearance."[69-124]

Communication is a two-way street, and listening is a major part of communication, but individuals frequently receive only the words that others utter or write; they have little understanding of the feelings and values that underlie the statements. As a result, an individual often misses the main points another person is trying to make, as in this exchange between a department head and a division officer.

DEPARTMENT HEAD: Jim, you're filling out your PMS forms all wrong. Didn't you read the notice? You're still doing it the old way, and that's what we are trying to get away from. Now the division is all fouled up. You'd better fill out the new forms and get your PMS up to speed.

Notice that the department head assumes that because the instructions were written and distributed, they were properly interpreted by the division officer. He assumes that the notice, which was, in fact, misunderstood, is clear. Notice also

that he expects bringing the notice to Jim's attention will make the situation clear to Jim. He was totally unprepared for what followed, however.

DIVISION OFFICER: Commander, this division has never been in trouble because of PMS. We've been doing just fine. Why did we change forms in the first place? I've been in this division over a year without problems. The previous method has worked just fine.

Notice that the division officer is responding to what he thinks is a personal criticism of him and how he runs his division, so he replies in a very defensive way.

DEPARTMENT HEAD: That's the trouble with you, Jim. You only think of yourself. I've made this change in the entire department. You're the only one complaining. As long as I'm the department head, we'll do it my way.

Now the department head sees the division officer's defense as an attack on his authority and responds blindly in terms of his own feelings.

This is a classic example of a breakdown in communication. Neither understands what the other is trying to say. Each is judging the other's statements in terms of his own attitudes and objectives. Little attention is being paid to the emotions the other is experiencing and expressing.

An officer who wants to improve his ability to communicate must take account of the other person's position and try to see the other point of view.

One key to effective verbal communication is to ascertain the characteristics of the audience in advance. Then the leader must adjust his speaking style and the message to fit the audience. He cannot necessarily communicate effectively, either up or down the chain of command, if he uses the same words and style of speaking in both directions. Admiral Carney cautions that,

when an officer delivers an order, he should observe the physical reaction as well as the verbal action it elicits, and he should pay attention to how the verbal response is given as well as to what the verbal response is. In other words, how something is said is as important as what is said. I was very aware of the negative attitude of one of my men, and my leadership helped turn the man into a fine sailor. I think you can sense a lack of sympathy or you can sense hostility. I had a sailor when I put the *Denver* in commission, he was from South Philadelphia, he was a troublemaker, and he was a bad actor. When we were crossing the equator and played a fire hose on his back, he came up with a knife and went berserk. He was overpowered, and I put him in the brig. So after he had served his bread and water, which in those days I could administer without the code of military justice interfering, I brought him back to mast, and before he said anything, I said, "I know exactly what you're thinking, and you're going to go back and do some more."

Well, I had a highly intelligent, loyal, first-class steward, and he went down on his own initiative and he talked to this bird and he explained to him that you can't have thirteen hundred people living elbow to elbow, cheek to cheek, on ship and have anybody who doesn't play along with the community rules. He accepted the steward's admonition, which he wouldn't have accepted had I used the very same terms to him. So the message came back that he'd like to see me. I brought him up to mast, he said he'd been wrong, he said the other man had talked to him and explained to him how he'd been wrong and that I wasn't going to have any more trouble with him. I said, "I'm going to tear that out of your record, but I'm going to keep it close by, and if you're sincere about what you say

that'll never show up in your record, but if you revert to your bad habits, I'll make sure it is in your records." He said, "No, Sir. You're not going to have any more trouble."

Time went on, we got out to the South Pacific, and one day we were under an air attack and he had a job in the forty-millimeter gun bucket right under the port side of the bridge, with a steel shield around it. This fellow came in strafing, pretty well peppering us, and the gun crew, quite within their rights and their instructions, ducked behind the steel shield. Except this one bird who was a loader, and he kept both those guns going with the ammunition that was in the magazines. I went on the loudspeaker to the ship and I told them about it. Well, you know from that day on, this troublemaker was the most loyal and valuable sailor I had on the ship. If anybody deviated from ship's pride and policy, he was right down their necks and it was a perfectly remarkable transformation.

An individual may be sending a message, but there is no communication unless the other person receives the message. What is said is important, but how it is said may be more important. Voice and inflection convey more than just words; they also denote enthusiasm, concern, elation, gloom, and anger. So, the officer should decide in advance how he is going to communicate. He should use the positive approach when he speaks. If he desires to gain approval of a new idea, he should not begin by criticizing the methods currently in use.

In written communications, unclear or improper sentences will cloud the message. Additionally, the manner in which the reader is addressed can greatly influence his perceptions and subconsciously create prejudice toward the subject matter and the communicator. In the following example, the officer is unmindful of the overtones that are present in his memorandum.

MEMORANDUM

From: B Division officer

To: B Division

Subj: LIBERTY

1. The cleanliness of B Division spaces—or lack of it—has been repeatedly brought to my attention by the XO following weekly zone inspections. Despite my fervent attempts to instill pride and professionalism in this division, the situation remains unsatisfactory. Therefore, by order of the XO, liberty is curtailed until all spaces meet established cleanliness standards.

2. The CO and Chief Engineer also know about this, so appeals to the Command Master Chief will be fruitless.

Although the division officer is obviously trying to motivate his division to clean the spaces, it appears that he is coercing them to do so. The underlying message is that he has lost control of his division and probably has little hope of regaining it. Even with the XO's decree that liberty is curtailed, he may not obtain the desired results over a sustained period.

The example also brings to light another fundamental precept of issuing orders; that is, the officer should be sure his language is understood. An officer should avoid "talking down" to the troops, but the officer who uses phrases such as "fervent attempts to instill" may not be understood by all members of the division. In addition, poor sentence structure detracts from any intended message.

66. Communication: A Two-Way Exchange of Information

By definition, communication can take place only if there is a two-way exchange of information. This implies the existence of a system in which senders and receivers are able to exchange roles. A good leader must be a good listener, and he can be, simply by applying the principle of do unto others as you would have others do unto you.[12-361] Sending and receiving functions are not used equally by all parts of the system. The amount of time spent in sending or receiving is a function of the purpose of the level in the chain of command that is being served by the communications system. If any component of the communications system is unable or unwilling to transmit, communication will not occur. Conversely, if any component is unable or unwilling to receive, communication with that component becomes impossible. To help ensure that the listener will want to take on board the message given, Admiral Larson suggests that

the first thing is to understand your audience. You have to understand their knowledge base and their interests and you have to talk right to them. Communicate with them honestly, openly, frankly, as if you were just talking to them one on one. Don't pontificate, don't strategize, don't talk in the lofty clouds, but speak to them and speak in a way that builds their knowledge base and involves them in what you're trying to do. Have a common frame of reference, have common interests. Now this will get difficult sometimes, when you're talking to an audience about things that may be controversial, that may not be easily accepted. On my ship and in my division, when I was a division officer, I used to involve my troops in the planning process. Before policy was formulated I would allow the dissenting views and all of the opinions to be gathered together. We would debate during policy formulation and then, once policy was formalized, I expected everybody to get on board once I had made my decision as a division or as a commanding officer. I expected them to get on board and support me firmly as we carried out our mission. If you are going to have to go before the whole crew or the whole division, it is useful to have that private policy planning session first, give that private explanation to some of the senior petty officers and junior officers, so that, when you go into that public forum with a controversial item, you will have their support immediately because they will understand where you're coming from, and then that support will capture the whole crew. But I think the important thing, I guess the bottom line, is just honest communication, as if you were talking to a friend or a contemporary, and talk to them, not down to them.

"Communications" is usually discussed in the context of communication between individuals: one-on-one, one-on-several, or one-on-many. Different techniques or approaches are effective in each of these three situations. For example, although a one-on-one private meeting and a one-on-many public oration both employ oral communication, complex ideas and problems are best discussed in detail in small groups. The spoken word becomes less useful, in a classic communications sense, as groups grow larger, such as when a general announcing system is used to address an entire organization. In this instance, communication exists only in a special sense, and only in one direction, because the receivers are not permitted to become senders except after the fact.

THE COMMUNICATIONS CLIMATE

The midshipman or young officer who understands the factors affecting his communications environment has an advantage over those who do not understand them. It is important for an officer to recognize and compensate for the fact that the chain of command in many instances impedes the flow of communications. Giving orders, sending directives, and establishing policy are easy—too easy. The inexperienced officer in the command structure can trap himself by assuming that communication is occurring because someone in the upper echelons of the organization hierarchy is transmitting frequently. Put another way, those in command are almost always the last to realize that the organization's communications needs are not being served well because the system lacks a well-exercised bottom-to-top communications capability. The ability to receive feedback is an essential ingredient in any unit or control system. The attentiveness of someone in conversation is an indication of how well a speaker is getting his ideas across.[12-356]

Organizations in which certain elements are always senders and other elements always receivers have allowed their communications system to become subverted. Variations on the "I know it all, I don't have to (and won't) listen" and the "You are too low in the organization to understand the problem, you don't know what you're talking about" syndromes abound in almost all organizations. Where the balance is struck between sending and receiving will govern the effectiveness of the organization's communications. The organization's leaders can enhance or degrade the communications environment by their apparent receptivity, by their response to legitimate stimuli, and by the climate of mutual trust and respect they help—or fail to help—develop.

Left to their own devices, bureaucracies tend to control and stifle rather than enhance or facilitate communications. "No, you can't talk to the division officer" or "The XO is too busy" are heard all too frequently. Turnoffs such as these convey the message that the command is not interested in what is happening on the other end of the totem pole. A positive communications "climate" can be turned off easily, while a negative climate is very difficult to turn around.

SHARING INFORMATION MEANS GIVING POWER

The chain of command concept provides a discipline that regularizes communications, but it also can isolate upper echelons from important information sources. Unregulated or unrecognized bureaucratic filtering deprives leadership of information that is frequently valuable, and the organization must remain sensitive to this possibility.

Knowledge is power, and while knowledge can be acquired from a variety of sources, that which is most valuable (and vital to the leader in an operating environment) is usually found among the subordinates in the organization. What kind of environment causes a person to want to tell the supervisor what is happening? What is it that makes that person want to share information and knowledge (and thereby power) with his seniors? Not surprisingly, the Golden Rule operates in the internal communications world, too. What motivates an officer to keep his boss informed will also motivate his subordinates to keep him informed. This motivation is provided by the knowledge or belief that seniors are interested in learning, that they will appreciate what the subordinate has to offer, and that they will act appropriately on the information passed to them. General Rice suggests that,

> to make sure that he is in fact receiving the intended message, a listener should, first of all, listen very carefully. And in order to make sure that people will listen carefully, a speaker must have something to say. Someone who holds meetings for the sake of holding meetings or hearing himself talk will find that people will not listen; they will come and they will take notes, but they will not really listen, because they will be thinking of other things.

An officer must use his judgment to determine whether it is better to ask a question during a briefing, in front of the group, or to wait and ask the question privately, after the briefing. It depends on the individual who is giving the briefing and on the circumstances. When I was in the U.S. Strike Command as a lieutenant colonel, the Commander in Chief's comments were taped. One time I happened

to be sitting in there when he talked, and I went back to my office and the major general called me in and gave me direction on what the CINC wanted. I just couldn't believe it, because I had sat there and listened to the CINC, and I knew what he wanted, and it wasn't close to what the major general said the CINC wanted. So, rather than counter the general, I went back and got the tape from the command center and played it back, and I heard what the CINC said, and it reinforced what I thought he said. So I went back to the general, an hour or so went by, and he said, "Well, maybe you're right. Go ahead and do it your way." I did it my way, and it happened to be right. So, you've just got to play it by ear.

I had the time and the opportunity to check my facts before I asked a question, but there are times, particularly in a combat situation, when a face-to-face immediate question is unquestionably necessary. An officer had better understand and know up front what the commander intends, and any commander worth his salt will either reinforce what he said or give the answer that is required. The worst thing an officer can do is just sit and mull. If he does not understand what is going on, he can get himself or someone else killed, simply because he was embarrassed to, or didn't want to, ask a question.

Every organizational level must be able to start the communications process, and while transmitting is usually the first step, receiving and listening to feedback is the second and more important step. The person who cuts off the head of the messenger bringing bad news will also miss out on a lot of "good" bad news. On the other hand, if the organization can see that the command puts feedback to good use, information sources flourish.

UNDERSTANDING AND EVALUATING

Listening is not a trivial task. It requires sensitivity, intelligence, understanding, and common sense. Aside from being sensitive, the listener must also be an astute judge who is able to evaluate the information he receives. A listener must either know the source of the information or have great faith in the reporter of it. Knowing the reporter's biases and special interests and how well the reporter evaluates the information acquired is essential. Harold J. O'Brien and Harold P. Zelko, professors of speech and communications, offer the following criteria for being an effective listener:

1. Attune yourself to the sender. An attitude of waiting to be sold or convinced may keep you in the dark. You must have a positive attitude of wanting to learn or understand.
2. Try to receive, no matter how poorly a message may be sent. Although a poorly organized talk, a rambling speech, a disjointed conversation, make listening difficult, try to understand.
3. Evaluate and analyze as you receive. People normally send what they want you to hear or they believe you want to hear.
4. Receive objectively. People tend to select senders who offer compliments or make life pleasant. This discourages the sender who has valuable though unpleasant information. Try to see the message from the sender's point of view.
5. Take appropriate action on what you receive. Receiving implies action.

The leader must know if the reporter is reporting facts he has acquired firsthand or is reporting "processed" data. If the latter, the leader must determine the attenuation factor. Does each successive layer in the chain put an increasingly benign face on bad news? Sometimes by the time the "problem" gets to a level in which people are capable of providing a solution, it does not seem to be a problem at all. This is a major source of frustration to subordinates who see and report real problems and have to live with these real problems on a daily basis. Admiral Burke notes that

a subordinate generally will not volunteer very much unless he believes his opinion is wanted. I did a lot of little things to obtain information from my people. For one thing, I had a Navy dinner, a mess dinner, every two weeks. I'd have some junior people, and the people who were connected with surface-to-air missiles, for example, and, if I could get them, one or two people who were opposed to surface-to-air missiles. I started off the dinner with drinks all the way round, and I went back to the old, old customs where the junior man speaks first. So the junior lieutenant would get up and he would make a proclamation of what he thought ought to be done, and he told this before anyone else said anything. No one would ever criticize him or any of the other subordinates directly. They would just talk about the subject. It was remarkable how well this always happened. The seniors leaned over backward to make sure they didn't cut the junior down just because they thought he was wrong.

Another thing I did was, sometimes when I put out an order, I got a flock of junior people, senior people, all the way up and down the line, and I said, "Let me know what happens, what is really done on this thing." So when I put out an order, I checked, maybe a couple of weeks later, as to what was happening here. I called lieutenants in, commanders in: "What about this work that's being done?" When my orders were not followed, it usually was not deliberate. The order was modified a little bit, or they interpreted it a little, or it just wasn't that important. In other words, things didn't happen the way you thought they were going to happen. I never did anything, I never took corrective action, except through the chain of command, but the information I got every way I could get it. I got information from wives, from secretaries, but I never used it except to check the thing officially.

For example, while I was commander of destroyers in the Atlantic before I became CNO, we were in Newport. Newport's a very easy harbor to get into, it's not bad, though sometimes it gets foggy. But I had a destroyer coming into port with a new captain aboard, and I guess he came from Norfolk or someplace. Anyway, he requested a pilot. Well, I had a rule on the staff and it was that I was the only one who could say no. If anyone asked for permission to do anything, asked for anything, no one else could tell them no, I would tell them no. If the answer was yes, they'd go ahead and do it, but only I said no.

Well, that rule worked as this thing came up. I said, "He shouldn't need a pilot and I'm going out and bring his ship in." "You can't do that," the staff said. I said, "The hell I can't," and so I went and met the ship with a barge and I climbed aboard and said, "I'll take over the ship." The captain said, "Admiral, I can take her in." I said, "No, Captain, you asked for a pilot, you got one. I'll take your ship in." And I took her in. I only had to do that once. I never had anyone ask for a pilot again. That went to the fleet in nothing flat.

A third thing I did was, every night when I was in destroyers, I drove my own car. No one in those days had quarters afloat, you lived on the economy. So on the way home I would pick up officers or blue jackets or whoever on the dock and talk to them on the way home. I kept a notebook in my pocket, and I always asked them certain questions. What ship

are you on? How is she? And what's she doing? Everything about her. I caught the name of each man, the ship and the captain's name, and maybe one line. Well, after two or three months I got a pretty good line on my ships, on the gripes. They wouldn't always tell me the truth, though they would sometimes, but I could get an awful lot of truth even when they weren't telling me all the truth. No one would ever say "My captain's a louse" or anything like that, but I'd get a half-damn praise.

I got a lot of dope about captains, so much so that when I was called out to be CNO, I had that book in my pocket, and they said, "You've got to have a flag lieutenant." I said, "I've got one, a junior lieutenant." They said, "You've got to have a commander." I said, "This boy's a good boy." They said, "No, he can't handle it, you've got to have more experience than this youngster has." Well, I looked in my book to find out what captain of what ship was best—I had these things by ship—and I went down and found a man, whom I did not know. I'd never seen him, but he had the best reputation from my own book. Everyone liked that ship, liked the skipper and what he had done. So I called his wife at Newport and said, "Is your husband in?" She said, "No, Sir, he's on the golf course." I said, "Would he like to be flag lieutenant to me?" And she said he would. "How do you know?" I asked. "I'll tell him to," she said. I said, "Can he be down here tomorrow morning?" "He'll be there." He was a hell of a good flag lieutenant, still is a very good friend, very fine man. But this came about strictly from asking anyone I found a lot of questions. You could ask other questions: What did you think about this ordeal? What do you think went wrong? Well, they'd tell you something,

345

and mostly it didn't matter much. Once in a while you'd get a pointer and it was damn good, though. What it does do is start people to think a little bit, and they would have something on their mind next time you talked to them, or the word spread that the commander asks his people questions, and so they would be interested in some things. Interest is one thing you've got to get.

The officer must be a perceptive listener, because frequently what is not said is more important than what is said. As he practices and gains experience, the young officer will develop a facility for asking "the right question."

Admiral de Cazanove suggests that
it is best if the officer can lead others to draw for themselves the conclusion that is his. The principal way this can be achieved is by ensuring that your people know your thinking and approaches to problem solution. The perfect command is not to give any command, because if your people know exactly what you are going to give as a command, they will take the necessary action without further directives having to be given. Sometimes I used to be asked to ask the admiral what he would say, and I would reply that there was no need to ask him that, and when asked why, I replied that I knew perfectly well what he would say, so why ask him? There is no need to ask the boss whether he wants the job done in the way that will give the best results, for that is obviously what he will want. In wartime this is particularly important, and officers must know both the desires and reasons therefore of their senior, as well as what action should be taken to gain the senior's objectives. You do this because you love your country and your boss. When you have the privilege of feeling this way about your boss, it is extraordinary, for you obey not only because he is your boss but also because you "like" him very much—you respect him, and know that you are being well led. Especially in action this is a great benefit and gives all a great feeling, but even if you do not feel this way about your boss, you will do what he wants because you are disciplined.

MCPON Sanders: *To be a successful officer you must work at being a good listener. As a leader, you should not only listen to your crew but, while giving them your message, see the nonverbal feedback that you are getting and determine whether they are listening and understand what you are saying. When they speak to you, direct your attention to them, for if you don't, they will automatically cut you off. Unless you are ready to listen, you will have fewer people coming to you, and speaking to you only when they have to. Be a good listener, take notes, mental notes at least.*

67. On the Receiving End of Effective Communications

One method of instruction is for the instructor to tell the class what he is going to help them learn, present the subject, and then tell them what they are supposed to have learned. Communication can be thought of as a teaching/learning process, wherein one individual has information he wants to impart to another individual, who wants to receive the information. Communication does not take place just because the person with a message to transmit has a desire for another person to receive the message, a fact that has not gone unnoticed by advertisers, who try to convey a message to the consuming public in a variety of ways, in the hope that one of the repetitions of the message will get through.

This is not to say that the Naval Service is involved in an advertising campaign, for naval units receiving information want the information and thus will exert effort to make sure they receive it. Officers try to communicate to others in terms they will understand, but they also determine whether the receiver is ready to receive the message and wants to do so.

The ability to convey messages from one person to another is dependent on attitude as well as physical presence. Between units, communication is also dependent on equipment capability, and it is the responsibility of the leader to make sure his receiving communications equipment and personnel are up to standard. In both cases, the motivation of the person receiving the message must be considered. It is obvious that if the receiving individual does not understand the language of transmission, the message will not get through, and it is just as true that if the individual does not want to receive the message, he will not. Admiral Fran McKee notes that

> counseling on fitness reports/evaluations is probably the best example that I can think of to illustrate the need for an officer to properly communicate that he or she has a subordinate's best interest at heart. This includes commending on strong points as well as sometimes getting an unwelcomed message across on some area of deficiency. While it is generally easy for people to accept praise, the reverse may be said for people when they hear of their shortcomings. Since most of us have delusions of our approaching perfection, it can be an enlightening moment to hear of any discrepancies in performance. It's therefore important that the individual being counseled be receptive to any discussion on this point. It is easy to listen to praise or to dispense it, but a productive discussion of below-par performance is sometimes difficult. It is the responsibility of officers to counsel and assist subordinates, and it must be done with skill and understanding to be effective. The best interest of the individual and the overall unit will then best be served.

A primary consideration in the communications process is to ensure that the individual not only is ready to receive the message but wants to do so, as well. This desire to receive a message depends partly on the receiver understanding both the importance of the message and the effect it can have on his unit. The receiver in this instance is the ultimate receiver, not the person or persons who transmit a message between sender and receiver. Obviously, everyone in the transmission process will not understand the importance of all the messages they send. The receiving commanding officer, therefore, must ensure that training and experience and equipment capability make it possible for the sender's message to be received on board.

Certainly it can be assumed that well-trained, disciplined, and loyal officers will want to receive another officer's message, but the sender should keep in mind that the receiver has many competing matters to consider. Thus, messages sent in a way that indicates to the receiver the value of receiving the entire message are more likely to get the receiver's attention. The leader must also be on the lookout to avoid words with ambiguous meanings. Some words may have many meanings, and it is best to avoid these unless it is perfectly clear what is meant when one is used. Semantics is the study of words and word usage and may help the officer in avoiding this problem.[35-581] Before messages are sent between people, the people usually have established a relationship by personal contact or by reputation. Pre-existing conditions such as this affect communications, and thus interfaces between groups and individuals set the stage for future communications between these same groups: communications generally are transmitted well between "friends." By communication style and personal contact, then, a unit or an individual develops a reputation of generally communicating something that is worthwhile to listen to. Receivers of a message from these individuals or units will want to listen, for they realize that they will benefit from what they hear.

This puts the onus on the sender to ensure that the message being sent is, in fact, important to the receiver and will be of help and value to him. It is necessary, then, for the sender to understand the mission and goals of the receiver; only then can he be assured that the messages he sends meet the needs of the receiver and will not become just more paper work for the receiver to process. There are five principles to help increase the accuracy of the message. They are:

1. Ensure that the message is relevant to the receiver.
2. Reduce the message to the simplest possible terms.
3. Organize the message.
4. Repeat key points (verbal messages).
5. Focus on essential aspects only.[35-563]

It is useful for individuals and organizations to review messages with those who sent them, whether through data links or in person, and to discuss the value of the messages sent and received. If an individual receives a message that does not seem to have any practical application to his operations, then he should raise a question with the sender as to the importance of what was sent, so that if the receiver missed the importance he can discover what it is. There is a dual responsibility in this relationship: not only is the receiver required to check with the sender if he does not understand the reason for the message, but the sender must double-check from time to time to make sure the receiver is getting the message that was intended.

The main point here is that messages are sent for a purpose: to convey information to others which may affect their actions. Messages will be better received if the receiver sees a value in the message (this is a responsibility of the sender), and the action of sending a message is only completed if the receiver receives the message and the sender knows that the receiver understands the meaning he intended the message to convey.

68. Setting the Example: One Form of Communicating

Consider the following clichés:

"Actions speak louder than words."
"I'm from Missouri. Show me."
"Do what I say, not what I do."

We tend to toss off these well-worn phrases, and we tend to answer them with a "Ha!" Perhaps because they are so often repeated, they have lost credibility, especially in today's verbal-video world, where "image" or reputation is frequently made in a few paragraphs or in 90 seconds on television. Disregarding the message behind these clichés is a trap into which naval officers should not and cannot fall if they expect to be effective in the hard, real world of the U.S. Navy or Marine Corps. One of the foremost responsibilities of a leader is to serve as the example or model for his followers in everything that he does or is.[32-49] The military expects that its officers will be an example to their troops in the performance of duty, in the sharing of hardships and danger with the troops, and, above all, in the high standards of moral and ethical behavior.[32-33]

This is not to say that verbal and written communication is not important. On the contrary, the talent to communicate effectively with language has been the mark of great leaders throughout history. The words of Winston Churchill and Franklin Roosevelt during World War II were a great inspiration to the people of their nations. General MacArthur and Admirals Nimitz and Halsey also knew how to use the language to great effect. But all of those leaders had something else in common: they acted on what they said. They backed up their words with behavior and performance that made the words they spoke and wrote true and therefore meaningful.

One key to effective communication in leadership, then, is being articulate—and that does not necessarily mean "fancy"—and matching articulateness with action. When actions and words are not combined effectively, they are out of synchronization. Everyone has met a great "embellisher," a person who has more big-fish stories than anyone else but who never seems to produce the fish—or even the fishing pole. The embellisher is wonderful at happy hours but not very good during working hours. That person is not someone with whom many would choose to go to war.

Then there is the person who says nothing, forcing everyone else to interpret his actions. It is not always bad to say nothing. However, actions in this complicated world are not always simple or clear-cut. They sometimes leave people saying to themselves, "What's going on?" Everyone has been perplexed by the unexplained actions of another at least once. A leader is above all a teacher, and, like all teachers, he is constantly under the very acute, and not always charitable, observation of his pupils. They will, perhaps instinctively, model themselves on him—even to the extent of copying his idiosyncrasies.[64-29]

So there is a simple formula: *Say it well* plus *do it well* equals *successful communications*. Right? Almost, but not quite. There are two intervening variables that make a big difference. First are the expectations of the officer's audience, whether it is made up of peers, crew members, or the general public. Second is the stereotype within which the officer operates (everyone operates within a stereotype). These two factors are separate and distinct, but they act together in the fine art of human communications.

An individual carries with him the stereotypes belonging to the career and lifestyle he has chosen as well as to the organizations he joins. These categorize him. Corporate presidents have different images or stereotypes than rock stars or professional football linebackers. People conjure up a mental image of an individual well before they meet him. Therefore, they expect that person to display a certain pattern of behavior and speech. These expectations are not always valid, but they are there. Admiral Taylor:

Actions speak louder than words is the expression, and I think that's true, but I don't think actions alone can do it, and I don't think words alone can do it. My style has been to keep the troops well informed. When you're in command of an aircraft carrier with 5,000 guys scattered out in 2,000 spaces, what keeps it all together from my experience is a commanding officer who gets out there on a regular basis for a few minutes. If he gets out there and he talks for too long, then he's losing the crowd, but if he boils it down to the right kinds of things, then people are going to listen.

You also have to get out among the troops, and you have to be true to your word, to what you tell them, and you have to set an example of leadership. You have to be up early, and up late, and work hard in the middle. And if you don't care about what time you get in there, what time you go home, if you don't have the philosophy of first in, last out, and I'm going to work hard in the middle, then you're going to get left by others, because that is the old work ethic. The leader has to set the example; that is something that junior officers must fully understand. There are an awful lot of people who know they're smart and sharp, and then they'll get whipped by the turtle who gets up early and stays up late. So your actions and what you do and making good on your word and setting a good example in every respect, of being personable, keeping the old positive attitude out there are important.

Let me relate an experiment I ran on *Coral Sea* with respect to actions and positive attitude. After a bad night with three or four hours of intermittent sleep, 20 phone calls, as we made our way through a lot of busy water, I finally got up at 5:30 and started walking on the bridge at ten minutes of six. As I walked through the pilot house, a boatswain's mate of the watch said, "Good morning, captain," "Good morning, troops. How we doing here? It looks like it's been in good hands tonight. You guys are all looking smiley faced here, I guess everything is in good shape, not a worry, right?" and I walked out on the bridge and I saw the OD and told him, "It's a great-looking day, and I think we're going to have a good day today." I set a tone of positive and good and everything's under control and smiley face, and all those guys on the sound powered hook ups, they're talking down into the ship saying "Look, captain's on the bridge, everything's going good." The tone is set. A positive tone.

But then on a couple other nights when there were two or three hours intermittent sleep, maybe I got a bad letter from home, bills were piling up, and the executive officer was not hacking it, and I walked on the bridge and they said, "Good morning, captain," and I said, "Same to you, fellow." You put on a little old glum face and the first thing you say to the OD is "Get the XO up here," then you get the XO out on the wing of the bridge and the guys are saying, "Hey, the skipper's up here chewing on the XO," and then all of a sudden there's another tone going out through the ship. But what you've done is squash enthusiasm.

As a leader you have to be able to absorb that shock, just take it and take it and take it. It's the greatest thing in the world, it makes you stronger and better for it. It's a great privilege and honor to lead troops, but it's a price you pay. You

have to be able to set a tone and keep it there every day, and you do that by your actions, just little subtle ones, but you have to have them, and if you're going to want the troops to be positive, you've got to be positive. Case in point, the 1980 presidential election, we have a leader with all his training who gets up and says everything's okay. We have another guy up there saying everything's terrible. Now, political philosophies aside, to me it said who do we want to lead, the guy with the smile who says everything's going to be okay, trust me, or the guy who says, hey, we're in a whole lot of trouble? Everybody's always in a lot of trouble. But your leadership has got to get in and say we're going to whip this problem, stay with it. The same thing is true at a breakfast table in the families of our country. If the mother and father are coming down to breakfast and there is a positive tone, then it goes out. And then achievement, you check back in at dinner time, and everyone has a positive glow there. But turn it around the other way. If the bills are piling up and there are internal problems in the family, you can squelch real enthusiasm for going out and whipping the world by just the tone that gets set at breakfast.

Naval officers who are graduates of the Naval Academy, as well as Academy midshipmen, are stereotyped immediately. The image or reputation of the Naval Academy follows its students and graduates, and its students and graduates reinforce or erode that image. The process is synergistic. The people naval officers interact with have expectations of them based on the stereotype of Naval Academy graduates. In order to communicate effectively, naval officers must understand their own stereotype, because what they say and do will be interpreted within their audiences' expectations, at least at first. The leader sets the moral tone for his subordinates by the example of integrity he provides in both his official duties and his private actions. Honesty cannot be instilled by contract—but may be enhanced by education about its importance to mission accomplishment and by example.[28–106]

This does not mean that an individual must be or live the stereotype. But the individual must understand the stereotype in order to carve his individuality from it, to redefine or enlarge the stereotype with his own image. In the process, he is able, ultimately, to communicate from a platform of his own making. The process begins, however, with an understanding of the expectations and the stereotypes that obtain.

One point must be made here. As each person redefines the stereotype with his own audience, he carries a responsibility not to tarnish, but rather to enhance, the fundamental stereotype within which he has chosen to operate (i.e., the Naval Service). Fulfilling that responsibility effectively brings individual benefits and institutional rewards.

How does this process work in practice? Lieutenant Bobby Goodman, USN, was a bombadier/navigator in an A-6 shot down by groundfire over Lebanon in 1983. His pilot was killed. Lieutenant Goodman was captured, taken to Syria, and held there for more than a month. He was released and returned to the United States with Reverend Jesse Jackson to a hero's welcome at Andrews Air Force Base. He was subsequently sought after by all of the television talk shows and other media from around the world. Heady stuff for a young officer to handle all at once, but he did exceptionally well. He handled himself in captivity extremely well, and when he returned, what he had to say about himself, the mission, and his captivity reflected a cool, deliberate, intelligent, and professional manner. What he said and how he said it matched his actions before, during, and after his captivity. What is more, all of these things fulfilled the expecta-

tions people have of a professional naval aviator who graduated from the Naval Academy. At the same time that Lieutenant Goodman carved for himself an individuality, he brought credit to himself and to his service.

Finally, when officers communicate verbally or nonverbally, they must be concerned with context. When, where, and how they say or do something make a great difference in the way it is interpreted. If someone yells "Beat Army" at a rally in front of Bancroft Hall, that is very positive. What if someone yells the same thing with the same intensity at the Tomb of the Unknown Soldier on Memorial Day? Same words, same volume, but a different message that generates a different image for the yeller. A ludicrous example? Perhaps. But the point is clear. Be aware of context. Be aware, too, that context is dynamic. As society and culture change, as events change, opinions and mores change style, so context changes. Consequently, no one can communicate well without being aware of his surroundings. Army Chief of Staff General Edward C. Meyer put it well in 1980 when he said "The obligation of service and commitment inherent in the military ethic imposes burdens not customary in the larger society, where obligations are normally contractual in nature and limited in degree of personal sacrifice expected. For the soldier, the obligation is complete: to the death if necessary."

Remember, then: Say it well. Do it well. Know your stereotype and yourself and your audience's expectations. Be aware of the context. Stay in synchronization or, in today's cliché: "Be a together person."

MCPON Sanders: *The crew must know your policies, not necessarily by you repeating them but by personally setting the standard, yourself, as well as requiring the crew to meet standards. It's really a matter of personal example in everything you do and how you approach your work. If you set a good example, others will follow.*

69. Communications as a Component of Planning

In the process of developing plans for the future, the officer is afforded the opportunity to communicate both formally and informally. To ensure the development of useful plans, the officer must engage in a continual exchange of ideas, requirements, and objectives with others. In fact, the process of planning is sometimes more valuable than the plan itself, and can be viewed as a communications exercise. Planning requires a thorough and common understanding of the organization's mission and function, and it formalizes the steps that will be taken to execute them in the future. Each word or group of words has different meanings and connotations, and does not convey the same ideas to every person; thus, special care must be taken in communications.[74]

The process of establishing organizational goals provides another opportunity for everyone concerned to discuss where the organization is going. Normally this process entails setting up long-term goals or objectives; a set of more specific, short-term objectives is established periodically. The establishment of objectives is a top-down evolution, with each organizational layer implementing the senior's objectives as they apply. Although an active exchange will result in understandable and achievable objectives, the leader ultimately sets the objectives. Again, the communication leading up to the actual setting of objectives is valuable. As Admiral Zumwalt points out,

> the importance of communication is (a) to make sure that what is wanted is understood, (b) to make sure that the understanding includes why the order or assignment makes sense, and (c) to make sure that the sense includes an explanation of how the specific assignment fits within the objective of the day or the month or the year. These three aspects of communications are sufficient to convey

an order, but the order is often followed better if in addition the officer can make it part of the fun of the day or the month or the year.

The officer who has first-hand contact with his people will be more successful than one who does not, because they will be familiar with the officer's style, and the officer will be aware of their capabilities. A commanding officer, for example, might get around daily to see what is going on in various parts of the ship, to drop into chief's quarters for that cup of coffee while he listens carefully amidst the banter to pick up where there is a problem that is not otherwise surfacing. He can then go back and ask a question through the chain of command that will lead to the necessary insights and changes. The successful leader analyzes the situation when something has not gone right, and determines whether or not in part or in whole it was the result of not communicating properly. If he concludes that that is the reason for the failure, then he should seek to improve his or his subordinates' ability to communicate.

Oftentimes the senior (rating officer) and the subordinate can use organizational objectives to establish individual objectives. The communication surrounding this procedure defines the future relationship of the two and determines the type of work the subordinate will do over the next rating period.

Following up on plans and objectives established for the future is a necessary part of discipline. The follow-up should be simple and avoid excessive paper work. The follow-up process must be well understood by both the senior and the junior, and it must permit the junior to ask questions concerning his progress. Without a follow-up system, human nature will lead individuals to expend all of their effort on immediate issues or crisis and neglect the direction of the organization. A means of measuring progress toward goals and objectives, or periodic plan assessments, is essential.

In some instances it is beneficial to formulate a method of measuring progress at the time a plan or program is approved. This technique avoids misunderstanding and allows future success or failure to be easily determined.

On the general subject of communication, Admiral Holloway makes the point that,

> when the officer deems the delivery and comprehension of a message to be very important, he should not hesitate to ask for an acknowledgment of the message. For example, if an air raid on a city was scheduled, but the commander received word from the White House not to deploy because a U.S. government envoy was arriving in the city that day for a peace conference, the commander's message to the front would probably read: "Cancel air operations tomorrow in Vietnam between 1000 and 1800 local time. Repeat, cancel scheduled operations. Acknowledge this message." Because it would be essential that no one missed that instruction—and end up sending a combat flight in there when the envoy arrived—the commander would request acknowledgment.

> On the other hand, many messages do not require an acknowledgment. The person who sends the messages can tell by the messages he receives within the next week or so whether the original message was understood.

> If he considers it necessary, the officer can always ask his senior to acknowledge a message. Say the leader of a unit is told to deliver an intelligence officer to a destroyer on the gun line, and it is very important that the intelligence officer get up there because he has some information. If the weather was bad, the unit leader would immediately send the word back: "Unable to deliver Lieutenant Jones to USS *Treadway* because of bad weather.

> Repeat, unable to deliver. Confirmation requested." The leader must be sure that the commander receives the message; if he does not receive it, he will assume that Lieutenant Jones delivered his very important information, and he will make his plans accordingly.

70. Written Communications

Much of the routine, day-to-day operation of the Naval Service is governed by written orders. U.S. Navy Regulations, OPNAVINST 3120.32A (the Navy SORM), Marine Corps Orders, and Uniform Regulations are examples of written orders that govern the way in which naval officers go about their business. Of particular importance is the detail these written orders contain and the frequency with which officers benefit from the guidance they provide. They deal with relatively complex, multifaceted issues and generally are not subject to rapid change or modification based on the circumstances surrounding their implementation.

The written instructions and notices published by a command or a higher headquarters usually fall into a similar category, but the scope of their coverage is less broad. Similarly, it is usually advisable to utilize written orders when citing or quoting a higher authority, thus eliminating the possibility of error or confusion through misinterpretation. Admiral Fran McKee states that,

> in general, written orders are for more complex tasks or tasks requiring detailed explanations. Standing orders, or orders that you want to place in a book of information or on bulletin boards, or things that you want to have or use for some time should also be written.

Admiral Larson:

> Written orders are very important when the orders are complicated, when they are extremely formal, when they are very important to the safety of the ship. Now

one example here are your captain's standing orders to the officer of the deck, or your captain's night orders. You don't want to rely on word of mouth passing from person to person, but you want to have certain basic principles in writing so they can be referred to, and referred to frequently. Written orders convey a sense of formality and provide a common frame of reference for all of your actions and all of your decisions. I think we all realize how easily the verbal word can be confused once it's passed from person to person. We've all played that old parlor game where you whisper around the table in somebody's ear and you don't recognize the result that comes after five or six people have passed a sentence. So I think that all the following should be written so you have that very important frame of reference: (1) very formal things that are the basis of your organization, (2) complicated orders, (3) things that will need to be referred back to and spot-checked because you want to make sure that you're doing it exactly right, (4) things in highly sensitive areas where you need to be sure, such as in rules of engagement or ships' actions, and (5) things that are critical to a ship's success. Verbal orders can be given to augment that foundation as you operate your command.

Operations Orders (OPORDs) written to govern the operations of a fleet or the conduct of a fleet exercise are documents that, because of the complexity of the evolutions they control, must spell out in detail what procedures are to be followed and how operational plans will be executed. Some sections of a OPORD, such as a schedule of events, are subject to change as an activity evolves, but the basic governing document normally remains in effect throughout the duration of the activity.

From these examples of written orders emerge several common features. The following char-

acteristics are normally associated with the use of written orders in the Navy:

1. The topic addressed by written orders usually is complex, is broad in scope, and requires a considerable amount of detailed explanation to be conveyed effectively.
2. Implementing changes to written orders requires time.
3. The guidance provided by written orders is usually of an enduring nature, governing an activity for a considerable period.
4. Personnel subject to a written order are strictly bound to adhere to its provisions; written orders leave little or no room for interpretation or personal preference.

The use of written orders is not restricted to matters of policy and broad interest, however. There may be occasions when it is in the best interests of a senior to provide written guidance to a junior. A complex task, a need for strict accountability, or a need to correct noted performance deficiencies are conditions in which the use of a written, rather than a verbal, order would be appropriate. The specific responsibilities of certain watchstanders, for example, such as sentries or sounding and security watches, should be clearly spelled out in writing.

The provision of policy and guidance through a written order is typified in shipboard orders such as the commanding officer's standing orders and the engineer's night orders. A junior officer can apply the concepts delineated in these orders when he writes his own orders for a unit as small as a division. In his orders, the junior officer can specify divisional policies, work and cleaning assignments, and operating procedures for the personnel concerned.

The concepts in the following list can help an officer determine whether written orders can be used effectively and efficiently to accomplish a specific mission.

Do use a written order to promulgate policies or assignments that have wide application.

Do use a written order to cover complicated issues, particularly when subordinates may need to refer back to the order for details or additional guidance.

Do use a written order when there is any indication that a subordinate might deviate, deliberately or otherwise, from verbal guidance and must be held strictly accountable.

Do use a written order when it is anticipated that its provisions will remain in effect for some time and that sufficient lead time will be available to issue any necessary changes to the order.

Do use a written order when continuity is needed and a succession of persons are involved.

Do use a written order when cooperation and coordination between several organizations, units, or work groups is required.

Do use a written order when it must be issued to persons or activities in widely separated locations.

Don't use a written order when timeliness is paramount.

Don't use a written order for very simple instructions.

Don't use a written order when rapid changes in tasking or circumstances are expected.

Don't use a written order as a substitute for leadership and instruction.

Admiral Long suggests that

it is very important for ships or squadrons or base operations to have written instructions, particularly those dealing with the operation of complex equipment. That equipment must be operated properly and maintained properly, and this includes such things as preventive maintenance schedules, operating procedures, safety precautions. There must also be written procedures and doctrines for essential personnel matters, such as how someone gets promoted or what someone's benefits are. There should be written guidelines for the necessary reports that are written and the inspections that are conducted, too.

Any organization needs to be careful, however, to make sure that written procedures, paper work, and check-off lists serve primarily as a guide or a reminder for most people. They should not become so indispensable that people cannot function without them. If people fail to follow the procedures, it will be harmful to their equipment or to themselves or to their own welfare or to morale, and people must understand this. But it is impossible to cover every situation, so it is essential that people try to adapt general principles to specific situations. An old tongue-in-cheek rule is: As a last resort, let's shift to common sense.

As an officer advances in his rank he will no doubt rely more and more on informal discussion. But when a senior command is communicating with a junior command, it is incumbent upon the senior command, regardless of the amount of informal staff discussion that takes place on a significant issue, to put their views in writing rather than passing it up and down the line by staff to staff on a telephone.

A leader must know what is going on, and clearly one way he can find out what is going on is to receive written and oral reports through a formal chain of command. An officer can also keep informed by inspecting the spaces or "walking the ship." Another very important way is to talk to his people.

MCPON Sanders: *I would recommend to the junior officers that they use written orders when (1) the orders of operation are important and need to be followed exactly, (2) you desire to hold an individual strictly accountable, and (3) there is complicated work or a lot of things to get done within a short period of time. In the last case it is also important to set a priority listing of what you want done by order of importance.*

71. Oral Communications

> And ye shall compass the city, all ye men of war, and go round about the city once. Thus shalt thou do six days . . . and when ye hear the sound of the trumpet, all the people shall shout a great shout; and the walls of the city shall fall down flat. (Joshua 6:2–5)

These are some of the earliest recorded oral military orders. According to the Bible, God spoke these orders to Joshua and directed the fall of Jericho. This biblical passage provides a good introduction to a study of oral orders.

An officer can expect to give and receive thousands of oral orders during his career. An order, according to the *Joint Chiefs of Staff Dictionary*, is "a communication, written, oral, or by signal, which conveys instructions from a superior to a subordinate." The situation dictates the manner in which this communication is made, but as long as the issuer of the order possesses the requisite authority to issue the order, any manner he deems appropriate is acceptable. Admiral Long suggests that,

> in communicating orally, leaders should adjust their style and their content to fit their audience. People who communicate in a monologue in most cases are not communicating as well as they could. Officers need to develop the ability, whether in a social environment or in a professional environment, to listen to people.

> It is especially important for officers to give subordinates an opportunity to express their views. Not only does the senior gather more information this way, but he also has subordinates who become a part of the organization and a part of the business of running such an organization because they are able to express their own views and know the senior is listening. Of course the responsibility still remains with the senior, but he will benefit if he can generate within his subordinates not only

candor but also loyalty to carry out his decisions after they are made.

It is impossible to have written orders on every aspect of professional life, and this is particularly true in an operational capacity, such as aboard ship or in an aircraft or in an organization of Marines. There used to be a saying within the submarine force, which probably has as many written directives and instructions and procedures as any military organization, "We do not have an instruction forbidding elephants down in the reactor compartment." This was just a way of saying all situations cannot be covered, and at some point those in command will have to make on-the-spot decisions.

Good orders meet three criteria. First, they point the way to a goal. To achieve this goal, the order describes a well-thought-out plan and specifically tasks each person with a job that contributes to the completion of that plan. The heart of an order is the plan it describes. A good order also clearly describes the role every person will play in the plan to achieve the goal. Furthermore, only orders that you intend to enforce should be instituted. Orders that are issued just for the record are useless.[47-655]

Second, orders have to be understood by the individuals to whom they are given. Helmuth von Moltke, in the 1800s, said, "An order that can be misunderstood will be misunderstood."[34-225] The heroic charge of the Light Brigade, made famous by Tennyson in his poem of the same name, was a military blunder caused by misunderstood orders. The 600 brave cavalrymen who rode to their deaths were carrying out an order from their commander to "Attack the guns!" The guns that the commander wanted them to attack were a small battery off to the side of the valley. Unbeknown to the commander, this battery was hidden from the brigade's view by a berm. The 600 men saw only the main battery of guns at the far end of the valley, presumed these were the guns they had been ordered to attack, and rode to their deaths, dutifully carrying out misunderstood orders.

Rarely is an order of such consequence given. As officer of the deck on a destroyer, however, an officer has responsibility for the safety of the entire crew, and he must word any orders he gives carefully. In an emergency, the helmsman who is issued an irregular order may misunderstand it, with disastrous consequences. The maintenance officer of a helicopter squadron who gives an order to "Replace a worn-out linkage" on a helicopter could cause the death of a crew six months later; the accident investigation will show that the wrong linkage was replaced. The decisions an officer makes and the orders he gives will, by the very nature of the job, affect the lives and safety of his fellow officers and the enlisted personnel. Orders must not be misunderstood.

The third part of a good order is timeliness. Personnel need enough time to carry out orders in accordance with the plan. Military evolutions are often complex, requiring long set-up times and coordination with other units. An order to launch a noon air strike given at 1145 is impossible to carry out, and if this strike is in support of a noon amphibious landing on the beach, the consequences, again, could be disastrous.

These are the three essential criteria of a good order. It clearly tasks each person with a job in accordance with a plan, it is easily understood, and it is timely. Orders may be in written, oral, or signal form, but oral orders are the oldest and by far the most common form of orders given. An officer will learn through experience when it is best to use oral orders, and he will discover the problems peculiar to their use, but the following are generally accepted guidelines for issuing oral orders. Four situations are particularly well suited for using oral orders: when there is a need to clarify written orders and provide minor details; during an emergency; during an ongoing operation; and when an officer is working with a thoroughly trained team.

Admiral Horatio Nelson, perhaps the greatest naval tactician who ever lived, was famous for his oral orders. He would gather his ship captains together before a battle and explain his plans and expectations for the upcoming battle. After these verbal briefings, written orders would be issued and the whole plan would be started by a simple numerical sign. The prebattle oral communication was the essence of the "Nelson Touch." It ensured a clear understanding of the written orders and gave Nelson's captains an opportunity to ask questions and clarify the details of the battle plan. Oral orders are still an excellent tool for clarifying written orders and for providing minor details to personnel.

Emergency situations often require verbal orders. Admiral Fran McKee comments: "Verbal orders are issued when you don't have a great deal of time or when the individual is very knowledgeable about the task and it takes very few words to delineate a task to that person and you think that they'll understand what you say without detailed explanation." In August 1814, President James Madison and several members of his cabinet observed the beginning of the battle of Bladensburg. Secretary of the Navy William Jones mentioned to the President that if the British were to win the battle and march on Washington, D.C., ships and stores at the Washington Navy Yard would fall into enemy hands. Jones recommended their destruction should the British advance. President Madison agreed. Later that same day, Secretary Jones visited Captain Thomas Tingey, commandant of the yard, and issued verbal orders to burn whatever the British could make use of should they reach the city. That night Tingey was forced to follow the secretary's command.

During an ongoing operation, timeliness is an important factor. Oral orders allow an officer to give instructions to his personnel quickly and without interrupting their work. A captain's verbal order to "Fire" in the midst of battle, or his rudder orders to the helmsman, could not effectively be written down and delivered. Oral orders ensure timely communication and minimize the interruption of the work at hand. They are an excellent way to give direction to personnel during an ongoing operation.

Lastly, verbal orders are well suited for directing a thoroughly trained team. An experienced boatswain knows what he and his team should do when he hears orders to "Single up the lines." A thoroughly trained crew knows where to go and what to do when general quarters sound over the 1MC. Thorough training beforehand enhances the communication and understanding between senior and subordinate and permits the effective use of verbal orders in virtually any situation. General Rice notes that

> time is one factor to consider in determining whether orders should be written or spoken. It is far better in terms of staff coordination to have written orders. A staff evaluation, for example, should be written, because the people have something they can turn to. In emergency situations, fast-breaking situations, verbal orders are called for. The key to successful verbal orders is for people to know the officer, to have worked with him and trained with him. If the officer and the troops have done things over and over again, have practiced different things, and the troops know that the officer can save time by giving a verbal order, they will respond to it quickly and well.

Problems associated with verbal orders stem from the same qualities that make them so well suited to the preceding situations. The speed and ease with which oral orders can be given make it easy for a commander to issue bad orders. A hastily given order can be misunderstood because it provides only partial or inaccurate information. Or a commander, under pressure to deliver an order quickly, could decide on a bad plan—for which there can be no good orders. An officer's people will know and measure him most by his orally delivered orders. He must be careful not to let the ease with which he can

deliver an order orally diminish the care he takes in leading his subordinates.

As a subordinate himself, he should recognize that the action he takes on verbal orders, should it lead to debacle, leaves him open to scapegoating. Safety cannot be found, however, by demanding that everything be in writing, but only by demanding that both seniors and subordinates command respect and display trust through their professional behavior. Without respect and trust up and down the chain of command, an oral communication system cannot function effectively. In his memoirs, Viscount Montgomery of Alamein wrote: "A commander must train his subordinate commanders, and his own staff, to work and act on verbal orders. Those who cannot be trusted to act on clear and concise verbal orders, but want everything in writing, are useless."[33-226]

72. Avoiding Communication Pitfalls

Orders are absolutely necessary; they tell individuals how to act in their formal positions.[63-53] When giving an order to subordinates, the leader must use a straightforward approach and the simplest of terms to convey what he wants them to accomplish. His orders should leave no room for interpretation and should contain no words with a hidden or "double" meaning. Too often the word *should* is used in orders when the officer really means *must* or *will*. Before issuing an order, an officer must always ask himself whether or not the order is explicit. As Admiral Holloway points out,

> orders are most likely to be misunderstood either when the senior who drafts them does not take the time or care to make them clear, concise, and unambiguous, or when a subordinate is unable, for some reason, to understand what he is being told. Very often an order is unclear because an officer relies on his aide or assistant to convey his wishes. The officer

who writes his own orders can be sure they are worded so they can be understood. An officer should instruct his staff to check with him if an order is unclear, because sometimes assistants are reluctant to disturb their boss for that purpose. On the receiving end, subordinates sometimes have difficulty understanding the intentions of their leaders, so officers must eliminate ambiguity from their messages, both written and oral.

If an explanation or background information is necessary for the proper execution of an order, and time permits, the officer should provide this information prior to issuing the order. Then he should issue the order as a checklist. Sea stories or superfluous materials are not required, and they will only create diversions and confusion for the crew or the troops. An order should not be entwined with an explanation or overview.

People work better when they understand the purpose of their efforts, so a leader can often achieve better results by providing subordinates with an overview. Giving subordinates sufficient background material will make them feel that they are "involved" and are taking an active part in the exercise or work effort. Subordinates who understand the reasons for an assignment are also better able to exercise their judgment and make adjustments as the situation changes or as problems arise. The officer who keeps everything to himself and practices the "mushroom" theory with his subordinates only creates problems. A leader cannot keep his people in the dark and expect them to function effectively and to their full potential or to feel that they are a part of the "team."

The leader must know what he is going to say. Unorganized thoughts result in an unorganized effort, so he should ask himself if his ideas are clear and concise, and, if he has time, he should bounce them off his roommate or colleague before expressing them to subordinates.

From the top on down, orders are sometimes given without thought to priority of accomplishment, redundancy, or consistency. Feedback and rapport up and down the entire chain of command is required if orders of this nature are to be avoided. Following the chain of command may act to slow down transmission. Despite the dangers of such a delay, as Chester Bernard put it, "a communication from the head of an organization to the bottom should pass through every stage of the line of authority."[63-42] Subordinates in the chain must continually discuss problems and priorities among themselves and with their commanding officer. Rapport among people will preclude them issuing conflicting orders and will permit an effective and coordinated effort.

Before issuing routine orders, a leader should discuss priorities with others. He must keep in mind that the desires of the commanding officer receive top priority, even though the commanding officer may not have made his task a top-priority item.

A leader must not take the drive out of his subordinates by chipping away at their egos. He has to avoid threatening the status or ego of a subordinate at all costs, and he must recognize a situation where this is likely to happen before he finds himself in the middle of it.

Giving false expectations, such as early liberty, a day off, or basket leave, for the accomplishment of a task that cannot be accomplished within the time frame or is beyond the subordinates' capabilities is damaging to the morale and cohesiveness of the unit. Goals have to be attainable, and a consistent policy, such as permitting the chief petty officer or staff noncommissioned officer to control leave or early liberty based on job accomplishment, promotes high morale within the division or unit. Work that has been done correctly and in a timely manner can always be rewarded with special privileges. This tends to keep the unit in a high state of readiness.

To avoid having his orders distorted as they pass through the chain of command, a leader should make sure his leading petty officers or noncommissioned officers use wheelbooks or notebooks at quarters. After quarters, the leader can observe and listen to his LPO/NCO putting out the same information the leader just provided him with. If there is a distortion or other problem, the leader should call the LPO/NCO aside and settle the matter as soon as possible. "Many administrative failures can be traced to discretionary orders to which absolutely strict compliance was expected."[63-57]

A leader must establish a rapport with his subordinates that permits them to ask questions without fear of receiving a sarcastic reply or a foul look from him. He must provide his LPO/NCO the opportunity to ask questions, either during a meeting or afterward in private.

If the leader must criticize or correct someone, he should do so in private, and he should always finish up the meeting by reminding the individual of some of his good points and recent accomplishments. Leaders have to treat subordinates as competent individuals until they prove otherwise. Additionally, leaders have to respect someone who is honest and sincere. Everyone wants to do well and to please the senior, and the senior should keep that in mind and treat his subordinates as he would like to be treated.

Chapter 7 Bibliography

1. Ageton, Arthur A. *The Naval Officer's Guide*. Annapolis: Naval Institute Press, 1970.
2. Anderson, C. J. L. F. "The Defense of Superior Orders." *Russi Journal of the Royal United Services Institute for Defence Studies*, June 1981, pp. 52–57.
3. Argyris, Christopher. *Interpersonal Competence and Organizational Effectiveness*. Homewood, Ill.: Dorsey Press, 1962.
4. Arrison, J. M. "Battle Orders." *Proceedings*, July 1984, pp. 62–67.
5. Asprey, Robert B. *The Battle of the Marne*. Philadelphia: J. B. Lippincott, 1962.
6. Aurner, Robert Ray. *Effective Communication in Business*. Cincinnati: Southwestern, 1967.
7. Bach, C. A. "Leadership." In *Selected Readings in Leadership*. Ed. Malcolm E. Wolfe and F. J. Mulholland. 2d ed. Annapolis: Naval Institute Press, 1960.
8. Balkind, Jonathan J. *Morale Deterioration in the United States Military during the Vietnam Period*. Ph.D. diss., UCLA, 1978. Ann Arbor, Mich.: University Microfilms International, 1978.
9. Ballou, Sidney. "Faulty Communications." *Proceedings*, Feb. 1929, pp. 89–98.
10. Becke, Archibald F. *Napoleon and Waterloo*. New York: Books for Libraries Press, 1971.
11. Bellows, Roger. *Creative Leadership*. Ed. Dale Yoder. Englewood Cliffs, N.J.: Prentice-Hall, 1959.
12. Brown, Leland. *Communicating Facts and Ideas in Business*. Englewood Cliffs, N.J.: Prentice-Hall, 1961.
13. Burrage, Henry. *Gettysburg and Lincoln*. New York: G. P. Putnam's Sons, 1906.
14. Cherrington, David J. *Personnel Management*. Dubuque, Iowa: William C. Brown, 1983.
15. Cherry, Colin. *On Human Communication*. Cambridge: MIT Press, 1966.
16. Clarke, Bruce C. *Guidelines for the Leader and Commander*. Harrisburg, Pa.: Stackpole, 1973.
17. Clarke, Jean Illsley. *Who, Me Lead a Group?* Minneapolis, Minn.: Winston Press, 1984.
18. Connelly, J. Campbell. *A Manager's Guide to Speaking and Listening*. New York: American Management Association, 1967.
19. Department of the Navy. *Quotable Navy Quotes*. Washington, D.C.: United States Office of Information, 1967.
20. "Effective Communications." *Approach*, Aug. 1971, p. 3.
21. Eisenhower, Dwight D. *At Ease: Stories I Tell to Friends*. Garden City, N.Y.: Doubleday, 1967, p. 323.
22. Faris, John H. "Leadership and Enlisted Attitudes." In *Military Leadership*. Ed. James H. Buck and Lawrence J. Korb. Beverly Hills: Sage Publications, 1981.
23. Fogel, Irving M., and Bell, Anne E. "Communicating Effectively in the Construction Industry." *Military Engineer*, Sept.–Oct. 1981, pp. 344–46.

Bibliography

24. Freeman, Douglas S. "Leadership." In *Selected Readings in Leadership*. Ed. Malcolm E. Wolfe and F. J. Mulholland. 2d ed. Annapolis: Naval Institute Press, 1960.

25. Furse, George Armand. *Information in War: Its Acquisition and Transmission*. London: William Clones and Sons, 1895.

26. Galdston, Iago, and Zetterberg, Hans. *Panic and Morale*. New York: International Universities Press, 1958.

27. Gibson, James L.; Ivancevich, John M.; and Donnelly, James H., Jr. *Organizations*. 4th ed. Plano, Tex.: Business Publications, 1982.

28. Goodwin, J. F. "Ship's Orders." *Proceedings*, 1940, pp. 78–82.

29. Gorden, Thomas. *Leadership Effectiveness Training*. New York: Wyden Books, 1977.

30. Hamilton, Andrew. "Where Is Task Force Thirty-Four?" *Proceedings*, Oct. 1960, pp. 76–80.

31. Hawkins, Wallace W. "Participate." *Proceedings*, Aug. 1966, p. 91.

32. Hays, Samuel H., and Thomas, William N. *Taking Command*. Harrisburg, Pa.: Stackpole, 1967.

33. Heinl, Robert Debs. *Dictionary of Military and Naval Quotations*. Annapolis: Naval Institute Press, 1966.

34. ———. *The Marine Officer's Guide*. Annapolis: Naval Institute Press, 1977.

35. Hellriegal, Don, and Slocum, John W., Jr. *Management*. 3d ed. Reading, Mass.: Addison-Wesley, 1982.

36. Henderson, George, ed. *Human Relations in the Military*. Chicago: Nelson-Hall, 1975.

37. Hubbell, John G. *POW*. New York: Reader's Digest Press, 1976.

38. Hudgins, L. E. "Ready for Fear." In *Selected Readings in Leadership*. Ed. Malcolm E. Wolfe and F. J. Mulholland. 2d ed. Annapolis: Naval Institute Press, 1960.

39. Hurlburt, J. S. Response to "Communications and Command Prerogative." *Proceedings*, July 1974, p. 96.

40. Jones, William. "Getting Things Done through Better Communications." *U.S. Army Aviation Digest*, Oct. 1974, p. 35.

41. Jurika, Stephen, Jr. *From Pearl Harbor to Vietnam*. Stanford, Calif.: Hoover Press, 1980.

42. Kaufman, Herbert. *Administrative Feedback*. Washington, D.C.: Brookings Institution, 1973.

43. Keena, E. Douglas. "Exploring Leadership." *Vital Speeches of the Day*, Aug. 1980, pp. 638–40.

44. Lawrence, James J. "Effective Communication." *Aerospace Safety*, Dec. 1977, pp. 2–5.

45. Leighton, A. H. *The Governing of Men*. Princeton, N.J.: Princeton University Press, 1946, p. 288.

46. Linver, Sandy. *Speak Easy*. New York: Summit Books, 1958.

47. McCracken, Alan. "When Is an Order?" *Proceedings*, June 1949, pp. 653–57.

48. Mack, William P., and Konetzni, Albert H., Jr. *Command at Sea*. 4th ed. Annapolis: Naval Institute Press, 1982.

49. Mack, William P., and Paulsen, Thomas D. *The Naval Officer's Guide*. 9th ed. Annapolis: Naval Institute Press, 1983.

50. "Manager Communications: Organization Lifeline." *Defense Management Journal*, Jan. 1973.

51. Markham, Felix. *Napoleon and the Awakening of Europe*. New York: Collier Books, 1965.

52. Marshall, D. J. "Communications and Command Prerogative." *Proceedings*, Jan. 1974, pp. 29–33.

53. Megginson, Leon. *Personnel: A Behavioral Approach to Administration*. Homewood, Ill.: Richard D. Irwin, 1967.

54. Mooney, J. D. *Principles of Organization*. Rev. ed. New York: Harper Brothers, 1947, p. 131.

55. Newman, Aubrey S. *Follow Me: The Human Element in Leadership*. Novato, Calif.: Presidio Press, 1981.

56. Newman, William H. *Administrative Action*. 2d ed. Englewood Cliffs, N.J.: Prentice-Hall, 1963.

57. Noel, John V., Jr. *Watch Officer's Guide*. Annapolis: Naval Institute Press, 1961, p. 139.

58. Plumb, Charlie, and DeWerff, Glen. *I'm No Hero*. Independence, Mo.: Independence Press, 1973.

59. Potter, E. B. *Bill Halsey*. Annapolis: Naval Institute Press, 1985, p. 290.

60. ———, ed. *Sea Power: A Naval History*. 2d ed. Annapolis: Naval Institute Press, 1981.

61. Puryear, Edgar F. *Nineteen Stars*. Washington, D.C.: Coiner, 1971.

62. "Realities of Clear Communications." *Army Logistician*, Mar.–Apr. 1977.

63. Redfield, Charles E. *Communication in Management*. Chicago: University of Chicago Press, 1958.

64. Roskill, S. W. *The Art of Leadership*. London: Collins Clear-Type Press, 1964.

65. Samovar, Larry A., and Mills, Jack. *Oral Communication*. Dubuque, Iowa: William C. Brown, 1972.

66. Selby, John. *The Thin Red Line at Balaclava*. London: Hamish Hamilton, 1970.

67. *Ship Organization and Personnel*. Annapolis: Naval Institute Press, 1972.

68. Smith, S. E. *The United States Navy during WW II*. New York: William Morrow, 1966.

69. Soper, Paul L. *Basic Public Speaking*. New York: Oxford University Press, 1949.

70. Staff, W. W. "Mission-Type Orders." *Army*, Jan. 1957, p. 71.

71. Thayer, Lee O. *Administrative Communication*. Homewood, Ill.: Richard D. Irwin, 1961.

72. Vaeth, J. Gordon. "Communications: A Lost Art?" *Proceedings*, Sept. 1976.

73. Valenti, Jack. *Speak Up with Confidence*. New York: William Morrow, 1982.

74. Van Dersal, William. *The Successful Supervisor*. New York: Harper and Row, 1974.

75. Vardaman, George T. *Effective Communication Ideas*. New York: Van Nostrand Reinhold, 1970.

76. Vardaman, George T., and Halterman, Carroll C. *Managerial Control through Communication*. New York: John Wiley and Sons, 1968.

77. Wakin, Malham M. "Ethics of Leadership." In *Military Leadership*. Ed. James H. Buck and Lawrence J. Korb. Beverly Hills: Sage Publications, 1981.

78. Weinhold, Barry K. *Transpersonal Communication*. Englewood Cliffs, N.J.: Prentice-Hall, 1979.

79. Woodham Smith, Cecil Blanche. *The Reason Why*. New York: E. P. Dutton, 1960.

8

Securing the Support of Subordinates and Providing Them with Job Satisfaction

Introduction

Encouraging Subordinates' Suggestions

One of the most effective ways for an executive to win his people's good will and promote the welfare of his organization is to encourage and take seriously suggestions. To keep the suggestions coming, follow these rules: (1) Be willing to accept the ideas of others. Everyone probably knows more about *something* than you do. (2) Don't expect only great ideas. A lot of little improvements will add up to a large saving. (3) Be courteous and unsarcastic in turning down even the silliest idea. That man may have a good idea next time, but he'll never come back if you ridicule his firstborn brainchild. (4) Also, when you turn down a suggestion, be specific as to why it's unworkable. (5) If an idea has workable features, but doesn't seem quite right, search for related ideas. If you find one of value, be sure to give the employee credit for his help. (6) Remember that suggestions must not be taken for granted. Human beings require credit and recognition if they are to produce their best work.

Roland Sandell, *Supervision*

How to Make a Worker Willing

Despite all the literature that has been written about motivating employees, there still remain only two basic things which you can do to spur better performance—to make a worker a willing worker.

You can allow your people to tackle as much— and more—than they can handle. Most people don't really begin to click until they are under some pressure. Good ideas, a better way to do things, are not the result of a mind working at half-speed. Further, people are happier with a full work load; they have more to be happy about.

Employees must be given the freedom to make

363

mistakes. A subordinate can win some and lose some. If a wild idea hits the mark, all to the good. If it's a bomb, it's important for you to be solidly behind him.

A good manager constantly asks himself this question about each employee: "What can I do to make it easier for him to work harder?"
Office Administration

73. Foreword

In order to gain his subordinates' support, the officer must be himself. He should never "put on an act" by attempting to be someone he is not. His subordinates will quickly see through any facade and will lose respect for the officer who is insincere. An officer cannot act one way toward subordinates and present a different personality to seniors. Leaders can, however, "be themselves" while at the same time integrating proven principles of leadership into their own personalities. John Paul Jones, in *Qualifications of the Naval Officer*, wrote at length about securing the support of subordinates:

Coming now to view the naval officer aboard ship and in relation to those under his command, he should be the soul of tact, patience, justice, firmness, and charity. No meritorious act of a subordinate should escape his attention or be left to pass without its reward, even if the reward be only one word of approval. Conversely, he should not be blind to a single fault in any subordinate, though, at the same time, he should be quick and unfailing to distinguish error from malice, thoughtlessness from incompetency, and well-meant shortcoming from heedless or stupid blunder. As he should be universal and impartial in his rewards and approval of merit, so should he be judicial and unbending in his punishment or reproof of misconduct. In his intercourse with subordinates he should ever maintain the attitude of the Commander, but that need by no means prevent him from the amenities of cordiality or the cultivation of good cheer within proper limits. Every Commanding Officer should hold with his subordinates such relations as will make them

constantly anxious to receive invitations to sit at his mess-table, and his bearing towards them should be such as to encourage them to express their feelings to him with freedom and to ask his views without reserve.

An officer who follows these principles of leadership, according to John Paul Jones, can expect to receive the support of his subordinates. However, Jones wrote, the officer who treats subordinates with "indiscriminate hauteur" and with "rude, ungentle treatment" will have a "sullen crew and an unhappy ship."

Admiral Zumwalt suggests that, to gain the support of his subordinates,

an officer must make sure that all the individuals in his command understand that they have been properly looked out for, properly cared for, and properly treated as individuals of merit. It is vitally important that they understand their seniors are looking out for them and for the solution of their personal problems. Individuals who have this understanding will more willingly make the sacrifices that are necessary in order for the mission to be a success.

Those who recognize the concern of their seniors are also likely to show concern for their subordinates. Many of the people who were enlisted personnel in the seventies and have left the Navy are now at the level of vice-presidents of corporations or in some cases presidents of corporations, and it has been interesting to hear their reaction to how it felt to have the feeling that somebody "up there" really was interested in them as individuals—it seemed to come somewhat as a breath of fresh air and made quite a difference to them in their subsequent attitude toward their own subordinates.

This does not imply that the leader must make an effort to be loved by everyone all the time. The leader who must be loved is putty in the hands of his troops. He will do anything to avoid face-to-face confrontation and unpleasantness with them. He will sell his soul for praise and approval and will easily be had.[110-87]

The officer who has worked to let his people know that he is interested in their welfare—but that he will not hesitate to get up on the loudspeaker as a commanding officer and announce, for example, that the ship has to spend two more months in the western Pacific than originally planned—will get the necessary support for an unpopular decision. His people will know that he is only making it because it is necessary, and that he has done everything he can for them.

Criticism of an individual should always be done in private, while praise of an individual is clearly more rewarding if it is given in front of his peers. When, on the other hand, an officer is critiquing an exercise in which his division or his ship did badly, he should address the group en masse, because it is not an individual performance he is criticizing but the performance of the team as a whole.

In rendering criticism, it is important not to end on a negative note. In criticizing a group effort, the officer should go through and hit as hard as he can on all of the failures, then make the suggestions that he thinks will be helpful, and conclude by pointing out, if it is true, that he knows that the people did their best and that those who are responsible for the training have to share the black mark with them. Dismissal should be on the order of "Now, let's all get with it and do better." By following these steps, the officer conveys the necessary criticism and encourages his people to do better the next time.

FIRM

The following guidelines for leadership are categorized into the acronym FIRM (Firm Principles of Leadership) for easy remembrance. They are all useful in helping a leader gain the support of subordinates.

F: Three *F*s: *Faith* in self, *Faith* in seniors and the Navy or the Marine Corps, and *Faith* in subordinates
I: Two *I*s: *Integrity* and *Idealism*
R: Two *R*s: *Mutual Respect* and *Golden Rule*
M: Two *M*s: *Moderation* and *Manners*

His *faith in himself* should be evident in all of a leader's actions. He must have self-confidence and exude that self-confidence to others. His subordinates do not expect him to be correct all the time or to know everything, but they do expect a leader to be secure in his sense of person and worth. They want to look up to their leader and be able to take problems to him without being saddled with their leader's personal problems in return.

Enthusiasm, not self-doubt, is the image to project to both seniors and juniors. An officer's willingness to learn from his mistakes, and an officer's sense of humor, particularly about himself, are also important. The leader must know himself, his strengths and weaknesses, and compensate for his weaknesses and exploit his strengths. He must never be daunted by a situation or tasking, but should look on each situation and tasking as a challenge. (The word *tasking* means both the task and the act of being assigned a task; thus, every tasking should be seen as an opportunity, as it [1] enables the subordinate to show the senior his willingness to support the senior and [2] permits the subordinate to demonstrate what he is capable of accomplishing.) He should be eager to learn and be receptive to learning anything he can from any source. He should not make excuses or try to shift blame to others. If he has self-confidence, the officer will find that all things are possible. Opinions of others should never be able to erode his self-confidence, though certainly they must be examined.

Having *faith in seniors and in the Navy or the Marine Corps* is another key to obtaining the support of subordinates. An officer's seniors want him and his subordinates to be successful. The officer must always keep that in mind. The Navy and the Marine Corps have designed several supplements to the chain of command to ensure successful communication up and down the chain, thereby also ensuring fairness and justice. For example, the master chief petty officer of the command or the command sergeant major, the command career counselor, and the human relations council, along with the special request chit and request mast procedures, are all designed to assist the chain of command in resolving leadership and administrative problems. The promotion system of the Naval Service has also been upheld as the epitome of fairness. The Naval Service's military judicial system is one under which anyone can put anyone on report for a violation of the Uniform Code of Military Conduct and under which every accused person is afforded extensive rights. An officer's subordinates should be encouraged to share his faith in the fairness, justice, and impartiality of the Navy and Marine Corps "systems."

Faith in subordinates is often found lacking in those who miss the mark of being a highly successful leader. Subordinates want to succeed, they want to be "winners," and they need leadership and sufficient resources to do so. Only an unsuccessful leader treats subordinates with disdain and a lack of trust or fails to create a climate in which they feel free to express their feelings and ideas to him. The few people who cannot be trusted will soon make themselves known, and appropriate action can be taken by the officer to correct their failing or to isolate them from the vast majority who do deserve his trust. The transforming leader tries to develop the wisdom to look into his troops and actually read their minds and understand what they want. Then he must use his knowledge to know what they need and how their goals and those of the service can be combined. Finally, he must implant these wants in the form of goals into their hearts and help them work toward these goals.[114-88]

The officer must have sufficient faith to foster his subordinates' initiative and delegate authority, along with accountability, to them. No officer can be a "one man band." Encouraging the free expression of ideas and questions is one way an officer can elicit the support of his subordinates. There is no such thing as a dumb question. Only ignorance and potential disaster are created by a climate in which questions are discouraged. Actually, the only dumb question is that which was not asked.

Of course, there are operational situations in which unquestioned instant obedience to orders is necessary, but these occasions are almost invariably evident to the giver and receiver of orders. The only other exception to the general rule of encouraging questions is when a decision has been made by the leader after he has given due consideration to various courses of action. Full support for such a decision is expected from subordinates.

It is crucial to differentiate between having faith in subordinates and personally keeping tabs on people. The leader should pay attention to detail and double-check everything. He should be out of his office and around his people. It is not a matter of a lack of trust, but a matter of his sense of "ownership" for everything for which he is responsible. By being among his people, the officer lets them know he is interested in them and their work, and he also helps establish his standards for performance of tasks assigned.

An officer must keep in mind that his influence extends beyond those who are currently under his control. Those enlisted personnel whose maintenance is supervised today will be responsible for equipment maintenance long after they have been transferred or the officer has gone on to another assignment. A leader should feel personally accountable for the maintenance and operability of equipment for which he is held responsible. If one individual neglects maintenance or fails to observe proper operation of shipboard or aircraft engineering or combat systems, the neglect may not immediately impact on the readiness of the ship or aircraft. However, those who depend on that equipment at a later date will suffer from the lack of a sense of "ownership" by their predecessors. Such supervisory failure is inexcusable in a leader and is easily traced back to the officer who failed in his responsibilities to those who came after him or to those to whom his enlisted were sent. As might be imagined, the service reputation of the officer who failed to be involved will certainly be damaged; in addition, he has let the rest of the Naval Service team down. Our combat capability must be constantly maintained, and this can only be accomplished if personnel and equipment are working properly. This is a primary responsibility of junior officers: to ensure that the unit is ready to swing into action at a moment's notice. In addition, many of our military operations are totally dependent for their safety on the proper meeting of standards—whether we are at war or peace. A submerged submarine patrol is as challenging during peace as it is during periods of conflict.

Some of the primary reasons given by enlisted personnel for leaving the Navy or Marine Corps are lack of recognition, suppressed initiative, and unfair treatment. An effective leader will work hard to eliminate these sources of dissatisfaction. Admiral Hayward suggests that responsibility for securing comfortable living conditions for personnel rests with officers at all levels. He described some of the steps officers can take to make sure personnel are taken care of in this regard:

There were many, many people who recognized that we needed to do much more in the various senior levels to show clear evidence that Washington was a friend of the sailor and not an enemy of the sailor, and I think we did a fairly good job of that over three or four years' time. But that comes about largely through working with the Congress and generating the necessary support from the senators and congressmen, who have to understand what service life is all about, and making certain that the sailor and the soldier and the airman and the Marine and the Coast

Guard are taken care of. Uniformed leaders must carry that load, they have got to accept it as a priority responsibility, and in many cases that means bucking the tide against some of the budget cutters, the people who simply don't have a good perspective of what it takes to run an organization like the military, the sacrifices the people make, the living conditions under which they generally operate, and that we have to generate support.

Now, having said that from the CNO level, you really have to get down to the leadership level. How do you come to grips with the issue of taking care of your people? That very basic leadership requirement of caring for your people is a critically important thing to do. It is perhaps easier for the Army and the Marines to face up to that as junior officers, because they are working so closely with their people and they're out in the field, generally speaking, and boy, they know how to generate loyalty and to take care of their people. In the Air Force and the Navy it is easier to avoid that or, let's say, fall into a lackadaisical attitude about caring sufficiently for your people. But a good officer who is really on top of it is going to be watching all the time to put his troops ahead of himself and always get them taken care of first.

If their living conditions are lousy, then work on it all the time; if their working conditions are poor, then you correct that sort of thing; if the food is a problem, then you get after that. You don't leave it up to the system to take care of it, because if the situation is bad, it's probably because the leadership has gotten slack and lazy and is not paying attention to the situation surrounding the division, the workshop, the living spaces. There's no excuse for that.

The responsibility of all of them might

rest with the first class and the chiefs. On a day-to-day basis, if the senior officers, if the division officers, if the junior division officers, aren't paying attention, then it's going to take an unusually strong senior petty officer to keep the place squared away or otherwise it's going to drift downward. So I don't care if you are an officer or an enlisted man, caring for your people is a fundamental requirement, and without that you're going to have poor morale, lousy cooperation, lack of pride. It's critical. Now there are loads of situations where the living conditions and the situation facing the command are difficult. Let's take Adak, Alaska, for instance, where a paint job doesn't stay on a building very long and the cement is cracking and all kinds of unique environmental situations confront leadership and the budget support isn't adequate and that kind of thing. Well, that's when innovation comes forward and people join forces and accomplish things together, and as a consequence of that they are able to maintain a very strong attitude favorable to the command and to their own participation in it because they're working together to solve the problem. Generally speaking, I've found that the more distant the assignment from the hub of civilization, from the big cities, the higher the morale. Quite unusual. Places like Adak or Midway Island or Scotland, where you think that it's pretty tough, well it's tough, but that brings out a lot of good character in people, and they pull together and they get things done. In those circumstances it's unusual to find where the leadership isn't paying attention. It is more apt to be in San Diego, where it's easy to be thinking about getting off the ship and racing out and having a great time with a friend or going to the ballgame or whatever, and

you've left a problem behind in your division that's yours and you've left it in somebody else's hands to take care of it. That's not loyalty down. That's not strong leadership.

Admiral Hayward discussed some of the reasons officers in today's Naval Service need to keep informed about the social problems affecting personnel and the services that are available to help them:

The change in social mores in this country over the last 20 years and some of the changing attitudes between generations underlie a new responsibility on military leaders. You see so many things available today that we didn't even think about when I was an ensign. We didn't have to worry about family service centers: the divorce rate among military people was very, very low, we didn't have drugs, we didn't have abuse of the family—or if we did, it didn't surface in a way that we were even cognizant of the problem. Today there's a great deal more awareness of the need to look out for these kinds of social ills that are a part of both military and civilian life.

Perhaps we aren't as well prepared for these things today as we used to be 50 years ago. Therefore, there's a constant requirement to be on the lookout for ways to bring the family on board, take care of the family, have access to solutions when the ship is gone and there's nobody close by and you've got a 21-year-old wife who is pregnant and has one child, and she's got some very serious family difficulties or financial problems or sickness or things of that sort. We have learned to deal with that much more realistically than we used to. We used to, I guess, just leave it up to family ties, which were stronger, I suppose, than the ones we have today.

It does mean that the young officers

need to be more aware of what's available and be certain that their people are aware of it, that there are programs established to follow up on difficult problems, to sense the humanitarian needs. It's part of our way of life, and it's a good part. The Navy has reason to be proud of what it has accomplished in these many, many effective programs.

One of the most difficult things for a junior officer to do is to talk to any one of his people in a straightforward, honest way, but it is a skill an officer ought to acquire very early in his career. He must develop the ability to fill out a performance report and discuss it with the individual in a constructive fashion so that it is helpful to everyone concerned. The individual should receive a good assessment of how he is doing, including learning what improvements he needs to make.

If the officer conducts this discussion in a constructive way, he can increase the incentive to improve instead of providing a disincentive. The individual who leaves the discussion with an attitude of, "Well, you know Ensign Jones is against me, and what the heck, no reason for me to try to fix this thing, no matter what I do, he's always going to be against me," has been hindered, not helped, by the officer.

The junior officer who has not previously counseled a subordinate generally will not have the skills to do it easily; he will be an amateur. But amateurs become professionals, and the only way to become a professional is to work at it. The danger emerges when the officer puts that kind of issue aside. He fills out a fitness report or an evaluation report, files it away, and never discusses it with the individual because he does not have the courage to lay it on the line or the ability to lay it on the line in a constructive way. He decides

that the easiest way to handle the problem is to avoid it, but if he does that long enough, he will be faced with some very serious issues.

Furthermore, the individual will be failing to take advantage of an opportunity to develop his own essential leadership capabilities, which he will need when he faces some tough decisions. If he develops that habit of avoiding issues, he will not have loyalty and he will be an ineffective officer.

One of the things a leader must do is treat everyone as an individual without appearing to favor one individual over another. The leader is going to have favorites—the person who is really working and performing and is never in trouble is going to be someone the leader is going to be attracted to more than the one who is late for work and always has a problem. But he cannot let his personnel know that he has favorites.

Dealing with each person individually and learning how to grapple with the leadership problem of not showing favoritism takes a great deal of hard work on a daily basis. The leader cannot just deal with the masses, nor can he only interact with the ones who are easy to handle. He has got to take on the ones who are hard to handle and develop the techniques that allow him to develop their potential. That will strengthen his own leadership skills, will build teamwork and loyalty, and the leader will be successful.

Decisions should never be made on the basis of popularity. A leader must make a decision because it is the right thing to do. It is natural for a leader to try to do things in a way that makes the organization work in a coherent, cohesive way as a team, and if he deals in the negative or does not seem to care what the troops think of him, odds are that, over time, there will be a very poor situation in that unit. But the leader's first concern should be making the *right* decision, not deciding on the basis of what the troops would like. By instilling in subordinates a sense of "winning" and a sense of "ownership" and participation in fulfilling the mission, goals, and tasking, the leader motivates them to extend themselves to their highest potential.

One way an officer can create an atmosphere in which people do their best is to establish specific goals for himself and his subordinates, in terms of both professional growth and his unit's performance. These goals should be written out and clearly understood. They should be quantifiable as much as possible, so that progress can be tracked and perceived. Of course, the organizational goals should be developed in participation with subordinates so that each person has a sense of ownership and responsibility toward achieving them. This is not "management by objective," but rather a leadership tool that provides a common sense of direction for the unit and an individual sense of direction for each person. Additionally, it is instrumental in developing the sense of success and confidence necessary for the officer, his people, and the organization as a whole to achieve the mission in the most effective manner. Friendly, constructive competition with other units provides one source for establishing goals and creating the winning climate. In developing these goals, the leader should always keep his mission in mind, so that the goals provide the stepping-stones heading in the proper direction.

These goals and their achievement (or lack thereof) can also be used for performance appraisal purposes. Subordinates should be kept informed on a routine basis as to their performance in relation to the mutually established goals and in meeting the officer's standards. A subordinate should never be surprised by the official evaluation. A quick reprimand and speedy congratulations are the most effective evaluations available. There is no confusion concerning what action the words are being spoken about, and the incident is fresh in the minds of everyone.[20-321]

By having faith in his subordinates, an officer integrates the sum total of all their talents and potential into a force primed for excellence.

Considered the *key* leadership trait, *integrity* is a personal attribute that a leader must make visible to his subordinates if he is to gain their support. Integrity, simply put, is the "hard right over the easy wrong." It impacts on every aspect of an officer's naval life; an officer must take a position on operational and staff issues, do what he says he will do, make sure his seniors are not surprised by something he has done, and make his personal moral conduct impeccable. Integrity is counterpoised by peer pressure. A leader should make it clear to subordinates that individual integrity is what counts with him, not excuses resulting from mistakes (professional or personal) caused by peer pressure.

The principle of *idealism* means being altruistic as much as possible, giving something of one's self to something larger than one's self. By serving his nation in the armed services, an officer is already following the principle of idealism. Most of the enlisted recruits coming in today are eager to learn a skill and do a job. The following quote exemplifies the attitude of recruits, upon which officers can build: "Please, give me direction; give me an objective; give me a sense of worth. I want to be a part of a team. Make me earn my rewards. I have tried the do-it-yourself, 'Now' generation. I have had all the freedom and mobility that I can endure. I now seek meaning in life, and I really do care what other people think about me."[58-68] It is far better to be in a service-oriented profession than to proceed through life merely making money. Similarly, there is always time for volunteer work, community service, and extending a helping hand to those less fortunate than one's self. A sense of commitment to his division, battalion, department, ship, or squadron is essential for an officer's success. If he is selfish, or if he thinks in terms of personal ambition, an officer will be quickly perceived as lacking idealism and will lose the support of his subordinates.

The two Rs are closely related. First, *mutual respect*. As every successful leader has realized, respect cannot be demanded from others. It must be earned. It must be mutual. An individual must treat others with respect if he wants to receive respect. Following the principles outlined above will help the officer earn respect. By demonstrating his sincere interest in the welfare of his subordinates, an officer can also earn respect. The Marine Corps's principle that stipulates that an officer not eat or sleep until after the troops have been fed and rested is noteworthy. In addition, an officer should never give an order that he would not be willing to carry out himself if the roles were reversed.

It takes nothing away from the dignity of his position for an officer to be courteous to his subordinates and to be friendly while at the same time avoiding familiarity. It also helps him gain his peoples' respect if he sets a high military standard for physical fitness, stamina, and personal appearance. If he works harder and more enthusiastically than any of his subordinates, he will certainly be respected. The officer should remember that he cannot expect his subordinates to achieve higher standards than those he achieves himself.

Of course, an officer does not earn respect by attempting to be "popular." His subordinates do not want him to run a popularity contest. What they do want in a leader is fairness, consistency, justice, impartiality, civility, high personal and institutional standards, and open communication. They want a leader who is interested in their morale and welfare, not because that is what is written in Navy regulations or on fitness report forms, but because the leader is sincerely dedicated to their well-being. Admiral Long notes:

> Loyalty for an officer involves something other than running a popularity contest. There are occasions when officers,

junior and senior, conduct their affairs with the idea of winning the approval of juniors and, certainly, of seniors, but an officer's relationship with others should be based firmly on mutual respect, not popularity. That means that not only does an officer treat his juniors with respect, but he insists that they treat him with respect, as well. It is a two-way street. Because of this, an officer needs to be very careful about becoming too familiar with his enlisted personnel, because this is a relationship that can be easily distorted.

An officer who is responsible for the performance, welfare, and safety of his people must treat those subordinates with genuine respect. He must have a sincere concern for their professional advancement and their health and safety. I remember years ago, when I had command of a ship and I was talking to one of my senior chiefs, that he brought up the question about a certain officer whom he really admired. He said, "He's always the same, and never slapping people on the back and always business, but we always know where he stands."

At the same time that they avoid being overly familiar, young officers should not act as if they are superior to their juniors. This can be very damaging to an officer today. People must respect one another if the job is to be done.

An officer's subordinates also want his respect, and he can use this innate desire to assist him in motivating them to achieve his high standards and mutually established goals. An organization composed of individuals possessing mutual respect for one another, not a mutual admiration society, is what is desired.

The second principle under the letter R is that of the *Golden Rule*. This principle for interpersonal relationships is considered desirable in all major cultures and religions. It may be the closest thing to a universally known basic truth that exists. An individual who bases his conduct on the Golden Rule cannot go wrong. Following this principle eliminates any basis for treating people differently because of their race, sex, creed, national origin, or age. This principle is the foundation for all the other principles outlined here. It is a simple rule, simply stated, but it is very hard to put it into consistent practice. However, a leader who is faced with personnel-related challenges should definitely follow the Golden Rule. He cannot show bias or favoritism, nor can he display a negative attitude toward others on any basis other than professional performance.

The next principle in the FIRM categorization of leadership principles necessary for gaining the support of subordinates is that of *moderation*. Subordinates will not fully support a leader who is radical in personal demeanor or in leadership decisions. In personal demeanor, being even-tempered and possessing self-control are highly desirable. No one likes working for a senior who yells and shouts. The work will usually not get done any better or faster for all the yelling, and frequently it will get done less well and less quickly for it.

An officer can be persistent and insistent without losing his temper. He can effectively express dissatisfaction without losing his temper. In actuality, losing his temper only indicates to his subordinates that the officer cannot maintain self-control, and, as a result, they will start to mistrust his abilities as a leader. Someone who works efficiently and effectively under extreme pressure without creating a crisislike atmosphere gains the support and respect of subordinates. If a leader can also do that in an even-tempered, unemotional manner (that is, displaying no emotion except enthusiasm), then personal dedication and loyalty become part of the subordinates' relationship with the leader. The best leadership is positive in nature—pulling a chain is more effective than pushing it. Leadership based on fear, threats, and mistrust is not leadership but is, rather, "pushership."

Naval warfare is based in part on taking calculated risks, and leaders must be capable of taking calculated risks and must practice taking them. No battle was ever won by waiting until all the available information was analyzed to eliminate all risks. But there is a vast difference between taking risks that are calculated and taking risks that are foolhardy. An effective leader will ensure that his subordinates know, and observe, that calculated risks are an integral part of the leader's method of operation while at the same time ensuring that they never get the impression that the leader is foolhardy, particularly when their own welfare and professional reputations are at stake.

Moderation is just another way of saying self-control. Without self-control there can be no self-discipline. Without self-discipline there can be no organizational discipline. Discipline is not punishment; rather, it is the basis for effective leadership. It ensures that individuals work toward a common mission as a team in the most effective manner possible given the resources available.

The final principle in the FIRM categorization of leadership principles is *manners*. There are two subsets of manners. First, there are personal manners. Civility, of course, is the backbone of civilization. Good personal manners, such as politeness, discretion, and prompt response in personal correspondence (including thank-you notes) are a hallmark of the successful leader.

The second subset of manners, which is not so widely recognized, is administrative manners. An effective leader will be known for proper, thoughtful manners in the administrative conduct of responsibilities. Examples are the timely response to tasking, the timely response to required due dates on reports, the prompt handling of telephone calls, and the prompt review of staff work drafted by other staff members or other commands and submitted for a "chop." Those leaders who do not exhibit professional administrative manners will soon lose the respect and cooperation of their subordinates.

Some people cannot follow these principles because they do not fit their personalities, but those people should attempt to modify their personalities to make them more positive. At a minimum, they should learn to avoid and compensate for their negative points and accentuate their positive points. A leader should not be a cynic, he should be enthusiastic and positive. When he has followed the FIRM principles of leadership, an officer can say that he has truly practiced "leadership through personal example."

General Wilson reminds us that

the military commander, by virtue of his commission and his overall qualities, is responsible for all his unit does or fails to do 24 hours a day, including family, morals, health, and pain. He is responsible for all the things that make for dignity and a self-fulfilling life, that make his troops enjoy their work, enjoy their service, and, in the end, accomplish the commander's mission. We must never fail to keep in mind mission and objective and quality of life.

Quality of life is important, and commanders are very influential in it. I know that I've had both good and bad, and the quality of life that I have is almost identical to the quality of the commander. I like to believe that I can go into a unit and in ten minutes I can tell you whether or not a commander is interested in his people and whether they are happy or whether they are resentful. This comes from experience, and any commander can do that who has spent a long time in the service. So right away the morale, the quality of a unit, reflects the commander, and it is so apparent you almost ask why the commander can't see it himself.

Let the junior commanders each one feel that he has a responsibility. The military service has the simplest form of command relationship and the most ideal form of command relationship in the world.

When you come right down to it, every commander has only about three or four people reporting to him in varying degrees, but down the chain of command, which is a pyramid, when you come down to find the basic squad, the basic fire team organization in the Marine Corps, the fire team has three men and therefore he's responsible for those, and the squad leader has three fire teams, and so on up the line.

If everyone would do his job, it would be the simplest thing in the world. Now, since we know human nature and we know that everyone is not going to do his job, people require supervision and a stern hand to insist that they do their jobs. This is tempered with compassion, understanding that people have problems. We try to bring the best out in them.

74. Overcoming Bias or Prejudice

Over the years, this nation has come to stand for many fine things, and the military services have often led the way, as they did by providing opportunities to all military personnel. Both the Naval Service and the United States have laws mandating that all individuals be treated equally; however, the leader must take an active part in seeing that all personnel in his command not only are treated equally, without regard to race, sex, or religion, but also are treated fairly as human beings. "Nothing destroys the efficiency of a military unit faster than partiality."[123-1476] Officers must be intimately familiar with all aspects of the organization's daily operation. A junior officer can see firsthand that the letter and the spirit of the law are being followed, and when an officer rises to a point where he cannot personally ensure compliance with the intent as well as the words of the rules and regulations, then he must see that subordinate leaders are complying with the law within their particular divisions, departments, and command. Admiral Fran McKee:

> A subordinate could get a set of orders and say, "Gee, I don't know why I got this assignment. What can you do?" Perhaps your knowledge of that individual's personal and professional background is as good as anyone else's and you feel that circumstances warrant reconsideration and your intercession in the assignment process. While there are usually general guidelines governing assignments, there may be justifiable reasons for exceptions. You can't always please everybody and there is a limit on what you can do. It is important to be intelligently responsive to the needs of your people, but it must be done in an equitable and unbiased manner so that the unit's effectiveness is not impaired.

It is not sufficient for the officer to be responsible for these matters; he must be accountable, as well. Thus, he will make sure that all members in the chain of command understand his policy, through both written and spoken words, and also that those at the bottom of the chain know that if his policy is not being followed by intermediary commanders, they should bring the matter up through the chain of command for resolution. While policies should be equitable, which means that they apply equally to all personnel, and consistent, which means that a particular act will always be handled in a particular way, it is not necessary for everyone to receive the same treatment for the same actions. No two individuals are the same, no two sets of circumstances are the same, and it is rare for the pressures and responsibilities affecting any two individuals to be the same, and these differences must be kept in mind when the interpretation and application of policies are considered. There are times when you should give out different types of treatment to different individuals. Fairness is another element without which leadership can neither be built up nor maintained. There must be that fairness which treats all people justly. A punishment that would be dismissed by one person with the shrug of a shoulder is mental anguish for another. An officer who for a given offense has a standard punishment that applies to all is either too indulgent or too stupid to study the personality of his troops.[74-89] Every officer must acquire the handling of personnel for himself, largely through the medium of personal experience.[123-1476]

The leader, then, reviews the requirements of his command; interprets the policy of higher headquarters; and develops policies of his own that make it apparent to everyone concerned that it is his desire to treat people positively, put trust in them, and give them the opportunity to know how and why the organization functions. For the most part, policies will apply to all individuals in all circumstances; however, the policies may have to be tailored to fit individual requirements and circumstances. The overriding consideration is to maintain preparedness for the unit's mission while doing all that is possible to provide personnel with satisfaction in their jobs, even-handedly applying discipline as necessary.

This country was founded by people with diverse religious, cultural, and ethnic approaches to life. It is the mixture of these differing backgrounds which has provided the country with its resiliency, its ability to safeguard its own freedom and help provide many other nations freedom to choose their own government rather than have it imposed on them. Some naval personnel, through education and experience, will have a very clear idea of the importance of the component parts of this nation's cultural heritage, and others will have learned concepts that are antithetical to the basis of national operations at this point in U.S. history. The leader cannot assume that all individuals can embrace an open-minded outlook; therefore, just as he does not leave it to chance that his personnel can operate their equipment and meet operational objectives, he does not leave equitable treatment of personnel to chance. Through meetings with supervisors and other members of the command, the officer can set the tone for involving all hands in such a way that operations not only seem to be but are independent of considerations other than capability to get the job done efficiently, on time, and in a way that supports the objectives of higher and lateral headquarters.

The Naval Service operates with a replacement pool of people, but training is the preferred method of providing for rotation of duties, replacement of casualties, and changes in personnel that may be required in a specific mission. When it becomes apparent that an individual or group of individuals is not able to perform a particular function, then a training program that will improve performance is to be provided. It is not acceptable for the leader to ship someone who is not performing well—and *performance* is the only acceptable criteria—off to another command. Rather, working with intermediary personnel in the chain of command, the officer must see that a training program is established which will overcome the deficiency. Only if, after a valiant effort, progress has not been made, should the officer try to put the individual out of the organization, and even then, only after the situation has been discussed with personnel experts in Washington, who are best qualified to determine whether further intensive training is required or the best solution is to relieve the individual from active duty.

Notwithstanding efforts to build an integrated team, minority groups do exist, because of differences in race, ethnic background, and sex. With this in mind, the leader should periodically meet with personnel in these groups. Through consultation with them and other members of the command, the leader can determine what steps must be taken to account for differences in perceptions. For example, if women were to indicate that they were not being given challenging enough assignments, the commander of the unit might sit down with the spokeswoman and senior aides to evaluate what additional operational assignments could be given to women so they could make an equal contribution to the overall well-being and mission capability of the unit. Women have made significant military contributions over the years in the service of many nations, and the strength of this country's efforts is dependent on the ability and willingness of the services to capitalize fully on the abilities of women in the services, so that women are able to serve in all positions other than those excluded by law.

For Admiral Taylor, fair treatment of subordinates means that the troops come first.

Look out for the troops, they're your greatest resource. In many areas, equal treatment is maybe not good enough, maybe top treatment is required. But certainly from the standpoint of the things that we measure as equal—equal opportunity for advancement, equal in all other respects—equal treatment is necessary. You can't tolerate the people in your lineup who have an uneven distribution. A favoritism by a chief to someone is wrong, and you have to find those things where he's letting a guy off one of the not-so-good details because he's a favorite. It creates a wrong impression.

Division officers have to be tough, and being a division officer is a tough job. You're fresh out of the Academy, or wherever your source is, and you check into a squadron or a ship and you're given a division of 30 men and women and you have a chief petty officer who has been around for 20 years and is used to running things. That's a hard transition, and all of us have to go through it. How do I get the chief to work for me? You have to use him as the conduit to the troops, but when you find that there's unequal treatment going on, you have to stop it, you have to squelch it. Take the subordinate off to the side and tell him it won't be tolerated.

I think that in each of our hearts there remains a bias or two, which must be kept under tight control. While things may be down in your heart, we won't tolerate a lack of self-discipline which allows those biases to come out and leads to discrimination. When you're an officer, you must set the example, you must stick to it and live the Ten Commandments plus the Golden Rule. Good, fair, unbiased, equal, solid treatment of all.

Don't get into an organization and right away start changing things. It's too traumatic, and you'll end up with lumps, and it will just be too hard. If command is not your initial goal in starting this business, then you must make command your goal. Flying airplanes was really what I had in mind, but I think I was a lieutenant when someone said "Command is what you want to do." So command is the goal, but in aviation you get a year and a half as an XO before you are a CO, so in the squadron you have a chance to have some impact on the way the rules are written, and it's a very smooth transition generally, only a few growls. In ships it's considerably different, because the personalities change and there are going to be some different ways of getting the job done from one CO to the other, just from the personality standpoint. So you want to be very careful about checking in with some wild ideas about the way you want to run this command. Maybe your long-term goal is to turn it over into something else, but you want to do it so gradually, so cleverly, so that people are just kind of moved over into that and they don't really know that there's a big change going on.

I had had command of a squadron, and

during my air wing tour I discovered that I needed a written philosophy of command. There's a fine little book, *Command at Sea*, that's available on the bookshelves, and buried in it is a short philosophy of command. Everyone needs to have a philosophy, and for my replenishment oiler and my carrier tour and wherever I go in the future, now I will have a philosophy of command that is dynamic. It basically states what I think are the important goals. You must put that out in the first two weeks of your command, and you could do the same thing on a division level. Just write a memo to all your troops saying here is what I see as our mission, and here is the way I think you ought to get there. You have established some common ground for the followers and the leader, and it just sets a better tone for achievement of the goals. So stating a philosophy of command that is easy is the first step; you haven't stated any big changes, probably, but a tone has been set. Now you have the groundwork to make those little transitions.

No matter what the level of harmony is in an organization, the commanding officer and the division officer leadership, at all levels, has to understand that drugs are always going to be a problem. At the same level with drugs you've got a little alcohol problem, and at the same time you have a race problem and you have a sex problem. These are biases that you have been trained in, and maybe it doesn't affect everyone, but someone in there has got it, so you have to know that you have a problem. Don't assume "no problem." It is a problem, and so you have to watch and you have to inform and you have to educate and you have to lay down a hard rule that breaches will not be tolerated.

Alcohol, you get help, drugs maybe get

a little help before you're out. That depends, because some people are worth the extra effort to save, others, sorry, that's too many times, you're out of here, we can't tolerate it. Sexism and racism, there's no place for in our business. If you have those kinds of biases, they absolutely have to be kept under control. What a division officer's got to be attentive to is knowing that these things are there, recognizing the symptoms early. For instance, down in the troops, in the berthing compartment, a white guy clipped out a cartoon from a magazine, it was anti-black, and he pinned it on the other guy's rack. Well, that's the kind of thing that can inflame people. Do you just look the other way or something like that? No, you've got to get in on those little things and see what's going on in this guy's mind, because it isn't right, it's going to lead to disharmony.

We're a team, we've got to be ready to pull together to fight, and if you're going to have someone who can't do that, you've got to get him out of there. As I heard the Secretary of the Navy say, gather up the recalcitrants and send them to re-education.

The Naval Service has many programs for the enlightenment of its people, and its leaders at all levels are exposed to concepts that work to eliminate racism and sexism in the services. Thus, when they join a unit, officers need to consult with the people already in the unit about what programs are in place and begin to consider what kinds of programs they might initiate. Through reading the various publications that are issued in the service, officers become aware of initiatives that can be taken. Certainly, it is important for all officers to appreciate that there is no place in the military service for anything other than 100 percent support of the equality of all people and the basic ability of everyone to contribute equally to this nation's defenses. Juniors must

realize that their seniors expect this kind of support, and senior officers must realize that their juniors are looking for positive leadership in this area. Overt or covert bigotry and intolerance are not acceptable in the Naval Service.

When considering where his sense of wrong takes him, and where it should take him, when he is aware of a major institutional wrong, an officer might keep in mind the way Admiral Zumwalt addressed a problem presented by one of his assignments.

As a commander, I was brought into the Bureau of Naval Personnel to be a detailer, an order writer for some four thousand surface lieutenants, and the verbal briefing that I was given when I took over was, "This is the way we handle the blacks: If you've got an officer who has gotten through the system, send him to recruiting duty." (In those days, that was the worst form of duty; now, fortunately, it's not.) "At the end of his two years there, extend him a third year. He's then almost certain to be passed over. If he should be promoted, send him to the worst ship you've got at sea."

Now, to me that briefing was an absolute atrocity. I did not carry out those instructions. I meticulously sought to give the minority officers the very best break that they could get, but I wasn't able to do anything about correcting the institutional problem until I became Chief of Naval Operations.

Now one could say I should have broken my spear and taken on the system as a commander, or one could say that I did right in waiting until I had a position where I could really make a change, or one could say that someone else might have done nothing about it either then or as CNO. I like to think that in my own case the long-term decision turned out to be right, but I don't intend to imply that it might not have been more ethical to have engaged in the battle and ended my career as a commander.

75. Keeping an Open Mind: Communications

The officer who makes himself available to subordinates encourages two-way communication and avoids oversupervising. General Charley Stone, a division commander in Vietnam, was known for his sincere concern for his men. On daily walks through the base he would stop and talk to them. In the evenings, he would write their parents or wives and inform them of their progress. Although he was a very busy man, he was never too busy or too proud to care for his men.[12] An officer can also make himself available by establishing a policy such as office hours or an open-door arrangement. Of course, the officer will be available at quarters, but he should also be available for group discussions, rap sessions, and one-on-one meetings as appropriate. Admiral McDonald suggests that an officer should seek the opinions/views of his juniors as often as seems practical.

An effective leader holds a daily meeting with the leading chief or platoon sergeant and leading petty officer or platoon guide. He listens to them because he acknowledges their experience, and he uses the answers to questions he asks them to help him make decisions. A good leader uses the experience of a senior enlisted, who is probably much older than him and possesses both technical and leadership experience from years of doing the job.

The officer should also meet periodically with various other groups of personnel, such as non-rated personnel, petty officers and noncommissioned officers, and chiefs and staff noncommissioned officers. Each of these groups has unique interests and problems.

The officer should take the opportunity offered by these meetings to state his policies and viewpoints as a means of reinforcement. It is also worthwhile for him to ask for the participants' recommendations and suggestions regarding policy. If the leader promises information or a follow-up session, he must make good on that promise, and he should feel free to bring professionals into a meeting when necessary.

After gaining the participants' go-ahead, the officer may want to publish information resulting from these meetings for the benefit of the rest of the organization. A commanding officer can use audio-visual equipment to communicate with his subordinates in larger commands. However, he should only address questions that are applicable to the entire unit when an audio-visual record of a meeting is being made.

Sailors and Marines appreciate the opportunity to interface directly with their bosses, and many of them will take advantage of the opportunity afforded. The leader should hold one-on-one sessions in a quiet, comfortable location, such as a stateroom or a private office, if possible. He must be careful to give individuals or groups adequate time to discuss their interests and concerns. He cannot appear impatient, because this will inhibit the subordinate and quickly bring the meeting to an end. The leader should show sincerity and interest in what is being said and express his personal concern if appropriate. To lead troops requires that the leader be responsive to *their* needs, be familiar with the frame of reference in which they face *their* problems, and be aware of the responsibilities, rights, and benefits accruing to *them*.[118-28]

Many people choke up in front of their bosses, particularly if they need to discuss an issue of a personal or embarrassing nature. It is the leader's job to make them feel comfortable enough to address such subjects. He can encourage the individual who is having difficulty in approaching the intended subject by listening patiently and attentively and asking the right questions.

The leader should not hesitate to cut an individual off and reexplain the rules of meetings if the individual is out of line, however. Examples of this are attempts to turn the meeting into a "bitch" session (a meeting in which no constructive comments are made) or to defame a third party's character. The leader must maintain control of the conversation. He should avoid developing overly personal relationships with individuals who continually seek personal audiences, and he should keep group meetings on a professional basis. Be the friend of your troops, but do not become their intimate.[6-45] General Barrow believes that leaders should not become overly dependent on suggestions from others:

If there is time, you are probably going to obtain suggestions from subordinates through the staff planning process and consider all the facts that go into your decision. They might even recommend the decision to you. But in making hasty decisions your experience and knowledge should tell you to move out with whatever it is you are going to do.

It is not necessary for an officer to have a gathering of subordinates and ask, "Does anyone have any suggestions or anything he wishes to inform me about?" to find out what is going on in his command. Commanders at all levels need to get out and see and hear what is going on. And you don't always have to hit them over the head with a blunt question. You can be subtle and still be very effective in your question to a subordinate, almost casual. You can ask insignificant, casual kinds of questions, and buried in there is a question that you want an answer to on something that is bothering you.

You are looking for staff views, staff suggestions, but you have to get around to do that. You can do some of that in your office, but in moving about with a very humanistic, easily approachable demeanor, talking not just to immediate subordinates but to subordinates of all levels in their work spaces, you will learn more. You will be surprised at the things they'll tell you. They'll say, "He looks like the kind of guy I can tell that we haven't

had this damn thing fixed since I've been on the job." So when you say, "How are things going?" he feels comfortable in saying, "Fine, Sir, except this valve doesn't work; never has worked, Sir. We've had work called in on this valve ever since I've been here, and I've been here nine months."

Even in combat, you go out and visit troops on the line, as we say, you go along foxhole to foxhole and say, "How's it going, Marine?" and pretty soon one of them is going to say something that rings a bell, like "We're doing fine, Sir, except we're short of ammo," which is one thing you've got to know.

I believe something could be gained from time to time by calling subordinates in one on one in your office. It makes them feel good to know that you value whatever it is you want them to talk about. You can do that selectively, you don't have to call in every subordinate, nor have to call in all at a certain level. You can say, "I'd like to see Captain Jones this afternoon," and he comes and you say, "Captain, I understand that you served in Kuwait," and pretty soon you get him started on something he knows something about and you can't shut him up, and then you sort of shunt him on to another subject, "How are things going?" and you find out one helluva lot. But you cannot lead without listening, and you can't listen if you don't make yourself available, by either going to the speakers or having the speakers come to you.

You cannot command by memorandum and telephone and Xerox machines, and in and out baskets, and third persons. There are people who do that, sit behind a desk with the accouterments of authority around them so they feel like they exude it. That's bad business. Command by being fixed someplace is pointless.

In meetings, as elsewhere, the leader must make the chain of command work. He must ensure that subordinates go through their work center supervisor to the chief or platoon sergeant before they come to him, except in unique situations of a personal nature. Likewise, the leader must go down the chain, allowing subordinates to exercise their authority and responsibilities. By utilizing the chain of command, the leader assures that his subordinates gain valuable experience in leadership, and he avoids real or perceived oversupervision. Admiral Long adds:

> An officer should very seldom bypass the chain of command in directing action, but information can come from a variety of places. In this context, communication with subordinates is very important because the leader will receive information and because the subordinates will benefit from knowing he is interested enough to seek their advice and their counsel.
>
> It is also very important for an officer to talk to his people and find out what their problems are. The Naval Service is not a nursery or a home for ill-prepared people, but people do have problems and questions. They are concerned about their own promotion, they are concerned about their dependents. Officers in positions of command have a responsibility for the welfare of their people, so it is important that officers make themselves available to hear what is troubling their people. Many of the problems that are presented are not problems at all, but questions that need an explanation. Sometimes problems are presented that are not solvable at that officer's level, but for the problem to be solved, the officer must be made aware of it. Officers should strive to develop the ability to communicate with their subordinates, not on a buddy-buddy basis, like "one of the guys," but on a basis of mutual respect.

The effective leader knows that he is probably the best-informed and most aggressive individual in one-on-one sessions with his personnel, and so he does not talk down to the less-educated individual. Rather, he carefully and gradually brings that individual toward his level of conversation. He does not dominate a conversation when an individual needs to talk and be heard, but he helps the individual toward a solution to his problem by leading him through a logical progression to the solution. If the conversation ends up with the individual developing his own solution to a problem, the officer has truly been successful.

One of the most difficult skills to acquire is the ability to get along with others in day-to-day relationships. One avenue to success is to become a "professional" listener. Regardless of what he wants to hear, the leader must be prepared to receive and take advice and suggestions which are contrary to his own views. There must be open-mindedness, a willingness to hear and consider other points of view. The prestige of any leader can be immeasurably enhanced by listening to the suggestions of his subordinates.[107-1286] Another approach is to put yourself in the other person's shoes. What would you do if you were in his place? This approach will earn the officer credibility and a reputation for being a reasonable individual. Subordinates are for the most part educated, caring, and concerned individuals. If the leader treats them as such, he will bring out the best in them and will gain the reputation of being a "people person." That is one of the highest compliments a leader could receive.

Admiral Larson summarizes by reminding us that

> every human being has thoughts and ideas, and they're very, very important to that human being, and it's important that you let those thoughts be heard. If he's not able to express himself, if he's not able to offer something to you or get those ideas into the chain of command or into

the division planning, he'll become frustrated, he'll assume he's not an important member of the team. When people make that assumption, they become withdrawn and, perhaps even worse than that, they start complaining and grousing and become a morale problem. So it's very important that you do listen to those troops; after all, there is a good reward for that, too. You get a lot of good ideas from some of the troops, regardless of their experience level. There's no premium on good ideas that go just with rank or just with experience. The other thing that's very important is that you listen to your supervisors, to your senior petty officers, to your chief, because when the troops see that you are listening to your chief and he has your ear and he can make recommendations, they will develop confidence in him and confidence in your internal chain of command and will function within that, because they know that they won't be filtered, that he will represent them, that they will be able to get their thoughts to the top. So the whole thing is a very healthy environment, and I think just out of mutual respect for any individual and his worth and his dignity, he deserves to be heard.

As far as oversupervising, you've really got to trust your subordinates, you've got to show that trust, and you've got to show it in everything you do. A couple of times in the past I even allowed someone to tell me something that I knew probably wasn't totally true, and I let it go on and something happened and I took the rap just to show them that I trusted them and they let me down. I didn't make a big deal out of it, but once they saw that, they understood that we better be totally honest with this guy in the future because he trusts us and he stood up for us and we let him down. So you show that trust by letting them do things, by not always peering over their shoulder, by not talking down to them, not checking up on them in a way that it really shows distrust. However, you still have to spot-check, move around and observe, because you have the ultimate responsibility to see that things are being carried out, but you can do that within that environment of open communications, listening to and trusting your subordinates.

76. The Participative Approach to Decision Making

Different styles of leadership may be necessary in different situations. In emergency situations, the leader must depend on his ability to be autocratic. There is no time for group participation in decision making during a crisis. Admiral Zumwalt makes the point that,

in an operational environment, an officer has got to make a fast decision if a fast decision is required, but where there is time, he should very carefully break a problem down into its parts and analyze each one of the parts, and the impact on the whole, and then build it back up. He must also put a priority on the problem. If he has very serious mission problems and is asked to grapple with something short of a mission problem, he must ask himself whether a solution to this problem will contribute to the solution of the overall problem. If so, he had better get on it right away. If not, he can give it a little lesser priority while he works on what needs fixing. It is counterproductive to spend an exorbitant amount of time fixing minor problems while ignoring the serious impediments to accomplishing the long-term objective.

Faced with an emergency, leaders make decisions for their subordinates that affect the unit's well-being as well as mission accomplishment. "How do you want to go about remedying this?" is not an appropriate question when the bilges are flooding and the ship is under fire. Admiral Carney makes the point that,

> unless the officer is certain that he knows completely and accurately all the factors of the problem in front of him, he should consult with others and obtain as many diverging opinions as he can. When he is called on for an opinion, the officer should be frank; he should not offer an involuntary "Yes, Sir," for that answer does not help the officer who is asking his opinion. Conversely, when a subordinate always agrees with an officer, the officer should consider whether the subordinate is frankly stating his opinion or just agreeing because he is reluctant, for some reason, to disagree.
>
> When an officer is asked a question and he is not sure of the answer, he should always state that he does not know the answer but he will find it out. I learned my lesson the hard way. Carl Vincent was the chairman of the Naval Affairs Committee, and I was called over there one day to testify, and he asked me a question. I took a shot in the dark, and Carl spit in the cuspidor very accurately and said, "Now, that's not the way I remember it." Well, he remembers so much more about the Navy than I had heard in a lifetime, I was really put in my place and put in short pants. I learned my lesson, and I came home and told Mrs. Carney, "I've made my last smart crack without knowing what I'm talking about."

A participative style—in which input is solicited from the group—is effective when an officer is considering how to do something in a non-emergency situation. No leader can perform effectively over a long period without a certain amount of participation from his subordinates. The participative approach does not mean that decision making is left entirely to subordinates, however. It means that the leader draws on the knowledge of the members of the work group to reach the objectives of the organization more effectively.

The sum knowledge of subordinates is often greater than that of their leader when all the facts concerning a situation are available to the unit. Admiral Hunt remarks:

> My principle is that a leader should consider his subordinates' ideas very, very carefully. They may be better than his own, and he should react constructively to them. Once he gets himself into an ivory tower, he's lost.

Leaders who consider and discuss the suggestions of others, including subordinates, avail themselves of experience, knowledge, values, and methods beyond their personal inventory. New ideas often surface as a result of the interpersonal exchange that takes place during collective problem solving. Listening to the ideas of others, then, entails more than just hearing what they say.

Considering the ideas and suggestions of others can be extremely effective in a variety of situations, and leaders will find that they have many opportunities to involve their personnel in decision making and planning. Having an input to the decision-making process often increases an individual's commitment to the objectives and goals of the organization. Subordinates believe their ideas are important—as, indeed, they frequently are—and they often are considerably more committed to decisions in which they have participated than they are to decisions in which they had no say.

The participative approach to decision making also increases satisfaction among subordinates and raises morale, which in turn encourages increased productivity. Subordinates whose input is valued develop greater self-esteem. Feeling that they "belong to" and are contributing to an organization, individuals are also more likely to display initiative. Admiral Holloway says:

The chain of command is put to best use when people who have ideas and thoughts communicate up the chain and when the commander or the officer makes certain that whenever someone expresses a legitimate fault, complaint, idea, or initiative, the people in the chain of command give it consideration. The leader must tell his leading chiefs and division chiefs and assistant division officers not to "turn the sailors off," because listening is part of leadership. Noncommissioned officers have to be concerned enough to listen to the sailor but smart enough to know what to pass and what not to pass on up the line. Every sailor who has an idea cannot tell it directly to the captain, because the captain does not have time to listen to all those ideas. But the sailor needs to know that his idea will be considered by his seniors. That is one reason the chain of command exists.

The feeling of being valuable to the organization often is in itself a reward to members of an organization, but tangible rewards are sometimes also needed to sustain high performance levels. Subordinates often need or want praise for "above average" work or accomplishments. Rewards of a compensatory nature, such as special liberty and special considerations, usually encourage increased productivity, but they should not be the basis for achieving involvement of the troops.

The conditions that lead to success in the area of participative decision making include acceptance by leaders of their responsibility and accountability to both seniors and subordinates, belief in the value of subordinate participation by everyone in the organization, and adequate time to allow leaders to anticipate and plan ahead for subordinate participation.

The four participative decision-making techniques are: (1) delegation, in which decisions are made at the lowest possible level; (2) question asking, which encourages subordinates to resolve problems in response to the questions; (3) formation of committees, in which dynamic interaction produces insights that cannot otherwise be gained; and (4) goal sharing, which results in a diffusion of responsibility throughout a unit or organization and a concomitant increase of authority for the persons whose responsibilities have been increased.

These leadership techniques are used in a leader's interactions with subordinates. An executive-level leader, one who is responsible for junior leaders and several hierarchical levels, uses these techniques, and he also contributes to the junior leader's effectiveness by allowing him to be accountable for his own actions and decisions. Inputs from the senior based on his knowledge and experience are more meaningful to the junior than are precise instructions on what to do and how to do it. Personal confidence, confidence of subordinates, and confidence of seniors all are more affected by a leader's decision-making ability than by his ability to carry out instructions.

A leader must exercise a certain amount of caution when employing a participative decision-making technique, however. Inclusion of subordinates in decision making must never be carried so far that it undermines the leader's right or ability to make the final decision. The needs, expectations, and inclinations of subordinates should be evaluated before their participation is solicited. Members of the unit may interpret his solicitation of ideas to mean that the leader does not know what to do or is unable to make decisions on his own.

Leaders must also retain responsibility for the decisions they make. They are obliged to report, explain, or justify any untoward occurrences and accept the consequences for their own actions as well as for the actions of their personnel. When the junior officer is confronted with a potential problem, he should ask himself these questions:

1. *"Is the problem clearly understood?"* Can he outline the implications and significance of the problem? If not, maybe more facts are needed

or the problem needs to be reinterpreted by the one who brought it in.

2. *"Is the stated problem the real one?"* Is he treating the symptom or the causes?

3. *"Does the problem 'feel' right?"* Was the report of the problem an accurate one? Does the problem occur consistently, or is it just a one-time thing?

4. *"Am I the right one to consider the problem?"* An officer can never forget the chain of command and must never assume more power than rightly given to his rank. In the same respect, the junior officer must realize the chain also goes downward and that some problems should be entrusted to his senior sergeants or chiefs.

5. *"Do I have an open mind?"* Do I fail to consider it a problem just because it is only a private or a seaman presenting it?[27-18]

The leader who has fostered teamwork through participative decision making and has retained control of his own responsibilities is not guaranteed to be successful; nor can rewards alone ensure timely and efficient results. The leader must also acquire the loyalty, commitment, and support of subordinates by displaying his own loyalty and commitment to and support of the mission—as well as his loyalty to his subordinates. To be dedicated, subordinates must consider their leader's values to be worthwhile.

Admiral de Cazanove secured the ideas of subordinates by, most importantly, giving them
confidence in themselves, and helping them to understand that they have good ideas and that they should not think to do like this all the time and think like that all the time. By showing them respect, you help them to fight against self-doubt and hesitation. While everyone may have a time of self-doubt in his life, it is important—especially in action—to have your personnel trained so that they take action without doubt and hesitation, and, in addition, this will help them lead a full life.

A leader who allows subordinates to partici-

pate in decision making improves the quality of his decisions and the quality and efficiency of the work performed by his subordinates. But the leader must never lose sight of the fact that, although he includes the ideas and suggestions of others in the decision-making process, the final responsibility for decisions is his.

MCPON Sanders: *It's important for the officer to make himself available to receive the ideas and suggestions of the crew. Of course, if he adopts someone else's idea, it is still the responsibility of the leader for choosing that plan of action, whether or not it works out. But, if you do use someone else's idea and it turns out to be a good one, make sure the other person receives some kind of praise or recognition, and make sure that your senior knows that Jim or Jane was the originator, that they get the credit.*

77. Accepting Responsibility for the Actions of Subordinates

The leader of any unit deals with success and failure as that unit strives to meet set goals. Successes are easy to deal with, and a good leader passes appropriate credit to his subordinates. Dealing with a failure to achieve an objective is not as easy, whether its cause was a unit member's mistake or just that the best efforts of the unit were not sufficient to accomplish the goal. How the leader reacts to failure, including whether or not he accepts responsibility for the unit's actions, is important to that unit and its leader.

Experienced leaders know that it is common sense to accept responsibility for the actions of subordinates, for doing so is part of being a good leader and helps the leader achieve his goals. In order to develop trust and loyalty, maintain morale, develop a successful unit, and earn his position as the unit's leader, an officer must accept responsibility for the actions of the people who work for him. A review of the great military leaders supports this. General Grant achieved success and recognition as a leader because his subordinates found him worthy of their loyalty and commitment. He surely displayed many attributes that earned him the loyalty of an entire army. One specific incident portrays one of those attributes. General Grant arrived at Fort Donelson after his army was suddenly attacked during the execution of an amphibious campaign. His army's right wing had been crushed and his force was on the verge of defeat. Quietly he said, "Gentlemen, the position on the right must be retaken."[31] A man of decision he was, but also important is what he did not say: he blamed no one. He accepted the responsibility for his unit and for the actions of his subordinates.

In accepting responsibility for the positive and negative accomplishments of subordinates, the leader furthers the unit's ability to succeed by demonstrating to his troops that they are all part of the same team, which he is glad to lead.

All officers in the Naval Service perform both as a manager and as a leader, but the distinction between leadership and management may be fuzzy at times. In general terms, management tends to be concerned with policies, procedures, organizational structures, and "pushing paper." Leadership tends to be concerned more with the interpersonal relationships between seniors and subordinates. Leadership can be broken down into two dimensions.[66-345] *Consideration* includes behavior indicating mutual trust, respect, and rapport between the leader and his subordinates, while *structure* includes behavior that organizes and defines activities, defines roles for subordinates, assigns tasks, and plans and pushes for goal achievement.

Taking responsibility for subordinates' actions is part of the consideration aspect of leadership. Sun Tzu states in his early writings on the art of war that there are five fundamentals of war; the first of these is maintaining the morale and trust of subordinates. Accepting responsibility for subordinates' actions enhances morale, trust,

and respect, and it influences how effective the leader can be in developing a successful unit. Admiral Uchida comments:

> An officer should, in principle, take responsibility for all that his subordinates do, although there will be differences in how far he takes this idea, depending upon the nature and the occasion of their actions, and whether he is taking on official or moralistic responsibilities. An officer should not forget to have the grace to bear the blame that he should bear.

A leader who does not develop the trust and respect of his subordinates will not be an effective leader. Subordinates of a leader who does not accept responsibility will lose respect and say, "He blamed us and he is the one who tells us what to do." It is human nature to attempt to transfer blame to someone else, but it is also human nature to share blame with someone who has accepted that blame. By accepting responsibility, the leader establishes rapport with, gains the trust of, and encourages confidence in his subordinates; the subordinates will comment, "The boss took that one, let's not let him down again." An officer should never for a minute think his comments to a senior on mission accomplishment do not travel as if by osmosis throughout the organization—they do. Besides, the senior was once in the same position and knows the challenge and pitfalls involved in supervision, thus obviating the need for any excuses. The senior knows the JO wasn't doing everything himself. As Secretary Webb remarks,

> Each individual is responsible for his own acts, but a leader is responsible for the success or failure of the mission. There is an old saying that responsibility cannot be delegated, but that does not mean that if an individual under his command disobeys the law or does not perform his duties because of his own personal inadequacies or failure, the officer should commit hari-kari. If an individual had an obvious flaw and the officer

failed to see it, then the officer shares the responsibility for the individual's misconduct. This is why anyone who is conducting plebe indoctrination on an individual whom he feels should not become an officer should speak up before that plebe becomes an officer and makes a mistake that results in an unnecessary death. In a purely military sense, however, an officer's responsibility is toward the success of the mission, and if he makes a grievous error of judgment, he is responsible. But if another individual does something that was totally unpredictable, the officer is not responsible in a military sense.

Another reason to accept responsibility is because behavior is one of the best teaching tools. Leaders want their immediate subordinates to be responsible and complete assigned tasks without offering excuses. Many studies have shown that subordinates tend to behave as their leaders behave. That is reasonable and makes sense. The leader is able to reinforce behavior by controlling privileges and evaluations. An officer's behavior communicates better than words. As previously pointed out, the old adage "Do what I say, not what I do" surely alludes to the importance of behavior as a strong method of communication. Therefore, in order to get his immediate subordinates to accept responsibility, the leader must accept responsibility.

Of course, a leader should accept responsibility—he is responsible. A leader defines roles and controls time, equipment, and direction for tasks. Understanding this helps a good leader to develop a closely knit unit with high morale, one that will accept a great deal of structure (strict definition of roles, plans, due dates, etc.) when doing so is necessary to get the job done. By accepting responsibility for the actions of his subordinates, a leader confirms his position as the leader of the unit. Having demonstrated his loyalty to the unit, the officer will find that loyalty will be returned. Admiral Moorer notes:

An officer is not directly responsible, or legally responsible, for what his people do ashore or on leave. But he is indirectly responsible if their conduct ashore or on leave is due to a lack of proper indoctrination and instruction. He should point out to them the need to maintain a very acceptable image in the eyes of the American public, which is paying their salary and buying the ship they live in, and the foreign public, for the sake of the image of the U.S. Navy and the United States.

Admiral Moorer related how he acted in a situation where he was not legally responsible for the welfare of the men, but he felt a responsibility to them, nevertheless.

In the Seventh Fleet, we had about eighty thousand sailors and a division of Marines, and this was right after the Korean War, and the Japanese came out with these very high-powered motorcycles. The sailors, after being at sea, would come in and jump on one of these motorcycles. I went over to the hospital when we had all these accidents—because in Japan they have many, many blind corners, and the streets were extremely narrow, and people would be going that way and a driver would come this way—I went over to the hospital and there were six boys there with nothing but basics. I mean they were going to be a ward of the government for the rest of their lives. One wasn't even 20 years old.

So I announced there would be no more motorcycles, nobody's going to ride motorcycles. Now I felt that that was my responsibility, since they were 10,000 miles from home. Of course, the motorcycle people almost had a fit, and I got a letter from a senator and he says he wants to know who do you think you are in violating their rights. So I just wrote him a letter and I said, Dear Senator, I received your letter about my decision on the motorcycles . . . and I told him about these boys being absolutely broken in places, and I said I'm only doing what I would expect somebody to do for my boy if I had an 18-year-old boy 10,000 miles from home. Well, that was the end of it, never heard anything more from him.

I was a personnel officer in a fighter squadron for three years, Fighter Squadron One, it was first aboard *Langley,* which was our first aircraft carrier, then we came on the old *Lexington* for a little while, and then to Norfolk on the *Enterprise* (the one that was so famous during World War II). We had about 80 enlisted men in that squadron in those days, because we had very simple aircraft, but in any event, during the three years I was personnel officer, we had not one single court martial, and we didn't take anyone to captain's mast, because I handled by delegating authority to the enlisted people. I gave the chief the authority to restrict a kid who came back a little late or didn't have his shoes shined when he came in for inspection. In those days all the sailors had a liberty card, and he would just take the liberty card away from him (he couldn't get out of the gate without the liberty card) and then give him some kind of unpleasant job, maybe like painting the head or something.

The main thing is contact. I tried to learn about their families, how many children they had, whether they were married, and so on. Of course, that was all in their service record. But the point is, you've got to maintain communications with people who are working for you and treat them as people, find out things that are troubling them and things that they're interested in aside from their work in the unit. I was real proud of them, not one court martial because we didn't have any offenses that warranted a court martial or even close to it.

MCPON Sanders: *We in the military must accept responsibility for the actions of our subordinates. This means that we should be aware of what our subordinates are doing, that we train them, that we let them know what we expect of them, that we set the standards and ensure their being met. However, there will be times when all your planning and all your training go awry, simply because someone did not do what he should have, but you're going to have to step up and take responsibility for the error. I guess if you're going to step up and accept the praise when things work fine and when the crew produces properly, you certainly have to step up and take the blame when things don't work out as wanted. It's always a learning process, and if someone fails to do something that he should have done and you had to step up and accept the responsibility, make sure that it's always passed on to the crew or the person who is involved, that they also are going to have to share the responsibility. For the officer, it is one of the things that certainly shows the growth of an individual: being able to be responsible for himself as well as others.*

78. The Components of Training

An officer in a military unit is in a position of trust and responsibility which has no equivalent in other fields of endeavor. The very definition of the word *officer* evokes the accountability, trust, responsibility, and authority that an officer carries. An officer is a shareholder in the "company" and is, thus, responsible for the accomplishment of his unit's mission. He will lead and direct some of the unit's enlisted personnel in the accomplishment of that mission, and often he will be responsible for some of the unit's hardware, as well. Leading machinery is no challenge, but leading people is tough! But the rewards of leadership are to be found in uniting a diverse group of people and working with and through them to excel in the tasks at hand.

387

Admiral Burke learned to handle a ship because a senior let him take over, and later, Admiral Burke let others take over so they could learn ship handling:

> When I was a destroyer executive officer and I went to sea, my captain was an ex-submariner. He was the best ship handler in port I had ever seen, but he had never been on a surface ship and he didn't know anything about tactics and he was afraid of his ship in high-speed maneuvers. I found that out after we'd taken a shake-down cruise. Well, I hadn't had any destroyer experience, either, but I figured that would be a very good thing, so after a little while we had an unspoken agreement that if I would take the ship under all tactics, operations or not, he'd appreciate it. I didn't actually volunteer to do that, but it actually was a very good thing for me, because I learned how to handle a ship, and it didn't matter to him, because he was a beautiful ship handler and there was no reason why he couldn't have done it.
>
> The worst thing a captain can do to the ship is not train his people. I think a good ship handler is essential, but when I was executive officer of a ship, I never got to take my ship alongside the dock at all. The captain always did it, he could do beautifully. No one on the ship could take the ship into dock in the harbor, and it was just magnificent, he wasn't going to ruin it. I decided I wouldn't do that, and so when I took over the *Mumford*, which I took over at seven o'clock in the morning (we were going to sea at eight), I gave a little speech of two or three minutes to the officers and said, "The one thing I promise you is that I will take the ship one-third of the time, the exec will take it one-third of the time, and the other officers of the deck will take it the other

> third, in rotation. This is my time today, I'll take her out." Well, I never regretted so much in my life any words, because it was a fixed schedule that I hadn't thought about very much, and naturally the time soon came when the most inexperienced officers of the deck had to take the ship out under very difficult conditions. I didn't want to break my promise, but I stood on the wing of the bridge ready to take over any time, and they knew that, but it was a hard thing to do. Yet those officers all became good ship handlers, and they all became good captains later.

AN OFFICER MUST TRAIN HIMSELF BEFORE HE TRAINS OTHERS

During his first tour, an officer lays the foundation for the rest of his career as an officer. He will use the skills he develops on that tour time and time again. He must: (1) know what his unit's mission is, (2) know what his subordinates are supposed to do in support of that mission, (3) be able to measure their performance, (4) learn how to give job performance appraisals, and (5) become familiar with and use the resources available to help him improve his group. The resources mentioned in item 5 are exhaustive. In fact, the officer will find resources to help him in each of the other four areas.

When he reports aboard his first command, one of the first things a young officer should do is begin thinking about designing and implementing his own training program. Chances are that when he gets to his first command, the new officer will take over from someone who already has a program in place. It is seldom necessary to reinvent the wheel, and the new officer should avoid trying to do so. Rather, he should build on what already exists. He will find it especially worthwhile to learn from the successes and failures of other individuals, officer and enlisted, whose professionalism he admires. There is something to learn from everyone, the plodders as well as the rising stars.

The new officer should tackle the available resources, refresh his memory concerning the things he heard in the training pipeline, and learn about the things that are unique to his new command. The unit's organization and regulation manual and current notices and instructions, better than anything else, tell him what goes on in his command. The young officer should develop the habit of reading them, because as he progresses through his tour, his ability to locate a description of a certain procedure or a set of rules in a directive will give him a positive edge in taking care of his subordinates.

Next in importance are the directives of his unit's seniors, such as the Navy type commander's regulation manual and directives. Operations orders will also affect what an officer does, even if he is the most junior officer in the command. There are technical publications that address the subsets of every unit's mission, and the officer need only read them to learn the details of his particular responsibilities. Knowledge is power; knowledge is the basic building block of an officer's professional foundation.

Another tier of resources is composed of the people in the officer's unit, from the commanding officer on down. He should talk to all of them and take advantage of what they have to offer. His seniors will give him guidance on *what* to do, and his enlisted personnel are knowledgeable in *how* to do it. An officer should not hesitate to tap into the knowledge and experience of his personnel.

Every ship and unit has all of the publications and all of the instructor talent that are found in any Navy or Marine Corps school, so the young officer can learn anything he sets out to learn. (The senior enlisted personnel could very well be school instructors on their next tour.) He need only ask for a "show and tell" from those who know. An officer will learn faster and his subordinates will feel better about him and about

themselves in this kind of setting. There is quite a contrast between a subordinate who can tell his family, "I taught Ensign Door 'such and such,'" and one who complains, "Ensign Door made me do 'such and such.' He was wrong and it's all screwed up." Not only is the latter angry, but his family thinks the command does not appreciate him. What effect will that have at reenlistment decision time? An officer should not be bashful. He should ask his troops to teach him.

The training pipelines an officer follows en route to his first command will give him only a rudimentary idea of what the enlisted personnel under his supervision do. The officer needs to learn the "rules" of the ship or unit and get his people to teach him, as discussed. He needs, also, to look at the type of work his people do and find out how they know how to do it. An officer should become familiar with every job his people do, even if the job is as simple as chipping paint (an entire chapter in the *Naval Ships Technical Manual* [*NSTM*] is devoted to a description of applying preservation coatings).

Sailors and Marines perform preventive maintenance on equipment ranging from the lowliest items of hardware to the most sophisticated weapons systems in the inventory. This PMS, as it is called, is performed using Maintenance Requirement Cards (MRCs). The MRCs are an excellent source of information regarding subordinates' technical duties—which, through his responsibility, are also the officer's duties. An officer should read the cards, especially when he is watching his people. He should look inside the gear; he should find out how the required tools are used. His search for knowledge will pay the dividend of making his people more interested in using the MRCs and thereby following proper maintenance procedures themselves. The paths to department heads' and company commanders' doors are well worn by young officers coming to explain that Seaman or PFC Jones just broke the "gizzframitz" by using a pair of vice-grip pliers instead of the tool required by the MRC.

DEVELOPING SUBORDINATES THROUGH TRAINING

A new division or platoon member, even if he is straight out of school, will need to be trained in the unit's policies, procedures, and equipment. Their commanding officer has the responsibility to tell new individuals just what he expects of them (qualification, advancement, deportment, etc.) and just what they can expect from him (support, fairness, high standards, etc.). The officer should ensure that his senior enlisted supervisors are doing the same thing. One of the joys of being a leader comes from watching subordinates develop personally and professionally. Every new sailor or Marine entrusted to an officer will pass through those critical maturation years (17–21) under his guidance and leadership—he has a national treasure in his hands. It is up to every officer to run a training program that develops the skills and expertise of personnel. Admiral Long explained how he determines how much supervision is required and how supervision should be carried out:

> Supervision is an area that requires a good sense of judgment. The degree of supervision is clearly not the same for all circumstances. On one end of the spectrum you will find that there are officers who feel that they have no responsibility to supervise the actions of their subordinates. Their idea is that if they supervise the actions of their subordinates then they show no confidence or trust in their subordinates. At the other end of the spectrum is the officer who essentially is back in the work spaces with tools in hand and is pushing the chiefs and the first-class petty officers and the others out of the way, and he is actually performing the work that should be done by subordinates.

I've always found that the degree of supervision depends, first, on my assessment of the importance of the task, second, on the qualifications of the people under me, and third, on the degree of my own expertise. I would say that officers in general need to give direction as to what they want to be done. It is entirely appropriate, if it is a rather critical or sensitive operation, to require subordinates to explain in some detail how they intend to tackle the problem, and it can also be appropriate, depending on the importance of the task, for the officer in charge to be present in the spaces in order to supervise personally the specific task that is underway. I reject completely the idea that supervision is unnecessary because it shows a lack of faith and confidence. This is completely contrary to my belief of responsibility residing in an officer, who must know what is going on.

There is another consideration in the question of supervision. Sometimes officers believe that they cannot contribute anything to the solution of a problem. You will find that, in most cases, one very important reason why officers need to be involved in what's going on in their divisions or spaces is that they can contribute to the solution of the problem. I have found over my years, particularly when I was a younger officer, that my knowledge of theoretical aspects of a problem many times could contribute to the practical solution of a problem. Whereas I could not handle the wrenches and the screwdrivers and the meters, I knew enough about the theory to be able to ask intelligent questions that actually assisted in developing the solution of the problem.

In addition to bringing along the new people, the training program must also aim at refreshing the knowledge of the old-timers. People's memories must be stimulated to recall the information they contain; thus, the established members of a unit must be retrained on basics in addition to receiving training on more sophisticated details. The excuse "We're too busy to train, Sir" is as old as it is dangerous. If members of a unit are too busy to train, then something is not right, and the officer needs to take a hard look at what his people are doing.

PLANNING AND IMPLEMENTING TRAINING PROGRAMS

One-on-one training, like Smith showing Jones how to light off an eductor (vacuum pump used on fluids) and pump out a space, is easy to do and is understood by most people. Training a group is more difficult, but most activities in the Naval Service are done in a group, and with a proper training program, even the most diverse group imaginable can work miracles. In order to do a good job training the team, an officer has to know the resources, rules, and personnel of his unit. Properly armed with this knowledge and the unit's objectives, the officer can institute a training program that utilizes a process of action, feedback, and correction. Good team training with feedback, so the team knows they are getting better (or worse), builds unit identity and pride, which build on themselves. Individuals can go a long way toward being good when they believe they are good.

Group training programs generally are composed of a mixture of formal (classroom) lectures, discussions, and unit exercises. The mixture depends on the unit's and the officer's short- and long-range objectives. Because the unit's objectives change with time, the officer must likewise change his objectives and adapt his training program. He will have to set and reset goals and milestones to do this.

An important part of any training program is recognizing achievement. That is where esprit de corps can work for the unit. When the necessary progress has not been made, that, too,

must be recognized. People know when they are doing poorly. Calling poor performance something other than what it is, is unwise, and people know that, too. Admiral Taylor suggests:

Management by objective is the first thing you do. You see it in all our athletic teams: We're number one, we're going to win the championship. It works in a division because all of the troops in a division are athletic or want to be, and so they will press on if you set the goals and you appeal to their competitive spirit. Having set an objective, then it's a case of getting the right people on the right job, so you have to understand who you have working for you, and how you organize.

You have a limited span of control, so you probably work through maybe as many as 6 individuals. In a division that's not a problem, normally you work through a chief, maybe you have a couple of second- or first-class petty officers. But, for instance, on the *Coral Sea*, a lieutenant checks in as the boiler officer with 12 boilers, and each fire room has some problems. How do you get all of these guys to get ready for an OPPE [Operational Proficiency Propulsion Exam]? The size of the division varies from maybe 400 guys in one division, down to 20 or 30 in another, but basically if you have an OPPE, and ORE [Operational Readiness Exam], the Battle E, you have some things coming up, and inside that line division in a squadron is a top-notch job because you have maybe one or two petty officers and then a bunch of third class maybe, and some nonrated guys. It is a good leadership opportunity to impress on them that we want to get every airplane to make a round trip, we don't want any airborne aborts, we want to have the airplanes ready with all the switches in the right places and all the reservoirs filled.

It's a case of the day in, day out, routine that is hung into a basic plan that goes to some long-range objective. One-minute management is what this is all about. You have set your goal, you are participating, you have your team in place, and now what you do is recognize achievement. Go out there and stroke the guy: "Hey, that's a great airplane." Find other little ways to reward a guy, not so much in time off or money, but in little emblematic things. Work to the pride in the unit and the pride in self that just fires the guy up. He doesn't want to go home, he wants to stay out there and work with this team that you've got.

I don't want to say it's like coaching a Little League team, but it isn't very far from it. You have a basic desire in everyone to excel, and you have to find some way to give them an outlet, and you have to give them encouragement, and when you get that working for you, it's momentum, it works. You don't lead with a two-by-four, you lead by finding ways to get the guys and the gals to want to do what they have to do, and that is team spirit. Have out in front of it always the fact that we've got to be ready to prevail against an enemy who is also ready. Get the country involved, get God involved, establish the long-range target. These are not fallacious principles at all, they really apply, particularly to the quality of the troops that we have in our Navy today.

In running a training program, it is very difficult to determine how much time to allow. In this area an officer can turn for advice to people with more experience than he has, including the commanding officer, the department head or company commander, and the senior enlisted personnel. The officer will benefit from their advice. As mentioned earlier, an officer can never afford to let his unit become too busy to train. Former commanding officers of naval vessels have

indicated that they would have done a better job as CO if they had realized beforehand that they should dedicate about 70 percent of their time to training their officers and enlisted personnel. Admiral McDonald comments:

While a commanding officer may be concerned, he should not avoid letting his executive officer, navigator, or the officer of the deck put the ship alongside the tanker to replenish. Yes, there might be a collision if anyone other than he does it, but training of subordinates and their being capable of handling emergencies require a certain amount of trust and allowing subordinates to gain experience.

If COs should be spending that kind of time training, then training should consume a large part of every officer's time.

The effectiveness of a training program reflects the quality of the management effort given to it. After laying out the command's goals and objectives, an officer must derive his own unit's goals. What kind of action to undertake (formal training versus exercises), how to measure the training's effectiveness (written quizzes, qualification progress, post-exercise critiques), and how to disseminate and obtain results from feedback (fine-tuning) are considerations. Different levels within a unit may have different training needs, and so, without going to extremes, the training must be tailored to the audience. An officer should be careful not to bore his people; he should, rather, challenge them, make them reach. Training, whenever possible, should be related to what the individuals do in the "real" world. That includes teaching them theory as well as reviewing the "nuts and bolts." An officer should be consistent and formal; he should use lesson plans and standard handouts; and he should keep in mind that quizzes do wonders for keeping people on their toes.

The officer who goes off by himself to devise a training program is taking a wrong approach. His chief petty officers or staff noncommissioned officers (SNCOs) have been trained and have been training others for a long time. The officer should get their ideas or, better, have them prepare the training program. For guidance in assigning this task, the officer should read through the Indoctrination and Training Program for new CPOs or SNCOs. It contains an excellent explanation of who does what in the officer–CPO/SNCO relationship. Officers, from junior division officer to fleet commander, must push the work as far down as it can go. An officer should get his leading chief or sergeant to devise a training plan, schedule, etc., then he should review it, discuss the changes he believes are necessary, and have his assistants finish it up. The officer supervises. His responsibility will in no way be diminished in this scenario, and his subordinates will feel ownership for the plan.

In implementing the plan, the officer can again use his senior supervisor's expertise. After the planning, getting underway is comparatively easy. The effectiveness of the program will, in large part, be a function of the quality of the people executing it. If he uses the person who breaks things to run his training program, the officer can expect the product to be people who have been trained to break things. Thus, the officer should use his best people to do the training. Using anyone less qualified is false economy.

A new officer has many knowledge and experience gaps that his senior enlisted personnel can help fill, but the officer is still in charge, and he still has the responsibility for the unit. What he has that they do not is a valuable and tailored education. He spent four tough years learning how to think and being exposed to ideas that required him to exercise that capacity to think. This education is his "ace in the hole" while he is gaining experience and filling those gaps in knowledge. He must involve his senior enlisted personnel and demand a product from them. Then he can use his knowledge and common sense to draw conclusions. Does the product measure up? Should it be improved, and how? This is what the officer has been educated to do.

Training is one of the toughest jobs in the Navy or Marine Corps, and one of the most important. The Naval Service must be ready to go to war tomorrow, and its personnel become and remain ready by training. Training begins with the junior officer. The elements of a good training program are straightforward: action, feedback, correction. Some officers and enlisted personnel try to make training more complicated than it needs to be; it should be kept simple and given the time it deserves. Time devoted to training will pay for itself.

MCPON Sanders: *In addition to managing and developing subordinates, it is important for the officer to develop the unit into a team, for there's not any one person who is going to get the overall job done; everyone has a part. But I do strongly believe that the senior enlisted should be the one primarily dealing with the work force, especially in the aviation field, where the officers have so many jobs, including flying, debriefings, etc., that a strong relationship must exist between the officer and his senior enlisted to ensure that the jobs get done. This means that the officer has to assign responsibility and delegate authority to the senior enlisted so that they can get the job done, and in this way the officer shows all of the crew that he trusts the senior enlisted and thus they in turn will get the job done. It's a little like when a spouse goes home after an extended deployment that the returning spouse does not take back all the responsibility and authority from the person who was leading the family unit, for if that is done, then some havoc is going to be created. As with the officer and senior enlisted—once having put faith and trust in someone else to do a job, don't take it back just because you have the opportunity.*

79. Loyalty: A Two-Way Street

The primary requirement for continuing success in mission accomplishment is effective leadership. Without it, no matter how sophisticated the machinery, procedures, and technology, regardless of how dedicated the people are, the chances for success are minimal. There are many definitions of leadership. An all-encompassing definition, as noted previously, was given by General Eisenhower: "Leadership is the ability to get people to do what you want them to do because they want to do it." That wise statement says a great deal, but most of all it brings up the importance of loyalty. Without loyalty from subordinates, the boss will always find the chances of success relatively slim and certainly short-lived. There is a two-way street of loyalty within a command or activity. Admiral Zumwalt agrees that loyalty is a very significant requirement in any institution:

> If an individual cannot feel loyalty to the overall objectives of the institution, then he becomes a negative factor and ought not to be in it. Loyalty must go a step beyond the traditional inclination of every commanding officer to take care of his people, of every division officer to take care of his people. When someone has performed extremely well in a given job, his leader will carry with him a piece of that person and an obligation to him to be helpful in other times and other places. I would suppose that over my 30 years in the Navy I've tried to be helpful to tens of thousands of individuals who have written me on this or that matter where I felt that their contribution to the team of which I was a part was such that they had earned that loyalty. One of the things in retrospect that I have concluded is that loyalty very definitely turns out to be a two-way street, and the fact that you have sought to try to carry that loyalty beyond just the time of your immediate exposure with an individual comes back and pays dividends in unsought ways.

No commanding officer could rest easily if he thought his command was not supportive of and loyal to him. Without that support, the difficult, unpopular decisions go down very, very hard. It is entirely right to expect that kind of loyalty, but it does not happen by accident. It is cultivated through mutual respect, trust, and concern. People are what leadership is all about. Many have erroneously believed that loyalty can be built on personal popularity, but that is certainly a totally false belief. Admiral Hayward related a story that he believed epitomized the kind of loyalty a naval officer should show to his senior officers and, as a result, to his organization:

> This case left an indelible mark with me when I was a junior officer in a fighter squadron. We had a commanding officer who was a pretty difficult person, plenty of talent but difficult. We had an executive officer who had been out of flying for a number of years, and after postgraduate work and other things, had come back into the squadron as an executive officer, having left as a jg or perhaps a lieutenant quite a number of years before: a difficult situation for any executive officer to be in. As a matter of fact, for a long while I was a jg and he was flying on my wing as a lieutenant commander.
>
> The situation was not a healthy one from the standpoint of the way in which the commanding officer dealt with the exec. It was obvious to everybody in the squadron that there was a real problem that existed at that level, and that the commanding officer had a "How did I get stuck with this guy?" kind of attitude. The exec has to be a strong person. It really impressed all of us that that executive officer never once said anything that was disloyal to the skipper of that unit, and he would often interrupt the junior officers when they would be busy talking about what the CO was doing. The exec always stepped in and chewed out the disloyal JO for not understanding the situation. He was showing the unique kind of loyalty

that is well worth remembering if you find yourself in circumstances from time to time that are very unmanageable. It takes a very strong character to be able to handle loyalty in the truest sense. This exec did that and had everybody's respect as a consequence.

Character determines how someone performs his duty. The officer who has a good character can expect also to have a good reputation, and a good reputation will gather influence and prestige. Reputation is like a bond. Professional ability determines how much discretion someone will be allowed. Add to the foregoing professional talent, and the characteristics of a leader begin to take shape.

Loyalty is the foundation of military character. It is easy for an officer to be loyal to his seniors, but it is difficult for him to develop loyalty to himself in his juniors. This must be done through demonstrated performance as a leader. Perhaps the best building block an officer has for the development of loyalty is standing up for his personnel as a group and as individuals—when they are right. The leader should not jump to conclusions when someone is accused, maligned, or charged. He should get the facts first, and even if the facts are overwhelmingly supportive of the accusation, he should consider well before deciding on a course of action. Many individuals have been condemned because of a faulty or an incomplete investigation. Standing tall with solid support for a junior in this instance will do more to foster loyalty up the chain of command than anything else the officer can do. Loyalty is a characteristic that must be developed to its fullest extent immediately. Without it, a naval officer cannot be a successful leader.

Personal loyalty frequently is tested. It is very easy to react to an allegation against a subordinate without getting all of the facts. It is even more tempting to form judgments when there are seemingly solid facts to support the judgment. In one instance within the Navy, an outstanding officer was relieved from a prestigious job because of allegations concerning his personal conduct. The evidence was overpoweringly against him, but the seniors and juniors who knew this fine officer were convinced that his character and professional make-up would not support the allegations, no matter what the evidence said. They were loyal to and supportive of him in the difficult period of investigation. He was subsequently entirely cleared and ordered to an even more prestigious job. This kind of situation tests every aspect of loyalty. It tests loyalty to (1) the Navy by an individual, (2) an individual by the Navy "system," and (3) an individual by others who know him and serve with him. A situation such as the one described should deepen the officer's appreciation for the critical importance of loyalty within any organization.

Loyalty is at the very core of leadership. It can never be legislated, bought, or commanded. It has to be earned and fostered through interactions with people, especially in leadership. The officer who is concerned, supportive, and interested in his subordinates and peers will instill a genuine sense of loyalty to himself in them. He would want no less of his seniors and, without question, *he owes it to them.*

MCPON Sanders: *If it appears that an enlisted has done something wrong, either on the job or off, it is very important to withhold judgment until all the facts are in and an investigation has been completed. If it's a situation that requires immediate action, certainly you have to go with it, but if it is not time sensitive, then be deliberative in your actions. If you don't, you are going to be known as a hip shooter, and your judgment will be questioned. It's perhaps easier to show loyalty up the chain of command, but just as important to show it down the chain, as well. If you have a situation where it appears that your work force did all they could, be loyal and stick up for them. However, if they did make a mistake, you should acknowledge the fact that there is a problem and you are going to solve it, never forgetting that the officer in charge has the primary responsibility for everything that happens within his unit.*

80. The Uses of Praise and Reprimand

The modern Navy and Marine Corps must function as a team, a finely trained and administered group of individuals working toward one goal. Each individual in the organization plays a vital role in the overall team effort. To ensure teamwork, naval officers must praise and reprimand subordinates at the proper time, in the proper place, and in the proper manner. Admiral Long agrees that a valuable element of leadership is recognition of performance:

> One responsibility of command, of officers in charge—whether they're division officers or commanding officers of ships—is that they must recognize performance, and that means good and bad performance. Officers do have the responsibility of handing out rewards and punishment, and an officer who only rewards and never punishes for poor performance is bound to lower the performance of his personnel as well as the esteem with which he is held by his subordinates and his peers.

Due to the complexity of today's Naval Service, an officer must know and follow guidelines that transcend simple social custom in order to praise and reprimand effectively. Admiral Nakamura comments:

> "Reward and punishment" is an important means of boosting morale or maintaining the discipline of the force. But if this method is not applied suitably, the reverse effect can be produced by causing discontent among personnel, and the unity of the force can be hurt very badly. Therefore reward and punishment should be administered with scrupulous care, considering the following matters.
>
> 1. Fairness, not only in a particular force, but also as a whole in the military.
> 2. Best timing, which means at least before the impression of that deed has disappeared.
> 3. Consideration of the effect of the reward or punishment upon other people to encourage good actions or to deter bad deeds, as well as the effect upon that person himself.

The officer must base both praise and reprimand on fact; hearsay cannot be used as a basis for military action. The officer must praise and reprimand fairly; friendships and animosities must be disregarded. Above all, an officer must never show favoritism or single an individual out and make an example of him. The repercussions can be very damaging and may even split the team into factions. General Rice observes:

> The basic rule is to censure in private and to give credit where credit is due in public, but there are exceptions, and the officer will know when those exceptions come up. Usually an exception is made for the good of the command, and generally it is embarrassing to the individual, but something tells the officer that it is the right thing to do, and he will sacrifice the feelings of an individual for the good of the command. Every commander has been in that position, where he did not want to do it, but he felt he had to.

One officer remembered an incident in World War II when his entire regiment fell out at 0400 as an individual was brought forward who had been AWOL seven hours and was on his way to the stockade for 30 days; that made an impression on that officer that lasted for the rest of his life. And General Rice remembered:

> On Okinawa, we had a little working party, extra police duty [EPD], and they would break rocks with sledgehammers. Corporal Crump was in charge, and I had my own little working party, and it was pretty embarrassing when the rest of the company was going on liberty. There

were never more than two or three out there with sledgehammers breaking rocks, because people got the word, and because it was humiliating. They were there for good and just reasons, small infractions of the rules, but they knew the rules of the ballgame and decided not to play, and so they were suffering the punishment.

In determining the extent to which an individual's family should be advised of his progress in the service, officers should, first of all, be sincere, which means there must be meaning behind what they do. This will keep them from going overboard, which they must avoid. When that happens, officers are signing letters, sending things out, but the actions have no meaning behind them.

It is important that promotions and medals be recognized, and the family should be encouraged to come in. A proud spouse will support the service person and make him or her a better Marine or a better sailor. On the other hand, an upset family will upset the soldier, sailor, or Marine, and that may result in poor performance or substandard duty. So the family is part of the team effort, and officers must work to keep them involved.

In his book *Games People Play* (New York: Ballantine, 1974), Erik Berne introduces a theory concerning the basic human need for both positive and negative strokes. This theory has been widely accepted and utilized by those who develop motivational techniques. Strokes, according to Berne, can be defined as "sudden actions or processes producing an impact." Positive strokes, or praise, can range from a simple pat on the back to a verbal "Well done" in private or in a public ceremony. Negative strokes can involve verbal correction of or disciplinary action against an individual. To be motivated, the young seaman or private may require many strokes each week from his supervisor, while the seasoned sailor or Marine may function perfectly

after receiving a single stroke from a respected senior. In dealing with new recruits who have erred, the leader, realizing that the person is a new recruit, should allow more tolerance, as new recruits are very impressionable, and should have their reprimand initially limited to use as a learning instrument.[125-487]

An officer should be able to recognize when praise is due and give it immediately if possible. Praise given should be apparent to and deserved by the individual receiving it. When it is administered correctly, praise is instrumental in building professional pride in the praised individual as well as in observers. Public recognition fosters the establishment of role models; those who have done well and have been recognized for their accomplishments become examples for others to emulate. In this regard, Admiral Hunt suggests:

> On the whole, public chocolate and private acid is a better arrangement. There are occasions, however, when public reprimands spread the message more easily; and similarly there are times when private praise is more effective than public praise. So "public chocolate and private acid" is no more than a general rule.
>
> I think if you know someone well and he's done a particularly good job in a particular field, it's probably much better to send for him and have a private informal chat, saying, "I thought you did it very well, and these are the reasons, and if there are any problems perhaps you could explain them," and so on. That on the whole is more productive than getting up in a meeting and saying, "I think Jones did a marvelous job yesterday." I think privately you can generally be more informal and you can cover more ground between you, which is more productive.

Officers must consider very carefully before administering a reprimand. The individual who is improperly reprimanded may be demoralized; he may even be outcast from his peer group. Public correction often produces results opposite to those intended. Rather than striving to improve, an individual may be intimidated, may lose motivation, or may build up resentment. Reprimands must be instructive. Admiral Burke suggests:

> There is no set rule for praising or reprimanding, because individuals are so different. What will work for one person will not work for another. But a leader has to make sure that people get credit for doing the little things. The big ones will take care of themselves, but the little things are important, too. When people do some little thing well, the leader need not make a big point, but he should recognize it in some way.
>
> On the other hand, the leader cannot let people do anything sloppy, nor can he just bawl them out. He has to find a way of making them realize that they have done a sloppy job. He can embarrass them if they deserve it, but in every case the punishment must fit the crime.

Administering timely and fair praise or reprimand is an important task of leadership. Responsibility and accountability are more important than ever before, which make guidance, encouragement, and recognition vital elements in today's Naval Service. All naval personnel, regardless of their rank, need instruction in order to grow professionally.

MCPON Sanders: *We have improved in giving credit to people for work well done. However, don't give false credit or build up someone to their family if in fact that individual has not performed properly. But I can tell you that there's no better feeling, and I speak as a father, than for someone to speak well of my son. Speak to the parent on an even level, and don't say "Your kid has done well," but, rather, tell the parent that his son or daughter is a good man or woman in the unit. When a subordinate is promoted, take the time to write to the family and tell them how important their son or daughter is to the team. We don't do enough of that. I have received very positive feedback during my visits around the country from parents who have received personal notes from the officers. I strongly encourage the use of the pen—it is so much better than a computer-generated form letter. Remember that when the family at home are happy with and understand the role their offspring or spouse plays in the service, they will be more supportive of that individual's staying on active duty.*

81. Administering Discipline in a Constructive Manner

Naval organizations, whether ships, divisions, or fleets, do not approach perfection any closer than other organizations do. Imperfection can be caused by institutional factors, administrative factors, factors related to equipment maintenance or design, or, simply, the human factor. Sometimes things do not work out the way they were supposed to because of the way the people involved responded to the other factors. But when things go wrong because a member of the unit clearly did not do his part or did not do it the way he knew it was to be done, some form of discipline is in order. Discipline, however, should not be a "stopper." It need not be a negative experience for the unit, or even for the individual. In fact, if the individual at fault is to become a better-motivated member of the organization because of the experience, discipline had best be positive, ergo motivational. Positive discipline may seem to be a dichotomy. But it is possible to be "called down" and yet to be motivated by the discipline at the same time; it all depends on the manner in which the discipline is applied.

Two different leaders can attain the same visible results from their respective units, yet their styles of leadership may differ totally. One unit may strive to achieve because of the positive personal leadership style of the boss, whereas the members of another unit may work hard mostly because they were driven to it by a style of leadership that gets results by applying duress. Some naval leaders have accomplished their goals by instilling in their unit a fear of reprisal if something goes wrong. Were they effective leaders? Very. Did they accomplish goals that were crucial to our national defense? Yes. Were they motivational leaders? No! Did people clamor to be in their organization? No. Great things can be accomplished under negative styles of leadership as well as under more positive styles; the choice depends on the human price those in the organization are willing to pay.

It is generally agreed that the human price paid in a system based on duress is, over time, too high. The payoff in everything done in operating units is combat effectiveness. There are many ingredients that go into combat effectiveness, and the administration of discipline is an important one. Applied discipline has a great impact on the overall morale and combat effectiveness of a unit.

FAIR, TIMELY DISCIPLINE

Unit members will have their own beliefs as to whether the discipline in the unit is fair or unfair. These beliefs will depend more on individual perceptions of single cases than on an analytical study of all cases. Therefore, consistency in judgment is the most important factor in administering discipline. Discipline that seems to vary depending on the mood of the captain or the length of time at sea or any other environmental or human variation is most disconcerting and cannot be construed as fair. F A I R to the hard-nosed chief may mean maximum punishment for almost any infraction, whereas F A I R to an immature and errant sailor may mean the lightest sentence possible. F A I R to the captain and the supporting chain of command must mean humane and consistent justice.

The accused must always have not just the right but also the opportunity to give his side of the story, to explain why he did what he did, or to claim that he did not do what he has been accused of doing. Sometimes the accused is wrongly advised, for any number of reasons, not to say anything, so it is often left to the administrator of discipline to encourage the accused to speak his fair mind. Fair discipline, therefore, takes time. The time involved may not seem long to the accused, because it probably is his only case, but many hours are spent by the unit's seniors, because the boss reviews all the cases. Nevertheless, giving the accused ample opportunity to state his views on the case is crucial to the reality and the perception of a fair hearing.

Timeliness is second only to fairness in administering discipline. An individual who knows he has violated the Uniform Code of Military Justice (UCMJ) or unit regulations truly wants to be dealt with to "clear the air." In units where discipline is held up because of "more pressing matters," a pall may hang over the members who are uncertain what is going to happen to them when discipline is finally meted out. This creates an environment that is not conducive to teamwork and aggressive mission accomplishment. Those awaiting punishment are not sure if they are still part of the team or are soon to be branded as outcasts. Some develop a defeatist attitude, commit other punishable acts, and cause an overall drop in the capability and morale of their work center or division because of their increasingly nonproductive work. Each infraction should be dealt with up to the appropriate level of the chain of command within two weeks. Settling some violations requires thorough investigation, but, generally, an infraction that is going to be dealt with at the division level should be concluded in 3 to 5 days; at the department head level, in 6 to 8 days; and by the Exec, in 9 to 11 days.

Factors such as unfairness or untimeliness or improper leadership (railroading) can cause the accused, rightfully, to feel bitter after the disciplinary experience. He will lose whatever respect he may have had for the organization and/or his chain of command, and although justice may have been (ill) served, he is likely to make contributions to his unit's mission accomplishment in the future only under duress. That scenario is very unhealthy, not only for the individual, but also for his division and the unit as a whole. If the chain of command practices fairness, timeliness, and positive, caring, helpful leadership, the individual will know he has been treated fairly. He will be relieved, almost glad, to serve punishment. He will also likely resolve not to repeat the infraction, and, most importantly, he will be motivated to "rejoin" his peers and bosses in accomplishing the mission at hand.

DISCIPLINE AT DIFFERENT LEVELS OF COMMAND

Administering discipline is often more difficult at some levels of the chain of command than at others. It is important to recognize this and to understand some of the reasons. Peer pressure, although not called discipline, is the most powerful force at work on young people in their first few years in the service. The leader who recognizes this can, through positive and motivational leadership, take advantage of peer pressure to help keep his division well trained and disciplined. Middle-grade petty officers are not, commonly, the best disciplinarians. Often they are more effective because they are peers than because they are seniors. It takes several years of experience for a middle-grade petty officer to acquire the leadership skills necessary to be a good disciplinarian in the work center or division. There is a wide variation in middle-grade petty officer leadership styles; some are too close to their subordinates (a buddy is almost always ineffective as a leader), and some are too authoritarian (which leads to overkill). The ones who show a firm, positive approach to leadership at an early stage are destined to advance higher in rank.

Division officers also often have difficulty personally disciplining subordinates, because of a combination of experience and proximity in age to most people in the division (or age inversion—that is, disciplining someone older). For these reasons, the division chief petty officer can

be invaluable in assisting, teaching, and administering the disciplinary process. He, too, must pursue the ideals of fairness, consistency, and timeliness in order to be effective. Since both the LCPO and the division officer are in the chain of command, heavy reliance on the LCPO is only acceptable for two or three months, while the division officer is gaining experience.

Discipline administered above the division officer level is usually more structured because of the experience of the individuals, the extent of their other duties, and the likelihood that the offense is more serious. Division officers should contribute significantly to the administration of discipline above them in the chain of command. If the individual has committed a serious infraction of the UCMJ but there are extenuating circumstances, he should be encouraged and advised to describe what happened. Some may be afraid to speak out when they are before the exec or the captain. The reviewing officer should ask the division officer to state his opinion of the individual. The division officer should not be shy, and he should not assume anything. He should speak in the absolute. If the accused individual contributes to division work and is a positive influence, the division officer should say so. If the individual is not a positive influence, the officer must not get caught in the trap of firmly adhering to the maxim that "a good division officer stands up for his men" when he and the rest of the division know that the individual detracts from mission accomplishment or is a negative influence. The division officer must stand up for the good members of his division (most of them) but require the others to retain his respect through their performance and attitude.

Admiral Holloway comments about the saying "Admonish in private, praise in public" that the rule almost always should be followed. Like most rules, however, this rule has exceptions. Admiral Holloway explained why he did not always follow the rule:

When I was commanding officer of the *Enterprise*, six thousand people were aboard that ship, living very close together with two or three thousand tons of high explosives and millions of gallons of aviation fuel. We had to be a disciplined organization, and when I held commanding officers' non-judicial punishment mast, I did it publicly and I did it in a very solemn fashion. Everyone was in their best uniform, everything went just by the book, and the punishments that were meted out not only were done in a very positive way, they were also published in the plan of the day because I believed that that was the best way to get everybody's attention and let them know what my standards were and this was my view of how the ship was going to be run.

RESPONDING TO IMPROPER CONDUCT AND TO CRIMINAL AND NONCRIMINAL ACTS

Notwithstanding the efforts of the officer to use positive leadership techniques, show personnel that he cares for them, and involve himself and his crew in a variety of programs designed to improve the functioning of the unit, the officer will at times have to discipline individuals because they fail to obey the rules or are involved in activities that are considered detrimental to good order and that can affect the overall mission capability of the unit and the morale of the command. Good people will for years meet all requirements without exception and go out of their way to make a major contribution to the unit and to help their fellow service people— and then suddenly will go wrong due to pressures they are under or due to a lapse in their sense of responsibility for their actions. The leader must react to a transgression by this kind of individual differently than he reacts to similar behavior by a "repeat offender." Determining how to respond to improper conduct is seldom a simple matter.

Possibly the simplest case would be one in which someone has failed to remember the requirement to drink responsibly. It is a responsibility of every level of command to ensure that all personnel receive instruction regarding what is expected in the way of responsible drinking and what the regulations are for drinking, as well as the many physical and social considerations involved—for example, 25 percent of all highway deaths and injuries are the result of a teenager drinking to excess and then becoming involved in an accident. The officer must be sure that all personnel have had an opportunity to participate in a program that explores why people drink to excess and, furthermore, that personnel are aware of the services that are available to military personnel to help them work out personal problems that may contribute to excessive drinking.

Even if a particular officer is derelict in duty and fails to install adequate programs within a particular unit, an individual has no excuse for becoming drunk and disorderly and having his behavior brought to the attention of the civilian or military authorities. In such a case, it is incumbent on the officer's senior to see that the officer reacts in a positive fashion to ensure that all hands know what their responsibilities are, know what sources are available for help, and know why irresponsible drinking cannot be tolerated: its adverse effect on the individual, the unit, the individual's family and friends, and the image of the military. The overall message sent to Congress as to the need for the people requested and the dollars required to train these individuals may also be adversely affected by individuals who drink to excess.

When an individual is reported for drunk and disorderly conduct, the officer should have the incident investigated and determine all of the facts. The investigation may uncover extenuating circumstances such as a death in the family or another personal tragedy that might have triggered an uncharacteristic response in an individual who otherwise is a fine performer. In a severe case where no one has been injured and no property has been damaged, restitution might consist of the individual's apology and counseling by the officer and/or a psychologist in the Naval Service. Where it is anticipated that this was both a first and a last incident, the punishment will be milder than if the incident had been preceded by similar incidents. The purpose of action taken is to avoid a repetition of the incident, and generally this is accomplished by providing counseling that will resolve the underlying cause of the drunkenness. Most serious cases of alcohol abuse need to be considered in light of court-martial regulations and the advice of a psychologist.

While extensive screening and boot camp and basic training are intended to furnish operating units with personnel who understand the requirements of military life, personnel who by attitude and ability are able to make a consistent contribution to the military, some individuals who emerge from basic training will have failed to make the transition from civilian to military life. The "do your own thing" philosophy that pervades some civilian subcultures, and a failure to learn responsibility for self and others, may produce problems with some personnel, as it does in the industries and cities of the United States. Problems caused by these attitudes are rare in the military, where a sense of ethics and purpose and willingness to work for the good of the team prevail. However, the officer has to understand that disciplinary action must be taken at times and that its purpose is to improve the individual as an operating member of the unit.

In the case of criminal acts, the criminal justice system in the military will be called into action. There will be noncriminal incidents, however, when, due to background and failure to integrate fully into the military, an individual makes a mistake in performance. Assuming it is a noncriminal act and the individual has basic worth and capability, constructive disciplinary action will enable the individual to remain in the unit and continue working with his peers as well as provide a degree of education that will help the individual avoid repeating the act. The person being disciplined must understand what he did wrong, why it was wrong, why such actions should not be done, and what steps he could have taken other than the one that got him into trouble.

DISCIPLINE: DISAPPROVAL OF THE ACT, NOT OF THE PERSON

As much as possible, disciplinary action should convey disapproval of the act and not of the individual who performed the act. In other words, officers must let the person know that he has been making a good contribution to the unit, that they are disappointed in the person's performance, that it is necessary to discipline the person for what he has done wrong so that in addition to him being punished for his mistakes, others will be reminded that unacceptable behavior cannot be tolerated in a unit, which must function smoothly if it is to prevail during peacetime or combat operations.

In some cases the discipline may even be considered positive in nature, such as sending an individual who is very capable to a school to increase his value to the unit. The schooling should not be seen as a reward for the misdeed; however, if the infraction was minor, the challenge might well be the ticket to bringing the individual around, as he realizes that his commanding officer does want him to be a performing and contributing member of the unit. When an officer talks to an individual about what he did wrong and why he should not have done it, and reminds him why everyone must work for the good of the group while sublimating personal needs and interests for the group, he often can bring the individual around as the individual realizes that he is needed and is reminded that he is capable of doing things properly. It can be assumed that all personnel want to be members of the team, and thus those who "step out of line" are, in some cases, those who failed to understand how much others depended on them.

There will be times when an officer is required to administer punishment, or negative discipline, as it might be called. No system is perfect, and every individual is not capable of changing his habits after being talked to. The Naval Service is in a serious business, and dangers and threats to individuals can at times cause them to perform acts that are counterproductive to the good order of a unit. All officers are provided with instruction in military discipline and punishment. Suffice it to say here that an officer must know what is required and what authority he has in these situations, as well as what the practice is within a particular unit and what is required by the Naval Service. A great deal of effort should be made to let the individual know that after he has served his punishment, he is welcome back as a full member of the unit and that he will be counted upon to make a contribution to supporting unit objectives and to work with his peers for the completion of the mission and the continuing welfare of all personnel.

Admiral Taylor sees the responsibilities of a commanding officer at a captain's mast as very demanding and important, because

this is a crossroad in each one of those trooper's lives. I did some captain's masts on TV for broadcast through the ship, well announced, so that those who did not go to a captain's mast would get a chance to see how fairly justice was meted out on the *Coral Sea*. During indoctrination, for the first two weeks the trooper was aboard ship, he got a chance to see a lot of things, including a film of what captain's mast is all about, so that he had an opportunity to see that, hey, you step out of line, fail to stick to the standards, there is going to be some punishment, but there's also going to be an opportunity for rehabilitation in almost every case.

I looked at about 400 cases at captain's masts in my last year on the ship. I ran about 40 cases a month when I first got to the ship, and then it was about 20 cases along toward the end. The drugs and the UA, they're the big ones. Drug usage in

the time frame went from about 25 percent positive on urinalysis down to as low as 2 or 3, and then we were at the shipyard in the end, got back up into the 8 and 9 percent. So a kid steps up there, he always came in his best uniform after a full bag inspection, and if he didn't have a full bag, he had to go buy a full bag, so you know right away there's a penalty for having to go to captain's mast, monetarily, just to get your bag up to limit. Not every captain does that, but the chief then had to get involved, the division officer had to get involved, and they solved a lot of problems without me putting it into a captain's mast and getting it in a guy's jacket.

I never had a captain's mast that I didn't go through the trooper's jacket to look for the value and the positive aspects of this trooper, because he's there for punishment, but when the punishment is over you've got to look him in the eye and tell him "You are a winner, you are not a loser. You are needed, you are wanted. Isn't that right, chief?" You've got to show that guy he's out of line but he's not forgotten and he's not gone forever. He's got to work to get back up there. I made mandatory requirements for those who were on restriction. One of the officers on the ship ran a program, which I recommend, it's by an ex-Naval Academy tac pilot, now Dr. Dennis Waitley, who has the philosophy of winning. It's a ten-hour set of tapes, and each trooper would have to take notes on this as a way of enforcing what I insisted, that they were all winners. Out of that length of time there were only two guys that I ever just fired out of the Navy. Even the guys who had had two or three drug busts and were going out, I'd remind them that they were smart, that they'd blown it, had lost an opportunity here. They were being fired by the Navy, but before they got out, I wanted them to finish up with honor, so they could get out feeling good about themselves.

It is a very, very important business, administering discipline and making sure it's balanced. It's the same for everyone and it'll stand scrutiny of an entire crew on TV, as well as at mast, and it all gets published in the POD. At captain's call, the master chief of the command and I looked the tube in the eye, took the phone calls, took the things out of the CO's suggestion box. There were no gripes about the quality of justice on the ship, because it was always up in the sunlight where everyone could see what was going on. You must demonstrate a sensitivity to these fantastic human beings who are your work force and your shipmates, and you must address each one of them, look him in the eye and tell him, "You've done wrong, but we think a lot of you. Now let's get cracking. Chief, listen up, he needs a little extra coaching, but he's a winner, make him so."

Admiral de Cazanove makes the point that in reprimanding, one should not be lax. Whether the commander has to say something good or bad it should be said firmly, but courteously and with tact, showing the individual is respected whether he be subordinate, peer, or senior. It is difficult to reprimand and punish, but it has to be done at times. Times are really not that much different than they were 20 or 30 years ago. When there are a number of people together, someone has to be in charge, or otherwise there will be difficulty. Even in civilian life there has to be a boss, though there is some difficulty with the concept of authority. Someone has to be in charge, and that individual must reward or punish as circumstances direct so that the rest of the people will understand that there is someone setting the direction of their efforts. Recognition of performance with awards and decorations is as important as it was three or four hundred years ago. People like to be recognized, and they work harder knowing that their efforts will be recognized. We say in France, as we did hundreds of years ago, that "A man is a man and will always be a man." That is what makes the Army, and you have to deal with man just as he was centuries ago. His efforts have to be recognized by his seniors.

82. The System of Reward and Praise

Efficient, effective, and on-schedule completion of assignments is expected of all personnel in the military, and thus a daily pat on the back or a letter of commendation for every completed assignment is not necessary. Individuals who do more than is required, who work later than others, who are more productive, who spend less money in completing their assignment, and who cause the unit to be positively recognized by higher authority, however, should receive recognition beyond the usual "Well done" that an officer gives all personnel upon their completion of an assignment.

Because the effective leader spends a great deal of time among his troops, it will be easy for him to find appropriate times to let subordinates know that what they are doing is important and appreciated. This attention from the officer is both appropriate and necessary.

Regarding exceptions that may be required within an organization, the leader must remain flexible and realize that the concept of showing no favoritism does not mean that every individual will be treated exactly the same for doing the same thing. For example, a seaman who is two days late in returning from leave in Atlantic City should be disciplined more harshly than a seaman who is two days late because his mother was killed in a car crash while he was home on leave. The officer is also likely to give greater recognition to a pilot who makes a carrier landing at night in rough seas after receiving fire that disabled a crew member than to the pilot who makes a night landing in smooth seas. It is important for an officer to show his humanness.

Up to this point, the idea of reward and praise has been discussed in the past tense. That is, after the deed has been done, the reward is doled out. But the system of reward and praise can also exist before the fact. This can be done simply in terms of letting people know what is expected of them and what is waiting for them when the task is complete—this goes a long way toward motivating subordinates. Napoleon Bonaparte illustrated this when, at the Battle of Austerlitz, he said to his men, "In future years, if you tell someone that you were at Austerlitz, they will say, 'There is a brave man.' " He was speaking to an as-yet untested army which had a muddy record of performance and was letting them know that he expected them to be brave, to be able to take on an army superior in numbers and training and win—and they believed in him and did just that.[75-200] This pre-reward has its value in motivating subordinates, for the fact is that sometimes subordinates perform better when they know what is expected of them instead of when they just have to "puzzle it out."

The primary function of a leader is to have under his command an effective unit capable of performing its mission, and the effectiveness of the unit directly reflects the leader's attitude toward and treatment of his personnel. The leader establishes the standards and ensures that these standards are observed and met, without justifiable exception, by every member of his unit. If he permits inappropriate exceptions to be made, then the leader is implying that the people who break the rules are more important than the people who meet the standards, and the discipline and integrity of the unit will quickly disintegrate.

Although conformity is required in a military organization, this does not mean that the leader cannot recognize and respect the individuality of each member of the unit. The greatest reward the leader can give his people is to recognize that each of them is a unique individual, not just a nameless member of the outfit. Some of the greatest needs of human beings are the needs to be recognized, to be respected, to be needed. The officer who meets these needs will find that his people will follow him through hell.

The reward and punishment capability of the leader will determine the effectiveness of his unit. A leader must respect his people, be strict, be tough, and, most important, be fair. Subordinates respect a leader for being tough but fair. To be fair, a leader cannot display any favoritism, either in rewarding exceptional performance or in punishing unsatisfactory performance. Nothing will destroy the effectiveness of a unit faster than favoritism. If favoritism is shown, the pride in the unit will disappear along with morale and esprit de corps. Instead of being respected, the leader will have to be tolerated and will be held in contempt, and the capacity of the unit to perform its missions will be degraded.

The leader who rewards his people for correct behavior will get the right results, and the leader who fails to reward correct behavior will get the wrong results. Admiral Holloway suggests that there are several ways of rewarding performance:

> One is in the fitness report, which usually is a factor when the person gets promoted, does not get promoted, or gets promoted early. An officer can also write a letter of recommendation for or present an award to a worthy individual. Awards and medals should be presented only to the most deserving individuals, however, so that the meaning of the honor is not diluted through overuse.

83. The Importance of Providing a Challenge to Subordinates

While having professional and technical knowledge is a prime requisite for the successful officer in the Naval Service, it must be kept in mind that every organization is only as good as its members, and thus one of the many responsibilities of an officer is training members of the organization so that they may prevail in both peacetime and combat operations. It is of paramount importance that every unit in the Naval Service be ready at all times to take on any mission assigned to it. The Naval Service can prevail only when its people are trained as a team and are all pulling in the same direction.

As a combat arm, the Naval Service must be prepared for losses that may take place by ensuring that individual casualties will not radically alter the effectiveness of operations. Thus, training and education for meeting current assignments must be augmented by cross-training and cross-education for meeting challenges in a hostile environment. Admiral Long notes:

> One of the most important responsibilities of an officer—whether division officer, commanding officer of a ship, group commander, force commander, or theater commander—is to train junior officers for greater responsibility. Division officers have the responsibility to train junior enlisted personnel, to get them in a position where they can take over more demanding responsibilities.
>
> The Navy is in a constant state of change. People are coming and going, people are leaving the Navy or being transferred, so the officer will never find himself in a static position where he has a fully trained crew for an extended period of time. It is not only important from the standpoint of the readiness of the squadron or ship that he has an extremely dynamic, active, and effective training program, but it is also very important for the morale and well-being of all personnel.
>
> Training programs must be realistic, and they must actually produce results. A

training program that is beautiful on paper but ineffective in practice is not worthwhile. For this reason, the officer must keep records so he can monitor the progress being made as a result of the training program. Officers establishing training programs need to have realistic goals and a way of measuring the progress they are making with each individual under them.

To a great extent, the requirements of being prepared for mission accomplishment and meeting the needs of personnel lead to the establishment of programs that are mutually supportive, in that as personnel improve, unit capability to meet mission requirements improves. The fact that there is a mission requiring support by personnel provides the impetus to place subordinates in challenging situations, which in turn develops their abilities and provides them with opportunities for growth and advancement.

Simply stated, a challenge is something that, when it is met, results in a feeling of accomplishment. Individuals who meet a challenge realize they have performed in a way that they may not have anticipated they were able to, at least without a tremendous effort. An individual can pay himself psychic income for work accomplished, because not only his self-worth, but also his satisfaction in his capability, increases.

Frederick Herzberg suggests that work must be enriched to bring about effective utilization of personnel, and that job enrichment is a continuous management function best accomplished on an immediate supervisory level.[51-17] To be able to place his subordinates in a challenging position, an officer must first know their interests and capabilities. Interests are mentioned first, because with proper training and guidance, most people can increase their capabilities. Knowing the capabilities of the individual allows the senior to look for areas to build on. For example, knowing that a sailor is a handy mechanic as well as an electronics technician allows the officer to suggest on-the-job training in motor generator repair with some sense of surety that the individual selected will be able to learn the new skills involved.

Admiral McDonald points out:

> One way an officer can see results of his labor is to help an individual find a job in which he will be content and perform well. Sometimes an officer will find that an enlisted person is not doing a good job because he is the "round peg in a square hole." If he can spot either the abilities or inabilities of the person who has not had the opportunities that the officer has had and re-train the person, the officer will be able to see that he has made a difference in an individual's life and in the service.

Boredom can strike anyone in any walk of life, in or out of the service. However, it should not happen in the service, because officers in the service have a responsibility to ensure that their subordinates not only are ready for battle, but also are "happy in their work." This is easily achieved if the officer takes the time and expends the effort to prepare a training program for each of the people in his unit. Such programs, while they require extra effort to establish, tend to become self-perpetuating, and their details are worked out so that in time there are a series of options available for individuals who come into the unit.

Of course, the most challenging situations are those concerned with an individual's primary assignment and the back-up position to which he will be assigned or which he will have to take over, when necessary, in time of combat. It is important for all hands to recognize, as pointed out elsewhere in this book, that doing a job is like playing a sport—individuals should use 100 percent of their capability, and in so doing, they will derive satisfaction, whether they are doing their job or contributing to a successful athletic effort. Just as no one would expect to become an accomplished athlete with infrequent practice, and no one who plays a musical instrument

can expect to develop skills without a great amount of practice, and no one can develop the ability to speak and write well without many years of practice, anyone doing a job—whether technical or nontechnical—must practice and strive in order to perform his job exceptionally. This point needs to be stressed, as the troops repeatedly go through the same drills and must be reminded that service people sometimes have to play for keeps, that they do not always have next Saturday to regain the upper hand; thus, as with sports, practice of tasks permits accomplishment of tasks faster, with greater accuracy, and with less expenditure of effort. By letting the troops know how they are doing and by providing sufficient practice, the officer ensures that their performance will improve, that individuals will be able to perform more than their own assignments, and that opportunities for advancement will be made possible by the increased capability of the individuals involved. Every person in the organization will come to realize that he is a member of a winning team whose possible achievements are limited only in some people's minds.

Admiral Larson:

> One of an officer's foremost responsibilities from day one as a division officer is the responsibility to help your people improve, to expand their education, their training, their advancement in rate, to make them more valuable for the Navy and to make them more valuable to your individual unit. Now you have to do this by, first of all, getting to know them. I met individually with each of the persons in my division when I first went on board as a division officer, and I would talk about their background, their educational background, both in civilian life and in the Navy. I would talk about their advancement status, about their practical factors, about their schools, about their goals and aspirations, qualification on the

407

ship, and really try to understand where they felt they were going or what their ambitions were, and where they wanted to go. Now it's human nature not to push yourself sometimes, so you're going to be responsible for encouraging, helping that person, pushing him on toward that advancement. I think too many junior officers say "Well, it's the troop's responsibility. He didn't fill out the paper work, he didn't request the course, he didn't sign up for the school. It's his fault." I say that's wrong. You've got a responsibility to start out and help them, help them with that paper work, help them order that school; you've got the knowledge, you can do it very quickly. I'm not saying you have to be a den mother for all the troops, but you get them started this way and you point them in the right direction, then they will pick up that motivation and they will go on and improve themselves.

You also have to instill in your unit the feeling that one of your responsibilities is to self. You've got a responsibility to country, to ship, to Navy, but also to self, and the responsibility to self is self-improvement. You need to convince the troops that they need to take some time each day to work on their personal advancement as well as their division business, and the best way to do that is to set that example yourself and set aside a time for yourself to work on your advancement, your training, your next higher level of qualification, so that you can show them that you're really serious about it, and then you're progressing together as a team.

MCPON Sanders: *We need to put subordinates in as challenging situations as possible. We have bright, hard-charging teams, that include very good individuals, in the Navy today. Some of them may not have extended formal educational* *backgrounds, but their ability to do things is not lessened thereby. As we challenge them, we can see these individuals grow, gain self-confidence, and produce even more. This is an area that all of us can work on.*

84. Developing Personnel and Boosting Their Confidence by Delegating Authority

A successful leader and manager, whether in the military or in the civilian world, must be able to delegate authority and assign responsibility to subordinates. In virtually all military organizations, this delegation is inherent in the formal structure of the command. Admiral Hunt echoes the point by advising: "The basic rule is, delegate as much as you possibly can." Admiral Itaya concurs:

It is good for the officer to delegate as much authority as possible. If he does this, subordinates will be enthusiastic, will use ingenuity, and will be more effective. However, delegation of authority does not mean delegation of responsibility. Naturally, the scope of this delegation is determined by the capability of the subordinates, the relative difficulty of the task, and the time constraints.

I used to give the following advice to carrier officers: "Even after you have become a leader, speak your mind without hesitation and create an atmosphere where the views of subordinates will find their way to the leader smoothly. This will foster mutual understanding and respect between leader and follower and will greatly facilitate the delegation of authority." It is said that a leader is friendless, for regardless of how large a staff and how many assistants he has, the decision is the leader's alone. The ultimate responsibility is his. Therefore, the leader must endure the loneliness with the feeling that

"Heaven is above me," and he must bravely make the decision which he feels is best. Also, he must stand ready to bear the responsibility for the outcome.

The senior is responsible for supervising his subordinates to ensure that authority, once delegated, is prudently applied throughout his command, as well as for training juniors and monitoring them in the discharge of their duties. Final responsibility for what goes on in a department must always remain on the shoulders of the individual in charge. When excellent work is achieved, the leader will receive credit; on the other side of the fence, if his department commits errors and blunders, then he must accept full responsibility. The fair supposition is that the leader trained those reporting to him; therefore, he is held responsible for their performance.[21-318]

Admiral de Cazanove makes the point that the officer must always keep in mind that one should conserve one's responsibility, and by that I mean that you may delegate authority, but you will never delegate responsibility. This means that you delegate authority in accordance with subordinates' capabilities, trying at the same time to develop their capabilities further, but you retain responsibility for everything they do or do not do. You must support subordinates in difficult times, not just when things go well. The mark of a leader is to what extent he will support subordinates during bad as well as good times. Without this accepting of good and bad results, there is no possibility of delegating authority, for subordinates will know that you only take on a job when good results are expected and leave to them those jobs that may go bad.

The question that a leader must consider is how he can direct subordinates so as to delegate to them a sense of authority and assign responsibility that is commensurate with their capabilities, experience, and position within the command. Admiral Ramage recommends delegating as much authority to subordinates as they can responsibly handle:

I always organized every one of my commands so that they would function as effectively with or without me. In other words, I made sure that every one of my staff officers understood my desires and my policies. Each one was given ample opportunity to exercise his responsibilities, thus showing that I had explicit trust in their good judgment at all times.

Regulations, organization books, and established directives delineate what is expected of each level in a military command. The leader, then, provides effective training in the overall mission of the command and the specific duties and responsibilities of individuals, and initiates review and feedback to ensure that leadership is properly executed within the command.

Effective assignment of responsibility and delegation of authority take place frequently within the Navy. Examples are the role given to Arleigh Burke and his " Little Beavers" in World War II destroyer actions in the Pacific, the patrol orders given to submarines for the wide range of sensitive operations required today, and the rules of engagement given to Navy units operating independently in the Persian Gulf. Admiral Burke points out:

The best orders I ever had in my life, or that any command could have, was when Admiral Halsey said "Thirty-one-knot Burke proceed. You know what to do." Those were the only orders I ever had. That's pretty good. I'd do anything for Admiral Halsey except unballast a ship in a storm. He was a wonderful commander. I have also found that what works in the Navy from a senior to a junior, a junior to a senior, works in civilian life, too. A man can't foresee everything that's going to happen, and so he's got to have the authority to do something, to make changes. Something that hasn't been

understood or something new—he's got
to be able to take quick action. Otherwise
it's bound to fail. You can't write back to
Washington for advice or for additional
orders.

On a smaller scale, examples within a command,
while less historic, are both crucial to the success
of the command and rewarding to the individuals involved. These include the relation between
a commanding officer and his engineer, the
authority and responsibility an officer of the deck
and a tactical action officer are expected to accept
on a command involved in a critical contingency
operation, and the effective operation, the maintenance, and the cleanliness of a propulsion space.
The principles in each case are the same: formal
delegation of authority (through an organization
book, in the case of the engineer and the propulsion space, and standing orders, in the case
of the OD and the TAO), training of the individuals commensurate with their experience and
the duties involved, and command supervision
and overview to ensure successful achievement
of the tasks assigned. General Rice makes the
point that

an officer determines how much authority
he should delegate to a subordinate by
how much confidence he has in the people who work for him. Different individuals are willing to delegate different
amounts of authority. It is difficult for
anyone to watch someone else do something he knows he can do better, faster,
and with improved results, but the officer
must learn to let his people do their jobs.
Obviously, the officer cannot let them
jeopardize themselves or the command,
and sometimes it is difficult to determine
how far to let an individual go over the
line in order to learn. But the more confidence he has in his people, the more he
has trained them, the more he can let
them get on with their job. And that, in
fact, makes the officer's job easier.

Senior officers should not be doing the

work of their juniors, i.e., colonels doing
majors' work, majors doing captains' work,
and captains doing lieutenants' work. That
is wrong, because lieutenants should do
lieutenants' work and, in fact, lieutenants
should be able to do captains' work if they
are worth their salt. Officers must give
subordinates the responsibility, give them
the authority, and let them get on with it.
They can correct subordinates when they
are wrong. Another aspect of this is that
young people should seek responsibility,
they should not stand in the corner and
wait for someone to call them.

In directing individuals, leaders at every level
must make the distinction between excessive
supervision and effective delegation of authority. Admiral Ernest J. King provided classic
guidance to this question immediately before
World War II in a general order which stated
in part:

It is essential to extend the knowledge and
the practice of "initiative of the subordinate"
in principle and in application until they are
universal in the exercise of command throughout all echelons of command. Henceforth, we
must see to it that full use is made of the echelons of command—whether administrative or
operative—by habitually framing orders and
instructions to echelon commanders so as to tell
them "what to do" but not "how to do it" unless
the particular circumstances so demand. The
corollaries are:

a. Adopt the premise that the echelon commanders are competent in their several command echelons unless and until they prove
themselves otherwise.

b. Teach them that not only are they expected
to be competent, but it is required of them that
they be competent.

c. Train them—by guidance and supervision—to exercise foresight, to think, to judge,
to decide, and to act for themselves.

d. Stop "nursing" them.

e. Finally, train ourselves to be satisfied with
"acceptable solutions" even though they are not

"staff solutions" or other particular solutions that we ourselves prefer.

Subsequently Admiral King sent out an amplifying order addressing the correct use of initiative, which stated:

> a. Initiative means freedom to act, but it does not mean freedom to act in an offhand or casual manner. It does not mean freedom to disregard or to depart unnecessarily from standard procedures or practices or instructions. There is no degree of being "independent" of the other component parts of the whole—the Fleet.
>
> b. It means freedom to act only after all of one's resources in education, training, experience, skill, and understanding have been brought to bear on the work at hand.
>
> c. It requires intense application in order that what is to be done shall be done as a correlated part of a connected whole—much as the link of a chain or a gearwheel of a machine.

The fundamental principles articulated by Admiral King remain valid, and they undoubtedly always will. They are among the challenges faced by all leaders. A frequent symptom of faulty working relations, for example, is the failure of relevant information to flow up and down the chain of command.[21-208]

The elements required for successful leadership also change little over time. They are: (1) training of subordinates, (2) formal delegation of authority commensurate with the situation and the capacity of the individuals involved, and (3) effective follow-up to ensure that tasks assigned are accomplished and to hold individuals accountable and responsible for the proper application of authority. There are no short cuts in this process, and each step is essential to success. Mastering the technique of delegating authority to the right individuals will gain the leader peace of mind and invaluable time that can be more efficiently used for planning or other activities.[8-268]

"Blind" delegation of authority without effective training and frequent follow-up by the command is often a path to failure. It makes routine tasks burdensome and impairs the development in subordinates of the skills they must cultivate to advance in their profession and become capable of greater responsibility. On the other hand, sensible delegation of authority with proper training and follow-up establishes the sense of confidence between juniors and seniors that is one of the most rewarding aspects of a military career for both.

85. Implementing Changes

"Active obedience implies initiative, and intelligence in the exercise of this initiative requires a knowledge of how the specific objective fits into the general plan."[77-131]

It was a beautiful day. The fleet ballistic missile submarine USS *Simon Bolivar* was coming home after a three-month deployment. The boat was on the surface, heading up the river estuary for her home port in Charleston. The captain was on the bridge, topside with the officer of the deck, who had the conn. Looking aft, the captain suddenly realized that the prop was churning up mud from the bottom and that the boat was moments away from becoming beached in the mud. Taking the conn, he barked "Shift your rudder." The crew responded immediately and brought the bow back into the middle of the constantly shifting river channel.

The crew did not question the sudden change in direction. Everyone on board knew the danger involved in bringing a boat up a narrow and shallow river channel. There was the danger of damaging the boat by grounding her on the bottom, but the reputation of the crew and the career of the captain were also on the line.

Most of the time reasons for change in direction are not that clear, and the changes themselves are not that urgent. Usually reasons for change are not so clearly focused or life or career threatening that an immediate understanding of them is guaranteed. As dangers and issues become blurred and less sensitive to time, changes become more difficult to justify to an officer's boss, his people, and himself. Complacency is an ever-present danger in the normal workday routine, because most people resist change and tend to settle into the more comfortable status quo. General Wilson notes:

> Changes will always be made, and I think whether a leader needs to justify the changes to subordinates depends on the extent of the changes. If you feel it's significant to justify, you should; on the other hand, there is a tendency for subordinates to feel that if you have to justify, you're not sure of yourself. The reaction depends on the way the justification is stated. You have to be careful not to appear to be on the defensive about it.

> As an example, when I was a Commandant—and I don't like that personal thing, but I suppose I'm known for a harder line in discipline than most people—and I came in, I said that there would be no overweight Marines and that we would maintain a standard of discipline of short hair and shined shoes and that our uniforms would be immaculate and that I welcomed the opportunity for anyone who wanted to challenge me on it. There were many who did, and the question inevitably was Why can't a Marine who is a computer operator and three thousand miles away from the battle zone be overweight? The reason is that he knows the requirements of the service, and that is a manifestation of his acceptance of regimentation. Furthermore, there are reasons having to do with his own health, his appearance.

> Second thing is that the American people expect more of the Marines than they do of other people. They expect Marines to be the epitome of soldierly virtue as part of the American fighting force. I believe that this is a good thing for the Marine Corps. It attracts better recruits.

The Marine people see on the street, or the recruiter in their hometown, is the Marine they seem to know, and so whether you like it or not, this is a policy we are going to follow, and you really don't have any opportunity but to follow. These are things you don't necessarily have to explain; say, "This is the way it's going to be." Only explain if you want to. Now I understand that this did not meet with a great deal of enthusiasm at the time and that there was great criticism of me, which was unimportant, because I believe that it was good for the Marine Corps and that was what I was getting paid for. That's the oath I took, and whether or not it has been successful, why, time will tell.

Many factors determine the speed and method an officer can use to bring about change. The degree of danger, the importance of the mission, the type of organization, the structure of ranks, and the experience level and background of personnel are some of the factors that must be considered. But the most important factor is people. "Any change in an individual's life—whether it is pleasant or unpleasant—requires some readjustment," thus causing stress. An explanation of a change in policy or procedure will usually reduce the stress that goes along with the change.[5-445] Regardless of how smart an officer is or what his rank is, he will always need his people to bring about change. The bottom line is that it makes good sense to give a great deal of consideration to how people will feel about and react to change. Admiral Taylor remarks:

> I would not explain to the troops the reason for a change only if I was told not to. In my philosophy and in my formula, my style of leadership—of which management is a subset, I might add—keeping everyone informed is paramount to achieving goals. I always told them, "Hey, here's the latest dope, guys, but I've got to tell you, this may not work out this

way." There are many leaders who won't get on until it's positive, it's hard copy, it's going to happen that way. Meanwhile, the butter cutters, as we call them, are down there starting all kinds of rumors, and the ship is rife with rumors, and now no one knows which way to go. If you want the division officer to have a handle on things, you've got to have internal communications. I'm not saying that this is the first amendment and that you have to say everything, but you want to be able to get the truth out, you want to cut off the rumors, so you must keep the crew informed. If you treat them like men and women, they'll be men and women. If you treat them like mushrooms, that's what you're going to get. You keep them in the dark, don't give them anything important, let them feed on whatever's down there, you have lost touch.

It's important to call it what it is, to say, "Latest rumor up here on the bridge is," or "Please don't write this in a letter home, but let me tell you what's happened with respect to the schedule." It greatly enhances the credibility of the leader, and from my perspective it doesn't violate any of the trust. Again, if there's a close hold requirement, a special instruction from a senior commander that says, "Here's a set of orders, keep it secret," then you just say, "Guys, we're turning to 270. We have a special mission. As this develops I'll let you know what it is, but let me tell you right now, it's important to our national interests. They picked the right ship and the right crew. We've got to be ready!" That's what you have to tell them, and they'll know right away that you can't tell them more, because always before you gave them the right kind of talk. I think the importance of a good flow of information is crucial to making the entire style work.

The following example illustrates the approach to instituting change by one of the Navy's fleet admirals. He was in the process of making some major organizational changes in the Logistics and Security Assistance Directorate on the USCINCPAC Joint Staff located at Camp Smith in Hawaii. The 85-person directorate was divided into eight divisions, each headed by a captain or a colonel and divided evenly between logistics and security assistance. Most of the officers were commanders or lieutenant colonels.

Shortly after signing into the command, the commanding officer got the impression that either there was not enough meaningful work to keep all of these officers gainfully employed, or they were not doing the right job. Since this joint staff assignment was his first job away from submarines in 25 years, he thought his perception might be the result of his inexperience in logistics and security assistance. He decided to talk with all the people and try to improve his understanding of just what it was that these logisticians and security assistance advisors were supposed to be doing. He began consciously to note which action officers came into his office, how many and what kind of issues came across his desk, and whether people looked busy. He tried to determine whether there were overlaps in missions or turf fights between divisions, how much interaction there was between the directorates, and what kind of reputation the unit had. One of his major concerns was whether the issues his boss, the commander in chief of the Pacific, considered important were being addressed.

In addition to observing the work in the headquarters, the admiral traveled throughout the directorates' geographic area of responsibility. They were involved in logistics issues and exercises in Korea, Japan, the Philippines, Australia, and Thailand. They also provided evaluation and assistance to 25 Security Assistance Offices in various locations in an arc from Korea to Madagascar. Feedback from these organizations gave him more information to use in his evaluation of the effectiveness of his directorates. The trips gave him a chance to talk one on one with the action officers away from the inhibiting constraints of headquarter offices. The trips also provided an opportunity for him to get some reactions to his ideas about the unit, find out how important other people believed their work to be, determine the direction the unit was going in, and decide if any changes were needed in the way it was doing business.

With each passing week it became clearer to him that basic changes in the organization would improve the directorates' efficiency. By combining the functions of the Logistics Plans and the Mobility divisions, since both were driven by the Joint Deployment System, he could eliminate overlap of effort there. He anticipated that if the two Security Assistance divisions were merged into one division, the work load would be more level and flexibility would improve. The Security Assistance Policy and Performance Evaluation divisions also could be made into one, which would provide better integration of the two functions.

These changes were going to disrupt many people in the unit and eliminate several positions. Were the changes necessary? He decided to hold four separate group meetings (nonattribution, open commander's calls) with action officers, enlisted personnel, civilians, and division chiefs. Everyone knew that major changes were being considered, and these meetings would give them the opportunity to express their opinions.

Information gathered in these open forums and in more informal contacts confirmed the admiral's suspicion that change was, indeed, necessary. He made every effort to reassure his people that his approach to reorganization was positive. No one would be fired or forced to move out of cycle. He allowed 45 days for developing a detailed plan in order to allow for individuals to make adjustments and in order to prevent the reorganization from dragging out. He also asked his deputy, who was charged with developing the plan, to solicit further recom-

mendations and to use his power of persuasion to convince people of the need for change.

Admiral Hayward explains that,

when a leader is forced to alter an order he has previously given, he should explain the reasons for the change when he has time and keep his people's confidence up when he does not have time to explain. He should never undercut the command in the process, even if he does not like the decision. If the decision is his, he should deal with it straightforwardly by leveling with his people, but he should get the job done.

The situation is going to determine how an officer ought to deal with a change in orders. By the situation, I mean the urgency of what has to be accomplished. Usually there's no reason not to explain to your people what they are supposed to do and why. The day of just telling somebody to go do it and don't ask, just get on with it, this may have worked years ago in the military and industry and everything else, because that's just the way people were able to deal with each other. That doesn't work today. I doubt if it really worked back in the days of John Paul Jones. My guess is that he kept his troops informed every minute of what was going on, and they were ready for emergencies and they could handle any task because they worked as a team and there was that sense of understanding.

If an officer must reverse an order that he gave, it may seem ridiculous under the circumstances, so, if he has time, he should explain it, tell his people why he has changed his mind. He should never blame his seniors for the change in any way, because of the damage that would do to the sense of loyalty.

A leader ought to be able to grapple with this difficult reversal, even if he does not understand it. That happens to officers; an officer can have an order reversed, and the reversal seems stupid to him, but he must execute it, and the way to do it is to execute it in the most constructive way he knows how and not say, "Well, you know the XO says, 'Go do this,' and he's all screwed up just like he always is, but let's go do it." The leader must execute the change in a constructive way, because the only way a leader can build solid, continuous support is through teamwork and loyalty.

Each commander, director, or manager has his own way of gathering information, making decisions, and implementing change. The speed and technique he uses to bring about change will be influenced by many different factors. The common denominator in all of these considerations, however, is people and how they will react to the changes they have to implement. Letting them know that he has taken them into consideration in his decision-making process could well be the difference between success and failure of the officer's next "Shift your rudder."

86. Physical Fitness

In the technically oriented modern Navy, sailors sit at complex control panels, monitor computers, and rest as nuclear fission propels ships through the water. No longer do men climb riggings, carry 16-inch shells, or adjust the trim and set of sails. Because the routine for today's sailor appears to be physically less demanding, some people believe that physical fitness is no longer a necessary component of service in the Navy. However, this is a misconception. General Rice believes that

an individual must be physically fit to meet the rigors of combat and of being a unit commander. He cannot lead from behind—you don't push the rope, you pull the rope. But the officer must not

mix up his priorities, he must strike a balance. A person who has pride in his ability to bench press a certain number of pounds and at the same time says he never reads and does not have time to read, and so is not current with world issues, has got his priorities mixed up. Naval officers must strike a balance, not going overboard in any of the attributes of leadership. Obviously, physical fitness is an important leadership attribute, but it is not the only one.

Today, more than ever, physical fitness is a vital asset for sailors and officers. The rigors of daily shipboard life, although they are different from those of one hundred years ago, can still only be withstood by a fit person.

Anyone who believes that "sailors today don't need to be in shape, because their jobs are easy," obviously has never

been a member of a working party loading stores; fired any type of large-caliber gun other than a MK45; worked aloft; worked in an engine room on a steam-driven ship; stood port-and-starboard watches for four hours on and eight hours off for a six-month deployment; tended a mooring line; worked on machinery; swabbed, scowered, or holystoned; manned a fire hose; run the length of a ship setting material condition behind you; crawled beneath a main engine; loaded an anti-submarine rocket; or carried revision three of that letter from the type commander from the captain's office through the chain of command for chop.[64-1]

In the shipboard environment, high morale and the ability to carry out duties competently are vital, and an individual's physical capabilities help determine his morale and his performance.

An out-of-shape person who, as a result, is constantly tired and sluggish cannot pull his own weight and becomes a burden on the rest of the crew. The unfit sailor turns in a poor performance in watch standing, work parties, and endurance in general. Furthermore, he serves to weaken the morale of his peers. Lack of enthusiasm and vigor can quickly spread through the crew and cause a sharp decline in spirit.

Physical fitness is indeed an indispensable trait in the modern sailor, and one definition is that physical fitness is "a state of mind as well as body. It is a determining factor in our overall health, attitude, and even character. The fit person gets more out of life. He does his job better, and enjoys himself more at leisure. He is less susceptible to fatigue, illness, or minor aches and pains, and has the self-satisfying reward of looking fit and trim."[64-1]

The challenge of promoting physical fitness involves more than just having people reach a state of conditioning which enables them to stand long watches and move heavy objects. People should also feel good about their health and their condition. Fortunately, being in shape makes almost everyone feel good, so the task at hand is not very difficult.

Before he begins a program to increase physical fitness in his people, the junior officer should meet two objectives. First, he should become thoroughly familiar with the subject of fitness. This includes not only exercise, but also proper diet and rest and restraint in the consumption of tobacco and alcohol.

Second, he must set an example by striving to display a neat appearance, an energetic attitude toward work, and an interest in sports. Becoming a model of physical fitness is crucial to promoting a program of exercise and diet in his division. An overweight officer will find it difficult to convince a petty officer to lose 20 pounds. Conversely, a trim, athletic officer may very well influence that same petty officer to try to match his level of physical aptitude. Fitness, like any other leadership problem, brings the leader under constant scrutiny, and for that reason he must practice what he preaches.

In order to become better educated on the subject of physical fitness, the officer should examine books containing basic information on diet and nutrition. Knowledge in the area of

nutrition is necessary because the effects of exercise are minimal when nutritional requirements are not met.

The theory behind food intake is, simply, that fuel, which provides energy for bodily motion, is found in all foods. Calories are units of fuel measurement, and whenever a person engages in an activity—such as exercising, walking, reading, sleeping, or even eating—calories are burned off. Any calories that are not lost through physical activity are stored in the body as fat. But fat people do not have more energy than skinny people; research conducted by physicians has determined that one pound of fat is more than sufficient energy to allow an athlete to complete a 26.2-mile marathon race.[103-124]

Research also indicates that weight control is an essential step in attaining physical fitness. "Uncontrolled weight gain not only is hazardous to health, but is also unsightly, demoralizing, and a cause of discomfort and fatigue."[64-6] While proper diet alone will not keep the body from building up fat layers, controlled caloric intake combined with a regular exercise program will.

It is clear that proper diet requires a good bit of planning and a certain amount of self-discipline. The major consideration in determining proper caloric intake is how many calories are burned off during normal daily activity. The individual must know approximately how many calories he can consume in a day without producing excess fat; this allows him to plan his daily meals. On board ship, the weekly menu is generally published in advance, which allows each fitness-oriented sailor to plan his caloric intake for an entire week. This vital aspect of a good physical fitness program should be stressed by the division officer.

Once he understands the importance of nutrition to physical fitness, the junior officer should learn about exercise. He may have to make special considerations and design flexible workout programs due to the limited space available on a ship. Obviously, personnel on an aircraft carrier have the opportunity to perform more types of exercise and recreation than their counterparts on a minesweeper do. However, any sailor who is serious about staying in shape can make do with what is available. Many routines can be carried out on a flat piece of deck.

Before organizing a program for physical fitness, the division officer must examine the facilities available. If the ship has a weight room, a basketball hoop, or a volleyball net, his task becomes much easier. Whenever it is possible to make an organized workout enjoyable through competition, the turnout will be high. Sparking the competitive nature of sailors in sports such as basketball or volleyball is relatively easy, but weightlifting and other individual sports also attract many participants.

Informal volleyball and basketball games in the division increase fitness in personnel. Enthusiasm for this type of activity can quickly spread throughout the crew, and an interdivision competition can result when the division officer challenges his fellow officers. The most benefit will be gained, as far as fitness is concerned, by playing the most games, so the officer should set up a tournament and promote it through newsletters. A round robin tournament, where every division gets the opportunity to play every other division, yields the best results. The team with the best win-loss record is the ultimate winner. This type of activity benefits personnel by increasing their physical activity, and it also boosts their morale. As members of the crew pull together to work as a team on the court, they will learn to become a more effective unit on the job.

The promotion of exercise is a more challenging problem for the officer whose equipment and space on board ship are limited. Because of their size, smaller ships encourage a sedentary routine, but this is all the more reason for the officer to develop a daily routine of exercise for his people.

A time must be agreed on for workouts to take place, before quarters or after the working day being optimal. A good move on the junior officer's part would be to let the crew decide on the time. If a watch rotation is in effect, then two sessions a day can be held.

Any exercise program should be gradually introduced in order to avoid injury to those who are in poor physical condition; workouts should take place on the largest available deck area. The outline for a model program follows.

For the first week, each session will be 20 to 30 minutes long and will consist of stretching exercises only. Increasing the flexibility of all muscles and tendons is vital for safe performance of more strenuous activity. This week will prove invaluable in preventing muscle pulls and tears later. Also, a program that initially appears easy will elicit more response than one that looks difficult.

During the second week, calisthenics—such as jumping jacks, toe touches, six-count pushups, jogging in place, and bouncing—are added to the workouts. At first individuals will be required to repeat the calisthenics a few times, but the number of repetitions will slowly be raised, increasing the difficulty of each exercise. Members of the division who are unable to keep pace will be encouraged to work at their own speed, while those in good shape will be encouraged to continue with individual workouts after each session.

By the fourth or fifth week, depending on the progress of the division members, more physically strenuous exercises, such as sit-ups and manual resistance exercises, will be introduced. Manual resistance is a revolutionary theory that substitutes the resistance of a spotter for the weight that is used in a weight room. Before embarking his people on manual resistance exercises in the fitness program, the division officer should hold one or two meetings solely to teach them about the exercises. The officer can select one of the stronger division members to demonstrate with, thereby proving that this type of workout can yield the same benefits as one using regular weights. By the end of the demonstration, the person chosen will be exhausted.

Two exercises serve to illustrate manual resistance techniques. The bench press and the military press are two common weight-room exercises, and each has a manual resistance equivalent. For the bench press, it is the push-up. The lifter assumes the upright push-up position, while the spotter straddles the lifter's lower back and places his hands on the lifter's shoulder blades. While the lifter is on the way down to the floor, the spotter applies upward pressure. On the lifter's way up, the spotter again constantly applies pressure, this time downward. The motion down is by four counts and on the way up a two count is used. This method—four seconds on the way down and two on the way up—is used for every exercise.

For the military press, the lifter sits on the floor. The spotter stands behind him and grasps each of the lifter's hands in his own. While the spotter applies constant downward pressure, the lifter presses his hands above his head as if he was lifting a bar stacked with weights.

The principle behind these exercises is not to allow the muscles to rest during the entire routine. One set of manual resistance exercises, consisting of 8 to 12 repetitions, is equivalent to a full three- or four-set workout of the same exercise with free weights. It is of the utmost importance that both the spotter and the lifter be knowledgeable in these techniques. The lifter will only gain as much from these exercises as the spotter demands.

To stimulate crew members to take full advantage of the opportunities available for increased fitness, a division officer can circulate information on diet and nutrition and material on proper exercise form and technique. He can provide a suggestion box for new ideas on exercises and meal planning. It is the division officer's responsibility to maintain a peak level of intensity and interest in this program. Personnel can also stimulate interest and strive for excellence, through push-up and sit-up contests, for example. The competitive spirit can thrive even in

limited space. The junior officer need only use his imagination.

When a ship spends time in its home port, crew members can enhance their physical fitness through recreational activities. Softball games, tennis matches, racquetball tournaments, and bowling matches are an enjoyable outlet of energy. The division officer can arrange these contests on any level: among the division, with other divisions on the ship, or with crews from other ships in port. Programs stymied by ship size, such as jogging or hiking, can be boosted at this time. A picnic combines a small amount of fitness-oriented activity with a lot of good food to serve as an overall lift in morale. Being in port provides access to many facilities that simply are not available at sea. Getting the most out of this opportunity is largely a product of the effort put forth by the division officer.

Finally, to round out a physical fitness and health plan, drinking and smoking must be held to moderation. This is perhaps the hardest part of a fitness program. Some individuals are set in their ways concerning drinking and smoking. Obviously, a division officer cannot order his personnel to stop drinking and smoking, but he can make them conscious of the tremendous harm they are doing to their bodies. Pamphlets, books, questionnaires, and guest speakers make up a good awareness program.

Today's technically sophisticated Navy needs physically fit sailors. Mental acuity and alertness are needed more than ever, and maintaining a peak mental condition requires being in top physical condition. The division officer is responsible for seeing that his people reach and sustain a high degree of fitness. The diet and exercise programs briefly discussed here provide the junior officer with a base to start meeting the challenge before him. However, no amount of knowledge can substitute for the example he sets in this program. By being in top physical condition and approaching conditioning enthusiastically, he will serve as the model sailors need.

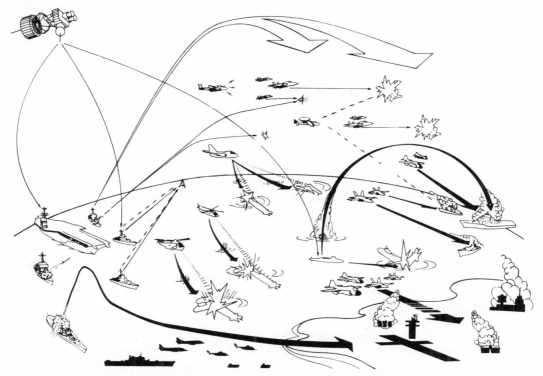

Teamwork does it!

The division officer will be amazed at the benefits resulting from a successful program. Sailors will have more energy on the job; be better able to enjoy their liberty; have pride in their trim appearance; and work more closely as a unit. Another important outcome will be the natural boost in morale among the crew. With a spirited, well-trained crew, any task is easier.

The importance of sports to the development of an officer is seen in the accompanying illustration, where the connection is made between the battlefield and the playing field. Through team sports, people learn that every player must do his duty, consider what everyone else is doing, know the desires of the team leader, and be prepared to help those in other positions if something goes wrong. Team players also come to understand, through the course of a season, that despite a momentary setback, each future engagement must be met afresh with confidence, effort, and vigor, and the team must come back and fight again toward ultimate victory. This is important because it is in the nature of war that every engagement is not a victory.

The essence of war is essentially one of trying to surprise the enemy, and this is much like action on the playing field, where team members, individually and collectively, learn to think about what the other side has done, is doing, and will do and thus take counter or evasive action. In the course of a sports contest, both sides are constantly surprised, and team members learn to recover quickly from unexpected actions by their adversaries. This bounce-back recovery from unforeseen incidents is a key to the training of officers, who, after being surprised in combat, must quickly return to the fray with renewed vigor and not mentally brood about what went wrong, other than to try to avoid future surprises by the other side.

Thus, if we are to be victorious in the air, on the sea or the land, and below the surface, we must remember that not only do sports benefit the self-development and general mental and physical fitness of our people, but sports and the teamwork developed are significant contributors to combat victory—and that is what the Naval Service is all about: victory in war and the development of a strong defensive force in peace. When a team is properly trained, a potential enemy will neither overlook nor miscalculate the team's strength or willingness to fight. As the inset in the photograph illustrates, Naval forces are very complex in their operation and involve many teams of individuals, and these teams in turn must operate as one very big team if the mission is to be accomplished.

MCPON Sanders: *Physical fitness is a concern not only for the junior officer's subordinates, but also for the junior officer. If we have people who are in good condition, they eat well, they sleep well, have good habits, we find that they also have good work habits and they're very, very productive. Physical fitness is here with us, it's not going to go away. Meeting the proper weight standards and body fat content is very important for the junior officers; it goes back to being a role model, a personal example. If you have a fat junior officer telling his or her division that they must run three miles and if they don't pass the test that their evaluation will suffer, then it really detracts from the authority of the junior officer. I think that we must stress physical fitness. The standards are already out there; you need to make your people aware that there are standards, what the standards are, and that they will be expected to adhere to those standards. Maintaining a proper physical fitness program is very, very difficult, especially aboard ship. We have individuals who work 10 to 14 hours a day in an environment where they cannot get out and readily exercise. We feed them three or four times a day, and they go from the job through the chow line, directly to bed and then get up and go to work the next morning. All that is counterproductive to being in good physical condition, so we should be very careful, and provide time and assets for the program. Individuals must be given every opportunity to work out and have recreation, to do things that are going to make them a little bit more physically fit. Sometimes we must make those opportunities ourselves, whether we are enlisted or junior officers.*

87. The Morale, Welfare, and Recreation Program

Admiral Uchida believes that

leave, liberty, and recreational activities are very important for the refreshment of the corps' spiritual as well as physical state. An officer also can reduce the number of careless mistakes his subordinates make by providing them with refreshment.

In determining how often he should give liberty or leave, the officer should also consider the frequency that is optimum for his own corps. Individuals come to depend on regularly scheduled liberty, but an additional, unexpected grant of shore leave, for instance, will greatly improve their morale.

Admiral Hunt states:

We should run an organization in a way which provides satisfaction to those who are part of it. They must be given responsibility, risk, adventure, and an environment in which they feel they are making a useful contribution. At the same time they must have enough time and freedom for leave, to spend with their families, and for recreation. In determining leave and liberty policy, the key is to achieve a balance. He is an unwise commander in my view who spends too much time working and too little playing. If in doubt, give more liberty; then, when the crisis comes, people will seldom fail to give you everything possible. To overwork when there is not a crisis, and

to adhere too strictly to what may be archaic, restrictive, or excessively generalized rules of liberty, leave, and recreation seems to me to be unproductive.

Admiral Long notes:

Morale affects the ability of an individual to do his job because it influences his attitude toward his job and toward the Navy. Reenlistment, loyalty, initiative, pride—all of the things that contribute to the ability of a ship or an aircraft squadron or a submarine or a Marine company to perform with excellence—are inseparable from morale. Clearly, then, one of the most important responsibilities an officer has is to maintain the highest state of morale among his people, not just because it is a "nice" thing to do, but because high morale normally equals high readiness, and every officer should be interested in the ability of his unit to perform its primary mission and to perform it as well as possible. Insofar as a person's ability to go on leave or liberty impacts his morale, that ability becomes very important to the organization. Thus, an officer's concern for the welfare—and therefore morale—of his people is demonstrated, in part, by how frequently and consistently he grants leave and liberty. Naval Service personnel, whether admirals or seamen, must have the opportunity to go on leave. Officers should schedule leave for their people over a period of time, trying to accommodate the people's personal wishes, and try to adhere to that schedule. In the Navy it is sometimes difficult to predict operations, but insofar as he is able, it is good for morale if the officer lays out a leave schedule and adheres to it.

An appropriate amount of liberty is also important. Some ships grant liberty sparingly, but generally it is not best to keep people on board when they have nothing to do. When the ships are in port, commanding officers should try to give the maximum amount of liberty. Now I'm not suggesting for an instant that liberty be granted at the expense of proper maintenance and training and readiness. I will observe that some of the best-run ships that I have seen, the best maintained ships, were also able to grant the maximum amount of liberty in port. Those ships did much of their work at sea, so when they came into port, many of the things were done. Obviously, certain things cannot be done at sea, they can only be done when machinery and weapons systems are shut down, in port. But I would urge any young officer to try to get most of his work done at sea so that when his people are in port they can spend the maximum amount of time with their families.

THE PROGRAM

The Morale, Welfare, and Recreation program makes a significant contribution to the quality of life in the military community and is directly related to recruitment and retention. For military personnel, the program offers activities that maintain a high level of esprit de corps and therefore enhance job proficiency and contribute to military effectiveness. Activities that help personnel make the transition from civilian to military life are also provided. By making military service an attractive career, the program facilitates recruitment and retention.

MWR benefits the larger community, as well. Its activities promote and maintain the physical, mental, and social well-being of military members, their families, and other eligible members of the community. Opportunities for acquiring new talents and skills that contribute to the military and civilian community are plentiful. Providing community support programs and activities for military families, particularly when the serv-

ice member is on an unaccompanied tour or is involved in armed conflicts, is another important aspect of the MWR program.

MWR ACTIVITY CATEGORIES

The activities in each of the eight categories of MWR activities are designed to ensure that the Morale, Welfare, and Recreation program is well rounded. The eight categories of activities designed to satisfy the free-time needs of service personnel are:

1. armed services exchanges;
2. resale and revenue-sharing;
3. military general welfare and recreation;
4. civilian employee general welfare and recreation;
5. open messes (clubs);
6. other membership associations;
7. common support service nonappropriated fund instrumentalities; and
8. supplemental mission services nonappropriated fund instrumentalities.

Leave and liberty must be granted to free military personnel from the exacting duties of military life. Periods of leave and liberty permit service personnel to arrange their own schedules—to do what they want to do during a specific period of time—without military supervision. A good leader properly plans his personnel's leave and liberty and informs the personnel and the command of these plans.

LEADERSHIP IN THE MWR PROGRAM

Good leaders help plan, program, administer, and manage the MWR program, and they demonstrate their enthusiasm for the program by personally participating in it. Their presence at any event encourages optimum individual attendance and participation. Demonstrated command interest is crucial for making the Morale, Welfare, and Recreation program in the armed forces meaningful and worthwhile. While remaining responsive to the mission of their commands, leaders must also be cognizant of the MWR needs of their commands' members and their dependents.

A good leader need not be an expert in all phases of the MWR program, but he should know the elements of the program and their related functions. He should determine the interests and needs of his personnel and take note when these change. The leader should consult with MWR activities managers about the activities his people would benefit from. He should work to establish a variety of programs so that interests are met through base activities or local civilian community programs. The leader should provide suggestion boxes and respond to every suggestion.

In implementing the MWR program, a leader should provide agendas for recreation councils and committees. He must provide training for the MWR work force and ensure that the work force is patron service oriented. The leader sees to it that sufficient equipment is available on a timely schedule and that hours of operation are scheduled to provide the maximum time available for patron use. He makes sure that events are preplanned and well publicized, so that patrons can take full advantage of them, He places notices in base newspapers, posts notices on bulletin boards, puts up posters at congregating places, and makes MWR announcements at staff meetings.

To complement the service-provided activities of the MWR program, the leader should establish a liaison with off-base community recreation leaders and cooperate with civil leaders in joint efforts to provide recreational outlets. Competitive sporting events and other physical activities that help military personnel remain physically fit and healthy are a prominent and important part of the program, and the leader should at all times provide for the safety and well-being of the participants. The leader should keep the command staff and organization commanders informed of the program, and he should see that new personnel and their dependents

are apprised of the program and encouraged to participate through orientation briefings.

Finally, the leader should conduct preplanned evaluations of this MWR program and effect necessary revisions as soon as possible to retain patron interest.

Leadership is the key to the presentation and operation of a viable Morale, Welfare, and Recreation program. The leader must recognize the importance of the program and ensure professional management of all MWR activities; determine patron interests and needs; offer viable programming; ensure that periods of leave and liberty are planned and publicized; and accept responsibility for improving the quality of life for service members and their families.

FUNDING OF THE MWR PROGRAM

Financial support for the MWR program is provided by appropriated funds and nonappropriated funds. Appropriated funds are allocated by Congress. The requirements and budgets for this type of funding are established by the military services within the specified limitations for each of the eight categories of MWR activities. Nonappropriated funds (NAF) are funds that are generated within the various MWR activities through sales in the military exchanges, resales, and locally imposed fees and charges for use of selected MWR activities and services.

One of the major challenges encountered by a leader in providing a well-rounded MWR program is attaining adequate financial support. How well he plans, budgets, and supervises the MWR program determines the activities and services that can be offered military personnel and their families.

MCPON Sanders: *In today's world, I think, everyone is aware that recreation and liberty are necessary. You will find that your better workers will avail themselves of recreational opportunities. We have discovered in recent years that some of our people do not know how to become involved in recreational activities, so the junior officer should encourage the crew to get involved in recreational activities. If the officer does this, he will have healthier individuals who will also be much better workers. However, there can also be a problem in the leave and liberty area if the junior officer does not keep a close watch on the books and ensure that proper records are kept and that enlisted know how much leave they have. Don't let them build up too much leave, unless they knowingly want to do*

that, nor allow them to do so if in the future you will not have enough people around to do the work. On the other hand, don't allow one person's job to become so important that he can never take all the leave that he has earned. You must stay on top of this, including providing cross-training as necessary, for if you don't make this a matter of priority and examine the entire leave and liberty policy within your division, you may be digging yourself into a hole.

Chapter 8 Bibliography

1. Andrews, Lincoln C. *Military Manpower*. New York: E. P. Dutton, 1920.
2. Anthony, William P. "Managing Incompetence." In *Supervisory Management*. New York: AMACOM, Division of the American Management Association, 1981.
3. Argyris, Christopher. *Executive Leadership: An Appraisal of a Manager in Action*. New York: Harper and Brothers, 1953.
4. *The Army Officer's Guide*. Update by Lawrence P. Crocker. Harrisburg, Pa.: Stackpole, 1960.
5. Atkinson, Rita L.; Atkinson, Richard C.; and Hilgard, Ernest R. *Introduction to Psychology*. New York: Harcourt Brace Jovanovich, 1983.
6. Bach, C. A. "Know Your Men, Know Your Business, Know Yourself." *Proceedings*, Apr. 1974, pp. 42–46.
7. Baldwin, Robert H., and Daula, Thomas V. "The High Cost of Quality Recruits." *Armed Forces and Society*, Fall 1984, pp. 96–115.
8. Bass, Bernard M. *Leadership, Psychology, and Organizational Behavior*. Westport, Conn.: Greenwood Press, 1960.
9. Beardon, William, and Wedertz, Bill. *The Bluejacket's Manual*. 20th ed. Annapolis: Naval Institute Press, 1978.
10. Bellows, Roger. *Creative Leadership*. Ed. Dale Yoder. Englewood Cliffs, N.J.: Prentice-Hall, 1959.
11. Bennett, Geoffrey. *Nelson the Commander*. New York: Charles Scribner's Sons, 1972.
12. Blumenson, Martin, and Stokesbury, James L. *Masters of the Art of Command*. Boston: Houghton Mifflin, 1975.
13. Bogardus, Emory S. *Leaders and Leadership*. New York: D. Appleton-Century, 1934.
14. Bowditch, James L., and Buono, Anthony F. *Quality of Work Life Assessment: A Survey-Based Approach*. Boston: Auburn House, 1982, pp. 1–20.
15. Boyarsky, Bill. *Ronald Reagan: His Life and Rise to the Presidency*. New York: Random House, 1981.
16. Caday, A. "Criticism: Tool or Tyrant?" *Proceedings*, Mar. 1969, p. 135.
17. "Calley." *Time*, 22 Sept. 1975, p. 75.
18. "Carnage in Beirut." *Time*, 31 Oct. 1983, p. 18.
19. Carnegie, Dale. *How to Win Friends and Influence People*. New York: Simon and Schuster, 1952.
20. Cherrington, David J. *Personnel Management*. Dubuque, Iowa: William C. Brown, 1983.
21. Chruden, Herbert J., and Sherman, Arthur W., Jr. *Readings in Personnel Management*. Cincinnati: Southwestern, 1961.
22. Clark, Charles E. *My Fifty Years in the Navy*. Boston: Little, Brown, 1917.
23. Clarke, Bruce C. *Guidelines for the Leader and Commander*. Harrisburg, Pa.: Stackpole, 1973.
24. Clexton, E. W., Jr. "Trust and Confidence." Commanding Officer's Memorandum no. 20, USS *Dwight D. Eisenhower* (CVN 69), 21 Feb. 1984.
25. Collins, Arthur S. *Common Sense Training*. Novato, Calif.: Presidio Press, 1981.
26. Commanger, Henry Steele. *The Blue and the Grey*. New York: Fairfax Press, 1978.
27. Cooper, Joseph D. *The Art of Decision Making*. New York: Doubleday, 1961.

28. Cope, Harley F. *Command at Sea*. Annapolis: Naval Institute Press, 1966.

29. Copeland, Norman. *Psychology and the Soldier*. Harrisburg, Pa.: Military Service Publishing, 1942.

30. Department of the Army. *Combat Leader's Field Guide*. Harrisburg, Pa.: Stackpole, 1980.

31. Department of Defense, Office of Armed Forces Information and Education. *The Armed Forces Officer's Guide*. Washington, D.C.: U.S. Government Printing Office, 1960.

32. "D.O.D. Renews Its Emphasis on Training and Education." Interview with Lieutenant General Edgar A. Chavarrie, USAF. *Defense Management Journal*, fourth quarter, 1984, pp. 2–7.

33. Dugan, James. *The Great Mutiny*. New York: G. P. Putnam's Sons, 1965.

34. Eller, Earnest. "Leadership in Navy and Industry." *Proceedings*, June 1948, pp. 544–71.

35. Fingarette, Herbert. *On Responsibility*. New York: Basic Books, 1967.

36. Ford, Robert N. *Motivation through the Work Itself*. New York: American Management Association, 1969, pp. 185–99.

37. Foulkes, Fred K. *Creating More Meaningful Work*. New York: American Management Association, 1969.

38. Frier, John M., Jr. "Leadership and Morale." *Proceedings*, Jan. 1960, pp. 109–10.

39. Gallin, A. L. "Effectiveness: The Basic Criterion." *Proceedings*, Apr. 1958, p. 110.

40. Gannon, Joseph C. *The USS Oregon and the Battle of Santiago*. New York: Comet Press, 1958.

41. Garraty, John. *A Short History of the American Nation*. New York: Harper and Row, 1985.

42. Gatchel, Theodore C. "Gunny, Put Up the Flagpole." *Marine Corps Gazette*, Feb. 1982, pp. 38–44.

43. Gibson, Charles C. "Leadership Is Not Enough." *Proceedings*, Aug. 1955, p. 917.

44. Glover, John Desmond, and Siomon, Gerald A., eds. *Chief Executive's Handbook*. Homewood, Ill.: Dow Jones–Irwin, 1976.

45. Gosnell, H. A. "As Before, Except." *Proceedings*, Jan. 1931.

46. Grassey, Thomas B. "Outcome, Essences, and Individuals." *Proceedings*, July 1976, pp. 72–75.

47. Hackman, Ray C. *The Motivated Working Adult*. New York: American Management Association, 1969, pp. 125–62.

48. Heinl, Robert Debs. *Handbook for Marine NCOs*. Annapolis: Naval Institute Press, 1977.

49. Hellriegal, Don, and Slocum, John W., Jr. *Management*. 3d ed. Reading, Mass.: Addison-Wesley, 1982.

50. Henderson, George, ed. *Human Relations in the Military*. Chicago: Nelson-Hall, 1975.

51. Herzberg, Frederick. "One More Time: How Do You Motivate Employees?" In *Job Satisfaction: A Reader*. New York: John Wiley and Sons, 1976, pp. 17–32.

52. Hodgkinson, Christopher. *The Philosophy of Leadership*. New York: St. Martin's Press, 1983.

53. Hunt, James G., and Larson, Lars L. *Leadership: The Cutting Edge*. Carbondale: Southern Illinois University Press, 1977.

54. ———, eds. *Leadership Frontiers*. Kent, Ohio: Kent State University Press, 1975.

55. Huppuch, M. C. "A Naval District's Recreation Program." *Proceedings*, Mar. 1945, pp. 299–301.

56. Jacobsen, K. C. *Watch Officer's Guide*. 11th ed. Annapolis: Naval Institute Press, 1979.

57. Jones, Arthur J. *The Education of Youth for Leadership*. New York: McGraw-Hill, 1938.

58. Kahar, Richard J. "The First Commandment of Leadership: Love Thy Soldier." *Military Review*, July 1980, pp. 65–68.

59. Kazmier, Leonard J. *Principles of Management: A Program for Self-Instruction*. 2d ed. New York: McGraw-Hill, 1969.

60. Knox, D. W. "Elements of Leadership." *Proceedings*, Dec. 1920, p. 1883.

61. Lahey, Benjamin B. *Psychology*. Dubuque, Iowa: William C. Brown, 1983.

62. Lawrence, William P. "Common Qualities of Good Leaders." *Marine Corps Gazette*, Apr. 1981, pp. 40–41.

63. Lord, Walter. *Day of Infamy*. New York: Bell, 1956.

64. Loren, Donald P. *Shape Up!* Annapolis: Naval Institute Press, 1980.

65. McCann, Tommy J., and LeBlanc, Grover. *Basic Military Requirements*. Washington, D.C.: U.S. Government Printing Office, 1981.

66. McCormick, Ernest J., and Fiffin, Joseph. *Industrial Psychology*. 6th ed. Englewood Cliffs, N.J.: Prentice-Hall.

67. Mack, William P., and Paulsen, Thomas D. *The*

Naval Officer's Guide. 9th ed. Annapolis: Naval Institute Press, 1983.

68. Mahan, A. T. *Types of Naval Officers.* Boston: Little, Brown, 1901.

69. Manchester, William. *American Caesar: Douglas MacArthur, 1880–1964.* New York: Bell, 1978.

70. "The Marine Massacre." *Newsweek*, 31 Oct. 1983, pp. 20–25.

71. Marvin, Philip. *Man in Motion: A Winning Game Plan for Executives.* Homewood, Ill.: Dow Jones–Irwin, 1972, pp. 47–69.

72. "Military Jobs: A Pretty Good Place to Start." *Changing Times*, May 1983, pp. 32–36.

73. Mitchell, Joseph B. *Decisive Battles of the Civil War.* New York: G. P. Putnam's Sons, 1955.

74. Moffat, Alexander W. "Leadership: A Process of Growth." *Proceedings*, Nov. 1973, p. 89.

75. Montgon, Ade. *Napoleon.* Paris: Bibliotheque de Paris, 1937.

76. Montor, Karel, and Ciotti, Anthony J., eds. *Fundamentals of Naval Leadership.* 3d ed. Annapolis: Naval Institute Press, 1984.

77. Mooney, J. D. *Principles of Organization.* New York: Harper and Brothers, 1947.

78. Morosky, Paul. "Physical Fitness in the Sea Services." *Proceedings*, Oct. 1971, p. 58.

79. Mumford, Robert E., Jr. "Get Off My Back, Sir." *Proceedings*, Aug. 1977, pp. 18–23.

80. "Naval Maneuver." *Newsweek*, 22 Sept. 1975, p. 32.

81. "The Navy: Collision Course." *Newsweek*, 8 Dec. 1975, p. 47.

82. Newman, Aubrey. *Follow Me.* Novato, Calif.: Presidio Press, 1981.

83. Newman, William H. *Administrative Action.* Englewood Cliffs, N.J.: Prentice-Hall, 1963.

84. Noel, John V., Jr., and Bassett, Frank E. *Division Officer's Guide.* 7th ed. Annapolis: Naval Institute Press, 1977.

85. Owen, John D. *The Price of Leisure.* Montreal: McGill-Queens' University Press, 1970.

86. Patton, George S., Jr. Third Army Speech. In *Patton Papers.* Boston: Houghton Mifflin, 1944.

87. Peabody, Robert L. "Perceptions of Organizational Authority: A Comparative Analysis." *Administrative Science Quarterly*, Mar. 1962.

88. "Personnel Problem Looms for USAF." *Jane's Defense Weekly*, 2 March 1985, p. 347.

89. Pocalyko, Michael N. "The Fleet Nugget." *Proceedings*, July 1983, pp. 70–72.

90. Pollock. *New Jersey Business.* Philadelphia: Herman Goldner, 1984.

91. Powers, Bruce F. "The United States Navy." In *The United States War Machine.* New York: Crown, p. 108.

92. Prange, Gordon W. *At Dawn We Slept.* New York: McGraw-Hill, 1981.

93. ———. *Miracle at Midway.* New York: McGraw-Hill, 1982.

94. Quester, Aline O., and Thomason, James S. "Keeping the Force: Retaining Military Careerists." *Armed Forces and Society*, Fall 1984, pp. 85–95.

95. Record, Jeffrey. "Why Our High-Priced Military Can't Win Wars." *Washington Post*, 29 Jan. 1984.

96. Reitzel, William A. *Background to Decision-Making.* Newport, R.I.: U.S. Naval War College, 1958.

97. Reynolds, James B. "The Key Man." *Proceedings*, Aug. 1970, p. 124.

98. Reynolds, Russell B. *The Officer's Guide.* Harrisburg, Pa.: Stackpole, 1965.

99. Ridde, Truman Post. "Recreation Camps for Enlisted Men." *Proceedings*, Dec. 1937, pp. 1765–70.

100. Ryan, Paul B. "U.S.S. Constellation Flair-up: Was It Mutiny?" *Proceedings*, Jan. 1976, p. 46.

101. Sarkesian, Sam C. "Military Leadership: Time for a Change?" *Military Review*, Sept. 1980, pp. 16–24.

102. Schine, Eric. "One That Works." *Harper's*, Jan. 1983, p. 25.

103. Shephard, Roy J., and Lavalle, Hugh, eds. *Physical Fitness Assessment.* Springfield, Ill.: Charles C Thomas, 1978.

104. Shepherd, David R. *Ronald Reagan: In God I Trust.* Wheaton, Ill.: Tyndale House, 1984.

105. Shepherd, Stephen, ed. *Reef Points, 1983–1984.* 78th ed. Annapolis: U.S. Naval Academy, 1983.

106. Sibson, Robert E. *Increasing Employee Productivity.* New York: American Management Association, 1976, pp. 170–85.

107. Small, James C. "Factors in Leadership." *Proceedings*, Dec. 1947, p. 1505.

108. Smith, H. E. "The Anatomy of Leadership." *Proceedings*, Dec. 1951, pp. 1285–87.

109. Smith, Hedrick, et al. *Reagan the Man: The President*. New York: Macmillan, 1980.

110. Smith, L. N. "Leadership Awakening." *Proceedings*, Jan. 1961, p. 116.

111. Soper, M. E. "Finding the Best among Us." *Proceedings*, Nov. 1977, p. 35.

112. "The Spectator." *Readings in Administration*. New York: Herman Goldner, 1984–85.

113. Spector, Ronald H. *Eagle against the Sun*. New York: Free Press, 1985.

114. Stephens, Rusty. "Building a Man-to-Man Relationship." Address presented at the U.S. Naval Academy, Annapolis, 1984.

115. Stern, David. *Managing Human Resources*. Boston: Auburn House, 1982.

116. Stockdale, James B. "Moral Leadership." *Proceedings*, Sept. 1980, pp. 86–89.

117. Stodgill, Ralph M. *Stodgill's Handbook of Leadership: A Survey of Theory and Research*. New York: Macmillan, 1974.

118. Swartz, Oretha D. *Service Etiquette*. Annapolis: Naval Institute Press, 1977.

119. Swarztrauber, S. A. "Take Care of Your Men." *Proceedings*, Dec. 1963, pp. 26–34.

120. Taylor, Jack W. *How to Select and Develop Leaders*. New York: McGraw-Hill, 1962.

121. Thebaud, Hewlett. "Authoritarian Paternalism." In *Leadership and Law Department NL 303 Book of Readings*. Ed. J. M. Kelly, G. D. Patton, J. F. Downs, and G. J. Corini. Annapolis: U.S. Naval Academy, academic year 1983–84.

122. Thebaud, L. H. *Naval Leadership*. Annapolis: Naval Institute Press, 1939.

123. Theobald, R. A. "Handling of Men." *Proceedings*, Sept.–Oct. 1915.

124. "There It Was: A Nightmare." *Time*, 8 Dec. 1975, p. 16.

125. Upham, F. B. "Leadership of Men." *Proceedings*, Apr. 1921, p. 487.

126. Vaeth, J. Gordon. "Communications: A Lost Art?" *Proceedings*, Sept. 1976.

127. Vroom, Victor H. *Work and Motivation*. New York: John Wiley and Sons, 1964.

128. Washbush, John B., and Sherluck, Barbara J. *To Get the Job Done*. Annapolis: Naval Institute Press, 1984.

129. Webb, Ewing T., and Morgan, John B. *Strategy in Handling People*. New York: Halcyon House, 1930.

130. "Who'll Fight for America?" *Time*, 9 June 1980, pp. 24–36.

131. Wolfe, Malcolm E., and Mulholland, F. J., eds. *Naval Leadership*. Annapolis: Naval Institute Press, 1983.

132. Wood, William J. *Leaders and Battles: The Art of Military Leadership*. Novato, Calif.: Presidio Press, 1984.

133. "Zulu Dawn." Paramount Pictures, 1978.

9

Equipment and Materiel Management

Introduction

Advice to *BRILLIANT* Young Officers—and Maybe a Few Older Ones, Too

Winning Naval Battles

The first thing to have in mind is that it is a good idea to win naval battles—or don't get in 'em. Losing naval battles is disheartening to the nation and quite unhealthy for the losers.

Naval battles are won by sinking enemy ships, shooting down enemy planes and missiles, destroying enemy submarines, and preventing the enemy from sinking our ships, shooting down our planes and missiles, and destroying our submarines.

To be able to do that, it is well to design, manufacture, and have afloat, ready to use, the best weapons systems, engineering systems, communications systems, and any other systems you need in battle that you can get with the money allocated to the Navy. It is also a good idea to have as much such stuff to destroy the enemy as is likely to be needed. It is not good to run out of ammo or ships or anything else you need in battle, for then you have to stop fighting.

All that good equipment must be operated with skill the way it should be, or it won't accomplish much.

All that equipment has to work the way it ought to, or it is simply excess baggage.

Busted equipment won't help in battle. If your gear won't work, it's no good to anybody.

If the systems operators know how to use their equipment, if they have kept the equipment in operating condition, there is a good chance we can win naval battles.

If the equipment doesn't work in battle, it doesn't make much difference how much else the officers know, the battle is lost—and so are the people in it.

So, it can be right handy to be a good engineer first—and a brilliant theorist after.

Admiral Arleigh A. Burke

This nation's success or failure in the first six months of a war will be determined by what the services do today, not by what they do in the first six months. When democracy goes to war, it goes in the suit of clothes it is wearing that day, because a democratic country is generally responding to an aggressive act on the part of another nation. This allows no time for buildup, and that is why keeping the Navy and the Marine Corps in a very high state of materiel readiness is so important. For this reason, the officer should understand the materiel side of the services and carefully manage his equipment and supplies.

Admiral James L. Holloway, III

88. Economy and Materiel Management

Historically, successful leaders have exhibited an understanding of and respect for economical equipment and materiel management, whereas failure has been the rule for those who did not learn this lesson. For example, Hannibal was defeated in the Second Punic War at Zama because he hadn't planned ahead to have enough water for his troops.[20-25] At Waterloo, Napoleon's army went to battle without breakfast,[17-134] while at Verdun, in World War I, millions of shells were fired due to not knowing exact target locations.[17-231] The concepts involved in this area of leadership should be familiar to all leaders. They facilitate operational planning and prevent expensive redundancies, which are counterproductive and diminish readiness.

Since officers lead from the front, they set the standard for accountability and responsibility in expenditures. Officers who are ruthless in their quest to protect the property and funds entrusted to their care set an example that others would do well to follow. Accountability is fundamental to effective management; officers must be as dedicated to accountability as they are to leading sailors or Marines effectively. Following the example of a conscientious senior, sailors and Marines will understand and embrace a spirit of responsibility and be more likely to protect their equipment from loss and damage.

Proper planning is fundamental to economy and effective leadership. At all levels of command, readiness and efficiency hinge on the plans for and equipment requirements of mission accomplishment. An organized plan and budget that are consistent with the organization's guidelines are necessary for achieving the goals of readiness and efficiency. Planning must be dynamic and nonlinear, drawn from and communicated to all subordinates.

Once he has determined his goals and plans, an officer must calculate funding requirements, taking into account the limits imposed by headquarters. An officer who exercises fiscal economy will prepare a realistic budget, which has a better chance of gaining approval. After his budget is approved, the officer must obtain authorized funds within the time period specified. He should review his budget periodically to ensure that funds are properly allocated in light of changing priorities. The review will also give him an opportunity to adjust funds to meet unexpected expenses, such as acquiring equipment or meeting training requirements that were not allocated funds in the original budget. The officer who manages his budget economically will not only achieve the goals identified earlier, he will also make the best use of surplus funds to cover contingencies.

Economical management of equipment and materiel dictates a prudent, judicious use of funds and supplies by the responsible officer. Excessive or indiscriminate use of supplies (the "use it or lose it" syndrome) involves waste, fraud, and abuse, which are inconsistent with leadership and integrity. Indiscriminate expenditures result in diminished materiel readiness, which can only be alleviated by requesting additional funds (assuming the funds are available and are not reserved to meet other requirements). In addition, time required to requisition and obtain the replacement supplies is time that is unavailable for other purposes.

Regardless of the size of the organization, a leader must continually review the table of equipment allowance lists. This process helps him balance the equipment requirements with the mission at hand. Should the mission be modified, the officer's request for increased funding or equipment must include a justification to support the requested increase. Conversely, if the listing contains a surplus of equipment, the officer who follows a sound, economical approach will redistribute the surplus to put it to the most effective use.

Although it is outside the defined parameters of economy in equipment and materiel management, the singularly effective tool that provides managers with both quantitative and qualitative economy is quality assurance. In essence, quality assurance prevents shortfalls and realigns maintenance requirements to avert bottlenecks that halt the operation. An effective quality assurance program does not hinder or harass personnel; rather, it assists them by ensuring a smooth and efficient operation.

The leaders of today must refine their planning and thought processes to capitalize on the most advanced methods of equipment economy and materiel management available. When properly executed, these methods generate tremendous advances in a unit's ability to respond, and ultimately in its organization and its service to the fleet. Admiral Taylor points out that

> the economical management of equipment and materiels is a big concern on a ship and an even bigger one in the Office of the Comptroller, where the responsibility for 26 billion dollars' worth of the operations and maintenance money of the Navy and the Marine Corps is to a degree. I think it goes back to the need to be able to ask the hard question. The taxpayer has

got to get his value for his dollar or he's going to come down on us, and we deserve to be held accountable for the failure to get the most out of those bucks. If you're responsible for resources, for materiel, you must, at all levels, ask, "Is this reasonable? Do I really need this? Is there a less expensive way to solve this problem that is not going to hurt anyone or damage equipment?" It's just a case, I think, of using good common sense and treating the taxpayer's money as you would your own, with a little bit of control. Don't goldplate things; do with what is absolutely necessary.

> Let me put it this way. When you spend money for little extravagances that make life a little bit smoother down in your outfit, does that come out of our war-fighting capability? Does it come from other programs in the Navy? We've got to conserve our resources, we don't want to waste money. We want to be vigilant so that we can buy good, solid hardware and training to make sure we know how to use it. There is a waste fraud and abuse hotline, which you want to keep in mind, and it goes back to something the CNO laid on us, which is, Can you answer these questions: How will this look in a newspaper column? and Can I defend myself in front of the American people? At every level, if we would use those kinds of rules, as a division officer on up through, we'd end up getting more for our buck. Don't waste a dime. We can't afford it anymore, because guess who's at the gates?

Economy in equipment and materiel management, then, goes hand in hand with accountability, responsibility, quality assurance, and innovative thinking. When they are properly orchestrated, these considerations provide the basis for success in leadership and goal and mission accomplishment. Ultimately they make a significant contribution to success on the battlefield.

89. Encouraging Resourcefulness in Materiel Utilization

The judicious application of materiel assets toward military capability requires resourcefulness at the national as well as the unit level. In a peacetime environment there are numerous competing demands for these assets by the civilian sector and other military organizations. In order to ensure the best possible utilization of these assets, an active and effective program of materiel management is essential.

For today and the foreseeable future, the Naval Service, along with the rest of the military establishment, must manage with a finite quantity of materiel assets while carrying out its peacetime mission and maintaining a high state of wartime readiness. Potential adversaries are intelligent, competent, and able to inflict significant damage on the U.S. fleet. Moreover, they would most likely dictate when, where, and how hostilities would be initiated. Fleet commanders, never content with the number of ships and aircraft assigned to them, are sensitive to the fact that critical munitions and other sustaining supplies are scarce commodities.

Senior military strategists have expressed considerable concern that the materiel assets that are available to them or could be rapidly produced by the industrial base may be inadequate to support the optimum execution of their operation plans (OPLANs). Modern munitions, which provide greater firepower with reduced delivery system vulnerability but at a unit cost that prohibits maintaining large inventories, make resourcefulness in managing scarce assets essential.

Resource availability considerations have become increasingly important to joint planners; in fact, the emerging tendency is to rely heavily on the logistician's assessment of an OPLAN's supportability. The joint planning system is working to ensure that inherent logistic risks to successful OPLAN execution are identified early, allowing the entire concept to be modified if necessary. This is especially important in a period when military commitments are increasingly being made to regions that have no immediate access to bases or materiel storage facilities.

The military success of a battle group or a Marine Air Ground Task Force (MAGTF) depends on an intricate sustainment infrastructure. Included in this infrastructure are strategic airlift assets, which move a small (from a national viewpoint) volume of essential items rapidly, and strategic sealift assets, which move a much greater volume of cargo but within a notably longer time. Naval Mobile Logistics Support Forces must then deliver these resources to the battle group. The efficient utilization of these lift assets is imperative if resupply materiel is to be delivered in a timely manner, especially during periods of conflict and when commitments are extended to more remote areas of the world.

Macro-level concerns for materiel allocation, distribution, and the accompanying infrastructure may seem far removed from the problems associated with the day-to-day demands of the division officer or platoon commander, yet the combat effectiveness of a division or a platoon will always be determined by the same combination of manpower, readiness, and materiel that affects the fleet overall. Resourceful application of materiel resources must not be relegated solely to the planners. When General John C. Meyer, USAF, was the Commander in Chief of the Strategic Air Command, one of the key points he made in a memorandum to the Air Force was the idea that every individual held some form of responsibility in promoting "better resource management."[23]

The ship, battalion, or aircraft squadron commander, like the commanders senior to him, is aware of the limitations associated with scarce repair parts, ammunition, or other special consumable goods, as well as the effort required to ensure reliable and timely delivery. The sophisticated and highly technical systems installed in ships, vehicles, and aircraft, while operationally superior to those of the past, nevertheless may become degraded or even inoperable should important sustainment items not be aboard.

To promote a division's or a platoon's proper materiel condition, an officer must commit himself to established maintenance programs, which serve to optimize the value of currently installed machinery. There is no better mark of commitment to optimum materiel utilization than personal involvement in the Maintenance and Materiel Management (3M) system. The officer who works with subordinates to formulate a maintenance program, conducts spot-checks to ensure that the scheduled preventive maintenance has been properly completed, and reviews the maintenance records regularly guarantees that equipment in the division is contributing to the materiel component of military capability. The naval officer must be able to manage as well as lead.[26-22]

After preventive and corrective maintenance has been completed and the paper work properly submitted, the officer should spend some time reflecting on the need to change a procedure, or to modify a piece of equipment for greater efficiency or ease of maintenance. The assumption that all wisdom concerning equipment design or maintenance procedures lies with senior engineers and designers in the bureaus of Washington, D.C., or that the problem has already been identified, is faulty. The officer should submit feedback reports, engineering field changes, or ship alteration requests, because these provide the Navy and the Marine Corps with a valued input on how to make equipment more efficient and serviceable.

The young officer must establish his own system of checks and balances to remain cognizant of all materiel problems that impact on mission accomplishment, and he must insist on frank and thorough reporting by subordinates. The first step toward familiarizing one's subordinates with prudent materiel utilization is to ensure that the task to be undertaken is well organized.[10-22] It would be unconscionable to have to report that gun mount 51 was out of commission just as the ship received an urgent call for shore bombardment, or that the platoon's squad automatic weapons were malfunctioning, if the failure was due to known but unreported materiel problems.

Once materiel problems are reported, the division or platoon officer must make sure that all reasonable efforts to obtain needed resources are underway. Insistence on prompt supply part status and follow-ups is almost always required. If an important spare part was placed on a truck for shipment the previous week and has not yet arrived, the officer must determine its whereabouts. If the division officer or platoon commander is not interested, his attitude will be reflected by his subordinates—with predictable results on equipment readiness.

Knowledge of equipment capabilities is crucial during those periods when sustaining supplies or repair parts are on order or in transit. Other equipment that has similar capabilities might be used to compensate for the loss of the primary, preferred equipment or as a substitute to extend the preferred equipment's service life. The capability regained might offset any loss of efficiency that results from using equipment in less than optimum roles. Work-arounds to a loss of equipment capability must be considered as an integral part of materiel management.

An officer who realizes that his influence can extend beyond his division or platoon has taken a step toward being selected for assignments of greater responsibility. His ability to influence optimum materiel utilization within the department or command will undoubtedly affect the command's overall readiness. Consider the officer who goes to the bridge to assume the watch as junior officer of the deck. As he climbs the ladder to the bridge area, he looks down and sees an electrical drill, rusty and awash in the motor whale boat. If he is responsible for boat maintenance or the electrical safety program, he will undoubtedly act to rectify this unsatisfactory situation. However, even an officer who seemingly is not directly affected by the rusty drill has a professional responsibility to make the electrical officer and the first lieutenant aware of such a wasteful and inefficient maintenance practice.

The naval officer knows that many aspects of materiel replacement and repair are beyond his control, but the effective officer makes every effort to ensure that his division, department, and command are in the highest possible state of materiel readiness. Contributing directly to military capability in this way is both part of his responsibility and within his scope of authority.

90. Organized Preventive Maintenance

Making sure that equipment and machines are ready for fighting or emergencies or just everyday work is an important goal for every officer. "The officer-in-tactical command . . . should be familiar with the characteristics, tactical doctrine, and limitations of each of the many different platforms under his command."[18-126] Establishing an aggressive program of preventing failures as well as finding and fixing the deficiencies that exist is a large part of this goal. Admiral Long notes:

It is not difficult to grasp the importance of leaders understanding the capabilities of their equipment when lives depend on that understanding. When an individual is flying an aircraft, if he wants to survive, he needs to understand very clearly the capabilities of that aircraft. If he is in a submarine, where his life and those of his shipmates depend on his knowledge of damage-control equipment and firefighting equipment, then he needs to have that knowledge. An officer needs to understand the equipment so that he

can operate or supervise its operation if that becomes necessary in an emergency. Aboard ship, in peacetime as in wartime, there are tragedies—fires, collisions, explosions—and the leader will have to draw on his knowledge for the survival of the ship and its crew.

There are other reasons for leaders to become very familiar with the operation of the equipment they are responsible for. They must understand the capabilities of the equipment of an aircraft or a ship or a submarine in order to optimize the performance of that equipment in carrying out the mission. An officer also needs to understand the capabilities of the equipment, whether in the engineering department, the operations department, or the weapons department, so he can supervise the training and the performance of the people under him. And, of course, as he moves up the line and starts dealing with ships and aircraft, it is important that he understand the capabilities of the group of ships or aircraft or submarines in aggregate.

It is also important, since being ready to fight wars is the naval officer's chosen profession, that he understand the capabilities of the equipment of the opposing forces, whether they be aircraft or ships or submarines, or air defense or even space systems. For years the U.S. Navy has been running war games, and those in the Atlantic have been particularly effective. One of the principal purposes of those war games is to teach naval officers not only the capabilities of the enemy forces, but also the capabilities of U.S. forces.

Admiral Long believes that understanding personnel capabilities is as important for an officer as understanding equipment capabilities.

I would strongly urge each young officer, as he proceeds to an operational unit, to set about and learn the capabilities of the equipment he has. Now, having said that, not only is it important to learn the capabilities of the equipment, whether it is electronic or mechanical or hydraulic, but also, certainly, it is important to learn the capabilities of the personnel operating that equipment. Unfortunately, we continue to have instances where the equipment is not operating to the optimal degree because of the lack of training of the personnel operating that equipment, and that, clearly, is a responsibility of the officer in charge. An officer in charge, to be truly responsible for an organization, must accept the responsibility; he must know what is going on, and he needs to understand the capabilities of the components under him. That principle is true whether an officer is in command of a division aboard ship or he is in command of a theater. The same principles are true: he is unable to perform as he should perform unless he understands the capabilities of the units—people and equipment—under his command. What I'm suggesting is the desirability of approaching one's job with a certain discipline, a certain outlook, that encompasses the concept of responsibility, that encompasses the concept of mutual respect for one's personnel, up and down, and also with a clear commitment to understand the capabilities of the people and the equipment that are under one's command.

The officer's ultimate goal should be to groom every piece of his equipment to the point that it will reliably do everything it is supposed to do, "every time." The officer's personal goal should be to have a unit that is known for its high standards of material readiness; he must be ready and willing to use the time and energy required to achieve this goal. Admiral Carney makes this point:

Equipment inspections within an estab-

lished period greatly reduce the possibility of breakdown. Otherwise maintenance does not take place until something happens, and by then there is a problem. Every piece of equipment should have a written check-off list, just as when the pilot steps in the plane and the copilot goes right down the list and checks everything, not trusting anything to memory. Periodic inspections using a checklist are essential in the maintenance of any equipment.

RATIONALE FOR AND COMPONENTS OF PREVENTIVE MAINTENANCE

You can well imagine the frustration an officer will experience if his division is ready to demonstrate superior teamwork in a man-overboard drill and the boat engine refuses to start! (The commanding officer may not find it amusing, either.) Of course if the engine does not work, the officer's team cannot perform, no matter how well prepared it is.

Needless to say, in a drill the problem can be found and fixed before the drill is run again, but imagine the agony if a life was lost because the emergency equipment failed when it was needed. Imagine being in battle and having to delay firing the battery for a few minutes because of a malfunction . . . that delay may provide just the time the enemy needs to win.

Obviously, gear that is broken will not do much, but even "minor" degradations can mean the difference between success and failure. For example, a radar operating at peak effectiveness will pick up small targets farther away than one that appears to work but is degraded by poor alignment, dirty and loose connections, and worn-out components. The same is true for all equipment. Therefore, the officer uses an organized preventive maintenance program to make sure the equipment is ready when it is needed and to help make it last longer and run better. An officer must be familiar with his equipment capabilities. This includes both basic operational knowledge—how to start equipment, operate it successfully, and turn it off—and maintenance ability, which is especially important to the modern naval officer, who is so dependent on highly technical equipment to transport and protect him and his troops. "It is obvious that his competence to judge whether certain equipment can or cannot operate safely or can or cannot be successfully repaired at sea affects his ship's safety."[4-3]

But how does the preventive maintenance program help? It is important for the officer to remember that the goal of the preventive maintenance program is *maintenance*—that is, the things done to the gear to make it work better. It is a mistake to let schedules, reports, procedures, and inspections of administrative skills fog goals. To be sure, the administrative aspects of the program are needed to keep track of the maintenance, but it is maintenance that is the real objective.

The types of maintenance programs to be performed on military equipment can be related to maintenance on something most people are very familiar with, a car. The effective officer will think of his maintenance in terms of what is done to the gear rather than in terms of moving scheduling symbols around on a chart or totalling statistics in a report.

Every car comes with an owner's manual that specifies what periodic maintenance is recommended when, and, possibly, how it is to be done. The things that can be done to cars to make them more reliable and last longer include

- checking the oil, because an engine without enough oil fails;
- changing the oil regularly to keep it clean and free of dissolved contaminants;
- changing the oil and air filters regularly, because they get clogged with dirt;
- checking the tires for air pressure and wear so they will not fail;
- aligning the front end to keep the tires from wearing out quickly;

- tuning the ignition system to make the engine run better;
- checking the level and freezing point of the coolant and changing the anti-freeze periodically to renew the corrosion inhibitor; and
- checking the battery and the voltage coming out of the voltage regulator so the car will start on a cold day.

These actions are organized and managed with the help of the checklists, records, and procedures in the owner's manual, and are an *organized preventive maintenance program*. A unit's maintenance program is very similar in principle, but, of course, it is more complicated, because the unit's equipment is probably more complicated than a car.

Preventive maintenance tasks usually fall into one of eight categories. Relating maintenance actions to these basic categories of maintenance will help the officer keep track of what needs to be done and will lead him to understand better how important maintenance is.

LUBRICATION: periodically applying or inserting grease and oil, checking oil levels, checking oil purity, sending oil in for analyzing wear products, checking lubrication systems for temperatures and pressures, changing or cleaning filters and strainers

COOLING: monitoring temperatures, pressures, and flows, checking for corrosion inhibitors, checking for fouling of heat-transfer surfaces, changing or cleaning filters and strainers

INSPECTIONS: for normal operation, for tightness of connections, for dirt, for broken or missing parts, for leaks, for burned-out lights

TESTS: of performance, of safety features, of set points, of automatic functions

ALIGNMENT: making adjustments to restore peak performance

CALIBRATION: testing and adjusting test equipment

CORROSION PREVENTION: painting and preservation

CLEANING: inside and out

All those checks might be fine for mechanical systems, but what about electronics? The officer should not assume that electronics is an esoteric field of wizardry that only highly trained technicians can understand. Electronics equipment is lubricated, cooled, inspected, tested for level of performance, aligned, preserved, and cleaned in ways not all that different from the way cars or other mechanical devices are. One way the officer can learn how to maintain the electronics equipment is to ask the technicians in the unit.

> A sound knowledge of practical electronics is almost a professional necessity; the fundamental principles of capacitances, inductances, relays, amplifiers, rectifiers, solid-state devices, and cathode-ray applications pervade our Navy today the way rope, tar, and canvas did a century-and-a-half ago. They are part of our professional equipment, and a basic understanding of their principles and applications will go a long way toward explaining the fundamental working of much of our new naval equipment. . . . More and more, the naval officer must understand the principles of metallurgy in order to make sound judgments about his ships, his planes, his missiles, and their capabilities and limitations.[4-4]

The unit's emergency and infrequently used equipment should not be neglected. It is easy to forget to check the air pressure in a car's spare tire—and a hard way to find out why it should have been done.

USING WRITTEN PROCEDURES FOR AN ORGANIZED PREVENTIVE MAINTENANCE PROGRAM

Written procedures available to the officer describe the maintenance required, when it should be done, and how to use the forms, schedules, and reports to manage the program. The effective officer studies these procedures

and becomes expert in them. By knowing how to use the procedures to get the maintenance done effectively and efficiently, the officer will rise above the average. By paying attention to the fine points, the officer and the unit can reach excellence in materiel readiness.

The procedures and records provide the officer with the following information necessary for effective maintenance.

1. The rules and requirements: what to do and how.
2. The officer's duties and the duties of other members of the team.
3. The step-by-step procedures for schedule planning and management.
4. The reports required and how and when to submit them.
5. The language and abbreviatons of the system.
6. How to request changes or correct errors.
7. How the program will be inspected by others; the common deficiencies; the results of the prevous inspections.

The procedures are written to help the officer and his people make the system effective. Maintenance procedures may not be easy to do, but they do work for the unit that puts in the time and the effort maintenance deserves.

THE OFFICER'S ROLE IN PREVENTIVE MAINTENANCE

Just what is the officer's role in making a preventive maintenance program effective? After all, the senior enlisted personnel do the work, and the department heads or company commanders manage the big picture. But the officer performs six key roles in a maintenance program. He is

a standard setter,
a coach and supervisor,
a planner and coordinator,
an advocate and provider,
a motivator, and
a problem solver.

As in all leadership situations, the exercise of command at the right level is very important. Too much involvement results in taking the job away from the members of the team, and not enough means someone else has to do the officer's work.

As the standard setter, the officer sets the tone. He establishes the discipline to reach the goals set. The officer establishes that he and the team are striving to be the best because they believe in the goals, not because they have been forced to perform.

As coach and supervisor, the officer helps his people get better and avoid making mistakes.

As planner and coordinator, the officer helps the senior enlisted supervisor by planning ahead and coordinating with other units. This role of the officer is important because of the pressures of the other tasks that compete with maintenance for time and manpower.

As advocate, the officer sees to it that his unit's interests are taken care of up the chain of command. As provider, he ensures that the necessary supplies, tools, training, and people are available to get the job done.

As motivator, the officer provides the incentive to do the job. Preventive maintenance is seldom fun, and very often the young technicians and workers do not appreciate how important the work is. If the unit has high standards of readiness, the youngsters may well be wondering why it is necessary to go to "all that trouble" when things go wrong so seldom.

As problem solver, the officer participates with his subordinates and the boss in solving problems. The officer should not underestimate detective skills, the value of resourcefulness, or the power of his office and rank to overcome problems that might otherwise be the reason (or excuse) for not being ready. In all instances, every effort should be made to clear up or eliminate any confusion or ambiguity which may occur when the task is communicated to one's subordinates.[26-22] Admiral Larson feels that

the role of the officer in the support of organized maintenance programs is a very important one, because you have the ultimate responsibility. To exercise that responsibility, first of all, you must know your equipment, you must understand how it operates, you must understand the maintenance procedures, and then you must oversee the scheduling. You can be a very nice internal audit, if you will, of the planned maintenance procedures. You can ensure that the maintenance of all of the equipment is properly scheduled, and you should spot-check to make sure that the work is being done. You should spot-check some of this by going on the scene and talking to one of the troops doing something, tell him you want to learn about that pump, this is the first time you've had the opportunity to see it taken apart, to look at the bearings on the inside, so you'd like him to explain to you how he's carrying out that particular planned maintenance, and in doing that, as you refer to that card, you'll have some confidence that he either is or is not properly carrying that out, and whether he is qualified to do that job. So you're the auditor, you're the scheduler, but you're also spot-checking around the scene to see that the work is really being done.

Now when problems come up, you need to be involved there, too, because you need to be involved in the solutions. When I was a division officer, I had an agreement with my division chief that whenever something went wrong, we both were called. The first thing we did was get together and try to decide on a plan of action. So if the chief would get called in the middle of the night, the first question he would ask is have you called Lt. (jg) Larson? And if I got called in the middle of the night, I would say have you called CPO Smith? By working together that way to ensure that people knew that we were a team, that I had ultimate responsibility but I had petty officer expertise that I needed to work with, that team concept carried over into scheduling and planned maintenance and preventive maintenance, and also into emergency repairs, and I think we got the whole unit working together and understanding that this was a critical part of our division.

The importance of firsthand knowledge. The more the officer knows about his gear, the more effective and helpful he can be in making sure each piece of equipment is in top condition. The officer certainly has a right to expect his top-notch enlisted technicians and supervisors to know more about the gear than the officer does. However, the more knowledge the officer has, the better he will be at his job.

The officer who takes care of his gear will succeed while others use "It broke" as an excuse for their failures. Also, occasionally a key person rises to his level of incompetency, and the officer must have enough knowledge to determine this, to tell the good people from the bad, before a disastrous "bottom-line" failure makes the situation all too clear.

The officer can become knowledgeable about the maintenance program by taking the following steps.

1. Have the troops make a list of every piece of equipment they "own."

2. Have the petty officers and noncommissioned officers gather the maintenance program procedures and records for the officer to study.

3. Acquire block diagrams of the systems. They may be readily available in the technical manuals or the unit's information books, or it may be necessary to have the technicians draw them.

4. Have the senior enlisted person take the officer on a tour of the unit to see and discuss each piece of equipment in the system. On this tour the officer should get to know

what each piece of equipment is called and what it does;

who operates each piece of equipment and how he learned to do so;

how the equipment is tested and to what standards;

how well the equipment is working now, including what the three most important things wrong with it now are; and

who performs the maintenance on the equipment and what problems are encountered in getting the maintenance done correctly and on time.

5. Repeat a visit to each piece of equipment, this time with maintenance personnel. Obtain a copy of maintenance procedures and

a. Read parts of each procedure to learn what the procedure says about when maintenance is required; what tools, personnel, parts, and supplies are needed; and the precautions to be taken.

b. Ask the maintenance personnel to describe in general terms what each maintenance action entails, how long it takes, what help they need, what coordination is required to schedule it, and what problems are anticipated with tools, supplies, and procedures.

c. Ask the maintenance personnel when the last major maintenance action was performed and what was found.

d. Ask how well the gear is performing now. (The officer will need to obtain a better answer than "Great." He needs to know more specifically by a measure such as power out, flow, temperature, etc., as applicable.)

e. Ask what is wrong with the gear now.

f. Ask the maintenance personnel the specific procedures followed when a problem is found. Of particular concern is whether the problem was recorded and the supervisor notified.

g. Ask about the maintenance that is performed before or after a key event or other situation. How do personnel remember to perform it? Has it been recorded?

6. After all of that, the officer should review the list of gear and ask the following questions.

Is the gear ready? How ready? Do you know how to tell if it will measure up when the chips are down?

EFFECTIVELY MANAGING AN ORGANIZED MAINTENANCE PROGRAM

The effective officer wants a good maintenance program. He educates himself about the equipment and about maintenance procedures, and he also does the following to be effective as a manager.

Most importantly, the officer must train and train his people. He cannot assume that they will learn by themselves or that the service has sent them to a school. Training in the performance of each maintenance action may well be a weak point in the unit because of the rapid turnover of personnel and the prevalent assumption that low-level tasks are so simple anyone can do them. In addition to having technical manuals on hand, units should use the maintenance procedures as lesson plans. They can be used to teach the language, the tools, the systems.

The officer must read the procedures and reread them often. He must do what they say, do it carefully, and require others on the team to do likewise.

Tour spaces often to look, listen, and feel.

Hold a planning session at least weekly with the troops to organize the work to be done around the questions When? Who? What tools? What permissions? What precautions? And so on. Coordinate training and maintenance.

Talk to his people often, especially as they work. Convince them he really cares about what they are doing and how well their gear works. Find out what he can do to help. For example, the officer can see that supply obtains that tool they need or get the executive officer to schedule the item to be down for a day.

Hold working-level inspections with his senior enlisted supervisors and the technicians. Look for problems instead of waiting for the boss or the CO to come and find the problems for him. The problems are the officer's problems,

and he is supposed to find them. Inspect himself the same way he will be inspected by the formal inspection team.

Keep his seniors informed. Tell them in routine reports, memos, or phone calls what is wrong and what help will be needed to set it right. The officer cannot assume they do not need or want to know.

Be sure he and his people look for early signs of failure. A parameter that is degraded but still "in spec" may be the first sign of failure.

Have his people test the gear that does not undergo formal tests. Just running it and noting its behavior, like road testing a car, is a great test.

Make sure the deficiencies are recorded and subsequently fixed. Corrective maintenance requires planning, training, preparation, and supervision. Most often neglected in this regard are planning and training.

Critique failure to find out why it occurred and determine what can be done to prevent recurrence. All too often failures are accepted as inevitable or "just accidents." The officer should assume all failures are preventable and do everything he can to prevent them.

Use the "first-team concept"; that is, use the best people available to look for trouble and teach the others. This approach is counter to a great deal of conventional wisdom that calls for the most junior and inexperienced people to do everything they might be able to do, even though they have not been trained and lack the maturity to recognize the pitfalls. The first-team concept requires the officer to start at the top and work down, instead of the reverse, to make the unit's watch and work assignment. A few senior enlisted personnel prefer assignments to be made from the bottom up because, if the seniors are clever, the unit will run out of important jobs before they are tasked, and then they can "hang out" in the senior enlisted mess and "let the junior people get some experience."

Get the day started early by making sure the

senior enlisted people have given the work assignments at the beginning of the day and that all of the necessary preparations have been made.

Be particularly concerned about the maintenance actions that are keyed to an event such as getting underway. These have frequently been neglected because they are not well managed by some systems. One good way to keep track of them is to post a list of the actions required under a heading for each event that calls for maintenance.

Be enthusiastic, because your enthusiasm is so very important. Because people want to believe their work is important, the officer should be careful to convince them he believes it is. They know by where he goes and what he does what his priorities are. He must show them he cares!

Aggressively use proper procedures to request changes to get errors corrected.

Look ahead for the difficult maintenance actions and make plans early to incorporate them.

Look for the procedures that appear as though they have not been used before. (Usually they are the white pages in a deck of various shades of brown.)

Determine the last time actions were deferred, why, and what is being done to complete them.

LEADING WITH A POSITIVE TONE AND GUARDING AGAINST PITFALLS

Enthusiasm, pride in being the best, and confidence in his personnel are cornerstones of a good leader, but good leadership does not include being naive about the common pitfalls. A truly effective leader actively leads his people away from common errors.

Some of the pitfalls discussed here are, of course, the consequences of not doing what was recommended in the previous section. However, these points are important enough to deserve emphasis.

Stressing the importance of preventive maintenance to personnel. While fixing things is often exciting and rewarding, preventive maintenance is often hard and seldom any fun. It is best to assume the officer's input is needed to help personnel believe their work is important. This must be done so that:

Corporal Smith won't use pliers to turn a nut because he forgot to bring the right wrench.

Seaman Jones won't skip a maintenance step because he is in a hurry.

PO3 Philips won't skip a step because he can't figure out what the words in the procedure mean and he is afraid to ask.

Private Daly won't report the change in the results because the change might be normal and he doesn't want to look stupid.

Maintenance training pitfalls. Not planning the training to meet the current needs of the people in the unit but picking formal training subjects from a list made up to meet the requirements of an administrative inspection produces personnel who are unable to perform all of their duties well.

Another pitfall is not using hands-on training for teaching maintenance tasks. When "how to" training is done in a classroom or by a teacher who demonstrates the task and does not let the students practice it until each one can do it correctly, training suffers.

Assuming that personnel already know is a common error. One of the worst ways to find out if a person knows how to perform a task is to ask him. How can sailors and Marines not be motivated to answer affirmatively?

Assuming the job is so easy that training is not necessary or assigning instructor duties to the most junior personnel instead of the best teacher results in personnel who are unprepared. Not holding the chief petty officers and staff noncommissioned officers responsible for the training of their people, and leaving training completely up to petty officers and noncommissioned officers, can have the same results.

Not supervising people who have just learned how to do a job, and leaving a new person to his own devices, invites trouble. How many people who are instructed to call if they have any trouble will readily admit it if they are having trouble?

Maintenance procedures are not without errors. Many errors in maintenance procedures go unreported for years. An effective preventive maintenance program includes an active search for errors and aggressive submission of requests for correction (feedback).

Common mistakes in maintenance programs. The effective officer is on his guard for the following pitfalls in maintenance programs.

When the wrong person decides that skipping a step or modifying a procedure or accepting a poor situation is good enough, he may be setting the stage for failure. *Remember that, in war, in emergency, and in competition, the very best is barely good enough.* The officer should seek wise counsel before accepting a recommendation to stop shy of the mark because of "good enough."

The officer cannot assume that personnel will go to the trouble of getting the right tools and setting the right plant conditions, negotiating the scheduling, etc. All too often the not-so-hot trooper will quit at the first resistance to progress.

Deferring maintenance because it is difficult to schedule is a common mistake. Some maintenance is very hard to schedule because it affects the whole unit in significant ways (for example, cleaning major electrical distribution panels in ships). The officer needs to be farsighted and aggressive to get things scheduled.

The officer should be very curious about equipment that fails often. It is easy, when the maintenance man fixes the gear over and over, to get used to that way of doing things. Discovering that "normal" may be wrong is very difficult.

While it is good for new people and junior people to learn to do the maintenance, it is a serious mistake to send them off to check on the readiness of equipment without supervision. The more experienced personnel will be much more sensitive to small and early indications of failure. The officer should require effective amounts of supervision for every task his unit performs.

DISCIPLINED EXECUTION IS THE KEY

Disciplined execution is the opposite of doing the job in a sloppy and careless manner. It is doing things exactly as planned without cutting corners or skipping steps. It is putting in the extra effort to make sure the job comes out right.

All the training, planning, and preparations are for naught if a sloppy approach is taken when the job is done. There are often excuses—not enough time, too tired, can't get the right parts or tools—but sometimes sloppiness is pure laziness. At other times sloppiness results from a lack of appreciation for the importance of the task at hand. Doing things right the first time is easier in the long run, though doing things in a sloppy way is often considered a convenient short cut. The troops may prefer the short cuts unless the officer instills in them a sense of responsibility and duty to do things well.

A disciplined execution is one that is deliberate, accurate, thorough, and in accordance with plans and procedures. It is one that receives the effort and the time it deserves. It is one that has been supervised and double-checked to make sure errors have not been made.

The officer who has trained himself, trained his people, led his people in planning and preparation, and helped them achieve disciplined execution will reach specific goals for improved material readiness and will enjoy the satisfaction of having equipment perform well when it counts the most.

Admiral Moorer, in talking about maintenance, notes:

The Navy has always published a complete set of maintenance booklets for equipment. When a new system is introduced into the Navy, these instructions are based on the experience that has been had so far, with the test program and the development program. As time goes on and problems crop up, changes have to be introduced, and these changes are sequentially numbered.

These changes, particularly if they involve safety of any kind, must be installed immediately. And anyone who has discovered a weakness or a problem in a piece of equipment must see that it is immediately broadcast to all the people who have the equipment so they can be on the lookout for it even before the material people disseminate the correction to it. An officer in charge of maintenance must keep very close tabs on these changes, make certain he keeps up with the experience others are having, and understand what he has to do to correct the deficiency in the equipment so he does not encounter the trouble they did. Conversely, if the equipment he is responsible for has the trouble, he has to pass along the information right away.

Another aspect of equipment maintenance is the necessity of keeping the maintenance facilities neat and orderly. You know, I can look at an outfit and I can tell you how proficient and effective it is just on the basis of how it looks. Now I'll tell you, I fly frequently to Atlanta, and there's one airline that goes down there to Georgia. You get down there and you taxi up to the gate, they call it, and all the baggage carts are painted just like they're brand new, the men are in clean, snappy coveralls, and the aircraft is just spotless. There's another airline that has just as many flights, but you get down there and the baggage carts are about to fall apart and the planes don't look very well, and sometimes I ride these planes because of the time schedule and I want to come on home, but one time I had two of them run together while they were taxiing, another time I had one get out on the runway and the radio did not work and they had to come back, had to get off and get on another airplane, and several times they never arrived at all. But the facts are

that there's just a general atmosphere of lackadaisical approach to the job and it's not neat and it's not clean and they're not smart looking, so in the maintenance business you'll find that the effectiveness of it is determined to a large degree by whether the people put the tools away and can keep everything in shipshape form. It's a form of discipline that's very important.

The maintenance officer should check on the experience and qualifications of his maintenance people to see if they have been to the proper schools. If they have not, he should arrange to send them to the school for their specialty.

The maintenance officer should also develop "usage figures," by determining how often he uses a particular spare and why. With these figures, he can equip his unit with the spare parts it requires in order to be able to function. When a ship gets to the Indian Ocean, it is difficult for the officer to get a spare part flown out of, say, Paterson, New Jersey, so he must have the necessary parts on hand. The extreme case is the submarine, which leaves Norfolk and never surfaces for 60 days, until it gets back. It must have 60 days of spare parts, and the maintenance officer must see that it does. If a piece of *urgently needed* equipment fails and the people assigned to it are unable to repair it and the officer is the only one around who can repair it, he should repair it. But these are the only circumstances in which an officer should do a job that belongs to a subordinate. If the regular maintenance people are struggling with a piece of equipment and are unable to fix it, then the officer's job is to fix the personnel, not the equipment.

In the Navy, exceptional electronic petty officers are often promoted to officers—six months previously they had been repairing equipment and now they are officers. Their tendency is to get "itchy fingers" and want to get in there and do it. As a matter of course, however, their responsibility is primarily to ensure that the people who are supposed to fix it know how to fix it.

The best training comes from the people with experience, experienced people who can take under their wing the others. For instance, I made a cruise to the Mediterranean one time on an aircraft carrier and we only had one first-class radarman. That was right after the war and everybody left, and so this one radarman, one first-class man, had to maintain all those radars, and he did it just by holding school when he wasn't working on the radar. By the time we got about halfway through that cruise, it was a six-month cruise, everyone could do the job. But that was expedient, where you didn't have any other. That's not the way to do it as a matter of practice, but if you get just one good person who understands, he can teach others.

A leader needs to be able to assume that everything is okay unless he is advised otherwise, and he should inform his staff that that is how he operates. The leader needs to be informed about those things that are in trouble and cannot be fixed right away, but he need not know about things that will be fixed by the next day.

Admiral Holloway points out:

It is essential that officers be familiar with equipment capabilities, because, although the enlisted people are responsible for maintaining equipment and repairing it, officers must know enough about the equipment to determine the accuracy of their people's status reports on it. When an individual reports to the officer that a repair cannot be done or will take

24 or 48 hours or a week, the officer must be able to tell whether that sailor himself knows his business or is just trying to cover up for his own shortcomings. When, on the night before a ship is supposed to get underway, the chief engineer on watch comes up and tells his senior the ship has a feed pump out and that will delay getting underway for 48 hours, the officer in charge must be able to determine if the report is true or is being exaggerated.

Admiral Holloway believes strongly that officers must understand their equipment and the principles of its operation, as well as how it is maintained and whether it can be repaired, although they need not know how to repair it.

When I was Chief of Naval Operations, we established what was known as the Senior Officers Material Maintenance Course in Idaho. This was a school that all commanders were to go to before reporting to their command, and by this I mean ship commanders, ship unit commanders, unit fleet commanders, so that they would understand the equipment with which they were dealing on the ships and be able to handle the problems of knowing what command actions to take to ensure the material readiness of their command, be it a ship, a task force, or a fleet. The importance of the decision to establish this school and conduct this course was all brought home to me in one incident that occurred when I was on the West Coast. I happened to be walking through an oiler, a fleet oiler, probably the ship was 35 to 40 years old, and I was in the engineering spaces and paused, and an old chief came up to me and there were tears in his eyes and he said, "Admiral, I want to thank you for that course you have that sends all the senior officers through." I asked why, and he said that in the past he would get a new skipper every year, and they knew nothing about ships—a lot of them were aviators—but they were there to learn about ships. The chief said, "I would tell them that this 35-year-old bucket had a leaky header or a feed pump had gone out, and they'd say, 'Get it fixed. Get it fixed in an hour.' I couldn't get it fixed in an hour, and I'd go back down, tell this to my kids down in the gang, and what did they do? They went over the hill because they knew they couldn't fix it and what was the point of working on it?" He said that recently this last skipper came aboard and he was a product of this Material School. "I had a severe engineering casualty," the chief said, "and instead of saying 'Get it fixed so I can get underway tomorrow,' he said, 'Chief, let me come down and take a look at it.' We went down there, 'We have a problem'—he didn't say *you* got a problem, *we* got a problem—'What can I do to help? If I go up to the local Navy Yard, do you think we can get it?' and instead of just getting demands that I couldn't fulfill, I got cooperation and support." The chief said that the morale in this ship's engineering gang had turned around totally, and the reason it had is because he had a skipper who understood and didn't cover up for his ignorance by being brutally insensitive.

In discussing an officer's knowledge of the equipment in his unit, Admiral de Cazanove expressed his belief that

the officer must know the principles of operation, though not necessarily the details, of the equipment under his command. Leave the screwdriver to the man trained for the screwdriver, first of all, because he knows much better than you the screwdriver, and also because you have other things to do. If you spend your time doing what you are not meant for, you have less time to do what you are

meant for. It is easy to make a job out of the level underneath you, because you used to do it and you are probably much better able to do it, which in turn resulted in your promotion. However, while you should be striving to learn the higher-level job, you should not abandon those now at the lower levels, and you probably have the ability to help them, and we must remember that we are still all working for the same cause.

We have both technical and generalist leaders, and the main chief (seniormost officer) must be the generalist type, which covers all aspects, including the technical aspect, of the mission. You cannot do anything without the technical people, but by themselves the technical people cannot run the show. While some ships may be commanded by the "technical" person, groups of ships or a squadron in the Navy can only really be commanded by the generalist. This does not mean that one group is less than the other, just that they have different training and experience, and the group commander must have a broad view of both his responsibilities and the mission to be accomplished. It may be seen that becoming an outstanding generalist is more difficult to achieve than becoming outstanding in technical proficiency.

MCPON Sanders: *Those who are in charge of an area that has any type of equipment, while not expected to be professional repairers or operators of that equipment, should know how and where it is used as well as knowing the maintenance history of the item. This is important so that the seniors will know what their subordinates are talking about, when discussing problem areas, as well as being knowledgeable about information they have to pass up the chain of command.*

Chapter 9 Bibliography

1. Aitken, Douglas B. "Professionalism: What That Overworked Term Means to Me." *Combat Crew*, June 1983, pp. 5–6.
2. Buell, Thomas B. "The Education of a Warrior." *Proceedings*, Oct. 1983, pp. 41–45.
3. Byron, John L. "Sea Power: The Global Navy." *Proceedings*, Jan. 1984, pp. 30–33.
4. Calvert, James. *The Naval Profession*. New York: McGraw-Hill, 1971. Chap. 6 reprinted in *Class of 1987: Fundamentals of Naval Leadership*. Annapolis: U.S. Naval Academy, 1983.
5. Chartrand, Joseph. "Rainy Day Warriors." *Proceedings*, Oct. 1983, pp. 134–55.
6. Chesarek, F. J. "New Techniques for Managing Men and Material." *Army*, Oct. 1967, p. 51.
7. Cooper, Leonard. *Many Roads to Moscow.* New York: Coward-McCann, 1968.
8. Dean, Merrell E. "Managerial Styles." *Air University Review*, Mar.–Apr. 1976, pp. 41–46.
9. Foord, Edward. *Napoleon's Russian Campaign of 1812*. London: Hutchinson, 1914.
10. Fowler, George O. "Resource Management and Its Implications for Forces Afloat." *Naval War College Review*, Oct. 1963, pp. 19–36.
11. Freidin, Seymour, and Richardson, William, eds. *The Fatal Decisions*. New York: William Sloane, 1956.
12. "GAO to Services: Use Resources Better." *Air Force Times*, 10 May 1982, p. 8.
13. Goodenough, Simon. *Tactical Genius in Battle*. Oxford: Phaidon Press, 1979.
14. "Harris Survey: Public Backs Bucher." *Air Force Times*, 19 Feb. 1969, p. 13.
15. Hausch, John. "What If the Pueblo Had Sailed on at Full Speed?" *Data*, 14 Mar. 1969, pp. 13–15.
16. "Iran Rescue Attempt." *Air Force Times*, 12 May 1980, pp. 1, 4.
17. Keegan, John. *The Face of Battle*. New York: Viking Press, 1976.
18. Laur, Joseph M. "Tactical Training, Tactical Testing." *Proceedings*, Oct. 1983, p. 126.
19. Leader, Charles A. "The Talent for Judgement." *Proceedings*, Oct. 1983, pp. 49–53.
20. Liddell Hart, Basil Henry. *Strategy*. New York: New American Library, 1974.
21. Lupfer, Timothy T. *The Dynamics of Doctrine: The Changes in German Tactical Doctrine during the First World War*. Fort Leavenworth, Kans.: Combat Studies Institute, 1981.
22. Mack, William P. "Education and Professionalism." *Proceedings*, Oct. 1983, pp. 40–47.
23. Meyer, John C. "Better Resource Management." *Air Force Comptroller*, Oct. 1972, back cover.
24. Peet, Raymond E. "As I Recall . . . Operating with the Little Beaver Squadron." *Proceedings*, Jan. 1984, pp. 119–20.
25. Schemmer, Benjamin F. "Presidential Courage and the April 1980 Iranian Rescue Mission." *Armed Forces Journal International*, May 1981, pp. 60–62.
26. Sims, Robert G. "Leadership and Management: A Conceptual Model with Definitions." *Air Force Journal of Logistics*, Spring 1982, pp. 22–24.
27. Wheeler, James J. "Professionalism: Where Does It Begin? Where Does It End?" *U.S. Army Aviation Digest*, Jan. 1983, pp. 18–19.
28. Wilson, Paul E. "Leadership: Rx for Improvement." *Marine Corps Gazette*, Feb. 1984, pp. 44–47.

10

Final Considerations for Naval Officers

Introduction

Thoughts on the Career of a Naval Officer

I guess foremost on my mind after having a full career in Navy is to say that there is simply no career that one could ask for that is more satisfying than the Naval Service. Now that's going to sound hollow to a lot of midshipmen or ensigns or junior officers—What the heck, he was CNO, why wouldn't it look good to him? But remember that that's a reflection of the whole career put together and the kinds of people you associate with, the experiences you have, the demands that are placed upon you, the satisfaction that you get for service to your country.

That doesn't come in the first year or second or third year. The first few years in the Navy are tough. I think they're tough on enlisted people, I think they're tough on officers. It's a toughness brought about by the entire lifestyle, and not being particularly prepared for it. You don't anticipate very well what shipboard life is like. It's usually the time when you fall in love and get married, and the first thing you know you're overseas and your spouse is back home and you've got a kid with a runny nose, and those are new experiences that you just aren't adjusted to. It takes time to adjust to that. Most people get over that readjustment very, very well.

Once you pass that, you get that real sense of belonging. That's the great strength in the Navy, and I'm sure it's true in the other armed services, where you have that real feeling that you're doing something for your country, you're doing something of a service nature that only occurs in a few careers. A naval career is one of those, and the longer you stay in, the more those experiences build on themselves and reinforce the positive aspects of a naval career to the degree that one has a positive attitude about the Navy and works hard at it, gets satisfaction out of serving. You can be sure that their whole view about that service is going to be self-reinforcing, with their families, with themselves, with their shipmates, which is not to say that there aren't plenty of tough times in the service. I don't think I would have stayed in if it wasn't tough. I don't think your good people would stick around if it wasn't tough, they would go find something else to do.

If you look at the world situation today . . . I will predict for anyone who is a midshipman presently or a junior officer, you're going to live through a lifetime, in all probability, that's loaded with very difficult times for the United States. The world's in a significant transition between North, South, East, and West, rich and poor, the haves and have nots, interspersed with ideological conflicts between socialism and Marxism and capitalism and free enterprise. I don't see any way in which the United States is going to avoid carrying the burden of responsibility of ensuring that the world stays reasonably stable and hopefully out of war.

If there is a war, we're going to be in it. So the profession itself is going to have plenty of challenges placed before the Naval Service, and the individual will have all the opportunity he would ever want to accept challenges, to do something great for somebody else, his country. So I really mean it when I say that there is no finer career, and I don't believe you'll find anyone who has stayed in for 20 years or more who will say much different than that. You'll even talk to people who will have 3 or 4 years of service, who have been out for a while, and ask them about their new careers and their lifestyle, and they'll say, "Gee, but do you know, the thing that I'll never forget are the few years that I spent in the service." So what I'd like to leave with aspiring young naval officers is that the opportunities abound in the Navy. One can find one's niche in several different places. I think you could find a successful, enjoyable career of self-satisfaction, and achievement in a variety of

ways, because it's a career filled with such a variety of expectations and demands.

There's no reason for an individual to serve this great country of ours without sensing that service on a day-to-day basis in a self-fulfilling way wearing the naval uniform. If one isn't getting that out of it, one's missing something, and one has to find out what it is that one is missing, because the opportunities are there. It's a life filled with positive experiences, surrounded by achievers who are determined to do the best they can to make this a great country and a great Navy, and everyone has a place in it, and if you can wear a naval uniform, you're lucky and you're probably very happy.

Admiral Thomas Hayward

91. Building a Military-Civilian Team

As the nature of naval warfare has changed significantly over the last 200 years, the Navy and Marine Corps have found themselves dependent on highly sophisticated technology. This dependence on technology necessitates a stronger relationship between the military and the civilian communities. In order to become fully functional at a performing level, a naval officer requires roughly 20 years of development. Scientists and engineers, in order to become fully proficient and reach the top of their disciplines, also require roughly 20 years. The 30-year career of a naval officer cannot be stretched to the 40 years required to make him both a competent, operationally oriented naval officer and an intellectually competent scientist. A naval officer has the capability to be both, but if the needs of the service demand two sets of skills with 20-year time frames for proficiency in each, it is obvious that in order to achieve the objectives of the service, a team of naval leaders and civilian scientists and engineers must be formed. Secretary Webb observed that, in the modern Naval Service,

officers can expect to work side by side
with civilians on occasion. These civilians

are generally very mission oriented. They are for the most part dedicated people who consider themselves a part of the service. Some civilians are archives, in a way, because in most cases they have remained in one place longer than the military people and they have a sense of history of the office; this makes them good people to go to when it is necessary to look at past actions.

It is important for the military leader who interacts with civilians to understand the differences between his own culture and the civilian culture. The military officer's culture is formed around execution. He is part of a process that involves centralized decision making relative to his career. His development is based on experience he gains through varied job assignments that have a common pattern. He competes for rank, not for jobs.

All naval officers go through somewhat similar education and training. Thus, when a group of naval officers meet, not only are a high percentage of them participating in a "class" reunion, but they can also share "sea stories" from a common set of experiences. They are a homogeneous group of people with a common point of origin, a common set of experiences, and a career focus toward execution. The visible rank on their uniforms and their sworn obedience to lawful orders from seniors make these officers and their service highly efficient. Efficiency is vital for people who serve in the face of danger, where time is a critical factor in making life-and-death decisions.

On the other hand, the civilians who are a part of the Navy and Marine Corps team are culturally a heterogeneous group, reflecting their many different backgrounds. In a group of 20 civilians, probably no 2 of them would come from the same university. Their development is self-directed rather than centrally managed. They compete for jobs, not for rank.

Civilians develop along narrow lines of professional specialization, such as a specific science or field of engineering. They do not get broad exposure to the Navy or the Marine Corps, as the officer does. The average naval officer changes jobs ten times before making flag or general officer rank. The average civilian only makes one and a half career moves in his life. The greatest strength of civilians is their ability to look at the various angles of a problem. They are taught as scientists and engineers to ask "Why?" whereas naval officers are taught in a disciplined process to ask "What?"

The great weakness of civilians is their tendency to "worry" a question forever, and therefore the execution drive of the uniformed military must impact on the decision-making process. The great weakness of the uniformed side lies in the power in rank, which requires officers to obey orders from a senior when in fact, on a technical question, the senior person may not know the correct answer. When there is a potential breach of discipline, the service requires that an order be executed without argument. Therefore, the ability of the civilian component of an organization to raise questions without breaching discipline is an effective complement to the execution efficiency of the uniformed military.

It is also important to understand management in general and to know where power lies when dealing with civilians. In an organization involved in performing unobservable tasks, in intellectual processes (such as trying to find a solution to a technical problem), power is in the mind of the person who understands the problem, not in the rank of the person who may be in charge. The formal authority may well be in the rank of the person, but the power to get things done resides in the person who understands how to do them. A strong military-civilian team takes the knowledge base of the naval officer, expands it through the specialized knowledge and experience of the civilian, and combines it with the formal authority of the naval officer to form an effective execution-oriented team that is capable of considering a technical question thoroughly, coming to a correct conclusion, and seeing that the solution is put to efficient use. Failure to build this team results in an ineffective organization, because the power of knowledge is not effectively coupled with formal authority to be applied to the needs of the command.

Teams made up of military people and civilians have long contributed to the strength of the Naval Service, particularly in research and development centers, where naval officers, who are in command of the centers, and scientists and engineers, who make up the bulk of the work force, work so well together. This cooperation extends throughout the material acquisition area in the Navy and the Marine Corps, where intellectual disciplines and the need for effective management and execution are combined in a powerful team.

The leader of both military and civilian members of government is the President. Civilians and military personnel view the President of the United States in different ways, according to Admiral Moorer:

> I think what is not realized by the public and even by the military people themselves is that the civilians in the government are "appointed" to high places in the Cabinet and elsewhere in the government. They look on the President as the leader of their political party. That's the way they deal with it all the time. The military people look on the President as set by the Constitution as the Commander in Chief. There's a big difference in looking on someone as Commander in Chief and someone as a leader of a political party, which is the way they generally deal with a President, no matter who he is.

> If the military were to have two loyalties, a military loyalty and a political loyalty, there would be all kinds of caucuses going on, and in the military, only one man can make a decision; decisions cannot be made by a committee. A leader cannot

take a vote in the executive pyramid system, he must make his own decision and tell his people why he is making it. For this reason, the military rule that forbids personnel from getting involved in politics is a necessary and a good rule.

MCPON Sanders: *The Navy of the future is going to see more and more military and civilians working side by side. My own experience has been one of learning to understand that the regulations and requirements under which civilians operate are significantly different than those governing military personnel. A resourceful military leader will make it a point of learning the special regulations under which civilians work, including the understanding that, while a military leader may give time off to deserving personnel to take care of a personal need, you cannot give a civilian that same time off without charging that time to his leave statement. It is important that we build a good, hard-working team, but you have to understand the differences before you can put the two groups together and make them work as a team.*

92. The Naval and Marine Corps Reserve

The all-volunteer force makes resource managers of all officers. As people are one key asset the Naval Service cannot maximize as to quantity and quality, to succeed in its mission, the service must maximize effectiveness for a given cost or minimize cost for a given effectiveness. In these days of building and sustaining ever-more-complex weapons systems and platforms, officers frequently find themselves working with civilian employees and reservists, and they must work with them—and with all members of the Navy and Marine Corps team—with pride and professionalism. A naval officer knows his mission cannot be completed without the commitment of his entire command, no matter where its members fit into the organizational matrix. Admiral Larson points out that

> we are one Navy here, the regulars and the reserves, and our country can't afford the resources necessary to have active duty forces of sufficient size to react to any contingency, so we have to have the capability to mobilize, to augment from our reserve forces, in order to expand rapidly in case of a contingency, national emergency, or even in time of war. The best way to do this is to have trained people, people who are involved, people who are familiar with our latest equipment, and with our goals and objectives. We do this by bringing good people into the Navy, by training them, and by encouraging those who do depart the Navy to stay active and to stay in that reserve area and to continue to train so that we can use them. I think, also, if you want to look at another dimension, I think politically it is very good for us to have people scattered throughout the country who are drilling reservists, who understand the Navy and understand the Navy's mission, so that in Kansas City, Missouri, or in Omaha, Nebraska, if someone asks questions about the Navy, you've got a spokesman there, someone who can explain to the taxpayers the need for a Navy and what the Navy provides to the country. This is a communication that we owe to the taxpayers, and these people can be very, very helpful in that area.

The mission of the Naval Reserve and the Marine Corps Reserve is to be trained and ready for mobilization, ready to be a part of the Naval Service that wins the war at sea or on land. The Reserve is an experienced arm of the service and is essential to the service's mission. It constitutes a key force in the resources available to fleet and Marine unit commanders who must execute war plans. Successful execution of these plans depends on the intelligence, skill, and best efforts of everyone on the Navy and Marine Corps team.

The Naval and Marine Corps Reserve is essential. Its ships, infantry, aircraft, squadrons, combat support, and service support organizations and augmenting personnel are vital, accounted-for elements of the national maritime strategy. Maritime patrol aircraft provide squadrons of trained crews and aircraft to counter the submarine threat; frigates, along with key mine warfare and auxiliary ships, are part of the Naval Reserve force. A number of complete carrier tactical air wings are presently embarked on a far-ranging modernization program. A "horizontal integration" policy assures the availability of fleet-compatible aircraft that are deployable aboard the U.S. fleet's mighty carriers wherever they are needed. Combat and combat support units provided by the Naval Reserve (NR) include naval construction battalions, cargo-handling battalions, inshore undersea warfare units, special boat units, and naval control of shipping units, as well as cryptological, intelligence, supply, medical, and other staff organizations.

The Marine Corps Reserve (MCR) is charged with the responsibility of providing rapid expansion of the force in war or national emergency. It has a mobilization capability second to none among the services; Marine Reserve forces can be quickly integrated into a total war effort. Provisions have been made to augment or reinforce active commands with everything from individual combat or support units to an entire Reserve Marine Air Ground Task Force. In a maximum effort, the Reserve can provide almost 33 percent of the manpower and a broad range of combat assets, including 100 percent of the civil affairs capability, 67 percent of force reconnaissance assets, 40 percent of the tasks, 33 percent of the heavy artillery, 33 percent of the anti-aircraft missile capability, and 30 percent of the light-attack aviation.

The Naval Reserve is *Navy*. The Selected Reserve has thousands of full-time Training and Administration Reserve (or TAR) officers and enlisted personnel. The balance are Navy men and women who find time in their civilian work or school schedules to drill two days each month and take active duty training two weeks every year. Many of the commissioned or "hardware" units put in 100 days or more every fiscal year through a combination of additional training drill periods or active-duty-for-training tours. Selected Naval Reservists are proud to contribute to meeting the challenge of the Navy mission.

As the Naval Reserve is Navy, the MCR is *Marine*. The wealth and depth of experience and expertise in the Reserve are impressive. The Marine Corps has developed a program to take advantage of skills developed in the business world. Mobilization training units (composed of officers and noncommissioned officers) in the Individual Ready Reserve (IRR) focus their expertise on special projects for operational sponsors throughout the United States. The technical credentials and completed projects of these Marines are catalogued for future reference.

All MCR units are closely tied to their active-duty counterparts in contingency planning. On the total force equipment side, the reservist modernization and structure growth parallels that of the active forces. The MCR receives the latest major new ground and air support equipments, as well as weapons systems, which are being introduced into the Marine Corps inventory. Training cements the relationship between active-duty Marines and reservists and transforms the individual Marine and his unit into "combat power." Tens of thousands of reservists are currently training in exercises around the world. The Marine Corps has substantial capability in its Reserve. Marrying their civilian pursuits with the needs of the service, these "civilian Marines" are a great source of pride to the service in peacetime, and if they are called on, they will be an indispensable source of strength for the national defense as part of the Marine Corps total force.

The Naval and Marine Corps Reserve is largely experienced. Most officers will have completed at least four years on active duty prior to affiliating with the Reserve; most petty officers and noncommissioned officers will have completed two years. A small but growing percentage will have no prior service, but will have been recruited through the Sea, Air Mariner (SAM) program or the Selected Marine Corps Reserve (SMCR). Many will start out their careers with enthusiasm; it is up to their leaders to keep them motivated. The opportunity to be part of a unit in which meaningful missions are accomplished, modern equipment is used, and goals are attainable is an incentive for people to join and stay in the Reserve. Participation and morale are inextricably linked within the Naval and Marine Corps Reserve. A very valuable by-product of the participation in training periods is the experience gained, often on state-of-the-art equipment. In mutual support of this type, personnel receive training, and the service benefits from having access to trained personnel.

93. The Junior Officer's Security Responsibilities

Myriad responsibilities are assigned to military personnel, but few are more critical, in the final analysis, than information and personnel security. History has demonstrated that, to be successful in fighting wars, a force must have knowledge of its opponent. Faulty information and lack of personnel security on one side provides the other side with an advantage in preparing for and executing the engagement.

Security procedures do not prevent spying, or even the flow of information to hostile governments. They do, however, significantly hamper intelligence gathering and halt the disclosure of classified information deemed critical to our national security. In an open society such as ours, a great deal of political, technological, and military information is naturally available to all. However, information vital to our defense cannot be made available to hostile countries if we are to protect our way of life. Information security procedures are designed to prevent the unauthorized disclosure of classified information found in publications, charts, pictures, blueprints, and elsewhere.

In a world plagued by terrorism, the personal safety of the officer and his subordinates must always be of great concern. Personnel security measures help minimize individual exposure to and risk from terrorist organizations.

INFORMATION SECURITY

The information security procedures currently in use were designed in response to the lessons of history. Almost every international event in recent years has been influenced by espionage. Therefore, it is necessary to take precautions to minimize espionage and its adverse effect on our national security. The threat of espionage cannot be overstated and should never be underestimated. Incalculable damage to the nation has been done in recent years by Americans who gave military secrets to other countries. The act of selling satellite secrets to a potential enemy is dramatically portrayed in the film *Falcon and the Snowman*. A CIA watch officer also sold satellite information to a foreign country. Another CIA official was found guilty in 1980 of disclosing to the same country the extent of our knowledge about its military equipment. One American passed highly classified material to this same country during his naval service. Following his retirement, he recruited family and friends to assist him in continuing his espionage activities. These are just a few recent espionage activities. How many individuals engaged in espionage have not been caught? How much highly sensitive information vital to our national defense is disclosed today to foreign governments?

In addition to deliberate espionage such as that noted above, presumed unimportant bits of information are disclosed inadvertently or otherwise at social gatherings, on the telephone, via the wastebasket, etc. This also can do significant damage to the nation. Also, classified information is occasionally "leaked" to the media by individuals whose motives are not usually connected with espionage. Because ours is an open society, this information invariably reaches our enemies and aids them in determining our capabilities and intentions.

Rigorous information security procedures, including strict accountability, control, and dissemination procedures, significantly hinder the collection efforts of hostile foreign intelligence agencies and help preclude the intentional disclosure of classified information. In addition, all military personnel are required to report all contacts with individuals who attempt to acquire classified information through casual conversation or other means. This requirement not only helps our counterintelligence efforts, it also protects our military personnel from the clever recruitment techniques of foreign espionage services.

For example, one nation's foreign agents have a standing order to search for Americans having access to classified information or holding key government positions who have exploitable weaknesses. Once these individuals are identified, these foreign agents attempt to exploit the greed, sexual preferences, psychological instability, or ideological views of these individuals. It has been estimated that one potential enemy country successfully recruits an average of one individual each year in the CIA alone.

The key to minimizing inadvertent disclosures is for all personnel handling classified material to be keenly aware of security. Although the commanding officer, through his security manager, is responsible for the effectiveness of information security procedures and security education within the command, it is imperative that each individual actively participate in the safeguarding of classified material. Determining the capabilities of an opponent is somewhat analogous to deciphering a picture puzzle of unknown size. The solution is obviously facilitated by accumulating as many pieces as possible. Our enemies can obtain a large number of unclassified pieces simply by scrutinizing information readily available in our open society. The picture cannot be understood, however, until some classified clues are garnered. Consequently, every unauthorized disclosure of classified information, regardless of its scope or apparent importance, aids our enemies in formulating a better evaluation of our capabilities and intentions. Therefore, our national security is eventually threatened by all deviations from established security regulations by individuals within our military organization.

PERSONNEL SECURITY

Certain risks have always been associated with the military profession. In recent years, however, terrorism has become a viable threat to all military personnel. Terrorists in pursuit of their objectives have increasingly targeted military personnel, as, for example, in the bombing of the Marine barracks in Lebanon in 1983 and the unprovoked murder of a petty officer traveling on a commercial airliner in 1985. American citizens and interests are today the prime target of terrorists throughout the world. Although there is no guaranteed method of averting terrorist violence, certain precautions can reduce an individual's vulnerability. The majority of the victims in past terrorism incidents became targets because they failed to follow even the most basic personal security precautions. In some documented cases, individuals were targeted only because more attractive potential targets utilized measures that eliminated them from consideration. Terrorists usually prefer to attack the weakest target with the most desired impact. Conscientious adherence to reasonable personal security measures will reduce an individual's chances of being selected as the next victim. General Rice provided an overview:

A study titled "Terrorism: The Warfare of the '80s" was recently released to the

Joint Chiefs. Terrorism is a form of warfare, and service personnel are deeply involved in it whether they like it or not. The United States, its ideals, and its citizens are under attack, and there is no clear-cut solution to terrorism for the individual serviceperson or the individual American.

Obviously, certain things, such as installation of bigger fences and electric fences and more guards, are being done to protect U.S. resources, but wherever Americans travel, wherever they're exposed, they are a potential target. No one knows when it might happen to them, so everyone must be aware of the threat and what self-protective measures can be taken to lessen the threat against the individual. Good judgment and common sense are called for. They are manifested in a variety of ways. For example, I made a change in routine to lessen my chances of being a target for terrorism. I just returned from a trip a couple of months ago to Central America; part of that time I was in the Mideast, and I just got back from Korea last week, so life goes on, and if it doesn't, then the terrorists are winning. But there are some basic, common-sense things that you do. As an example, I used to carry a beautiful camouflaged hang-up bag with the big eagle globe, an anchor on it, and my name emblazoned, Major General Rice. I am very proud to be a major general of the United States Marine Corps, but it's kind of dumb because, obviously, I was carrying a big neon sign around with me to identify myself as a major general of the United States Marine Corps. So I don't carry my camouflaged bag. I now have a gray nondescript hang-up bag like thousands of other people have. It's a small point, but it's the kind of thing that you think about.

There are some basic things people can do to protect themselves. For example, when people wear unit colors on their tee shirts, it draws attention to them, and while no one wants them not to be proud of their unit, when they are on an airplane flying to Greece, they probably should not wear that tee shirt. It is necessary to use a little sense and good judgment.

Terrorists are going to strike again, there's no question about it, because terrorism is the warfare of the eighties. Everyone is susceptible, and the U.S. government cannot protect everyone all the time everywhere, so people must take protective steps on their own.

The following guidelines for personal security summarize the information found in various publications on the subject.

Maintain a low profile in personal appearance, demeanor, and activity. Decreasing your visibility also decreases your chances of being selected as a target.

Vary your routine. Unpredictability makes you an elusive subject of surveillance, which increases the vulnerability of the potential terrorist to discovery and apprehension. In addition, unpredictability makes it much more difficult for the potential terrorist to plan his attack. A terrorist organization that cannot discern a reliable pattern of activity in a possible target often will shift its focus to easier prey.

Be alert to surveillance. Most terrorist incidents have been preceded by extensive surveillance (lasting several days to several months). The purpose of this surveillance is to choose a feasible target and a suitable time, place, and method of attack.

Be wary of revealing personal information or itinerary. This type of knowledge is invaluable to both potential terrorists and ordinary criminals.

Know your surroundings. Be able to rec-ognize abnormal conditions. Terrorists sometimes clear untargeted individuals from the planned attack location prior to acting. The absence of street vendors, for example, may indicate impending terrorist activity. When transiting high-threat areas, constantly imagine what you would do if an attack took place. This mental preparation will likely result in a more effective and timely response should an attack actually occur. Also, effective preparation will help you remain calm in a crisis situation.

Use available passive protection devices. Several military officers have died as a result of terrorist violence because they did not use bullet-proof windows or other equipment in their automobiles.

Conduct contingency planning with family and friends. Make sure that all vital documents (insurance policies, wills, etc.) are kept up to date. Discuss with family and friends the actions you want them to take if you are kidnapped. Proper preparations will help alleviate the anxiety of the loved ones of someone who is taken hostage.

Report all unusual or suspicious activity immediately to appropriate security personnel.

Be constantly alert. More than six hundred terrorist acts occur each year. As an American, you are a very attractive target to a number of terrorist groups in the United States and around the world. Terrorists have become increasingly sophisticated in their methods, but constant vigilance has proven to be one of the best defenses against them.

It may be difficult to consider the possibility of a terrorist incident being directed at you or at your personnel. Although increasing each year, the chances of such an occurrence are relatively small. However, the prudent individual will take necessary precautionary measures to minimize its likelihood. As in other forms of warfare, effective and timely preparation promotes success against terrorism.

94. Spiritual Welfare

INTRODUCTION

Sitting at anchor in the harbor at Athens, Greece, on a bright calm Sunday morning, the USS *Adams* (DDG-2) reflected the tranquility of the surroundings. The officer of the deck had just dispatched the captain's gig with the ensign lay leader to fetch a civilian Catholic priest who had kindly volunteered to come aboard to conduct mass for the crew. The command duty officer appeared on the quarterdeck and told the OD, "Go ahead and bong the captain off; he's on his way down." The OD's heart sank! "Sir, the lay leader just left in the gig to get the priest. He said the captain told him he could use the gig." The captain arrived on the scene just in time to observe two very embarrassed officers watching the gig, which was well beyond hailing distance, speed for the dock. The captain, of course, had intended to take the lay leader ashore with him and allow the gig to return with the priest. Noting that the two officers were inflicting enough pain upon themselves for the error, the captain, as he turned to proceed back to his cabin, said, "Well, I guess the spiritual welfare of the crew *is* more important than the captain's liberty. Let me know when the gig returns—and you might tell the priest that the lay leader needs prayer."

This true story directs attention to an area of leadership that is often neglected. Spiritual welfare is lumped together with morale and esprit de corps most of the time, or it is cast in the category of "religion" and ignored in a misguided effort to keep church and state "separate." The leader needs to understand the spiritual needs and drives of subordinates in order to lead the whole person effectively. Spiritual welfare is an area of leadership that requires sensitivity, insight, compassion, and courage, regardless of the religious background of the leader. Understood, spiritual welfare can contribute to an atmosphere of justice, morality, integrity, and ethics within a command, which promotes uncommon success. Misunderstood, spiritual welfare issues can separate and isolate the leader from subordinates in a most destructive way.

WHAT IS SPIRIT?

Spirit is most often thought of as a nonreligious word. Like the wind, spirit is powerful, mysterious, and directed. It is under control, but just barely. *Proceeding* is too dull a word for the action of spirit. A spirited horse or team spirit doesn't proceed—it surges. There is purpose and intention to spirit. There is also a sense of intelligence to spirit. It's alive. Hailstones don't have spirit. Horses have more spirit than mosquitos. Ghosts have too much mystery and not enough intelligence to have real spirit. The French incorporate in their work *esprit* a touch of verve, wit, and elan, perhaps adding a further dimension of spirit. Spirit is a fundamental attribute of human beings.

Individual spirit. In the modern world, the word *holistic* is used with great frequency. *Holistic* means that a human being is a unit, not three parts: mind, body, and spirit. The physical affects the mental, and vice versa.

Vitality—life itself—is somehow wrapped up in the unity of mind, body, and spirit. But even within this unity, the word *spirit* has come to reflect the totality of the individual person. What makes persons different from animals is that persons can make themselves the object of their own action. Persons can transcend themselves and look at themselves objectively. The relationship between self as subject and self as object is linked by spirit. In a sense, the spirit reflects the unity of an individual person. The point of all this is that spiritual welfare is the glue that makes an individual whole. It is from "wholeness" that effectiveness as a subordinate springs. For the leader, then, spiritual welfare for self and for subordinates is a key to success.

Group spirit. Spirit has a function for groups of people. Just as the human spirit plays a role in the interconnectedness of mind, body, and spirit, so human spirits reaching out form a collection that yields team spirit, school spirit,

American spirit, and others. When such collections form, the need for communication is diminished, because oneness exists. Humans belong to many units or collections, such as families, nations, churches, divisions, crews, and watch sections. In collections where a caring spirit is nurtured, morale develops. Where there is morale based on caring, a high sense of justice develops. Where there is justice, a high degree of morality develops. Where these concepts do not develop, there is disintegration.

The wise leader recognizes the need to balance individual spirit and group spirit to derive a total spirit that is constructive and productive for both the individual and the group. The individual thus contributes to and benefits from the group. One of the interesting things about human spirit is that it does not seem to stand well on its own.

INTERACTION BETWEEN SPIRITS

It is by the interaction of spirits that we know each other and are known by each other. The truth of the matter is that there are conflicts between spirits more often than not. The human spirit is eager to mingle with other human spirits. It is fulfilled by love and stifled by pride. There are always Romeos and Juliets caught up in the spiritual warfare of the Montagues and Capulets. The spirits of state conflict with the spirits of family. The spirits of family conflict with the spirits of church. We search in these conflicts for an absolute or ultimate spirit to lay its claim upon the conflicts and point out to us a clear course of action.

In the midst of the conflicts, representative persons come forth to summarize and maximize group spirit. In fact, a healthy group produces such leaders. One of the functions of a leader is to encourage the emergence of these representative persons. We need those who will show us and others what aspect of our group is true and desirable. We need those whose human spirit typifies what is true and desirable in our group spirit.

In addition to individuals, the representation of group spirit emerges in other forms. Art often translates the essential reality of spirit so we can understand it. The theologian Karl Barth said of Mozart that he was "someone who hears not the silence of the world, but the eternal music of the eternal divine comedy." Some would even say that life is the mirror and art the reality.

Morality, like art, emerges to represent group spirit. The prophet, leading the quest for good, seeks justice, perhaps not knowing what justice is. Prophets drive the group beyond conventional moral insight. Without the prophet saying "Something is wrong," morality could become conformance with the custom of the group. The prophet moves the group to a new understanding, to a better morality.

Wisdom is another product of group spirit. Philosophers and wise persons come out of spirit-filled groups. Certain members are inspired by a group with a sense of untruth and are driven in search of truth.

Unfortunately, both individuals and forms such as art, morality, and wisdom which emerge from group spirit are not always positive. Adolph Hitlers also emerge. Forms of disorder, injustice, and mischief arise. Life in the spirit is deeply ambiguous.

HOLY SPIRIT/ABSOLUTE SPIRIT

The human spirit, facing the ambiguity found in group spirit, needs an absolute leader. The leader concerned about the spiritual welfare of subordinates will find a variety of responses to this need. Some will simply claim the strongest voice as absolute. Some will be convinced that no fixed absolute can exist; nothing can claim human spirit in a unique way. In other words, "All things are relative." Some, through religious experience or conviction, will have a sense of God in the form of Spirit and will express the fact that, for them, an Absolute that transcends humanity has come into relation with them. In this case, *spirit* with a small *s* is ready to move beyond itself. Thus, the word *Spirit*, the concept of the Holy or Absolute, has its roots in the nonreligious word, *spirit*, connected to human spirit and group spirit. In a sense this Holy Spirit is like human and group spirit, in that spirit is that which produces unity in the human and the group, as Spirit is that which relates or produces unity between humanity and the Absolute or God.

SPIRIT IN THE WORLD

Just as human spirit and group spirit represent the way humans and groups reach out and interact with the world, so Holy Spirit reflects the way the Absolute or God reaches out to the world. Our holistic person is vital and alive. So the person who experiences the Holy Spirit experiences a living God. This God raises up prophets, philosophers, and wise men to represent his Absolute. Individuals with this understanding of Holy Spirit, whatever their faith, know an individual relationship to the Absolute that transcends their human spirit and the group spirit. This Holy Spirit represents a God of action, a God who is moving out in the world. Thus, creation is moved step by step through the ambiguities surrounding human and group spiritual activity.

SPIRIT VERSUS SPIRIT

The leader concerned with the spiritual welfare of subordinates must recognize that human spirit and group spirit cannot be *replaced* by the Holy Spirit. What the leader seeks to do is direct the human and group spirit to reflect the Holy Spirit in the sense that morality, integrity, ethical standards, and justice prevail. While this sounds simple, it obviously is not. There are, however, some practical avenues the leader can take to enhance the possibility of success.

1. *Build upon what you start with.* One can presume that *most* Americans are exposed in their youth to religious practices in a family/church setting. While religious practice is certainly not the only access an individual has to absolute values of morality, integrity, ethical

standards, and justice, it is *one* access. Just as they might recognize the number-one graduate of an A-school as having potential, leaders should expect high standards from those who have highly developed religious values. More important is the need to provide a continuing opportunity for reinforcing those values. In a shipboard setting, that encouragement often comes through providing time at least one day a week for worship. That time does not necessarily have to be 10:00 on Sunday morning.

Concern for environment, for lay or ordained leadership, and for worship material is part of this practical effort to enhance spiritual welfare. If the ship or unit is blessed with ordained clergy, or if access is available to shore-based religious counselling, such support can build upon existing value systems or can resolve ambiguities that arise. One captain, for example, made his sea cabin available to the chaplain in port as an office to provide a quiet, private place for value reinforcement.

2. *Set a moral tone.* If the spiritual welfare of individuals is to be nourished and to flourish, the leader must set a moral tone that honors morality, integrity, ethical behavior, and justice. However, if the leader by action and deed contributes to the ambiguity that exists between human spirit and Holy Spirit, subordinates have three choices: (a) they can choose to follow another human absolute who represents the sum of what they believe the group spirit reflects; (b) they can follow the Holy Spirit as they conceive it standing as a lonely prophet against the tide of ambiguity; or (c) they can follow the leader's human spirit as the organization disintegrates in ambiguity.

Moral tone is set in a command first in the example of the leader's own behavior and second in the example of the leader's action in relation to subordinates. A leader is called to be a prophet in the organization, to reveal and correct immoral behavior, lack of integrity, unethical behavior, and injustice. If the leader neglects this responsibility by failing to establish a moral tone

457

or by failing to hold subordinates accountable for their responsibility to maintain it, the moral tone will foster disintegration as the human spirits cope with the ambiguous.

This moral tone is best set in the indoctrination of newcomers to a command. It is maintained by an attitude of consistency. For example, while the well-placed expletive is often good for stress relief, a continuous stream of expletives as a substitute for normal communication has no place in the moral tone of a command. One crusty CPO, rather famous within the command for well-chosen expletives delivered in a timely manner, instructed a seaman, "Son, in this command we may occasionally use that kind of language, but we don't talk with it."

Moral tone is set in terms of attitude that discourages such things as pornography, drug use, promiscuity, drunkenness, brawling, and misconduct ashore. In short, that which separates the human spirit from a group spirit (which enhances unity with the common absolute) is destructive. The leader should not be afraid to use the word *I* to describe the moral tone expected.

"Captain's Mast" is often the most visible setting for the prophetic voice. It is the event in which an accounting is made when other checks on morality, integrity, ethics, and justice have failed. It is a place where standards and absolutes are revealed to the human spirits present. Many times a chaplain is invited to Mast. Frequently, it is obvious that the underlying reason for a sailor's presence at Mast is a bankrupt human spirit confused by misguided group spirit or false absolutes. In other words, the spiritual welfare of the person at Mast is at stake. The chaplain, working with the division officer, can on many occasions deal with the real problem after justice is dispensed at Mast. Prophetic leaders must be as concerned with spiritual welfare as they are with justice.

3. *Take spiritual temperatures directly and often.* The leader *can* delegate the responsibility for measuring the spiritual welfare of subordinates. When that is done, spiritual welfare is degraded. The sensitivity, insight, compassion, and courage of the leader make up the only thermometer that can properly record spiritual temperature. Even at that, spiritual temperature is hard to take. But there are some practical principles for measuring spiritual welfare:

a. *Measurement is best taken in the environment of the subordinates.* Talk to the engineer in the engine room.

b. *Listen first and talk second.*

c. *Know enough about the subordinate (because you care) to relate.* What is the current status of the individual's watch qualification, advancement preparation, work center responsibility, and family situation? Know this before beginning to measure. Human spirit wilts without relatedness.

d. *Don't take spiritual temperatures if you don't plan to deal with an out-of-specification reading.* The prime cause of out-of-specification readings in spiritual welfare is separateness. Individuals who feel separate from the group spirit or from their concept of the absolute spirit need to be directed or to have ambiguities resolved. Only rarely is a kick in the tail a cure for deteriorated spiritual welfare. Most often it is cured by a return to unity with group spirit and with the Absolute or Holy Spirit.

e. *Take extraordinary measures in extraordinary circumstances.* Shipyard overhaul is a prime culprit in corrupting spiritual welfare. Nonstandard things, such as fire watches, occur and often contribute to a sense of separateness. This separateness leads to a perception of lessened moral restraints. Major competitive inspections may contribute to a lowering of ethical standards or integrity as fear of failure forces the human spirit to draw away from absolutes. The point is that the leader needs to anticipate ambiguities and to deal with them with insight and courage. The spoken word of the leader is often the cure for ambiguities of spirit in extraordinary situations. Again, the word *I* used to express the leader's human spirit is invaluable in unifying group spirit and relating that spirit to the absolute.

4. *Work on individual spirit.* The human spirit causes individuals to reach out to relate, to seek unity with something or someone beyond themselves. If there is no human spirit, there can be no relatedness. The leader may find that individuals are directed in war so far that there is no evidence of spirit, only mind and body. The proverb is correct: "Where there is no vision, the people perish." The task of the leader in this case is to try to bring the individual to an understanding of the importance of relatedness. Often the place to start is the family or the church, in the sense of the individual's recollection of being related to the absolute in these institutions. It is no accident that military organizations promote themselves as "familylike" in orientation by stating: "The Navy takes care of its own."

The Navy learned early in the development of the drug culture in America that the arrival of the new recruit aboard ship created a sense of separation in that individual which was relieved by a welcome into the drug culture where it existed. The establishment of a strong "I"-division, well led by a caring human, countered this threat to human spirit.

5. *Lift up the leaders.* As human spirit, group spirit, and absolute spirit fuse, spiritual welfare blossoms. From this environment leaders emerge who reflect this unity in the sense that they can articulate the sense of excitement, the desirable qualities, and the power of the group. These emerging leaders who can stand above the group and constructively assess it need to be encouraged and supported. Communication channels need to be established to allow articulation of ideas and prophetic voices. While this can filter up to the leader through a proper chain of command, it is still important for the leader to allow an opportunity for direct interaction with emerging leaders. These leaders will have proven themselves worthy of occasional direct access to the leader because of their own example of morality, integrity, ethics, and justice.

CONCLUSION

One cannot long be on, above, or under the sea without experiencing a sense of a power or force beyond self and beyond the group. The same human spirit that generates this conclusion senses a relatedness to this Absolute. With this relatedness comes a desire for unity, and that unity comes in the form of morality, integrity, ethics, and justice. All these values are recognizable to the leader as essential elements of organizational success. Where the organization reflects standards of morality, integrity, ethics, and justice in harmony with the absolute values humans seek beyond themselves, the ambiguity of interactions between spirits is reduced, and spiritual welfare results. Where these values differ, ambiguity is exacerbated and disorganization results.

The wise and prophetic leader works to stimulate the growth of human spirit within subordinates and the growth of group spirit within the organization in the direction that enables unity with this Absolute or Holy Spirit.

For some, the path is through religious experience. For *all* who find a sensitive, insightful, compassionate, and courageous leader willing to set a personal example in lifestyle and action, a sense of spiritual welfare develops that produces uncommon unity, purpose, and direction in an organization. This is not a mystical, mysterious activity. It is rooted in practical, time-tested experience of leaders throughout history. While it is not easy to accomplish because of the complexity of the interaction of so many forces, spiritual welfare, like a vector, has magnitude and direction. It can be measured, enhanced, and redirected, and it starts with the key to the success of any organization: an individual. Building upon a Biblical theme: Physical, mental, and spiritual welfare abide, but the greatest of these is spiritual welfare.

95. Senior Officers Express Their Thoughts

MATTERS OF SPECIAL INTEREST TO THOSE JUST STARTING A SERVICE LIFE

Admiral Uchida: Junior officers seem particularly interested in the leadership in the battlefield. I used to tell them my experiences obtained during World War II. I said to them that fighting is creating.

What I mean is that we sometimes encounter in battle instances in which any regulation is useless, because the situation there changes so rapidly and in a manner that has never happened before. So, an officer must always be ready to create new tactics by his originality, according to the situation on the spot.

General Wilson: Officers can best prepare themselves through, first, a dedication to their profession. This dedication will take the form of attributes such as initiative, enthusiasm, belief in their work, a commitment. They should be in good physical condition, because that may be required. They should understand the moral aspects of don't do as I say, do as I do, know that their actions are always subject to visibility, especially as they get more senior in rank. Therefore they must be like Caesar's wife, and not put themselves in the position where their presence or their actions are questionable.

Admiral Holloway: An officer should live every day of his professional career with the thought that he might have to go to war tomorrow. He cannot permit himself to get run down physically, and he cannot allow his skills to become dull. He should face every day with two ideas. First, that he will not have time to get himself retrained and reinvigorated when the time comes to perform against a live enemy. And second, that how well he has trained over the past years will determine how well he will perform in the first month of combat.

When I traveled as Chief of Naval Operations, young officers asked me, What sort of a career pattern should we follow? Should we go to postgraduate school? Should we concentrate on operations? Is duty in the training command a good duty? What's the best path to the top? and I always told them the same thing. I said, "The best path to the top is to take one day at a time. Don't worry about what you're going to do next year or your next duty station. You'll never get there unless you do a good job today and tomorrow on this duty station. If you do your very best today and plan for tomorrow to do your very best, your future's going to take care of itself."

I remember when I had command of the Seventh Fleet. I had served in the Seventh Fleet a total of seven times, the first time was in 1943 as an ensign on a destroyer during World War II, and here I was, my seventh occasion back, as Commander, Seventh Fleet. I called on the British governor, the lord governor of Hong Kong, and he said, "When you were an ensign on that destroyer back in 1943, did you ever think you'd be Commander of the Seventh Fleet?" and I said, "Sir, back in those days I wasn't sure I was going to make it." I think that's what we have to face: one step at a time and that will get you there.

Admiral Carney: Along about 1921, I was about five years out of the Naval Academy, I applied for the postgraduate instruction in ordnance. I got a very nice letter saying that they had to assign the available billets to people who had associated themselves with the gunnery and ordnance business in the very beginning and they very much regretted they didn't have a spot for me. Well, I felt terribly let down. I had picked that as a possible specialty because it was the one specialty that permitted you to alternate with sea duty. So I was pretty much down in the dumps. My uncle was Chief of Staff to Commander in Chief, Atlantic, and I went over and had lunch with him one day and I told him that I'd been turned down and I just felt that this condemned me to sort of a journeyman's position for the rest of my life and I was very upset about it. He said he had another thought that he'd like me to consider. He said, "There's another specialty, which I don't think they can deny you, but it's a very good one." I was still skeptical. I asked what this wonderful thing was and he said, "Command." He said, "You grab command of everything that passes your file." Well, it turned out to be pretty good advice, and he followed it himself and he finally became a four-star himself one day. This opened up a whole new line of things to me.

Vice Admiral Ruge: After the war it was repeatedly said that Rommel was no more than a good tactician, a military leader who was lucky. I, however, am of a quite different opinion. I came to his headquarters after a long career, in which I had met many high-ranking officers and leading personalities. I had extensively studied history and written about historical topics as well as having led a number of commando raids. When a naval officer is ordered to join a new division he first sits back and critically observes, which is what I did when assigned to Rommel. What I first noticed was his natural manner with his subordinates. He easily made contact with most of the people he met or worked with. The soldiers immediately felt he was interested in them as human beings, and his relationship with his staff was the same. He never showed off and was only proud of the fact that he was able to achieve his successes with minimal losses. He was a good listener and liked good jokes but never "bad" ones. . . . Hitler's murder of Rommel demonstrates his absolute disrespect for the German people whose fate he so selfishly decided.

Admiral Hayward: Let me start out by saying that, while one ought always to strive to be first in his class, it isn't necessarily the guy who is first in his class who is the only person who can succeed. I sure wasn't the first in my class. As a matter of fact, I didn't expect to get through the first year. What I learned fairly quickly in the Navy is that the Navy allows one a great deal

of opportunity to perform, and all you have to do is just work your tail off. Hard work accomplishes an enormous amount, and my own experience showed me that again and again. I found that just by determination and sticking with it, if you could learn a job, then you could perform that job, then you probably would perform it well if you tried hard enough. I just kept struggling, just kept working the problem. Some people are said to be very lucky. I think I was lucky, and there are many people whom I think were lucky. But I've also decided that luck generally falls to people who are successful, they're working hard at it, they take advantage of an opportunity.

The first real break that I would look back on occurred during the Korean War when I was a lieutenant junior grade and a division officer. The opportunity was presented by the emergencies generated over the loss of life, pilots being killed, and crises being faced by the command. I was chosen by the commanding officer or the exec to fill in for a senior and take the responsibility of that senior. That undoubtedly came about in a fortuitous sense—fortuitous for me, certainly not fortuitous in the event of the individual who lost his life or his family—but the event came about almost certainly because of the effort that I had been putting into that squadron up to that point without particularly knowing that I was separating myself in the eyes of others as someone whom they were going to call on if they had to.

That was the first break in my naval career. Things of that sort over a period of time undoubtedly led to my first preselection, and that first preselection led to people starting to pay attention to Who are these guys who had been preselected? And so you end up getting a better assignment than someone else. Someone might say that's a little unfair. On the other hand, if you're constantly challenged and you constantly work hard at it and you constantly perform well, that's what the system's supposed to do. It is supposed to keep identifying those people who will perform well under difficult circumstances, who can take on an additional load and move ahead a little bit faster. And that can come just from hard work. I can guarantee you it could come from hard work, because you can go back to the Academy and break out my record and you'll see where I stood in my class. I mean, I worked hard at surviving.

The leader's responsibility to see that his people are comfortably housed is one of his most important responsibilities. I have never forgotten a time when I overlooked this responsibility. I feel so strongly about this basic requirement to worry about everybody in your organization and looking out for their well-being, and generally I think I was successful in doing that. I must have been, because divisions usually work well together and so forth, but I remember a time when I did not and a lot of the people aboard the ship did not. I had command of an AF and we went into a shipyard for about a four-month period of time. It was wintertime in San Francisco, and we tore the ship apart quite a bit to pull out some main machinery equipment; had to cut holes in the side of the ship. It's a pretty crummy life in a shipyard, there's no way to describe it other than that, it's crummy. We've done a lot since then to try to improve upon that by getting barracks ashore, moving the crew off the ship, but this was a private shipyard and there was no place to do that and our crew had to live aboard throughout this period of time. I was well into the ship repair work, the third month or so, when the ship was being put back together again before it struck me as to what a poor job I had done as skipper, and the exec and division officers, to look out for our people who had to live aboard. Most of us had families, and we went home and put that thing out of our minds for the time being, but some of those fellows had no place to go except stay aboard and live there night after night after night in this very cold, damp environment.

I don't look back on that with any pride in my own performance. It could have been fixed, it

would never have been good and comfortable, but one thing I'm sure of, and that is that the young enlisted aboard that ship had no reason to take pride at that moment in that ship, certainly didn't have any reason to take pride in their skipper or their exec or their division officer, because if we had been doing our job they'd have felt our presence all the time, they'd have felt our awareness of their circumstances. Even though we couldn't have fixed it perfectly, the fact that we were doing our best would have been adequate. One thing you find is that people don't have to be patted on the back very much, but they do have to be patted on the back from time to time; they don't have to have a lot of attention, but they have to have some attention. They'll respond enormously positively to a little positive awareness, and if you give them a lot, you can accomplish almost anything. It's just an illustration, I have not ever forgotten that, it was not one of those things that I could easily forget. How I allowed myself to get in that position is a reflection of carelessness and brought me back to one of those fundamental factors of leadership: If you aren't thinking about your people right now, then that factor of leadership is not adequately ingrained in your subconscious and conscience; it has got to be well ingrained that it's there all the time.

Secretary Webb: Soon after I had taken over my platoon in Vietnam, which I took over in the field, the second patrol I took out got trapped in the middle of a paddy. We were taking fire from three different sides, and my decision at the time was to split my platoon in half because we were completely exposed. I split my platoon in half to have one half of it provide a base of fire on the nearest tree line where we were taking fire, and have the other half assault to the safety of a tree line. They were to set up a base of fire so the other half of the platoon could assault and join us, which worked very well.

When I came back to our company perimeter, a fellow who was one of the machine gunners who had been involved with this thing must have decided it was "time to test the lieutenant." He came up to me while I was pounding a stake in the ground trying to build a hooch, and he said loud enough for the whole platoon to hear, "Excuse me, Sir. I have something I would like to ask you, Sir." I said, "Yes?" and he said, "Sir, I have been wounded twice in the service of my country. I am a man. I don't need to listen to this man (the team leader)." I thought, the machine gunner has a problem and he wants a lot of people to know he has a problem, and what am I going to do? And I said, "Yes, that's right." He said, "Well, Sir, you know today out in that paddy, you said open fire on the whole tree line? Well (the team leader) says we don't open fire on that tree line. He says maybe we got something else in the tree line, what are we shooting at in the tree line? He tells me not to. Now I did it. Now wasn't I right? That's what I want to know."

I sat there and I said, "Well, I gave the order, yes, you were right, you did what I said, you did a good job, nobody got hurt, I'm really, really proud of the job you did." He thought that was pretty good, and said, "This man is always making fun of me. He tells me I'm stupid. He says I can't read a map. He can read a map, but nobody ever taught me to read a map." And I said, "I'll tell you what, you know you come up here some day, as a matter of fact this afternoon, I'll start showing you how to read my map." "You really would, Sir? You really would?" And I said, "Yes," and he started to get mad again—I guess the (team leader) was still watching him, you know—and he said, "What I want to know is, do I still have to serve under him? What am I supposed to do? I won't serve under him anymore!"

When I went through basic school, we would see a film and it would always end, "What are you going to do now?" Okay, so now here you have your first real problem, and it's easy looking back on it now, at the time I was twenty-two years old, and had a nineteen year old who was a very good guy, who has told me he's not going to serve under his team leader, and my whole platoon was watching. Here were my alternatives: order him to go serve under the team leader; call them up and counsel them both at the same time and resolve it; or maybe this guy just needs one more stroke. It worked before, so I figured, well, nothing's going to be lost if I just try the smallest thing first, and so I said to him, "Why don't you just go try to get along with him? He's not bad. You want to read a map? I'll help you read a map," and he said, "Yes, Sir, I think you're right," and he went on back down, and that was the end of it.

The very important lesson I learned is that whenever you've got a leadership situation where you haven't time to think about it, the first step should always be the small step. Too many people are going to get in and they're going to say this is what used to be done, and they're going to reach over and create a bigger problem. If I had ordered him to go down there and get along with his team leader, I would have had a miserable situation.

General Rice: Living overseas and traveling overseas is one of the great fringe benefits of being a professional officer. It offers the opportunity to see countries that prior to the visit the officer has only read about or seen in the movies; to associate with this country's allies and, in some cases, adversaries; to see how people in other countries live; and to learn a foreign language in some cases. The Naval Service sends thousands of officers to the language school to understand other cultures and customs. All officers should strive for overseas assignment, because it is a tremendous opportunity. When it is possible for an officer's family to travel with him, the family can benefit from the experience, as well.

I've been very fortunate. I've visited almost every country in the world—not every, but a significant number of the countries. And I was fortunate enough to live in England with my family, with the Royal Marine Commandos, and those professional and social relationships of twenty years ago are still there. So I encourage people to travel and take advantage of their overseas tours and the opportunities. It's just a great opportunity to see and learn and be exposed to other cultures of the world, because the United States is not in a vacuum. Our livelihood depends on our interface, interaction, with the different countries of the world. You know you're an ambassador, you represent all that is good in the United States as a lieutenant in the United States Navy or a lieutenant of Marines. You represent the government, you represent something special, the United States Navy, the United States Marine Corps.

MCPON Sanders: Our program needs to be improved to prepare people to work and live in a foreign environment. Once a person is assigned a duty station overseas, I think that he should immediately start grooming himself and learning about that particular country, its customs, traditions, and culture. I have found through experience that most foreigners hold officers more accountable for their actions than they hold enlisted personnel. Many of our foreign friends will overlook something that an enlisted person would do, where they will not overlook the things that an officer would do. An officer can find himself in a compromising position very, very fast if he is not careful. The officer needs to be extremely aware of where he is and what he is doing at all times. Officers must understand how important this is.

Admiral Ramage: I would say that I always got challenging assignments. When I came back after the war I was assigned to the Guided Missile Division and at that time we didn't have anything that even resembled a guided missile. My first job was to get the German V-1 into production and then modify two fleet submarines to carry and launch this missile now called the Loon. The next step was to build a radio-controlled drone with a radius of 100 miles, capable of carrying the big atom bomb. This was called the Regulus. Several of these were built

and taken to sea for a short time but were soon superseded by later developments. Admiral Gallery, for whom I was working at that time, had captured the German submarine U-505 during the war and subsequently had found a home for it out in Chicago. I was assigned the job of seeing that it got out there. Moving it to Chicago was no problem. But it required a cut through Michigan Boulevard to get the submarine from Lake Michigan up alongside the museum where it now resides. Next we looked into the possibility of designing a submersible tank capable of being towed by a submarine which would carry the German V-2. The idea being to surface the tank, bring it to a vertical launch position, open the hatch and fire the missile. That idea was soon abandoned after the attempt to launch a V-2 off the carrier Midway turned out to be a complete failure. Well, these were all challenging assignments.

As a matter of fact, the same is true of practically every other assignment I had. There's always something new and different coming along. Before Pearl Harbor, I was the communication officer of the submarine force staff. I decided maybe it was time to see whether we could receive radio signals underwater. We experimented with various types of coils and antennas until we found the then-installed direction finder loops on the new fleet submarines were able to copy very low frequency signals most effectively while submerged. However, as soon as any antenna was submerged below 20 feet all signals cut off abruptly. As a result of these experiments, fixed loops were installed high up in the periscope shears in all submarines. It is doubtful if they were ever used during the war as all submarines had to surface each night and there was no difficulty copying the regular schedules which were repeated several times. Later, when the Polaris submarines came along, they adapted this principle in their trailing wire antennas enabling them to receive radio traffic without having to surface. So you find your own challenges, you look around for something that has never been done before. Use your imagination and strike out into new areas, that's the main idea I would like to leave with you.

When Pearl Harbor was attacked, one of the first things that happened as I recall was that I was called in the following morning by Admiral Withers and told to meet Earl Thacker at the main gate and escort him in to discuss leasing the Royal Hawaiian Hotel as a R&R center for submariners. That was on the eighth of December and it was one of the best moves ever made. Subsequently, rest camps were established in Midway, Brisbane, Perth, and Guam. So when you returned from patrol a bit shaky and tired you looked forward to a few days R&R at these spas while the relief crews moved aboard and made all necessary repairs and readied everything for sea again. On returning from R&R we normally had a week to check out all the work that had been accomplished. Then you were ready to load out and sail. Surprisingly, not too many submarines sustained any severe battle damage, but the relief crews managed to cope with all such problems expeditiously.

The difference between readying a crew for combat as opposed to a training exercise was that after each patrol we had about a 25 to 30 percent personnel turnover. So there was always quite a large injection of new blood into the crew which necessitated a lot more basic training to ensure they all understood their jobs and responsibilities. In addition, all new members had to be given some idea as to what to expect. I only had two occasions where a crew member buckled. The first one was down in Perth, where we had come in after an extensive patrol. Most of the crew had gotten well acquainted with the natives. The morning before we were to depart on patrol my pharmacist's mate came in and complained of low back pains and requested to be relieved. Well, I wasn't surprised knowing the company he had been keeping but we got a relief for him. Then the next morning I was down on deck as

the OD was getting the ship underway. As he backed away from the tender he almost backed into a Dutch submarine moored astern. Then as he started ahead the current caught him and we almost drove into a big gaping hole in a merchant ship docked ahead of us. I got up on the bridge just in time to salvage the situation. But just as we were pulling clear there came a loud shout from the upper deck of the tender, "So long, suckers." I was never so mad in my life and was ready to go back and get that pharmacist's mate but I said, "Well, we are all clear and we'll go on," and we did.

The other case occurred out in the South China Sea. We had been on station for some time and our pharmacist's mate began complaining about pains in his belly, that he had appendicitis. He was in his bunk, applying ice packs, moaning and generally carrying on. Actually, he was chickening out and wanted us to abort the patrol. After our big shootout was over, I went down to see him in his bunk and asked him how he felt. Well, he felt a whole lot better, and I said, "We got two choices, we are heading back now, we can go to Saipan, where the tender is just moving in. It isn't there yet, but it will be there in a day or two, and they haven't really secured Saipan but we can get in there. Or we can go all the way back to Pearl Harbor." He said, "Oh, I think I can make it back to Pearl now." Well, about an hour or two later, I guess he had second thoughts. To make his sham more credible he changed his mind and told me he thought we had better go into Saipan. So on to Saipan we went. They were shooting at us from the beach with rifle fire as we pulled in alongside the *Holland*. After dropping him off, we proceeded to Pearl Harbor and guess who was jumping up and down on the dock to greet us upon arrival. That guy never had an operation and was in better health than most of us. So the only two softies I had were pharmacist's mates, quite surprisingly. On the other hand, two pharmacist's mates received the Medal of Honor during WWII, one of whom was a conscientious objector. He went through all kinds of hell and never fired a shot. So it all depends on the individual. There is no way of telling what a man will do under trying conditions. Only time will tell.

Admiral de Cazanove: I started my schooling at the Royal Naval College at Dartmouth during World War II. While there were other programs to make one an officer in six months, and these individuals were able to go on and command small boats—and even, a few, ships such as submarines or small destroyers—this is not enough school to prepare an officer to go outside of his field of specialization. It is good for the immediate requirements of war, but there is also the need for the Naval Academy, which prepares people to be the bosses of their respective services, and while only a few may reach the highest levels of command—if they start preparing themselves by learning all they can at their service academy—they will have a start which, when added to what they later learn, will qualify them through knowledge and experience to run their service's operations.

We can more or less agree that leadership is an art rather than the direct result of learning or teaching. However, much has to be learned as part of the profession. The greatest immorality is to carry on a profession one does not know. These are not my words but rather those of Napoleon, and while this is true for any profession, it may be of much more importance in our profession, for the leaders of the Army and the Navy. A primary quality is that of self-respect, that is, both respect of oneself and respect of others, and not only as to appearance, general behavior, and integrity—but everything. With self-respect and respect of others, I put also rigor in the sense of strictness, exactness, not to be rude to others, and a sense of respecting the rules and the exactness of things. I believe that a priori we need a good opinion of others, even if we need to be circumspective. Of course, we may be deceiving ourselves, but I believe that, to start with, we must have confidence in our-

selves; the leader needs to have confidence in himself and in others, for if you start doubting others, you may not go very far. One of the first requirements is always trying to improve oneself, to increase one's knowledge and knowledge of others. Realize that nothing comes automatically, and that nothing can be taken for granted. Always stop to make things out and reflect on things to be sure to come to the right truth, if there is any truth. A statement of General de Gaulle comes to mind, "The true school of command is general culture, not only to learn techniques but to learn to work with things in general and to understand what is moral." This I believe even more now than in the beginning of my naval career, that one learns through involvement in the general culture and in the school of having command. Repeating myself, I would note that it is important to have faith and confidence in oneself, in others, the profession, the team, and the country.

We have all seen in our lives people, including leaders and chiefs, knowingly or not, playing a game. These men never last. The leader is not a conductor or a committee; he has to be himself and not try to be someone else. But in any case, one cannot play games, or deception will soon follow. Deception can never last, for we work as a team and others depend upon us. It is very rare for someone to be able to be successfully deceptive in dealings with others. While having character is important, it is especially so in times of crisis and difficulties, though it is not so easy in normal life. In fact, it is more difficult to be a man of character in normal life, where one tries to keep things simple and avoid challenges. In a crisis you have to take a chance, whatever it is, and, thus, being a man of character at those times is made easier than during normal life. Another thing I believe is important is for staff officers to dare to say no before the final orders are given, for afterward may be too late. It is certainly easier to say yes, but dare to say no when it is important to do so. To say no, you must be sure of yourself, you must know exactly what you're talking about. Thus, the importance of having as much experience as possible. Of course, when orders are given, you have to obey. Courtesy, tact, and politeness are important, though more easily realized during normal times. Unfortunately, some young petty officers and even young officers forget to be courteous, tactful, and polite—and this is a change from the past. I used to practice these virtues with seniors, peers, and subordinates for, while they held different stations in life, they were on the same level from a human aspect. It is important for the young officer to start his career with these traits, and treat all people as human beings.

Another area of importance is that of communication. I've often seen people mistaken in the belief about what was said to them—what was meant by the person doing the communicating. So as to avoid this kind of communication problem, it is best to ask the person to repeat his words or to tell him what you understood the words to mean. One way of avoiding such problems is to use written orders, but even there exists the possibility of misunderstanding as to the meaning of the words used. Thus, asking a person what he understood by the written order is also useful at times. In times of peace there is the luxury of being able to do this, and by so doing, all will better understand one another, and when war comes, there is a greater probability that people will continue to understand one another during crisis situations.

While the President, these days, has the capability to call directly to anyone in the chain of command, that may not be all that good, for not so many are prepared to say to the President: "Would you please say that again, Mr. President?" It puts a great strain on the ultimate leader to be perfect in all that he does for all the armed forces, for he is the one giving the orders. It was surely simpler years ago, when the naval commander left the country for six months at a time and it was not possible to receive orders at sea, and everything was relying on the ship's captain. Of course, it is not like that anymore, and can't

be that way ever again, but maybe it was a better way to make leaders, for they had to rely on themselves and not on others. It is so easy nowadays to pick up the phone and ask: "What should I do?" The officer as much as possible should take the initiative and do what has to be done, without constantly asking for guidance, for if that is his way of operation—why do we need him?

(The following short quotes are taken from Admiral de Cazanove's retirement ceremony):

The duty of a subordinate is to help his command. The duty of the chief is to command.

Strictness does not exclude good spirits and having joy in living. Passionate people live.

Every sailor must have a certain idea of the functions he occupies.

Be yourself in all circumstances.

Be intellectually prepared for daily action as well as war.

Be a man of will and action.

Admiral Taylor: The effective officer gets a good philosophy and then, as he studies other great military captains and leaders, as he gains experience, as he watches good COs, bad COs, good XOs, bad XOs, good division officers, he takes these lessons and doctors his philosophy. After thirty years, I still can say it's been a great adventure and it just is without parallel for opportunity at being with people and leading troops and going places and doing important things and being ready to look the enemy in the eye, if it comes to that. But there is a philosophy that I have which has five tenets. This is my message, to encourage everyone to do something like this. First of all, work hard. Get up early, stay up late, and work hard in the middle, because with the assets that God has given you and that you've trained in and that you have working for you, if you do that you're going to do a good job and you're going to be successful. Knock out any of the three, and you're in trouble, because there's going to be some turtle out there who didn't have as much to start with, who's going to use it better than you, and you won't be the top performer that you want to be, that you think you are.

Second one is have fun. If you're not having fun, you're not doing anything right. No matter where you go you can find ways to have fun in what you're doing. There will be a lot of days when you have to tell yourself "I am having a good time," and maybe you aren't, but the leader must keep the old smiley face. You can get serious a few times to get the troops serious, but don't make it a habit and don't do any frowning; it's bad for business.

Three, be positive. I was lucky. When I was young, I heard a Burl Ives record, never will forget it, it's worked great: "As you go through life, make this your goal, watch the donut, not the hole." There are always a lot of problems, they are the holes, but there are a lot of good things, and when you have a bunch of troops and you're looking at the donut, the solid part, it's good for you. When you start to lose your focus and you're getting bogged down on all the problems, think about the fact that you've got ten toes and ten fingers, great opportunity, and a lot of things working for you, so be positive and exude that positive attitude.

Four, live the Golden Rule. Think about other people before you think about yourself. Do unto others as you'd have them do unto you. Make it a dynamite habit and, first thing you know, they are doing unto you and you feel good and you work for them, and that's team effort. You have to set the example.

And, finally, you've got to be proud. Proud of your country. We are just expending natural resources at great pace to make the world—and I guess it's our historical destiny—a better place, to give people self-determination. We are the number one experiment in democracy in the history of the world, and we are expending ourselves to do that. Our country is always there with moral principle beyond anything any other civilization has ever seen. The Navy carries a heavy burden. First in, last out, is the basic way

you've got to look at the employment of our battle groups. You've got to be proud of them, you've got to feel like you're part of them, you've got to be proud of your unit. You've got to be so proud that you inspire others to achieve the kinds of goals that you've set, and most of all, you've got to be proud of yourself, proud for the achievements that you've accumulated to this point, and just feel so good and so proud of who you are and what you've been that everyone can see your military bearing. When you have that, then you're setting an example, and you have others to go with you.

So, get that philosophy and maybe work on it from something your dad or mom said to you, or some other important person in life who is in the clergy or whatever, read the great leaders. Patton did all the readings for all the previous years, so when you read Patton he figured a new way to say what they said, so now you can learn an awful lot from how he did things. Work hard, have fun, be positive, live the Golden Rule, and be proud. It's a very simple philosophy. Put it to work and you'll do well.

REMEMBRANCES OF SPECIAL EVENTS IN NAVAL CAREERS

Admiral Hayward: As an officer advances through the ranks, his perceptions change, and his perspective changes. An ensign looks at the lieutenants and wonders why they are so inept, and the lieutenants wonder the same thing about the lieutenant commanders and the commanders. This is a natural inclination because, as he advances, the officer sees things from a different level of responsibility and a different level of awareness. He has more information about what is going on.

One of the ways senior officers determine whether an officer is capable of going on to very senior positions is how well that person deals with that change in perspective that occurs when he assumes new responsibility. Is he able to handle that in a way that does not create a negative competence below him because he is so uptight about suddenly "having it all"? Maybe he was always great at working for someone, but how is he to work for?

An officer's perception is always changing. It changes with age, it changes with experiences, the environment you've been through, your awareness of what's going on. That means you're always learning, you're learning from mistakes, you're learning from successes, hopefully you're always looking around for new lessons to learn and believing you'd go on all the way through to being CNO. I learned something new every year as CNO, and if I could stay on as long as Admiral Gorshkoff, I could probably get fairly good at the job, but there's just so much to know that it's constantly challenging your total capacity to do the job better. Of course it's true to say that a captain forgets what an ensign's perspective is, and as a consequence of that forgetting makes mistakes, and that's probably true of a division officer forgetting what an eighteen-year-old boot thinks about when he walks aboard that ship, if he ever did know. It's not easy for us who graduated from college to remember what it was like when you were in the eighth or ninth or tenth grade. As an officer, put yourself in that person's position at least often enough to be able to deal in a leadership way with that individual's surroundings. That person's going to react to stimuli on the basis of his own frame of reference, and that frame of reference is certain to be limited. As one gets more and more senior and has more experience, that frame of reference gets broader and broader.

Our ability to deal effectively with others is going to be conditioned by our awareness and our ability to recall how that individual sees his or her own problem and then be able to help him or her come to grips with that problem and solve it in a successful way instead of trip up and fail in the process. I have spent almost forty years in the Navy and was learning something all the time. I was forgetting things I should have remembered all the time, and my own perception of what had to be done was constantly

changing, but I came out of it with a reflection of a career being around a unique group of professionals, most of them you can really rely on.

One of the major programs that you hopefully remember is our Pride and Professionalism Program, which we stress so hard. That program was developed because of my perception as CNO that the Navy needed to regain a more positive attitude about its own competence. Its competence is very high. The way to regain a positive attitude was to put the responsibility and the authority back in line with the professionals; by professionals I distinguish between years of experience and responsibility. The chiefs would admit it, they were the first to come on board with this program before we instituted it; they said, "Give us more authority back and hold us responsible for getting the job done. We've gotten soft and sloppy," and so they knew they weren't doing their job. When it was put back on their shoulders, they ate it up, they started really taking hold.

This question came up again and again with junior officers I would meet with, they'd ask how to deal with chief petty officers. A real hot-shot aggressive ensign or jg wants to get in there and really get the job done. It's not easy for him to let the chief get the job done and take all the credit. Most chiefs can do the work of a lieutenant, if they're any good they can, so that ability to live with the chief petty officer and ensigns and jg's is not simple; it's tough. I often used to tell the chiefs, "You know, you've got a job, you've got to train those ensigns." They always chuckled, but they understood it. That really is true, the ensign and the jg have so much to learn that a smart ensign or jg is going to learn from that warrant officer and that chief petty officer, that E-8 and that E-9, that E-7, they're really going to teach him a lot. But if the ensign tries to do it all, the chief will go down to the Chief's Mess and he'll drink his coffee and say okay, that's the way they are. So it's a difference of perceptions. It's always going to be that way, and the best of the good leaders will try to remember how it used to be so they can relate as much as possible and bring people along as much as possible.

Admiral Moorer: Well, I think the first thing you've got to realize when you get to Washington is, the next person you contact up the line may be a civilian, and many of them have never been to Washington before, and the average time they stay in is about two and a half years. Of course, you have to deal with the Congress continuously, and sometimes there's a big bruhaha gap between the Congress and the Chief Executive, and so it's a really new experience to move out of the general circuit of the military and move into this one, because you are the dividing line between the airborne people and the civilian. But I think the main thing to remember is that, regardless of what kind of laws they pass or what kind of wiring diagram they draw, the way things function depends almost entirely on the personalities in the executive branch, beginning with the President and the President's relationship with the Secretary of Defense and the people you have to deal with in the National Security Council and the State Department and so on. For instance, Mr. Johnson was suspicious of military people for some reason, because he didn't even have any official meetings, although he had some with the National Security Council. He had what you call a Tuesday lunch, and all the decisions about the Vietnam War, for instance, were made during the Tuesday lunch. If we wanted to get authority to do something in Vietnam, they'd tell us "Wait until the Tuesday lunch," and sometimes the military people would be invited over there, sometimes they wouldn't. On the other hand, when Mr. Eisenhower was president, he had a very structured system for handling issues and various decisions about every department in the executive branch, including the Defense Department, and so when Nixon, having been Eisenhower's vice-president, came into office as President, he more or less set up the same structure that Eisenhower had, which put the National Security Council back in the

official functioning agency or activity. So the thing is that, when you become CNO, you've got to recognize the things that go in to move along according to the personnel who happen to be in the job at the moment. I think you've got to be very careful about testifying before the Congress, as I told you, sometimes a certain Congressman will try to get you to criticize your boss.

An officer should never answer a question if he does not know the answer. If you [as CNO] tell Congress, "I don't have the answer to that, I'll send it over to you tomorrow," that will satisfy them completely, but if you answer the question and it's wrong, then you can spend hours and hours undoing that one.

There is a discussion that Congress and the media have about the Joint Chiefs of Staff relative to the idea of having just one individual presenting the President with a military view. I think it's very important that he find out what the Chief of Naval Operations thinks and what the Chief of Staff of the Air Force and Chief of Staff of the Army think, and why. Because these aren't black-and-white problems they're dealing with, and the Joint Chiefs of Staff represent a wide service of 150 years, and naturally they are qualified or they wouldn't be there to point out the contributions the Navy has made.

To go back to World War II, there was a very strong argument between Admiral King and General Marshall over whether all assets were to go into the Atlantic end of Europe or whether some should begin to be devoted to the Pacific against Japan. Now I guess according to present customs, when people say that the Supreme Court delivers and the Congress debates and the Joint Chiefs of Staff bicker, people would say that General Marshall and Admiral King were bickering and that there was interservice rivalry there, and so on. The facts are that the problems the Joint Chiefs of Staff face, as I said, are not black and white, and the expertise that one acquires operating on the ground or at sea or in the air is very valuable to the President. Of course, if

I was in a position as President, I would certainly want to hear more than one view, so I think our system of military command is good. I think it would weaken the system if you just had one military view taken up to the President. The President's got to know that there are experts or experienced people who have been appointed by the President and confirmed by the Senate who have some different views about certain aspects of the solution. He finally has to decide what he's going to do.

Admiral Holloway: (A story Admiral Holloway related illustrates the need for knowledge and experience and background.)

In 1970, I was commander of the Attack Carrier Striking Force of the Sixth Fleet (it would now be known as the Battle Force Sixth Fleet), and Admiral Ike Kidd was Comm Sixth Fleet at the time, and a fracas developed in the Near East, I think the Syrians invaded Jordan with a tank column. Sixth Fleet was ordered down to the eastern Mediterranean, and Admiral Kidd moved his flag aboard the aircraft carrier where I was flying my flag, and we had arrived on station and Admiral Kidd got a message that the President wanted to talk to him on the radio telephone (which was a brand-new capability). Admiral Kidd was a very gracious gentleman, and he said to me, "Come on down with me," and he picked up the phone and he put his hand over the mouthpiece and said, "The President is getting ready to make a proclamation that the United States is going to send the Sixth Fleet to the eastern Mediterranean to contain the explosive situation between Syria and Jordan, to protect American lives in the area, and to do everything necessary to protect the sovereignty of the Jordanian state, and the President wants to know before he makes his announcement, are we, the Sixth Fleet, capable of doing all these things?" and he said, "How about it?" and I said, "Admiral, give me time to work on that one a little." I was mumbling, and Admiral Kidd said, "You've got ten seconds. The President is holding on the other end." So I said, "Yes, we can,"

and he told the President we could and the message went out.

Admiral Kidd and I talked about that because it was not a snap judgment out of thin air, it was based on a number of things that ran through that little computer known as the human brain. First, I had spent, in 1958, thirty days flying three flights a day around Lebanon and through the Middle East at the time of the Lebanon crisis, and I knew the area like the back of my hand. Second, I knew most of the pilots on the carrier that I was embarked on and the others, because I had come from command of the *Enterprise*, and most of these people were combat veterans of the conflict in Southeast Asia and I knew what they could do. And finally, I had kept myself professionally abreast of the battles of the Arab forces in the Middle East. When I put it all together, I knew what they could do, I knew what we could do, and therefore I could make virtually an instant judgment that what the President was asking us to ensure, we were capable of doing. But I couldn't have done it unless I had been an experienced naval officer.

Admiral Uchida: In January 1971, the *Fuji*, the icebreaker of the Japan Maritime Self-Defense Force, was caught in the ice pack in the Antarctic Sea and had a propeller blade broken by the iceberg. There seemed little hope for her to move out soon by breaking the thick ice carpet. At that time, I was Chief of Staff, JMSDF, and I had scheduled an official visit to the United States, South America, and Europe, and my departure had been settled to be in a few days.

I was in a quandry to estimate the situation rightly; should I cancel all trips ahead, or should I entrust my subordinates for the rescue of the *Fuji*, and start? Would the cancellation of the trip be a rash decision based on a minor accident, or would the accident be so serious a moment for me that I must give up the trip entirely?

I further examined the situation and surveyed the documents of the past. Then, I found a short remark of the captain of the *OB*, USSR icebreaker, about the nature of the icepack around

471

the *Fuji*. It reported that although the ice pack there seems solid and tight, the pack is loosened and the open sea appears in one night of southerly winds and that such winds prevail until April every year.

I started on the trip with some unrest in my mind. When I arrived in Beirut two weeks later, I got a report from my officer in Tokyo. It said that the *Fuji* had safely gotten out of the ice with the blessed southern breeze. Knowledge and experience in the hands of a seasoned officer equal power and correct decision-making capability.

Admiral Ramage: Do the best job you possibly can, wherever you're at. I've seen so many people who tried to do their own career planning, plan their own careers, and they spent more time worrying about where they were going next than they did where they were at, and I found that the Bureau of Personnel, the Personnel Command, as it's now called, did a fine job of detailing me without me worrying about it; in other words, if you do a good job where you're at, you're bound to get another good assignment. But if you don't do well where you're at, forget it, you're not going anywhere. So you better concentrate on where you're at, doing the best job.

There were two things I ever requested. The first was Submarine School rather than going to the Service Force. But here the first hurdle was the physical exam. I had one eye that I had injured wrestling at the Naval Academy and it was about 10/20 and of course 20/20 vision in both eyes was required. Fortunately, I was able to have that road block waived and as it turned out my bum eye was an asset. Once at sea I found that I could see perfectly through the periscope when the focusing knob was against the stop and, of course, the periscope had to be in perfect focus to see anything at night. So I was in luck and never had any trouble in that respect. Later, when I was due for shore duty, I requested postgraduate school rather than being assigned to some routine administrative job. I

was not eligible for gunnery, engineering, or any of the desirable courses, so I had to settle for Applied Communications. Right after the end of the first year, war broke out in Europe and within a week we all had orders back to sea. All I got out of that year was credit for the one-year General Line course.

One more comment about the eye requirements. After I made flag rank and was on duty in Washington I found many very eligible young men were being turned down by the Navy because of eyes. The old 20/20 requirement was still taking a heavy toll. So I prevailed upon the Bureaus of Medicine and Personnel to review this problem. After making the point that everyone is going to wear glasses sooner or later, the requirement was changed so that now anyone with vision as bad as 20/100 that is correctable to 20/20 with glasses is acceptable.

For officers to improve their administrative and management abilities you've got to state the problems and the objectives of your command, you've got to request suggestions, recommendations, and comments from appropriate staff members and you've got to incorporate their input into final decisions, if practical, and you've got to give everyone a chance to contribute and thereby enhance their own self-esteem and encourage more active participation in the actual decision-making process. It's very heartwarming to see that those people who have worked under me have continued to be successful. It's a rewarding experience, because there you try to reward their loyalty in every way possible, but I've never really had anyone who went against me or tried to buck me or anything like that, because we always would come to some modus operandi that would be satisfactory to each. You never can be sure that you're always right, that's for sure, you don't want to take that position or that things that you suggest can't be improved upon.

To ensure that the Navy and Marine Corps work as closely as possible to assure mission accomplishment, you've got to become more familiar with the capabilities, the limitations, and problems of the other services, and the more personally acquainted you get with the Marines or they with the Navy, the better, because you've got to work hand and glove, and there should be no friction, there should be the same mutual confidence and respect for each other.

Secretary Webb: The individual who always tells the unvarnished truth will have to meet himself coming and going. He might make people angry, however, and he should try to develop tact. But the individual who is known as a person of principle and sincerity has little to worry about in terms of his reputation. It is much better for a person to get in trouble for saying what he believes than to get in trouble for saying something that is not true or for trying to be different people for different audiences.

When someone speaks badly of someone else to an individual, that individual should consider saying, "Well, you're entitled to your opinion, but I happen to think that Webb (or whoever) has these good characteristics." An individual who is loyal enough to do that will probably tell the truth in other areas, as well.

Even exchanges between adversaries can be helpful as long as each person is truthful. The United States is the most unusual society on earth in terms of being a multi-cultural society in a state of continuous abrasion. On any issue that has any relevance, citizens have different moral perspectives, and this leads to creativity, politically and in every other way. But even though there is nothing wrong with disagreement, someone must have the strength to make a decision in an operating environment. Setting an ultimate goal may not always be a good idea, because an individual is likely either to undershoot it or overshoot it or find it irrelevant somewhere down the line. Setting an immediate goal is essential, however. The individual who can give 100 percent to that goal will find that things happen for him or her. Someone who cannot give his heart to what he is doing at the moment will probably not give his heart to other things

that come along. But if the officer commits himself to something and gives it everything he has, then the future will take care of itself.

Admiral Carney: As Chief of Naval Operations, I had deputies and extensive organizations under each of the deputies with subdivisions; these were my direct responsibilities and accountability. But I also had a responsibility to the Secretary of the Navy and, as a member of the Joint Chiefs of Staff, I had a responsibility to that organization. To my deputies, my instructions had to be clear. If the deputy couldn't carry out those instructions, the fault was his for lack of initiative and force, or it was my fault for lack of clarity in my directives.

My immediate staff did not require any exposition, because they knew what I wanted and they had to do it. I did pick my own people. I had one man who was with me for a total of 12 years, and he took it upon himself after I had trusted him with it to keep things away from me that somebody else could do. Sometimes he ruffled some feathers, but the feathers weren't mine, they were somebody else's. In my relationship with the Secretary of the Navy, he had his responsibilities, which were not only military but political, and so there were many things that he wanted to do that perhaps I didn't agree with, and we had to hammer that out somehow. Sometimes he would stick his nose into assignments that I wanted to make, into military assignments in the force load or elsewhere. We finally came to an agreement that if he had specific and overriding evidence that the person of my choice for this job under consideration was disqualified by reason of conduct or whatever, I would go along with him, but when it came to assignment of billets at sea in the military organization, unless he had that sort of information, he wouldn't mess around with my assignments. So whereas the commandants of the district were primarily responsible to the Secretary of the Navy, they did have military responsibilities in the event of emergencies or whatever, so after we had hassled that one around for a while we came to that agreement and it was satisfactory, but it was a question of persuasion rather than force leadership.

In the budgeting, the governing first parameter is the outside limit for defense expenditure that is assigned by the White House. That in turn has to be parceled out to the services in accordance with an original analysis within the Department of Defense. The amount each service receives is usually subject to further argument, but once that is settled and X number of dollars have been allocated to the Navy Department for a certain fiscal year, the Navy prepares a budget. The Navy has to allocate the funds to cover all its various needs. The first priority in funding is difficult to determine, and the budget is continually revised. Often 15 or 20 variations of a budget are made before a final budget is approved.

Admiral Ruge on why Rommel could not stop the invasion: In 1943 the situation for Germany worsened considerably. Stalingrad, North Africa, Sicily, Southern Italy, Kursk, are a demonstration of it. A huge landing operation by the Allied troops in northwestern Europe became more and more probable. In this situation, Field Marshal Erwin Rommel was given the order to plan the defense against the Allied forces. He had spent the summer at Hitler's headquarters, and they did not use his talents there at all. In October he commanded forces in northern Italy. For his new task I was ordered to assist him as naval expert [councellor]. I reported to his headquarters on November 10, 1943, at Lake Sarda [northern Italy]. Prior to my arrival at Rommel's office, I had worked with minesweeping and then mine-defense forces, and I therefore knew the coasts and harbors from Skagen down to the Spanish border.

In my first conference with Rommel, he discussed Hitler's order NR41. He did this in a very clear and natural manner. I quickly became acquainted with him. OKW (high command in the west) ordered us to constitute ourselves and

start operations [inspections] in Denmark in the beginning of December.

A combined landing of the Allied troops was not likely there because of the distance to the airports in England. The operations [inspections] in Denmark, however, provided us with valuable and useful suggestions, especially for the construction of landing obstacles, the fortifications of the coastal lines, which should at least make the landing procedures more difficult. Our work in this regard started at the end of December in France at Fountain Bleau.

The attempt to form a unified plan for the defense against an Allied landing was unexpectedly met with opposition and difficulty. The opinions as to the location for the operation differed widely. OKW expected the landing in the Channel zone (near Boulogne-Calais); they were influenced by a fictitious army of 20 divisions, which the Allied forces very cleverly pretended to have in southern England. (This was based on intercepted communications. Wrong data, of course.)

The Field Marshal in the West, Runstedt, expected the landing near the Somme River estuary. This area had excellent landing conditions and was completely open to the west. I, myself, have noted in my war diary of June 1, 1942, after the attack on St. Nazaire in assessing the situation, that I believed the target of the Allied invasion would be the Seine Bay [inlet], since it was geographically suitable for such an attack. Rommel first was inclined to follow Field Marshall Runstedt's idea [Somme], but then decided for the Seine Bay. At the Channel zone many divisions were stationed so that a landing was unlikely. Also in regard to the method [how to defend], how to *repulse* such a landing, not *one* opinion could be formed. At all meetings on that subject, Rommel always pointed out three areas that were important (decisive) for him. (1) A landing operation has its weakest point at the phase of the actual touchdown on land. (2) Orderly tank movements at daylight are impossible if the enemy has a superior air support. (3) The Germans are unable to maintain a *third front*. On the basis of these three realities, Rommel developed his plan, which should according to the available forces and their team play (unified actions) make a landing as difficult as possible. The infantry should in the majority be placed right behind the *coastline* barricaded in "Stacheldraht" [barbed wire] and land mines in a strip of a few kilometers. The coastline itself and the strip before the coast [into the sea] should be mined and fortified to make a landing difficult. In order to maintain good coverage, the tanks ought to be forward enough so that they were within striking distance of the coastline. This way they could be used when needed and yet remain movable. Deeper out in the sea, the navy was to lay mines of all types, including minesweeping-difficult [counter-minesweeping] devices. This meant utilizing all existing forces effectively, but Rommel did not succeed in implementing it before the actual invasion. Field Marshall Runstedt did not consider the landing itself that decisive. His plan was to organize the available tanks in such a way as to force the enemy back into the sea. He was supported by General Geyr von Schweppenburg, who commanded the armored forces [tanks], and he was supported by OKW, although Hitler's order 40 and 41 was to fight the enemy before it, at the latest, at the landing itself.

In the west we had about 50 infantry divisions among which were some rather weak divisions, which were recently put together from air force personnel without fighting experience. The armored [tank] divisions were increased to 10 by June 1944. Almost one-third of these forces were located south of the Loire and would need some time to relocate in order to be effective in the Normandy area or north of it.

At the end of December 1943 Rommel started to visit the units in Belgium first, then in the Netherlands and the Channel Zone, and then he went to the Normandy area. He learned that some sort of defense system which one could call an Atlantic Wall really only existed between Dunkirk and Le Tougnet, south of Boulogne. Farther to the west the defense system became weaker and weaker. The western Normandy area, where later the landing took place, was completely neglected [not prepared to be defended at all]. The whole stretch of beach where the landing took place was 50 kilometers long and was only secured by a weak auxiliary (second line) division with only a few positions.

Rommel continuously, according to his plans, pleaded for an effective defense system. He established immediate contact with his troops (they liked him immediately), and they listened to his plans and started working in this direction [toward Rommel's goals], but *their* seniors were only partially for him. He complained about this to OKW and was given total authority over the troops at the coast from Bretagne to the Netherlands at the end of January. However, Rommel's authority was limited at the highest command headquarters. He could only redirect the infantry divisions within the area with a part of the armored division directly commanded by OKW and serving as a reserve force. West of Normandy there was only the 21st armored division near Caen, where they could be used immediately if needed at the coast. The excellent division "PanzerLehr" and "Hitler Youth," however, were far back [inland]. He also had difficulty moving the flak corps [Air Defense Artillery]. The Pickert Flak Corps were moved to the coastline—they guarded frequently destroyed bridges in the hinterland. However, he was able to move the newly revived 352d infantry division to the coast, where they took over the portion of the 716th division which was very weak. The small and weak 90th air landing division he moved to the peninsula of Cotentin, north of Cherbourg. Both divisions were in place on June 6. Rommel had no influence on the Navy, and he was not able to convince the Navy group west to mine the Seine Bay. They relied on "Blitzsperren" mines that could be laid at a moment's notice, when the danger of the invasion was imminent. As we expected, we did succeed to do that almost everywhere, only *not* where it was most necessary.

On June 6, Rommel was on his way to Berchtesgaden to try to get the order to move the armored divisions and the Flak Corps to the coast. His presence at our headquarters, which had been established at La Rouche Guyon [near Normandy], would not have made much difference anymore. The tank division in the hinterland needed three days to be able to attack at the coastland. The enemy flew 11,000 sorties (attacks) daily. The Germans succeeded in sending up to 500, yet one could see what we could have done had we been prepared at the 352d division. The Americans pondered whether they should attack. They landed only 20 tons of material instead of the 2,400 tons planned on the first day. At Caen, still in the afternoon, the 21st armored division almost succeeded in driving the British back into the sea. It did not help, since they did not receive any reinforcement in order to utilize their successes. Nevertheless, the Allies captured four beachheads, which were combined later with Cherbourg, giving them a big harbor.

Rommel's clever tactic only postponed the obvious for about six weeks. Still, on July 17, an attempt of the British to break through near Caen cost them the loss of more than 500 tanks. But on the same day, Rommel's car was surprised by an air attack and his driver was killed. Rommel was the only one who could have succeeded in getting the army in France to rise against Hitler. An end of the war in 1944 would have saved the world a lot, but fate wanted it differently. The dictator Hitler forced Rommel to commit suicide. With that, the free world lost a man with a great ability to see things clearly, a man with a great sense of sympathetic understanding and great decency. He could have given the free world a lot.

I was ordered by Hitler to represent the navy at Rommel's funeral. I reached Ulm on the day of the funeral [October 11, 1944]. The whole city was in mourning, with flags lowered and huge masses of people in the streets. Field Marshall von Rundstedt spoke as the representative of Hitler. It was a good speech, yet strangely impersonal and untrue. Until the funeral I had assumed that Rommel's death was caused by his recent car accident. Now it became clear to me that something was wrong. At the entrance to the crematorium I succeeded in talking to his personal assistant, Aldinger, in private and said, "What's going on here?" Tears came down and he only managed to say "On Saturday they came." Then I knew enough. . . . Later on, still in Ulm, I found out that Hitler had sent Generals Burgdorf and Maisel to put an ultimatum to Rommel—either be tried before a people's court or take poison. Should he decide for the latter his family would not be touched. Now I understood Rommel's remarks to me earlier, that if he had gone to Berlin, he would have had an "accident."

Admiral Burke: Different individuals have different obligations, but they all must accept their obligations and fulfill them to the best of their ability. A naval officer has many conflicting obligations, including to his family and to the service. I made it very clear to my girl that the Navy would come first and she would be second. She understood that, she accepted it, and she leaned over backward to make sure she did. Well, that's fine until you retire, then it shifts. The obligation now is primarily to her, that's the way it should be. So obligations aren't fixed, and they are not the same for each individual. When you're saying the Navy is number one, you're really saying the country is number one, and if you ask my good wife, that's still number one in her point of view.

Officer's spouses play a large role in the officer's career. Wives are very important. I know my own has done more for me than I've ever done for myself, because she's got a hell of a lot of wisdom. But a drinking wife, for example, can be disastrous. You have got to know about it, because if you don't she can create so much hell and do so much damage before it's discovered. I checked everyone's wife. Everyone knew I was checking wives and I kept a dossier on wives. (It was burned.) Well, that got me into a lot of trouble. I didn't do it properly. Spouses aren't in the Navy.

So I learned how, after awhile, to let the wife do it. I let the wives into the command, for example, by asking them to make recommendations about housing in Newport. I got the chief's wife, happened to be a wonderful person, and she brought in three or four people. I appointed them as a committee, they made recommendations, I got them typed. It was good, and instead of making a presentation to the city myself, I had them present it, and I presented them. They had that thing squared away in a hurry, so I told the city council or whatever, I said, "I have got the strongest weapons. I'm not going to fool with you, these are women, they are wives, and they are powerful, and they think this thing is a mess and it is a mess and you've got to do something to fix it." Well, they did right quick. Those women would do anything, and it worked. Wives' clubs formed, all sorts of things. These little things don't matter a dime on a particular incident sometimes, it's just that it shows that people are part of the outfit, all people, and they've got something to say. If they've got something to say, something can be done about it.

(Editor's note: The following is an example of the multiple careers of a naval officer.)

I was on the board at Texaco a good many years after I retired. The Texaco people had a big refinery in Cuba, and they came down to see all the State Department people and the White House and everyone else when Castro was first starting his march to Havanna. They had gone to see everyone, and I knew Gus Long, who was chairman of Texaco, and he came into the office with some of his people and told me what his problem was and he said, "What would you do?" and I said, "I would get every person, every bit of equipment, out of Cuba you can get

out, but get all your people out as fast as you can except those that you have to leave." I said, "I would put dynamite under your important equipment and be ready to blow it all because you'll never get it back, this has gone too far, you'll never get it back." Well, he pulled his people out, he got a lot of material out of there in a week.

When I retired, he called up and said, "I want you on the board." I said, "I don't know a thing about oil." He said, "You're a chemical engineer." I said, "Yes, but I've forgotten it all." He said, "I want you on the board." I said, "Okay, it's your board, if you want to put up with me."

Well, later, oil struck in the North Sea, and Texaco, as all these big oil companies, bought as much as we thought was right. We had a lot of surveys made, we did a lot ourselves, and we had big holdings in England and big holdings in Germany and Norway, and we bid on a lot of things in the North Sea. Everyone knows the North Sea is a rough, damn area. It's cold up there and the wind blows, and the pressures in the northern channels are really terrific, and they vary.

We had all kinds of studies made on how to make those rigs and how to protect people in times of emergency. How do you take them off? The only way you can take them off sometimes is with helicopter, and sometimes you can't do that, so rigs ought to be made so that there's some part of it that will float so people can be safe in that part. It ought to be made so that no matter what direction the winds come from, not just the normal or the unusual conditions in the North Sea, it will probably hold. They put out anchors and scope chain to hold these. The whole thing is very carefully computed, and I looked at this thing and I said, "I don't think there's enough anchor." They said, "It's computed that way," and I said, "The statistics are probably correct, except for one thing, the input may be greater." I said, "They've got 150 knots or something like that, and no one really knows what happens with winds like that, but it may be greater so we ought to put a safety in all the way around. Let's put some more anchors out. It doesn't cost us that much." Our rigs were saved, and a lot of other rigs were not.

Now the people who were making those decisions were the top people of the company, and they accepted their responsibility completely, and they knew their stuff. Well, right after I went on the board they wanted to increase our manufacturing capability in England. To do that we wanted to put a refinery at the best location in England with all the factors involved. They chose a point in Wales, a very good spot, and they said, "You're a sailor. Take a look at this." It was on the coast, they showed the depth of the water and where they had 300 acres or something like that, what they were going to do, and where they were going to build a refinery. I looked at that thing and I couldn't find anything wrong with it until I got an idea, and I said, "I'll get some data on winds."

So they got normal winds and other things and I took a look at the currents and all the other and I said, "I don't think your refinery's in the right place, because you're putting it in a very exposed place. If you move just about a mile down the coast, there's a little point of land that comes out, and your tankers can stay there." That saved them, they say, all of my salary for all the years I was on the board, because that's what they did. Exxon has a refinery right nearby, and their tankers have a hell of a lot of trouble. They used to come over to Texaco docks across the bay.

I was on a lot of boards. There are some exceptions to this rule, but generally when a big decision would come up—on what to do with Libya, for example—the top people in the companies wanted to know the position of the relationships between the country and Libya. They would go down and check with the State Department, get their ideas, get their views, and they would make a decision, lots of times, to do things that cost them money to support the United States Navy. They did this without the government knowing anything about it. They do this in the building of their ships, their tankers, even in the design of tankers. They said, "What do you know about tankers?" I said, "Very little," and they said, "Is there anything we can do with our tankers, anything that we can put in now that might help if the government wants to take them over?" "Yes, a little bit, not much, but I think your shipbuilder's already got it in there. Make it easy so you can strengthen the decks, and a few things like that," I said. "You don't really have to change anything, you just have to think about it now." They did all that. They were the ones who thought about that. I didn't say, "You ought to do this." They were the ones.

What I believe is that in a lot of companies there is more consideration for the government by the companies than there is by government officials themselves.

Now you take the protection of these rigs in the North Sea. They are right close to the Soviet Union, they can be destroyed fairly easily, so to the best of their ability those rigs are built so that additional protection can be used, that additional steps can be taken. Everything that they can think of that can be done in advance has already been done. I was on the board of one company whose motto was: "We'll build good ships at a profit if we can, but we will build good ships." They meant it. They would build good ships, that was the proudest thing they could ever do. Well, I went down and worked with the company, with the people, with the supervisors, and to make sure I knew what the company was doing, as all directors did, I went clear through the company. Those people were trying very hard. Bill was the chairman, and I said to Bill, "Bill, your organization is wonderful as long as you are here, but you're not as young as you ought to be, and who's your successor? Who is being trained here as your successor?" He said, "How am I doing?" and I said, "You're doing fine. It's no criticism of what you're doing, but you ought to have somebody." He said, "No." There wasn't anyone in that company who was being trained, who had the knowledge of how he got his information, what he was doing. They should not have trained just one person, but three or four, several people, who could flight up if they had to. This bothered me, so I went to some other noncompany board members (usually they have two or three company executives on the board, but about three-fourths of the board have no connection with the company, they're outsiders) and I said, "What about Bill? He gave me hell because he didn't like part of that," and they said, "Well, we think you're right," and I said, "Talk to him about it," and they said, "No, no, you can't do anything. He won't listen. We've tried it before, too. He just won't listen, and he won't do it, he doesn't believe in it."

We asked him, and he did go so far as to put two people in as sort of executive vice-presidents who would be given a little more instruction, but he died before they were in. When he found he had cancer, at the board meeting he said to the whole board, "Damn, you were right as hell. It's too late now." Now, that man was probably the best shipbuilder by instinct, what the factors were that he used to make so many right decisions we'll never know, but he made a lot of very fine decisions. He had the support of everyone, but there was no one after he died to take that company over from the inside. That's the worst thing that can happen to a company, of course; so within a month we had to find someone to make a friendly acquisition. Well, we found Tennaco, and Tennaco took it over and they've done a good job. The first thing that Tennaco did was to take that damn motto down that used to be on the gate. It's not there anymore, and they are building ships for a profit, period.

Before the war General Motors was into the gun mount manufacturing business up in Erie, and they did a very good job, though not nearly as good as some of the others. One of the others was a very enthusiastic, hard-working man. He was brilliant himself, he had a lot of money, he went out and got things, he was ruthless.

I was gun mount inspector, 5-inch thirty-eights,

and we needed a plant that had a new concept, because we were turning out at the naval gun factory 24 gun mounts a month. Twenty-four gun mounts is five ships, five destroyers, and we needed a hell of a lot more than destroyers, we needed the gun mounts for cruisers and battleships and carriers and everything else, and they couldn't possibly do that. So we went out to see who could do this, and Northern Ordnance, Northern Pump at that time, was building hydraulic drives, and they were excellent, and they were in competition with another hydraulic company. It was an old-timer, but it impressed us, so we asked this man, Hally was his name, "Would you be interested? Would it be possible for you to take this whole gun mount, start from scratch?" and he said, "I'll do it."

Things happened fast then. Hally went around to every company and he hired from every company the most expert man in the gun mount business he could get. One of the critical things in the manufacturing of those gun mounts in that time was, they had great big rings of bearings, really big bearings, they were about 10 or 12, 15, depending upon the size of the gun mount, feet in diameter, and they had to be held to a thousandth of an inch. The machining of that was very, very difficult, and that was one of the bottlenecks. He put people to the designing of a piece of equipment—no matter what it cost, no matter what they had to do—to make those things automatically, without people. He made it in a month. He did this with all of the other parts. We gave him all the bottlenecks, he knew all of the bare data. If he found someone whom he thought he could hire, and he needed, he could get him. The net result was that he lived up to his promise. He built a factory in nothing flat, and in an almost impossible time he had gun mounts coming out. The gun mounts used to cost about eighty or ninety thousand dollars apiece, that was a lot in those days. At the end of the war he had made all of those gun mounts at about twenty-four thousand dollars apiece, so his profits were just stupendous. Well of course the government said, "You can't make a profit three or four times what it cost you. That's not fair," and he said, "The hell it ain't." Well, anyway he lost his suit, and he got cut way back on his profits, but his profits were still great, he was a multimillionaire.

He did everything he could to support the government. He made better gun mounts than the gun factory ever made. If he could get an idea from someone else, he'd buy it or he would work around it somehow, but he would use anything that he could use. For example, at the end of the war, I was down in the gun factory here, I was a lieutenant commander, I think, and he called me up about four o'clock one afternoon, and he said, "We're stuck at the back door." I said, "What's the matter?" He said, "Mounts ought to be coming out the back door and they aren't. They aren't passing inspection. You've got to get out here right now." I said, "What's wrong?" He said, "If we knew what's wrong, you wouldn't have to come out. I don't know what's wrong, the damn things won't work, so get out here." I said, "I can't. I'll come out in the morning." He said, "No." I said, "I've only got an hour to catch a plane. The plane leaves at five o'clock." He said, "I've got reservations on the plane. They'll hold the plane for a little while. You get over there." I said, "I don't have any gear." He said, "You don't need any gear," so I said, "All right, I'll be there."

My secretary called my wife. I grabbed a hydraulic pump on the way out, which happened to be a competitor's pump, because hydraulics is usually the trouble with the accuracy of a gun mount, and I took this, which was new design, out with me. That's the only baggage I had. I was met by a little German band in Minneapolis at about midnight, I had to change planes in Chicago. We went out to the plant, and we stayed in that plant for about fifty hours, and I had one suit, a Navy uniform, and we crawled under that gun mount and we worked on it as two mechanics, he and I. We couldn't find what was wrong, we just couldn't find it. I

had insulted him, of course, by bringing out his competitor's pump, and the pump wouldn't fit on this mount, so the pump was just a useless thing, but I said, "It's got to be in the hydraulics." He would say that, too, but we couldn't find anything wrong with the hydraulics.

Finally I said, "Let's build this thing. Take the hydraulic system apart piece by piece, and we'll build it, you and I. We'll check every dimension on everything." Well, what we found out was, on those things there was a little bit of a release hole, about an eighth of an inch in diameter. It was just a release, it didn't have anything operating in it, but that little hole served a purpose of giving relief to high pressures. I said, "Well, it won't do any harm," so we reamed that out quite a bit. It worked, and we started rolling out gun mounts.

We went right back to his house. It was the first time I had ever been in his house. He had a great big mansion, he said, "Here's your room." Of course we were both dead tired, we hadn't had any sleep—we'd sleep under the gun mount for an hour or something like that while the other one worked—we were filthy dirty. We walked into this house with oily shoes. I started taking mine off. He said, "The hell with it, you don't have any time, here's your room." I took my clothes off and put them in the bathroom, took a shower, about four showers, but still I couldn't get all the dirt off, and of course I went to sleep and slept. When I got up I had a civilian suit, he tailor made it, all that complete equipment, everything else, he was that kind of a man. Now that man felt that the government cheated him right and left, but he did everything he could to do what he thought was right for the government. The point that I'm trying to make is that the top civilians of the country do remarkable things for their country.

Admiral de Cazanove: For three years I commanded our forces out of Brest and put the word out not to phone Paris asking questions, for if I do something wrong, they will tell me very quickly. So we did not phone except in exceptional cases, and this worked well with Paris, because they often did things without asking what to do. After a while the word went in Paris, among the staff, that I knew what I was doing, and they were glad that I was not bothering them every day. In any case, when you phone to headquarters, you don't generally get the person in charge, but end up talking to someone on the staff who doesn't know much more than you do. So I think one has to be careful with the use of modern communication capabilities, for they can have both positive and negative results in their use.

I should also like to stress that to be a leader you must wish to be a leader, for without that desire you will never be a leader. It's not because you have been through such and such a school or academy or that you get stripes or stars that you will be a leader, and if you don't have the desire, then why not choose another profession? Commanding is a necessity for a leader, and for many it is much easier to obey than to command. There are people who think it is easy to command and say: "I am the boss," and then quickly find that it is much easier to obey. Basically, it is the duty of the person having the authority to act and command. Do not fear to be wrong, for in the final analysis is it not the leader who donates his life to formal difficulties? There is no such luxury as being able to choose the possibility which will give no trouble—that is not the way of command. In peacetime I've seen people, some in the highest ranks, who had no trouble or difficulties, just because they didn't have much character and always did the thing with the least amount of risk, and, fortunately for them, luck or not, they have not been confronted with a crisis. They are really not leaders, they are just men. Unfortunately, in peacetime there is a temptation to choose people who will not take risks, will not place the government, the minister, in difficulty—even though this lack of taking on the difficulty now may cause even greater difficulties in the future. In other words, some are inclined to choose those who have not

much character, and this is terrible, because if difficulties come, if a war happens, this is certainly not the one to deal with the difficulties of war. I should like to stress the importance of preparation, planning, and, of course, responsibility and speed of action, which you cannot have unless you have thought a great deal about it before the action becomes necessary. Make the time, in your cabin, on the bridge, wherever you are, to reflect; "What if this happens . . . what will I do?" It is true that things never happen exactly as they have been planned, but all the same, they have to be planned and planned and planned, because planning is a matter of making you reflect on your work, on your responsibilities, and will give you the maximum chance when the unexpected comes that you will have thought of so many contingencies that you will have a reasonable chance of taking the right action the first time, for in war there often is not a second chance to recover from mistakes.

(The following are taken from the writings of Admiral de Cazanove while he was Commandant Chief of the Atlantic Theater):

Draw your strength from yourself, from your will, your energy, and from the experience you have gained year after year from the responsibilities you have assumed.

You have to dare and you don't have to be afraid to command.

To command is maybe also to know when to disobey, without necessarily having to be one-eyed and named Nelson.

(Admiral de Cazanove believes the following, though he doesn't claim to have been the first to say them):

The legitimacy of your authority will be as great as your sense of duty will be high and your loyalty to the state is deep.

Discipline in the fleet is based on the spirit of the wardrooms. (Admiral Jervis)

It is necessary that captains be great-hearted men. (Richelieu)

To command is first to convince.

The chief, like the artist, needs talent shaped by practice.

96. Conclusion: Professionalism and Ethics

This book has examined the actions and ideals required of officers who want to make a positive contribution to the Naval Service. In the final analysis, officers are known by the professional and ethical approach they use in meeting their responsibilities; in this section, the components of these approaches are reviewed.

Webster's dictionary defines the adjective *professional* as "of, engaged in, or worthy of the high standards of a profession; engaged in a specified occupation for pay or as a means of livelihood." A *professional,* the noun form, is defined as a "person having much experience and great skill in a specified role," and this definition is most important in the Naval Service. *Ethics,* as defined by Webster's, is "the study of standards of conduct and moral judgment; moral philosophy; a treatise on this study; the system or code of morals of a particular profession." These two terms, no matter how long or short a naval officer's career, constitute the most important factors in the officer's physical and mental makeup.

Military professionalism is a unique "way of life." On the one hand, military leaders are citizens who are responsible to the entire population for the nation's defense. On the other hand, they are responsible, ultimately, for mission accomplishment and, just as important, for their personnel and, at times, their personnel's lives. One day your decision, like Eisenhower's on D Day, 6 June 1944 at Normandy, when he ordered tens of thousands of men possibly to their deaths for the Allied invasion of Europe, may carry an awesome responsibility. Eisenhower no doubt weighed the risks carefully, but he also was doubtlessly relieved when he received word that the landing had been successful and the Allies had gained a foothold on the beach.

Military professionalism and ethics are closely aligned. Individuals in the Naval Service who are professionals and live by a code of ethics have developed certain personal characteristics, maintained high standards of conduct, and developed an ethical and professional judgment, philosophy, and morality.

WHERE DO ETHICS COME FROM?

As many of us have learned in other courses or from our own experiences, we are what we come from. Our specific culture has sought to ingrain in us certain mores that have been considered conducive to the good of the group or society we were raised in. These are standards set up by people for the benefit of all. People in the Naval Service come from all walks of life, and their status, standards, and personal characteristics determine their behavior. Their guidelines for living may need little alteration, or they may need a great deal.

Exposure to ethical considerations starts in childhood and continues throughout life. From their earliest learned ethics, individuals can pursue an infinite number of directions. All people have their own ideas of how ethics fit into their lifestyle. Some people are cold and callous and care little, for example, about poor people who live on the streets without food or shelter; others show humility and compassion and seek the welfare of all people. It is ludicrous to say that a person "will always" be virtuous, do what should be done over what is popular, or impose self-denial instead of permitting self-indulgence.

Today's generation, like others before it, is a melting pot of the rich and the poor, the happy and the frustrated, the leader and the follower, the strong and the weak. The economic conditions in our society have led thousands to join the Naval Service just to survive. The Naval Service must continue to grow, but it can ill afford to allow the military ethic to erode or diminish in any way. For all of these reasons, officers in the Naval Service must work to instill ethical standards and military professionalism.

WHAT WE CAN DO

Some people have the misconception that ethics as they pertain to civilian life do not constitute professional military ethics; in fact, however, many ethical standards, no matter where they were acquired, influence sailors and Marines. If high standards are found to be rare or nonexistent in their subordinates, then professional leaders in the Navy and Marine Corps must ensure that standards of proper conduct or behavior are established and honed. They should undertake this task for many reasons, some of them going back in naval history hundreds of years. The Naval Service is rich in traditions and values such as loyalty, esprit de corps, and service to country. These are concepts that have made this country and the Naval Service what they are today.

Unfortunately, this train of thought seems to be declining somewhat. Therefore, those in the Naval Service must be on guard to ensure that the qualities necessary for their profession are not diminished. Their ethical responsibilities are unparalleled by those of any other profession; few individuals in other professions—if any— have the responsibility of the country or the lives of subordinates in their hands or are recognized by the public to be absolutely necessary. The Naval Service, no matter how you slice it, is clearly a profession, and as such it must establish minimum standards of behavior.

In order for the Naval Service to contribute to the defense of this nation, individuals serving in it must have moral values. Human nature itself dictates this. Because people come from different cultures and have different values, naval leaders must indoctrinate all personnel in the value system of the Naval Service.

Order is a necessary concept in the Naval Service. Without it as part of the whole, there would be chaos and confusion; without it as part of the individual, the same result. Order leads to prioritizing, and prioritizing leads to values, which, as stated above, are necessary in the service. The values of the Naval Service have changed little over time. The following values reflect the thinking of today's military leaders: integrity; duty, honor, and country; competence; teamwork; and authority, responsibility, and accountability.

Can a person be ethical and a professional without embracing the aforementioned values? Positively not! In many cases these values must be taught, and there is no better place for this indoctrination to take place than at naval recruit depots, officer candidate schools, NROTC units, and the Naval Academy. A genuine leader and a professional must embrace these values.

INTEGRITY

The hallmark of all professionals is integrity. Without it there is no viable officer corps. Slogans such as "Can Do," "Semper Fidelis," and "Duty, Honor, Country" are meaningless without integrity. Naval traditions and codes dictate that officers exemplify this basic honesty.

The officer corps must at all times set the example for others to follow. Any statement, whether official or unofficial, from an officer is considered to be "fact" by an enlisted person. Officers cannot afford to let their subordinates down, for when the chips are down and officers lead these sailors and Marines into battle and possibly death, the troops must have faith in the officers, respect them as leaders, and perform for them. The responsibility is unique and involves awesome moral judgment.

The naval profession is very stressful, and under stressful conditions anyone who is not disciplined may bend under pressure and lose his integrity. Don't let it happen to you!

DUTY, HONOR, COUNTRY

Perhaps during a first tour, military service is just an adventure; some people join simply because there was nothing else available for them. But once individuals make the commitment and are part of the Navy or Marine Corps, they will realize the importance and truth of the statement "It's much more than just a job!"

Hearing the National Anthem, military personnel get goose bumps, and they realize how special they, their service, and their country are. They realize the purpose, necessity, and importance of their duty in safeguarding this nation's ideals. The ideal of freedom is enjoyed by Americans daily. Too many take this freedom for granted. Without freedom and the other American ideals, this nation will fail miserably. And when a service person no longer gets goose bumps when the National Anthem is played, the time has come for him to move to another profession or retire.

COMPETENCE

Competence is required of officers in a wide range of areas, but in the Naval Service three main themes emerge. They are: being technically and tactfully proficient (knowledge), being a leader of people (leadership), and keeping standards high (set the example). These three areas encompass nearly all aspects of the Navy and Marine Corps. An officer who lacks competence in one of these areas can be in jeopardy and place others in jeopardy. If officers do not know the technical or tactical aspects of their jobs, there is a distinct possibility that lives will be lost in combat. If officers cannot lead their personnel effectively, lives can be lost. If they fail to set a proper example at any time, they risk having their subordinates believe that the standards that have been set by the government, service, or commanding officer "don't mean anything." These risks are unacceptable, and therefore competence in these areas is mandatory. Secretary Webb suggests that

> a leader should never give a personal benefit to an individual if it impacts on the unit's mission. By the same token, he should never put a burden on an individual that does not relate to the unit's mission. Procuring better rations for personnel is a benefit that will affect them only positively, while allowing them to bunch up in fighting holes so more of them can get sleep can affect the entire

mission. The officer is not doing anyone a favor when he "cuts" his people the sort of "slack" that impacts on the unit's mission. In most cases in an officer-enlisted relationship, the enlisted person does not need a friend (which does not mean the officer cannot be his friend), he needs someone knowledgeable to lead him and give him directions and accept responsibility.

TEAMWORK

In order to engage in war and win, the Naval Service must make a cooperative effort. In the Naval Service, as in most sports, businesses, and large organizations, "success" can only be achieved when the *team* is formed, tuned, motivated, and performing at its peak. The most successful team in the world is the United States Navy and Marine Corps. It can remain effective, but will it? The Naval Service can ill afford to leave the answer to chance.

Naval personnel must always feel and be a part of the group and have a clear sense of responsibility to their fellow sailors and Marines. The whole of the service—the team—must be the most important aspect of whatever they do. It must be the center of their thought. How they practice in peacetime, no matter how boring or repetitious practice may be, determines how they will react when the real thing comes along. For things to "fall in place" as naval personnel expect them to, the team must become self-reliant, believe its job is significant, and be recognized by seniors in the chain of command.

Sometimes officers forget the team because they are so interested in themselves. Sometimes it is extremely difficult to get the team properly tuned because turnover is so rapid, and keeping the troops motivated may become a laborious task. However, remembering the team, tuning the team, and motivating the team are all part of being a leader. The old axiom "A chain is only as strong as its weakest link" is of paramount importance to the Navy and Marine Corps team.

To make and keep this team "the best," officers must be able to focus on the big picture and exhibit those uncommon qualities that are absolutely necessary and that set them apart from individuals in other professions. The vital link is a simple one: teamwork. Admiral Larson makes the point that

> excellence in a military unit is achieved through having high standards, through having people who believe in those standards and support them. They do this through good communications, by having their troops understand the mission of the ship, and by taking pride in being united in carrying out that mission. You have high standards by having officers who set a good example, who meet those high standards themselves, who are willing to work hard and sacrifice for the good of the unit, and who will take care of those troops and make sure that they are treated fairly and that they are given a maximum opportunity for training and advancement. Probably the hardest thing in setting a high standard for a unit is to discipline people. We all like to give medals, we all like to give rewards, we all like to tell people they've done a job well. The tough thing in holding a high standard is to take those who don't meet the standard and discipline them. There are many different ways to do this, but it is important that those who don't meet the standard are disciplined, are weeded out, and that all are encouraged to meet that standard, because if you don't set a high standard and you don't achieve it, you will not have excellence.

AUTHORITY, RESPONSIBILITY, AND ACCOUNTABILITY

A professional who lives by an ethical philosophy understands the importance of assuming authority, fulfilling responsibilities, and being accountable for his actions. These three characteristics are part of the interchange of thoughts and feelings between people and are the essence of military fiber. Without them the walls would surely crumble. Command and authority are very closely intertwined. Command is the authority (the legal basis) of a person in the military to exercise control of subordinates through the chain of command. Authority, therefore, is the legitimate power of leaders to control and direct the subordinates under them and cause subordinates to react to their commands, if in fact those commands are within the scope of the leader's position.

Directly related to authority is responsibility. Naval officers receive certain responsibilities along with each assignment. Some responsibilities, such as discipline, morale, training, and troop well-being, are inherent in every job assigned. Others come from the authority bestowed on officers, petty offiers, and noncommissioned officers alike. Responsibilities also originate from guidelines such as orders, regulations, directives, and manuals.

Commanders are accountable for their own actions and the actions of their personnel, and that accountability is based on the authority delegated and responsibility assigned to commanders as a result of their past performance, experiences, and judgment. Responsibility and authority increase with rank. In the Navy and the Marine Corps, they go hand in hand, and as an officer increases in rank, he must not lose sight of their importance, always remembering that he is 100 percent accountable for all of his actions 24 hours per day.

A FINAL THOUGHT ON LEADERSHIP

Quality is an acquired trait, an accomplishment, a capacity that is distinctive and characteristic. In a naval sense, *quality* embodies the precepts of performance, readiness, and professionalism and the degree to which they are achieved. It is a trait that is quantifiable by experience and examination.

To a great extent, a unit's *quality* will be

assessed during the many evaluations and inspections conducted by external agencies. A unit will be under almost constant observation and appraisal, requiring an undiminished effort to attain and maintain superior quality.

QUALITY connotes excellence; excellence is our mark!

Spirit is that special attitude or frame of mind peculiar to and animating a particular ship or unit. In a sense, it is the breath of life of a ship or unit. It is the distillation of the diverse personalities of the crew or unit members, mirroring their collective dispositions. Although intangible, *spirit* is apparent in every ship and unit.

Leaders must endow their ships and units with a *spirit* that provides the inner structure, dynamic drive, and creative response to cope with the demands they will encounter. They must generate a sense of belonging; they must understand and appeal to personal pride; and they must define their unit's purpose explicitly. The characteristics of *spirit*, such as enthusiasm, energy, vivacity, ardor, courage, cheerfulness, and firmness, must be focused in a productive and positive manner in support of the organization's primary goals.

SPIRIT is a vital principle; we must nurture it!

Character is the stamp of individuality impressed on a ship or unit. It is the aggregate of the moral qualities of each person serving in the unit. In a manner of speaking, it is the "style" of the ship or unit.

Character should be strongly marked and should serve to distinguish ship or unit, crew, and individual. Leaders must be forceful and resolute, exhibit self-discipline, demonstrate high ethics, utilize superior judgment—not only in their day-to-day conduct of business and associations with each other, but also in their outside activities.

The reputation of the Naval Service will be founded on *CHARACTER*; we must engender a strong, moral vigor!

QUALITY, SPIRIT, AND CHARACTER are mutually supportive traits. It is self-defeating to concentrate on one and neglect the others. Collectively, they are the properties that leaders should consider while making decisions in order to provide frames of reference vis-á-vis their chosen goals.

As Admiral Hayward said in the beginning of this chapter, have a full career in the Naval Service supporting your country. You will find it enjoyable and rewarding.

Recommended Readings

1. *Above and Beyond: A History of the Medal of Honor from the Civil War to Vietnam*. Boston: Boston Publishing, 1985.

2. Armbrister, Trevor. *Matter of Accountability: The True Story of the Pueblo Affair*. New York: Coward-McCann, 1970.

3. Baldwin, Hanson Weightman. *Battles Lost and Won: Great Campaigns of World War II*. New York: Harper and Row, 1966.

4. Barclay, C. N. *Upon Their Shoulders*. London: Farber and Farber, 1963.

5. Barnett, Correlli. *Desert Generals*. Bloomington: Indiana University Press, 1982.

6. Becton, F. Julian. *Ship That Would Not Die*. Missoula, Mont.: Pictorial Histories, 1987.

7. Blanchard, Kenneth. *Putting the One Minute Manager to Work*. New York: William Morrow, 1984.

8. Blumenson, Martin, and Stokesbury, James L. *Masters of the Art of Command*. Boston: Houghton Mifflin, 1975.

9. Boettcher, Thomas D. *Vietnam: The Valor and the Sorrow—From the Home Front to the Front Lines in Words and Pictures*. Boston: Little, Brown, 1985.

10. Bradden, Russel. *The Siege*. New York: Viking Press, 1969.

11. Byron, John L. "The Captain." *Proceedings*, Sept. 1982.

12. Caesar, C. Julius. *Caesar's Conquest of Gaul*. New York: AMS Press, 1911.

13. Calvert, James. *The Naval Profession*. New York: McGraw-Hill, 1971.

14. Carnegie, Dale. *How to Win Friends and Influence People*. New York: Simon and Schuster, 1952.

15. Carr, Edward Hallett. *Twenty Years' Crisis, 1919–1939: An Introduction to the Study of International Relations*. New York: St. Martin's Press, 1956.

16. Catton, Bruce. *Glory Road: The Bloody Route from Fredericksburg to Gettysburg*. Garden City, N.Y.: Doubleday, 1952.

17. ———. *Grant Moves South*. Boston: Little, Brown, 1960.

18. ———. *Mr. Lincoln's Army*. Garden City, N.Y.: Doubleday, 1951.

19. ———. *Stillness at Appomattox*. Garden City, N.Y.: Doubleday, 1953.

20. Chamber, James. *Devil's Horsemen*. New York: Atheneum, 1979.

21. Churchill, Sir Winston Leonard Spencer. *Marlborough: His Life and Times*. New York: Scribner, 1968.

22. ———. *River War: An Account of the Reconquest of the Sudan*. London: Eyre and Spottiswoode, 1933.

23. ———. *The World Crisis*. New York: Charles Scribner's Sons, 1951.

24. Clausewitz, Karl Von. *On War*. Trans. Michael Howard and Peter Paret. Princeton, N.J.: Princeton University Press, 1976.

25. Collins, Arthur S. *Common Sense Training: A Working Philosophy for Leaders*. Novato, Calif.: Presidio Press, 1978.

26. Cooper, James Fenimore. *History of the Navy of the United States of America*. Upper Saddle River, N.J.: Literature House, 1970.

27. Crane, Stephen. *Red Badge of Courage*. New York: Macmillan, 1962.

28. Cross, Wilbur. *Naval Battles and Heroes*. New York: American Heritage, 1960; distributed by Golden Press.

29. Davis, Burke. *Marine! The Life of Lieutenant General Lewis B. (Chesty) Puller*. Boston: Little, Brown, 1962.

30. DeBono, Edward. *New Think*. New York: Basic Books, 1968.

31. de Gaulle, Charles. *Edge of the Sword*. Westport, Conn.: Greenwood Press, 1975.

32. Denton, Jeremiah A. *When Hell Was in Session*. New York: Reader's Digest Press, 1976; distributed by Crowell.

33. Devereux, James P. S. *The Story of Wake Island*. New York: J. B. Lippincott, 1947.

34. DiMona, Joseph. *Great Court-Martial Cases*. New York: Grosset and Dunlap, 1972.

35. Downey, Fairfax Davis. *Indian-Fighting Army*. New York: Bantam Books, 1957.

36. du Picq, Ardant. *Battle Studies*. Harrisburg, Pa.: Stackpole, 1946.

37. Earle, Edward Mead. *Makers of Modern Strategy: Military Thought from Machiavelli to Hitler*. Princeton, N.J.: Princeton University Press, 1943.

38. Eccles, Henry. *Military Power in a Free Society*. Newport, R.I.: Naval War College Press, 1979.

39. Eggenberger, David. *Dictionary of Battles*. New York: Dover, 1985.

40. Emery, Noemi. *Washington: A Biography*. New York: Putnam, 1976.

41. Flanagan, Edward M. *Before the Battle: A Common Sense Guide to Leadership and Management*. Novato, Calif.: Presidio Press, 1985.

42. Forester, Cecil Scott. *Admiral Hornblower in the West Indies*. Boston: Little, Brown, 1958.

43. ———. *Beat to Quarters*. Boston: Little, Brown, 1942.

44. ———. *Commodore Hornblower*. New York: Grosset and Dunlap, 1945.

45. ———. *Flying Colours*. London: M. Joseph, 1938.

46. ———. *Hornblower and the Atropos*. Boston: Little, Brown, 1953.

47. ———. *Hornblower and the Hotspur*. Boston: Little, Brown, 1962.

48. ———. *Hornblower during the Crisis, and Two Stories: Hornblower's Temptation and The Last Encounter*. Boston: Little, Brown, 1967.

49. ———. *Lieutenant Hornblower*. Boston: Little, Brown, 1952.

50. ———. *Lord Hornblower*. Boston: Little, Brown, 1946.

51. ———. *Mr. Midshipman Hornblower*. Boston: Little, Brown, 1950.

52. ———. *Ship of the Line*. Boston: Little, Brown, 1938.

53. Forrestel, Emmet P. *Admiral Raymond A. Spruance, USN: A Study in Command*. Washington, D.C., 1966. For sale by the Superintendent of Documents, U.S. Government Printing Office.

54. Freeman, Douglas Southall. *Lee's Lieutenants: A Study in Command*. New York: Charles Scribner's Sons, 1942–44.

55. ———. *R. E. Lee: A Biography*. New York: Charles Scribner's Sons, 1934–35.

56. Fuller, J. F. C. (John Frederick Charles). *Generalship: Its Diseases and Their Cure—A Study of the Personal Factor in Command*. Harrisburg, Pa.: Military Service, 1936.

57. Fussell, Paul. *Great War and Modern Memory*. New York: Oxford University Press, 1975.

58. Gilbert, Martin. *Winston S. Churchill: Finest Hour*. Boston: Houghton Mifflin, 1983.

59. Goldman, Peter Louis. *Charlie Company: What Vietnam Did to Us*. New York: Morrow, 1983.

60. Goodenough, Simon. *Tactical Genius in Battle*. London: Phaidon Press, 1979.

61. Grant, Ulysses Simpson. *Personal Memoirs.* Cleveland: World, 1952.

62. Grechko, Andrei Antonovich. *Armed Forces of the Soviet State: A Soviet View.* Washington, D.C.: U.S. Air Force, 1975. For sale by the Superintendent of Documents, U.S. Government Printing Office.

63. Gugliotta, Bobette. *Pigboat 39: An American Sub Goes to War.* Lexington: University Press of Kentucky, 1984.

64. Gullickson, Gregg G., and Chenette, Richard D. *Excellence in the Surface Navy.* Monterey, Calif.: Naval Postgraduate School, Department of Administrative Sciences, 1984.

65. Hamilton, Nigel. *Monty: The Making of a General.* New York: McGraw-Hill, 1981.

66. Haskell, Franklin Aretas. *Battle of Gettysburg.* Boston: Houghton Mifflin, 1958.

67. Hays, Samuel H., and Thomas, William N. *Taking Command.* Harrisburg, Pa.: Stackpole, 1967.

68. Heinl, Robert Debs. *Soldiers of the Sea: The United States Marine Corps, 1775–1962.* Annapolis: Naval Institute Press, 1965.

69. Heinlein, Robert Anson. *Starship Troopers.* New York: Putnam, 1959.

70. Hemingway, Ernest. *Men at War: The Best War Stories of All Time.* New York: Crown, 1942.

71. Henderson, George Francis Robert. *Stonewall Jackson and the American Civil War.* New York: Longmans, Green, 1936.

72. Hersey, John. *Hiroshima.* New York: Knopf, 1985; distributed by Random House.

73. Hersey, Paul. *Management of Organizational Behavior: Utilizing Human Resources.* Englewood Cliffs, N.J.: Prentice-Hall, 1972.

74. Holm, Jeanne. *Women in the Military: An Unfinished Revolution.* Novato, Calif: Presidio Press, 1982.

75. Horsfield, John. *The Art of Leadership in War: The Royal Navy from the Age of Nelson through World War II as a Case History.* Westport, Conn.: Greenwood Press, 1980.

76. Hough, Richard. *The Great Admirals.* New York: William Morrow, 1977.

77. Howarth, David Armine. *1066: The Year of the Conquest.* New York: Viking Press, 1978.

78. ———. *Trafalgar: The Nelson Touch.* New York: Atheneum, 1969.

79. ———. *Voyage of the Armada: The Spanish Story.* New York: Viking Press, 1981.

80. ———. *Waterloo: Day of Battle.* New York: Atheneum, 1968.

81. Hubbard, Elbert. *Message to Garcia: Being a Preachment.* East Aurora, N.Y.: Roycroft Shop, 1899.

82. Huntington, Samuel P. *Soldier and the State: The Theory and Politics of Civil-Military Relations.* Cambridge: Belknap Press of Harvard University Press, 1957.

83. Icenhower, Joseph B. *Submarines in Combat.* New York: Franklin Watts, 1964.

84. Isely, Jeter Allen. *The U.S. Marines and Amphibious War: Its Theory and Its Practice in the Pacific.* Princeton, N.J.: Princeton University Press, 1951.

85. Janowitz, Morris. *New Military: Changing Patterns of Organization.* New York: Russell Sage, 1964.

86. Kahalani, Avigdor. *Heights of Courage: A Tank Leader's War on the Golan.* Westport, Conn.: Greenwood Press, 1984.

87. Keegan, John. *Face of Battle.* New York: Viking Press, 1976.

88. Kellerman, Barbara. *Leadership: Multidisciplinary Perspectives.* Englewood Cliffs, N.J.: Prentice-Hall, 1984.

89. King, W. J. *The Unwritten Laws of Engineering.* New York: American Society of Mechanical Engineers, 1944.

90. Knightley, Phillip. *First Casualty: From the Crimea to Vietnam—The War Correspondent as Hero, Propagandist, and Myth Maker.* New York: Harcourt Brace Jovanovich, 1975.

91. Krulak, Victor H. *First to Fight: An Inside View of the U.S. Marine Corps.* Annapolis: Naval Institute Press, 1984.

92. Kozlov, S. N. *Officer's Handbook: A Soviet View, Moscow, 1971.* Washington, D.C., 1977. For sale by the Superintendent of Documents, U.S. Government Printing Office.

93. Laffin, John. *Links of Leadership: Thirty Centuries of Military Command.* New York: Abelard-Schuman, 1970.

94. Lea, Homer. *The Valor of Ignorance.* New York: Harper and Row, 1942.

95. Leckie, Robert. *Helmet for My Pillow.* New York: Random House, 1957.

96. ———. *March to Glory.* Cleveland: World, 1960.

97. ———. *Strong Men Armed: The United States Marines against Japan.* New York: Random House, 1962.

98. Lederer, William J. *All the Ships at Sea.* New York: Sloan, 1950.

99. Legg, Stuart. *Trafalgar: An Eye-Witness Account of a Great Battle.* New York: John Day, 1966.

100. Lewis, Lloyd. *Sherman: Fighting Prophet.* New York: Harcourt, Brace, 1958.

101. Liddell Hart, Basil Henry. *The German Generals Talk.* New York: William Morrow, 1984.

102. ———. *History of the Second World War.* London: Cassell, 1970.

103. ———. *A History of the World War, 1914–1918.* London: Faber and Faber, 1934.

104. ———. *Reputations: Ten Years After.* Boston: Little, Brown, 1928.

105. ———. *Strategy.* New York: Praeger, 1967.

106. ———. *Sword and the Pen: Selections from the World's Greatest Military Writings.* New York: Crowell, 1976.

107. Livingstone, Sir Richard. *Thucydides: The History of the Peloponnesian War.* Harmondsworth-Middlesex, England: Penguin Classics, 1954.

108. London, Jack. *Sea-Wolf.* New York: Grosset and Dunlap, 1931.

109. Long, David Foster. *Nothing Too Daring: A Biography of Commodore David Porter, 1780–1843.* Annapolis: Naval Institute Press, 1970.

110. McDonough, James R. *Platoon Leader.* Novato, Calif.: Presidio Press, 1985.

111. Machiavelli, Niccolo. *Prince.* New York: Dutton, 1958.

112. Mackay, Charles. *Extraordinary Popular Delusions and the Madness of Crowds.* Boston: L. C. Page, 1932.

113. McKenna, Richard. *The Sand Pebbles.* New York: Harper and Row, 1962.

114. Mahan, Alfred Thayer. *Life of Nelson: The Embodiment of the Sea Power of Great Britain.* Boston: Little, Brown, 1943.

115. ———. *Naval Strategy Compared and Contrasted with the Principles and Practice of Military Operations on Land.* Lectures delivered at the U.S. Naval War College, Newport, R.I., 1887–1911. Westport, Conn.: Greenwood Press, 1975.

116. Malone, Dandridge M. *Small Unit Leadership: A Common Sense Approach.* Novato, Calif.: Presidio Press, 1983.

117. Manchester, William Raymond. *Last Lion: Winston Spencer Churchill, Visions of Glory, 1874–1932.* Boston: Little, Brown, 1983.

118. Manstein, Erich von. *Lost Victories.* Chicago: Henry Regnery, 1958.

119. Marshall, Samuel Lyman Atwood. *Men against Fire: The Problem of Battle Command in Future War.* Gloucester, Mass.: Peter Smith, 1978.

120. ———. *Officer as a Leader.* Harrisburg, Pa.: Stackpole, 1966.

121. ———. *Soldier's Load and the Mobility of a Nation.* Quantico, Va.: Marine Corps Association, 1965.

122. Masters, John. *Bugles and a Tiger: A Volume of Autobiography.* New York: Viking Press, 1956.

123. Mattingly, Garrett. *Armada.* Boston: Houghton Mifflin, 1959.

124. Miller, John Grider. *Battle to Save the Houston, October 1944 to March 1945.* Annapolis: Naval Institute Press, 1985.

125. Millett, Allan Reed. *Semper Fidelis: The History of the United States Marine Corps.* New York: Macmillan, 1980.

126. Monsarrat, Nicholas. *Cruel Sea.* New York: Knopf, 1951.

127. Montross, Lynn, and Miller, William Marshall. *The United States Marines.* Cambridge, Mass.: Riverside Press, 1962.

128. Morris, Donald R. *Washing of the Spears: A History of the Rise of the Zulu Nation under Shaka and Its Fall in the Zulu War of 1879.* New York: Simon and Schuster, 1965.

129. Morrison, Matt R., and Tibbits, Keith A., Jr. "To Be The Best: A Study of Excellence in United States Marine Corps Infantry Battalions." Master's thesis, Naval Postgraduate School, Monterey, Calif., 1985.

130. Mrazek, James. *The Art of Winning Wars.* New York: Walker, 1968.

131. Murphy, Audie. *To Hell and Back.* New York: H. Holt, 1949.

132. Myrer, Anton. *Once an Eagle.* New York: Holt, Rinehart and Winston, 1968.

133. Newman, Aubrey S. *Follow Me: The Human Element in Leadership.* Novato, Calif.: Presidio Press, 1981.

134. O'Brien, William Vincent. *Conduct of Just and Limited War.* New York: Praeger, 1981.

135. O'Connor, John Joseph. *Chaplain Looks at Vietnam.* Cleveland: World, 1968.

136. ———. *In Defense of Life.* Boston: St. Paul Editions, 1981.

137. Patton, George S., Jr. *War as I Knew It*. New York: Bantam Books, 1980.

138. Peters, Thomas J. *In Search of Excellence: Lessons from America's Best-Run Companies*. New York: Harper and Row, 1982.

139. Plutarch. *Lives of the Noble Grecians and Romans*. New York: Modern Library, 1932.

140. Porter, David. *Journal of a Cruise Made to the Pacific Ocean*. New York: Wiley and Halsted, 1922.

141. Potter, John Deane. *Fiasco: The Break-out of the German Battleships*. New York: Stein and Day, 1970.

142. Puryear, Edgar F. *Nineteen Stars*. Washington, D.C.: Coiner Publications, 1971.

143. ———. *Stars in Flight: A Study in Air Force Character and Leadership*. San Rafael, Calif.: Presidio Press, 1981.

144. Reeman, Douglas. *Destroyers*. New York: Putnam, 1974.

145. ———. *Greatest Enemy*. New York: Putnam, 1971.

146. ———. *His Majesty's U-Boat*. New York: Putnam, 1971.

147. ———. *Pride and the Anguish*. New York: Putnam, 1969.

148. ———. *Rendezvous—South Atlantic*. New York: Putnam, 1972.

149. ———. *Ship Must Die*. New York: William Morrow, 1979.

150. ———. *Strike from the Sea*. New York: William Morrow, 1978.

151. ———. *Torpedo Run*. New York: William Morrow, 1981.

152. ———. *Winged Escort*. New York: Putnam, 1976.

153. Remarque, Erich Maria. *All Quiet on the Western Front*. Boston: Little, Brown, 1958.

154. Reynolds, Clark G. *Famous American Admirals*. New York: Van Nostrand Reinhold, 1978.

155. Richardson, James O., and Dyer, George Carroll. *On the Treadmill to Pearl Harbor: The Memoirs of Admiral James O. Richardson*. Washington, D.C.: Naval History Division, Department of the Navy, 1973. For sale by the Superintendent of Documents, U.S. Government Printing Office.

156. Rickover, H. G. *Eminent Americans: Namesakes of the Polaris Submarine Fleet*. Washington, D.C.: Superintendent of Documents, 1972.

157. Roberts, Kenneth Lewis. *Arundel*. Garden City, N.Y.: Doubleday, 1956.

158. ———. *Battle of Cowpens: The Great Morale-Builder*. Garden City, N.Y.: Doubleday, 1958.

159. ———. *Captain Caution: A Chronicle of Arundel*. Garden City, N.Y.: Doubleday, Doran, 1953.

160. ———. *Northwest Passage*. Garden City, N.Y.: Doubleday, Doran, 1937.

161. ———. *Rabble in Arms*. Garden City, N.Y.: Doubleday, 1947.

162. Robertson, John Henry. *Auchinleck: A Biography of Field Marshal Sir Claude Auchinleck*. London: Cassell, 1959.

163. Robertson, Terence. *Escort Commander*. Garden City, N.Y.: Doubleday, 1979.

164. Rommel, Erwin. *Attacks*. Vienna, Va.: Athena Press, 1979.

165. Rosenbach, William E. *Contemporary Issues in Leadership*. Boulder, Colo.: Westview Press, 1984.

166. Ruge, Friedrich. *Rommel in Normandy: Reminiscences*. San Rafael, Calif.: Presidio Press, 1978.

167. ———. *Scapa Flow 1919: The End of the German Fleet*. London: Allan, 1973.

168. ———. *Seekrieg: The German Navy's Story, 1939–1945*. Annapolis: Naval Institute Press, 1957.

169. Russ, Martin. *Last Parallel: A Marine's War Journal*. New York: Rinehart, 1957.

170. Sassoon, Siegfried. *War Poems of Siegfried Sassoon*. London: Faber and Faber, 1983.

171. Scullard, Howard Hayes. *Scipio Africanus: Soldier and Politician*. Ithaca, N.Y.: Cornell University Press, 1970.

172. Semmes, Raphael. *Confederate Raider, Alabama: Selections from Memoirs of Service Afloat during the War between the States*. Gloucester, Mass.: P. Smith, 1969.

173. Shaara, Michael. *Killer Angels*. New York: McKay, 1974.

174. Sheehan, Neil. *The Arnheiter Affair*. New York: Random House, 1971.

175. Sherrod, Robert Lee. *Tarawa: The Story of a Battle*. Fredericksburg, Tex.: Admiral Nimitz Foundation, 1973.

176. Shirer, William L. *Rise and Fall of the Third Reich: A History of Nazi Germany*. New York: Simon and Schuster, 1960.

177. Sims, Edward H. *Greatest Aces*. New York: Harper and Row, 1967.

178. Smith, Gene. *Lee and Grant: A Dual Biography*. New York: McGraw-Hill, 1984.

179. Solzhenitsyn, Aleksandr Isaevich. *Mortal Dan-*

ger: Misconceptions about Soviet Russia and Its Threat to America. New York: Harper and Row, 1980.

180. ———. *World Split Apart*. Commencement Address Delivered at Harvard University, 1978.

181. Southey, Robert. *The Life of Nelson*. London: Bickers and Son, 1884.

182. Stockdale, James B. *In Love and War: The Story of a Family's Ordeal and Sacrifice during the Vietnam Years*. New York: Harper and Row, 1984.

183. ———. *Vietnam Experience: Ten Years of Reflection*. Stanford, Calif.: Hoover Press, 1984.

184. Summers, Harry G. *On Strategy: A Critical Analysis of the Vietnam War*. Novato, Calif.: Presidio Press, 1982.

185. Sun Tzu. *Art of War*. New York: Delacorte Press, 1983.

186. Suvorov, Viktor. *Inside the Soviet Army*. New York: Macmillan, 1982.

187. Tacitus, Cornelius. *Works*. Cambridge: Harvard University Press, 1980.

188. Taylor, Robert L. *Military Leadership: In Pursuit of Excellence*. Boulder, Colo.: Westview Press, 1984.

189. Toland, John. *No Man's Land: 1918, The Last Year of the Great War*. Garden City, N.Y.: Doubleday, 1980.

190. Touchstone Books. *Patton's Principles: A Handbook for Managers Who Mean It*. New York: Simon and Schuster, 1982.

191. Tuchman, Barbara. *Distant Mirror: The Calamitous Fourteenth Century*. New York: Knopf, 1978.

192. ———. *Guns of August*. New York: Macmillan, 1962.

193. ———. *Practicing History: Selected Essays*. New York: Knopf, 1981.

194. ———. *Stilwell and the American Experience in China, 1911–45*. New York: Macmillan, 1971.

195. ———. *Zimmermann Telegram*. New York: Viking Press, 1958.

196. Turley, Gerald H. *Easter Offensive: Vietnam, 1972*. Novato, Calif.: Presidio Press, 1985.

197. United Services Automobile Association. *Return to Iwo Jima*. Videotape, 1986.

198. ———. *The Unknown Soldier*. Videotape, 1986.

199. United States Department of Defense. *Soviet Military Power*. Washington, D.C.: 1985. For sale by the Superintendent of Documents, U.S. Government Printing Office.

200. United States Infantry School. *Infantry in Battle*. Washington, D.C.: Infantry Journal, 1939.

201. United States Office of Armed Forces Information and Education. *Armed Forces Officer*. Washington, D.C.: 1960.

202. Van Creveld, Martin L. *Command in War*. Cambridge, Mass.: Harvard University Press, 1985.

203. ———. *Fighting Power: German and U.S. Army Performance, 1939–1945*. Westport, Conn.: Greenwood Press, 1982.

204. ———. *Supplying War: Logistics from Wallenstein to Patton*. New York: Cambridge University Press, 1977.

205. von Schell, Adolf. *Battle Leadership*. Quantico, Va.: Marine Corps Association, 1982.

206. Walker, Keith. *A Piece of My Heart: Stories of Twenty-Six American Women in Vietnam*. Novato, Calif.: Presidio Press, 1986.

207. Walt, Lewis W. *Strange War, Strange Strategy*. New York: Funk and Wagnalls, 1970.

208. Warner, Philip. *The Soldier: His Daily Life through the Ages*. New York: Taplinger, 1975.

209. Webb, James H. *Country Such as This*. Garden City, N.Y.: Doubleday, 1983.

210. ———. *Fields of Fire*. Englewood Cliffs, N.J.: Prentice-Hall, 1978.

211. ———. *A Sense of Honor*. Englewood Cliffs, N.J.: Prentice-Hall, 1981.

212. *Webster's American Military Biographies*. Springfield, Mass.: G. and C. Merriam, 1978.

213. Werner, Herbert A. *Iron Coffins: A Personal Account of the German U-Boat Battles of World War II*. New York: Holt, Rinehart and Winston, 1969.

214. Wheeler, Richard. *Iwo*. New York: Lippincott and Crowell, 1980.

215. Whiting, Charles. *Massacre at Malmedy*. New York: Stein and Day, 1971.

216. Willenz, June A. *Women Veterans: America's Forgotten Heroines*. New York: Continuum, 1983.

217. Williamson, Porter B. *Patton's Principles*. Tucson: Management and Systems Consultants, 1979.

218. Winslow, Walter G. *Ghost That Died at Sunda Straight*. Annapolis: Naval Institute Press, 1984.

219. Wood, William J. *Leaders and Battles: The Art of Military Leadership*. Novato, Calif.: Presidio Press, 1984.

220. Woodham Smith, Cecil Blanche. *The Reason Why*. New York: E. P. Dutton, 1960.

Recommended Readings

221. Wouk, Herman. *Caine Mutiny: A Novel of World War II*. Garden City, N.Y.: Doubleday, 1951.

222. Yeager, Chuck. *Yeager: An Autobiography*. New York: Bantam Books, 1985.

223. Young, Peter. *Great Generals and Their Battles*. Greenwich, Conn.: Bison Books, 1984.

224. Yukl, Gary A. *Leadership in Organizations*. Englewood Cliffs, N.J.: Prentice-Hall, 1981.

Appendix

Contributions by Leaders

Ailes, Rear Adm. Robert H., USN (84)*
Aitcheson, Rear Adm. George A., USN (69)
Armstrong, Rear Adm. Clarence E., Jr., USN (23)
Arthur, Rear Adm. Stanley R., USN (28)
Aut, Rear Adm. Warren E., USN (76)

Baciocco, Vice Adm. Albert J., Jr., USN (intro. chap. 5)
Baker, Capt. Brent, USN (64)
Baldwin, Capt. Edwin M., USN (90)
Barrow, Gen. Robert H., USMC
Baumann, Lt. Comdr. C. W., USN (65)
Bodensteiner, Rear Adm. Wayne D., USN (46)
Brandon, Lt. B. D., USN (65)
Breast, Rear Adm. Jerry C., USN (30)
Browne, Midshipman 2/C Michael E., USNA '87 (53)
Bulkeley, Rear Adm. John D., USN (9)
Burke, Adm. Arleigh Albert, USN (4, intro. chap. 9)
Burkhardt, Rear Adm. L., III, USN (36)
Butcher, Rear Adm. P. D., USN (39)

Cadman, Lt. Col. George, III, USMC (6)
Campbell, Rear Adm. N. D., USN (65)
Carlson, Vice Adm. Dudley, USN (71)
Carney, Adm. Robert Bostwick, USN
Catola, Rear Adm. S. G., USN (49)
Ciotti, Lt. Col. Anthony J., Jr., USMC (32 and 96)
Clarkson, Col. E. J., USMC (87)
Clausen, Rear Adm. Karl, FGN
Clexton, Rear Adm. E. W., USN (81)
Colley, Rear Adm. Michael C., USN (83)
Colvard, Distinguished Navy Exec. James, Ph.D. (91)
Cooper, Lt. Gen. Charles G., USMC (27)
Cowhill, Vice Adm. William J., USN (89)
Cox, Maj. Gen. John V., USMC (56)
Curran, Comdr. Donald J., Jr., USN (2)

de Cazanove, Vice Adm. d'escadre Paul de Bigault, FN
DiCampli, Midshipman 2/C James, USNA '86 (86)
DiRenzo, Lt. Joe, III, USN (1)

*Numbers in parentheses are section numbers.

Emery, Rear Adm. T.R.M., USN (73)

Finneran, Rear Adm. William J., USN (25)
Fiske, Rear Adm. Harry K., USN (10)
Flatley, Rear Adm. James H., III, USN (17 and 24)
Fox, Rear Adm. Thomas R., USN (38)
Furlong, Rear Adm. G. M., Jr., USN (75)

Garrow, Rear Adm. Jack A., USN (68)
Greene, Gen. Wallace M., Jr., USMC

Hammond, Col. James W., Jr., USMC (61, intro. chap. 7)
Harlow, Rear Adm. David L., USN (62)
Hayward, Adm. Thomas Bibb, USN (intro. chap. 10)
Herberger, Rear Adm. Albert J., USN (77)
Holloway, Adm. James Lemuel, III, USN
Howe, Rear Adm. J. T., USN (16)
Hunt, Adm. Sir Nicholas, RN

Itaya, Adm. Takaichi, JMSDF

Johnson, Lt. Comdr. David A., USN (93)

Kelley, Gen. P. X., USMC (6)
Kelso, Vice Adm. Frank B., II, USN (19)
Kempf, Rear Adm. Cecil J., USN (15 and 92)
Kersh, Rear Adm. J. M., USN (18)
Kile, Capt. Tom, USN (35)
Kirkpatrick, Rear Adm. J. H., USN (29)
Kirksey, Vice Adm. Robert, USN (26, intro. chaps. 2 and 3)
Kitterman, Lt. Samuel A., JAGC, USNR (20)
Koenig, Rear Adm. J. Weldon, USN (85)
Kristensen, Comdr. Edward, USN (58)

Landersman, Lt. Comdr. Stuart D., USN ("Damn Exec," 17)
Larson, Rear Adm. Charles R., USN (5)
Lautermilch, Rear Adm. Paul A., USN (66)
Lawrence, Vice Adm. William P., USN (7)
Layman, Rear Adm. Lawrence, USN (63)
Long, Adm. Robert, USN
Looney, Brig. Gen. E. P., Jr., USMC (88)

McArthur, Rear Adm. John, USN (60)
McCauley, Vice Adm. W. F., USN (22)
McDonald, Adm. David Lamar, USN
Mack, Vice Adm. William P., USN (42)

McKee, Rear Adm. Fran, USN
MacKinnon, Rear Adm. Malcolm, USN (35)
Maloney, Lt. Gen. W. R., USMC (51)
Martinson, Capt. A. M., MC, USN (31)
Meyett, Comdr. Fred, USN (35)
Montor, Professor Karel, Ph.D. (12, 13, 21, 37, 44, 50, 54, 57, 67, and 74)
Moorer, Adm. Thomas Hinman, USN
Murphy, Col. James W., USMC (51)

Nakamura, Adm. Teiji, JMSDF
Nakayama, Adm. Sadayoshi, JMSDF
Newell, Rear Adm. Bruce, USN (94)

Pandzik, Lt. Jan, USN (55)
Patterson, Comdr. Perry S., Jr., JAGC, USNR (20)

Ramage, Vice Adm. Lawson P., USN
Ramsey, Rear Adm. William E., USN (26, intro. chaps. 2 and 3)
Rice, Maj. Gen. W. H., USMC
Rich, Rear Adm. Roger L., Jr., USN (34)
Ripley, Col. John W., USMC (47)
Rowden, Vice Adm. William H., USN (59)
Roze, Maj. Robert, USA (82)
Ruge, Adm. Friedrich, FGN

Sagerholm, Vice Adm. J. A., USN (43)
Sanders, Master Chief Petty Officer of the Navy Billy C., USN
Service, Rear Adm. James E., USN (14)
Shepherd, Gen. Lemuel C., Jr., USMC (intro. chap. 1)
Simon, Rear Adm. Roger O., USN (40)
Slack, Brig. Gen. Paul D., USMC (41)
Sutherland, Rear Adm. Paul E., Jr., USN (79)

Taggart, Capt. Don, USN (25)
Taylor, Rear Adm. Jeremy D., USN
Trucco, Lt. (jg) John A., JAGC, USNR (20)
Truly, Rear Adm. Richard H., USN (80)
Tuttle, Rear Adm. Jerry O., USN (8)
Twomey, Lt. Gen. D. M., USMC (33)

Uchida, Adm. Kazuomi, JMSDF
Ustick, Rear Adm. Richard C., USN (3)

Wallace, Comdr. Ray A., USN (78)
Walsh, Rear Adm. William A., USN (78)
Watson, Capt. J. F., USN (14)

Webb, Assistant Secretary of Defense for Reserve
Affairs James
Wilson, Gen. Louis, USMC
Wynne, Capt. Dave, USN (29)
Wyttenbach, Capt. Richard H., USN (73)

Young, Rear Adm. H. L., USN (52)

Young, Capt. Sue E., USN (11)
Yow, Rear Adm. J. Samuel, USN (45)
Yusi, Comdr. Frank, USN (72)

Zeller, Rear Adm. R. G., USN (70)
Zirbel, Rear Adm. W. D., USN (48)
Zumwalt, Adm. Elmo Russell, Jr., USN

Contributions by Midshipmen

Alexander, Marc R. '85
Allen, Douglas R. '86

Banister, Grady '87
Bates, Troy R. '85
Beach, John A. '85
Browne, Michael '87
Bryan, Scott R. '85

Caisse, Bryan '85
Campbell, Eric '85
Carlson, Scott '85
Challender, James P. '85
Chambers, Steven D. '85
Clark, William W. '85
Clouse, Richard '85
Cochrane, James R. '85
Cooper, Don N. '85

Dayoub, Gretchen M. '85
Derrane, James P. '87
Dorrell, Russell E., III '85
Duzan, Rob '85

Garay, Roger '86
Glavy, Matthew G. '86
Goehler, Barry J. '85
Graf, Holly Anne '85
Gunning, Edward '85

Harrison, D. E. '85
Hartman, Richard M. '85
Hauman, Mark H. '85
Hobbib, Thomas P. '85
Holmes, Steven W. '85
Holt, Timothy S. '85
Howell, Terry '85
Hudson, J. Neil '85
Huey, Joel '85

Ivey, Robert J., Jr. '85

Jackson, Edward Keith '86

Kessler, Michael L. '85
Klooster, Michael C. '85
Kramer, Timothy J. '86

Lankau, Paul A., Jr. '85
Ledbetter, Brian '85
Locher, O. G. '85
Lyter, Curtis E. '85

McElroy, Terry '86
McEnroe, Martin '85
McGinn, Elizabeth '85
Maraoui, Anne-Marie '85
Medve, Martin S. '85
Meisch, Paul J. '87
Merriman, Richard '85
Miller, Todd '86
Milliman, John C. '87
Mitchell, Don '85
Monk, Charlotte '85
Mudd, Michael W. '85

Noel, Jack S., II '85

O'Brien, Seamus M. '85

Petruncio, Emil '85
Pimpo, Stephen J. '85
Polinchock, F. Todd '85
Preddy, Joseph P. '85

Reiber, Deanna Lyn '86
Robinson, David M. '87
Rosmilso, Paul A. '85
Ruttenberg, John J. '85

Sanchez, Adrian A. '86
Schaeffler, Mark A. '85
Sham, Robert R. '85
Sizemore, Robert '87
Slyh, Paul '85
Smith, F. W. '87
Smith, Robert J. '85
Steffan, Joseph C. '87
Stonaker, Daniel '87
Sullivan, Charles F. '87
Sweeney, Greg S. '85

Thola, Forest D. '85

Van Cleave, John A. '85

Walls, Kenneth C. '85
Weist, Kathleen '85
Wells, S. K. '85
Wilson, Chet '85
Wright, Lloyd A. '85

Index

The individuals below contributed their thoughts on the topics covered in this book. Their comments begin on the pages indicated. Section numbers, which precede page numbers, are included for the reader who wishes to learn what an individual said regarding a particular subject. (*A* and *B* signify left-hand and right-hand columns, respectively.)

*Indicates quotations begin in both left- and right-hand columns.
†Indicates multiple quotations in left-hand column.
‡Indicates multiple quotations in right-hand column.

*Indicates quotations begin in both left- and right-hand columns.
‡Indicates multiple quotations in right-hand column.